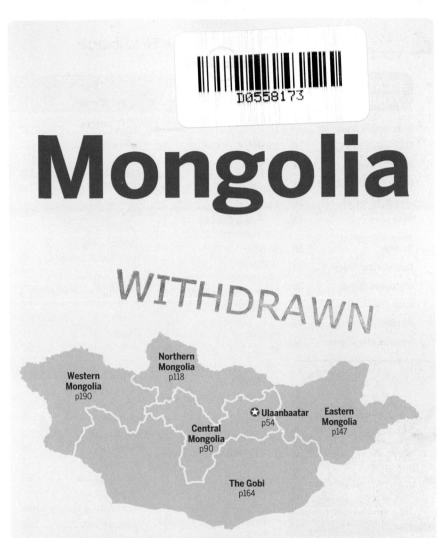

# Mongolia

WITHDRAWN

Western Mongolia
p190

Northern Mongolia
p118

Central Mongolia
p90

⭐ Ulaanbaatar
p54

Eastern Mongolia
p147

The Gobi
p164

Trent Holden, Adam Karlin, Michael Kohn,
Thomas O'Malley, Adam Skolnick

# Contents

## PLAN YOUR TRIP

NOMADIC CUISINE P238

TRADITIONAL GER P232

TOM O'MALLEY/LONELY PLANET ©

TOM O'MALLEY/LONELY PLANET ©

## ON THE ROAD

# Contents

OLIVIA POZZAN/LONELY PLANET ©

CAMEL TREKKING P35

# Welcome to Mongolia

*Rugged Mongolia is an adventure destination where travellers can experience nomadic culture and vast, untouched landscapes.*

## An Open Country

Mongolia existed in a Soviet bubble for most of the 20th century. Now a generation beyond the fall of communism, Mongolia has emerged as a young democracy with a promising economy based on mining, agriculture and tourism. Some revenue is being funnelled back into improving tourist facilities, including a new international airport near Ulaanbaatar. Visas are relatively easy to acquire; a handful of nationalities won't even require one. Competition among the tour operators has led to better services. Despite the warm welcome, travel can be rough at times, with only basic facilities in many areas.

## Mongolian Wilderness

Mongolians are fully aware of the unique beauty of their country. Ask locals and they will probably gush about the spectacular countryside, vast steppes, rugged mountains, clear lakes and abundant wildlife and livestock. Some areas are so remote you could drive a full day and see almost no signs of human habitation. It's this true wilderness experience that many people find so appealing. City residents from Ulaanbaatar have also started to discover their own country and camping is now popular among urban locals. Protected areas cover almost a fifth of the country and the government is looking to increase that figure.

## Nomad Hospitality

Mongolia's nomadic culture is famous – visitors can sleep in a herder's ger (traditional felt yurt), help round up the sheep, ride horses and simply 'get back to nature'. The legacy of Chinggis Khaan and resurgent nationalist pride sharpens the experience. A culture of tremendous hospitality makes locals more accessible. In a world beset by locks and gates, it's refreshing to meet people willing to open their doors to strangers. When travelling in Mongolia, however, keep in mind that guests are expected to reciprocate any forms of generosity, so when visiting families, always have a ready supply of gifts for the kids.

## Not Just Grass & Horses

Once half nomadic, Mongolia is changing rapidly, with its citizens flocking to Ulaanbaatar and other big cities for work and study opportunities. Indeed, many Mongolians have bought wholeheartedly into the global economy, capitalism and consumerism. Whether they are rural or urban, Mongolians take pride in their country's democratic institutions of civic participation. Eager to be part of the global community, Mongolia sends its troops on peacekeeping missions around the globe, and promoting itself as a country to host northeast Asian peace talks. Visiting now puts you right in the middle of these dramatic transformations.

## Why I Love Mongolia

By Michael Kohn, Writer

Over a period of 20 years I've explored every corner of Mongolia, writing about the history of Buddhism in the Gobi Desert, searching for cattle rustlers in the northwest and witnessing ancient shamanic ceremonies in the east. I love criss-crossing the country, enjoying the untouched landscapes, clear rivers and ger-dotted valleys. Each trip brings new adventures and unexpected encounters. While its nature and fascinating culture are things to treasure, my love for Mongolia is mainly for its hospitable and generous people – always there to welcome strangers, share news, gossip and jokes, and to show me the best of the human spirit.

**For more about our writers, see p295**

Above: Camels in Altai Tavan Bogd National Park (p198)

# Mongolia

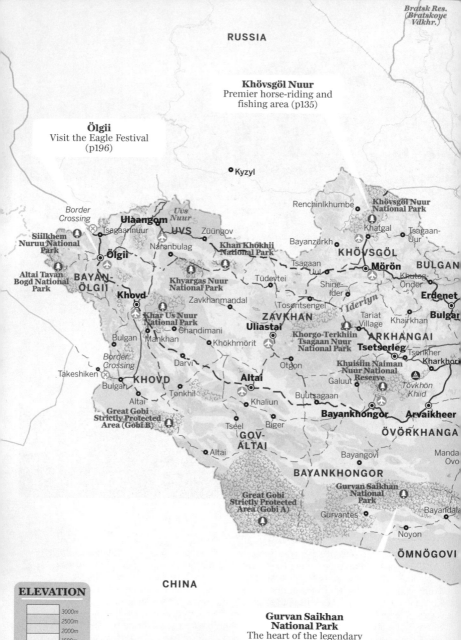

RUSSIA

Bratsk Res.
(Bratskoye
Vdkhr.)

**Khövsgöl Nuur**
Premier horse-riding and
fishing area (p135)

**Ölgii**
Visit the Eagle Festival
(p196)

Kyzyl

Renchinlkhumbe

**Khövsgöl Nuur
National Park**

Border
Crossing

Tsagaannuur

Ulaangom
Uvs
Nuur
UVS

Züüngov

Bayanzürkh

Khatgal

Tsagaan-
Uur

**Siilkhem
Nuruu National
Park**

Naranbulag

**Khan Khökhii
National Park**

Tsagaan
Uul

**KHÖVSGÖL**

Mörön

BULGAN

Ölgii

**Altai Tavan
Bogd National
Park**

BAYAN-
ÖLGII

**Khyargas Nuur
National Park**

Tüdevtei

Shine-
Ider

Khutag-
Önder

Erdenet

Khovd

Zavkhanmandal

Ider iyn

Tariat
Village

Khairkhan

Bulgan

**Khar Us Nuur
National Park**

Tosontsengel

ZAVKHAN

Uliastai

**Khorgo-Terkhiin
Tsagaan Nuur
National Park**

ARKHANGAI

Tsetserleg

Tsenkher

Kharkhor

Bulgan

Mankhan

Chandimani

Khökhmörit

**KHOVD**

Darvi

Otgon

**Khuislin Naiman
Nuur National
Reserve**

Galuut

Tövkhön
Khiid

Border
Crossing

Takeshiken

Bulgan

Altai

Tonkhil

Altai

Khaliun

Buutsagaan

Bayankhongor

Arvaikheer

**Great Gobi
Strictly Protected
Area (Gobi B)**

Tseel

Biger

GOV-
ALTAI

ÖVÖRKHANGA

Altai

**BAYANKHONGOR**

Bayangovi

Manda
Ovo

**Great Gobi
Strictly Protected
Area (Gobi A)**

Gurvantes

**Gurvan Saikhan
National Park**

Bayandal

Noyon

ÖMNÖGOVI

CHINA

## ELEVATION

| |
|---|
| 3000m |
| 2500m |
| 2000m |
| 1500m |
| 1000m |
| 500m |
| 0 |

**Gurvan Saikhan
National Park**
The heart of the legendary
Gobi Desert (p179)

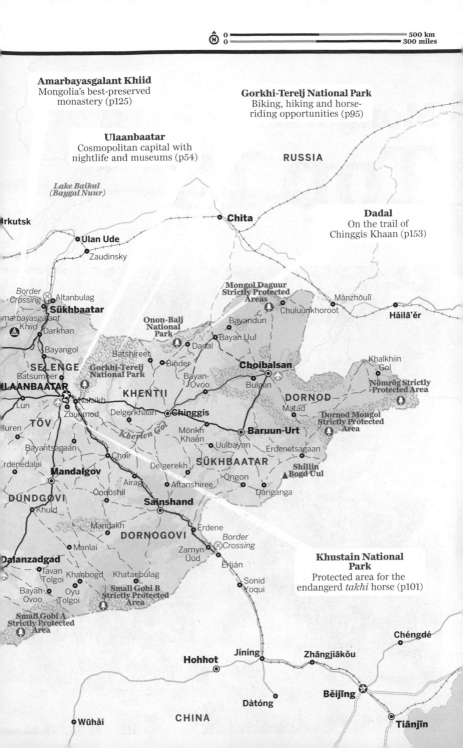

**Amarbayasgalant Khiid**
Mongolia's best-preserved monastery (p125)

**Gorkhi-Terelj National Park**
Biking, hiking and horse-riding opportunities (p95)

**Ulaanbaatar**
Cosmopolitan capital with nightlife and museums (p54)

**Dadal**
On the trail of Chinggis Khaan (p153)

**Khustain National Park**
Protected area for the endangerd *takhi* horse (p101)

0
500 km
0
300 miles

RUSSIA

*Lake Baikal
(Baygal Nuur)*

Irkutsk

Chita

Ulan Ude

Zaudinsky

Mănzhōulǐ

Hǎilā'ěr

Mongol Daguur
Strictly Protected
Areas

Chuluùnkhoroot

*Border
Crossing*   Altanbulag

Sükhbaatar

*marbayasgalant
Khiid*   Darkhan

Bayandun

Bayan Uul

Khalkhiin
Gol

Bayangol

Nömrög Strictly
Protected Area

SELENGE   Batshireet

Gorkhi-Terelj
National Park

Onon-Balj
National
Park

Dadal

Choibalsan

Batsumber

Binder

Bayan-
Ovoo

Bulgan

DORNOD

ULAANBAATAR

Nalaikh

KHENTII

Matad

Lun   Zuunmod

Dornod Mongol
Strictly Protected
Area

Buren   TÖV

Delgerkhaan   Chinggis

Mönkh
Khaan

Baruun-Urt

Bayantsagaan

Uulbayan

Erdenetsagaan

Choir

Delgerekh

SÜKHBAATAR

Shiliin
Bogd Uul

rdenedalai

Mandalgov

Ongon

Airag

Dariganga

DÚNDGOVI   Ondoshil   Altanshiree

Khuld

Sainshand

Mandakh

Erdene

DORNOGOVI

*Border
Crossing*

Manlai

Zamyn-
Üüd

Dalanzadgad

Tavan
Tolgoi   Khanbogd   Khatanbulag

Erlián

Bayan-
Ovoo   Oyu
Tolgoi

Small Gobi B
Strictly Protected
Area

Sonid
Yoqui

Small Gobi A
Strictly Protected
Area

Chéngdé

Hohhot

Jíníng

Zhāngjiākǒu

Běijīng

Dàtóng

Tiānjīn

Wūhǎi

CHINA

# Mongolia's
# Top 13

## Naadam Festival

**1** Mongolians love naadam (p47). With two or three days of serious wrestling action, awesome horse racing and dazzling archery, who wouldn't? While 'naadam' literally means games, the celebration is much more than that. It's all about fun, getting together with friends and relatives, eating a lot of *khuushuur* (mutton pancakes) and emptying a bottle or two of vodka. The most traditional festivals happen in villages such as Khatgal (p135) in northern Mongolia, where every member of the community is somehow involved. These village naadams are also ultra-photogenic – with all wrestlers, archers, jockeys and festival-goers set against stunning backdrops. Below left: Horseback archers, Naadam, Ulaanbaatar (p68)

## Hiking

**2** With its rugged mountains, serene river valleys and fields of wild flowers, the Mongolian back country is begging to be explored on foot. Hiking is a new activity in Mongolia, but it's certainly possible at places like Gorkhi-Terelj National Park (p95; pictured below), Bogdkhan Uul and Khövsgöl Nuur National Park. Although there are no warming huts and few marked trails, you'll find shelter in gers and encounter locals who are more than willing to show you the way. There are no Sherpas, but a pack horse (or yak) will do nicely. Good maps, a sturdy tent and a sense of adventure will help see you through.

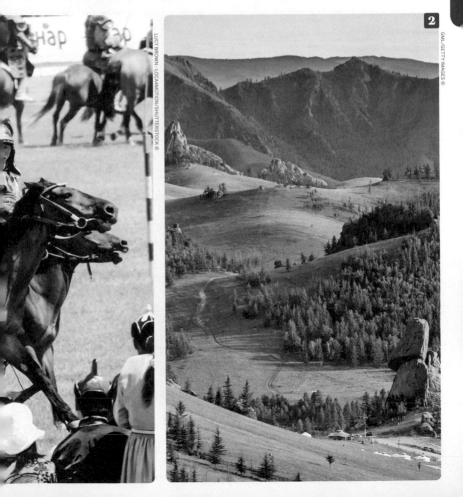

LUCY BROWN - LOCAMOTION/SHUTTERSTOCK ©

GML/GETTY IMAGES ©

## Monasteries

**3** The time-worn Buddhist monasteries *(khiid)* that dot the landscape are the most immediate window on Mongolia's spiritual roots. Lamas young and old sit quietly in the pews, while visiting laypeople pay homage with the spin of a prayer wheel and whispered mantras. As well as being places of pilgrimage, the monasteries are also rare slices of tangible history, filled with precious Buddhist icons, Sutras and the delicate paintings that grace their ancient walls. Amarbayasgalant Khiid (p125; pictured above), the country's best-preserved monastery, is dedicated to the great sculptor Zanabazar.

## Staying in a Ger

**4** Of all the experiences you are likely to have in Mongolia, the most memorable will be your visits to gers (p234), traditional felt yurts. From the outside, gers look like simple tents, but step inside and you'll be surprised by the amount of furnishings and modern appliances a nomadic family can have – not just furniture but also TVs, DVD players and smartphones. Visitors are always welcome inside a ger and you don't even need to knock (Mongolians never do). Instead, when approaching a ger, call out 'Nokhoi khor', which means 'Hold the dog'.

## Horse Riding

**5** Mongolians have been traversing their country on horseback for thousands of years – why not do the same? Short day rides are possible around Ulaanbaatar – but the best areas are Gorkhi-Terelj National Park (p97) and Bogdkhan Uul Strictly Protected Area (p91). Multiday horse treks can be made at Khövsgöl Nuur, the Darkhad Valley, Khan Khentii Strictly Protected Area and Naiman Nuur. Some adventurers have mounted their own cross-country expeditions. It can take some getting used to Mongolian horses and their short stocky build – pay attention to local guides and follow their lead.

**6**

**7**

## Eagle Hunters

**6** For centuries, using eagles to catch prey has been a traditional sport among Central Asian nomads. Even Marco Polo mentioned the great raptors kept by Kublai Khaan. The sport is alive and well today, but you'll only find it in a small corner of Mongolia. Travel to Bayan-Ölgii and link up with the Kazakh hunters who capture and train these magnificent birds. Hollywood has even taken notice with a major motion picture about a young female eagle hunter. The best time to visit is in early October, when you can attend the colourful Eagle Festival (p196) in Ölgii city.

## Gobi Desert

**7** The idea of going to the Gobi for a vacation would probably have Marco Polo turning in his grave. The Venetian traveller, and others like him, dreaded crossing this harsh landscape. Thankfully, travel facilities have improved in the past 800 years, and it's now possible to make a reasonably comfortable visit. A paved road even reaches Dalanzadgad from UB. Once there, ride a two-humped camel and explore dinosaur bone yards. The real highlight is the scenic Khongoryn Els in Gurvan Saikhan National Park (p179; pictured above) – towering sand dunes that whistle when raked by winds.

## Khövsgöl Nuur

**8** The natural highlight of Mongolia is Khövsgöl Nuur (p135), a 136km-long lake set on the southernmost fringe of Siberia. For Mongolians the lake is a deeply spiritual place, home to powerful *nagas* (water spirits) and a source of inspiration for shamans. For foreigners, Khövsgöl is a place for adventure, with horse riding, fishing, kayaking, trekking and mountain biking a few of the possibilities. Hard-core adventurers can even embark on a 15-day trek around its glorious shoreline. Launch your expedition from Khatgal, a quaint village of log homes, tourist camps and shops.

## On the Trail of Chinggis Khaan

**9** Don't miss your chance to track down Chinggis Khaan. Pack a copy of *Mongoliin Nuuts Tovchoo* (The Secret History of the Mongols), climb into your jeep and head east. Start at the place where Chinggis found his famous golden whip, Tsonjin Boldog, which is now a hill topped with a huge statue (p91) of the great conqueror. Continue on to Khökh Nuur, the site of his coronation before 100,000 soldiers. The trail gets wilder the further you go, until reaching Dadal (p153; pictured above), the great conqueror's alleged birthplace.

FOTOQLICK/GETTY IMAGES ©

## Wildlife Watching

**10** Mongolia provides an ideal landscape for watching wildlife. In the east you'll spot hundreds (sometimes thousands) of gazelles streaking across the plains. In mountainous areas, especially in the Gobi, there's argali sheep and ibexes, and in the taiga (subarctic coniferous forest) north of the Darkhad Valley you can see majestic reindeer. The easiest place to watch wildlife is at Khustain National Park (p101), home to *takhi* (wild horses) and wolves. And no matter where you travel, there are huge eagles, falcons and vultures circling overhead.

## Mongolian Food & Drink

**11** When it comes to cuisine, Mongolians make the most of limited ingredients. Meat (especially mutton), flour and milk products, such as dried curd and cheese, feature prominently in traditional dishes (p238). The best meals tend to be at gers, where a family feast includes animal organs, intestines and even the head. Other dishes include as *buuz* (dumplings, pictured above right) and *tsuivan* (steamed pasta), which you can find in every city. Drinking *airag* (fermented mare's milk) is a uniquely Central Asian experience, one your belly won't soon forget.

## Ulaanbaatar

**12** Once a quiet Soviet backwater, Ulaanbaatar (p54) has grown up to become a dynamic hub of commerce, culture and entertainment. The traffic and crowds can be overwhelming, but for travellers most of the main sights are within walking distance of downtown. After you've toured the museums, don't miss out on UB's heady nightlife and surprising range of cafes and restaurants. The city has a peaceful side too. Turn a prayer wheel at Gandan Khiid, or climb up Zaisan Hill to take a break from this bewildering and ever-changing city.
Top right: Choijin Lama Temple Museum (p62)

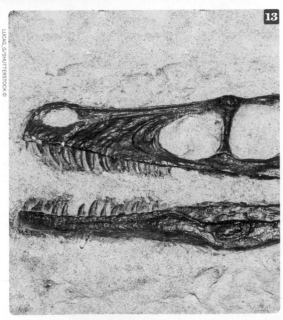

LUCAG_G/SHUTTERSTOCK ©

## Dinosaur Fossils

**13** Time travellers setting their destination to 70 million years ago would find the Gobi Desert lusher and wetter than it is today. The wildlife would be different too – instead of wild asses and gazelles, the landscape would be alive with herds of Protoceratops, hissing Velociraptors (pictured right) and the fearsome Tyrannosaurus Bataar, a cousin of the T-Rex. Their bones can be found buried in the sands and cliffs of the Gobi, awaiting discovery by the modern-day palaeontologist. In Ulaanbaatar, the best examples are to be housed in a new Museum of Dinosaurs (p63).

# Need to Know

**For more information, see Survival Guide (p247)**

## Currency
Tögrög (T), also spelt tugrik

......................................

## Language
Mongolian, Kazakh, Russian

......................................

## Visas
A 30-day tourist visa is required for some foreign nationals, although a number of countries can visit visa free, including citizens of the USA, Canada and Germany.

......................................

## Money
ATMs are widely available. Credit cards are accepted in most hotels, restaurants and shops. Money changers are easily accessible and give better rates compared to hotels.

......................................

## Mobile Phones
Use local SIM cards for better rates and to avoid roaming charges.

......................................

## Time
Ulaanbaatar and most of the country is GMT/UTC plus eight hours. The three western aimags (provinces) are GMT/UTC plus seven hours.

## When to Go

Khövsgöl Nuur National Park
GO Jun–Aug

Altai Tavan Bogd National Park
GO Jun–Sep

Ulaanbaatar
GO Jun–Aug

Dornod
GO May–Sep

Ömnögovi
GO May, Aug–Oct

- Warm to hot summers, cold winters
- Mild summers, cold winters
- Dry climate
- Desert, dry climate

### High Season
(Jun–Aug)

➡ Expect warm and mostly dry weather in June and July, with some thunderstorms.

➡ Late August sees cooler temperatures and more rain.

➡ Book flights and accommodation in advance, especially around Naadam.

### Shoulder
(May & Sep)

➡ Some ger (traditional yurt) camps may be closed.

➡ Weather can be changeable so plan for a cold snap.

➡ Fewer tourists means more available train and plane tickets.

### Low Season
(Oct–Apr)

➡ Most ger camps and some guesthouses close; discounts available.

➡ Frigid in December/January, air pollution in Ulaanbaatar. Winds and dust storms March/April.

➡ Activities like dog sledding, ice skating and skiing.

## Useful Websites

**Gogo.mn** (www.gogo.mn) Mongolia's leading news portal.

**Lonely Planet** (www.lonelyplanet.com/mongolia) Destination info, hotel bookings, traveller forum and more.

**Mongolia Expat** (www.mongoliaexpat.com) Slew of articles on living in Mongolia.

**Mongolia.travel** (www.mongolia.travel) Events, sights and trip planning.

**News.mn** (www.news.mn) Good site for news and information.

## Important Numbers

| | |
|---|---|
| Country code | ☏976 |
| Directory assistance | ☏109 |
| Ambulance | ☏103 |
| Police | ☏102 |
| Immigration Office | ☏1882 |

## Exchange Rates

| Australia | A$1 | T1785 |
|---|---|---|
| Canada | C$1 | T1778 |
| China | Y1 | T344 |
| Euro zone | €1 | T2636 |
| Japan | ¥100 | T21 |
| New Zealand | NZ$1 | T1710 |
| Russia | ₽1 | T39.8 |
| UK | UK£1 | T3003 |
| USA | US$1 | T2357 |

For current exchange rates, see www.xe.com.

## Daily Costs
**Budget: Less than US$50**

➡ Dorm bed: US$6–14

➡ Double room at a guesthouse: US$20–45

➡ Countryside camping: free

➡ Meal at a simple restaurant: US$3–6

➡ A 650km bus ride: US$18

### Midrange: US$50–140

➡ Double room at a standard hotel: US$30–70

➡ Midrange ger camp with room and board: US$45–65

➡ Meal at a restaurant in Ulaanbaatar: US$7–14

➡ Jeep hire with driver per day (without fuel): US$60–80

### Top End: More than US$140

➡ Top-end hotel or ger camp (only found in a few areas): from US$100

➡ Meal at a fancy restaurant: US$15–30

➡ Horse trek with professional outfitter per day: US$100–200

➡ Land Cruiser with driver per day (without fuel): from US$150

## Opening Hours

Operating hours in Ulaanbaatar are generally consistent, but are more loosely followed in the countryside. For more see information on Opening Hours in Directory chapter (p248).

## Arriving in Mongolia

**Chinggis Khaan airport (UB)** A desk situated beside baggage pick-up can organise taxis to downtown for T20,000. Private taxis usually overcharge foreigners. Alternatively, organise a pick-up through your guesthouse or hotel.

**New Ulaanbaatar International Airport** When it opens in 2018, shuttle buses should connect to downtown.

**Ulaanbaatar train station** The station is located close to the city centre – from here you can catch a bus or walk. It's best to organise a pick-up with your hotel or guesthouse. A taxi should cost US$3 to US$6 to most downtown areas.

## Getting Around

Public transport in Mongolia is slow, and destinations are limited to cities and towns. Hire a guide and driver to go further afield. Book tours several weeks prior to arrival. Occasional outbreaks of the plague and foot-and-mouth disease can quarantine areas and affect travel plans.

**Train** Useful for getting in and out of the country, unnecessary for domestic travel. One exception is for a side trip to Sainshand (for Khamaryn Monastery). Local trains are also good for a trip to Zamyn-Üüd for travellers heading to the Chinese border.

**Car** The main way to get around the countryside. Hiring a car and driver is actually cheaper than hiring a car without a driver. Drive on the right. A 4WD is essential for most destinations outside UB.

**Bus** The provincial capitals are accessible by bus and services run daily to most cities. Connections to the western aimags are less regular.

## What3words

In 2016 the Mongolian postal service adopted the What3words (https://what3words.com) address system. The What3words app identifies 3m x 3m squares across the planet with a unique three word address. This navigation system is particularly useful in Mongolia, where many businesses (such as ger camps) don't have a street address. The What3words are presented using the following icon: ///

To use: download the what3words app and enter the three words (found in a practicalities string in this guidebook) into the app and the location will appear on your device. The system even works offline.

For much more on **getting around**, see p260

# If You Like...

## Hiking

Mongolians are increasingly interested in hiking, and trails south of Ulaanbaatar are busy on weekends.

**Renchinlkhumbe Trail** One of the best multiday hikes in the country goes from the gorgeous shores of Khövsgöl Nuur over the mountains to the quaint village of Renchinlkhumbe. (p144)

**Bogdkhan Uul** For a long day hike or an overnight walk, start at Mandshir Khiid and walk over the mountain to Ulaanbaatar. (p91)

**Gorkhi-Terelj National Park** The main valley in the park is crowded with ger camps but hike over a mountain or two and you'll be in total isolation. (p95)

**Burkhan Khalduun** Foreigners are not allowed to climb up the actual peak, but a new 'observation route' will take you up a nearby mountain. (p152)

**Otgon Tenger Uul Strictly Protected Area** The locals don't want you climbing this mountain (it's sacred) but it's perfectly OK to hike around its base. (p214)

**Altai Tavan Bogd National Park** This park has a lot of varied terrain to tackle. You can hike along the side of the glacier at Tavan Bogd, or go down to the lake area for a trek around Khoton Nuur. (p198)

## Monasteries

**Gandan Khiid** The cultural and religious highlight of Ulaanbaatar. The incredible Migjid Janraisig statue looms 26m over the pious visitors below. (p64)

**Amarbayasgalant Khiid** Set in a wide valley, this magnificent complex has whiled away the centuries in almost complete obscurity. Camp by its walls and you'll have it almost to yourself. (p125)

**Baldan Baraivun Khiid** Lost in the wilderness of Khentii aimag, this remote, ruined monastery was once one of the largest in the country. (p154)

**Khamaryn Khiid** The home monastery of Danzan Ravjaa, a poet-monk who established Mongolia's first theatre here in the mid-19th century. (p174)

**Tövkhön Khiid** Recently revived, this former workshop of Zanabazar receives crowds of visitors who march uphill to discover this spiritual nook. (p112)

**Aglag Khiid** Recently built (in 2014), this monastery, located in a pretty pine forest 100km from Ulaanbaatar, was created by master Buddhist artist G. Purevbat. (p100)

## Spotting Wildlife

**Ikh Nartiin Chuluu Nature Reserve** One of the best places in the country to spot wildlife in its natural habitat, including argali sheep and ibexes. (p175)

**Mongol Daguur B Strictly Protected Area** Excellent place for ornithologists hoping to spot a white-napped crane. (p156)

## CLUBBING

**Ulaanbaatar** (p75) has surprisingly good clubs, with everything from jam-packed mini-clubs to massive event halls. The home-grown hip-hop scene features local DJs, rappers and folk-rock fusion bands. Special events are sometimes organised, including salsa nights and fashion shows. The locals are friendly and may invite you to their table to share a beer or something harder; just take care not to overdo it as some places can be a bit rough. Dress codes sometimes apply, so clean up as best as possible after a trek in the wilderness.

**Khustain National Park** Easily accessible from Ulaanbaatar, this is the place to visit for sightings of the *takhi* (Przewalski's horse). (p101)

**Khövsgöl Nuur National Park** Inhabited by moose, bear, argali sheep, wolves and several hundred species of bird. (p135)

## The Obscure

A lot of strange stuff happens in Mongolia. One day you're strumming a guitar in the shadow of John Lennon, the next day you're feasting on sheep-head stew. Keep your itinerary loose and expect the unexpected.

**Techie nomads** From the outside, the simple gers in far-flung corners of the steppe may appear oh-so-12th-century, but inside the 21st century is all too apparent, as weather-beaten nomads text, tweet, surf and maybe fling an angry bird or two on their mobile devices. (p233)

**Camel beauty pageants** How the judges determine a winner, we don't know. These happen as part of camel festivals held in late winter near Ulaanbaatar (p54) and the Gobi. (p179)

**Khar Temis** Dig your toes in the sand and listen to the seagulls caw at this oddball beach located 2000km from any ocean. (p211)

**Barefoot Paul McCartney** The bewildering monument to the Fab Four in Ulaanbaatar is just a few years old but has already become a local landmark. Paul's bare feet are a tribute to the cover of *Abbey Road*. (p64)

**Sheep-head stew** The Mongolian experience isn't complete without trying the local delicacy – boiled sheep offal and eyeball. Try it at Mongolian restaurants in Ulaanbaatar, or at a countryside ger. When in Mongolia... (p74)

PLAN YOUR TRIP IF YOU LIKE...

**Top**: Gandan Khiid (p64)

**Bottom**: Ibex (p244)

# Month by Month

## January

Cold. Darn cold. Frozen-toes-and-eyelashes cold. Ulaanbaatar can suffer severe levels of air pollution and is best avoided. If properly prepared, this is a good time for short winter walks in Terelj.

## February

Icy temperatures across the country (typically -15°C during the day and -25°C at night), although skies are usually clear. Deep snows can block roads but driving over lakes and rivers is possible. Pollution still lingers in Ulaanbaatar.

### ⭐ Bulgan Camel Festival

This festival features camel polo, camel racing, traditional music and other camel games. (p179)

### ⭐ Nomadic Culture Festival

Traditional games and other events associated with nomadic culture held at the Secret History Ger Camp in Töv aimag.

### ⭐ Tsagaan Sar

The Lunar New Year. This is a good time to meet Mongolians and, if you're lucky, get invited to a family celebration. Note: this may occur in late January or early March.

### ⭐ Ulaanbaatar Winter Festival

The festival features ice ankle-bone shooting, a competition similar to curling, except with ankle-bones (of goats or sheep) replacing the blocks of Scottish granite. (p68)

### 🏃 Winter Sports

Long-distance ice skating and dog sledding are possible at Khövsgöl Nuur (p135) – check with tour companies – or try downhill skiing at Sky Resort (p68).

## March

March sees strong winds, subzero temperatures, snow and dust storms. You may get all four seasons in one day and the inclement weather often cancels flights. Melting snows will reveal a brown, harsh landscape. The long winter and lack of fodder will make livestock thin – a bad time for horse riding.

### ⭐ Khatgal Ice Festival

A celebration that includes ice skating, horse-sledding races, ice fishing and thickly dressed locals. It'll be bitterly cold but skies are usually clear. (p135)

### ⭐ Navrus

The Kazakh spring festival begins in Bayan-Ölgii on 22 March. Visit a family feast and watch traditional games and contests. (p200)

## April

April sees frequent dust storms and cold snaps, but warmer weather later in the month. If the winter has been severe, livestock will die off rapidly at this time, causing hardship for herders. Melting snow can cause flooding and vehicles are prone to falling through ice. Air pollution in Ulaanbaatar is mostly gone.

## May

The weather will be warming up this month and the tourist season will start tepidly as some ger camps open. Snowfalls may still occur, especially in the north. Central areas will see a rainstorm or two.

### 🏃 Ulaanbaatar Marathon

The citizens of Ulaanbaatar take over the streets on a car-free day that includes running races of various distance (5km to 42km) as well as a bike parade and other events. Might happen in June. More info at: www.ub-marathon.ub.gov.mn.

### 🎎 Yak Festival

Held in Gurvan Saikhan National Park in Ömnögov, this festival features yak racing and yak games.

## June

Temperatures will reach the mid to high 20s (Celsius), allowing for more comfortable travel conditions. The weather tends to be dry this month but an occasional rainstorm will bring relief to the parched grasslands.

### 🎎 Mongol Nomadic Naadam

Mini naadam for tourists, including horse riding, wrestling and archery, located near Khustain National Park. Check 'Nomadic Naadam' on Facebook for dates or check with a tour agent.

### ☆ Roaring Hooves Festival

Often held in a remote part of the country (but starting in Ulaanbaatar), this international music festival (www.roaringhooves.com) features artists from around the world.

## July

This is peak travel season. Weather is good although a heatwave usually hits around this time; temperatures in the Gobi can reach 35°C.

### 🏃 Fishing Season Starts

Fishing season kicks off on 15 July in Mongolia.

### 🎎 Altai Nomad Festival

This festival in the third weekend in July in Altai Tavan Bogd National Park features traditional Kazakh horse games like *kokbar* – tug of war with a goat. (p198)

### 🎎 Naadam

Mongolia's premier summer sports festival erupts in July. The date is fixed in Ulaanbaatar (11–12 July) but will change from year to year in other cities and towns. Good village naadams can be found at Dadal and Khatgal.

### 🏃 Sunrise to Sunset Ultramarathon

A 100km race (there's also a 42km segment for wimps) is held on the shores of Khövsgöl Nuur. Check www.ultramongolia.org. (p135)

## August

In terms of weather, this tends to be the best month in Mongolia. Temperatures are pleasant and there is enough rainfall to keep the dust down and turn the grasslands an electric green. On the downside, heavy rains can turn jeep tracks into mud pits, causing vehicles to get bogged.

### 🎎 Danshig Naadam

The annual Danshig Naadam and Tsam Dance Festival combines religious ceremonies and traditional naadam sports events, usually in the first week of August. It's held outside Ulaanbaatar at Khui Doloon Khudag.

### 🎎 Gongoriin Bombani Hural

Religious festival held at Amarbayasgalant Monastery. Bring your tent and camp in the fields with the other festival-goers. (p126)

### 🏃 Mongolia Bike Challenge

Event that brings together serious mountain bikers for a cycling rally (www.mongoliabikechallenge.com).

### ☆ Playtime

Two-day alternative music fest in Gachuurt. A great chance to meet Mongol music fans of all ages. Sometimes held late July. (p68)

## September

As summer comes to an end, expect changeable weather. Temperatures will still be fair, but you should bring a fleece layer and light jacket with you just in case. A cold snap may occur and you might even see a brief snowstorm.

### 🏃 Fishing

September is a great time for fishing. The weather is good and rivers are calm after the August rains.

### 🦅 Altai Kazakh Eagle Festival

One of several eagle festivals held in Bayan-Ölgii. This one is held in Sagsai in late September. (p197)

### 🏃 Gobi Marathon

Go for a 42km run in one of the world's most inhospitable deserts.

## October

October is cool and sees snow flurries up north but is still fine for travel, especially in the Gobi. By now most ger camps are closed, except for a few around Terelj.

### 🦅 Eagle Festival

The Eagle Festival in Bayan-Ölgii is an annual highlight. (p196)

### 🏃 Swan Migration

Visit Ganga Nuur in Sükhbaatar aimag to watch thousands of migrating swans. (p162)

## November

The mercury dips below zero and will continue to plummet. Despite the cold there are still a few visitors around – some take trips down to the Gobi where it's a touch warmer.

### 🦅 Chinggis Khaan's Birthday

Birthday celebrations for CK are held on the first day of the first winter month, usually early November but the date changes each year. It's an official bank holiday.

### 🦅 Eagle Hunting

November is a good time to visit Bayan-Ölgii and watch the eagle hunters in action.

## December

Brace yourself, the Mongolian winter is upon you. Sky Resort near Ulaanbaatar will open (good for beginning skiers). The air pollution in Ulaanbaatar can be unbearable.

### 🦅 New Year's Eve

Mongolians celebrate New Year's Eve enthusiastically, usually with lots of beer, vodka and fireworks.

# Itineraries

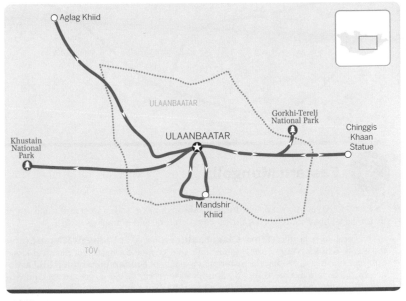

## Around Ulaanbaatar

Short trips from Ulaanbaatar can offer a taste of the countryside without having to invest too much time travelling along endless country roads.

From **Ulaanbaatar**, head to **Khustain National Park** for the night to watch the wild *takhi* horses. Back in UB, catch a ride to **Mandshir Khiid** in Töv aimag, from where you can hike back over the mountain to Ulaanbaatar. This can be done either as a full day trip or as an overnight hike.

Next, head east to **Gorkhi-Terelj National Park**. There are a number of activity options here, including mountain biking, horse riding, rock climbing, hiking and river rafting. Here you can also taste local cheese and house-smoked meats prepared by Bert, the Dutch cheesemaker.

If you have your own vehicle, push on a little further east to see the enormous **Chinggis Khaan Statue** at Tsonjin Boldog.

Back in Ulaanbaatar, leave one day for visiting the **National Museum of Mongolia**, **Gandan Khiid** and the **Winter Palace of the Bogd Khan**. If you have time for one more day trip, visit **Aglag Khiid**, located 100km north of Ulaanbaatar.

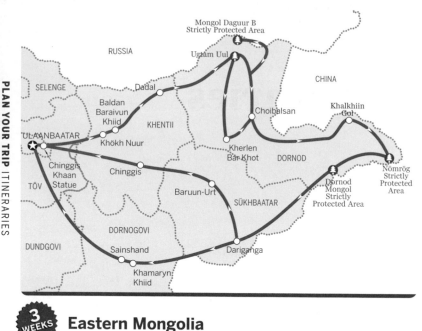

## 3 WEEKS Eastern Mongolia

Eastern Mongolia offers a delightful romp through grasslands, forest and some unique historical sights. Best of all, it's almost completely devoid of tourists.

In a hired jeep, head east from **Ulaanbaatar** and pass the **Chinggis Khaan Statue** on the way to **Khökh Nuur,** a pretty alpine lake that saw the coronation of the great khaan. Continue northeast, visiting the restored monastery of **Baldan Baraivun Khiid** and nearby sights as you travel through Khentii's scenic countryside. There are ger camps all along this route where you can stop for horse-riding trips in the mountains. Take a break in **Dadal,** a handsome village with horse-trekking options and an excellent naadam.

Following the Ulz Gol further east, you'll pass pretty Buriat villages and nature reserves including **Ugtam Uul**. If you're interested in meeting a shaman you may be fortunate enough to get the opportunity by asking around in this area. It's possible to continue northeast towards Chuluunkhoroot to visit **Mongol Daguur B Strictly Protected Area**, a protected area for wader birds. From northern Dornod, sweep south towards **Choibalsan**; some routes go via the ancient ruins at **Kherlen Bar Khot**.

The adventurous can push further east across the empty steppes to **Khalkhiin Gol**, a remote landscape of lakes, rivers, wildlife and historical sights. Highlights include a giant Buddha statue carved into a hillside and numerous WWII memorials.

You'll need another couple of days to visit the lush **Nömrög Strictly Protected Area**. From Nömrög, tackle the rough terrain in **Dornod Mongol Strictly Protected Area** to spot some truly massive herds of gazelles.

The **Dariganga** region, with its sand dunes, cinder cones and scattered stone statues, requires two or three days. Horse trekking is possible here. If you're in the area in early October, you'll catch the large migration of swans at Ganga Nuur.

Return to Ulaanbaatar via **Baruun-Urt** and **Chinggis**, or travel via **Sainshand** for a taste of the Gobi and a visit to **Khamaryn Khiid** monastery.

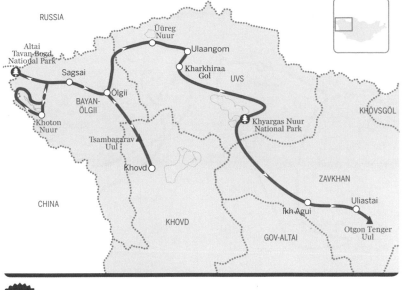

## Western Mongolia

The western aimags offer adventurous travel and exploration. Adrenalin junkies can break out the mountain-biking, kayaking or mountaineering gear.

Start with a flight to **Khovd** or **Ölgii**, hire a vehicle and motor out to the beautiful pastures and valleys around **Tsambagarav Uul**. You'll find eagle hunters and opportunities for white-water rafting. You could easily spend a couple of days here before moving on to Ölgii, a great place to recharge your batteries.

Heading west from Ölgii, spend three to four days around **Altai Tavan Bogd National Park**. With proper equipment and permits it's even possible to scale Mongolia's highest peak, the 4374m Tavan Bogd, though a visit to the base camp and glacier is more feasible. Malchin Peak is also climbable with help from local guides. With more time, consider doing a horse trek around **Khoton Nuur**. Around the area you'll spot interesting *balbal* (stone men) rock carvings and ancient burial mounds.

On the way to or from Tavan Bogd, stop in at **Sagsai**, an authentic Kazakh village that offers a taste of life in the Wild West. A few families here keep eagles and it may be possible to meet them. From Sagsai it's even possible to go rafting back to Ölgii. The best time to make this journey is in late September or early October, which gives you the chance to watch the spectacular Eagle Festival in Ölgii or Sagsai.

From Ölgii, the main road winds northeast, passing **Üüreg Nuur**, another gorgeous camping spot, en route to **Ulaangom**. Allow a week for trekking around **Kharkhiraa Gol**. An experienced driver can get you from Ulaangom to Uliastai, visiting **Khyargas Nuur National Park** and **Ikh Agui** en route. If you arrive at Khyargas Nuur before mid-September, you'll have a chance to see hundreds of squawking cormorants at Khetsuu Khad.

From **Uliastai** you can take a horse-riding or hiking trip to **Otgon Tenger Uul**. Flights from Uliastai are few and usually booked out so you may need to bus it back to Ulaanbaatar via Tosontsengel and Arkhangai.

 **The Big Loop**

 **Northern Mongolia**

The big loop combines desert and steppe scenery, and some of the country's top historical sites. It's a great area for horse or camel treks, dune walking and spotting wildlife.

From **Ulaanbaatar**, head south to the eerie rock formations of **Baga Gazryn Chuluu** and the ruined castle at **Süm Khökh Burd**.

At least three days are needed to explore Ömnögov: check out the spectacular ice canyon at **Yolyn Am**, the massive sand dunes at **Khongoryn Els** and the dinosaur quarry at **Bayanzag**. From here, go north to the ruined desert monastery of **Ongiin Khiid**, a perfect place to organise a camel trek.

Leaving the Gobi, your first stop is **Erdene Zuu Khiid**, the country's oldest monastery. Head west up the Orkhon valley to **Tövkhön Khiid**, a monastery in pine forest, and then on to the **Orkhon Khürkhree**. The waterfall is the perfect place to unwind after a long trip to the Gobi, so spend a couple of nights here (and wash away the Gobi dust in the falls).

On your way back to Ulaanbaatar, spend a night at **Khustain National Park**.

Mongolia's northern aimags blend Siberia and steppe, a vast region of rolling grassland, mountains and lakes. Experiences include encounters with the native Shamanic faith and reindeer herders.

Start week one by flying from **Ulaanbaatar** to **Mörön**. Hire a vehicle in Mörön and drive to **Tsagaannuur**. Drop into the TCVC here and hire a guide and horses to get you out to the taiga and **Tsaatan camps**. Plan for a week of travel in the area.

In week two, get a lift to **Renchinlkhumbe** and then trek to the shores of **Khövsgöl Nuur**. Walk down the lakeshore until you reach **Jankhai**. Spend a few days relaxing and then continue to **Khatgal**.

From Khatgal, the adventurous will make their way all the way up to **Khankh** on the northern shore of the lake. Alternatively, there are some gorgeous areas east of the lake in the **Chandman-Öndör area**. You'll need another week to explore this region.

The trip back to Ulaanbaatar runs via the pleasant aimag capital of **Bulgan**. After passing through **Erdenet**, make a short detour to visit the magnificent **Amarbayasgalant Khiid**.

Top: Yolyn Am valley
(p180)
Bottom: Aglag Khiid
(p100)

## Plan Your Trip
# Trans-Mongolian Railway

The Trans-Mongolian Railway is part of the vast network of track that links Běijīng and Moscow, a crucial piece of the world's longest continuous rail route. For rail enthusiasts, a journey on the Trans-Siberian is the railway equivalent of climbing Mt Everest.

## Trip Preparation

### Best Pretrip Movie
*Transsiberian* (2008) is a Hollywood thriller staring Woody Harrelson and Ben Kingsley. The film even includes a cameo by a Lonely Planet guidebook.

### Best Ways to Meet the Locals
Pack Chinese-, Mongolian- and Russian-language phrasebooks to meet and greet with the locals. Card or chess games can pass the time, or break out a stash of food and booze to share with new-found friends. Head to shop.lonelyplanet.com to purchase a downloadable PDF of Lonely Planet's Chinese or Russian phrasebooks.

### Best Online Tool
Google has uploaded the entire Moscow to Vladivostok rail journey online. It even comes with a soundtrack of Russian books and music. Go to www.google.ru/intl/ru/landing/transsib/en.html.

### By the Numbers
The gauge of the Mongolian railway is 5ft wide, as it is in Russia. This is slightly wider than the 4ft 8.5in used in most other parts of the world (including China). Mongolia has 1810km of railway track (ranking it 76th in the world).

## History of the Trans-Mongolian Railway

The idea of building a rail route from Moscow to the Pacific Ocean was hatched in the mid-19th century. This was the age of imperialism, when the powers of Europe were expanding across continents in a race to gobble up as much land and as many resources as possible. In 1916, after 25 years of planning and building, the final link along the Moscow–Vladivostok route was complete. The section across Mongolia, on the other hand, was only completed in 1956.

## Line Names

The names of the rail lines can be a bit confusing.

➡ The Trans-Mongolian Railway goes from Běijīng through Ulaanbaatar (UB) and on to a junction called Zaudinsky, near Ulan Ude in Russia, where it meets the Trans-Siberian line and continues on to Moscow.

➡ The Trans-Siberian Railway runs between Moscow and the eastern Siberian port of Vladivostok – this route does not go through either China or Mongolia.

➡ The Trans-Manchurian Railway crosses the Russia–China border at Zabaikalsk-Mǎnzhōulǐ, also completely bypassing Mongolia.

# General Train Information

**Station vendors** At the stations in Mongolia and Russia, there may be someone on the platform selling basic food (dumplings, soft drinks, snacks and fruit). Vendors in China offer a better variety of foods.

**Restaurant cars** The restaurant cars on the Russian and Chinese trains have decent food and drinks on offer for around US$3 to US$5.

**Toilets** Remember that toilets are normally locked whenever the train is pulled into a station and for five minutes before and after.

**Showers** Showers are only available in the deluxe carriages. In 2nd and 1st class, there is a washroom and toilet at the end of each carriage – which gets filthier as the trip progresses.

**Charging devices** Keeping your electronic devices charged can be a challenge as outlets are limited. The attendant's cabin usually has a decent outlet and you can ask to use it.

**Security** The trains are reasonably safe but it's still a good idea to watch your bags closely. For added safety, lock your cabins from inside and make use of the security clip on the upper left-hand part of the door. The clip can be flipped open from the outside with a knife, but not if you stuff the hole with paper.

**Non-Ulaanbaatar stops** If you want to get off or on the Trans-Mongolian at Sükhbaatar, Darkhan or Sainshand, you'll still have to pay the full Ulaanbaatar fare. If you're not actually getting *on* the train in Ulaanbaatar, you should arrange for someone (your guesthouse manager, your guide or a friend) to let the attendant know that you'll be boarding the train at a later stop to ensure your seat is not taken.

**Arrive early** Tickets list the train's departure time. Get to the station at least 20 minutes before *arrival* to allow enough time to find the platform and struggle on board, as the train only stops in Ulaanbaatar for about 30 minutes.

**Timetable** A timetable of stops hangs inside the carriage but times can shift so it's wise to double-check departure times with the *provodnista* (on-board attendant) if you get off at a station to stretch your legs.

**Bringing a bike** In Běijīng, take the bike to the train station one day prior to departure. No box is needed, they just wheel it onto a cargo car. If you are in Ulaanbaatar, bring your bike to the train station two days prior to departure with the bike packed in a box. A cargo fee of around T3000 is usually charged.

**MOVING ON?**

For full coverage on the Trans-Mongolian, Trans-Siberian and Trans-Manchurian routes, head to shop.lonelyplanet.com to purchase a downloadable PDF of Lonely Planet's *Trans-Siberian Railway* guide.

# What to Bring

**Currency** It is handy to have some US dollars in small denominations to buy meals and drinks on the train, and to exchange for the local currency so you can buy things at the train stations. It's also a good idea to buy some Russian roubles or Chinese yuan at a bank or licensed money changer in UB before you leave Mongolia.

**Food** Stock up on bread, cheese, salami, pickles and fruit before you depart, and bring some bottled water and juice. A small samovar at the end of each carriage provides constant boiling water, a godsend for making tea and coffee, as well as instant meals of packet noodles or soup.

**Sleeping-bag liner** Train cars are heated in winter and sheets and blankets are provided so a sleeping-bag is not necessary. However, it's a good idea to bring along a sleeping bag liner, which offers a little added comfort and warmth.

**Other essential items** Thongs (flip flops) or slippers, torch (flashlight), toiletries, a mug or coffee tumbler, toilet paper, a jumper (sweater), a washcloth (or towel), some plastic cutlery, plenty of reading material, a deck of cards (or travel chess set) and comfortable long pants. Tracksuits are a must for blending in with the locals.

**Baggage allowance** On Chinese international trains it's 35kg (20kg on domestic trains). On all Russian trains it's 36kg. You can store your luggage inside the base of a bottom bunk (you can lift up the bunk) or in the space above the door.

# Classes

With a few exceptions, all international trains have two or three classes. The names and standards of the classes depend on whether it is a Mongolian, Russian or Chinese train. Smoking is not allowed in any of the cabins but many travellers will smoke at the ends of the train cars.

# Trans-Mongolian Railway

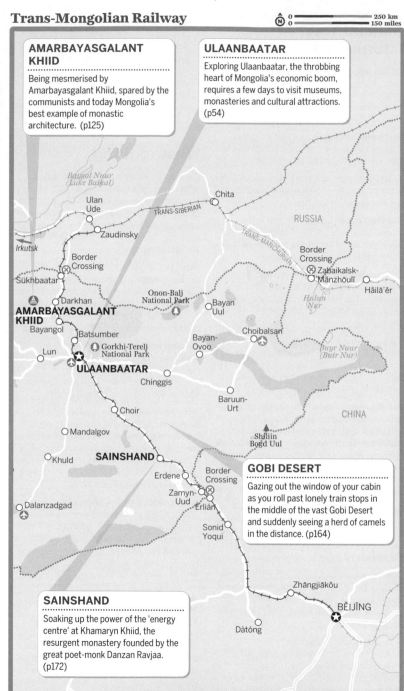

**AMARBAYASGALANT KHIID**

Being mesmerised by Amarbayasgalant Khiid, spared by the communists and today Mongolia's best example of monastic architecture. (p125)

**ULAANBAATAR**

Exploring Ulaanbaatar, the throbbing heart of Mongolia's economic boom, requires a few days to visit museums, monasteries and cultural attractions. (p54)

**GOBI DESERT**

Gazing out the window of your cabin as you roll past lonely train stops in the middle of the vast Gobi Desert and suddenly seeing a herd of camels in the distance. (p164)

**SAINSHAND**

Soaking up the power of the 'energy centre' at Khamaryn Khiid, the resurgent monastery founded by the great poet-monk Danzan Ravjaa. (p172)

0 — 250 km
0 — 150 miles

**Second class** On the Russian (and Mongolian) trains, most travellers travel in 2nd class – printed on tickets and timetables as '1/4' and known as 'hard sleeper', 'coupé', or *kupeynyy* in Russian. These are small, but perfectly comfortable, four-person compartments with four bunk-style beds and a fold-down table.

**First class** Sometimes called a 'soft sleeper', or *myagkiy* in Russian, this is printed as '2/4'. It has softer beds but hardly any more space than a Russian 2nd-class compartment and is not worth the considerably higher fare charged.

**Deluxe class** The real luxury (and expense) comes with Chinese deluxe class (printed as '1/2'): it involves roomy, two-berth compartments with a sofa, and a shower cubicle shared with the adjacent compartment. The deluxe class on Russian trains (slightly cheaper than the Chinese deluxe) has two bunks but is not much different in size from 2nd class and has no showers.

---

# Customs & Immigration

There are delays of three to six hours at both the China–Mongolia and Russia–Mongolia borders, usually at night. The whole process is not difficult or a hassle, just annoying because they keep interrupting your sleep. Your passport will be taken for inspection and stamping. When it is returned, inspect it closely – sometimes they make errors such as cancelling your return visa for China. Foreigners generally sail through customs without having their bags opened, which is one reason people on the train may approach you and ask if you'll carry some of their luggage across the border – *this is not a good idea*. During stops, you can alight and wander around the station, which is just as well because the toilets on the train are locked during the inspection procedure.

---

# Tickets

**Breaking the journey** The only practical way to break a journey is to buy separate tickets. For example, if you're travelling Moscow–Běijīng and want to stop in Irkutsk and Ulaanbaatar, it's best to take a Russian domestic train to Irkutsk and then pick up the twice-weekly K23/24 between Ulaanbaatar and Běijīng.

**Book early** The international trains, especially the Trans-Mongolian Railway, are popular, so it's often

---

### BOGIES

Don't be concerned if you get off at Èrlián (on the Chinese side of the border) and the train disappears from the platform. About an hour is spent changing the bogies (wheel assemblies) because the Russians (and, therefore, the Mongolians) and the Chinese use different railway gauges. Train buffs may want to see the bogie-changing operation. Stay on the train after it disgorges passengers in Èrlián. The train then pulls into a large shed about 1km from the station. You can watch the whole operation from the window of your train car.

---

hard to book this trip except during winter. Try to plan ahead and book as early as possible.

**Leaving from UB** If you are in Ulaanbaatar and want to go to Irkutsk, Běijīng or Moscow, avoid going on the Běijīng–Moscow or Moscow–Běijīng trains; use trains which *originate* in UB. In UB, you cannot buy tickets in advance for the Běijīng–Moscow or Moscow–Běijīng trains, because staff won't know how many people are already on the train. For these trains, you can only buy a ticket the day before departure. Get to the ticket office early and join the Mongolian scramble for tickets. With that said, it's worth touching base with **Mongolia Train Tickets** (☑8880 6963; www.mongoliatraintickets.com) which has a good track record in securing Trans-Mongolian tickets in UB to Beijing or Moscow.

## Booking Agents

Overseas branches of **China International Travel Service** (www.cits.net) can often book train tickets from Běijīng to Ulaanbaatar. However, the best company for Trans-Siberian rail tickets is Hong Kong–based **Monkey Shrine** (www.monkeyshrine.com). Or, try the following places:

**Gateway Travel** (www.russian-gateway.com.au)

**Intourist** (www.intourist.com)

**Lernidee Reisen** (www.lernidee-reisen.de)

**Mir Corporation** (www.mircorp.com)

**Regent Holidays** (www.regent-holidays.co.uk)

**The Russian Experience** (www.trans-siberian.co.uk)

**Mongolia Train Tickets** (www.mongoliatraintickets.com)

# Plan Your Trip

# Outdoor Activities

Mongolia is a gigantic outdoor park. With scattered settlements, few roads and immense areas of steppe, mountain and forest, the entire country beckons the outdoor enthusiast. There are excellent opportunities for hiking, fishing and long-distance cycling, and any journey in Mongolia always includes a bit of horse riding.

## Top Activities

### Most Popular Activity

Mongolians practically invented horse riding, making it one of the most iconic activities you can do here. Extended horse treks are best made in Arkhangai, Khövsgöl and Khentii, while Terelj is good for day trips.

### Best Off-Season Activity

Visit Mongolia in winter and you can try your hand at dog sledding. French tour guide Joel Rauzy (p40) harnesses up teams of strong huskies to pull your sled through the Mongolian wilderness.

### Best Area for Adventure

The varied terrain of Khövsgöl is ideal for horse riding and mountain biking. This is also one of the premier areas for fishing and kayaking. For mountaineering try Uvs or Bayan-Ölgii.

### Best Adventure near Ulaanbaatar

A nice option is a float down the Tuul Gol on an inflatable kayak or canoe. Several tour operators can facilitate this. Hiking is possible on Bogdkhan Uul.

## Planning Your Trip

Almost anywhere you go in Mongolia involves some form of off-road adventure. However, only a few areas (for example Khövsgöl Nuur, Terkhiin Tsagaan Nuur and Gorkhi-Terelj National Park) are set up to handle independent travellers. Signing up with a tour group, on the other hand, gives you instant logistical help. Tour agencies can act like mobile support centres, using vans, trucks and helicopters to shuttle clients and their gear around. Independent travellers hoping to explore remote areas of the country will need to be completely self-sufficient, although access to supplies is improving.

## When to Go

Summer offers the best weather for horse riding, hiking and mountain biking but winter sports are also possible – think ice fishing, dog sledding and long-distance ice skating. Independent travellers arriving in summer will have a good chance to link up with others to share costs.

### Best Times

**July and August** Weather is fair across the country and summer rains will bring life back to the pasturelands. This is an especially good time for horse trekking.

**September** This is perhaps the best month for fishing. It's also a great time for trekking in northern Mongolia where you can watch the leaves change colour.

**February** If you are considering a winter sport like cross-country skiing, February is a good time to do it. There will be a decent amount of snow cover by now and temperatures will be warming slightly by the day.

### Times to Avoid

**March and April** Spring weather is plagued by strong winds and dust storms. This is not a good time for horse trekking as animals move about after the long winter. The landscape – bare, brown earth – is at its least photogenic.

**December and January** These are the coldest months of the year and you'll get the least amount of daylight. Temperatures can plummet to -35°C at this time.

# Bird-Watching

Mongolia is rich in bird life and the Ministry of Environment & Tourism has identified this activity as a priority for development. Start your online research with the **Mongolia Ornithological Society** (☑8818 0148; www.mos.mn). These are the best places to get out your binoculars and telephoto lens:

**Ganga Nuur** (p162) Migratory swan.

**Khar Us Nuur and Khar Nuur** (p205, p206) Goose, wood grouse, relict gull and migratory pelican.

**Khyargas Nuur and Airag Nuur** (p211) Migratory cormorant and pelican.

**Sangiin Dalai Nuur** (p168) Mongolian lark, eagle, goose and swan.

**Uvs Nuur** (p209) Spoonbill, crane and gull.

# Cycle Touring

For cyclists, Mongolia is a country with lots of open spaces and sparse traffic, although conditions can be rough in some areas. Paved roads now reach most cities, while roads to smaller towns mainly consist of jeep trails so the going can be slow. Cycle tourists need to be totally self-sufficient in terms of tools and spare parts. Other factors include washed-out bridges, fierce dogs, trails that disappear into rivers or marshland and, in late summer, heavy rain and mud. Locals will be pleasantly intrigued by your bike and you'll have lots of inquiries to test it out, but don't forget to show them how to use the brakes! Specialist tour operators include Mongolia Expeditions (p39).

## Routes

The following trips require several days. They can be made solo provided you are equipped with a tent, a sleeping bag, food and spare parts. Another option is to use vehicle support: hire a jeep and driver to take you out to the best biking areas and keep all your gear in the vehicle while you ride unhindered. Gobi areas, due to their lack of water and facilities, are places to avoid.

---

### SAFE-CYCLING TIPS

➡ Dogs can be ferocious and will chase you away from gers. If you stop and hold your ground they will back off; it helps to pick up a rock. The faster you cycle away, the more they want to chase you.

➡ Cyclists usually follow river valleys. However, in Mongolia it's often better to go over the mountains. Roads along rivers are usually sandy or consist of loose stones that make riding difficult.

➡ Most cyclists consider the best trip to be a cross-country adventure but in Mongolia (where there are vast areas of nothingness) consider focusing on one small area and doing a loop. There are great routes to explore in Khövsgöl and Bayan-Ölgii aimags.

➡ Bring all the spare parts you may need, including brake pads, cables and inner tubes. Spare parts are hard to find in Mongolia, but you could try the Seven Summits (p252) or **Cycling World** (☑7711 0444; www.cyclingworld.mn; Khan-uul District, Tuul River St 79, ⊞sharper.clusters.fluffed; ◷10am-7pm), both in Ulaanbaatar.

**Chinggis Khaan Trail** This trail in northern Khentii offers plenty of cultural heritage and nice riding terrain. Get a ride from Ulaanbaatar to Tsenkhermandal in Khentii aimag, then cycle north to Khökh Nuur, in the Khentii Mountains. Continue northwest to Khangil Nuur, Baldan Baraivun monastery, Öglögchiin Kherem, Bat-shireet, Binder and, finally, Dadal. This trip takes four to six days.

**Khövsgöl aimag** A nice route leads south from Mörön to Tariat in Arkhangai, via the towns of Shine-Ider, Galt and Jargalant. The more popular route is from Mörön up to Khatgal and then along either side of Khövsgöl Nuur. The slightly more adventurous could cycle in the spectacular Chandman-Öndör area.

**Ölgii to Ulaanbaatar** This mammoth 1450km expedition will take three or four weeks. In summer, the prevailing winds in Mongolia travel from west to east, which means that you'll enjoy tailwinds if you start in Ölgii and end in Ulaanbaatar. The northern route, via either Mörön or Tosontsengel, is more interesting than the southern Gobi route.

# Fishing

With Mongolia's large number of lakes *(nuur)* and rivers *(gol)*, and a sparse population that generally prefers red meat, the fish are just waiting to be caught. Several shops in Ulaanbaatar sell fishing equipment, including **Ayanchin Outfitters** (Map p58; ☑11-319 211; www.ayanchin.mn; Seoul St 21, *///* reporting.kneeled.limit; ⊙10am-8pm Mon-Sat, to 7pm Sun).

## Lake Fishing

The season is mid-June to late September. The best places to dangle your lines are Khövsgöl Nuur (p135) for grayling and lenok, and **Terkhiin Tsagaan Nuur** (Great White Lake; winadequately.dissections.bone-less), which has a lot of pike. For the truly intrepid, visit either lake in winter for some hard-core ice fishing.

## River Fishing

Serious anglers will want to try out Mongolia's rivers. The major target is taimen, an enormous salmonoid that spends its leisure time hunting down unfortunate rodents that fall in the rivers. These monsters can reach 1.5m in length, weigh 50kg and live for 50 years. Taimen are a sensitive species and the authorities have taken care to protect them from habitat degradation and poaching. To avoid any problems, you must fish for taimen with a reputable outfitter. Catch and release is mandatory, using only single, barbless hooks (never use treble hooks). Outfitters run fishing trips on the Ider, Chuluut, Selenge, Orkhon, Onon and Delgermörön rivers.

## Permits

For national parks, you can get a fishing permit from the park office. Permits are valid for two days or 10 fish, whichever comes first. While it's relatively easy to get a fishing permit in a national park, buying one for other areas is much more difficult. Anglers must have a special permit authorised by the **Ministry of Nature and Tourism** (Map p58; ☑51-261 966, 51-266 171; www.mne.mn; United Nations St 5/2, Government Bldg II, Ulaanbaatar, wdampen.carbonate.doped), which costs US$330 a week. As a tourist you cannot get one on your own – you must get one through a tour operator (and only a few operators qualify to receive them). Before signing up, make sure your outfitter has the necessary permits; some take the risk of fishing illegally, which can get you in big trouble if you're caught.

## Fishing Operators

The per-person cost for a 10-day package trip runs at least US$5000, more if you take a Cessna flight direct to the camps from UB. Mongolia River Outfitters (www.mongoliarivers.com) is a responsible fly-fishing tour operator, as is Sweetwater Travel (www.sweetwatertravel.com).

# Hiking

A few marked hiking trails have been set up on Bogdkhan Uul, near Ulaanbaatar. In other areas of the country, hikers need to plan their own routes and have good navigational skills (plus maps, GPS and a compass). Pay any fees and procure any permits that are required by local authorities. Be aware of local laws, regulations and etiquette relating to wildlife and the environment. Be prepared to encounter mosquitoes and midges; the situation is at its worst during spring and early summer, with the marshy lakes and canyons in the western deserts the most troublesome areas.

**Western Mongolia** Prime hiking areas include Altai Tavan Bogd National Park, around Khoton Nuur and between the lakes and Tavan Bogd. In Uvs aimag try the Kharkhiraa and Türgen Uuls, which are good for three to seven days of backcountry hiking.

**Northern Mongolia** There is great hiking in the Khövsgöl Nuur area.

**Central Mongolia** Try the Naiman Nuur area. Nomadic Journeys (p40) runs trips here using yaks as pack animals.

**Near Ulaanbaatar** You can explore the valleys north of Terelj or hike over Bogdkhan Uul.

# Horse & Camel Trekking

Horse treks range from easy day trips with guides to multiweek solo adventures. Inexperienced riders should begin with the former, organising initial rides through a ger camp or tour operator.

**Cost** The prettiest, most accessible places to try are the camps at Terelj and Khövsgöl Nuur, where you can normally hire a horse for around T25,000 a day. Per-hour costs are around T10,000. Note that you will also have to cover the cost of your guide, if you have one. Horse hire in a less-touristy area will run around T20,000 per day.

**Equipment** If you need to buy a saddle or other equipment, the best place is the Naran Tuul Market (p81) in UB.

**Lessons** Even the most experienced riders will benefit from a lesson on how to deal with a Mongolian horse. The local breed is short, stocky and half-wild; Mongolian horsemen can provide instruction on saddling, hobbling and caring for your horse. You'll also get tips on the best places in which to ride and where to purchase saddles and other equipment. Try Stepperiders (p94) in Töv aimag.

## ZEN & THE ART OF HORSE MAINTENANCE

➡ Mongolians swap horses readily, so there's no need to be stuck with a horse you don't like, or which doesn't like you, except perhaps in April and May, when all animals are weak after the long winter and before fresh spring plants have made their way through the melting snows. The best time for riding is in the summer (June to September).

➡ Mount a horse (or camel) only from the left. They have been trained to accept human approach from that side, and may rear if approached the wrong way.

➡ The Mongolians use the phrase 'chu!' to make their horses go. Worryingly, there is no word for 'stop'.

➡ If you are considering a multiday horse trip, remember that horses attract all kinds of flies.

➡ A saddle, bridle, halter and hobble can all be bought at the Naran Tuul Market (p81) in Ulaanbaatar. An English hybrid saddle can be bought for around T150,000, packsaddles for half that. Riders with long legs might consider bringing narrow stirrup leathers from home.

➡ Buying a horse is best done with the help of a Mongolian friend. A decent-quality horse will run to between T500,000 and T1 million. Herders will be reluctant to sell their best (ie quiet and calm) horses and may try to sell you a nag. Buyer beware. Test ride any horse you are considering and try loading up potential pack horses to make sure they don't crumple under the weight.

➡ The most important thing to consider when planning a trip is where to get water. Following a river is a good idea, or you can ask around for a well, though these can be dry. As a rule of thumb, where there are animals and people, you'll find water.

## Treks

Of the dozens of possible horse treks, several are popular and not difficult to arrange.

➡ The most popular horse-trekking area is Khövsgöl Nuur, largely because there is such a good network of guides and available horses. Some travellers have horse-trekked from Terkhiin Tsagaan Nuur to Khövsgöl Nuur. By land (following the twisting river valleys) it's around 295km and takes at least two weeks by horse.

➡ Tsetserleg to Bayankhongor is a rugged wilderness trip that crosses a series of alpine passes.

➡ In the east, try the Binder area of Khentii aimag, which can include a ride to Dadal near the Siberian border.

➡ Closer to Ulaanbaatar, the areas of Terelj and Bogdkhan are both excellent if you don't have a lot of time.

➡ In western Mongolia there is great horse trekking around Otgon Tenger Uul; it can take six days to circle the mountain.

➡ In Altai Tavan Bogd National Park, try a horse trek around Khoton Nuur. There is also horse trekking around Tsast Uul and Tsambagarav Uul. Tour operators in Ölgii can help set something up, or just turn up in any nearby village and ask around for horses.

➡ Some of the ger camps at Ongiin Khiid can arrange one-hour camel rides. Multiday camel treks can be arranged at Bayanzag and Khongoryn Els for a minimum of T35,000 per camel per day. A trip between the two places takes about five days.

## Kayaking, Canoeing & Rafting

Mongolia's numerous lakes and rivers are often ideal for kayaking and rafting. There is little white water but, during the summer rains, rivers can flow at up to 9km/h. The best time for kayaking or rafting is July to September, after some decent rain. There is nothing stopping you from heading out on your own. Seven Summits (p252) rents inflatable kayaks and **Mongolia Canoeing** (☑11-685 503, 9982 6883; www.mongoliacanoeing.com) rents canoes.

➡ One of the most popular river trips is down the Tuul Gol, from the bridge at the entrance to Terelj back to Ulaanbaatar.

➡ There are more adventurous options that begin in Khövsgöl aimag. Boat or kayak trips on the Eg Gol can start at Khatgal.

➡ In Bayan-Ölgii it's possible to raft down the Khovd Gol from Khurgan Nuur, past Ölgii city and on to Myangad in Khovd aimag.

## Operators

Avoid cowboy outfitters that may not be qualified to run boating trips. Rafting and kayaking is organised along the Tuul Gol and Khovd Gol by agencies based in Ulaanbaatar, including Goyo Travel (p39) and Nomadic Journeys (p40). MS Guesthouse, Garage 24 and Bond Lake, all in Khatgal (p135), rent kayaks and may have rafts.

**Mongolia Canoeing** (☑9982 6883, 11-685 503; www.mongoliacanoeing.com) Runs trips on the Chuluut, Eg, Orkhon and Yeroo rivers. They also rent canoes if you want to mount your own expedition.

**Mongolia River Adventures** (MRA; ☑9950 1685; www.mongoliariveradventures.com) Run by experienced American river guides, MRA has trips in both western and central Mongolia, using both rafts and kayaks. Contact Pat Phillips.

# Mountaineering & Rock Climbing

Mongolia offers spectacular opportunities for mountain climbing. In the western aimags there are dozens of glaciers, and 30 to 40 permanently snow-capped mountains. You must have the necessary experience, be fully equipped and hire local guides. The best time to climb is July and August. Mongolia Expeditions (p39) is a leader in this area. There is also good potential for rock climbing in Mongolia – Wind of Mongolia (p40) can organise rock-climbing trips.

# Winter Sports

**Ice Skating** In winter you won't have to worry about falling through the ice, as many lakes and rivers freeze right down to the bottom. Many

## MONGOLIA'S HIGHEST PEAKS

**Tavan Bogd; 4374m** (p199) In Bayan-Ölgii, on the border of Mongolia, China and Russia. This mountain cluster is full of permanent and crevassed glaciers.

**Mönkh Khairkhan Uul; 4362m** (Мөнх Хайрхан Уул; Tavan Khumit; ⫟ symbolists. analyst.artiste; park entrance T3000) On the border of Bayan-Ölgii and Khovd aimags. You will need crampons, an ice axe and ropes.

**Tsambagarav Uul; 4208m** (p201) In Khovd; it is relatively easy to climb with crampons and an ice axe.

**Tsast Uul; 4193m** (p202) On the border of Bayan-Ölgii and Khovd aimags. It's accessible and the camping here is great.

**Sutai Uul; 4090m** (p188) On the border of Gov-Altai and Khovd aimags.

**Kharkhiraa Uul; 4037m** (p210) In Uvs; a great hiking area.

**Türgen Uul; 3965m** (p210) One of the most easily climbed with spectacular views; in Uvs.

**Otgon Tenger Uul; 3905m** (p214) Mongolia's holiest mountain, located in Zavkhan aimag. Its sacredness means that climbing is strictly prohibited.

**PLAN YOUR TRIP** OUTDOOR ACTIVITIES

Mongolians are keen ice-skaters – at least those who live near water, or in big cities with rinks. The National Amusement Park (p63) in Ulaanbaatar has ice-skating and skate hire.

**Long-distance skating** With proper planning, long-distance skating is possible on Khövsgöl Nuur (the tour operator will need to dig the toilet holes in August). Nomadic Journeys (p40) is most qualified to run this trip.

**Skiing** The only downhill ski resort in Mongolia is Sky Resort (p68), which offers a couple of beginner and intermediate slopes. There is much potential for cross-country skiing, although there are no developed trails and hiring equipment is difficult. If you have your own equipment, the best places to try are Nairamadal (about 20km west of downtown Ulaanbaatar), Khandgait and Terelj. The best months for skiing are January and February – but be warned: the average temperature during these months hovers around a very chilly -25°C.

**Dog sledding** Trips, organised by Wind of Mongolia (p40), are offered in Terelj (December to February) for US$60 to US$80 per day, and in Khövsgöl Nuur (March to April); cross-lake trips take eight days (all-inclusive US$2600).

Plan Your Trip

# Organised Tours

Mongolia's limited public-transport network makes independent travel challenging because the best sights can only be reached by private vehicle. Most travellers wisely opt for a tour in order to see more of the country in a limited period of time. Guided trips range from budget camping tours to high-end hot-air-balloon trips.

## Best Horse Treks

Everyone and their uncle runs horse treks, but if you are a serious rider consider going with a specialist company. Leading outfitters include Stepperiders (p94), Stone Horse (p40) and Horseback Mongolia (p39).

## Best for Budget Travel

Most budget travellers will sign up for a tour with their guesthouse but it's a good idea to compare prices with bona fide travel companies with proven track records for service and sustainability, including Meg's Adventure Tours (p259) or Rinky Dink Travel Mongolia.

## Best for Adrenalin Junkies

A few companies specialise in serious adventures on bike trails, mountains and rivers. Try Wind of Mongolia (p40) or Mongolia Expeditions (p39).

## Best Way to Enhance Your Tour

Set aside time for some independent travel. Take advantage of bus routes to popular destinations like Terelj, Khövsgöl and Kharkhorin to get a feel for what it's like to travel like a local.

## In Mongolia

There are dozens of travel agencies in Ulaanbaatar (UB) although many are little more than cowboy outfits, happy to take your money and drive you around the countryside for a few days, but with little knowledge of quality customer service or sustainable tourism.

**Cost** Per-day costs start at around US$100 (for two people), including food, accommodation, tickets to sights, a guide (who will double as a cook), a driver and a jeep. These costs can go up or down depending on several factors (eg whether you're staying in tents or a ger camp, type of vehicle).

**Guesthouse tours** The tours run by guesthouses get mixed reactions from travellers. Although lacking in professionalism, they are recommended for day trips in and around UB and Töv aimag as prices are usually much lower than what the bigger companies charge.

**Outside UB** Note that nearly all tour operators are based in Ulaanbaatar. The exception is Bayan-Ölgii where you can find a handful of independent tour companies, the best of which is Kazakh Tour (p194).

# Professional Tour Operators

The agencies we review are recommended for their reputation and experience. These include the following, all based in Ulaanbaatar:

**Active Adventure Tours Mongolia** (Map p67; ☑11-354 662; www.tourmongolia.com; Erkhuu St, Macro Center Bldg, 5th fl, ⦻blending. bugs.unpainted) Good for bike and horse trips, this eco-conscious Mongolian-run outfit also runs traditional homestays (US$15 per night including full board) and employs sustainable tourism practices by hiring local guides rather than shipping them out from Ulaanbaatar.

**Cycling World** (☑7711 0444; www.cycling world.mn; Khan-uul District, Tuul River St 79, ⦻sharper.clusters.fluffed; mountain-bike hire per hour/day/overnight US$3/11/17; ◷10am-7pm) Run by passionate owner Joel (who's the consul of Belgium), this bike shop hires out quality mountain bikes and runs tailor-made cycling tours. It sells a range of bikes and accessories, does repairs and has plenty of good ideas for mountain-bike trails around UB. Check the website for upcoming tours and meet-ups.

**Drive Mongolia** (Map p58; ☑11-312 277, 9911 8257; www.drivemongolia.com; Bayangol District, 3rd Khoroo 24-1, ⦻presuming.belief.insist) This unique company specialises in driving tours of the countryside (as in you drive the car). You can head off by yourself or bring along a guide. Motorbike tours are also available.

**EcoVoyage Mongolie** (Map p58; ☑English speaking 9901 5171, French speaking 9500 3242; www.ecovoyagemongolie.com; Apt 19A-D16, 2nd Khoroo, Chingeltei District, ⦻duke.fairness. resembles; ◷8am-7pm Mon-Fri) French-run tour operator that specialises in horse and walking treks, Buddhism tours and visits to shamans. It can also organise food and cooking tours.

**Goyo Travel** (Map p58; ☑11-313 050; www. goyotravel.com; Golomt Town, Peace Ave, tower A, door 1a, ⦻shirt.critic.stealthier; ◷9.30am-6pm Mon-Fri) An experienced and reliable British-Mongolian outfit, Goyo offers a variety of countrywide trips and some unique tours that may include hot-air ballooning and kayaking on the Tuul Gol (Tuul River). Particularly good with film and media groups or high-end travel. Well regarded for personal service and tailored trips.

**Horseback Mongolia** (Map p58; ☑11-331 098; www.mongolia-trips.com; Chingeltei District, Khoroo 1, apt 38, door 1, ⦻appointed.liberty. rely) French-managed company that offers horse trips around the country. Quality saddles, horse tack and equipment is available. Very competitive rates. The office is not far from the Zanabazar Museum, but you need to call to make an appointment as there's often no one there.

**Hovsgol Travel Company** (Map p67; ☑11-460 368, 9911 5771; www.hovsgoltravel.com; Namyanjugiin Gudamj, ⦻trickle.reader.asterisk) Runs countrywide tours, but specialises in boat, cycling and horse trips around Khövsgöl. Operates the popular Camp Toilogt at Khövsgöl Nuur. Works with the Taimen Conservation Fund as a responsible fishing outfitter. Also sponsors the annual 100km ultramarathon at Khövsgöl.

**Juulchin** (Map p58; ☑11-325 326, 11-328 425; www.juulchin.com; Embassy Rd, ⦻topics. staging.storm; ◷9am-1pm & 2-6pm Mon-Fri) Mongolia's oldest tour operator, Juulchin has been in business since the 1950s. It offers 15-day group tours departing on six different dates each summer. Well regarded for its experienced staff and good-quality vehicles. The office is just east of the Japanese Embassy.

**Khövsgöl Lodge Company** (Map p58; ☑9911 5929; www.boojum.com; Renchin St, apt block 2, ⦻migrate.cornfield.changed) This experienced outfit is part of the US-based Boojum Expeditions and has been running trips in Mongolia since 1994. It offers countrywide tours, but is particularly experienced in the Darkhad valley and Khövsgöl region. Good for horse treks in northern Mongolia. The office is in an apartment block behind the Drama Theatre, but you are better off calling first to get someone to meet you.

**Mongolia Expeditions** (Map p58; ☑9909 6911, 11-329 279; www.mongolia-expeditions. com; Jamyngun St 5-2, ⦻tinsel.orbit.inspects) Specialises in adventure travel, including cycle touring, downhill skiing, mountaineering, caving and rafting trips, as well as less vigorous options such as bird-watching tours. This is a good option if you are planning a climbing trip to Tavan Bogd or if you want to do a tour by bike.

**Mongolia Quest** (Map p58; ☑11-319 747; www.mongoliaquest.com; Jamyngun St 5-2, ⦻pressing.acids.scramble) Offers a range of interesting themed cultural and educational tours, from following the footsteps of Marco Polo or visiting dinosaur fossil sites to trips designed for art and architecture lovers. Tour guides include archaeologists and palaeontologists. It also offers a bunch of action-based tours, including motorcycle trips and horse treks.

**Nomadic Expeditions** (Map p58; ☎11-313 396; www.threecamellodge.com; Peace Ave 76, ⓦinhaled.truckload.apricot) This is the Mongolian office of the US-based travel company. Runs countrywide tours, but is especially good for the Gobi, where it runs the excellent Three Camel Lodge. A leader in environmental conservation and work with Mongolian scientists to protect plant and animal species in the Gobi.

**Nomadic Journeys** (Map p58; ☎11-328 737; www.nomadicjourneys.com; Olympic St 7/3, Tselmeg Tower, 5th fl, ⓦwidely.herds.snooping) A joint Swedish-Mongolian venture, this business concentrates on low-impact tourism, environmental protection and community development. It runs fixed-departure yak, camel and horse treks and can also arrange rafting trips on the Tuul Gol. Its trip in Terelj is unique – you walk while yaks haul your own portable ger on a cart. Also good for taimen (a salmon-like fish) fishing trips. If you are looking for a standard jeep tour this operator may not suit your needs as it caters to travellers seeking unique experiences.

**Nomads** (☎7011 9370; www.nomadstours.com; off Industrial St, ⓦlots.cupboards.hiked; ◷9am-6pm Mon-Fri, 10am-4pm Sat Jun-Sep, 9am-5pm Mon-Fri Oct-May) In business since 1992, this is a well-established company known for its horse-trekking tours. It offers a wide range of fixed-departure trips, including popular horse treks in Khentii and through Terelj, visiting Günjiin Süm. Also good for hiking and trekking in western

Mongolia. Has English-, French-, German- and Russian-speaking guides. The office is located in Khan Uul district, 600m south of the train station.

**Stone Horse Expeditions** (☎9592 1167; www.stonehorsemongolia.com; Chinggis Ave, Gutal Office, room 606, ⓦbonds.airbase.looked) Offers horse treks in the Khan Khentii Mountains (trips start from just one hour out of Ulaanbaatar) and Gorkhi-Terelj National Park. Professional outfit with well-tended horses and eco-conscious policies. Also offers reasonably priced homestay opportunities with herders near Ulaanbaatar.

**Tsolman Travel** (Map p58; ☎9911 4913, 11-322 870; www.tsolmontravel.com; btwn Peace Ave & Seoul St, ⓦdate.graced.candidate; ◷9am-6pm Mon-Fri, to 5pm Sat) Established in 1993, this is one of the oldest private tour operators in Mongolia. It runs a wide variety of trips at competitive rates and operates two ger camps, one in Terelj and a second at Khorgo-Terkhiin Tsagaan Nuur National Park.

**Wind of Mongolia** (☎9898 0593, 9909 0593, 11-316 222; www.windofmongolia.mn; Dilav Khutagt Jamsranjav's St, 7th fl, apt 45, ⓦreckoned.shadows.abolish) This French-run tour operator offers creative and offbeat trips, including rock climbing, mountain biking, kayaking and tours that focus on Buddhism, archaeology and botany. Owner Joel Rauzy is perhaps best known for his winter dog-sledding trips in Terelj and Khövsgöl. Call ahead before turning up as there is not always someone there.

## FREELANCE GUIDES

Few people in the countryside speak anything other than Mongolian and Russian, so a guide-cum-translator is very handy, and almost mandatory. A guide will explain local traditions, help with any hassles with the police, find accommodation, explain captions in museums and act as a linguistic and cultural interpreter.

**Finding a guide** In Ulaanbaatar you can find guides through travel agencies and guesthouses. In the countryside, there is nothing to do but ask – try the hotels and schools. Guides are easier to find between 15 June and 1 September, when schools and universities are on summer break. The pickings are slimmer at other times of the year.

**Pretrip meeting** It's a good idea to meet your guide before setting off on a two-week trip to the Gobi. Try to spend a little time with him/her to gauge if the match will be a good one. If you sense a personality clash or if language skills may be a problem, request another guide.

**Cost** For getting around Ulaanbaatar, a nonprofessional guide or a student will cost a negotiable US$15 to US$25 per day. To take one around the countryside from the capital you will have to include expenses for travel, food and accommodation. In an aimag capital, a guide (if you can find one) costs about US$10 to US$20 per day, plus any expenses. For a professional guide who is knowledgeable in a specific area, such as bird-watching, and fluent in your language, the bidding starts at US$40 to US$60 per day.

# Start-Up Tours

Some of the more entrepreneurial guides, fed up with working for tour operators and guesthouses, have set up their own mini companies – some official, some not.

**Finding a start-up** Guides advertise their services using word of mouth, a website, social media, ads at cafes and business cards passed out at the train station to new arrivals. Some recommendations appear on Lonely Planet's Thorn Tree.

**Negotiating** Many of these guides offer top-notch service at a low cost by cutting out the middle-man. However, there are obvious risks in dealing with a transitory company, so don't hand over all your money up front; ask to pay a little before the trip and the rest at the end of the tour (if all goes well). They usually ask for a 50% deposit.

**Research** Do some homework first by asking for references or search online to see what past travellers have posted. Also check that they have a 4WD vehicle and proper camping and cooking equipment.

## Guesthouse Tour Operators

Almost every guesthouse in Ulaanbaatar also runs tours, grouping together solo travellers and couples that wash up on their doorsteps. The guesthouses offer bargain-basement prices and run no-frills jeep tours of the countryside.

**Rivalry** Competition is stiff between guesthouses and some will be none too pleased if you stay at their guesthouse and then take a tour with a rival outfit. We have even heard of people getting thrown out of their guesthouse after booking a tour with another company.

**Cost** For the most basic driving tour, prices start at around US$50 per day per person, provided you have four or more people.

**Inclusions** Some budget tours don't include food or accommodation; however, they usually include stoves for cooking your own food and tents for camping out. The guesthouses rarely offer special activities such as biking, kayaking or horse expeditions, so for that it's better to try an actual tour operator.

**Guides** Guides employed by the guesthouses are often students on a summer break, who may have limited knowledge of Mongolian history or off-the-beaten-path destinations. If you think you might need a guide who can offer some in-depth knowledge about the country the best place to look, again, is the professional tour operators.

**Fishing** If you want to fish, note that some low-end companies take tourists fishing without a permit – if you are concerned, check with the operator before signing up for the trip or steer clear of the cheaper options. As a general rule of thumb, sustainable tourism is not a high priority of the guesthouse tours.

**Recommended tours** It's difficult to recommend one guesthouse tour over another because the drivers and guides change frequently and the tours are often almost identical (following the same standard itinerary of the Mongolian highlights, ie the Gobi, Kharkhorin, Terkhiin Tsagaan Nuur and Khövsgöl). What sets the tours apart is their levels of organisational skill and the ease of doing business with the guesthouses themselves. The guesthouses that tend to get the most consistently good feedback include UB Guesthouse (p71), Khongor Guest House (p70), LG Guesthouse (p70) and Idre Hostel (p71). Check two or three and compare prices and itineraries, meet the guide/driver and carefully scrutinise their payment and refund policies.

# Outside Mongolia

Reliable agencies outside Mongolia can help with the logistics of travel in Mongolia, including visas, excursions or the whole shebang, including tickets, individual itineraries or group packages. These include travel agencies, adventure-tour operators and homestay agencies.

These companies are particularly good at handling multination trips, for example if you plan to combine Mongolia with a trip to China or other countries in the region. They are also useful for door-to-door service, where you can meet the guides in your home country before setting off.

Overseas tour operators include the following:

**Boojum Expeditions** (☑406-587 0125, 1-800-287-0125; www.boojum.com)

**Geographic Expeditions** (www.geoex.com)

**Peregrine Adventures** (www.peregrine adventures.com)

**Regent Holidays** (www.regent-holidays.co.uk)

**Lernidee Reisen** (www.lernidee-reisen.de)

**Intourist** (www.intourist.com)

**Gateway Travel** (www.russian-gateway.com.au)

## Plan Your Trip
# Road Trip

Travelling around Mongolia with your own car or motorcycle has the makings of the adventure of a lifetime. The open prairies and deserts are begging to be explored by travellers willing to take on the world's most sparsely populated country with their own wheels.

## Best Experiences

### Best Driving Routes

Off-road adventures can be had almost anywhere. Do a loop around eastern Mongolia, down to the Gobi or through Arkhangai to Khövsgöl Nuur. Most Mongol Rally (p44) cars make the cross-country trip from Bayan-Ölgii to Ulaanbaatar (UB) before going on to Ulan Ude.

### Best Mongolian Phrases for Drivers

The tyres need air (duguindaa hii nemuulie); fill the tank to the top (durgei); I am lost (bi tuurson); we're out of petrol (benzin duussan); may I park here? (int mashin tavij boloh uu?); where is a petrol station? (benzin colonk khaana baina ve?)

### Best Ways to Pass the Time

Diversions to pass the time across long stretches of nothingness might include listening to traditional Mongolian music CDs or car games like yak counting.

### Guides

Guides can communicate with locals for directions and road conditions, and give advice on destinations. Consider a guide with vehicle experience as it's handy to have another body around in case of a breakdown.

## Road Conditions

What look like main roads on the map are often little more than tyre tracks in the dirt, sand or mud, and signposts only exist along paved routes. In Mongolia, roads connect nomads, most of whom by their nature keep moving, so even the roads are seminomadic, shifting like restless rivers.

Remote tracks quickly turn into eight-lane dirt highways devoid of any traffic, making navigation tricky. Expect to get lost.

While conditions are rough in most parts of the country, the government has been busy paving roads from Ulaanbaatar to the provincial capitals. The entire 1000km between the northern border at Altanbulag and the southern border at Zamyn-Üüd has been paved. Paved roads from Ulaanbaatar now reach Arkhangai, Bayankhongor, Mörön, Choibalsan and Dalanzadgad. The road from Mörön to Khatgal is also paved.

Shortages of petrol and spare parts are uncommon, except in remote regions. To avoid accidents, try to avoid travelling at night, when unseen potholes, drunk drivers and wildlife can wreak havoc. Driving in the dark is also a great way to get completely lost.

# Vehicle Hire & Purchase

**Self-drive** If you want to hire a car (and drive it yourself), contact Drive Mongolia (p270), a tour operator that rents out Land Cruisers and other suitably rugged vehicles. Another options is Sixt (p270), which has a range of vehicles including compacts for driving in UB, and off-road vehicles for the countryside.

**Car and driver** In Ulaanbaatar, the best place to organise such an arrangement is at the various guesthouses. These guesthouses will take a commission, but you'll get a driver and/or guide who should know tourist routes and be able to locate hard-to-find attractions such as caves, deer stones and ruined monasteries.

**Vehicles** The type of car you hire will depend on the size of your group. Four or more passengers (plus driver and guide) usually fit in a van. Smaller numbers can take a Japanese 4WD.

**Cutting costs** You can save money by using public transport to major regional gateways – that is Mörön for Khövsgöl Nuur, Khovd for the west, Dalanzadgad for the south Gobi and Choibalsan for the far east. Then, from these places rent a jeep and driver from the market, though drivers outside Ulaanbaatar will have little experience dealing with tourists. You will likely need an interpreter to help communicate your plans to the driver and negotiate costs. Finding an English-speaking guide in the countryside is difficult so bring one from Ulaanbaatar.

**Village hire** Villages are less likely to have vehicles for hire as they may not be available or running.

**Return fare** Note that when hiring a vehicle in the countryside to take you to another rural city you will have to pay for the return fare, because the driver will have to go back with an empty van. This does not apply when travelling to Ulaanbaatar as the driver can find passengers there. The upshot is that it will cost almost the same to hire a driver to take you from, for example, Ulaangom to Mörön as it would from Ulaangom to Ulaanbaatar.

**Purchase** Ulaanbaatar has several used car lots (guesthouse owners may have ideas on where to shop). An old Russian 4WD could go for around US$3500. A good condition, used Ij Planeta – the Russian-made motorcycle you see all over the countryside – sells for around US$1000. These tend to break down often but people in the countryside can help with repairs. A Japanese motorcycle will be more reliable. In markets the sign *zarna* (Зарна) on a jeep means 'for sale'.

## Costs

➜ On a long-distance trip, tour operators will have a per-day charge, from around US$80 to US$150 depending on the vehicle. This may be more if they throw in camping and cooking gear. For this price, petrol is usually not included. Some tour operators will build the cost of petrol into the price.

➜ Russian vehicles that you hire on your own (from a market) usually charge US$60 per day without petrol. Russian jeeps have terrible fuel economy: you'll need 20L to travel around 100km. Petrol was around T1850 per litre at the time of research.

➜ Some drivers may want to charge a per-kilometre rate; in the countryside this is around T800 to T1000. Vehicle hire is more expensive the further you get from Ulaanbaatar.

## Agreeing on Terms

It is vital that you and the driver agree to the terms and conditions – and the odometer reading – before you start.

Ask about all possible 'extras' such as waiting time, food and accommodation. There are several private bridges and tolls around the countryside (each costing about T1000), which are normally paid for by you. If you arrange for a jeep to pick you up, or drop you off, agree on a reduced price for the empty vehicle travelling back one way.

# Trip Preparation
## Supplies

**Food** Drivers from tourist agencies will assume that you will feed them along the way. On a longer trip it's easiest for everyone to cook, eat and wash up together. If you don't want to do this, you will have to agree on a fee for the driver's food or supply the food yourself. This shouldn't cost more than T20,000 per day.

**Cooking gear** Experienced drivers will have their own Soviet-era petrol stove, though it's a good idea to bring your own stove as a backup, and to boil water for tea while the other stove is cooking dinner. If you are cooking for a group you'll need a big cooking pot and a ladle. Everyone should bring their own penknife, cutlery, bowl and torch. Avoid drinking from the same water bottles as this spreads viruses around the group.

## THE MONGOL RALLY

In an age when getting from point A to point B has been simplified to the point of blandness, the Mongol Rally attempts to put a bit of spark back into the journey to Mongolia. According to rally rules, the London-to-Ulan Ude (via Mongolia) trip must be made in a vehicle that has an engine capacity of 1L or less. In other words, you have to travel 16,000km (10,000 miles) across some of the world's most hostile terrain in an old clunker barely capable of making it over the A83 to Campbeltown.

The wacky idea of driving from London to Mongolia in a clapped-out banger was dreamt up in 2001 by Englishman Thomas Morgan, whose own attempt to accomplish the feat failed miserably somewhere east of Tabriz. Morgan had more success on a second trip in 2004 and the Mongol Rally became an annual event. In recent years the finish line has been moved to Ulan Ude (in Russia) to lower the cost of shipping cars back to Europe.

The journey begins by selecting a vehicle. Gutless wonders such as old Fiat Pandas and Citroëns are suitable (so long as it's a 1.0ish-litre engine). Next, assemble your team – you can have as many people as you can squeeze into the darn thing. For the truly insane, there is the option of riding a moped.

Next, pay your dues: it's £650 to enter and then you must raise another £1000, which will go to a charity in Mongolia or another country en route (the Mongol Rally has raised over £2 million in charity money so far). Moped riders pay just £250. Finally, zoom out of London with 500 other like-minded drivers in July.

The organisers give absolutely no advice on how to actually get to Mongolia; that you've got to figure out on your own. Teams have travelled as far north as the Arctic Circle and as far south as Afghanistan on their way across the Asian landmass. This is by no means a race – whether you arrive first or last, your only reward is a round of free beers at the finish line. Some teams make the trip in around five weeks, while others have taken as long as three months, stopping off at places en route. From Ulan Ude, vehicles must be shipped back at your own cost.

The rally is organised by the grandly titled League of Adventurists International (www.theadventurists.com). If you want to sign up, contact the organisers early as spots can fill up a year in advance.

In addition to the Mongol Rally, a second rally, the Mongolia Charity Rally (http://mongolia.charityrallies.org), has also formed. Participants must raise £1000 for charity and vehicles cannot be more than nine years old.

**Camping gear** Breakdowns may force you to sleep by your car, so be sure to have camping equipment.

**Other gear** For long expeditions, also equip your vehicle with the following items. Most of these can be purchased from the Naran Tuul Market (p81) in Ulaanbaatar.

➡ jerrycans, for extra petrol

➡ water drum

➡ wide-mouthed plastic drum (useful for storing food, as boxes will rapidly disintegrate)

➡ resealable bags (useful for opened bags of sugar, pasta etc)

➡ water- and dust-proof bag (your backpacks will get filthy so it's a good idea to put them in one)

➡ bungee cords/luggage straps (handy for storing gear in a luggage rack)

➡ jack and lug wrench

➡ torch (flashlight)

➡ jumper cables

➡ standard toolkit

➡ steel wire rope with hook ends (handy for hauling a jeep out of the mud)

➡ fire extinguisher

## Fuel

Three types of Russian fuel are available: **A76** fuels Russian vehicles and trucks, while **A92** and **A95** are used for imported vehicles.

# Repair & Maintenance

**Flat tyres** These are a time-honoured tradition in Mongolia and it's essential that you know how to deal with one. The best solution, of course, is to have a good-quality spare tyre in your car. In fact, taking two spare tyres is not a bad idea as it's quite possible that you could incur two flats before finding a repair shop. Test the jack before setting off.

**Tyre repair** Just about every town in the country has a tyre-repair shop and these are even available at small villages along main routes.

**UB repairs** In Ulaanbaatar, a good place to start with repairs is the **Oasis Café & Guesthouse** (☑9996 0696, 11-463 693; www.intergam-oasis.com; Nalaikh Gudamj, ⁄/⁄ apparatus.doped.nozzles; dm & ger per person T28,000, s/d without bathroom T78,000/90,000; P🛈), which has a big yard for parking and caters to overlanders.

## Breakdowns

Serious mechanical breakdowns are a definite possibility. Should your vehicle break down irreparably in a rural area, you'll be faced with the task of trying to get back to civilisation either on foot (not recommended), by hitching, or by whatever means is available.

Hitching is never entirely safe, and we don't recommend it. Travellers who hitch should understand that they are taking a small but potentially serious risk.

The safest solution is to travel with a small group using two jeeps. Make sure your driver has tools and at least one spare tyre.

## Getting Bogged

Most of Mongolia is grassland, desert and mountains. You might think that mountain driving would pose the worst problems, but forests cause the most trouble of all. This is because the ground is often a springy alpine bog, holding huge amounts of water in the decaying grasses, which are instantly compacted under tyres, reducing a wildflower meadow to slush.

Mongolian drivers have one of two reactions when they get bogged. Some will sit on their haunches, have a smoke and then send word to the nearest town for a tractor to come and tow the vehicle out. Other drivers will get out a shovel and start digging; you can help by gathering flat stones to place under the wheels (drivers usually try to jack the tyres out of the mud).

# Navigation

**Telephone lines** Some of the best navigation tools are the telephone lines strung across the steppes, as these (almost) always lead to the next town.

**Local advice** Mongolian drivers like to stop and ask for directions and road conditions from families along the way, partly to stay on the right track and partly to have a rest and chat with the locals.

**GPS** Of course, the best way to navigate is with a GPS device. For ease of use, bring along a dashboard mount to keep the unit secured. A GPS is not foolproof as it won't be able to tell you if there's a muddy bog or flooded riverbed ahead, so you'll need to constantly correct.

**Maps** Good maps are essential and readily available in Ulaanbaatar.

# Road Rules

**Drive on the right** Where there are paved roads, Mongolians will drive on the right side.

**Right-hand-drive vehicles** More than half the cars on the road have right-hand-drive configuration (due to the preference for Japanese imports). As Mongolians drive on the right, this can make passing cars on the highway somewhat hazardous.

**Traffic infringements** In Ulaanbaatar, traffic police can pull you over for any number of traffic violations (although most locals flaunt the rules regularly). If you are pulled over, be prepared to show a driving licence, car registration and insurance. Fines start from around T50,000.

**Accidents** If you are involved in an accident, don't move your car. The traffic police will eventually arrive on the scene and make a report based on the position of the vehicles.

### SELF-DRIVE OR HIRE A DRIVER?

A self-drive tour is hard work and potentially hazardous. You have to deal with breaking down, getting bogged and getting hopelessly lost.

Most travellers hire a car *and* a driver. In terms of price, it can often work out to be the same as or even cheaper than renting without a driver.

An experienced driver will also know the best ways to reach towns and places of interest. Most travellers carefully inspect their appointed vehicle but don't bother to question the abilities of the driver. Truth be told, a seasoned driver with years of rural driving experience is the much better option compared to a young inexperienced driver, even if the latter has a flashier vehicle.

## Legal Requirements

A licence from your home country can be used within 30 days of your arrival. If you plan to spend more time driving in Mongolia, it's best to carry an international driving licence (IDP), which you can get in your home country for a nominal fee.

Expat residents need to apply for a local licence. If you buy a vehicle, inquire about registration with the traffic police. Insurance is also mandatory and travellers can purchase an insurance plan at the border.

## Hiring a Minivan or Jeep with Driver

The following section describes road-tripping in a hired car with a driver (as opposed to self-drive trips).

➡ Shop as a group when you reach a city or town. If you are travelling with strangers, it's a good idea to keep everyone happy by rotating seats so that everyone (including the guide) has a go in the front seat.

➡ Don't push the driver or guide too hard; allow them (and the vehicle) to stop and rest. However, regular and lengthy stops for a chat and a smoke can add time to the journey.

➡ Lastly, if you are on a long trip, you'll find morale boosted by a trip to a bathhouse (hot water!) in an aimag capital. Another morale booster is the occasional meal in a decent *guanz* (canteen). If you are camping a lot then add in at least one night in a decent hotel to clean up and sort out your stuff.

### Shortcuts

The quickest distance between two points is a straight line, and the only thing that can put off a Mongolian jeep driver from taking a shortcut is a huge mountain range or a raging river. If renting a jeep by the kilometre, you will welcome a shortcut, especially to shorten an uncomfortable trip.

If you have an experienced driver, allow them to take shortcuts when they feel it is worthwhile, but don't insist – they are the expert. The downside of shortcuts is the possibility of breaking down on more isolated roads.

# Plan Your Trip

# Naadam

Mongolia's penchant for war games comes to a head each summer on the vast grasslands, where competitors show off their skills in wrestling, archery and horse racing. The annual Naadam Festival is the much-anticipated culmination of these events, and it's a colourful spectacle enjoyed by locals and tourists alike.

## The Events

### Horse Racing

Mongolians hold a special place in their hearts for horse racing, and naadam is the best time of year to watch this sport.

Jockeys – traditionally children between the ages of seven and 12 years – race their horses over open countryside rather than around a track. Distances range between 15km and 28km and are both exhausting and dangerous – every year jockeys tumble from their mounts and horses collapse and die from exhaustion at the finish line.

Winning horses are called *tümnii ekh* (leader of 10,000). Riders and spectators rush to comb the sweat off the best horses with a scraper traditionally made from a pelican's beak. Pelicans being quite rare these days, most people use a wooden curry-comb called a *khusuur*.

The five winning riders must drink some special *airag* (fermented mare's milk), which is then often sprinkled on the riders' heads and the horses' backsides. During the naadam festival, a song of empathy is also sung to the two-year-old horse that comes in last.

To get a good feel for it all, consider camping out at the horse-race area one night during naadam. You'll have more time to explore the area in the evening and morning when the crowds are smaller. Most people visit on 12 July to see the end of the popular five-year-old horse race, which finishes around 10am.

## Need to Know

### Best Places to See a Naadam

While most tourists see the naadam in Ulaanbaatar (p68), smaller naadams are held in nearby towns including Erdene (8 July), Zuunmod (8 July) and Sergelen (15 July). Further away, you can see a naadam in Dalanzadgad (9 to 10 July) and Mörön (11 to 12 July). Khatgal, near Khövsgöl Nuur, has naadams on 11 and 12 July and a second 'mini naadam' on 11 August.

### Best Party During Naadam

Around 9pm on 11 July, half of Ulaanbaatar piles into Sükhbaatar Sq for the biggest party of the year. Light shows, fireworks, music and family fun.

### Traditional Food at Naadam

The favourite treat at a naadam is *khuushuur* (mutton pancakes) and everyone lines up at food stalls to get a stack. Expect to pay T700 to T1000 per *khuushuur*. As for beverages, don't miss trying some fresh *airag* (fermented mare's milk)

### Going Online

Dan Golan's blog (tomongolia.blogspot.co.il) is a great resource with a schedule of events for the Ulaanbaatar Naadam. He lists some countryside naadam dates but you'll need to confirm the dates with locals (try the nearby ger camps).

## Wrestling

Mongolian-style wrestling *(bokh)* has no weight divisions, so the biggest wrestlers (and they are big!) are often the best.

Out on the steppes matches can go on for hours, but matches for the national Naadam have a time limit – after 30 minutes the match goes into 'overtime' (the referees give the leading wrestler a better position from the get go). The match ends only when the first wrestler falls, or when anything other than the soles of the feet or open palms touches the ground.

The unique outfit *(jodag shuudag)* worn by the wrestlers needs some explaining. A Mongolian legend recounts that ages ago a particularly brawny female entered a wrestling competition and thrashed her male competitors. In order to prevent such an embarrassing episode from happening again, the wrestling jacket was redesigned with an open chest, 'exposing' any would-be female contenders.

## Archery

After the horse races and wrestling, the third sport of naadam is archery, which is performed by both men and women. Archers use a bent composite bow made of layered horn, bark and wood. Arrows are usually made from willow and the feathers are from vultures and other birds of prey. Targets are small leather cylinders placed 4m across and 50cm high. Judges, who stand near the target, emit a short cry called *uukhai,* and raise their hands in the air to indicate the quality of the shot. The first archer to knock down all their cylinders is the winner of that round.

The website www.atarn.org has a number of informative articles on Mongolian archery.

## Ankle-bone Shooting

Ankle-bone shooting, included in the naadam program, entails flicking a square-shaped projectile made of reindeer horn at a small target (about 3m away) made from ankle bones. It's a sort of Mongolian version of darts. The competition is held in the Ankle-Bone Shooting Hall near the archery stadium.

# Ulaanbaatar Naadam Basics

Countryside naadams are easy – just turn up and enjoy, as all the action will occur in one area. In Ulaanbaatar, the Naadam events are a little more spread out and may need more preparation.

**Dates** While Naadam officially kicks off on 11 July, other events get underway several days before. Uriankhai- and Buriat-style archery is held on 7 and 8 July while a children's archery tournament is held on 9 July. On 10 July, two horse races are held and the archery tournament officially begins, as does the ankle-bone shooting competition.

**Banner march** The festival officially begins at 9.30am on 11 July at Sükhbaatar Sq when an honour guard marches the nine horse-tail banners to the stadium.

**Opening ceremony** The opening ceremony, which starts at 11am at the Naadam Stadium, includes a speech from the president and a 40-minute show featuring traditional music, dancing and colourful costumes.

**Wrestling** The wrestling starts in the stadium about 20 minutes after the ceremony and continues all day.

---

### FOREVER TITAN BAT-ERDENE

The greatest naadam wrestling champion of all time was Badmaanyambuu Bat-Erdene, who won 11 straight naadams from 1988 to 1999. In 2000 he did not lose the naadam but rather stepped aside in order to give younger wrestlers a chance at the championship. His title, 'Dayar Dursagdah, Dalai Dayan, Tumniig Bayasuulagch, Darkhan Avarga Bat-Erdene', translates loosely as 'Renowned by All, Oceanic, Joy-Giving, Forever Titan Bat-Erdene'. Following his career in wrestling Bat-Erdene entered politics and he currently serves as a member of parliament representing his native Khentii aimag. In 2013 he ran for president, losing to ex-President Elbegdorj.

## WHICH NAADAM?

Every village and city has a naadam; some (including the one in Ulaanbaatar) are held on 11 and 12 July, coinciding with Independence Day. Other rural naadams are held a few days before or after this date, so some planning is required if you want to see one. Once you find one, hunker down, as shops and restaurants close and transport grinds to a halt.

If you must choose between a city naadam and a country one, choose the latter. Country naadams are friendlier, more photogenic and actually easier from a logistical point of view (you won't have to deal with big crowds or traffic). These smaller festivals also feel more authentic and traditional, although they too are showing signs of modernising.

Naadam in Ulaanbaatar has all the trappings of a big sporting event, with jostling crowds, souvenir salespeople, traffic and screeching loudspeakers. Most locals will simply watch the events at home on TV. Although it's less intimate than small naadams, during Ulaanbaatar's naadam it is nice to see the city in a more relaxed mood with plenty of associated concerts and theatre events.

**Horse races** The horse racing is held about 40km west of the city on an open plain called Hui Doloon Khutag. Buses and minivans go there from the road north of the Naadam Stadium for around T1000. The races can be disappointing from a spectator's point of view because although the race lasts about two hours you can only see the finish. Be prepared for some traffic bottlenecks to and from the racecourse. What is nice about the event is not so much the race itself but the generally festive atmosphere around the horse-race grounds. A cultural area near the finish line shows off traditional Mongolian music and games.

**Other events** Most people file out of the stadium after the opening ceremony to catch a little archery or ankle-bone shooting. Around the stadium are carnival games and rides for kids, as well as food tents. On the night of 11 July, a concert and fireworks display is held on Sükhbaatar Sq.

**Closing ceremony** By comparison with the opening ceremony, almost nothing happens at the closing ceremony. The winning wrestler is awarded, the ceremonial horse banners are marched away, and everyone goes home. It is held at about 8pm on 12 July, but the exact time depends on when the wrestling finishes.

**Post-Naadam events** Quite a few events now happen on 13 July at the horse-race area. A mini-naadam is held for the benefit of trainers; you'll see cultural performances and wrestling. You could even ride your own horse to the racing grounds. Stepperiders (p94) does four-day trips from its base near Bogdkhan Uul.

**Program** To find out what is going on during the festival, look for the events program in the *UB Post* newspaper.

**Information** The website http://naadam.viahistoria.com has pictures and historical information on naadam and the associated sporting events.

## Ulaanbaatar Naadam Tickets

Admission to the stadium (except for the two ceremonies), and to the archery and horse racing, are free, but you'll definitely need a ticket for the opening ceremony and possibly the last round or two of the wrestling and the closing ceremony.

**Cost** Ticket costs vary per section; the north side of the stadium (which is protected from the sun and rain by a roof) is more expensive with tickets going for US$40 or more. The cheapest ones are around US$12.

**Buying tickets** Tickets are sold at the Naadam Stadium and at the Cultural Palace (p57). They usually go on sale on 6 July but can be nearly impossible to get on your own as locals stand in line for hours to scoop them all up. The guesthouses and hotels always manage to get a few for their guests and this is the best way to get one. You can try to buy one from a scalper outside the stadium before the opening ceremony, but the going price is around T50,000.

Top: Archer at Naadam in Ulaanbaatar (p68)

Bottom: Wrestling during Naadam, Ulaanbaatar (p68)

# Regions at a Glance

Most first-time travellers to Mongolia spend a day or two in the capital, Ulaanbaatar, before setting off for the countryside. The most popular destination is the iconic Gobi; a trip here usually loops in part of central Mongolia as it's fairly easy to combine the two regions. Northern Mongolia, specifically Khövsgöl Nuur, is the second most popular destination. All three of these areas have built up a solid tourist infrastructure, with lots of ger camps along established routes.

Western Mongolia sees fewer visitors, largely because of its great distance from Ulaanbaatar and the cost of getting a flight there. However, the west does offer some spectacular scenery and is a great place for the adventurous. The east is Mongolia's least-known and least-visited region (only 3% of tourists head this way), a blessing for explorers wanting an off-the-beaten-path experience.

Note: the existence of two places – Mongolia and Inner Mongolia – can be confusing. The latter is a province of China bordering the independent republic of Mongolia.

## Ulaanbaatar

Shopping
Entertainment
Museums

### Art & Clothing

Ulaanbaatar is the best place for shopping. Pick up cashmere jumpers, artwork, crafts, antiques, traditional clothing, CDs and souvenirs. Visit galleries and buy directly from the artists.

### Culture & Nightlife

Options include Mongolian culture shows, operas, dramas, concerts and fashion shows, especially during the summer tourist season. Bars and nightclubs cater to both foreigners and locals.

### Mongolia's Best Museums

Mongolia's best museums are a must for a deeper understanding of the country. Some are neglected; others recently renovated and modernised. The National Museum is a must-see.

**p54**

## Central Mongolia

Historic Sites
Nature
Horse Riding

### Ancient Art

Arkhangai aimag has deer stones and ancient Turkic monuments carved with runic script. Some ancient monasteries survived Stalin's purge; the best is Erdene Zuu, with walls built from the ruins of Karakorum.

### Lakes & Mountains

There's marvellous scenery in the Khan Khentii Strictly Protected Area. Or head west to the Khangai Mountains to explore the Orkhon waterfall, Terkhiin Tsagaan Nuur (the Great White Lake) and the remote Naiman Nuur.

### Lakeside Rides

The Orkhon valley is great for horse trekking, especially from the Orkhon waterfall to Naiman Nuur. Terkhiin Tsagaan Nuur is also good, or closer to UB try the forests north of Terelj.

**p90**

# Northern Mongolia

Hiking
Fishing
Culture

### Backcountry Trips

There is wonderful back country in Khövsgöl aimag. Hikes can last from one day to more than a week. One of the most popular is along the west shore of Khövsgöl Nuur and through the mountains to Renchinlkhumbe.

### Fishing Holes

Fishing holes in northern Mongolia are world class. The big prize here is taimen, the world's largest salmonoid. Help protect this endangered species and go with an experienced guide.

### Tsaatan People

Khövsgöl is a culturally distinct part of Mongolia. The aimag features the unique Tsaatan, a tribe of reindeer herders, and if you're lucky you can visit a shaman ceremony while in the north.

p118

# Eastern Mongolia

Historic Sites
Wildlife
Horse Riding

### Chinggis Khaan

In Khentii take a trip along the Chinggis Khaan Trail, visiting sites associated with his life. The adventurous can head to Khalkhiin Gol to see the enormous Janraisag Buddha and WWII battlefields.

### Gazelle Spotting

Spotting gazelles on the eastern steppe rivals any wildlife experience you can have in Asia. Nömrög, in the country's far east, is another place to see wildlife, including moose, otters and bears.

### Mountain Rides

The horse trekking through the mountains of Khentii, especially around Dadal, is among Mongolia's best. Follow rivers, camp amid gorgeous scenery and learn horse-handling skills from local Buriats.

p147

# The Gobi

Palaeontology
Off-The-Beaten-Track
Camel Riding

### Dinosaur Bones

The palaeontological record in the Gobi is astounding – a little digging and you might find a cache of fossilised bones or dinosaur eggs. Try Bayanzag, where Roy Chapman Andrews uncovered hundreds of dinosaur skeletons in the 1920s.

### Gobi Desert

The Gobi Desert is the most sparsely populated region of Mongolia and there are huge areas where the number of yearly tourists can be counted on one hand. Head for Khermen Tsav or southern Gov-Altai.

### Sand-Dune Camel Treks

Trekking across sand dunes on a camel is the iconic Gobi experience. Pack camping gear and plenty of water – you can trek at Khongoryn Els and Ongiin Khiid.

p164

# Western Mongolia

Historic Sites
Eagle Hunting
Hiking

### Bronze Age Art

The Altai Mountains are rich in Bronze Age sites, many unmarked and undocumented. Altai Tavan Bogd National Park has petroglyphs, massive burial mounds and ancient stone statues of warriors. The rock-art gallery at Tsagaan Sala is one of the most impressive in Central Asia.

### Kazakh Eagles

Visit Bayan-Ölgii from November to March and you may see Kazakh eagle hunters in search of prey. A stunning experience, it requires time, patience, a good guide and luck.

### Tough Treks

Western Mongolia is ripe for experienced hikers in search of a challenge. Try the lakes in Altai Tavan Bogd National Park or in the Kharkhiraa Uul region of Uvs.

p190

# On the Road

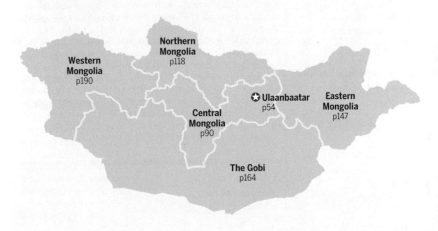

# Ulaanbaatar

☎ 011, 021, 051 / POP 1.4 MILLION

## Best Places to Eat

➡ Luna Blanca (p72)

➡ Hazara (p75)

➡ Tenger Restaurant (p75)

➡ Rosewood Kitchen + Enoteca (p73)

➡ Millie's Espresso (p72)

➡ Bull (p74)

## Best Places to Stay

➡ Zaya's Hostel (p70)

➡ Lotus Guesthouse (p71)

➡ Urgoo Hotel (p71)

➡ Best Western Tuushin Hotel (p69)

➡ Hotel Nine (p69)

## Why Go?

If Mongolia's yin is its pristine countryside, then Ulaan-baatar (UB; Улаанбаатар) harmonises as its vibrant yang. It's a sprawling, industrialised city of pulsating commerce, wild traffic, sinful nightlife and bohemian counterculture. The contrasts within the city are intriguing: Armani-suited busi-nessmen rub shoulders with mohawked punks and *del*-clad nomads fresh off the steppes; one minute you're dodging the path of a Hummer H2 and the next you're entranced by chanting Buddhist monks at Gandan Khiid. It's the coldest capital in the world, but come summer the city bursts into life after slumbering through a long winter.

Ulaanbaatar is not always the easiest city to navigate, but with a little patience travellers can take care of all their logistical needs, visit world-class museums, watch tradition-al theatre, sample international cuisine and party till three in the morning. Indeed, this ever-changing city may be the biggest surprise of your Mongolian adventure.

## When to Go
### Ulaanbaatar

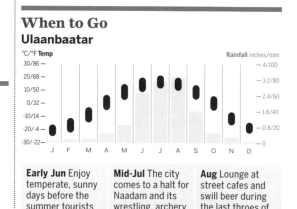

**Early Jun** Enjoy temperate, sunny days before the summer tourists arrive en masse.

**Mid-Jul** The city comes to a halt for Naadam and its wrestling, archery and horse racing.

**Aug** Lounge at street cafes and swill beer during the last throes of summer.

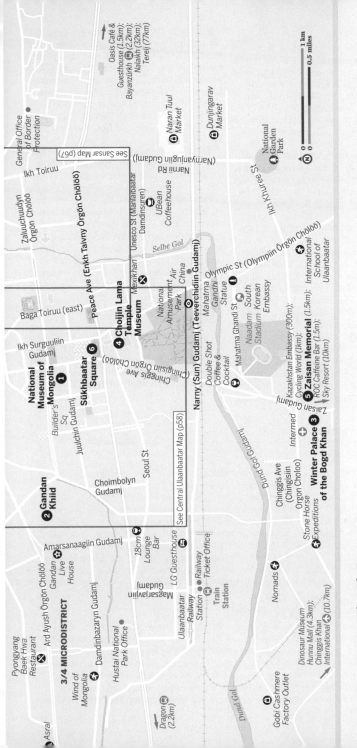

## Ulaanbaatar Highlights

**1** Weaving through Mongolia's ancient past at the impressive **National Museum of Mongolia** (p57).

**2** Walking the prayer circuit around **Gandan Khiid** (p64), the country's largest monastery.

**3** Pondering the eccentric collection of curios and artefacts at the 19th-century **Winter Palace of the Bogd Khan** (p65).

**4** Stepping back in time with a tour of **Chojin Lama Temple Museum** (p62) surrounded by the modern downtown.

**5** Ambling up the steps to **Zaisan Memorial** (p66) for sweeping views of the city.

**6** Soaking up the atmosphere of downtown Ulaanbaatar at **Sükhbaatar Square** (p57) under the watchful gaze of Chinggis Khan, surrounded by futuristic and neoclassical architecture.

## History

The first recorded capital city of the Mongolian empire was created in 1639. It was called Örgöö and was originally located at the monastery of Da Khuree, some 420km from Ulaanbaatar in Arkhangai aimag (province). The monastery was the residence of five-year-old Zanabazar who, at the time, had been proclaimed the head of Buddhism in Mongolia. Because it consisted of felt tents, the 'city' was easily transported when the grass went dry. Some 25 movements were recorded along the Orkhon, Selenge and Tuul Gols (rivers). Throughout these movements the city was given some fairly unexciting official and unofficial names, including Khuree (Camp) in 1706.

In 1778 Khuree was erected at its present location and called the City of Felt. Later the city became known as Ikh Khuree (Great Camp) and was under the rule of the Bogd Gegeen (Living Buddha). The Manchus, however, used Uliastai as the administrative capital of Outer Mongolia.

In 1911, when Mongolia first proclaimed its independence from China, the city became the capital of Outer Mongolia and was renamed Niislel Khuree (Capital Camp). In 1918 it was invaded by the Chinese and three years later by the Russians.

Finally in 1924 the city was renamed Ulaanbaatar (Red Hero), in honour of the communist triumph, and declared the official capital of an 'independent' Mongolia (independent from China, not from the Soviet Union). The *khangard* (garuda), symbolising courage and honesty, was declared the city's official symbol. In 1933 Ulaanbaatar gained autonomy and separated from the surrounding Töv aimag.

From the 1940s the Soviets built the city in typical Russian style: lots of large, brightly coloured theatres and cavernous government buildings. Tragically, the Soviets also destroyed many old Russian buildings as well as Mongolian monasteries and temples. Today the city heaves with construction projects fuelled by Mongolia's mining boom. It has also enjoyed a cultural resurgence with many museums, galleries, theatre performances and clubs bringing out the best in 21st-century Mongolian culture.

## ◉ Sights

Most sights are located within a 15-minute walk of Sükhbaatar Sq. The Winter Palace of the Bogd Khan and the Zaisan Memorial are a short bus or taxi ride south of the city. Gandan Khiid is about 2km to the west.

### ULAANBAATAR IN...

#### Two Days

Ulaanbaatar's main sights can be seen in a couple of days. On your first morning in town pay a visit to the impressive **National Museum of Mongolia** (p57) and discover Mongolia's ancient past, then take a turn around **Sükhbaatar Sq** (p57). After lunch visit the **Choijin Lama Temple Museum** (p62) in the middle of downtown Ulaanbaatar. Watch a Mongolian cultural show in the evening. Rise early on day two to visit **Gandan Khiid** (p64) in time to catch the monks chanting. Head down to the **State Department Store** (p80) to shop for Mongolian souvenirs and to check out restaurants around **Beatles Sq** (p64). After lunch, head south to the **Winter Palace of the Bogd Khan** (p65). In the evening climb the steps to the **Zaisan Memorial** (p66) to watch the sun set over the city, then hit lively Seoul St (p77) for a night out on the town.

#### Four Days

On day three visit the **Zanabazar Museum of Fine Arts** (p61) to see a superb collection of paintings, carvings and sculptures, then head over to **Naran Tuul Market** (p81). Celebrate your stay with a cocktail at rooftop **17 Sky Bar** (p76) or craft beer at **Hops & Rocks** (p77), before hitting **iLoft** (p78) nightclub. On day four take a day trip out of town to mountain bike to the **observatory** (p66) or hike over the **Bogdkhan Uul** (p91). Have a delicious Mongolian feast at **Modern Nomads 2** (p74) or go for vegetarian food at **Luna Blanca** (p72), then catch a local indie band at **Gandan Live House** (p79).

## ⊙ Sükhbaatar (Chinggis Khan) Square

★**Sükhbaatar Square**　　　　SQUARE
(Сүхбаатарын Талбай; Map p58; ⅢⅠ indeed.
strapped.unite) In July 1921 in the centre
of Ulaanbaatar, Damdin Sükhbaatar (the
'hero of the revolution') declared Mongolia's final independence from China. A
square later built on the spot now bears his
name and features at its centre a bronze
**statue** of the revolutionary astride his
horse. In 2013 the city authorities changed
the name of the plaza to Chinggis Khaan
Sq, but in 2016 Sükhbaatar's descendants
won a court battle to restore the original
name.

Peaceful anti-communism protests were
held here in 1990, eventually ushering in
the era of democracy. Today, the square
*(talbai)* is occasionally used for rallies,
ceremonies, rock concerts and festivals,
but is generally a relaxed place where kids
drive toy cars and teens whiz around on
bikes. Near the centre of the square, look
for a large **plaque** that lists the former
names of the city – Örgöö, Nomiin Khuree,
Ikh Khuree and Niislel Khuree. The large
**warehouse** on the square houses temporary exhibits. Poke your head inside to see
what's on.

The enormous marble construction at
the north end was completed in 2006 in
time for the 800th anniversary of Chinggis Khaan's coronation. At its centre is a
seated bronze **Chinggis Khaan statue**
(Map p58; Sükhbaatar Sq, ⅢⅠ confirms.breathing.
slouched). He is flanked by Ögedei (on the
west) and Kublai (east). Two famed Mongol
soldiers (Boruchu and Mukhlai) guard the
entrance to the monument.

Behind the Chinggis monument stands
Parliament House, which is commonly
known as **Government House** (Засгын
Газрын Ордон, Parliament House; Map p58;
Sükhbaatar Sq, ⅢⅠ unwound.blinking.guarded).
An inner courtyard of the building holds a
large ceremonial ger used for hosting visit-
ing dignitaries.

To the east of the square is the 1970s
Soviet-style **Cultural Palace** (Map p58; Sükhbaatar Sq, ⅢⅠ nuzzling.facelift.crinkled), a useful
landmark containing the Mongolian National Modern Art Gallery (p63) and several
other cultural institutions. At the southeast
corner of the square, the salmon-pinkish
building is the State Opera & Ballet Theatre

(p79). Just south of the opera house is the
symbol of the country's new wealth, **Central Tower** (Map p58; www.centraltower.mn;
Peace Ave, Sükhbaatar Sq, ⅢⅠ shocks.daydreams.
weddings), which houses luxury shops including Louis Vuitton and Armani.

The light-coloured colonnaded building
to the southwest is the **Mongolian Stock
Exchange** (Map p58; Sükhbaatar Sq, ⅢⅠ pinch.
scrubbing.keyboards), which was opened
in 1992 in the former Children's Cinema.
Across from the Central Post Office is
a **statue of S Zorig** (Map p58; Peace Ave,
ⅢⅠ pity.post.shrugging), who, at the age of 27,
helped to lead the protests that brought
down communism in 1990 (he was tragically assassinated in 1998).

## ⊙ West of Sükhbaatar Square

★**National Museum
of Mongolia**　　　　MUSEUM
(Монголын Үндэсний Музей; Map p58;
☎7011 0913; www.nationalmuseum.mn; cnr
Juulchin Gudamj & Sükhbaataryn Gudamj,
ⅢⅠ wonderful.successes.devoured;　　adult/child
T8000/1000, photography T10,000; ◷9am-7pm,
5.30pm mid-May–mid-Sep, 9am-6pm daily Tue-
Sat, 4.30pm mid-Sep–mid-May, last entry ½ hour
before close) Mongolia's wonderful National
Museum sweeps visitors from the Neolithic
era right to the present day. It's UB's only
genuine blockbuster sight, offering an unparalleled overview of Mongolian culture,
ranging from stone-age petroglyphs and
exquisite gold ornamentation to, arguably
the highlight, the full gamut of traditional
ceremonial costume – which unmistakably
inspired the look of characters from the
*Star Wars* prequels.

The 1st floor has some interesting exhibits on Stone Age sites in Mongolia, as well as
petroglyphs, deer stones (stone sculptures of
reindeer and other animals) and burial sites
from the Hun and Uighur eras. Look for
the remarkable **gold treasure** (including
a golden tiara), found in 2001 by archaeologists digging near the Kul-Teginii Monument in Övörkhangai.

The 2nd floor houses an outstanding
collection of costumes, hats and jewellery,
representing most of Mongolia's ethnic
groups. Take a gander at some of the elaborate silverwork of the Dariganga minority
or the outrageous headgear worn by Khalkh
Mongols. Some of the outfits contain 20kg to
25kg of silver ornamentation.

# Central Ulaanbaatar

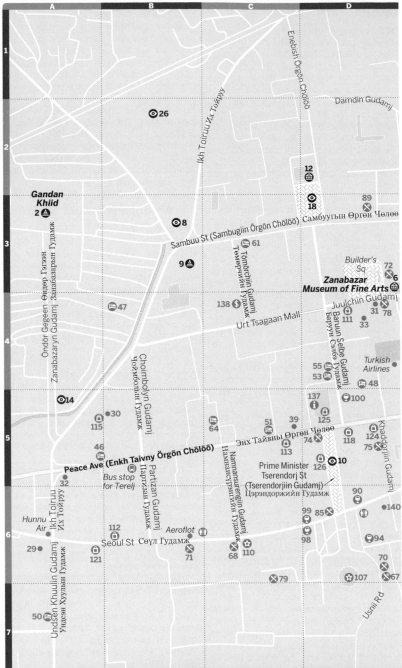

Gandan Khiid

Zanabazar Museum of Fine Arts

Builder's Sq

Juulchin Gudamj

Turkish Airlines

Enebish Örgön Chölöö

Damdin Gudamj

Самбуугийн Өргөн Чөлөө

Sambuu St (Sambugiin Örgön Chölöö)

Urt Tsagaan Mall

Ikh Toiruu Их Тойруу

Öndör Gegeen Занабазарын Гудамж Zanabazaryn Gudamj

Tömörchiin Gudamj Төмөрчийн Гудамж

Baruun Selbe Gudamj Баруун Сэлбэ Гудамж

Choimbolyn Gudamj Чойлболын Гудамж

Peace Ave (Enkh Taivny Örgön Chölöö)

Bus stop for Terelj

Partizan Gudamj Партизан Гудамж

Enkh Taivny Örgön Chölöö Энх Тайвны Өргөн Чөлөө

Namansürengiin Gudamj Намансүрэнгийн Гудамж

Prime Minister Tserendorj St (Tserendorjiin Gudamj) Цэрэндоржийн Гудамж

Khaddorjiin Gudamj

Hunnu Air

Ikh Toiruu Их Тойруу

Seoul St Сөүл Гудамж

Aeroflot

Undsen Khuulin Gudamj Үндсэн Хуулийн Гудамж

Usnii Rd

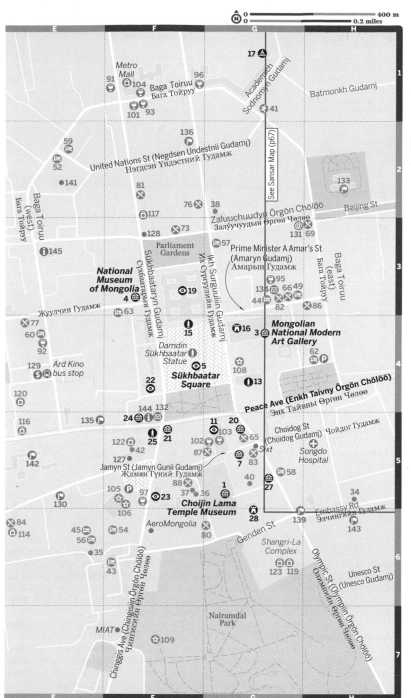

0 400 m
0 0.2 miles

17

91 104 96
Metro
Mall Baga Toiruu
Бага Тойруу
101 93

Academch Sodnomyn Gudamj
41

Batmonkh Gudamj

136

59
52

141
United Nations St (Negdsen Undestnii Gudamj)
Нэгдсэн Үндэстний Гудамж

81

76 38

117

128 73

Zaluuchuudyn Örgön Chölöö
Залуучуудын Өргөн Чөлөө

See Sansar Map (p67)

133

Beijing St

131 69

145

Parliament
Gardens

57

Prime Minister A Amar's St
(Amaryn Gudamj)
Амарын Гудамж

95
134 66 49
82 86
44

National
Museum
of Mongolia
4

Жуулчин Гудамж

63

19

16
3

Mongolian
National Modern
Art Gallery

Sükhbaataryn Gudamj
Сүхбаатарын Гудамж

Ikh Surguuliin Gudamj
Их Сургуулийн Гудамж

15

77
60
92

129 Ard Kino
bus stop

Damdin
Sükhbaatar
Statue
5

22

Sükhbaatar
Square

108

13

62

Peace Ave (Enkh Taivny Örgön Chölöö)
Энх Тайвны Өргөн Чөлөө

120

116

144 132

135 24

11 20

Choidog St
(Choidog Gudamj) Чойдог Гудамж

Songdo
Hospital

122 42
127
142

25 21

102 103
87 65
Sixt
7 83

40

58
27

105
130 106

97 23

88
37 36

1
Choijin Lama
Temple Museum

34

139
143

Embassy Rd
Элчингийн Гудамж

84
114

45
56

54

35

AeroMongolia
80

28

43

Genden St

Shangri-La
Complex

123 119

Unesco St
(Unesco Gudamj)

MIAT

Chinggis Ave (Chingisiin Örgön Chölöö)
Чингисийн Өргөн Чөлөө

Nairamdal
Park

109

Olympic St (Olympiin Örgön Chölöö)
Олимпийн Өргөн Чөлөө

# Central Ulaanbaatar

The 3rd floor is a must-see for fans of the Mongol horde. The collection includes real examples of 12th-century Mongol armour, and correspondence between Pope Innocent IV and Guyuk Khaan. Written in Latin and Persian and dated 13 November 1246, it bears the seal of the *khan*. There is also a display of traditional Mongolian culture with, among other things, a furnished ger, traditional herding and domestic implements, saddles and musical instruments. In the 20th-century-history section, look out for D Sükhbaatar's famous hollow horsewhip,

inside which he hid a secret letter written in 1920 by the Bogd Khan enlisting the aid of the Russian Red Army. It also covers the Soviet era, including the suit of cosmonaut Jügderdemidiin Gurragchaa, the first Mongolian in space.

The final hall contains a rousing, self-congratulatory display of Mongolia's recent history and the 1990 democratic revolution, with no mention of the breadlines of the early 1990s or other hardships of the transition from communism to democracy.

75 Khaan Deli Central ........ D5
76 Le Bistro Français ........ F2
77 Loving Hut ........ E4
78 Luna Blanca ........ D4
79 Merkuri Market ........ C6
80 Millie's Espresso ........ G6
81 Modern Nomads ........ F2
82 Modern Nomads 2 ........ G3
83 Rock Salt ........ G5
84 Rosewood Kitchen + Enoteca ........ E6
85 Sakura Bakery ........ D6
Shashlik Stands ........ (see 125)
86 Shilmel Buuz ........ H3
87 Spicy Street ........ G5
88 Veranda ........ F5
89 Zochin Cafe ........ D3

**Drinking & Nightlife**
17 Sky Bar ........ (see 13)
90 Basement ........ D6
Blue Sky Lounge ........ (see 103)
91 Chinggis Beer Club ........ F1
92 D.d / h.z ........ E4
93 Dund Gol ........ F1
94 Hops & Rocks Brewery ........ D6
95 iLoft ........ G3
96 Matchbox Cafe ........ F1
97 MB Beer Plus ........ F5
98 Mojito Cocktail House ........ D6
Peaberry ........ (see 98)
99 Revolution ........ D6
100 Revolution ........ D5
101 Salm Brau Pub ........ F1
102 Terrace Bar ........ G5
103 Vegas ........ G5
104 VLVT Lounge ........ F1

**Entertainment**
105 National Academic Drama Theatre ........ F5
106 Puppet Theatre ........ F5
107 State Circus ........ D6
108 State Opera & Ballet Theatre ........ G4
109 Tumen Ekh National Song & Dance Ensemble ........ F7
110 UB Jazz Club ........ C6

**Shopping**
111 Amarbayasgalant Antique ........ D4
112 Ayanchin Outfitters ........ B6
113 Books in English ........ C5
114 Butchery by Rosewood ........ E6
115 Cartography Co Map Shop ........ A5
116 Cashmere House ........ E5
117 Egshiglen Magnai National Musical Instrument Shop ........ F2
118 Hi-Fi Mega Store ........ D5
119 LHAMOUR ........ G6
120 Mary & Martha Mongolia ........ E4
121 Mongolian Quilting Shop ........ A6
122 Seven Summits ........ F5
123 Shangri-La Centre ........ G6
124 Souvenir House ........ D5
125 State Department Store ........ D5
126 Tsagaan Alt Wool Shop ........ D5

**Information**
127 Air Market ........ F5
128 Air Trans ........ F3
129 Ard Kino Money Changers ........ E4
130 Australian Embassy ........ E5
Canadian Embassy ........ (see 13)
131 Canyon Centre ........ G3
132 Central Post Office ........ F5
133 Chinese Embassy ........ H2
134 FedEx ........ G3
135 French Embassy ........ E5
136 German Embassy ........ F2
137 Guide Tourist Information Centre ........ D5
138 Ikh Naiman Sharga ........ C4
139 Japanese Embassy ........ G6
140 Legend Tour ........ D6
141 Ministry of Nature & Tourism ........ E2
142 Russian Embassy ........ E5
143 Swiss Consulate ........ H6
144 Tourist Information Booth ........ F5
145 Ulaanbaatar Information Centre ........ E3

**★Zanabazar Museum of Fine Arts** MUSEUM
(Занабазарын Уран Зургийн Музей; Map p58; ☎11-326 060; www.zanabazarfam.mn; Juulchin Gudamj, ///aimed.fills.measuring; adult/student/child T8000/2500/1000, audio guide free, photography T45,000; ⏰9am-5.30pm Apr-Sep, 10am-4.30pm Oct-Mar) This fine arts museum has a superb collection of paintings, carvings and sculptures, including many by the revered sculptor and artist Zanabazar. It also contains other rare religious exhibits such as scroll *thangkas* (paintings) and Buddhist statues, representing the best display of its kind in Mongolia. A bonus is that most of the exhibit captions are in English, to go with a very comprehensive audio guide.

On display are some fine examples of the sculptor's work, including five Dhyani, or Contemplation Buddhas (cast in 1683), and Tara in her 21 manifestations. Also worth checking out are the wonderful *tsam* masks (worn by monks during religious ceremonies) and the intricate paintings, *One Day in Mongolia* and the *Airag*

*Feast,* by the renowned artist B Sharav. These paintings depict almost every aspect of nomadic life.

The building itself carries some historical value. It was built in 1905, making it one of the oldest Manchu-era commercial buildings in the city. It was first used as a Chinese Bank, Soviet troops stayed here in the 1920s, and it later served as Ulaanbaatar's first State Department Store. It has been an art museum since 1966.

## ⊙ South of Sükhbaatar Square

### ★ Choijin Lama Temple Museum  MUSEUM

(Чойжин Ламын Хийд-Музей; Map p58; ☑ 11-324 788, 11-328 547; www.templemuseum.mn; Genden St, [///]should.indulgent.surviving; adult/student/child incl audio guide T8000/3000/1500; ⊙ 9am-5.30pm Tue-Sat) This temple museum smack in the middle of downtown Ulaanbaatar was the home of Luvsan Haidav Choijin Lama ('Choijin' is an honorary title given to some monks), the state oracle and brother of the Bogd Khan. Construction of the monastery commenced in 1904 and was completed four years later. It was closed in 1938 and probably would have been demolished had it not been saved in 1942 to serve as a museum demonstrating the 'feudal' ways of the past.

Although religious freedom in Mongolia recommenced in 1990, this monastery is no longer an active place of worship.

There are five temples within the grounds. As you enter, the first temple you see is the **Maharaja Süm**. The **main temple** features statues of Sakyamuni (the historical Buddha), Choijin Lama and Baltung Choimba (the teacher of the Bogd Khan), whose mummified remains are inside the statue. There are also some fine *thangka* paintings and some of the best *tsam* masks in the country. The *gongkhang* (protector chapel) behind the main hall contains the oracle's throne and a magnificent statue of *yab-yum* (mystic sexual union).

The other temples are **Zuu Süm**, dedicated to Sakyamuni; **Yadam Süm**, which contains wooden and bronze statues of various gods, some created by the famous Mongolian sculptor Zanabazar; and **Amgalan Süm**, containing a self-portrait of Zanabazar himself and a small stupa apparently brought to Ulaanbaatar by Zanabazar from Tibet.

The audio guide offers detailed information, and there are also volunteer guides who can answer your questions.

The complex is located off Jamyn St, with the entrance on the south side. The T50,000/100,000 fee for photography/video means it's mainly one for professionals.

### National Library of Mongolia  LIBRARY

(Map p58; ☑ 8602 5675; www.nationallibrary. mn; Chinggis Ave, 2nd fl, [///]gems.parrot.stud; museum T3000; ⊙ 9am-5pm Mon-Fri Jun-Sep, 9am-8pm Mon-Fri, 9am-5pm Sat & Sun Oct-May, museum 9am-5pm Mon-Fri year-round) Mongolia's neoclassical National Library houses the world's largest collection of Buddhist texts, of which a select few are on display within its **Museum of Rare and Valuable Books**. Here you can see Unesco-recognised Buddhist manuscripts and gold- and silver-leaf Sutras from ancient Tibet, India and Mongolia. Most of the collection was built from the mid-1960s to the 1980s, several decades after the Buddhist purge destroyed nearly every monastery in the country. Researchers started collecting the Sutras from families that had hidden them during the purge.

### Mongol Costumes Centre  GALLERY

(Map p58; ☑ 11-328840; Olympic St 3, [///]resources. volunteered.tummy; adult/child T3000/1000; ⊙ 10am-6pm Mon-Sat, to 3pm Sun) This place designs and manufactures many of the fabulous *dels* (traditional coats) that are worn during the Naadam opening ceremony and at other state events. You can see the different varieties of *del* and even dress up in traditional Mongolian gear for a professional photo shoot (T10,000). The highlight of the centre is a small **museum** that features traditional Mongolian garments, as well as ethnographic artefacts, old chess sets, jewellery and replica 13th-century battle gear.

### Mongolian Artists' Exhibition Hall  GALLERY

(Монголын Зураачдын Үзэсгэлэнгийн Танхим; Map p58; ☑ 11-327 474; www.uma.mn; cnr Peace Ave & Chinggis Ave, [///]glides.engulfing. shift; ⊙ 10am-6pm) FREE If you want to see Mongolian art, and perhaps buy some, head into the Mongolian Artists' Exhibition Hall, on the 2nd floor of the white-marble building diagonally opposite the CPO. The gallery has a rotating collection of modern and often dramatic paintings, carvings, tapestries and sculptures, and a good souvenir shop.

### Victims of Political Persecution
### Memorial Museum                          MUSEUM

(Улс Төрийн Хилс Хэрэгт Хэлмэгдэгсдийн Дурсгалын Музей; Map p58; ☑7011 0915; Olympic St, ⬚unsettled.aura.stated; adult/child T3000/1000; ◷10am-5pm, closed Sat & Sun Nov-Feb) This little-known museum houses a series of haunting displays that chronicle the communist purges of the 1930s – an aggressive campaign to eliminate 'counter-revolutionaries'. During the campaign, intellectuals were arrested and put on trial, then sent to Siberian labour camps or shot. Mongolia lost its top writers, scientists and thinkers. At the time of writing it was closed for renovations, scheduled to reopen in 2018 or 2019. The neglected building that houses the museum is one of the oldest in Ulaanbaatar.

### 976 Art Gallery                          GALLERY

(Map p58; ☑9905 1127; www.976artgallery.com; Jamyn St, Chojin Suites, 1st fl; ◷11am-7pm) **FREE** This well-established contemporary art gallery features established and emerging Mongolian artists, along with a small gallery/gift shop. It's run by Ms Gantuya, a passionate advocate for the local arts community. At the time of writing it was relocating to the Choijin Suites building in the city centre, across from the Blue Sky Tower.

### National Amusement Park     AMUSEMENT PARK

(Үндэсний Соёл Амралтын Хүрээлэн, Children's Park; cnr Olympic St & Narny Gudamj, ⬚tiles.alien.baguette; adult/child T1000/free; ◷11am-11pm; 🚻) Known to almost everyone as the Children's Park, this small amusement park features a roller coaster, among other rides, games and paddle boats. The target audience is the 12-and-under set, so it's perfect if you're travelling with small kids, but it's good fun for anyone to stroll about. For the rides you buy individual tickets, for around T4000 to T6000 a pop. It's open year round; in winter there's ice skating, too.

The park entrance is on the southeast corner, and there's another to the west.

---

### ◉ East of Sükhbaatar Square

### ★Mongolian National
### Modern Art Gallery                      GALLERY

(Монголын Уран Зургийн Үзэсгэлэн; Map p58; ☑11-331 687; www.art-gallery.mn; Sükhbaatar Sq 3, Central Cultural Palace B, ⬚spells.

competent.suggested; T2000; ◷10am-6pm Jun-Sep, 9am-5pm Oct-May) Sometimes called the Fine Art Gallery, this place contains a large and impressive display of modern and uniquely Mongolian paintings and sculptures, with nomadic life, people and landscapes all depicted in styles ranging from impressionistic to nationalistic. The Soviet romantic paintings depicted in *thangka* style are especially interesting, but the most famous work is Ochir Tsevegjav's 1958 *The Fight of the Stallions* (aka *Horse Fighting*).

---

### ◉ North of Sükhbaatar Square

### Central Museum of
### Mongolian Dinosaurs                      MUSEUM

(Map p58; ☑7000 0171; www.dinosaurmuseum.mn; Sambugiin Örgön Chölöö, Freedom Sq, winstilled.diamonds.remix; adult/student/child T3000/1000/500, photography T5000; ◷10am-7pm mid-May–mid-Sep, 9am-6pm mid-Sep–mid-May) Dinosaurs of all shapes, sizes and appetites once roamed the Gobi Desert. Their fossilised bones and eggs were first uncovered by American explorer Roy Chapman Andrews in the 1920s. Today you can come face-to-skull with some of the best examples of Mongolian dinosaur fossils in this museum. The centrepiece of the museum is the UV-lit 4m-tall, 3-tonne, flesh-eating Tarbosaurus bataar (a cousin of the Tyrannosaurus rex) and the smaller Saurolophus, with its distinctive cranial crest.

The Tarbosaurus bataar made international headlines in 2012 when it sold for over US$1 million at an auction in Texas. The Mongolian government protested that the fossil had been illegally smuggled out of Mongolia and demanded its return. The legal battle ended when a US judge ruled in favour of Mongolia.

The museum also includes Velociraptor and Protoceratops examples, and a nest of Oviraptor eggs. It's housed inside the former Lenin Museum, constructed in 1974. While there are plans to expand it into a world-class institution, for now it's still a bit limited in specimens. There's also another **dinosaur museum** (Airport Rd, Hunnu Mall, ⬚couches.lungs.unloading; adult/child T3500/1500; ◷11am-7pm), bizarrely located in the Hunnu shopping mall on the road to the airport, which has some impressive fossils on display.

### Dashchoilon Khiid — BUDDHIST MONASTERY

(Дашчойлон Хийд; Map p58; ☑ 11-352 007; www.dashichoiling.mn; Academich Sodnomyn Gudamj, ⓜ pelting.ringside.permanent) **FREE** Originally built in 1890 and destroyed in the late 1930s, this monastery was partially rebuilt and is now located in three huge concrete gers that once formed part of the State Circus. In the main temple a hefty string of 108 prayer-beads lies at the Buddha's feet, donated by monks from Japan; each bead weighs 45.5kg, making it the largest length of prayer beads in the world.

## ◎ State Department Store Area

### Beatles Square — SQUARE

(Tserendorjiin Gudamj; Map p58; Prime Minister Tserendorj St, ⓜ blurred.suspect.mouths) The plaza located between the State Department Store and the Circus has an unofficial name – Beatles Square, so named after the **monument to the Fab Four** located close to its northern end. The monument features bronze images of John, Paul (barefooted), George and Ringo on one side, and on the other, a sculpture of a young man sitting in a stairwell strumming a guitar.

The sculpture recalls the 1970s era in Ulaanbaatar when groups of teenagers would gather in apartment stairwells and sing Beatles songs, which they learned from contraband records smuggled in from Eastern Europe. The plaza – surrounded by cafes, restaurants and cashmere shops – is a popular meeting place and hub of activity in summer when locals relax by the fountains.

In August 2017 locals hit the street in protest against plans to bulldoze the square for commercial development; though regardless of how it plays out, the Beatles statue is expected to remain.

## ◎ Gandan Monastery Area

### ★ Gandan Khiid — BUDDHIST MONASTERY

(Гандан Хийд, Gandantegchinlen Khiid; Map p58; Öndör Gegeen Zanabazaryn Gudamj, ⓜ upstarts. gangs.shuffle; T4000; ☉ 8.30am-7pm) Around the start of the 19th century more than 100 *süm* (temples) and *khiid* (monasteries) served a population of about 50,000 in Urga (the former name of Ulaanbaatar). Only a handful of these buildings survived the religious purges of 1937. It wasn't until the early 1990s that the people of Mongolia started to openly practise Buddhism again. This monastery is one of Mongolia's most important, and also one of its biggest tourist attractions. The full name, Gandantegchinlen, translates roughly as 'the great place of complete joy'.

Building was started in 1838 by the fourth Bogd Gegeen, but as with most monasteries in Mongolia, the purges of 1937 fell heavily on Gandan. When the US vice president Henry Wallace asked to see a monastery during his visit to Mongolia in 1944, Prime Minister Choibalsan guiltily scrambled to open this one to cover up the fact that he had recently laid waste to Mongolia's religious heritage. Gandan remained a 'show monastery' for other foreign visitors until 1990, when full religious ceremonies recommenced. Today more than 600 monks belong to the monastery.

As you enter the main entrance from the south, a path leads towards the right to a courtyard containing two temples. The northeast building is **Ochidara Temple** (sometimes called Gandan Süm), where the most significant ceremonies are held. As you follow the *kora* (pilgrim) path clockwise around this building, you see a large statue behind glass of Tsongkhapa, the founder of the Gelugpa sect. The two-storey **Didan-Lavran Temple** in the courtyard was home to the 13th Dalai Lama during his stay here in 1904 (when he fled Lhasa ahead of a British invasion of Tibet).

---

## ULAANBAATAR FOR CHILDREN

Ulaanbaatar is a very child-friendly city, with plenty of playgrounds, parks and plazas with motorised toy cars and fun-fair stalls etc. The **National Amusement Park** (p63) is a must-visit, with rides for children of all ages. Kids will also be into watching the Naadam events, such as horse riding, wrestling and archery. While many of the history museums may be on the dry side (though they'll love the traditional costumes), the **Central Museum of Mongolian Dinosaurs** (p63) and **International Intellectual Museum** (p67) are essential viewing for kids.

At the end of the main path as you enter is the magnificent white **Migjid Janraisig Süm**, the monastery's main attraction. Lining the walls of the temple are hundreds of images of Ayush, the Buddha of Longevity, which stare through the gloom to the magnificent Migjid Janraisig statue.

The original statue was commissioned by the eighth Bogd Khan in 1911, in hopes that it might restore his eyesight – syphilis had blinded him; however, it was carted away by Russia in 1937 (it was allegedly melted down to make bullets). The new statue was dedicated in 1996 and built with donations from Japan and Nepal. It is 26m high and made of copper with a gilt gold covering. The hollow statue contains 27 tonnes of medicinal herbs, 334 Sutras, two million bundles of mantras, plus an entire ger with furniture!

To the east of the temple are four **colleges of Buddhist philosophy**, including the yellow building dedicated to Kalachakra, a wrathful Buddhist deity.

To the west of the temple is the **Öndör Gegeen Zanabazar Buddhist University**, which was established in 1970. It is usually closed to foreigners.

You can take photos (camera T7000, video T10,000) around the monastery and in Migjid Janraisig Süm, but not inside the other temples. Try to be there for the captivating ceremonies – they generally start at around 9am, though you may be lucky and see one at another time. Most chapels are closed in the afternoon.

### Badma Ega Datsan                              TEMPLE

(Gesar Süm; Map p58; cnr Sambuu St & Ikh Toiruu W, [m]bagpipes.sympathy.flickers; ☺9am-8pm) **FREE** Belonging to Gandan Khiid, Badma Ega is a small, ramshackle place on a busy intersection. While Badma Ega is the original name for the temple, many know it by the alternative name of Gesar Süm (Gesar was a mythical Tibetan king). It is a popular place for locals to request, and pay for, *puja* (a blessing ceremony). Allegedly the temple was placed here to stop the movement of the hill behind it, which was slowly creeping towards the centre of the city.

**Tasgany Ovoo** ([m]torches.reprints.wicked), about 300m north of Gesar Süm, is worth a look if you haven't yet seen an *ovoo*, a sacred pyramid-shaped collection of stones.

### Centre of Shaman Eternal Heavenly Sophistication      RELIGIOUS SITE

(Мөнх Тэнгэрийн Шид Бөө Шутээний Төв; Map p58; ☎9929 8909; Öndör Gegeen Zanabazaryn Gudamj, [m]bump.points.amplified; ☺11am-5pm Sun-Fri) **FREE** Ulaanbaatar's official Shaman Centre is a ramshackle ger teetering on the slope that leads to Gandan Khiid. While not particularly mystifying at first sight, this is the real deal, with a bona fide shaman at its helm holding court daily. The main ger contains a smattering of icons, from fake stuffed tigers to deer heads and bear rugs. Ceremonies (T50,000) can be arranged through the resident female shaman, Bayaremae. Call ahead to confirm.

## ◉ Khan Uul District & Zaisan Area

### ★ Winter Palace of the Bogd Khan       MUSEUM

(Богд Хааны Өвлийн Ордон; ☎7000 1926, 11-342 195; www.bogdkhaanpalace.mn; Bogd Javzandamda's St, [m]dawn.elections.punctured; adult/student/child T8000/3000/1500, photography/video T50,000/70,000; ☺9am-7pm daily mid-Apr–mid-Sep, 9am-6pm Thu-Mon mid-Sep–mid-Apr) Built between 1893 and 1903, this palace is where Mongolia's eighth Living Buddha, and last king, Jebtzun Damba Hutagt VIII (often called the Bogd Khan), lived for 20 years. For reasons that are unclear, the palace was spared destruction by the Russians and turned into a museum. The summer palace, on the banks of Tuul Gol, was completely destroyed. There are six **temples** in the grounds; each now contains Buddhist artworks, including sculptures and *thangkas*.

The white, Western-looking building to the right as you enter is the **Winter Palace**. Within you'll encounter a room showing the king and queen's unusual living arrangements, and a collection of gifts received from foreign dignitaries, such as a pair of golden boots from a Russian tsar, a robe made from 80 unfortunate foxes and a ger lined with the skins of 150 leopards. Mongolia's Declaration of Independence (from China in 1911) is among the exhibits.

The Bogd Khan's penchant for unusual wildlife explains the extraordinary array of **stuffed animals** in the palace. Some of them had been part of his personal zoo

– look out for the photo of the Bogd's elephant, purchased from Russia for 22,000 roubles.

The **exhibition hall** in the northern part of the complex has temporary displays from the palace's collection; visit the website to see what's showing.

The Winter Palace is a few kilometres south of Chinggis Khaan Sq. It is a bit too far to walk, so take a taxi or catch bus 7 or 19.

### ★Zaisan Memorial                MONUMENT

(Зайсан Толгой; Zaisan Hill, ///blanked.octagonal. blanking) **FREE** Built by the Russians to commemorate 'unknown soldiers and heroes' from various wars, the Zaisan Memorial features stirring socialist realism imagery with Soviet mosaics and reliefs, including that of Stalin and Lenin. Accessed via steep stairs, the monument sits atop the hill south of the city with wonderful views of Ulaanbaatar and the surrounding hills – although these have been blighted by recent high-rise commercial development. Take bus 8 or 52 from Bayangol Hotel or Baga Toiruu.

### Buddha Park                PARK

(Zaisan, ///vans.wildfires.liquid) **FREE** Buddha Park is harder to appreciate these days since the construction of a high-rise, commercial development that encompasses the 23m-high Sakyamuni statue. Below the statue is a small room containing *thangkas,* Sutras and images of the Buddha and his disciples. When it was erected in 2007, five tons of juniper were placed inside.

To get there, catch bus 8 or 52 from the Bayangol Hotel.

### National Garden Park                PARK

(Ikh Khuree St, ///factored.snooty.spoke; T1000; ⊙8am-midnight) In the southern part of Ulaanbaatar is the sprawling National Garden Park, a popular place for locals to unwind and get some fresh air after work and on weekends. The park is still a bit raw and forlorn, but as the trees grow it should improve over the years. It has a scenic mountainous backdrop, and there are food vendors, funfair games, open-air sculptures and sporting facilities. You can take a kitschy bike for a lap (per person T2000).

### Asral                BUDDHIST SITE

(☏11-304 838, 9595 2272; www.asralmongolia. org; ///trade.bond.nicely) Located in the northwest corner of the city, Asral is an NGO and Buddhist social centre that supports impoverished families. Its main aim is to stop disadvantaged youths from becoming street children. It also provides skills and jobs for unemployed women; an on-site felt-making cooperative Made in Mongolia (www.madeinmongolia.net) turns out some lovely products to purchase.

Asral encourages travellers to visit the centre. You can meet the felt-makers, learn to make felt products (workshops from US$20), buy items from its shop or volunteer. The centre is always looking for English teachers or gardeners to work on a small farm in Gachuurt or at its felt-making branch in Dundgov aimag in the Gobi region.

The Buddhist arm of the organisation has classes on Buddhism and meditation, although for now these are only offered in Mongolian. In summer, a high Tibetan Lama, Panchen Otrul Rinpoche, visits the centre and provides religious teachings.

The centre is in the 3/4 district opposite the Gobi Sauna, slightly off the main road. It's best to call before you visit. Take trolley bus '3,4 Horoolo' from Peace Ave to the last stop and continue walking for 300m. Asral is a two-storey cream-coloured building on your right.

---

## MOUNTAIN-BIKING NEAR ULAANBAATAR

The best short bike ride from Ulaanbaatar goes from Zaisan to the **Observatory** (Map p96; ///clinic.invisible.viewers). From the city centre, travel south to the **Zaisan Memorial** (p66). From Zaisan, continue in an easterly direction. The road follows the southern bank of the Tuul Gol for 11km until you reach the ski hill, **Sky Resort** (p68). The Observatory is a little bit further along; follow the switchbacks uphill until you reach it. It's a two- to three-hour return trip.

Get in touch with **Cycling World** (p68) for ideas on possible mountain-bike trails in UB and beyond. It also hires and sells mountain bikes and accessories, does repairs and arranges tours.

# Sansar

## ⊙ Sansar

### ★ International Intellectual
**Museum** MUSEUM

(Оюун Ухааны Олон Улсын Музей, Mongolian Toy Museum; Map p67; ☎ 11-461 470; www.iqmuseum.mn; Peace Ave 10, ⊞ overused.replays. dwelled; adult/child incl guide T8000/6000; ⊙ 10am-6pm Mon-Sat; ☺) This museum contains an intriguing collection of puzzles and games made by local and international artists. One puzzle requires 56,831 movements to complete, says curator Zandraa Tumen-Ulzii.

There are dozens of handmade chess sets and ingenious traditional Mongolian puzzles that are distant cousins to Rubik's Cube. An enthusiastic guide will show you how the puzzles operate and will even perform magic tricks. A fascinating place for both kids and adults.

# 🏃 Activities

## ★Cycling World
CYCLING

(☑7711 0444; www.cyclingworld.mn; Khan-uul District, Tuul River St 79, wsharper.clusters.fluffed; mountain-bike hire per hour/day/overnight US$3/11/17; ⊘10am-7pm) Run by passionate owner Joel (who's the consul of Belgium), this bike shop hires out quality mountain bikes and runs tailor-made cycling tours. It sells a range of bikes and accessories, does repairs and has plenty of good ideas for mountain-bike trails around UB. Check the website for upcoming tours and meet-ups.

## Sky Resort & Mt Bogd
## Golf Course
SKIING, GOLF

(☑7700 0909, 9100 7847; www.skyresort.mn; �░undercuts.allowable.elastic; ⊘11am-9pm Mon-Fri, 9am-10pm Sat & Sun; 🖫) Between mid-November and March this small ski resort operates a couple of beginner runs, two chairlifts, full ski services (equipment rental, lessons, cafeteria) and even night skiing! A three-hour lift ticket including ski rental costs T44,000. Snowboards are for hire, too. An 18-hole golf course operates here in summer (nine/18 holes from T180,000/265,000), but it's pricey. There's also a classy bistro that does quality lunches.

## Federation for the Preservation
## of Mahayana Tradition
BUDDHISM

(FPMT; Map p58; ☑11-321 580; www.fpmt mongolia.org; Juulchin Gudamj, Builder's Sq, �░rural.shiver.tour; ⊘9am-6pm Mon-Fri) The centre is involved in the regeneration of Buddhist culture in Mongolia and offers free lectures and courses on various aspects of Buddhist tradition, yoga and meditation. Lectures are mostly given in English. Look for the pink-tiled building with a stupa in front.

# 🎉 Festivals & Events

## Tsagaan Sar
CULTURAL

Lunar New Year festival held sometime between late January and early March, depending on the lunar calendar.

## Ulaanbaatar Winter Festival
SPORTS

(⊘Feb) The city hosts the Ulaanbaatar Winter Festival at the National Garden Park on the first Sunday of February with an ice ankle-bone shooting competition (something like bowling on ice, but with a ball made of cowhide), along with ice archery, dog sledding and figure skating.

## Ulaanbaatar Marathon
SPORTS

(www.ub-marathon.ub.gov.mn; ⊘late May) This event closes all the streets in downtown Ulaanbaatar as thousands of runners race around the city. Runners can participate in 10km, 21km or 42km races.

## ★Naadam
CULTURAL

(⊘11-15 Jul) The biggest event in Ulaanbaatar is undoubtedly the Naadam (festival). Some visitors may not find the festival itself terribly exciting, but the associated activities during the Naadam week and the general festive mood make it a great time to visit.

## Silence White Party
MUSIC

(National Garden Park; ⊘Jul) Mongolia's biggest dance-music festival takes place in July with local and international DJs entertaining revellers all dressed in white.

## Playtime
MUSIC

(www.playtime.mn; ⊘Jul or Aug) This annual two-day music festival features the country's top rock bands and hip-hop artists, as well as a few international acts. It's held at a venue outside the city, usually in July.

## Tsam-Mask Dancing
CULTURAL

(⊘Jul or Aug) On a date set by the lunar calendar (late July or early August) you can see *tsam*-mask dancing, usually held at Gandan Khiid.

# 🛏 Sleeping

There is a wide range of places to stay in the capital city, in particular budget guesthouses. There's some fantastic upmarket hotels, too, but quality midrange options are limited. During the week surrounding Naadam accommodation may be in short supply and prices are often higher; book well in advance if you're here in July.

## 🛏 East of Sükhbaatar Square

## Puma Imperial
HOTEL $$

(Map p58; ☑7711 3043; www.pumaimperialhotel. mn; Ikh Surguuliin Gudamj, wdevours.unframed. flushed; s/d incl breakfast T170,000/210,000; 🅿@🕸) This property is popular with visiting journalists and diplomats wanting to be close to the square, so you are paying more for the location than the quality of the rooms. It comprises two separate buildings: a modern, high-rise business-chic hotel (building B); and an original, Soviet-style hotel (building A).

It has courteous and accommodating staff and, in building B, a good in-house cafe and rooftop restaurant on the 17th floor.

### Ulaanbaatar Hotel
HOTEL $$

(Map p58; ☎11-320 620; www.ubhotel.mn; Baga Toiruu, 🏠skippers.regime.myths; s/d incl breakfast from T150,000/180,000; P✳@🛜) The Ulaanbaatar Hotel is the grand old dame of Mongolia. Opened in 1961, this was where Soviet dignitaries stayed during their visits to the 'Red Hero'. It still carries an air of the Khrushchev era with its high ceilings, chandeliers, marble staircase and lavish ballroom. Rooms are well appointed, but some are a bit small.

### ⭐ Best Western Tuushin Hotel
HOTEL $$$

(Map p58; ☎11-323 162; www.bestwestern mongolia.mn; Prime Minister A Amar's St 15, 🏠grapevine.unto.duties; r incl breakfast from T562,000; ✳@🛜) Ulaanbaatar's premier upscale hotel is this five-star gem with a prime location steps away from all the downtown museums and theatres. Spacious, tastefully decorated rooms have incredible city views, and facilities include a spa, a fitness centre, a couple of restaurants and a cocktail lounge on the 25th floor with more epic views.

### ⭐ Hotel Nine
BOUTIQUE HOTEL $$$

(Map p58; ☎7711 4334; www.hotelnine.mn; Prime Minister A Amar's St 8, 🏠lunge.feeds.courier; s/d incl breakfast from T232,500/308,000; ✳🛜) One of UB's more stylish options is this designer hotel in a prime downtown location. As with many boutique hotels, rooms are boxy, however they feature plenty of contemporary touches such as rain shower heads, Scandinavian-style shelving and business desks. Ask for a room with a view, unless you want be looking onto apartment blocks.

## 🛏 South of Sükhbaatar Square

### ⭐ Chuka's Guesthouse
GUESTHOUSE $

(Map p58; ☎9422 5672, 9999 5672; chuka927@ gmail.com; Bldg 33, entrance V, 🏠vibrating.pocket. chum; dm US$10-15, s/d US$25/35; 🛜) This popular guesthouse enjoys a central location in a quiet courtyard set behind the National Academy Drama Theatre. It's pricier than some of its competitors, but the quality of the rooms stands out. Furnishings

---

**ℹ LEFT LUGGAGE**

Most hotels and guesthouses can store luggage while you are off getting lost in the Gobi. There is usually no fee if you've stayed a few nights.

---

are modern and the bunk beds are soft and warm. It has a fully equipped contemporary kitchen and a cosy lounge.

### ⭐ Modern Mongol Hostel
HOSTEL $

(Map p58; ☎9910 1861, 7705 2255; www.hostel. mn; Chinggis Ave 14, 🏠diverting.evenly.cooked; dm US$10-15, r from US$35; 🛜) This contemporary hostel is a budget choice with a difference. Its lobby has the polish of a boutique hotel, and while it's all a bit squashy, the rooms are tidy and comfortable. Dorms range from capsule-style sardine tins to four-bed configurations. Private rooms are spacious and immaculate. There's a kitchen, simple breakfast and complimentary filter coffee.

### Mongolian Vision Guesthouse
GUESTHOUSE $

(Map p58; ☎9511 9399, 11-322 369; www.mongolian visiontours.com; Bldg 33, door 65, 🏠forum.operating.baths; dm/r incl breakfast US$7/25; @🛜) A fresh renovation in 2017 has given new life to this hostel, with sparkling, modern rooms, thick mattresses and a Western-style kitchen. Dorm beds are kitted out with power points and curtains. Rooms in the older wing are dated, but have more character. The friendly English-speaking staff keep the place tidy, and run a tour company with trips across Mongolia.

### Mongolian Steppe
GUESTHOUSE $

(Map p58; ☎9919 4331; www.mongoliansteppe. com; off Peace Ave, 🏠overhead.tides.graph; dm US$5-10, r US$14-20, apt US$35-80; 🛜) English-speaking owner Eiggy has established two guesthouses in two separate locations, both equally difficult to find. One is within an unsigned apartment (you need to call) behind the State Department Store, the other (🏠tasks.clipped.blocks) across the street from the central post office, accessed via the courtyard of the main building. Both have more of a homestay feel than a hostel, but gets a thumbs up from guests.

**Springs Hotel**                    HOTEL $$$
(Map p58; ☎11-320 738; www.springshotel.mn;
Olympic St 2A, ✉gazes.tidal.unicorns; r incl
breakfast from US$120; @🛜) This hotel's best
features are its helpful staff, good quality
wi-fi connection and central location just a
short walk from Sükhbaatar Sq. Prices in-
clude use of the fitness room. It's a popular
place for business travellers, does a good
breakfast spread and has an in-house Ko-
rean restaurant.

**Bayangol Hotel**                    HOTEL $$$
(Map p58; ☎11-328 869; www.bayangolhotel.mn;
Chinggis Ave 5, ✉blatantly.bulge.sway; s/d incl
breakfast T225,000/290,000; P✱🛜) One of
Ulaanbaatar's biggest and most reliable hotels, the Bayangol consists of two separate
towers that are located a five-minute walk
south of Sükhbaatar Sq (along a very busy
road). It was built in 1964 to accommodate
overseas tour groups and the structures
are a bit dated, but Tower B is newly renovated, and the much better option.

---

## 🛏 State Department Store Area

**★Zaya Hostel**                    GUESTHOUSE $
(Map p58; ☎11-331 575, 9908 9478; www.zaya
hostel.com; off Peace Ave, ✉clustered.elder.re-
minds; s/d/tr without bathroom US$25/36/45,
s/d with bathroom US$30/40; @🛜) While
most guesthouses in town are located
in crumbling old Russian flats, this one
is in a modern building with hardwood
floors, sparkling bathrooms, a comfortable
lounge, fresh paint and smart furnishings.
Owner Zaya speaks English, enjoys a good
conversation and is happy to help travellers. Eggs on toast and proper filter coffee
are available for breakfast.

**★Khongor Guest House**                    GUESTHOUSE $
(Map p58; ☎11-316 415, 9925 2599; www.khongor-
expedition.com; Peace Ave 15, apt 6, ✉pupils.hu-
mid.delivers; dm/s/d/f US$10/15/20/30; @🛜)
This popular guesthouse in an apartment
block is run by a friendly, knowledgable
team who work overtime to help guests
with logistical matters, and it remains one
of the best to arrange countryside tours.
The guesthouse is a basic affair with small
private rooms and slightly larger dorms
equipped with curtains, lamps and power points. There's a kitchen and a homey
lounge with computers.

**Golden Gobi Guesthouse**                    GUESTHOUSE $
(Map p58; ☎9665 4496, 11-322 632; www.golden
gobi.com; off Peace Ave, ✉upstarts.goodbye.flip-
ping; dm US$7-10, r with/without bathroom from
US$39/33; ✱🛜) This family-run place has
a fun, youthful vibe, with colourful noise-
proof walls, comfortable lounges and lots
of soft sofas. Dorms and private rooms
are clean and comfortable, and the bathrooms are kept tidy. On the downside, it
can get very crowded in summer. It's inside
a courtyard about 100m east of the State
Department Store.

It also has an adjoining apartment with
equally nice rooms.

**Meg's Guesthouse**                    HOSTEL $
(Map p58; ☎7709 3242, 9964 3242; www.meg
mongolia.com/guest-house; off Peace Ave, ✉heavy.
hindered.teams; dm US$6-12, s/d US$20/25, apt
US$40-60; 🛜) Run by Meg and an all-female
Gen Y staff, this breezy little guesthouse has
a homey atmosphere and a prime position
behind the State Department Store. Objects
collected by Meg in her far-flung travels
provide plenty of colour, and the single-sex
dorms are cosy and clean. Its apartment
next door is great value, with cable TV and
fast wi-fi.

Meg's is a reliable place to organise
tours, and there are also volunteering opportunities, from teaching English to crick-
et coaching.

**Four Season Guesthouse**                    GUESTHOUSE $
(Map p58; ☎8989 8389, 7733 8989; www.four
season.mn; Peace Ave, ✉handover.vocal.retract;
dm/s/d incl breakfast US$8/15/20; 🛜) Affil-
iated with Khongor Guesthouse is this
newish hostel, run by brother-sister team,
Tooro and Orgra: both experienced travellers and seasoned tour operators. Spartan
rooms are cosy and clean, while dorms
come with the benefit of curtains, power
points and lamps. There's fast wi-fi, jam-
and-toast breakfast and book exchange.
Highly recommended for both tours and
car hire. Entrance is via the rear courtyard.

---

## 🛏 Sun Bridge (Narny Guur) Area

**LG Guesthouse**                    GUESTHOUSE $
(☎9912 1096, 9100 2311; www.lghostel.com; Teever-
chdiin St, ✉cuff.electrode.sushi; dm from US$7, s/
tw US$20/30, d with bathroom US$40; @🛜) The
newly renovated LG is the largest guest-

house in the city. It has five floors of rooms, with dorms of varying sizes and some spacious private rooms that are hotel standard. There's a common area, a kitchen for self-caterers and clean bathrooms with reliable hot water. It's a little out of the centre, however, on the road towards the train station.

### Idre Hostel
GUESTHOUSE $

(Map p58; ☑9911 2575; www.tours2mongolia.com/hostel; Narnii Guur St 22, ⊞stockpile.shrimp.total; dm US$8, r with/without bathroom US$28/24; 🛜) The single-floor hostel is on a busy road near the new bridge over Narny Zam – not the flashest neighbourhood in town. It gets good reviews, however, with several dorms and small private rooms, plus a central lounge, small kitchen and book exchange. Bathrooms are small and slightly decrepit. It's about a 20-minute walk from the hostel to the centre of the city.

It's also a popular place to arrange a tour.

## 🛏 Gandan Monastery Area

### Gana's Guest House
HOSTEL $

(Map p58; ☑9911 6960, 11-319 325; Gandan Khiid ger district, house No 22, ⊞joints.implanted.archduke; dm/s/d/tr incl breakfast US$6/15/20/25; ☺Apr-Oct; @🛜) One of UB's most unique sleeping options is this longtime backpacker hang-out where you can stay in a ger on the rooftop. Gana's also has private rooms inside a main block, but here it's all about the gers; otherwise it's a pretty ramshackle place. Centrally located, it's part of a ger district close to Gandan Khiid.

## 🛏 Sansar

### Kempinski Hotel Khan Palace
HOTEL $$$

(Map p67; ☑11-463 463; www.kempinski.com/en/ulaanbaatar; E Cross Rd, ⊞bridge.crank.perfect; s/d incl breakfast US$190/210; 🅿🌡@🛜) This Kempinski-managed venture on the east end of Peace Ave is one of the best-run places in town. Rooms are plush, with a tasteful design and little niceties such as humidifier, robes and slippers. The hotel also has a fitness centre and sauna, upmarket restaurants (both Mongolian and Japanese) and a classy cocktail bar.

## 🛏 West of Sükhbaatar Square

### ★Lotus Guesthouse
GUESTHOUSE $

(Map p58; ☑9909 4943, 11-325 967; www.lotuschild.org; off Baga Toiruu W, ⊞endearing.reforming.

tiptoes; dm US$10-15, r/apt US$30/$50; @🛜) This homey place almost feels more like a boutique guesthouse than a hostel. Rooms are individually styled, some with traditional Mongolian furniture. It has a cosy, traditional atmosphere, but some parts can be a little dim. The location is central and quiet. It's run by the Lotus Children's Centre, an NGO that helps orphaned children and employs Mongolians who used to live in the orphanage.

### Sunpath Guesthouse
GUESTHOUSE $

(Map p58; ☑9914 3722, 11-326 323; www.sunpath-mongolia.com; Baga Toiruu W, bldg 37, door 56, ⊞comforted.perfume.tint; dm US$7, r with/without bathroom US$36/24; @🛜) This bright, family-run guesthouse offers spacious dorms and private rooms across a couple of stairwells. The facilities are clean and well-maintained and it occupies a cute downtown location. There's the usual guesthouse services including wi-fi, a jam-and-toast breakfast and countryside tours. Some travellers have also reported pressure to book a tour through the guesthouse.

### UB Guesthouse
GUESTHOUSE $

(Map p58; ☑11-311 037, 9119 9859; www.ubguesthouse.com; Baga Toiruu, bldg 41, entrance 2, door 21, ⊞classmate.masterful.pretty; dm/s/tw/d/apt US$8/20/22/25/50; 🛜) This well-established and central guesthouse has several rooms stretching around a Soviet-era apartment block. It's clean and there are plenty of bathrooms, but the common room is a bit small and the place does get very busy in summer. Owner Bobbi has plenty of experience in helping backpackers with logistics and trip planning. Enter from the back of the building.

### ★Urgoo Hotel
BOUTIQUE HOTEL $$

(Map p58; ☑7011 6044; www.urgoohotel.com; Tourist St 6, M100 Bldg, ⊞proper.bashed.creatures; d/ste incl breakfast from T185,000/225,000; 🌡🛜) This boutique hotel has just 10 rooms, each one decked out in brown and beige furnishings, with flat-screen TVs and modern, albeit small, bathrooms. The prime selling point here is the location, overlooking a little park near the National Museum. There's a suave European restaurant downstairs.

### UB Inn Hotel & Gallery
HOTEL $$

(Map p58; ☑7736 6666; www.ubinnhotel.com; Sambuu St 35, ⊞puppets.pits.regrowth; s/d incl breakfast T150,000/170,000; 🌡🛜) Opened in 2016, this modern business hotel comes with comfortable rooms featuring boutique touches, kitchenettes and city views. There's an art gallery, a rooftop terrace and professional English-speaking staff.

## ✕ Eating

You'll eat well in Ulaanbaatar, with a good range of local Mongolian restaurants and international options. There's Japanese, Italian, Indian, Ukrainian, French, Mexican, American and even North Korean restaurants to name a few. Vegetarians are well represented, too, with a surprising number of meat-free, vegan restaurants. Most pubs and bars also serve food (some of it quite good).

### ✕ Juulchin (Tourist) Gadamj

**Loving Hut**     VEGAN $
(Map p58; ☑9101 8889, 11-321 396; www.loving hut.com/mg; Juulchin Gudamj, ✉exchanges. grad.confined; mains T4500-12,500; ☺11am-8.30pm Mon-Sat; ✐) This popular cafe's all-vegan menu offers a good variety of healthy and tasty dishes. Try the *mogul* (a veggie stir fry served on a sizzling platter), one of the half-dozen soups, the veggie *gyoza* or the *buuz* (steamed dumplings). Ask to see the special menu featuring fruit shakes and herbal teas.

**Luna Blanca**     VEGAN $$
(Map p58; ☑5515 9651, 11-327 172; www. facebook.com/lunablancarestaurant; Juulchin Gudamj 16, FPMT Buddhist Centre, 1st fl, ✉remarried.lighter.tools; dishes T6000-13,000; ☺11am-10pm Mon-Fri, noon-9pm Sat & Sun; ✐🛋) ✐ Famous for being the first vegan restaurant in Mongolia, this place remains very popular for its consistently tasty and healthy food. The kitchen whips up classic Mongolian dishes such as the Flour Power *(tsuivan)* and Mongol Combo Plate (with *buuz* and *khuushuur*), as well as Asian- and European-inspired fare. The atmosphere is refreshingly clean, alcohol-free and kid-friendly, and it's great value for money.

**Green Zone**     CAFE $$
(Map p58; ☑9553 9766; www.facebook.com/ thegreenzoneub; Juulchin Gudamj, Builder's Sq, ✉spirit.outgrown.jiffy; mains T6900-23,800; ☺10am-midnight; 🛜✐) Appropriately named Green Zone is a lush oasis, where plants seem to grow from walls and col-

ourful, fresh ingredients appear in front of hungry diners. The cafe-style menu features sandwiches, burgers, quiche and soups. There's hummus, freshly baked bread, mini pizzas and salads with ingredients grown in the restaurant's hanging garden. Our go-to favourites are the broccoli soup, tuna melt and lasagne.

### ✕ West of Sükhbaatar Square

**Millie's Espresso**     AMERICAN $$
(Map p58; ☑11-330 338; Marco Polo Plaza, ✉putts.start.backs; mains T10,000-18,000; ☺8am-8pm Mon-Sat, 9am-4pm Sun; 🛜✐🛋) Since it first opened its doors in 1998, Millie's has been a favourite among expats seeking American comfort food. The owners – Daniel and Densmaa – warmly greet patrons to their sunlit restaurant and promptly serve up tasty burgers, sandwiches and soups. Special treats include smoothies, lemon pie and a delicious chocolate cake (which sells out early). Don't miss Daniel's famous Cuban sandwich, only available on Tuesday.

**Pyongyang Baek Hwa Restaurant**     NORTH KOREAN $$
(☑9553 9363, 9140 5152; Daco Bldg, 15th fl, ✉abandons.hopes.bigger; mains T13,000-27,000; ☺11am-11pm) This North Korean restaurant delivers in the weirdness stakes, with its classic DRPK kitsch and a memorable stage performance held each evening at 8pm. Hidden atop a high-rise building, there are fantastic city views, and it's decorated with fake birch trees. There's an art gallery (all works for sale), and a menu offering regional dishes and classics such as *bulgogi* and *bibimbap*.

Wash it down with a North Korean beer or soju, though the former will set you back T18,000! There's a bunch of intriguing propaganda material to peruse while you await your meal. All staff are from Pyongyang and speak reasonable English. It's a little out of the way, located in the Daco building behind the Urgoo-1 cinema.

**Veranda**     MEDITERRANEAN $$$
(Map p58; ☑7710 2992; www.veranda.mn; Jamyngun St 5/1, ✉woverdone.scared.finishers; mains T17,000-39,000; ☺noon-midnight; ✐) While it's not particularly old, this fine-dining restaurant has an almost colonial air to it, with couch seating inside and a big porch overlooking the Choijin Lama Temple Museum.

## ULAANBAATAR CHEAP EATS

There are dozens of Mongolian budget restaurants (guanz) and they can be found on every block in the city. Some are chain restaurants and you'll start to recognise prominent eateries, including Zochin Buuz (Зочин Бууз), **Khaan Buuz** (Хаан Бууз; Map p58; Peace Ave, *[w]*moon.flops.guideline; mains T6000-8500; ⊘24hr) and **Zochin Cafe** (Зочин Кафе; Map p58; ✆11-327 277; Sambugiin Örgön Chölöö, *[w]*lend.trending.possible; mains T3000-14,900; ⊘9am-9pm). They serve up buuz (steamed mutton dumplings) and tsuivan (fried noodles) plus soups and various meat-based creations. They are often quite dire – think globs of mashed potatoes, chunks of fatty mutton, and rice topped with ketchup – so keep your expectations at ground zero. Some of the chains operate 24 hours. Meals cost between T3000-14,900.

The food is surprisingly good, with a menu featuring an array of delectable main dishes that fuse Italian and French recipes served by bow-tie uniformed waiters. Reserve ahead if you want a patio table.

## ✗ Seoul Street

### Sakura Bakery
JAPANESE $

(Map p58; Prime Minister Tserendorj St, Beatles Sq, *[w]*canines.mascot.mothering; mains from T8000; ⊘7.30am-7.30pm Tue-Sat, to 3.30pm Sun Aug-Jun) This authentic Japanese cafe has a dedicated following who come for the simple curry lunches, fried chicken, ramen noodles, excellent cakes (try the famous cheesecake and cream puffs!) and friendly atmosphere. Manga fans will appreciate the collection of comic books. Note this place is usually closed in July.

### Bosco Verde
ITALIAN $$

(Map p58; ✆7011 7715; www.boscoverde.mn; Usnii Rd 37a, *[w]*radiating.lease.cowboy; mains T8000-12,000; ⊘11am-9pm; 🅙) This popular little trattoria does tasty vegan Italian pastas and pizzas, using dairy-free and meatless toppings. There's other Western mains as well, along with Mongolian dishes.

### Caucasia
CAUCASIAN $$

(Map p58; ✆7711 9900; www.modernnomads. mn; Usnii St, *[w]*scanty.economies.sidelined; mains T9900-31,900; ⊘11am-midnight Mon-Sat, to 11pm Sun; 🅙) Another offering from the Modern Nomads empire is this atmospheric restaurant specialising in food from the Caucasus. Expect the likes of khachapuri (cheese bread), eggplant rolls, lamb pita and plenty of vegetarian dishes from Georgia, Azerbaijan and Armenia.

### Rosewood Kitchen + Enoteca
ITALIAN $$$

(Map p58; ✆9402 0561; www.facebook.com/ rosewoodkitchenenoteca; Seoul St, Mandal Bldg, *[w]*guarded.prawn.defenders; mains T16,000-37,000; ⊘7.30am-10pm Mon-Sat; 🕾🅙) Hidden behind an ugly facade is this popular bistro that does homemade pastas, pizzas, sandwiches and salads, all made with high-quality local and imported ingredients. Many items are made in-house, including the breads. The atmosphere is smart and businesslike, and it's popular with expats.

It's tucked off the street in the ground floor of a five-storey grey building next to a large ger. There's also its **Butchery** (Map p58; ✆9401 0561; www.facebook.com/thebutcheryub; off Seoul St, *[w]*cone.keyboards.donates; ⊘11am-8pm), a small grocery that sells its bread, locally sourced meats and gourmet treats.

## ✗ East of Sükhbaatar Square

### Shilmel Buuz
MONGOLIAN $

(Map p58; ✆8881 0518; Prime Minister A Amar's St, *[w]*slopes.fended.starring; buuz T700, salads T1500; ⊘8am-9pm Mon-Fri) This small guanz (canteen), with plastic tablecloths and bare walls, may not have much atmosphere, but it's well known for serving some of the best buuz in the city (nearly homemade quality). Unlike most other cafes, the dumplings here are not overly fatty and come piping hot from a special steamer. Try a few with süütei tsai (Mongolian milk tea with salt).

Look for the picture of the two kids gorging on a big plate of buuz.

### Black Burger Factory
BURGERS $

(Map p58; ✆7711 4664; www.facebook.com/ blackburger.mn; Prime Minister A Amar's St 2, *[w]*pizzas.pines.joints; burgers from T7900;

## SELF-CATERING

For self-caterers, there are many shops around the city that sell food imported from China, Korea, the US and Europe. Fresh fruit and veggies are also available; some items are home-grown in Mongolia, although most of what you'll find is imported from China. Some tasty local products include yoghurt, cheese, apples, berries, tomatoes and cream. Most markets are open from about 8am to 10pm daily. The supermarket on the ground floor of the **State Department Store** (Map p58; ☑11-319 292; Peace Ave 44, ⊞conductor.nearing.given; shashlik T7500; ⊙8.30am-10pm) has a well-stocked selection, while **Good Price** (Map p58; Seoul St, ⊞: mull.direction.drawn; ⊙9am-midnight) is good for imported international items.

Bread is available everywhere, but the best is found at small bakeries such as **Butchery by Rosewood** (p73) and **Le Bistro Français**.

⊙10am-midnight; 🛜🍴) UB's first foray into a hipster-style eatery is this burger joint with exposed brick, low-hanging lamps, subway tiles and bench seating. As well as its signature black-bun burgers, there's all the expected classics, as well as veggie and vegan options. There are beers on tap and wines by the glass, too.

### ★Bull 3 HOTPOT$$
(Map p58; ☑7710 0060; Baga Toiruu E, Blue Mon Bldg, 3rd fl, ⊞amps.heads.harmony; T4500-9000; ⊙11am-10pm; 🍴) Within the upmarket Blue Mon Building is this elegant restaurant that's always busy with well-dressed folk here for hotpot. Order an array of raw vegetables, sauces and thinly sliced meats, which are brought to your table on platters, then cook the ingredients in your personal cauldron of boiling broth. It also has two branches on Seoul St – **Bull 1** (Map p58; ☑7710 0060; Seoul St, ⊞avoid.whimpered. broth; per piece T4500-9000; ⊙10.30am-midnight Mon-Fri, from 11.30am Sat & Sun; 🍴) and Bull 2.

### Modern Nomads 2 MONGOLIAN$$
(Map p58; ☑7012 0808; www.modernnomads. mn; Prime Minister A Amar's St, ⊞knots.jolt. regulate; meals T8600-30,000; ⊙10am-midnight Mon-Fri, to 11pm Sat & Sun) One of UB's best places to sample a feast of classic Mongolian dishes; try the *khorkhog* (lamb cooked on hot stone), *khuushuur* (meat pastries), *buuz* (steamed meat-filled dumplings), Mongolian soups or even sheep's head. Portions are insanely large. It's part of a chain of restaurants, but this branch seems to do slightly better than the others. A picture menu makes ordering easy.

## 🍴 North of Sükhbaatar Square

### Hashi JAPANESE$$
(Map p58; ☑9196 0523; Sambuu St, ⊞bandstand. walnuts.jolly; udon soup T10,000; ⊙10am-10pm Sun-Fri; 🛜) This small restaurant offers tasty, high-quality Japanese food at reasonable prices. Try the udon soup served in a small metal pot or add a side of tempura for T5000 extra. Has a handy location just behind Government House.

### Le Bistro Français FRENCH$$$
(Map p58; ☑11-320 022; www.facebook.com/ bistrotfrancaisUB; Ikh Surguuliin Gudamj 2, ⊞mildest.expectant.hint; mains T21,000-41,000; ⊙9.30am-11pm Mon-Fri, from 11am Sat & Sun; 🛜) The soft lighting, cream-coloured walls and French art give this bistro a peaceful, romantic ambience. Try the lamb goulash or beef fillet, washed down with a French red wine. It bakes its own croissants and baguettes, and classic French delicacies such as frogs legs and escargot are sometimes available. It's popular with expats and Mongolian corporate bigwigs looking for some Rive Gauche style.

## 🍴 Sansar

### Mongolians MONGOLIAN$$
(Map p67; ☑9909 7716; Ikh Toiruu 93, Barilga Mega Store, ⊞equity.remove.arena; mains T8600-30,000; ⊙11am-10pm; ♿) This upmarket Mongolian restaurant has walls lined with traditional antiques and old photos, and a menu of contemporary local cuisine. Expect stir-fried meats, dumplings and boiled mutton, along with some Russian and European influences and cold beer on tap. It's a bit out of the way, however.

★**Hazara**                                    INDIAN $$$

(Map p67; ☑ 9919 5007, 11-480 214; www.hazara.
mn; Peace Ave 16, ⊞ transmit.composts.spurned;
dishes T17,700-26,200; ⊙ noon-10pm; 🌶)
Tucked behind the Wrestling Palace, this
North Indian restaurant has consistently
been one of the best restaurants in Ulaan-
baatar for over 15 years. Each table is cov-
ered by a colourful Rajasthani tent, where
you sit back and enjoy tandoori baked
delights. Try the chicken tikka, *aloo gobi*
(potato and cauliflower) or *raan-e-hazara*
(lamb marinated in rum).

Prices are on the high side, but the por-
tions are massive.

**Tenger
Restaurant**          MONGOLIAN, INTERNATIONAL $$$

(Map p67; ☑ 11-463 463; www.facebook.com/
tengerkempinski; Kempinski Hotel Khan Palace,
⊞ always.inflating.exhaled; mains T16,000-
35,000; ⊙ 7-10am & 11.30am-midnight; 🌶) This
Mongolian restaurant on the ground floor
of the Kempinski Hotel has a reputation
for offering some of the highest standard
Mongol cuisine this side of the Great Wall.
Professional staff, crisp white tableclothes
and a good wine list go with well-made
dishes such as *khorkhog*, *khuushuur* and
*tsuivan* (noodles; including vegetarian
varieties), along with European mains, imported steaks and a house burger.

Its European-American buffet breakfast
(T37,000 plus tax) is one of the best in town.

---

🍴 **South of Sükhbaatar Square**

**Merkuri Market**                          MARKET

(Мэркури; Map p58; wdeflated.measures.
method; ⊙ 10am-7pm Mon-Sat, to 6pm Sun) At
Merkuri food market, private vendors sell
imported goods, meat, cheese, fruit and vegetables – easily the best selection of fresh
food products in the country. The door is
small and there is no sign, but you can find
it by walking to the right side of the large
'Minii Delguur' supermarket (or just follow
the crowds and ask for 'Merkuri').

The complex itself is hidden behind
apartment buildings about 200m west of
the State Circus.

**Khaan Deli Central**                   AMERICAN $$

(Map p58; ☑ 8846 3354; www.khaandeli.com;
Khaddorjiin Gudamj, bldg 31-44, ⊞ collides.mir-
acle.spelling; mains breakfast T5000-13,000,
dinner T15,000-17,000; ⊙ 8am-8pm Sun-Thu,

to 10pm Fri & Sat; 🌶) Owner and Michigan
native Darren has done his best to bring
American heartland food to Ulaanbaatar.
The speciality American breakfasts and ba-
gels are the perfect cure for a hangover, or
if you've come for lunch, there's a range of
burgers, hot dogs, salads and pulled-pork
sandwiches. It also serves some surprising-
ly good Mongolian dishes, including *tsuiv-
an* and *khuitsai*, a beef and vegetable stew.

**Arig & Anya**                             RAMEN $$

(Map p58; ☑ 7000 7020; Jamyn St 10, ⊞ duke.
clinic.tall; ramen T9200-12,000; ⊙ 10am-mid-
night; 🌶) A popular city Japanese ramen
bar featuring delicious spicy noodle
broths; try one with sausage, a speciality of
the house, and polish it off with a passion-
fruit smoothie, served in a jar. It has a cosy
atmosphere indoors and a small porch for
summer seating.

**Spicy Street**                         PUB FOOD $$

(Map p58; ☑ 8977 8977; www.facebook.com/
spicystreetub; Jamyn St, ⊞ resolves.moats.smart-
er; dishes from T11,000; ⊙ 11am-late Mon-Fri, noon-
late Sat & Sun; 🌶) Festooned with colourful
umbrellas, Spicy Street is a vibrant bar and
bistro that does a menu of burgers, pizza,
wings, ribs and Korean barbecue. Grab a
drink and head to its inviting courtyard
beer garden with exposed bricks and crate
furniture.

**Rock Salt**                          INTERNATIONAL $$$

(Map p58; ☑ 7700 1881, 8877 2662; www.rocksalt.
mn; Jamyn St, 4th fl, ⊞ prowl.users.cherished;
mains T15,000-65,000; ⊙ noon-midnight Mon-Sat;
🌶) This chic city restaurant channels Manhattan with its low-lit contemporary decor,
curved ceiling and smooth jazz. Steaks and
seafood are the speciality, which you grill
on hot stone boards brought to your table.
There's also Mongolian dishes, along with
pizza and pasta, and an outdoor terrace for
summer evenings.

🍷 **Drinking & Nightlife**

There are numerous good, clean and safe
bars and pubs in Ulaanbaatar; most of
them are located downtown around the
Drama Theatre or on Seoul St. For beer
lovers, there are several microbreweries
that have taprooms, while for cocktails,
hit one of the swanky rooftop bars. There
are plenty of clubs, too, for those looking
to kick on.

## South of Sükhbaatar Square

**★17 Sky Bar** BAR

(Map p58; ☑11-310 707; www.facebook.com/sky 17barulaanbaatar; Sükhbaatar Sq 2, Central Tower, 17th fl, ⊞represent.coaching.wriggle; ⊙noon-2am; ☎) One of UB's best spots for a cocktail is this ritzy rooftop bar atop the Central Tower, featuring wonderful views of the city and surrounding hills. Drinks are well made by friendly bar staff, though order off the menu if you're after something more classic. There's also bar food and international cuisine (mains from T17,000). DJs and live music on weekends.

**MB Beer Plus** PUB

(Map p58; ☑11-326 741; Chinngis Ave, ⊞wove. weep.digs; ⊙11am-2am Mon-Sat, from 4pm Sun; ☎) This popular city microbrewery produces four beers on-site, with the standout being its amber ale; it also does a lager, weiser and dark ale. It gets packed on weekend evenings with young professionals here for beers accompanied by plates of pub food, and it has a terrace beer garden for summer.

**Blue Sky Lounge** LOUNGE

(Map p58; ☑8000 2323; Peace Ave 17, Blue Sky Tower, 23rd fl, ⊞calm.grins.acute; ⊙5pm-2am; ☎) This cocktail bar at the top of the iconic Blue Sky Tower is a stylish place for a drink. There's great views, as expected, and it also does a menu of pizzas, burgers and the like.

**Terrace Bar** BEER GARDEN

(Map p58; ☑8810 9393; Peace Ave 17, Blue Sky Tower, ⊞screening.singing.weaved; ⊙5pm-1am Jun-Sep; ☎) Only open when the sun is shining, this sneaky outdoor beer garden does charcoal-barbecued meats and has

cold beers on tap. It's on the 2nd floor of the Blue Sky Tower.

**Vegas** CLUB

(Map p58; ☑7010 9889, 8810 9393; www. facebook.com/vegasmn; Peace Ave 17, Blue Sky Tower, ⊞blasted.winded.ordeals; cover T10,000-20,000; ⊙9pm-4am Wed-Sun) Located in the basement of the landmark Blue Sky Tower is this bunker-like nightclub that runs a variety of events through the week. Expect anything from R&B, to electro and salsa. It attracts a good mix of foreigners and locals.

## Khan Uul District & Zaisan

**ROC Caffeine Bar** COFFEE

(☑9999 0563, 9904 1165; www.roc.mn; Zaisan, Gerelt Khotkhon 17/10, ⊞drilling.strapping.spotted; ⊙7am-10pm Mon-Fri, from 8am Sat & Sun; ☎) Hidden away in an affluent south UB neighbourhood, this hip coffee roaster uses seasonal beans sourced from around the world. As well as knocking out a great flat white (T5000), you can get Aeropress, siphon and pour-over coffees to enjoy with avocado on toast for brekkie or the likes of Korean fried chicken burger for lunch (mains from T10,000).

Pop art decorates the walls and it attracts a cool local clientele. There's a glassed-in gallery to watch the coffee roasting.

## North of Sükhbaatar Square

**★Dund Gol** BAR

(Map p58; ☑8827 8017; www.facebook.com/ dundgol; Baga Toiruu, ⊞schematic.liked.workforce; ⊙noon-midnight; ☎) One for lovers of obscure, indie music, Dund Gol is a hip little bar that doubles as a record store, stocking an impressive collection of Soviet and post-communist vinyl. You'll come across some fascinating genres, from Polish psychedelic to Russian disco, all for purchase or to listen to. It's a cool place to hang out with retro lounge decor and an art-filled front beer garden.

**Matchbox Cafe** BAR

(Map p58; Baga Toiruu 30, ⊞sums.flames.compacts; ⊙11am-midnight; ☎) Catering to the local student crowd, Matchbox is a cool bar decked out with crate furniture, an old-school Sega console (with a heap of games), a foosball table and a good selection of board games. A guitar sits side of stage awaiting any budding musos. As well as cold beer and locally roasted coffee from UBean Coffeehouse (p78), it's popular for food.

### D.d / h.z
GAY & LESBIAN

(Map p58; ☑9400 8658; www.facebook.com/didihzub; Baga Toiruu, ⌘flame.blogs.pipe; ☺6pm-late) Ulaanbaatar's main hang-out for the local LGBT community, this relaxed neighbourhood pub has a friendly and welcoming atmosphere. Its owner Zorig Alima also ran Hanzo before its controversial forced closure, but this is a more laid-back incarnation. There's no clear signage, so look out for the bar named 'Kelvin's'.

### VLVT Lounge
BAR, CLUB

(Map p58; ☑9914 1980; www.facebook.com/vlvt.lounge; Baga Toiruu N, ⌘reclaim.drama.spruced; ☺5pm-midnight Mon-Wed, to 4am Thu-Sat; ☎) In this dimly lit den of luxury, Ulaanbaatar's young entrepreneurs cut business deals over pricey cocktails (from T10,000) and platters of sushi while sitting at a translucent bar made from marble. In a separate room, revellers arrive late for DJs spinning the latest hip-hop and dance mixes (cover charge T10,000). Dress code is smart casual.

### Chinggis Beer Club
BREWERY, PUB

(Map p58; ☑7011 5820, 11-325 157; www.chinggisbeer.mn; Sükhbaataryn Gudamj 10, ⌘assurance.phantom.dragging; ☺11am-midnight; ☎) Enjoy a pint of Chinggis while watching the brewers in action at this German-style tavern that produces this popular brand of Mongolian beer. There's also a full menu of hearty pub food (mains T13,000 to T27,000).

## 🍷 Seoul Street

### ★ Basement
BAR

(Map p58; ☑9520 7050; www.facebook.com/basementhouze; Seoul St, ⌘impulses.yachting.hobbit; ☺6pm-4am) Head downstairs to this cool, grungy basement club in Seoul St to hang out with the local indie kids. There's regular live bands and DJs, and it's a good place to meet a friendly, alternative crowd.

### ★ Hops & Rocks Brewery
CRAFT BEER

(Map p58; ☑8800 3506; www.facebook.com/hopsandrocksbrewery; Usnii St, ⌘purifier.flitting.staples; ☺6pm-2am Tue-Sat) Mongolia's first genuine producer of craft beer is this bar set up by a team of locals who brew a Crazy Shaman IPA, a Two Rams pale ale and a

Red Cheeks amber ale. There are also a few seasonal brews, along with bar food. It's in the same entrance as the Ikh Mongol beer hall, northeast of the circus.

### Revolution
BEER GARDEN

(Map p58; Seoul St 23, ⌘decency.loud.neckline; ☺noon-late) Playing its part in revitalising Seoul St is this happening pub fronted by an inviting terrace beer garden where owner Nasaa can usually be found behind the bar. Inside it's decked out with a dark-wood English-pub decor and a stage for regular live music, DJs, comedy and open-mic nights. It's equally popular for food, with Mongolian and Western dishes served in huge portions.

It also has a more cosy local **pub** (Map p58; ☑9918 8434; Baruun Selbe Gudamj, ⌘dentures.chip.perfectly; ☺11am-2am; ☎) across from the State Department Store.

### Mojito Cocktail House
COCKTAIL BAR

(Map p58; ☑7710 0808; Seoul St, Exquisite Centre, 2nd fl, ⌘composers.blame.clasping; ☺11am-11.30pm) A hip spot for drinking and meeting Ulaanbaatar's young urbanites. Unsurprisingly, mojitos are the house speciality, but there's some good tiki concoctions, too. The swanky interior, soothing playlists and sophisticated drinks make this a must-visit if you are painting the town red.

### Peaberry
COFFEE

(Map p58; ☑9925 0876; www.thepeaberry.mn; Seoul St, Exquisite Centre, ⌘rigs.select.rafters; ☺8am-10pm; ☎) One for those who take their coffee seriously, this cool microroastery brews beans from across Africa and Latin America. Coffees (T4500) are made by expert baristas using your choice of Aeropress, siphon, drip, cold brew or old-fashioned espresso, including flat whites and long blacks.

## ♀ Sansar

★**UBean Coffeehouse**                           CAFE
(✆9638 2326; www.ubeanroasterie.com; Man-laibaatar Damdinsuren St, wtastier.snap.skewed; ⊗8.30am-8pm Mon-Fri, to 2pm Sat; 🖥) Ul-aanbaatar's best spot for coffee, the stylish American-owned UBean specialises in pour-overs using single-origin beans sourced from farms from Ethiopia to Honduras. All coffee beans are roasted on-site, and prepared by knowledgable baristas; there's also 12-hour cold drip for summer. Food is another reason to drop by, with homemade bagels, dough-nuts, BLT sandwiches and cakes on offer (mains from T8000).

## ♀ East of Sükhbaatar Square

★**iLoft**                                        CLUB
(Map p58; ✆9909 0528; off Prime Minister A Am-ar's St, wshows.greyhound.tooth; cover T20,000; ⊗10pm-4am; 🖥) This multi-use venue trans-forms into a pulsing nightclub after dark. There's leather seating, a large dance floor, techno beats and a mature crowd. It's locat-ed behind the Best Western Tuushin Hotel.

## ☆ Entertainment

Both the *UB Post* and the *Mongol Messen-ger* English-language newspapers contain weekly events listings. Theatres and galler-ies sometimes post English ads outside or you could just buy a ticket and hope for the best. Also visit the Easy Ticket website (www.easyticket.mn) to see what's showing.

★**Tumen Ekh National Song
& Dance Ensemble**          TRADITIONAL MUSIC, DANCE
(Map p58; ✆11-322 238; www.tumenekh.word-press.com; Nairamdal Park, State Youth & Chil-dren's Theatre, wreadily.wealth.squashes; tick-ets T25,000, camera/video T20,000/100,000; ⊗4pm & 6pm daily; 🚑) The Tumen Ekh Song & Dance Ensemble at the State Youth & Children's Theatre is the most popular tourist cultural show in town, featuring traditional singers, dancers and contor-tionists. It's a great chance to hear *khöömii* (throat singing) and see some fabulous cos-tumes. Shows last just over an hour, and are held daily outside of winter months; check the ensemble's Facebook page for the schedule.

---

### MODERN MONGOLIAN MUSIC MASH-UPS

There is a thriving live-music scene in Ulaanbaatar. While you're in town, make sure to pick up some CDs of the newest artists; **Hi-Fi Mega Store** (p81) has a good selection. Even better, try to catch a live performance. You can hear live music at many downtown bars, but the best spots for gigs are **Gandan Live House** (p79), **Basement** (p77) and **Salm Brau Pub** (Map p58; ✆7711 5544; Baga Toiruu, ⊞left.betraying.clipboard; ⊗4pm-late; 🖥). At these venues you can catch local indie bands, punk, rap and hip-hop, as well as a totally Mongolian brand of folklore-rock fusion music that includes drums and guitars along with traditional instruments.

For folklore-rock, Altan Urag is regarded as one of the best. Their mash-ups of West-ern percussion and Mongolian string instruments will have you entranced. Check out YouTube for videos such as 'Raakh II' and 'Abroad'. Other bands worth checking out are Boerte Ensemble, who fuse all sorts of instruments into a mellow sound (good for long road trips), and Khusugtun, who were recorded by the BBC's *Human Planet* series.

Indie rock groups include the Lemons, Pips, Nisvanis and the Colors. For mellow R&B, try BX, Maraljingoo and Bold. Nominjin is a talented R&B voice on the international scene; she sings in both English and Mongolian.

If you are into hip-hop, look out for Opozit, Quiza, Tatar and Tsetse. The emulation of American inner-city gangsta rap speaks volumes about Mongolia's eagerness to embrace Western culture; however, if you can get someone to translate the lyrics you'll hear a distinct Mongolian flavour, with popular topics including lost loves, mothers, wild nature and blue skies.

This breakout in Mongolian rap has not gone unnoticed. Australian filmmaker Benj Binks has documented the phenomena in the film *Mongolian Bling* (www.mongolian bling.com). Not to be outdone, American Lauren Knapp created *Live From UB* (www. livefromub.com), a documentary exploring Mongolian rock music.

**Gandan Live House**  LIVE MUSIC

([📞]7010 4040, 7010 4004; www.facebook.com/gandanlivehouse; Amarsanaagiin Gudamj, [🌐]woven.envy.attention; ⊙noon-late) UB's premier live-music venue is this boozy club that hosts local bands playing anything from indie rock to electronica. Music is on Friday and Saturday nights, and during the week it's a rock bar and restaurant. There's an inviting outdoor terrace in summer, and it's part of an entertainment complex of bars, clubs and restaurants.

**UB Jazz Club**  JAZZ

(Map p58; [📞]7700 0138; www.facebook.com/UbJazzClub; Seoul St, bldg 44, [🌐]intruders.dampen.inherits; ⊙11am-4am) As the name suggests, this is a dedicated jazz club – the only one in Ulaanbaatar. There's live music nightly at around 9pm. A rotating group of bands play here (check the Facebook page for upcoming events). You don't need a ticket to get in, unless it's a special event. The unfiltered house beer is another reason to drop by.

**State Opera & Ballet Theatre**  OPERA, BALLET

(Map p58; [📞]7011 0389, 9690 7010; www.opera-ballet.mn; Sükhbaatar Sq, [🌐]media.congested.rock; tickets T8000-15,000; ⊙box office 10am-2pm & 3-6pm Wed-Sun) Built by the Russians in 1932 (look for the Soviet stars on the columns), the State Opera & Ballet Theatre is the salmon-pinkish building on the southeast corner of Sükhbaatar Sq. On Saturday and Sunday evenings throughout the year, and sometimes also on weekend afternoons in the summer, the theatre stages stirring ballet and Mongolian-language opera. It's closed in August.

**National Academic Drama Theatre**  THEATRE

(Map p58; [📞]7011 8187, 7012 8999; www.drama.mn; cnr Seoul St & Chinggis Ave, [🌐]converged.nurtures.satin; tickets T10,000-50,000; ⊙ticket sales 10am-7pm) During most of the year this large, red-hued theatre shows one of a dozen or so Mongolian-language productions by various playwrights from Mongolia, Russia and beyond. You can buy tickets in advance through Easy Ticket (www.easyticket.mn) or at the booking office, which is inside the small concrete guardhouse on the right-hand side of the theatre.

**Puppet Theatre**  PUPPET THEATRE

(Map p58; [📞]11-321 669; cnr Seoul St & Chinggis Ave, [🌐]glorious.likening.eased; tickets T5000-15,000; ⊙ticket office 9am-6pm; [👶]) Great if you are travelling with children, with three performances a week. Days and times change monthly, so call ahead.

**Wrestling Palace**  SPECTATOR SPORT

(Map p67; [📞]11-456 978; www.undesniibukh.mn; Peace Ave, [🌐]assures.leotard.blunders; tickets T5000-10,000) For wrestling outside of Naadam, check out the schedule at the Wrestling Palace, which is the ger-shaped building south of the Chinggis Khaan Hotel.

## 🛍 Shopping

The antique trade is booming in Mongolia, but you need to be careful about what you buy, as some of it is illegal to export. Make sure the seller can produce a certificate of authenticity. Some dealers will suggest shipping the antiques in the mail to avoid customs at the airport – if you get caught, you may end up in prison.

The numerous souvenir shops in town sell landscape paintings, wool slippers, Mongolian jackets, felt dolls and Chinggis Khaan T-shirts. On Sükhbaatar Sq and in the central post office you will undoubtedly encounter amateur artists selling watercolours for US$1 to US$5. Contemporary Mongolian artworks can be purchased at a small number of galleries around town. The biggest souvenir outlet is on the 6th floor of the State Department Store (p80).

Traditional musical instruments make perfect gifts for friends who are musically inclined. The *morin khuur* (horse-head fiddle) is particularly nice as a piece of decorative art (and Mongolians consider it good luck to have one in the home).

Cashmere also makes good gifts. The major cashmere and wool factories are Goyo, Gobi Cashmere and Altai. The State Department Store has cashmere on the 2nd and 6th floors. Some shops around Beatles Sq also deal in cashmere.

Be aware that Western-quality camping gear is not cheap in Mongolia, so you may want to bring stuff from home. Cheap Chinese-made products are available if you're desperate, though don't be surprised if it breaks down before you even leave the city. There is a decent camping section on the 3rd floor of the State Department Store. For secondhand stuff, check noticeboards at guesthouses.

For a country with such a rich tradition in horse riding there is a surprising lack of shops selling saddles and tack. The best selection is still at the Naran Tuul Market (p81). You may also be able to pick up a secondhand saddle from another traveller (check guesthouse noticeboards).

English-language bookshops are small and limited. Your best bet is the secondhand Books in English.

## South of Sükhbaatar Square

**Seven Summits** SPORTS & OUTDOORS
(Map p58; ☑9942 9989, 11-317 923; www.activemongolia.com; btwn Peace Ave & Seoul St, Ⓜabsorb.inkjet.whisk; ☺10am-7pm Mon-Fri, to 6pm Sat & Sun) Stocks German-made Vaude gear, GPS units, maps, stoves and gas, and travel books and accessories. It also hires outdoor gear, including tents, sleeping bags, gas stoves and inflatable kayaks.

**LHAMOUR** COSMETICS
(Map p58; ☑7712 0256; www.lhamour.mn; Shangri-La Centre, 2nd fl, Ⓜpublic.emulating.growth; ☺10am-10pm) Set up by a Mongolian woman, this classy cosmetics store specialises in organic body products and accessories made using local products from sea buckthorn to sheep's tail.

**Gobi Cashmere Factory Outlet** CASHMERE
(☑7013 9977; www.gobi.mn; Khan-Uul District, Industrial St, wfairway.shots.ratio; ☺9am-9pm) Has slightly lower prices than the cashmere shops in the city centre, although much of it is last year's stock. Next door is the flagship shop with a full range of items, and regular fashion shows during summer. It's in the industrial suburbs, so it's best to get a taxi here.

## West of Sükhbaatar Square

**Mongolian Quilting Shop** GIFTS & SOUVENIRS
(Map p58; ☑9909 9930, 9511 9930; www.mongolianquilts.org; Seoul St 39, Ⓜpayout.prefer.concluded; ☺9am-6pm Mon-Fri, 10am-5pm Sat & Sun Apr-Oct, 10am-6pm Mon-Fri, to 5pm Sat Nov-Mar) ✎ Sells handmade quilts produced by low-income families. The money earned here goes to the New Life NGO, which directly supports the women who produce the quilts.

**Cartography Co Map Shop** MAPS
(Map p58; ☑9115 6023; Ikh Toiruu, Ⓜcourtyard.studs.laugh; ☺9am-1pm & 2-6pm Mon-Fri, 10am-4pm Sat) For up-to-date road maps of Mongolia try this shop near the Elba Electronics centre.

## State Department Store Area

**★Mary & Martha Mongolia** GIFTS & SOUVENIRS
(Map p58; ☑9972 5297; www.mmmongolia.com; off Peace Ave, Ⓜdust.goods.flamingo; ☺10.30am-7pm) ✎ Fair-trade shop selling handmade traditional handicrafts, felt products, clothing (including men's and children's), toys, jewellery and modern Kazakh wall hangings. Has some innovative little products such as computer bags and mobile-phone cases made with traditional designs. As well as cashmere products, it has yak- and camel-wool products.

**★State Department Store** DEPARTMENT STORE
(Их Дэлгүүр; Map p58; ☑1800 2888; www.nomin.mn; Peace Ave 44, wbravo.hexes.steamed; ☺8.45am-10pm Mon-Fri, 9am-10pm Sat, to 9.30pm Sun) Established in 1921, the State Department Store, known as *ikh delguur* (big shop), is a local institution and virtually a tourist attraction in itself. Here the best products from around the city are squeezed into one building, and it's the place to come for quality cashmere (2nd floor), Erdenet carpets (4th floor) and a wide range of souvenirs, traditional clothing and books about Mongolia (6th floor).

**Tsagaan Alt Wool Shop** GIFTS & SOUVENIRS
(Map p58; ☑11-318 591; www.mongolianwoolcraft.com; Prime Minister Tserendorj St, Beatles Sq, Ⓜreleased.bystander.grandest; ☺10am-7pm Mon-Sat, to 6pm Sun) ✎ This nonprofit store, which sends money directly back to the craftspeople, has all manner of wool products, including toys, clothes and artwork.

**Cashmere House** CASHMERE
(Map p58; Peace Ave, Ⓜstiffly.altering.formation; ☺10am-8pm) Excellent cashmere and wool garments can be purchased here, with all of Mongolia's big brands represented, including Gobi, Goyo, Altai and Blue Sky. It's opposite the Russian embassy.

**Books in English** BOOKS
(Map p58; ☑9903 6703; Peace Ave, Ⓜhorizons.huts.hexes; ☺noon-8pm Mon-Fri, to 7pm Sat, 10am-6pm Sun) Sells and exchanges used books in English, including fiction, books on Mongolia and guidebooks.

### THE BIG SMOKE

Ulaanbaatar means 'Red Hero'. However, in winter a more apropos name would be 'Kharbaatar', the 'Black Hero', as the city is often cloaked in a thick cloud of noxious smoke that can linger for days until a strong wind blows it away.

By 2011 the air pollution had reached such epic levels that the World Health Organization (WHO) rated Ulaanbaatar the world's second-most polluted city, after Ahvaz in western Iran. While other cities have since displaced it with higher levels, in 2016 reports indicated Ulaanbaatar had reached levels of pollution five times that of Beijing, a city notorious for its red smog alerts.

However, unlike many cities, which are polluted year round, Ulaanbaatar's pollution is packed into the winter months, from November to March, when families in the ger districts furiously burn coal to fend off the extreme cold. Around 92% of the smoke in UB comes from stoves in the ger districts.

In the worst affected areas of the city, the levels of PM2.5 (particulate matter that is 2.5 micrometres or less) can exceed an appalling 2500. According to WHO, 300 or above is considered 'hazardous'. Levels in the city centre aren't quite so horrific but can still regularly exceed 1000 in winter.

To help cut pollution the government has sold around 120,000 subsidised Turkish-built stoves to families in ger areas. The stoves are more fuel efficient and cleaner burning than the traditional Mongolian stove, but they still emit some smoke so the project is considered just a temporary fix.

The longer-term solution is to bring central heat and apartments to the gers areas. But with a short building season and 180,000 families needing modern housing the project could be years, if not decades, in the making.

To see the latest PM2.5 measurements in Ulaanbaatar see www.ub-air.info/ub-air/en.

**Souvenir House** GIFTS & SOUVENIRS
(Map p58; ☎11-320 398; cnr Peace Ave & Khaddorjiin Gudamj, ///method.blessing.amaze; ⏰10am-8pm) One of the largest souvenir shops in town.

**Hi-Fi Mega Store** MUSIC
(Map p58; ☎11-333 111; www.hi-fi.mn; Peace Ave 5, ///dentistry.author.stocks; ⏰10am-9pm) The definitive spot to pick up local, contemporary music, stocking anything from Mongolian indie bands to Top 40, as well as traditional CDs.

## North of Sükhbaatar Square

**Egshiglen Magnai National Musical Instrument Shop** MUSICAL INSTRUMENTS
(Map p58; ☎11-328 419; www.egshiglen.mn; Sükhbaataryn Gudamj, ///blogs.brambles.jazzy; ⏰9am-6pm Mon-Sat) A great little shop for those interested in buying handmade Mongolian instruments. It sells *morin khuur* (horse-head fiddles; from T180,000), *yattag* (zithers) and two-stringed Chinese fiddles, as well as CDs of traditional Mongolian music. All instruments are made instore.

**Amarbayasgalant Antique** ANTIQUES
(Map p58; ☎11-310 000; Juulchin Gudamj 37/31, ///animated.texts.clothed; ⏰10am-5pm) A quality shop for the serious buyer, it sells enormous Sutras, traditional headdresses, Buddhist statues and other rare items. Some of the items are creations of Zanabazar and not for sale. Great for browsing.

## East of Sükhbaatar Square

★**Naran Tuul Market** MARKET
(Наран Туул Зах; Narnii Rd, ///satin.liquid.impresses; ⏰9am-6pm Wed-Mon) Also known as the Black Market (Khar Zakh), this is a must-see spot for those wanting to pick up traditional Mongolian clothing, carpets, horse-riding gear and souvenirs. It's notorious for pickpockets and bag slashers, so wear your backpack on your front and stash valuables in your money belt.

A covered area with a decent selection of clothes and accessories is one of the cheapest places to get traditional Mongolian garments, such as a simple *del*, starting from around T80,000, or *huruum* (Mongolian jacket), for around T50,000. There's also Western-style bags, jeans and fake North Face jackets.

Carpet sellers are also in the covered area, including Mongolian carpets from Erdenet. Just to the west of this section are stalls for the hat and boot sellers, where furry winter hats start from T60,000 and traditional boots start at around T65,000. All these make great gifts.

Towards the back of the market you'll find saddles (T80,000 for a soft Russian saddle or T165,000 for a Mongolian saddle), riding tack, Mongolian furniture and all the parts needed to build your own ger. The back area is also where you'll find antique and coin dealers, but they don't issue any official documentation (unlike the antique shops in town), making it illegal to export their stock. New items, such as the snuff bottles (made in China anyway), can be purchased without worry. You can also buy authentic shaman drums starting from around T85,000.

A taxi to the market should cost about T6000 from the centre of town. To walk from Sükhbaatar Sq will take about 40 minutes. Try to avoid the area on weekends, when the crowds (and traffic) can be horrendous. Though it opens at 9am, it doesn't really get going till around 11am.

**Dunjingarav Market** MARKET
(Ikh Khuree St, 🏿puns.operating.slap; ⊘10am-8pm Tue-Sun) Just south of Naran Tuul is this similar market, but with the difference of being indoors and organised in a more orderly layout. It's less atmospheric (and photogenic) than Naran Tuul, but a good alternative if it's raining. There's a decent food court serving Mongolian-style fast food.

## ℹ️ Orientation

Most of the city spreads from east to west along the main road, Enkh Taivny Örgön Chölöö, also known as Peace Ave. Confusingly, locals refer to this road as Töv Zam (Central Rd).

At the centre is Sükhbaatar Sq (aka Chinggis Khaan Sq), often simply known as 'the square' (talbai), which is just north of Peace Ave. Sprawling suburbia is limited by the four mountains that surround the city: Bayanzürkh, Chingeltei, Songino Khairkhan and Bogdkhan.

The city is divided into six major districts, but there's a multitude of subdistricts and microdistricts. Mongolians rarely use street names and numbers (because of their nomadic roots, they prefer to use landmarks), so tracking down an address can be difficult. Another problem is that many buildings are not on any road at all, instead located behind another building (sometimes behind a number of buildings).

A typical address might be something like: Microdistrict 14, Building 3, Flat 27. However, you are unlikely to know which microdistrict it refers to, building numbers can be hard to spot and most street signs are in Mongolian Cyrillic. As a result, most locals will give you an unofficial description, such as 'door 67, building 33, last door of a white-and-red building, behind the Drama Theatre'. Because of the confusing state of affairs, business cards usually have small maps on the back.

In 2016 the Mongol post service adopted the What3words address system, which is slowly being adopted by the city as a means of navigation using its smartphone app. For more information on this see pxxx.

If you think your destination might be hard to find, call ahead. The staff will send someone out to meet you at a nearby landmark. Most places you are likely to call (tour operators, hotels etc) will probably have an English speaker.

## ℹ️ Information

### DANGERS & ANNOYANCES

Ulaanbaatar is a fairly carefree and easygoing city, but there are a few concerns to keep in mind.

### Theft

Pickpockets and bag slashers are still a problem, though the situation is not as dire as it was a few years ago. When it happens, robbery is seldom violent against foreigners, just opportunistic.

Be particularly vigilant on Peace Ave between the post office and the State Department Store, or other main streets where tourists wander. Pickpockets also target public buses and the Naran Tuul Market. Keep an eye on your bag when sitting in cafes. Be very careful around the stadium during Naadam.

➜ Pickpockets often work in teams, often made up of street kids. One perpetrator may distract you while their friend picks your pocket.

➜ Leave passports, credit cards, large amounts of cash and valuables locked up in your hotel (preferably a safe). Just carry the cash you need for food, admission fees and incidentals. Carry this small cash in a shirt pocket rather than a trouser pocket.

➜ If carrying a backpack, clip the zippers together with a luggage lock or caribeener.

➜ Money belts are handy but not fail-safe (thieves might slice the belt with a razor).

➜ If you are robbed, you will need to file a report with the police to satisfy your insurance company. Immediately report the incident to the police station in the district it occurred.

➡ Use an official taxi – as opposed to a private vehicle – late at night; some foreigners have reported being assaulted and robbed in an unofficial taxi.

## Alcoholism

Alcoholism is a big problem in Ulaanbaatar, especially among out-of-work middle-aged and older Mongolian men. It's worse around Naadam time, but drunks are usually more annoying than dangerous.

## Traffic

Probably the most dangerous thing you can do in Ulaanbaatar is cross the street. Pedestrians are given no special treatment, so expect that you could get run over at any given moment. A green man or a zebra crossing are not safe either because at some intersections the right-turn arrow turns green simultaneously, so as you step onto the road a car will come around the corner into your path. Look out!

### EMERGENCY & IMPORTANT NUMBERS

It might take a few minutes to get hold of an English speaker for these numbers.

| | |
|---|---|
| Emergency Aid/ Ambulance | 📞103 |
| Fire | 📞101 |
| Police Emergency | 📞102 |

### GAY & LESBIAN TRAVELLERS

Though city folk are by far more liberal and modern thinking then the rest of the country, widespread intolerance to homosexuality remains firmly in place, keeping Ulaanbaatar's LGBTI community largely underground. With that said things have come a long way in the past few decades thanks to local advocate groups lobbying against discrimination and hate crimes. These days you'll find several bars and clubs that cater to the LGBTI community, where you'll find no hassles whatsoever.

While gay and lesbian travellers are very unlikely to encounter any problems, in recent years there have been violent attacks by neo nazis on locals – hence it's best advised to keep things discrete if walking around at night.

The LGBT Centre Mongolia (www.facebook.com/LGBTtuv) is a great resource for any queries or info about upcoming events.

### INTERNET ACCESS

Widespread use of wi-fi has killed off most of the internet cafes (Интэрнэт Кафэ) in Ulaanbaatar, but there are still a few around; just look for the signs, which are usually in English. Hourly rates are reasonable at about T800, but double that price at hotel business centres. Connections are generally good.

**Canyon Centre** (Map p58; Baga Toiruu E, 🌐blinking.comment.surfacing; per hour T800; ⊙8am-8pm)

### Wi-fi

Your hotel or guesthouse will most likely offer wi-fi, and nearly all cafes and restaurants in UB also offer free access. There are several public wi-fi hotspots, mainly in public squares and parks, as well as at the airport.

### LAUNDRY

Almost all of the hotels in Ulaanbaatar offer a laundry service for about T5000 per load.

**Metro Express** (📞7014 1004) has 30 branches scattered across the city, including one next to the Minii Delguur supermarket. It also has a kiosk on the ground floor of the State Department Store. A load of laundry costs T8500 and turnaround time is about four hours. It's cheaper and more convenient to go through one of the local guesthouses.

### MAPS

Several maps of Ulaanbaatar are available; a good one is the 1:10,000 *Ulaanbaatar City Map*. The most extensive selection of maps is at **Seven Summits** (p80). The **Cartography Co Map Shop** (p80) is another place to check.

### MEDIA

**Magazines** *That's Ulaanbaatar,* a free magazine published yearly and packed with updated tourist information, is available at hotels and tourist offices.

**Newspapers** Ulaanbaatar's two English-language newspapers, *Mongol Messenger* (weekly) and *UB Post* (www.theubpost.mn; thrice weekly), are well worth picking up for local news and entertainment information.

**Radio** You can listen to the BBC World Service on 103.1FM.

### MEDICAL SERVICES

For life-or-death emergencies you'll need to be sent to Seoul or Běijīng.

Pharmacies (*aptek;* Аптек) are common in Ulaanbaatar, stocking Mongolian, Russian, Chinese and Korean medicine. Check expiry dates carefully. The US embassy website (https://mn.usembassy.gov) has an extensive list of medical services.

**Degfim Dentist** (📞9916 2930, 7733 1313; www.degfim.com; Unesco St, Union Bldg, 3rd fl, 🌐twkling.sank.chainsaw; ⊙9am-5pm Mon-Sat) A modern, recommended dentist office with some English-speaking staff.

**Intermed** (📞7701 1111; www.intermed.mn; Chinggis Ave 41, Khan-Uul District, 🌐stands.pushover.kickers; ⊙8am-5pm Mon-Fri, to 1pm Sat) Hospital with 24-hour emergency and specialist doctors trained in South Korea. Rates to see a specialist start from T38,000.

**Songdo Hospital** (Map p58; ☑ 7011 1163; www. songdo.mn; Choidog St, ⓦ sampled.cool.sub-merge; ☺ 8.30am-5pm Mon-Fri, 8am-noon Sat) Modern Korean-run hospital with examinations starting at T20,000.

**SOS Dental Clinic** (Map p67; ☑ 11-464 330; www.sosmedica.mn; Big Ring Rd, 4a Bldg, ⓦ native.surround.trembles; ☺ 9am-6pm Mon-Fri) The best place for dental work. In the same building as SOS Medica Mongolia Clinic.

**SOS Medica Mongolia Clinic** (Map p67; ☑ 11-464 325, emergency 9911 0335; www. sosmedica.mn; Big Ring Rd, 4a Bldg, ⓦ native.surround.trembles; ☺ 9am-6pm Mon-Fri) The best place for most of your healthcare needs with Western expat doctors. It's very expensive, though (consultations cost around US$200), so you'll need to ensure you have travel insurance.

### MONEY

Banks, ATMs and moneychangers are wide-spread. Banks with the best services include Golomt, Khan Bank and Trade & Development Bank. ATMs (you'll find them in department stores, minimarkets and hotel lobbies) dispense tögrög; you can get dollars or euros from a bank teller, with your debit card and passport (expect a fee of around 1% to 3% from your home bank). The moneychanger on the ground floor of the **State Department Store** (p80) is handy, but rates here are not the best. The moneychangers at Ard Kino and Ikh Naiman Sharga generally have the best rates:

**Ard Kino Money Changers** (Map p58; Baga Toiruu W, ⓦ laces.craft.vans; ☺ 9am-7pm Mon-Fri, 11am-5pm Sat & Sun)

**Ikh Naiman Sharga** (Map p58; Tömörchiin Gudamj, ⓦ relies.tuck.slang; ☺ 9am-7pm) This building contains several moneychangers on the ground floor. The sign on the building says: Их 8 Шарга.

### OPENING HOURS

Operating hours in Ulaanbaatar are generally consistent throughout the year.

**Banks** 9am–6pm Monday to Friday, 10am–3pm Saturday

**Government offices** 9am–5pm Monday to Friday

**Restaurants** 10am–10pm daily

**Shops** 9am–10pm daily

### PERMITS

If you are travelling to border areas in Mongolia you'll need to arrange a permit through the **General Office of Border Protection** (☑ 51-266 638; Border Defence Bldg, ⓦ extensive. bunkers.gadgets; ☺ 10am-12.30pm & 2-5pm

Mon-Fri). You'll require a permit if visiting the following areas: Altai Tavan Bogd National Park in Bayan-Ölgii, Renchinlkhumbe, Tsagaannuur, Khankh, Dadal, Buir Nuur, Khalkhiin Gol, Nömrög and Dariganga. For Altai Tavan Bogd National Park, it's easier and quicker to arrange this in Ölgii, however for all others it generally needs to be done in Ulaanbaatar. Check this before you set out.

Most travellers get their tour guide to do this in advance, but if travelling independently you'll still need a Mongolian to apply on your behalf. Permits are free, but it can take three to five days to process (and it's closed on weekends). The office requires a passport photocopy and a map showing your route. If hiring a car with a driver you'll also need all the car documents and driver's passport, too.

The office is in a green-yellow building just west of the Mongolian Military Museum.

### POST

**Central post office** (CPO, Töv Shuudangiin Salbar; Map p58; ☑ 11-313 421; cnr Peace Ave & Sükhbaataryn Gudamj, ⓦ wicked.greet. conjured; ☺ 7.30am-9pm Mon-Fri, 9am-8pm Sat & Sun) Located near the southwest corner of Sükhbaatar Sq. The postal counter hall is the place to post mail, packages and check poste restante (counter 7). EMS express (priority) mail can also be sent from here. On Sunday, although it's open, most services are nonexistent. Express services such as FedEx are more reliable if sending important documents. There is also a good range of postcards, small booklets about Mongolia in English and local newspapers for sale. Upstairs is the small **Stamp Museum** (☺ 9am-1pm & 2-6pm Mon-Fri).

**FedEx** (Map p58; ☑ 11-320 591; www.fedex. com/mn; Prime Minister A Amar's St 15, ⓦ appoints.self.lads; ☺ 9am-6pm Mon-Fri) Located next to the Best Western Tuushin Hotel is this local FedEx contractor, Tuushin (www. tuushin.mn/eng). A 500g letter to most Western countries costs around $45.

### SMOKING

A strict ban on smoking was passed by parliament in 2013, so don't even think about sparking up in any public places, including bars, restaurants and hotel lobbies. Smokers seen in public places have been shouted at by local vigilantes.

### TELEPHONE

Many tourists end up buying a local SIM for their phone, but otherwise you can use the phone at your hotel for local calls, often for free. Other hotels, including those with business centres, charge T400 for a call to a landline (six digits) or a mobile number (eight digits). Where available, internet cafes are equipped with headsets and webcams for Skype calls.

## TOILETS
There are a handful of public toilets in UB.

## TOURIST INFORMATION
**Guide Tourist Information Centre** (Map p58; ☑ 7010 1011; www.touristinfocenter.mn; Peace Ave, State Department Store, 1st fl, ⚹ bravo.hexes.steamed; ☺ 9am-9pm Mon-Fri, 10am-9pm Sat & Sun May-Sep, to 6pm Oct-Apr) Privately run tourist information centre within the State Department Store; offers maps, brochures and tours. It's located up the stairs on the western side of the building.

**Tourist Information Booth** (Map p58; Central Post Office, Peace Ave, ⚹ wicked.greet.conjured; ☺ 8am-8pm; ☎) Privately owned tour company has a tourist information booth within the **central post office**. It offers brochures, maps, guesthouse booking, general info and wi-fi access.

**Ulaanbaatar Information Centre** (Map p58; ☑ 7010 8687; www.tourism.ub.gov.mn; Baga Toiruu W15, ⚹ float.unscathed.snippets; ☺ 8am-5pm Mon-Fri) Located in the Ulaanbaatar Bank building (door is on the north side). This office (run by the city) has a rack of brochures, but the staff here seem pretty indifferent to visitors.

## TRAVEL AGENCIES
Staff at backpacker guesthouses can help with visa registration and train tickets. For a small fee, some guesthouses even help visitors staying at other hotels.

**Air Market** (Map p58; ☑ 11-305 050; www.airmarket.mn; cnr Seoul St & Chinggis Ave, ⚹ outright.composers.umbrellas; ☺ 9am-10pm Mon-Fri, 10am-4pm Sat & Sun) Good for organising air tickets.

**Air Trans** (Map p58; ☑ 11-313 131; www.air-trans.mn; cnr Sükhbaataryn Gudamj & Sambuu St, ⚹ stow.dare.branching; ☺ 8am-8pm Mon-Fri, 10am-4pm Sat & Sun)

## 🛈 Getting There & Away

### AIR

**Chinggis Khaan International Airport** (☑ 1900 1980; http://en.airport.gov.mn; ⚹ inspects.roaring.nags; ☎),16km southwest of the city, will remain Mongolia's main gateway until the full completion of the New Ulaanbaatar International Airport. The airport has an ATM (though it's not always reliable), a post office, free wi-fi, mobile phone operators and car rental. A tourist booth operates inside the baggage hall when planes arrive.

At the time of writing, the **New Ulaanbaatar International Airport** (www.nubia.mn; ⚹ loaves.clipping.ministers) , 50km south of Ulaanbaatar near Zuunmod in Töv Province, was scheduled to begin operations in August 2018. It will service flights from Europe, North America and Asia.

Mongolia has two domestic carriers: **Hunnu Air** (Map p58; ☑ 7000 1111; www.hunnuair.com; cnr Ikh Toiruu & Seoul St, Rokmon Bldg, wcovenants.spoiler.outgoing; ☺ 9am-6pm Mon-Fri, 10am-5pm Sat & Sun) and **AeroMongolia** (Map p58; ☑ 7010 3030; www.aeromongolia.mn; Chinggis Ave 15, Monnis Tower, 1st fl, wecho.smuggled.alleyway; ☺ 9am-6pm Mon-Fri, 10am-5pm Sat) On domestic routes with Hunnu Air and AeroMongolia you are allowed 10kg to 15kg of baggage (combined carry-on and check-in). You'll pay around T3000 per kilogram over the limit. Flight days always change, so check updated schedules. The airlines accept credit cards for international and domestic flights.

**Aeroflot** (Map p58; ☑ 11-320 720; www.aeroflot.ru; Seoul St 15, ⚹ opponent.prank.crust; ☺ 9am-5pm Mon-Thu, 8am-4pm Fri, 10am-1pm Sat)

**Air China** (☑ 7000 9933; www.airchina.com; Narny Gudamj 87, ⚹ weekends.steady.hoping; ☺ 9am-noon & 1-5pm Mon-Fri, 9am-noon & 1-3pm Sat & Sun)

**Korean Air** (Map p67; ☑ 11-317 100; www.koreanair.com; Tokyo St, Chinggis Khaan Hotel, 3rd fl, ⚹ outs.mimed.bracelet; ☺ 8.30am-12.30pm & 1.30-5.30pm Mon-Fri)

**MIAT** (Mongolian Airlines; Map p58; ☑ 11-322 144; www.miat.com; 13 Chinggis Ave, ⚹ cools.shelters.cashiers; ☺ 9am-7pm Mon-Fri, 10am-3pm Sat & Sun)

**Turkish Airlines** (Map p58; ☑ 7585 9999; www.turkishairlines.com; Baga Toiruu-17, JJ Tower, 1st fl, ⚹ swooned.viewer.guesswork; ☺ 9am-6pm Mon-Fri)

### BUS
Two stations handle most bus traffic. The eastern depot, **Bayanzürkh Bus Terminal** (Баянзүрх Авто Вокзал; Bayanzürkh Avto Vaksal; ☑ 1900 1234; ⚹ destroyer.destined.recliner), is 4.5km east of Sükhbaatar Sq, located at Tenger shopping centre. The western bus station, the **Dragon Bus Terminal** (Dragon Avto Vaksal; ☑ 1900 1234; www.eticket.transdep.mn; Peace Ave, ⚹ wouts.solve.enlarge; ☺ 7.30am-7.30pm), is 7km west of Chinggis Khaan Sq.

In addition to the buses listed, minivans run daily to many of the same destinations (at a similar price), departing when full. It's best to have a Mongolian friend call the bus station to inquire about the minivans, as schedules change frequently. An online schedule can be found at www.transdep.mn (in Mongolian), where you can book tickets online.

Buses are always full, so buy your ticket as early as possible; tickets can be bought up to one month in advance from the station.

### MINIVAN & JEEP

The national bus network is now fairly comprehensive, but if you're unable to get a ticket, the fall-back option is to take a privately operated jeep or minivan.

Vehicles heading for destinations in the north and west (but not east) leave from the **Dragon Bus Terminal** (p85), the same place as the main bus departures. For eastern destinations, use the **Bayanzürkh Bus Terminal** (p85). Minivans are also available from the **Naran Tuul Market** (p81), but it's a fairly chaotic place and far less user-friendly compared to the bus stations. Note that there are no vehicles at Naran Tuul on Tuesday, when the market is closed. Shared cars to Darkhan can sometimes be found across the street from the train station.

Minivans are privately run, so drivers will try to stuff as many people and as much luggage as they possibly can into their vehicle. There is no set schedule; never expect to leave straight away, even if the van is full. Some might not be leaving for another day. If you can find out when it will leave, you could ask the driver to save your seat, and return later. For destinations reachable by paved road you might find a Korean compact car.

Van destinations are posted on the dashboard (in Cyrillic). Prices are usually about 10% to 15% higher than the bus trip. Most travellers prefer buses, as they tend to leave on time and are considered safer and more reliable.

### TRAIN

The very Soviet-looking **railway station** (Narny Gudamj, [///] ethic.pursuing.baking) has a left-luggage office (T1000 per piece), an ATM, a foreign exchange, mobile-phone companies, an information centre and a restaurant.

From Ulaanbaatar daily trains travel to northern Mongolia and on to Russia, via Darkhan and Sükhbaatar, and southeast to China, via Choir, Sainshand and Zamyn-Üüd. There are also lines between Ulaanbaatar and the coal-mining towns of Erdenet and Baganuur.

To buy a ticket you must show identification; a passport or driver's licence will do (student ID won't work).

### Domestic

Tourists seldom use the train in Mongolia to travel domestically as buses are faster, cheaper and more reliable.

The **domestic railway ticket office** ([⌇] 21-24109, 21-24137; www.ubtz.mn; Narny Gudamj, [///] engrossed.veal.abacus; ⊙ 8am-9pm Mon-Fri, 9am-5pm Sat, 11am-5pm Sun) is located in the modern-looking building on the east side of the train station. Boards inside the office show departure times (in Cyrillic) and ticket prices. There's also a full timetable at the information desk on the station platform. Times and schedules are available at www.ubtz.mn (in Mongolian), however it's rarely updated, especially given timetables are always changing.

Tickets can be booked for a seat (niitin obshe), hard sleeper (untlagiin obshe) or a soft sleeper (tasalgat).

### International

Upstairs from the domestic railway ticket office is the **International Railway Ticket Office** ([⌇] 2124 4367, 2124 3848; Narny Gudamj, 2nd fl, [///] engrossed.veal.abacus; ⊙ 8am-8.20pm). Here you can buy tickets to Irkutsk and Moscow in Russia, and to Běijīng, Èrlián and Hohhot in China. Timetables are listed in English.

## ⓘ Getting Around

### TRANSPORT TO/FROM THE AIRPORT

If it's your first visit to Mongolia, the best way to get into the city from Chinggis Khaan International Airport is to organise a pick-up from your hotel/guesthouse (just email them with your flight details). This may be free (usually if

## DOMESTIC TRAINS FROM ULAANBAATAR

| DESTINATION | TRAIN NO | FREQUENCY | DEPARTURE | DURATION (HR) | FARE (SEAT/HARD SLEEPER /SOFT SLEEPER) |
|---|---|---|---|---|---|
| Darkhan | 271 | daily | 8.35pm | 6 | T5950/13,950/19,850 |
| Erdenet | 273 | daily | 8.35pm | 11 | T8400/17,000/25,800 |
| Sainshand | 286 | 2 daily | 10.10am, 5.20pm | 9-10 | T9100/18,000/27,100 |
| Sükhbaatar | 263 | daily | 8.35pm | 7¾ | T7900/16,400/24,200 |
| Sükhbaatar | 271 | daily | 10.45am | 7¾ | T7900/16,400/24,200 |
| Zamyn-Üüd | 276 | daily | 5.20pm | 12 | T11,950/21,850/33,950 |

you book a few nights' accommodation) or cost around US$15 to US$20. Otherwise there are plenty of official taxis waiting at the terminal that charge a fixed price of around T20,000 into the city. Be certain to confirm the price before taking off as otherwise they will likely rip you off.

If you don't mind walking a little, you can use bus Ch-7 (T500) that connects with the city centre and the district of Nisekh, close to the airport. At the airport, go out of the terminal and across the parking lot to the main road (a 500m walk). At the main road turn right and walk about 400m, until you reach the bus turn-out (there is no sign, but you'll see others waiting). Only do this during daylight (for safety reasons). A bus comes by every 15 minutes or so until 8.30pm. You'll need to purchase a U Money card (T3600) before you embark, available from the small kiosk at the bus shelter. Once in the city you can get off at the bus stop near the main library (opposite the Drama Theatre).

To the airport, bus Ch-7 will stop at **Ard Kino** (Map p58; Baga Toiruu, 🎬 movies.stealthier. jump), and also near the Bayangol Hotel, but again it won't drop you at the terminal. You still have to haul your luggage 500m from the bus stop on the highway.

### TRANSPORT TO/FROM THE TRAIN STATION

It's a 25-minute walk from the train station to the State Department Store. International trains arrive early in the morning while the city is still quiet, so with a backpack it's easy to walk into town. Guesthouses and hotels may pick you up if contacted ahead of time (some hostel owners will be at the station anyway, trawling for guests).

The nearest bus stop is across the street from the station. Bus 29 or trolleybus 4 will get you to the State Department Store and Sükhbaatar Sq. To the train station, bus 29 takes Seoul St so you won't see it if waiting near the State Department Store. In this direction you should take trolleybus No 4.

Some taxi drivers at the station, like those at the airport, may agree on one price and then charge more once you reach the hotel. If this happens, stay calm and be patient and polite. Don't give in to their demands. Eventually they will get bored with trying to rip you off and will just accept a reasonable price. Keep your luggage with you in the car so they can't hold it hostage in the boot. If you must use a taxi, head out of the station and up the road to escape the sharks, then flag down a taxi and pay the standard rate of T800 per kilometre. Expect to pay around T10,000 for a ride into town.

### BICYCLE

Mongolian drivers are downright dangerous, so riding a bike around town can be hazardous to your health. There are no bike lanes and you should never expect to have right of way. **Cycling World** (p68) hires out mountain bikes for US$11 per day and also sells quality bikes. For cheaper bikes try the **State Department Store** (p80) or the **Naran Tuul Market** (p81); the market sells new and used bikes.

### BUS

Local public transport is reliable and departures are frequent, but buses can get crowded. Cash payment is no longer accepted on board, so you'll need to purchase a **U Money** card (T3600), available from bus kiosks around town. Be sure to touch on when boarding and touch off upon exiting. Bus trips cost T500, and T300 for trolleybus.

Pickpockets and bag slashers occasionally ply their trade on crowded routes. Seal up pockets, hold your bag on your chest and be careful when boarding.

The route number is next to the (Cyrillic) destination sign on the front of the trolleybus or bus. The route is often marked on the side of the bus. For short trips it's just as cheap to take a taxi, especially for two or more passengers.

### Main Bus Routes

Outlying destinations can be reached by bus from downtown Ulaanbaatar. Routes are constantly changing, however, so it's imperative to double check what bus goes where before setting off. A map of updated bus routes (in Cyrillic) can be found on http://transport.ub.gov. mn; scroll down to select the 'Чиглэлийн зураглал' tab. You could also try downloading the UB Smart Bus app (in Mongolian), but it's not guaranteed to be up to date.

**Bayanzürkh Bus Terminal (Eastern Bus Station)** Take trolleybus 4 from anywhere on Peace Ave heading east.

**Chinggis Khaan Airport** Take bus 7 from Bayangol Hotel.

**Dragon Bus Terminal (Western Bus Station)** Take bus 1 and 59 from Peace Ave, heading west.

**East Cross Road** For Intellectual Museum and Kempinski Hotel; take bus 1, 3 and 37, or trolleybus 2.

**Naadam Stadium** Bus 34, 7 and 55 from Ard Kino or Bayangol Hotel.

**Naran Tuul Market** Bus 3 goes here from anywhere on Peace Ave to the rear of the market.

**Three/Four District** Take bus 2 or trolleybus 5 from Peace Ave, bus 51 or 52 from Tengis cinema, or 58 from Bayangol Hotel; bus 51 from Dunjingarav past the Chinese Embassy and Tengis cinema.

## BUSES FROM ULAANBAATAR
### From Dragon Bus Terminal

| DESTINATION | PRICE (T) | DURATION (HR) | FREQUENCY | DEPARTURES |
| --- | --- | --- | --- | --- |
| Altai (Алтай) | 66,000 | 25 | Wed, Fri & Sun | 1pm |
| Arvaikheer (Арвайхээр) | 20,000 | 8 | 3 daily | 8am, 2pm, 6pm |
| Bayankhongor (Баянхонгор) | 27,000 | 15 | 3 daily | 8am, 2pm, 6pm |
| Bayan-Ölgii (Баян-Өлгий) | 80,000 | 45- 60 | Mon, Wed, Fri & Sun | 3pm |
| Bulgan (Булган) | 16,500 | 8 | daily | noon |
| Darkhan (Дархан) | 10,000 | 3½ | 8-9 daily | 11.30am-7.30pm |
| Erdenet (Эрдэнэт) | 15,000 | 6½ | 6 daily | 9am, 1pm, 1.30pm, 2.30pm, 4pm, 5.30pm |
| Kharkhorin (Хархорин) | 17,000 | 8 | 2 daily | 11am, 2pm |
| Khovd (Ховд) | 68,000 | 36 | weekly | 1pm |
| Mandalgov (Мандалговь) | 8700 | 4-5 | 2 daily | 8am, 2pm |
| Mörön (Мөрөн) | 32,000 | 18-22 | 3-4 daily | 8am, 3pm, 6pm |
| Tsetserleg (Цэцэрлэг) | 27,000 | 12 | Thu & Fri | 8am, 6pm |
| Ulaangom (Улаангом) | 63,000 | 46 | daily | 3pm |
| Ulan Ude (Улаан-Үд) | 67,000 | 11 | 1 or 2 daily | 7.30am, 7.30pm |
| Uliastai (Улиастай) | 48,000 | 20 | 2 daily | 11am, 4pm |
| Zuunmod (Зуунмод) | 2000 | 1 | hourly | 8am-6.30pm |

### From Bayanzürkh Bus Terminal

| DESTINATION | PRICE (T) | DURATION (HR) | FREQUENCY (DAILY) | DEPARTURES |
| --- | --- | --- | --- | --- |
| Baganuur (Багануур) | 6100 | 2½ | 4 | 11am, 2pm, 4pm, 7pm |
| Baruun-Urt (Баруун-Урт) | 21,400 | 10 | 2 | 8am, 5pm |
| Chinggis Khot (Чингис Хот) | 13,200 | 6 | 2 | 8am, 4pm |
| Choibalsan (Чойбалсан) | 31,000 | 12 | 3 | 8am, 1pm, 6pm |
| Dalanzadgad (Даланзадгад) | 23,000 | 10 | 2 | 10am, 4pm |
| Èrlián (二连) | 56,200 | 10-12 | 2 | 7am, 9pm |

**Train Station** Bus 29 goes here from Bagshiin Deed (near Ulaanbaatar Hotel), via Seoul St; trolleybus 4 comes here from Peace Ave.

**Winter Palace and Zaisan** Take bus 8 and 52 from Bayangol Hotel; bus 52 also leaves from Ard Kino.

### CAR

**Drive Mongolia** (p270) offers driving tours of Mongolia, allowing you to drive the car with a backup support vehicle. **Sixt** (Map p58; ☑ 8600 7259; www.sixt.mn; Jamyn St, ICC Tower, ⃞ selection.pegged.dynamics; ☺ 8am-9pm) is another company that has vehicles for hire in the city.

### TAXI

In Ulaanbaatar there are official and unofficial taxis. The official ones are noticeably labelled on the exterior and inside may or may not have a meter. The unofficial taxis are simply locals trawling for passengers.

All charge a standard T800 per kilometre (check the current rate, as it increases regularly). Don't agree to a set daily price because it will always be more than the standard rate per kilometre.

Before you get in the cab always have the driver reset the odometer to zero and agree on a per-kilometre rate before setting off. It also helps to have some idea of the route and the price.

To find a taxi, just stand by the side of a main street and hold your arm out with your fingers down. After dark, avoid using a private car – stick to an official taxi.

**Help Cab & Tours** (☑ 9965 2371; www. help-tours.com) Has an English-speaking dispatcher and a reputation for being reliable, safe and honest. Its main clients are expats and the prices are slightly higher than other companies. Booking fee is T1000 and flagfall is T5000 for the first 2km and then T1000 per kilometre. A ride to or from the airport to the city centre is T40,000. You can also hire a car for a half-/full-day city tour for T80,000/120,000.

**Noyon Zuuch Taxi Company** (☑ 1950) Reliable service with English-speaking dispatchers.

ULAANBAATAR GETTING AROUND

# Central Mongolia

POP 294,800

## Best Places to Eat

➡ Fairfield Cafe & Bakery (p115)

➡ Ayanchin Four Seasons Lodge (p100)

➡ Arvaikheer Palace Hotel Restaurant (p104)

➡ Ikh Khorum Hotel (p109)

## Best Places to Stay

➡ Maikhan Tolgoi (p117)

➡ Fairfield Guesthouse (p115)

➡ Ecotourism Ger Camp (p99)

➡ Ayanchin Four Seasons Lodge (p99)

➡ Family Guesthouse (p109)

➡ Khögnö Khan Resort Mountain Camp (p111)

## Why Go?

Roll out of Ulaanbaatar (UB) in a Russian jeep, or even just on a public bus, and you'll only need to put a hill or two between yourself and the city before the vast steppes of central Mongolia begin to unfold before your eyes.

Verdant swaths of empty landscapes are sprinkled with tiny gers (traditional yurts) stretching to the horizon, while magical light plays across the valleys. This is the Mongolian heartland, loaded with both historical sites and natural beauty, with plenty of scope to horse-trek over forested mountains, camp by pretty lakes or soak in hot springs.

Because the region is relatively close to Ulaanbaatar (and many sights are right beside the city), infrastructure is a little better than in other areas, with many places reachable by public transport. The most scenic sub-region is the Khangai Mountains, but you'll find beautiful scenery even if you only venture as far as Terelj.

## When to Go
### Tsetserleg

**Feb** Experience Tsagaan Sar (Mongolian New Year) with a family of herders.

**Jul** Naadam festivals in many *sums* (districts) and aimag capitals.

**Aug** Good for horse treks, hiking and biking.

## History

The many deer and 'animal-art' stelae found in the valleys of Arkhangai aimag are evidence of tribal existence here around 1300 BC, but the region really came into its own in the 3rd century BC, when the nomadic Xiongnu set up a power base in the Orkhon valley. Various 'empires' rose and fell in the Xiongnu's wake, including the Rouran, the Tujue, and the Uighurs, who built their capital at Khar Balgas in AD 715. These Turkic-speaking peoples held sway over vast portions of inner Asia and harassed the Chinese (whose attempts to defend the Great Wall were never really successful). They had their own alphabet and left several carved stelae that describe their heroes and exploits. The most famous is the Kul-Teginii Monument, located relatively close to Kharkhorin.

Chinggis Khaan and his merry men were only the latest in a string of political and military powers to use the Orkhon valley as a base. Chinggis never spent much time here, using it mainly as a supply centre for his armies, but his son Ögedei built the walls around Karakorum (near present-day Kharkhorin) in 1235, and invited emissaries from around the empire to visit his court.

Centuries after the fall of the Mongol empire it was religion, rather than warriors, that put the spotlight back on central Mongolia. Erdene Zuu Khiid (Buddhist monastery) was built from the remains of Karakorum and, with Manchu and Tibetan influence, Buddhism pushed the native shaman faith to the fringes of society.

### Getting There & Away

If travelling direct from Ulaanbaatar you can reach Kharkhorin, Tsetserleg, Arvaikheer and Terelj via good sealed highway roads, though travelling between these areas will involve plenty of off-road shortcuts along unsealed roads driving through the steppe.

If you're coming from western Mongolia to Ulaanbaatar, the route through Arkhangai is more interesting than the journey via Bayankhongor.

If you are travelling in the Gobi and heading towards northern Mongolia, go to Bayankhongor and pick up the scenic 210km road over the mountains to Tsetserleg. Local vehicles are rare on this route so it's best to have your own vehicle.

Mongolia's new **international airport** (p85) is located 14km south of Zuunmod in Töv aimag. At the time of writing, it was due to commence operations in late 2018.

### Getting Around

Töv aimag has a network of good unpaved and paved roads, so you can easily use public transport to make day or overnight trips from the capital.

Further afield, you can also reach places such as Kharkhorin, Tsetserleg and Tariat by public bus.

Off the main paved roads, though, traffic is light. In Övörkhangai, for example, you'll need your own transport to visit Tövkhön Khiid or Orkhon Khürkhree falls, and horse is the best way to reach Naiman Nuur.

# TÖV — ТӨВ

POP 90,400

Töv, otherwise known as the 'Central' province, surrounds Ulaanbaatar, and its forested mountains offer a welcome escape from the city. Popular but picturesque Gorkhi-Terelj National Park is great for horse-trekking, hiking and camping, and it's only an hour or so away by bus. Further afield, you can spot *takhi* (wild horses) at Khustain National Park. For something a little surreal, check out the 40m-tall silver statue of **Chinggis Khaan** (wbacklashes.snakes.gremlin; GPS: N47°48.494', E107°31.860'; adult/child T8500/3500; ⏲9am-8pm mid-May–mid-Oct; 10am-6pm mid-Oct–mid-May) outside Nalaikh.

## Bogdkhan Uul — Богдхан Уул

ELEV 2122M

The **Bogdkhan Uul** (Богдхан Уул; ///evaporated.blockaded.loadings; T3000) is said to be the world's oldest nature reserve. Established in 1778, the park was guarded by 2000 club-wielding lamas. Animal poachers were hauled away in chains, beaten within an inch of their lives, and locked inside coffin-like jail cells.

These days it's perfectly safe and legal to walk on the mountain, and you can enjoy some terrific **hiking** and **horse-riding** trails. Wildlife is more difficult to spot than it used to be, but you still stand a chance of seeing red deer.

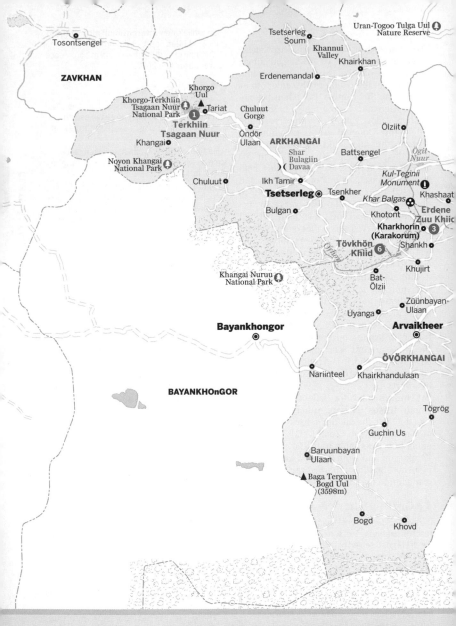

Tosontsengel

**ZAVKHAN**

Tsetserleg
Soum

Khannui
Valley

Khairkhan

Uran-Togoo Tulga Uul
Nature Reserve

Erdenemandal

Khorgo
Uul

Khorgo-Terkhiin
Tsagaan Nuur
National Park

Tariat

Chuluut
Gorge

Ölziit

**Terkhiin
Tsagaan Nuur**

Öndör
Ulaan

Khangai

**ARKHANGAI**

Shar
Bulagiin
Davaa

Battsengel

Ögii
Nuur

Noyon Khangai
National Park

Chuluut

Ikh Tamir

*Kul-Teginii
Monument*

Khashaat

**Tsetserleg**

Tsenkher

*Khar Balgas*

Khotont

**Erdene
Zuu Khiid**

Bulgan

**Kharkhorin
(Karakorum)**

**Tövkhön
Khiid**

Shankh

Khujirt

Khangai Nuruu
National Park

Bat-
Ölzii

Züünbayan-
Ulaan

Uyanga

**Arvaikheer**

**Bayankhongor**

**ÖVÖRKHANGAI**

Nariinteel

Khairkhandulaan

**BAYANKHOnGOR**

Tögrög

Guchin Us

Baruunbayan
Ulaan

▲ Baga Terguun
Bogd Uul
(3598m)

Bogd

Khovd

## Central Mongolia Highlights

❶ Camping, hiking and swimming your way around the stunning volcanic lake at **Terkhiin Tsagaan Nuur** (p116).

❷ Taking a break from Ulaanbaatar and heading to the nearby hills and valleys of **Gorkhi-Terelj National Park** (p95), best explored on a hike or via horseback.

❸ Visiting history-laden Kharkhorin for the ancient temples and ruined remains of **Erdene Zuu Khiid** (p105), Mongolia's first Buddhist monastery.

**SELENGE**

⦿ **Bulgan**

*Khan Khentii*
*Strictly Protected Area*

Jargalant
Bornuur
▲ Asralt Khairkhan
(2800m)

Tseel
*Aglag*
*Khiid*
Altan-Ölgii
Uul (2656m)

Ugataaltaidam
**Gorkhi-Terelj**
**National Park**

Zaamar
▲ Jalman Uul
(2051m)

ULAANBAATAR
*Günjiin*
*Süm* ②

**ULAANBAATAR** ✪
Terelj
Village

Lun
*Chinggis Khaan*
*Airport*
Bogdkhan Uul Strictly
Protected Area

**Khustain**
**National Park** ④
Nalaikh

Altanbulag
Zuunmod

**Khögnö Khan Uul**
**Nature Reserve**
**TÖV**
*New*
*Ulaanbaatar*
*Airport*
Sergelen

Öndörshireet
Baganuur

Mongol
Els ⑤

*Övgön*
*Khiid*
Rashaant
Erdenesant
Bayan

Batkhaan Uul
Nature Reserve

Burd
Buren
**Bayan**
**Önjuul**
Bayantsagaan

⦿ Esönzüil

Bayan-
Öndör
Delgerkhaan

Sant

⦿ Bayangol
⦿ **Mandalgov**

**DUNDGOVI**

Ⓝ 0 ————— 50 km
0 ————— 25 miles

④ Searching for the rare *takhi* (Mongolian wild horse) in the wildlife-rich **Khustain National Park** (p101).

⑤ Exploring the boulder-strewn landscape of **Khögnö Khan Uul Nature Reserve** (p110) before hopping on a camel at the nearby sand dunes of Mongol Els.

⑥ Hiking up through a pine forest to the atmospheric **Tövkhön Khiid** (p112) mountain monastery, with its awe-inspiring panoramas.

## ◉ Sights

**Mandshir Khiid**                    BUDDHIST MONASTERY
(Мандшир Хийд; [m]passports.derives.stalling; GPS: N 47°45.520', E 106°59.675'; adult/child T1000/500, photography T2000; ☺9am-1pm & 2-6pm Mon-Fri, 8am-noon & 1-7pm Sat & Sun) For the 350 monks who once called this place home, the gorgeous setting around this monastery (elevation 1645m) must have been a daily inspiration. Like most monasteries in Mongolia, Mandshir Khiid was destroyed in 1937 by Stalin's thugs, but was partially restored in the 1990s.

The main temple has been restored and converted into a museum, but the other buildings remain in ruins. The monastery and museum are not amazing in themselves, but rather it's the beautiful forest setting that makes a visit worthwhile.

## 🏃 Activities

### Hiking

Bogdkhan Uul has a broad and flat summit, so many routes cross it. Most hikers get dropped off on one side and hike to the other on a day or overnight hike. The summit, known as **Tsetseegün Uul** ([m]cartload.billionths.gallantly; GPS: N 47°48.506', E 107°00.165'), reaches 2256m and is a popular destination, but including this part of the mountain requires a bit more time.

Don't underestimate the weather up top. Even in summer strong thunderstorms can tear across the mountain without much warning. Hikers have died of hypothermia after getting stranded on the mountain during a major thunderstorm. Even if you are just doing it as a day hike, bring warm, waterproof clothing, a compass, food and water. Yellow paint on the trees marks the trail, but it can be hard to spot.

Some scrambling over fields of granite boulders is necessary, and the chance of slipping and injuring yourself should not be taken lightly.

It's wise to inform a friend or guesthouse owner in Ulaanbaatar of your itinerary and the time of your expected return.

#### Mandshir Khiid to Ulaanbaatar

This approach to Tsetseegün from the south side is the easiest route by far. As you face the monastery, cut over to your right (east) until you get to the stream. Just follow the stream until it nearly disappears and then head north. About three hours' walking should bring you out over a ridge into a broad boggy meadow, which you'll have to cross. If you've walked straight to the north, the twin rocky outcrops of the summit should be right in front of you. When you start to see Ulaanbaatar in the distance, you're on the highest ridge and close to the two large *ovoo* (a shamanistic pyramid-shaped collection of stones as an offering to the gods) on the summit. From the *ovoo* you can return to Mandshir or descend to Ulaanbaatar.

A second route from the monastery begins from the left (west) side of the temples, passing a stupa on the way up to the ridge. This route, marked with yellow tags, is faster, but you'll miss the *ovoo* on Tsetseegün.

Coming down from Tsetseegün the quickest way is to head due north, towards the Observatory (p66) ('Khureltogoot' in Mongolian), and descend to the valley where you'll cross the train tracks. You can catch a taxi from here to town for around T10,000. A route from the Observatory goes downhill and then west one valley to the Sky Resort, where it's possible to hike or hitch on a new road to UB along the southern bank of the Tuul river.

Another route takes you to the Zaisan Memorial (p66), on the southern fringe of the city. Be careful not to drop down too soon or you'll end up at **Ikh Tenger**, one valley short of Zaisan. Ikh Tenger is where the president lives with machine-gun-wielding guards, who will be none too pleased if you drop by unannounced. If you see a barbed-wire fence you are in Ikh Tenger; to get out, just continue west along the fence and over the next ridge.

From Mandshir Khiid straight to Zaisan, plan on walking about six to seven hours. From Mandshir Khiid to the Observatory, figure on six hours.

### Horse Riding

★**Stepperiders**                    HORSE RIDING
([☎]9412 5965, 9911 4245; www.stepperiders.mn; [m]buckled.open.buxom; GPS: N 47°43.649', E 106°47.418') A leader in horse-riding trips near Ulaanbaatar, this wonderful camp is hidden away in a beautiful secluded valley. It caters to riders of all levels, and arranges treks from one-day jaunts (US$50 per day including food) to two-week countryside expeditions. Its most popular trip is the three-day trek into Bogdkhan Uul (US$280); rates include pick-up from Ulaanbaatar.

## 🛏 Sleeping

**Ovooni Enger Ger Camp**   TOURIST GER CAMP **$$**
(📞 8313 2011;  🌐 expenditure.recreations.potbelly; ger per person T60,000-100,000, r T80,000-240,000) Larger and better equipped than neighbouring Mandshir Ger Camp, Ovooni has a holiday-camp atmosphere with a choice of ger accommodation or (less preferable) lodge rooms, a modern shower block with sit-down flush toilets, and a restaurant ger (mains T5000 to T14,000) with terrace seating. Avoid weekends, if possible, as it's popular with folk from UB here for karaoke.

## ℹ Getting There & Away

The most accessible entrances to the park are reached from the ger camp at the southern end of Zaisan valley, the Observatory and Mandshir.

The monastery is easy enough to visit on a day trip from Ulaanbaatar, via Zuunmod (from where it's a 7km drive). From Zuunmod you can get a taxi to Mandshir Khiid for around T20,000, including waiting time.

If you're walking from the north of Zuunmod, it's 6km; you can either walk along the main northern road, or save some time by walking directly north from Zuunmod, eventually joining up with the main track which heads up the valley to your left.

At Mandshir, wranglers from the nearby ger camps rent horses for around US$5 to US10 per hour.

# Terelj Area   Тэрэлж

Only 55km northeast of Ulaanbaatar, the Terelj region makes up part of **Gorkhi-Terelj National Park** (🌐 embarrasses.envy.sphere; T3000), offering great opportunities for hiking, rock climbing, swimming (in icy-cold water), rafting and horse riding. At 1600m the area is cool, and the alpine scenery magnificent, and for hard-core extreme-sports fanatics, there's skiing and dog-sledding in the depths of winter.

Terelj was first developed for tourism in 1964 and 30 years later it became part of the national park. It's a bit crowded with ger camps these days, but you can easily get away from the hustle and bustle. Be prepared for mosquitoes, especially in late summer.

Pay the admission fee at the park entrance. Note, passengers on the public bus from Ulaanbaatar rarely have to pay this as the bus usually drives past the entrance without stopping.

### TRAIL RIDE DAY TRIPS NEAR ULAANBAATAR

A number of tour operators can organise horse-riding day trips near Ulaanbaatar. They are usually in Gorkhi-Terelj National Park, which can get crowded on summer weekends. A handful of companies offer specialised day trips on horseback in the backcountry, away from the ger camps. These are some of the best:

**Stepperiders** (p94) in Bogdkhan Uul.

**Xanadu** (p97) near Gachuurt and Terelj.

**Stone Horse** (p98) near Gachuurt to Terelj route.

Terelj village (🌐 rephrasing.inclusions. wrongful; GPS: N 47°59.193', E 107°27.834') is about 27km from the park entrance, at the end of a paved road.

## 👁 Sights

**Günjiin Süm**   BUDDHIST TEMPLE
(Гүнжийн Сүм; 🌐 skit.delivering.fizzled; GPS: N 48°11.010', E 107°33.377') Surrounded by magnificent forest and not far from a lovely river, the Baruun Bayan Gol, this Buddhist temple (elevation 1713m) was built in 1740 by Efu Dondovdorj to commemorate the death of his Manchurian wife, Amarlangui. Once part of a huge monastery containing about 70 sq metres of blue walls, five other temples and a tower, Günjiin Süm is one of very few Manchurian-influenced temples in Mongolia to survive over the centuries. Only a couple of buildings and walls remain.

Unlike most other monasteries in Mongolia, Günjiin Süm was not destroyed during the Stalinist purges, but simply fell into ruin from neglect, vandalism and theft.

The temple is not a must – there are many better and more accessible temples and monasteries in Ulaanbaatar and Töv – but more of an excuse for a great **overnight trek**, on horse or foot, or as part of a longer trip in the national park.

Günjiin is about 25km by foot (or horse) from the UB-2 (p99) hotel, heading in a northwest direction. The jeep trail is longer (about 40km in total), as you need to skirt around the mountains (only accessible in dry months and only with a reliable 4WD),

# Terelj Area

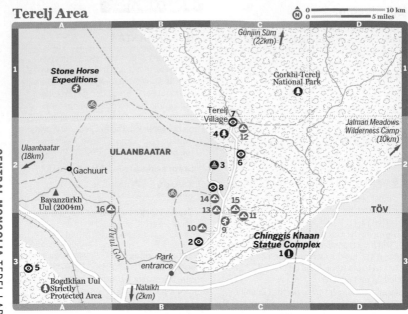

N 0 — 10 km
0 — 5 miles

Günjiin Süm
(22km)

Stone Horse
Expeditions

Gorkhi-Terelj
National Park

Terelj
Village

Jalman Meadows
Wilderness Camp
(10km)

Ulaanbaatar
(18km)

ULAANBAATAR

Gachuurt

Bayanzürkh
Uul (2004m)

TÖV

Chinggis Khaan
Statue Complex

Park
entrance

Bogdkhan Uul
Strictly
Protected Area

Nalaikh
(2km)

Tuul Gol

but easier if you don't want to walk the hills. You can do the trip on your own with a good map and compass (or GPS), but it's best to take a local guide.

### 100 Lama's Cave CAVE

(schemes.nougat.appeasing) Right by the side of the road in the south of the national park is this rocky outcrop that you can scramble up to squeeze within its cavernous space. It's where 100 lamas hid in an attempt to escape the communist purge in the 1930s. Tragically, however, they were found and executed.

### Khan Khentii Strictly
### Protected Area NATIONAL PARK

(Khentii Nuruu, eggs.solubility.feigning; T3000) To the northeast, Gorkhi-Terelj National Park joins the Khan Khentii Strictly Protected Area, comprising more than 12,000 sq km of the Töv, Selenge and Khentii aimags. The Khan Khentii park is almost completely uninhabited by humans, but it is home to endangered species of moose, brown bear and weasel to name but a few, and to more than 250 species of birds. If you come from Terelj, the fee at the gate there covers this protected area as well.

## 🏃 Activities

### Hiking

If you have good maps, a compass and some experience (or a proper guide), hiking in the Terelj area is superb in summer, but be prepared for mosquitoes and unpredictable weather.

For more sedate walks in the Terelj ger camp area, follow the main road and pick a side valley to stroll along at your leisure. From the main road, look out for two interesting rock formations: **Turtle Rock** (Melkhi Khad; luxuriously.balloon.packer; GPS: N 47°54.509', E 107°25.428') in a side valley to the south of Terelj, which really looks like a terrapin from a certain angle; and the less dramatic **Old Man Reading a Book** (Monk Praying Rock), which can be spotted on the left side of the road when travelling south from Terelj village. Head north 3km from Turtle Rock to reach the **Aryapala Initiation & Meditation Centre** (extroverts.book.unaccountable; GPS: N 47°56.121', E 107°25.643; adult/child T2000/500; 8am-7pm), set on a spectacular rocky hillside. The **temple** at the top of the hill is a new creation. If you're lucky, you might arrive during a prayer session, when you can sit and hear monks chanting.

# Terelj Area

Some suggested easier hikes are to Günjiin Süm or along the Terelj or Tuul Gols towards Khan Khentii. This is a great area for wildflowers, particularly rhododendron and edelweiss.

Places of interest on more difficult, longer treks in Khan Khentii include **Altan-Ölgii Uul** (2656m), the source of the Akhain Gol; **Khagiin Khar Nuur**, a 20m-deep glacial lake, about 80km up Tuul Gol from the ger camps at Terelj; and **Yestii Hot Water Springs**, which reach up to 35°C, and are fed by the Yeroo and Yestii Gols. Yestii is about 18km north of Khagiin Khar Nuur.

## Horse Riding

Travelling on a horse is the perfect way to see a lot of the park, including Günjiin Süm and the side valleys of Tuul Gol. To travel long distances, you will need to have experience, or a guide, and bring most of your own gear. Horses can be hired through any of the ger camps, but you'll pay high tourist prices (around US$35 to US$40 a day). A mob of horse boys hang

around **Turtle Rock** offering horse riding at around US$5 per hour, or somewhere between US$12 and US$20 for the day. Alternatively, approach one of the Mongolian families who live around the park and hire one of their horses, though they may not be much cheaper. Bert the Dutch cheese maker, who owns Ecotourism Ger Camp (p99), can help you hire horses from nearby herdsmen for around $7 per hour. Horse-rental guys sometimes hang out in front of Terelj Hotel (p99), offering horse rides for T10,000 per hour, or T40,000 per day.

## Rafting

Tuul Gol, which starts in the park and flows to Ulaanbaatar and beyond, is one of the best places in the country for rafting. The best section of the river starts a few kilometres north of Terelj village, and wraps around the park until it reaches Gachuurt, near Ulaanbaatar. Nomadic Journeys (p40) and Dog Sledding Mongolia run rafting trips here, or you can also hire rafts or kayaks from Seven Summits (p252), a good-quality camping shop in UB, and Goyo Travel (p39).

## 🕝 Tours

Most foreign and local tour companies include a night or two in a tourist ger at Terelj in their tours. Local agencies based in Ulaanbaatar, such as Nomadic Journeys (p40) and Nomads (p40), run some of the more interesting trips around Terelj.

In winter there's also snow dog-sledding tours; both Wind of Mongolia (p40) and Dog Sledding Mongolia can arrange short trips or week-long expeditions.

**Xanadu**  ADVENTURE SPORTS
(☑ 9975 6964, 9987 2912; www.mongolienomade. mn) Frenchman Côme Doerflinger runs adventure trips in the countryside adjoining Terelj through his outfit based in Gachuurt. He mainly runs horse treks, including all-inclusive multiday trips, but also has kayaks and canoes that you can use to float down Tuul Gol, and mountain bikes that are great for excursions up Gachuurt's side valleys towards Terelj. There's also accommodation at his ger camp (T25,000 per person, meals from T6000).

**Dog Sledding Mongolia**  DOG SLEDDING
(☑ 9916 2233, 9900 5181; www.facebook.com/mongoliansleddingdogs) This local adventure

CENTRAL MONGOLIA TERELJ AREA

## MOUNTAIN BIKING AROUND TERELJ

Depending on your fitness levels, Terelj is about half a day's cycle from the capital. The road is paved the whole way, but mostly uphill. **Cycling World** (p68) in Ulaanbaatar is the best place to hire mountain bikes. Otherwise in Terelj you can rent a bike from **Xanadu** (p97) en route, or from **Dog Sledding Mongolia** (p97) or **Terelj Hotel** (p99).

### Terelj to Gachuurt (Central)

This rugged route takes in two passes along the way. Get a ride all the way to the town of Terelj and then start riding on the road that heads west; it's about 2km to the next small settlement of gers. The trail continues west and starts heading into the wilderness, up a valley with a forest to your left. The ridge tops out at 1859m and descends to another valley. The trail climbs again, slightly to the right, to another 1859m ridge, from where you begin a long descent towards Gachuurt. At the end of the valley (it's about 15km) you'll reach Tuul Gol, which you follow to Gachuurt town. All up it's a 30km ride and should take around five hours.

### Turtle Rock Loop

This convenient route begins and ends at **Turtle Rock** (p96) in the Gorkhi valley. From Turtle Rock ride west down the slope until the road goes right into a ger camp (the camp was built over the trail). Go around the camp and then it's a 30-minute climb to the top of the hill. From the top you get some great views of the rock formations in the next valley. The trail continues south past several ger camps and eventually leads back to the main road and back to Turtle Rock. This loop is 15km.

operator is most notable for its dog-sledding trips that zip through the snow from November to the end of April. You can sign up for shorter runs (per person US$40 for 5km), day trips (US$150 for 35km) or longer journeys that last for a week or more. Rates include guide, transfers and food.

**Stone Horse Expeditions**　　　HORSE RIDING
(☑9592 1167; www.stonehorsemongolia.com) This Western-run company offers a variety of trips into Gorkhi-Terelj National Park and the Khan Khentii mountains. Tours are mostly one week or longer (up to 14 days), and include lodging at the staging area and camping equipment when on the trail. Occasionally it arranges day trips (US$100 per person).

## 🛏 Sleeping

During the peak season of July and August, it's not a bad idea to book ahead. From October to May, it's a good idea to ring ahead to make sure the camp is open and serves food. A few places stay open in winter.

Unless you hike out into the hills, it's best to get permission for camping, either from the nearest ger or, for a fee, a ger camp. Pitch your tent away from the main road, don't use wood fires and take all of your rubbish out.

## 🛏 Road to Terelj Village

**Otgoo Family Ger**　　　TOURIST GER CAMP $
(☑8915 6391; 🌐 musically.luge.incisively; per person incl meals US$25) There are a few family gers as you approach the Buuveit Camp, offering cheap, bare-bones accommodation. One is Otgoo Family Ger, which is run by a lovely nomadic family. Rates include a one-hour horse ride.

**Mirage**　　　TOURIST GER CAMP $$
(☑11-325 188, 9902 2979; www.mongolaltaitravel.com/mirage_tourist_camp; 🌐 shortlived.performers.pinpoints; per person incl meals T90,000; 🛜) Mirage is a relaxed ger camp with a scenic location set beneath picturesque boulders. Gers are fitted out in traditional style, there are Western toilets and hot-water showers, and you can book horse treks and other activities in the park. Staff will light fires for you and there's a lively ger restaurant for meals.

**Guru Camp**　　　TOURIST GER CAMP $$
(☑9909 6714; 🌐 trumpets.idyllic.humankind; per person with/without meals T100,000/80,000) Located 14km along the main road from the Gorkhi-Terelj National Park entrance, Guru

makes for a lovely choice of ger camp, with thick mattresses, clean, modern bathrooms, a comfortable restaurant-bar and sweeping views. There's also a small art shop and a foot-massage centre. Boya, the manager, speaks some English.

**Buuveit Camp**  TOURIST GER CAMP **$$**
(☑ 9911 4913, 11-322 870; www.tsolmontravel.com/en/our-camps/buuveit-camp;  ///leases.clenched.whoops; per person with/without meals from US$55/20) About 13km along the main road from the park entrance, Buuveit is in a beautiful secluded valley with a rocky backdrop. It's a sprawling camp with a choice of ger accommodation or rooms in its lodge. It's 3km east of the main road; walk past Chinggis Khaan Country Club then turn right and bear left.

**★Ayanchin Four**
**Seasons Lodge**  TOURIST GER CAMP **$$$**
(☑ 9909 4539; www.ayanchinlodge.mn;  ///woodwork.overcook.horns; ger/yurt or r incl breakfast from T250,000/300,000; 🛜) This luxury American-built camp comprises a mix of Western-style lodge rooms with alpine views, Mongolian gers and Colorado-built yurts with a modern shower and toilet block, a children's play area and a top-notch restaurant (p100). It's about 10km from the main Gorkhi-Terelj National Park entrance, marked with a big billboard. Open year-round.

**Tuul Riverside Lodge**  TOURIST GER CAMP **$$$**
(☑ 7011 9370; www.tuulriverside.com;  ///outsource.paternal.overdrive; s/d/tr ger incl breakfast from US$90/150/180) This riverside, family-friendly option has upmarket en suite gers that include bath and shower. It's good for a short break from Ulaanbaatar (total driving time is one hour) or family holiday. It's about 10km past Gachuurt, at the foot of Bayanzurkh mountain, on the back roads to Terelj. There's a bunch of activities on offer, including guided hikes, kayaking, mountain biking and bird-watching. Lunch/dinner costs US$20/25.

Pick-up from Ulaanbaater costs US$25/30 per group of two/four people.

## 🛏 Terelj Village Area

**★Ecotourism Ger Camp**  TOURIST GER CAMP **$$**
(☑ 9973 4710, 9973 4815; bergroo@hotmail.com;  ///displayed.insulate.proteins; GPS: N 47°58.722', E 107°28.907'; per person incl meals $42) For an offbeat experience, cross Terelj Gol for this pleasant ger camp run by an eccentric Dutchman named Bert and his lovely family. The meadow location here is gorgeous, and there's great hiking opportunities in the surrounding hills. The family makes a range of Dutch cheeses to go with hand-made sausage and house-smoked bacon to enjoy at breakfast or lunch. Reservations essential.

Bert organises horse trips up to Günjiin Süm (T50,000 per day, plus T20,000 for a guide) or can just help you arrange a quick ride on a neighbour's horse (€6 per hour). A trekking guide is T6000 per hour, and he can also arrange canoe trips.

The property is located 2.5km from the UB-2 hotel, and to get here you need to call well ahead so Bert can pick you up for free, or if he's not around he can arrange a transfer from UB-2 hotel, possibly on one of his neighbours' ox-carts (T10,000 one way). Otherwise it's a 40-minute walk; call or email ahead for directions.

**★Terelj Hotel**  HOTEL **$$$**
(☑ 9999 2233, 9900 7206; www.tereljhotel.com;  ///arranges.progenitors.conserves; s/d incl breakfast from T330,000/396,000; 🛜✉) Mongolia's first luxury hotel and spa is an incongruous neoclassical building set on the edge of tiny Terelj village. Opened in 2008, this five-star hotel is a class act with corridors lined with thick carpet and antiques, a palatial indoor swimming pool, several restaurants, a professional spa, a library and a children's play centre. Rooms are immaculate, but not exceptional.

**UB-2**  HOTEL **$$$**
(☑ 9977 4125; www.ub2hotel.mn;  ///headlamps.moviegoer.jumpstart; ger s/d/tr/q T35,000/60,000/80,000/95,000, s/d from T80,000/110,000; 🛜) This place – a branch of the iconic Ulaanbaatar Hotel – is not bad on its own, but looks a little sad compared to the swanky Terelj Hotel next door. The whole place is bit of a relic, and in desperate need of general maintenance, but rooms are fine and spacious. There's a gaudy pink restaurant (8am to 9pm; mains T3000 to T30,000) with decent vegetarian options.

Adding to its faded colonial atmosphere is its billiard room, par-three golf course (nine/18 holes T30,000/50,000, club hire T18,000) and golf-driving range.

## 🏕 Northern Terelj

### Jalman Meadows Wilderness Camp TOURIST GER CAMP $$$

(📱11-330 360; www.nomadicjourneys.com; Ⓜ searched.competitor.disobeyed; per person incl meals US$125) Run by Nomadic Journeys (p40), this remote and low-impact ger camp in the upper Tuul valley makes a nice base if you're headed to Khagiin Khar Nuur, an eight-hour horse ride away. The camp has a library of books on Mongolia and a number of great activities – including horse riding, mountain biking, yak carting and river boating – and even has portable saunas!

You'll need to book well in advance for these trips. The price includes transfers to and from Ulaanbaatar (around three hours, each way).

## 🍴 Eating

### ★ Ayanchin Four Seasons Lodge INTERNATIONAL $$$

(📱9909 4539; www.ayanchinlodge.mn/restaurant; Ⓜ woodwork.overcook.horns; mains T25,000-45,000; ⓧ7am-10pm; 🛜) This American-owned, architecturally designed lodge (p99) is a worthy stop for a meal. As well as serving the likes of cheeseburgers, steaks and pepperoni pizza, it does excellent Mongolian dishes including inventive takes on traditional dishes, such as a Mexican *khuushuur*. Its full English and American breakfasts are another reason to stop by.

### Terelj Hotel INTERNATIONAL $$$

(📱9999 2233, 9900 7206; www.tereljhotel.com; Ⓜ arranges.progenitors.conserves; mains T30,000-50,000; ⓧ7am-10pm) *The* place to come if you want to splurge on a fancy meal, with its posh Morin Khuur restaurant and classy

---

### OFF THE BEATEN TRACK

### AGLAG KHIID

The brainchild of G Purevbat, a lama and world-renowned master of Buddhist sculpture and painting, **Aglag Khiid** (Ⓜrefresher.noblewoman.slideshow; adult/child T5000/1000; ⓧ8am-7pm, museum closed Mon) was built in 2014 as a meditation and education centre. Yet following the trails of this mountain monastery, overlooking pine forest and dotted with boulders carved with Buddhist reliefs, you'd be forgiven for mistaking it for a 300-year-old temple. Located 100km from Ulaanbaatar, it's become an increasingly popular day trip for locals and tourists alike seeking fresh air with a dose of spirituality.

After a steep 10-minute hike from the car park, your first stop is the monastery complex, which houses several museums. Collectively they contain interesting local artefacts and Buddhist relics that have been shifted here from the original museum in nearby Bornuur. Some exhibits are a bit gruesome, including a stack of human skulls pulled out of a mass grave. They are the skulls of local lamas who were executed by communist forces in 1937. There's also a rather frightening collection of stuffed animals, both real and fabricated – from five-headed fish to a unicorn!

After viewing the monastery museum, follow the signed path that loops up above the monastery to view G Purevbat's series of exquisite Buddhist rock carvings. This walk is the highlight of a visit here, and you'll encounter atmospheric stupas and sacred rock formations (including fertility rock sculpture) as well as fantastic panoramas to the surrounding forest. There's no English signage (so bringing along a guide is recommended), but otherwise there's an informative, glossy book for purchase (T20,000) from the museum.

For food there's a very basic *guanz* (canteen) on-site that sells cold drinks and beef *khuushuur* (T1000), but a better choice are the lovely ger restaurants nearby with great steppe views and local food and *airag* (fermented mare's milk; available late June to August).

The site is around 100km northwest of Ulaanbaatar, along the Ulaanbaatar–Darkhan road, about 5km south of Bornuur (Борнуур). There's no public transport here, so you'll need to arrange your own vehicle or join a tour.

outdoor terrace bistro that overlooks the river; look out for the imposing Lenin statue that once stood in Ulaanbaatar. Note that a 19% tax is added to the bill.

## ℹ️ Getting There & Away

### BUS

The road from Ulaanbaatar to Terelj village, which goes through part of the national park, is in pretty good nick. A bus (T2500, 2½ hours) departs daily at 4pm, from a **stop** (Map p58; Peace Ave, ☷wins.energetic.interrupt) opposite the Narantuul Hotel. It then stops at every bus stop heading east along Peace Ave. Get there with 15 minutes to spare as they sometimes depart early. Going the other way, it leaves Terelj at 8am Monday to Friday and 11am on weekends; catch it near Hotel Terelj. You may have to pay an extra T2500 for a bike or heavy luggage.

Another option is to take one of the frequent buses between Ulaanbaatar and Nalaikh (T900, every 10 minutes), and then hook up with one of the shared minibuses that shuttle between Nalaikh and Terelj village (T1500, roughly every hour). A taxi to Terelj from Nalaikh costs about T25,000.

### TAXI

A taxi from Ulaanbaatar (T70,000 one way) is easy to organise; jeeps aren't necessary because the road is paved all the way. The driver may understandably want more than the one-way fare because their taxi may be empty for part of the return journey. You can also arrange with your taxi to pick you up later.

When there's enough demand, shared taxis to Terelj sometimes leave from Naran Tuul Market jeep station in Ulaanbaatar. This is more likely on summer Sundays when locals make a day trip to the area.

---

# Khustain National Park
Хустайн Нуруу

Spanning over 506 sq km, this **national park** (Хустайн Нуруу; Khustain Nuruu, Birch Mountain Range; ☎9323 0169, 21-245 087; www.hustai.mn; ☷fancy.hesitations.respond; T18,000, Mongolians free) was established in 1993 to protect Mongolia's wild horse, the *takhi,* as well as the reserve's steppe and forest-steppe environment. In addition to the *takhi,* there are populations of *maral* (Asiatic red deer), steppe gazelle, deer, boar, Pallas's cats, wolves, lynx, marmot and some 223 species of birds. It's located about 100km southwest of Ulaanbaatar,

and a visit to the park is a popular overnight excursion from the capital.

Wildlife watching is best at dusk and at dawn, so it's worth spending at least one night in the park in order to see *takhi* and other wildlife.

The park is run by the self-financed **Hustai National Park Trust** (☎21-245 087; www.hustai.mn; Hustai Bldg, 2nd khoroo, Bayangol District, ☷flux.exonerate.refrain; ⊘8.30am-5.30pm Mon-Fri). Its information centre (p102) at the entrance to the park at Hustain Tourist Camp offers an excellent overview of the national park.

## ◉ Sights & Activities

Horse riding (T12,000/70,000 per hour/day), hiking and jeep excursions (T2000 per kilometre, plus T65,000/100,000 for a guide per half/full day) are all good ways to explore the park.

Park regulations require you to take a park guide (free within the park) who can direct your driver to the best spots. You must stick to the existing tracks, and keep 200m from the *takhi.*

## 🛏 Sleeping

There are several ger camps that are either within or just outside of the park boundaries. Hustain Tourist Camp and Molit are the most popular options, both managed by the Hustai National Park Trust in Ulaanbaatar. In August there are also opportunities to stay with nomadic families.

**Bayansonginot**     TOURIST GER CAMP $
(☎9188 8533; per person incl meals US$29; ⊘Jul-Aug) If you're looking to experience daily life in the countryside, this place offers the chance to stay with a nomad community. As well as staying in a ger and eating traditional food you can arrange to ride horses and learn felt-making, among other things.

**Hustain Tourist Camp**     TOURIST GER CAMP $$
(☎21-245 087, 9323 0169; ☷hike.topple.cardigan; per person incl meals & park entry T146,000, incl breakfast only T56,500) The most popular spot to stay in Khustain is this sprawling tourist ger camp, located at the park's entrance. It has friendly, hard-working staff, clean facilities, a good restaurant and the fantastic information centre. It gets full with tour groups, so book well ahead.

## TAKHI – THE REINTRODUCTION OF A SPECIES

The year was 1969 and a herder in western Mongolia spotted a rare *takhi* (wild horse) in the distance. It was an extraordinary find as so few *takhi* were left in the wild. Alas, it was also the final sighting; with no new reports thereafter, scientists had to declare the species extinct in the wild – the result of poaching, overgrazing by livestock and human encroachment on their breeding grounds.

All was not lost for the *takhi*, however, as a dozen individual horses were known to exist in zoos outside Mongolia – their ancestors had been captured by game hunters in the early 20th century. A small group of conservationists dedicated themselves to breeding the animals with the hope that one day they could be reintroduced to Mongolia.

The conservationists did not fare so well with Mongolia's suspicious communist government, but when democracy arrived in the early 1990s they were welcomed with open arms. By that time the worldwide population was around 1500, scattered around zoos in Australia, Germany, Switzerland and the Netherlands.

From 1992, *takhi* have routinely been reintroduced into Mongolia at Khustain National Park, Takhiin Tal in Gov-Altai, and Khomyn Tal in Zavkhan. Today there are more than 350 *takhi* in Khustain, 80 in Takhiin Tal and 12 in Khomyn Tal. Given the political and logistical challenges to the project, their reintroduction is nothing short of miraculous, making it one of the most successful conservation stories of our times. In 2013, 40 new foals were born in Khustain alone. For US$125 you can 'adopt' a foal, which you'll get to name and obtain its official certificate.

The *takhi*, also known as Przewalski's horse (named after the Polish explorer who first 'discovered' the horse in 1878), are now descended from the bloodline of three stallions, so computerised records have been introduced to avoid inbreeding. They are the last remaining wild horse worldwide, the forerunner of the domestic horse, as depicted in cave paintings in France. They are not simply horses that have become feral, or wild, as found in the USA or Australia, but a genetically different species, boasting two extra chromosomes in their DNA make-up.

Within the parks, the laws of nature are allowed to run their course; an average of five foals are killed by wolves every year in Khustain. The park gets locals onside by hiring herders as rangers, offering cheap loans to others, and offering employment at a cheese-making factory on the outskirts of the park.

### Moilt Camp
CABIN $$

(✆ 21-245 087, 9323 0169; ⊞ stipulating.plunking.swimmers; per person incl meals & park entry T136,000, incl breakfast only T46,500) Inside the national park, 18km southwest of the park entry's and information centre, Moilt Camp is run by Hustai National Park Trust. It comprises basic wooden cabins, plus two gers, all clustered in a pretty valley. Prices are similar to Hustain Tourist Camp, although facilities aren't as good. The location, though, is far nicer.

### ℹ Information

**Khustain National Park Information Centre**
(✆ 9323 0169, 21-245 087; www.hustai.mn; ⊞ hike.topple.cardigan; ⊗ 7am-9pm) Offering a comprehensive overview of the park, this excellent information centre is located at the Hustain Tourist Camp. As well as detailed captions, you'll get an English-speaking guide to take you through the park's story, including that of the *takhi* and other wildlife and birdlife that reside in the park. There's also a documentary to watch on the horses.

It publishes a lovely series of books on the park that you can purchase from its souvenir shop.

### ℹ Getting There & Away

To get to the park, travel 100km west from Ulaanbaatar, along the road to Kharkhorin, where there is a signpost pointing you 13km south to the park entrance.

If you don't have a car, there's a minivan (one way US$15) that travels from the park to Ulaanbaatar and back twice a week, departing the park at about 10am on Friday and Sunday, and returning from Ulaanbaatar at 5pm on the same days. The van only has 10 seats, and is really for workers and volunteers, so you'll need to make an advance booking. In UB it leaves from the **Hustai National Park Office** (p101).

# ÖVÖRKHANGAI
# ӨВӨРХАНГАЙ

POP 112,400

Övörkhangai contains one of Mongolia's top attractions, the Erdene Zuu monastery in Kharkhorin. This is Mongolia's oldest monastery and it has become a regular stop on most tour circuits. But while travellers flock to this site and then rush off to points further west, many miss some of the best parts of Övörkhangai, including the stunning Naiman Nuur area, the impressive Orkhon Khürkhree Falls and the mountain-top monastery, Tövkhön Khiid. The southern part of the aimag, past Arvaikheer, is less interesting desert steppe.

# Arvaikheer   Арвайхээр

POP 25,600

A nondescript but friendly aimag capital, Arvaikheer is mainly used by travellers as a place to eat and rest, refuel the jeep or arrange onward public transport.

Note, there is no need to go to Arvaikheer if you only want to visit Kharkhorin and northern Övörkhangai, as a paved road runs to Kharkhorin from Ulaanbaatar.

## ◉ Sights

**Gandan Muntsaglan
Khiid**                    BUDDHIST MONASTERY

(Гандан Мунцаглан Хийд; [m]flame.unfilled. trials) This comparatively large monastery contains a fine collection of *thangka* (scroll paintings), including one depicting the original monastery, which was destroyed in 1937. The current monastery was opened in 1991, and now has about 40 monks in residence. It is located 900m northwest of the town square, through the ger districts.

**Övörkhangai Province Museum**   MUSEUM

([☎]1322-22075;  [m]mystery.rigs.pups;  T5000; ⊙9am-1pm & 2-6pm) Since Övörkhangai lies partly in the forested Khangai region and partly in the Gobi Desert, the aimag museum boasts a better-than-average selection of taxidermied mountain and desert animals. There are also some fossils and arrows, local artwork, leftovers from Karakorum, Soviet-era military pieces, and a feature on local identities – from writers to wrestlers. Entrance to the next-door Museum of Zanabazar is included in the price of admission.

**Museum of Zanabazar**          MUSEUM

([m]cookie.tenses.mouse;  free with Övörkhangai Province Museum ticket;  ⊙9am-1pm & 2-6pm) Has a small collection of religious artwork connected to the master sculptor. Ask at the Övörkhangai Province Museum for someone to open it up.

## ⊨ Sleeping

**Kharaa Hotel**                  HOTEL $

([☎]7032 3655;  [m]rocky.mailings.larger; tw& tr per person T10,000, half-lux twper person T20,000, lux d T30,000; [☎]) In a town where there's not much competition, Kharaa remains one of the better-value options. It's a bit rough around the edges, but rooms are spacious, with clean en suite bathrooms and hot water. It has a fairly uninviting restaurant downstairs. Staff are very friendly, but don't speak much English. There's wi-fi, but it's patchy at best.

---

**NOMADIC NAADAM**

For those unable to make it to Mongolia in July for **Naadam** (p68) – one of the world's great festivals – you no longer have to worry about missing out. The team from **Nomadic Naadam** ([☎]9908 9730, 9911 8573; www.facebook.com/NomadicNaadam; US$19-38) have come together to regularly host a mini version of the event, showcasing all of the iconic Mongolian sports and activities.

While it may be a condensed version, it's a spectacle that doesn't compromise in quality, with the same talented representatives who take part in the main event.

It's held on the Mongolian steppe around 60km from Ulaanbaatar, and you'll get to see multiple rounds of wrestling, horse racing and archery, to go with traditional dance performances, *khöömii* (throat singing) and back-bending contortionist acts. There's also yak carts, camels and plenty of traditional costumes for photo ops, as well as beauty contests and traditional food.

Check its Facebook page for the schedule, but events generally take place between one and four times a month from May to September. The cost is US$38 per person, but is reduced significantly if higher numbers are in attendance, and includes transport to/from UB.

# Arvaikheer

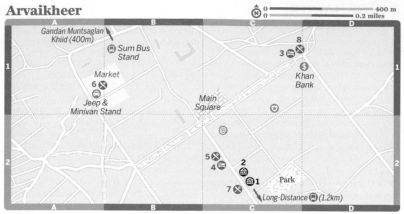

## Arvaikheer

### ◉ Sights
1 Museum of Zanabazar ........................C2
2 Övörkhangai Province Museum .........C2

### ⬤ Sleeping
3 Arvaikheer Palace Hotel ....................C1
4 Kharaa Hotel..........................................C2

### ⊗ Eating
5 Altan Holbo ............................................C2
  Arvaikheer Palace Hotel
  Restaurant ...................................(see 3)
6 Container Market................................. A1
7 Jargalan..................................................C2
8 Nomadic Irish Pub ............................. C1

★ **Arvaikheer Palace Hotel**   HOTEL $$$
(☏7032 6598; arvaikheerpalace_hotel@yahoo.
com; ⧈chose.muddle.throwaway; tw/tr incl break-
fast from T60,800/90,000, lux T120,000; 🛜) If
you want to swank it up, look no further
than this six-storey hotel. Its business-style
rooms are enormous, immaculate, and fea-
ture modern en suite bathrooms. There's
wi-fi access, and the on-site restaurant is
one of the best in town.

### ✗ Eating & Drinking

There's a couple of quality restaurants
in town – namely Arvaikheer Palace Ho-
tel Restaurant and Nomadic Irish Pub –
otherwise there are *guanz* (canteens)
around town, several of them in the **con-
tainer market** (⧈exclaim.agreement.broom).

**Jargalan**   MONGOLIAN $
(⧈tripled.caskets.truffles; mains T2000-4000;
⊙8am-8pm) A warm, friendly canteen that
opens earlier than most for breakfast. It
serves *buuz* (T600 per dumpling), goulash
(T3500), various soups (from T2500) and
warming mugs of *süütei tsai* (salty milk tea;
T200). No English sign or menu.

**Arvaikheer Palace
Hotel Restaurant**   ASIAN $$
(⧈chose.muddle.throwaway; mains T6000-11,600;
⊙8am-10pm; 🍴) Arvaikheer's smartest restaurant is on the ground floor of its best hotel, with a fabulous range of Mongolian and
pan-Asian dishes, including soups, salads,
kebabs, chicken dishes and plenty of vegetarian options. It's excellent value, spotlessly
clean and the menu has English translations
and photos.

**Nomadic Irish Pub**   PUB FOOD $$
(☏9981 0904; www.facebook.com/pg/uvfreedom;
⧈recruited.combos.butternut; mains T7000-
20,000; ⊙10am-midnight) For those who've
endured a long, dusty day in the car, this
Western-style pub is a bit of a godsend, with
a menu of international and Mongolian
mains to go with cold beers on tap.

**Altan Holbo**   MONGOLIAN $$
(⧈handbags.lemmings.cyclones; mains T6500-
16,500; ⊙10am-midnight; 🛜) This once humble eatery has undergone a major facelift
to be transformed into a rather flash restaurant upstairs. It does mostly Mongolian
cuisine, and there's a bar if you're looking
to unwind after a long day on the road.

## SHANKH KHIID MONASTERY

The secluded, atmospheric **Shankh Khiid Monastery** (Шанх Хийд; [*III*]aftercare. unleaded.half; GPS: N 47°03.079', E 102°57.236'; T2500) was founded by the great Zanabazar in 1648 and is said to have once housed Chinggis Khaan's black military banner. At one time the monastery was home to more than 1500 monks. Shankh Khiid, once known as the West Monastery, and Erdene Zuu Khiid are the only monasteries in the region to have survived the 1937 purge.

As elsewhere, the monastery was closed in 1937, temples were burnt and many monks were shipped off to Siberia. Some of those that survived helped to reopen the place in the early 1990s. Today there's around 25 monks in residence; if no one is around you may have to poke around to find someone to let you inside the temples.

The monastery is about 26km south of Kharkhorin. You'll see it on the right side of the road as you approach the village of Shankh.

## ℹ Information

**Internet Cafe** ([*III*]croak.goes.shippers; per hr T800; ⊙8am-6pm) In the Telecom office, along with the post office.
**Police station** ([*III*]trample.palms.deeds) Southeast of the town square.
**Khan Bank** ([*III*]never.commenced.plastic; ⊙9am-1pm & 2-6pm Mon-Fri) The town's largest bank. Has money-changing facilities and an ATM.

## ℹ Getting There & Around

You can travel quickly along the 430km paved road between Ulaanbaatar and Arvaikheer. The paved road continues for more than 100km west of Arvaikheer, towards the next aimag capital of Bayankhongor. With a jeep, an experienced driver and lots of time you could venture south to Dalanzadgad, 377km away in Ömnögovi aimag, either via Saikhan-Ovoo or (more adventurously) via Guchin-Us, Khovd and Khongoryn Els.

### BUS

Three daily buses travel from Arvaikheer to Ulaanbaatar (T20,300, eight hours), departing at 8am, 2pm and 6pm. The **bus station** ([*III*]total. using.rejoiced) is southwest of the centre, near the highway, in a two-storey grey building.

The local bus stand, or **sum bus stand** ([*III*]lamenting.straw.glides), has minivans that ply set routes to other *sums* within the aimag, including Kharkhorin (T12,000, three hours).

### TAXIS, JEEPS & MINIVANS

Minivans, jeeps and taxis run along the paved road between Arvaikheer and Ulaanbaatar daily (T22,000 per person, seven to eight hours). Look for them at a **stop** ([*III*]exclaim.agreement. broom) on the west side of the market. Shared vehicles travel to Khujirt (T9000, two hours), Kharkhorin (T12,000, three hours) and Bayankhongor (T15,000, 3½ hours).

### MOTORBIKE TAXIS

Motorbike taxis charge T1000 per person to take you between the town centre and the bus station.

## Kharkhorin     Хархорин

🖉 013258, 7032 / POP 9000 / ELEV 1476M

While this is the site of Mongolia's famed 13th-century capital Karakorum, don't come expecting the glories of the Middle Ages – Kharkhorin itself is a gritty, nondescript Soviet-built town. What does pull in punters by the busload, however, are the remains of the 16th-century monastery, Erdene Zuu Khiid, and the impressive museum, both of which offer some evocative insights into the region's golden era. The scenic valley surrounds, along with the strong selection of horse-trekking outfits and numerous accommodation options, ensure plenty of people linger for a while.

Kharkhorin is also within striking distance of a number of worthwhile sights – the stunning lakes of Naiman Nuur, Orkhon Khürkhree waterfall, the secluded hilltop monastery, Tövkhön Khiid, the sand dunes known as Mongol Els, and the magnificently stark rocky nature reserve, Khögnö Khan Uul – making this the best place to base yourself for a tour of Övörkhangai aimag.

## ◉ Sights

★**Erdene Zuu Khiid**    BUDDHIST MONASTERY
(Эрдэнэ Зуу Хийд; 🖉9926 8286; [*III*]fattening. monotony.reformation; temple admission & tour adult/child T5000/free, grounds free, photography T20,000; ⊙9am-6pm May-Sep, 10am-5pm Oct-Apr) Founded in 1586 by Altai Khaan, Erdene Zuu (Hundred Treasures) was the first Buddhist monastery in Mongolia. The

# Kharkhorin

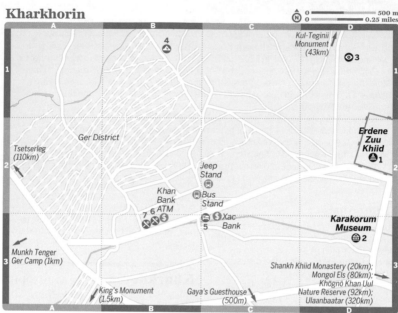

## Kharkhorin

monastery went through periods of neglect and prosperity until finally the Stalinist purges of 1937 put it completely out of business. The monastery remained closed until 1965, when it was permitted to reopen as a museum, but not as a place of worship. It was only with the collapse of communism in 1990 that religious freedom was restored and the monastery became active again.

Today Erdene Zuu Khiid is considered by many to be the most important monastery in the country, though there's no doubt it's a shadow of what it once was. At its peak, it had between 60 and 100 temples, around 300 gers inside the walls, and up to 1000 monks in residence. All but three of the temples in Erdene Zuu were destroyed during the purges and an unknown number of monks were either killed or sent to Siberian gulags. A surprising number of statues, *tsam* masks and *thangkas* were saved, however – possibly with the help of a few sympathetic military officers. The items were buried in nearby mountains, or stored in local homes (at great risk to the residents).

Entrance to the walled monastery grounds is free. If you want to see inside the main temple, you'll have to buy a ticket, which includes a guided tour of the site with an English-speaking guide.

The main temples date from the 16th century. Most of the artefacts you'll see – wall paintings, *thangkas*, masks etc – are from the 18th century. Many are in excellent condition. The monastery is an easy 2km walk from the centre of Kharkhorin.

➡ Temples

The monastery is enclosed in an immense walled compound. Spaced evenly along each wall, about every 15m, are 108 **stupas** (108 is a sacred number to Buddhists). The three temples in the compound – Zuu of Buddha, Zuun Zuu and

Baruun Zuu – which were not destroyed in the 1930s, are dedicated to the three stages of Buddha's life: childhood, adolescence and adulthood.

**Dalai Lama Süm** was built in 1675 to commemorate the visit by Abtai Khaan's son, Altan, to the Dalai Lama in Tibet. The room is bare save for a statue of Zanabazar and some fine 17th-century *thangkas* depicting the Dalai Lamas and various protector deities.

Inside the courtyard, **Baruun Zuu**, the temple to the west, built by Abtai Khaan and his son, is dedicated to the adult Buddha. Inside, on either side of Sakyamuni (the historical Buddha), are statues of Sanjaa (Dipamkara in Sanskrit; the Past Buddha), to the left; and Maidar (Maitreya in Sanskrit; the Future Buddha), to the right. Other items on display include some golden 'wheels of eternity', *naimin takhel* (the eight auspicious symbols), figurines from the 17th and 18th centuries, and *balin* (wheat dough cakes, decorated with coloured medallions of goat or mutton fat), made in 1965 and still well preserved. Look out for the inner circumambulation path leading off to the left, just by the entrance.

The main and central temple is called the **Zuu of Buddha**. The entrance is flanked by the gods Gonggor on the left and Bandal Lham (Palden Lhamo in Sanskrit) on the right. Inside, to the right of the statues of the child Buddha, is Otoch Manal (the Medicine Buddha), while to the left is Holy Abida (the god of justice). The temple also contains statues of Niam and Dabaa, the sun and moon gods respectively, a few of the *tsam* masks that survived the purges, some carved, aggressive-looking guards from the 16th and 17th centuries, and some displays of the work of the revered sculptor and Buddhist, Zanabazar.

In the temple to the east, **Zuun Zuu**, there's a statue depicting the adolescent Buddha. The statue on the right is Tsongkhapa, who founded the Yellow Hat sect of Buddhism in Tibet. The figure on the left is Janraisig (Chenresig in Tibetan, Avalokitesvara in Sanskrit), the Bodhisattva of Compassion.

As you walk north you will pass the **Golden Prayer Stupa**, built in 1799. The small locked temple next to it, with a blue-tiled roof, is thought to pre-date the monastery itself by around 200 years.

The large white temple at the far end is the Tibetan-style **Lavrin Süm**, where ceremonies are held every morning, usually starting at around 11am; the times vary so ask the office. Visitors are welcome, but photographs during ceremonies are not. This temple is the most active and atmospheric part of the whole complex.

★**Karakorum Museum** MUSEUM
(www.kharakhorummuseum.mn; ⊞awkward.mowing.unordered; adult/student/child T8000/3000/1000, photography/video T15,000/35,000; ⊗9am-6pm daily Apr-Oct, 10am-5pm Mon-Fri Nov-Mar) Kharkhorin's museum is small, but highly impressive – probably the country's best museum outside Ulaanbaatar. Everything is beautifully designed and well displayed.

The exhibits include dozens of artefacts dating from the 13th and 14th centuries that were recovered from the immediate area, plus others that were found from archaeological sites in other parts of the aimag, including prehistoric stone tools. You'll see pottery, bronzes, coins, religious statues and stone inscriptions. There's also a half-excavated kiln sunk into the museum floor.

**King's Monument** MONUMENT
(⊞wades.maturing.invalidated) This hilltop monument is *the* place to head for sunset, with magnificent 360-degree views overlooking Kharkhorin and its encompassing valley. The imposing monument comprises three colourful mosaic panels that each represent the empires of the Hunnu, Turkic and Mongol periods.

**Stone Turtles** HISTORIC SITE
(Turtle Rocks; ⊞brighten.alpha.adjective) Outside the monastery walls of Erdene Zuu Khiid are two stone turtles. Four of these sculptures once marked the boundaries of ancient Karakorum, acting as protectors of the city (turtles are considered symbols of eternity). Each of the turtles originally had an inscribed stone stela mounted vertically on its back.

One is easy to find: just walk out of the northern gate of the monastery and follow the path northwest for about 300m. This location is also the site of an archaeological excavation led by a German team.

You'll probably need a car to get to the other **turtle** (w informed.exodus.rasped), which is on the hill south of the monastery – otherwise it's a 45-minute walk. It has a more scenic location, but is blighted by being within a caged enclosure. En route you'll encounter the **Penis Stone** (w ham-sters.attachments.compasses), a historical stone phallic sculpture used as a reminder for young monks to remain celibate.

## ☞ Tours

Most of the ger camps can help to arrange horse trips around Kharkhorin. Family Guesthouse, Gaya's Guesthouse and Morin Jim all organise horse treks and jeep tours to surrounding sights in the region.

### THE ANCIENT CAPITAL

In the mid-13th century, Karakorum was a happening place. Chinggis Khaan established a supply base here, and his son Ögedei ordered the construction of a proper capital, a decree that attracted traders, dignitaries and skilled workers from across Asia and even Europe.

The good times lasted around 40 years until Kublai moved the capital to Khanbalik (later called Běijīng), a decision that still incites resentment among some Mongolians. Following the move to Běijīng and the subsequent collapse of the Mongol empire, Kar-akorum was abandoned and then destroyed by vengeful Manchurian soldiers in 1388.

Whatever was left of Karakorum was used to help build, in the 16th century, the enor-mous monastery, Erdene Zuu Khiid, which itself was badly damaged during the Stalinist purges.

Mongolia's ancient capital may be gone, but Karakorum is certainly not forgotten. By piecing together the accounts of the city written by visiting missionaries, ambassadors and travellers, we have some idea of what the imperial capital once looked like.

The missionary William of Rubruck (1215–95) dismissed the city as being no bigger than the suburb of Saint Denis in Paris. Giovanni de Pian Carpine (1180–1252), an envoy sent to the Mongols in 1245 by Pope Innocent IV, described the city vaguely as 'at the distance of a year's walk' from Rome.

The city never had much time to expand; it was only active for 40 years before Kublai moved the capital to Khanbalik. Interestingly, few Mongols lived there, most preferring to stay in their gers several kilometres away on the steppe. It was mainly inhabited by artisans, scholars, religious leaders and others captured by the Mongols during their foreign raids.

Its main feature was a brick wall with four gates that encircled the city. Each gate had its own market, selling grain in the east, goats in the west, oxen and wagons in the south and horses in the north.

The Mongol khaans were famed for their religious tolerance and split their time equally between all the religions, hence the 12 different religions that coexisted within the town. Mosques, Buddhist monasteries and Nestorian Christian churches competed for the Mongols' souls. Even powerful figures such as Ögedei's wife and Kublai's mother were Nestorian Christians.

The centrepiece of the city was the Tumen Amgalan (Palace of Worldly Peace) in the southwest corner of the city. This 2500-sq-metre complex, built in 1235, was the palace of Ögedei Khaan. The two-storey palace had a vast reception hall for receiving ambassadors, and its 64 pillars resembled the nave of a church. The walls were painted, the green-tiled floor had underfloor heating, and the Chinese-style roof was covered in green and red tiles.

A team of German archaeologists recently uncovered the foundations of the palace, close to one of the stone turtles. You can see a model of the palace in the **National Museum of Mongolia** (p57) in Ulaanbaatar, while inside the **Karakorum Museum** (p107), in Kharkhorin itself, there is a model of the whole ancient city.

Arguably, the most memorable aspect of the city was a fountain designed in 1253 by the French jeweller and sculptor Guillaume Bouchier (or Bouchee) of Paris, who had been captured by the Mongols in Hungary and brought back to embellish Karako-rum. The fountain was in the shape of a huge silver tree, which simultaneously dis-pensed mare's milk from silver lion heads, and wine, rice wine, *bal* (mead) and *airag* (fermented mare's milk) from four golden spouts shaped like snakes' heads. On top of the tree was an angel. On order, a servant blew a pipe like a bugle that extended from the angel's mouth, giving the order for other servants to pump drinks out of the tree.

## 🛏 Sleeping

### ★ Family Guesthouse    TOURIST GER CAMP $

(🖀 9645 8188, 9931 2735; www.horsetripganaa. com; ⓌΙΙ incinerated.exacting.restoration; GPS: N 47°12.496', E 102°49.151'; dm incl breakfast US$8, d per person incl breakfast & dinner US$12; 🛜) Offering a good insight into local life is this friendly family home on the outskirts of town, with several gers in its compound, offering excellent-value budget accommodation. Its Western-style rooms are less appealing. Ganbaatar and his wife Suvd both speak good English, and it's the definitive place for local information, onward travel and arranging jeep tours and horse treks in the surrounding region.

The food here is excellent and vegetarians can be catered for. Showers are in the bathhouse next door, but don't expect reliable hot water. The shared toilets are clean, but in an outhouse, so it's one for those seeking a more local experience. As well as the five kids who live here, there's a host of other relatives spanning generations. Free pick-up from the bus station.

### ★ Gaya's Guesthouse    TOURIST GER CAMP $

(🖀 9633 3809, 9989 3809; www.gayas-guest house.strikingly.com; ⓌΙΙ unwholesome.facilitating. coincidence; dm/s/d/tr from US$8/25/28/36; 🛜) This popular, family-owned guesthouse is run by Gaya, who has been providing travellers with a local experience since 2003. Take your choice between gers (dorms or private) or rooms in the newly built guesthouse. It's a good place to organise tours in Kharkhorin and beyond. There's also an on-site shop selling Mongolian felt products made by Gaya and her mother; lessons available.

There is free pick-up from the bus stop, and Gaya can arrange bus tickets to and from Ulaanbaatar..

### Morin Jim    HOSTEL $

(🖀 9924 2980; www.horsetrails.mn; ⓌΙΙ overstated.blubbered.speedway; ger/dm $6/11, d $37; 🛜) Attached to the Morin Jim Café are these comfortable Western-style hostel rooms and dorms in a fairly scrappy building. There's also a handful of fairly uninspired gers in the lot, in which you'll have to pay use the shower (T4000). Management speak English, and it's popular with those here to arrange horse treks, which are professionally run and highly recommended.

### Misheel Camp    TOURIST GER CAMP $$

(🖀 9901 2943; www.misheeltour.com; ⓌΙΙ lift.pestle. configuring; per person incl meals T85,000; 🛜) One of several options set in this beautiful grassy valley, this relaxed camp has 15 gers set below the mountain and close to the river. All the facilities, including bathrooms, are well maintained, and it's endorsed by visiting German archaeologists who are repeat clientele.

### Ikh Khorum Hotel    HOTEL $$$

(🖀 7032 7007; www.ikhkhorum.com; ⓌΙΙ nervous.hairpieces.actively; s/d incl breakfast from T220,000/280,000; ❄🛜) The arrival of this four-star business hotel is bit of a game changer in Kharkhorin. While you won't get a local experience (for that you'll need to stay in a ger), for those wanting Western-style comfort, it's a class act across the board, from the elegant business-chic rooms and professional staff to the suave on-site restaurant.

## 🍴 Eating

### Morin Jim Café    MONGOLIAN $

(🖀 9924 2980; ⓌΙΙ overstated.blubbered.speedway; mains T4000-7500; ⏱ 9am-midnight; 🛜) Simple, but excellent-value menu containing mostly Mongolian dishes, but also salads, fried chicken and vegetarian stew. There's roadside terrace seating out front, and it serves French wine and fresh coffee as well as beer. It has a full-sized billiard table and table tennis.

### Ikh Khorum Hotel    INTERNATIONAL, MONGOLIAN $$

(🖀 7032 7007; www.ikhkhorum.com/rest.html; ⓌΙΙ nervous.hairpieces.actively; mains T10,000-25,000; ⏱ 6am-midnight; 🛜) Whether you're in the mood for traditional Mongolian dishes or a cheeseburger, this upmarket hotel-restaurant is your best bet for a nice meal on the town. Portions are huge, and the professional uniformed staff and crisp white tablecloths create a somewhat refined atmosphere. It also has a rooftop terrace for alfresco dining, drinks and watching the sunset.

### King Restaurant    PUB FOOD $$

(🖀 9901 5120; ⓌΙΙ outweigh.hotel.rasped; meals T5500-18,000; ⏱ 10am-10pm Mon-Sat) A casual pub-style hang-out with booth seating, foosball table and live music to go with a menu of pizzas, Mongolian dishes and cheap beer.

**WORTH A TRIP**

## NAIMAN NUUR

The area of Naiman Nuur, which was created by volcanic eruptions centuries ago, is now part of the 115-sq-km **Khuisiin Naiman Nuur Nature Reserve** (Найман Нуур, Eight Lakes; 🔲behaves.consumes.kebabs; GPS: N 46°31.232', E 101°50.705'). Despite the name, there are actually nine, not eight, lakes. The lakes are about 35km southwest of Orkhon Khürkhree (waterfall), but the roads are often virtually impassable. Locals around the waterfall can hire horses for the two- to four-day trip to the lakes (around T15,000 per horse per day, plus the same again for your horse guide).

This area is environmentally fragile; vehicles that attempt to make the trip end up tearing new tracks through the grasslands, so local communities are working on ways to prevent cars from coming here. If your driver says he can make it all the way to the lakes by car, insist on going by horse.

From Kharkhorin, **Family Guesthouse** (p109) and **Gaya's Guesthouse** (p109) can organise horse treks here for around US$180 per person (minimum two people) for a three-day trip, which is inclusive of the jeep transfer from Kharkhorin. Ulaanbaatar-based companies such as **Nomads** (p40), **Nomadic Journeys** (p40) and **Nomadic Expeditions** (p40) also run tours here, including horse-riding trips.

## ℹ️ Information

**Khan Bank ATM** (🔲privations.eyebrows. deceived) Foreign-card friendly.

**XacBank** (📞1800 1888; 🔲season.relearning. stacking; 🕘9am-5.30pm Mon-Fri, ATM 24hr) Changes money, but accepts Visa card only.

## ℹ️ Getting There & Away

Two daily buses go to Ulaanbaatar at 10am and 2pm (T17,300, six to seven hours). You can buy tickets from the ticket office at the **bus stand** (🔲duties.selectors.eyeing; 🕘ticket office 9am-2pm & 3-6pm) two days in advance, and it's wise to do so if possible, though UB-bound minivans wait to sweep up ticket-less passengers, so you won't get stranded.

It's sometimes possible to snag a seat on an Ulaanbaatar to Tsetserleg bus if you wait on the main road at around 1pm to 2pm and flag it down as it passes. Otherwise, try to find a shared minivan heading west. You may have to charter your own vehicle, though (about T80,000 plus petrol).

Across from the bus station is the **jeep stand** (🔲extras.hoedown.foothold) from where minivans and jeeps run daily to Ulaanbaatar (T17,300, seven hours). The road is tarmac the whole way. There are far fewer vehicles going to Khujirt (T7000) on Monday, Wednesday and Friday, and Arvaikheer (T12,000) – maybe once a day if at all.

Coming here, buses from Ulaanbaatar to Kharkhorin leave from the **Dragon Bus Terminal** (p265) at 11am and 2pm.

## ℹ️ Getting Around

Erdene Zuu and the nearby sights are a 2km walk from town; otherwise ask around for a lift (about T700).

# Khögnö Khan Uul Nature Reserve
Хөгнө Хан Уул

The 469-sq-km Khögnö Khan Uul Nature Reserve centres on a large, boulder-strewn rocky mountain that rises up surreally from its semidesert surrounds. The arid terrain is good for short hikes (there's plenty of rock clambering to be done), and there are old temples to explore, both ruined and active. In terms of wildlife, as well as majestic red deer, you might also spot ibexes, various varieties of hawk, and even wolves.

The mountain is in Bulgan aimag, but is most easily accessed from the Ulaanbaatar–Kharkhorin highway.

## 👁 Sights

**Erdiin Khambiin Khiid**                    RUINS
(🔲fairytale.crusts.vowels; GPS: N 47°25.561', E 103°41.686') At the southern foot of the mountain are these ruins, with a couple of new temples and the remains of one older temple. About five monks reside here in the summer months.

**Övgön Khiid**                               RUINS
(Өвгөн Хийд; 🔲lightest.forecast.equinoxes; GPS: N 47°26.267', E 103°42.527') These 17th-century ruins are a lovely 45-minute (2km) walk along a rocky path (follow the pink dots painted on the rocks) up the valley to the right of Erdiin Khambiin Khiid. The monastery was built in 1660 and destroyed (and the monks massacred) by the armies of

Zungar Galdan Bochigtu, a rival of Zanabazar's, in 1640. The ruins are no more than the remaining brick foundations, but arriving here has the feel of being an explorer who's stumbled upon a hidden, long-lost world.

**Mongol Els**                               DUNES
(Монгол Элс, Elsen-Tasarkhai; [m]droves.nursemaids.blameless; GPS: N 47°19.819' E 103°41.618) On the road from Kharkhorin to Ulaanbaatar, one surprising sight that livens up a fairly boring stretch of road is the sand dunes of Elsen-Tasarkhai. Better known in Ulaanbaatar's tourist industry as Mongol Els, these large dunes stretch for some 70km, and are worth stopping off at if you're not planning to visit the much more spectacular Khongoryn Els (p180) in the Gobi Desert.

The dunes are located on the approach to Khögnö Khan Uul Nature Reserve. At the turn-off to the sand dunes there is a group of camel herders who hang around and sell camel rides. Expect to pay T5000 to have your photo taken on a camel, or T10,000 for a one-hour ride across the dunes.

### 🍽 Sleeping & Eating

**Ider-Tsogt's Family Ger**    TOURIST GER CAMP $
([J]9579 0048; [m]enthralled.leafing.cruiser; GPS: N 47°22.553' E 103°40.961'; per person T10,000, meals T5000) Ider-Tsogt is one of a number of herdsmen who rent out guest gers to travellers visiting the national park. He doesn't speak English, but is warm and friendly. His gers are between the main mountain and the sand dunes known as Mongol Els. Turn up to your left as you approach the mountain from the main road.

Ider-Tsogt also rents horses (per hour/day T7000/15,000, plus the same again for your horse guide) for treks in and around the mountain range. It takes three days to complete a circuit of the mountain by horse or by foot.

### ★ Khögnö Khan

**Resort Mountain Camp**    TOURIST GER CAMP $$
([J]9910 2885; www.naturetours.mn; [m]rescue.impressed.shroud; GPS: N 47°24.430', E 103°40.364'; per person T38,000, meals T17,000-22,000) In an attractive setting at the foot of the mountain, 4km southwest of Övgön Khiid, this comfortable camp has traditional ger accommodation, a large log-cabin restaurant, a clean and spacious shower block and great rock-clambering opportunities all around it.

It's run by the lovely Nara who speaks excellent English and German, and has been the manager here for 20 years.

**Övgön Erdene Tour Camp**    TOURIST GER CAMP $$
(Monastery Ger Camp; [J]9927 2873; [m]rumbled.rubble.fiscal; per person with/without meals US$80/30) This well-maintained ger camp and wood lodge is just beside the entrance to the Erdiin Khambiin Khiid temple. There are hot showers and a restaurant, and its position at the foot of the monastery makes it the perfect spot for those wanting to explore the area; plus having no generator ensures a peaceful atmosphere.

### ⓘ Getting There & Away

To get to Khögnö Khan Uul from Kharkhorin by jeep, turn north off the main road, 80km east of Kharkhorin, just past the huge sand dunes known as Mongol Els. From the turn-off, the track passes several herders' gers (Ider-Tsogt's Family Ger is up to your left from here) until, after 8km, you reach Khögnö Khan ger camp, where you turn right for the remaining 4km or so to the monastery ruins. There is a shortcut if you are coming from Ulaanbaatar (the turn-off is marked by a sign that says 'Ar Mongol', 1.2km after the Bichigt Khad ger camp).

There is no public transport to Khögnö Khan Uul, but you can take a Kharkhorin-, Khujirt- or Arvaikheer-bound minivan from Ulaanbaatar, get off at the turn-off on the main road and then hitch (or more likely walk) the remaining 12km.

# Orkhon Valley
## Орхоны Хөндий

If you've come to Mongolia to experience its vast mountainous steppe, then travelling through the Orkhon Valley region should be on your itinerary. Here you can drive all day and hardly see another vehicle, passing through flocks of goat and sheep that scurry out of the way, while herds of semi-wild horses graze in the distance. Crossing this vast nothingness of undulating hills you'll encounter the occasional ger camp of nomadic herders, who'll wave you on in the direction you're heading.

It's a route that's popular with tourists making their way from Kharkhorin, invariably stopping at Orkhon Falls. From here you can embark on a horse trek to Khuisiin Naiman Nuur Nature Reserve, or continue east to the scenic Khangai Mountains, where you'll find one of central Mongolia's most atmospheric monasteries.

## KUL-TEGINII MONUMENT

When Chinggis Khaan decided to move his capital to Karakorum, he was well aware that the region had already been the capital of successive nomad empires. About 20km northeast of Khar Balgas lies the remainder of yet another of these, the Turkic *khaganate* (pre-Mongol empire). All that's left of the *khaganate* is the 3m-high inscribed monument of **Kul-Teginii Monument** (Кул-Тэгиний Хөшөө; [⊕]seafront.tripe.insinuates; GPS: N 47°33.837', E 102°49.931'; museum T5000; ⊙9am-6pm), the *khagan* (ruler) of the ancient empire, which is exhibited within the Turkish-funded archaeological museum at the site.

All the outdoor monuments are replicas and the originals have been moved inside the museum.

The monument was raised in 732 and is inscribed in Runic and Chinese script. You can see a copy of the stela in the entrance of the National Museum of Mongolia (p57) in Ulaanbaatar.

Nearby is another **monument to Bilge Khagan** (683–734), older brother of Kul-Tegin. Ten years after the death of Bilge, the Turkic *khaganate* was overrun by the Uighurs.

The museum and monuments are 45km north of Kharkhorin, on a paved road.

## ⊙ Sights

### ★ Tövkhön Khiid
BUDDHIST MONASTERY

(Төвхөн Хийд; [⊕]oppositely.ogling.toasty; GPS: N47° 00.772', E102° 15.362'; T3500) Hidden deep in a pine forest in the mountainous **Khangai Nuruu National Park** ([⊕]netted. scarring.endorphin; T3000), this scenic monastery has become a major pilgrimage centre for Mongolians. Zanabazar founded the site in 1653 and lived, worked and meditated here for 30 years. The monastery was destroyed in 1937, but rebuilt with public funds in the early 1990s.

The monastery is situated at the top of Shireet Ulaan Uul, and Zanabazar apparently liked the unusual formation of the peak; the rocky outcrop looks like an enormous throne. It was here that Zanabazar created many of his best artistic endeavours, some of which can be found now in the Zanabazar Museum of Fine Arts (p61) in Ulaanbaatar.

Six or seven monks live here year-round, although sometimes more are here. Several **pilgrimage sites** have grown up around the temple and hermits' caves, including one that is said to be Zanabazar's boot imprint. There's another temple further up top, accessed past the two wells (signed with plaques) to the right of the temple; take the path past the *makhala* tree and round the rear up to Naga Temple. From here you can scramble up even further (though only males are permitted beyond this point), where there's an *ovoo* (shamanistic collection of stones) and incredible 360-degree panoramas.

The monastery is around 60km from Kharkhorin and is best reached with your own vehicle. Just follow the Orkhon Gol southwest for around 50km and turn north, up a side valley. This brings you to a couple of ger camps and the trailhead up the eastern side of the mountain. A good 4WD can drive the steep road up to the monastery in 20 minutes, but old Russian jeeps and vans can't make the trip so you'll have to walk (one hour) up the hill through the forest. From the car park it's 3km. The route is obvious and in summer locals offer horse rides (T10,000 one way) to the top and back. It's a pleasant hike to the top, although swarms of flies can plague your ascent in summer; wrap a T-shirt, bandanna or towel around your head to keep them away.

Note that if you are coming from Orkhon Khürkhree, you will arrive at the western slope of the mountain and will end up taking a different trail to the top. From this side you'll also find basic ger camps and herdsmen offering horse rides to the monastery.

### Orkhon Falls
WATERFALL

(Orkhon Khürkhree, Орхон Хүрхрээ; [⊕]splints. screened.sneezing; GPS: N 46°47.234', E 101°57.694') After a strong rain the magnificent seasonal Orkhon Falls is one of the best sights in central Mongolia. About 250m downstream from the waterfall you can climb down to the bottom of the gorge; it's 22m deep and dotted with pine trees.

Ask your tour operator about the status of the falls. The water doesn't run all year and will only start to flow after the first good summer rain. Late July and August are the best times to see it, although it's still a very attractive spot in autumn. If you arrive when the waterfall is not in flow, take solace in the fact that the region is still gorgeous, and a fine area for swimming, camping and horse riding.

There are a few different ways to approach the waterfall; all of them involve rough travel in parts, on very rocky roads. Coming directly from Ulaanbaatar, most traffic will go on the road via Khujirt (around 35km from the falls). You'll pass a lovely **viewpoint** (GPS: N 46°53.465' E 102°22.762') on this track, as the river skirts a cliff face it helped carve into the steppe. One or two kilometres further along you'll pass a remarkable collection of large, Bronze-Age **square graves** (GPS: N 46°53.465' E 102°22.762') on your left. The road from Kharkhorin is longer, but by taking this route you can stop at Tövkhön Khiid (p112) on the way. From Arvaikheer, it's possible to take a remote backcountry road via Züünbayan-Ulaan and Bat-Ölzii; but you'll need an experienced driver and a very sturdy 4WD to attempt it.

### 🛏 Sleeping & Eating

You'll find tourist ger camps close to Orkhon Falls, charging around T10,000 to T30,000 per person. It's best to have a look at a few to decide the one that's best for you.

At Tövkhön Khiid there are some family-run ger camps at the bottom, by the entrance to the national park. Expect to pay around T20,000 per person including meals.

All tourist camps offer inexpensive meal options, either served in your ger, or in the on-site restaurant. At Orkhon Falls there are a few grocery stores selling provisions for self caterers, along with cold drinks. Note that fishing is prohibited in the national park.

**Shar's Guest Ger**  TOURIST GER CAMP **$**
(☑ 9571 2038, 8832 7388; 🌐 moments.humbly. fuzzily; per person T10,000, breakfast T6000, lunch/dinner T5000) This guest ger near the falls is run by a herdsman known as Shar, and comprises a row of five or so gers. Like all family nomad gers, the long-drop toilets are a bit of a trek away (and shared among the community). Food is traditional and tasty, often featuring yak cream from Shar's own herd.

Shar also hires out horses (T10,000/15,000 per hour/day, plus the same again for the guide). The three- or four-day round trip to Naiman Nuur (p110) is popular from here.

**Orkhon Waterfall**
**Tourist Camp**  TOURIST GER CAMP **$$**
(☑ 9999 2067; 🌐 hooks.hazed.tingling; per person with/without meals T65,000/30,000) Easily the best option in the cluster of ger camps near the falls, with 14 clean, atmospheric gers, hot showers (T10,000 for nonguests) and a large ger restaurant (meals from T6500 to T15,000). There's also a shop (open 8am to 10pm) selling basic groceries, snacks, cold beer and soft drinks.

### ℹ Getting There & Away

There's no public transport to the Orkhon Valley region, so you'll need to hire a vehicle to access the area. Most of the guesthouses in Kharkhorin can arrange a car, or you can hire a vehicle from the jeep stand. It's about a four-hour drive from Kharkhorin to Orkhon Falls, and about five hours to Tsetserleg.

Orkhon Falls is the starting point for trips to **Naiman Nuur** (p110), only reachable on horseback.

# ARKHANGAI  АРХАНГАЙ

POP 92,100

Arkhangai is something of an oasis in the centre of Mongolia's harsh climatic zones; to the south lies the hot Gobi Desert and to the north lies the frigid Siberian taiga. Arkhangai is right in the middle, a mixed landscape of rugged mountains, peaceful forests, rushing streams and rolling steppe. All this wild nature and mixed topography makes for some interesting independent travel options: horse riding, mountain biking, fishing and trekking are all possible here.

Most travellers make stops at the Tsenkher Hot Springs and Tsetserleg before heading off to Tariat for Terkhiin Tsagaan Nuur (Great White Lake). From the White Lake there are trails north to Khövsgöl aimag. With a few extra days up your sleeve you could dangle a fishing line at Ögii Nuur and check out the historic Turkic-era stone monuments of Kul-Tegin.

# Tsetserleg  Цэцэрлэг

☑ 01332, 7033 / POP 20,600 / ELEV 1691M

Nestled comfortably between rugged mountains, and with a charming temple overlooking the town, Tsetserleg is one of the country's more appealing aimag capitals.

It's a perfect place to break up your journey between Kharkhorin and Tariat,

# Tsetserleg

Gangin Gol
(1.5km)

Museum of Arkhangai Aimag

Khan Bank ATM

Town Square

Khan Bank

Taikhar Rock (22km) ←

Bus Station

Tsenkher Hot Springs (27km)

especially if you manage to snag a bed at the stand out Fairfield Guesthouse. Nature lovers will appreciate the hiking opportunities and good camping spots in the surrounding area.

## ◉ Sights

★ **Museum of Arkhangai Aimag**    MUSEUM
(☎1332-22281; 🌐deliveryman.gaslight.fortifies; adult/child T5000/1000, photography T5000; ⊙10am-7pm daily Apr-Oct, 9am-6pm Mon-Fri Nov-Mar) This is one of the best aimag museums in the country, not least because it is housed in the charming courtyard-temple complex of **Zayain Gegeenii Süm**, which was first built in 1586 but expanded in 1679, when it housed five temples and up to 1000 monks. Miraculously, the monastery escaped the Stalinist purges because it was made into a museum. The main hall concentrates on traditional Mongolian lifestyle, with exhibits of costumes, traditional tools, a ger, musical instruments, weaponry and saddles.

**Galdan Zuu Temple**    TEMPLE
(🌐renewing.contemplate.vents) An unmissable landmark overlooking town is this spectacular temple perched high up the hill above the aimag museum. It stands behind an impressive 7m statue of the Buddha. Behind the temple is a large, near-vertical, rocky hill called Bulgan Uul, where there are some large Buddhist inscriptions and paintings.

**Taikhar Rock**    NATURAL FEATURE
(Тайхар Чулуу; Taikhar Chuluu; 🌐sesame.ambassadors.swung) Located 22km northwest of Tsetserleg, this rock formation is the subject of many local legends, the most common one being that a great *baatar* (hero) crushed a huge serpent here by hurling the rock on top of it. Locals claim there are some ancient Tibetan inscriptions on the rock, though you'll be lucky to spot them through 30 years of modern graffiti (including some interesting 1980s Soviet-era scribble). There is even an *ovoo* at the top.

## 🛏 Sleeping

**Naran Hotel**    HOTEL $
(☎9949 6679; 🌐contoured.graces.nappy; r with/without bathroom T60,000/30,000; 🛜) Next to the Fairfield Guesthouse, this inexpensive hotel has Soviet-style rooms with private bathroom and TV. There are also cheaper options with shared toilets, but no showers.

★ **Fairfield Guesthouse**    GUESTHOUSE $$
(☎9908 7745, 7033-3036; www.fairfield.mn; 🌐passes.turns.recounted; ger with/without breakfast per person T35,000/28,000, r with shared bathroom T45,000/38,000; 🛜) Attached to the excellent cafe-restaurant of the same name, this nine-room guesthouse, is run by an Australian guy called Murray, his young family,

and their team of friendly local staff, It's a hugely popular choice and one of the only hotels in the countryside where you need a reservation in summer. Rooms are stylish, clean and comfy, while shared showers are always hot.

During summer there's a ger option, too. Staff can also arrange horse-trekking trips (guides T55,000 per day, horses T27,000 per day), and there's a fleet of good-quality Trek mountain bikes for rent (T10,000/30,000 per hour/day). They also hire out camping and cooking equipment, and fishing gear (T10,000 per day) and guides (T80,000). Laundry costs T8000, and the free wi-fi extends into some of the rooms. They can arrange bus tickets to get here from Ulaanbaatar and back, and arrange homestays with nomads and tours around Mongolia.

**OD Hotel** HOTEL $$
(⏺8811 9004; ⏹silverware.sparkled.knotted; s/d T60,000/70,000) This reasonably stylish hotel is decorated with art, and has smart rooms with attached bathrooms, but is still seriously overpriced. There's an English sign, but no English is spoken.

 **Eating**

★**Fairfield Cafe & Bakery** CAFE $$
(⏺7033-3036, 9908 7745; www.fairfield.mn; ⏹passes.turns.recounted; mains T7000-9500; ⏺7am-9pm Mon-Sat; ⏹⏹⏹) A godsend for those who've done the hard yards in the countryside, this Australian-run cafe-restaurant offers a fantastic menu of international cuisine. The cafe bakes its own bread and cakes, to go with full English breakfasts (T15,500), egg-and-bacon rolls, roast beef with Yorkshire pudding, a monstrous Aussie burger, and vegetarian and Mongolian dishes to boot. There's proper fresh espresso-machine coffee, too.

**Tamir Hotel** KOREAN $$
(⏹subsystem.funk.playwriting; mains T6000-20,000; ⏺10am-9pm) Hidden behind a dreary facade is this Korean restaurant doing spicy chicken dishes, with the usual *bibimbap, bulgogi* and grilled-meat options served on lazy-Susan tables. There's a fridge full of cold beer, as well as Mongolian dishes including a few yak-meat choices.

🛍 **Shopping**

For souvenirs, try the small **Nooslog Wool Shop** (⏹boogie.contagious.spells) or the **Art Shop** (⏺9933 9902; ⏹separator.appreciates. gracing; ⏺10am-4pm).

If you need to stock up on supplies head to the **market** (Khunsnii Zakh; ⏹learnings. papaya.brimming) area, which has several supermarkets.

---

**WORTH A TRIP**

## TSENKHER HOT SPRINGS

Set between forested hills, **Tsenkher Hot Springs** (Цэнхэрийн Халуун Рашаан; ⏹discards.sparkled.bedbug; GPS: N 47°19.241', E 101°39.411') are a popular detour from the main road. If you're expecting to soak among pristine, natural surrounds, however, you'll be disappointed, as the hot water is pumped into splash pools at the ger resorts built around the springs. For nonguests it costs around US$10 to enter.

If you're already in Tsetserleg, it's possible to head south on a jeep trail 27km to get here. It's around T45,000 return in a taxi from Tsetserleg. You could also consider cycling. This rewarding 27km countryside ride from Tsetserleg to Tsenkher Hot Springs includes three tough climbs over passes at 1768m, 1820m and 1943m respectively (Tsetserleg, by comparison, lies at 1691m). The rural scenery is lovely, though, and the promise of a soak in a hot spring helps spur you on.

Bike rental from Fairfield Guesthouse costs T30,000 per day. Ask Murray at Fairfield Guesthouse for detailed directions, but basically, turn right out of the guesthouse and keep cycling straight out of town until the road bears right at the river. Follow the river for a couple of hundred metres, then cross it over the wooden bridge. Continue across the grassland, cycling south (roughly straight on) as you follow the main tracks up and down the three passes before bearing very slightly right as you descend to the springs. Expect to take around 3½ hours one way.

If you're coming from Ulaanbaatar, the turn-off is at Tsenkher *sum*. From the *sum* centre it's 24km to the hot springs.

## ❶ Information

**Khan Bank** (▦ fitting.heady.exceptions; ⊘ 9am-6pm Mon-Fri, ATM 8am-midnight) Overlooking the town square. Changes cash and has an ATM.

**Internet cafe** (☑ 01332-21110; ▦ entrusted. decoys.chronology; per hour T900; ⊘ 8.30am-8pm) In the Telecom office, along with the post office.

## ❶ Getting There & Away

There are two routes between Tsetserleg and Ulaanbaatar – northeast via Ögii Nuur (453km) or along the longer but better road via Kharkhorin (493km).

Tsetserleg to Tosontsengel is 350km to the northwest, but the paved road only stretches around halfway towards Tariat.

### BUSES & MINIVANS

Buses depart Tsetserleg **station** (▦ fittings. strap.gripped) daily at 8am, 2pm and 7pm for Ulaanbaatar (T23,400, 12 hours). Purchase the ticket at least one day ahead. **Fairfield Guesthouse** (p115) will arrange your ticket for a small commission, and it can also book your ticket here from Ulaanbaatar. The driver may impose a 20kg limit and charge you T5000 for an extra bag.

There's a minivan to Tariat (T10,000 to T12,000, 4½ hours) on Wednesday, Friday and Sunday at 5pm. Expect to pay around T15,000 for Kharkhorin (three hours, 115km).

---

# Khorgo-Terkhiin Tsagaan Nuur National Park Region

One of central Mongolia's standout sights is the 773-sq-km **Khorgo-Terkhiin Tsagaan Nuur National Park** (▦ offers.recalibrate.overshoes; park entry T3000), where the expansive, freshwater Terkhiin Tsagaan Nuur (Great White Lake) glistens against a dramatic volcano backdrop. It's a wonderful place to relax by the lake, pitch a tent, swim, fish, and go hiking and horse trekking. The extinct volcano stands among pine-clad lava fields, and is easily climbed for excellent views.

The dusty village of **Tariat** (Тариат) is the jumping-off point for the national park, where you can find an ATM, basic supermarkets, *guanz* (canteens), a backpacker guesthouse and buses to Ulaanbaatar.

The **national park headquarters** (▦ ritually.account.bereft; GPS: N 48°09.777' E 99°53.312'), where you'll pay your entry fee, is located by the bridge that crosses the river as you exit the village of Tariat.

## ◉ Sights & Activities

Terkhiin Tsagaan Nuur is excellent for **swimming** (if a little cold). Hidden along the shore are stretches of sandy beach, perfect for lounging with a book or fishing line. One nice spot is the beach on the sandy spit that juts out from the northern shore at the northeast corner of the lake.

The **fishing** is great, including the prized taimen (catch and release). Ask for a fishing permit (US$3) at the park entrance. You can hire gear (US$5) from Tunga Guesthouse, or Fairfield Guesthouse (p115) if you're coming from Tsetserleg.

There is also the option of exploring the lake by boat. Khorgo I and Maikhan Toilgoi ger camps both have row boats for rent.

★ **Khorgo Uul**                    VOLCANO
(▦ scallion.lecture.recurrence; GPS: N 48°11.187', E 99°51.259') With its surrounding lava field, this 200m-tall extinct volcano dominates the area to the east of the lake. From its west side there are stairs leading up to the rim of the crater, a short 15-minute trek that leads to fabulous views. Its desolate surrounds are littered with black volcanic rocks – making it look like it's erupted more recently than the estimated 10,000 years ago.

## 🛏 Sleeping & Eating

Except for a few annoying flies, Terkhiin Tsagaan Nuur is an excellent place for camping. It's free to camp, but you'll need to get permission from the rangers, and pitch a tent on the designated camping area on the northern shore – close to the ger camps. There is good fishing, endless fresh water, and flat ground for pitching a tent. And there are very few mosquitoes, even in summer. The area can be cold at night, year-round, and is often windy, so a good sleeping bag is important. There are a few basic long-drop toilets and rubbish dumping points.

### Khorgo-Terkhiin Tsagaan Nuur National Park

**Terkh Enkh**                 TOURIST GER CAMP $
(☑ 9918 8369; terkh_enkh@yahoo.com; wavoiding. tightly.auditoriums; camping T8000, ger per person incl meals T80,000) The first ger camp you'll encounter if coming over the mountain from Tariat is this decent option overlooking the lake. Staff are friendly, but don't speak English. Mongolian dishes are served in its small ger restaurant, and the bathrooms are modern with flushable toilets and hot-water showers.

# Khorgo-Terkhiin Tsagaan Nuur NP

0 _____ 4 km
0 _____ 2 miles

### Khorgo I
TOURIST GER CAMP $

(☑11-322 870, 8869 2847; ///song.pamphlet.lia-bility; GPS: N 48°12.246', E 99°50.834'; per person with/without meals T90,000/29,500) In a lovely mountainous, grassland location in the Zur-kh Gol Khundii (Heart River Valley), around an hour's walk from the lake (and 30 minutes to the volcano), Khorgo I is an immaculate ger camp. There are hot showers, a cosy restaurant ger with a bar, staff who speak good English, and excellent hiking nearby.

### ★Maikhan Tolgoi
TOURIST GER CAMP $$

(☑9909 3339; www.facebook.com/maikhan tolgoi; ///possessions.transferred.soulless; GPS: N 48°10.821', E 99°45.725'; per person US$23; ☎) Set on a pretty headland on the northern shore of the lake, Maikhan Tolgoi is easily the most attractive camp on the lake. The well-maintained gers are right on the water, and there are clean flush toilets and hot showers. The cosy restaurant-bar (open 7am to 10pm; mains T5000 to T15,000) does a tasty *tsuivan* (noodles) that goes great with a cold beer.

### Tariat

### Tunga Guesthouse
GUESTHOUSE $

(☑9983 6144, 9928 5710; www.tungaguesthouse.com; Tariat, ///insert.hermit.observed; per person incl breakfast US$10; ☎) Backpacker central in Tariat, this family guesthouse is pretty basic, but is run by the welcoming Tunga, who speaks perfect English and has great knowledge on the area. Rooms are clean and comfortable and she'll let you camp in the yard if the guesthouse is full. There's an outdoor long-drop toilet, makeshift hot shower and free laundry. Enter from the side gate.

The guesthouse is at the far eastern end of the main strip in Tariat, just a short walk from the bridge into the park.

Tunga and her husband Amaraa can organise horse riding (US$10 per day per horse, plus US$20 per guide), help with onward transport, car and motorcycle repairs, and fishing gear (US$5 per day). Local traditional meals can also be ordered for T6000. They can also arrange free tent hire, and have a summer-only **family ger** (☑9928 5710; ///arched.noise.ungoverned; GPS: N 48°09.318' E 99°45.206'; per person incl breakfast US$8; ☉mid-Jun–mid-Sep) on the quiet south side of the lake.

## ℹ️ Information

At time of writing, **Tunga Guesthouse** in Tariat and **Maikhan Tolgoi** on the lake were the only places to offer wi-fi access.

There's an ATM at **Khan Bank** (///acorn.pa-vilion.delinquent) in Tariat, but it's best to bring enough cash to last the duration of your stay.

## ℹ️ Getting There & Away

Tariat's bus stand is located just beyond the western end of the main drag, by the compound with animal statues. A bus leaves three times a week on Wednesday, Friday and Sunday for Ulaanbaatar (T31,600, 12 hours) at 9am, via Tsetserleg (T10,000 to T12,000) and Kharkhorin (T25,000). The days of travel are not fixed, so ask at Tunga Guesthouse for the latest.

Minivans run the same route daily, if demand warrants it.

Heading north or west will probably require chartering your own vehicle (about US$60 per day plus petrol). The road west of Tariat is unpaved and in poor condition. Heading east, the road is paved all the way to Ulaanbaatar.

# Northern Mongolia

POP 496,000

## Best Places to Eat

➡ Bulgogi Family (p124)
➡ Jargalan Restaurant (p133)
➡ Eternal Springs (p128)
➡ Garage 24 (p140)
➡ Traktir (p129)

## Best Places to Stay

➡ Nature's Door (p140)
➡ Saraa's Guesthouse (p132)
➡ Toilogt (p139)
➡ Bata Guesthouse (p132)
➡ Jargal Jiguur (p146)

## Why Go?

When we open our Mongolian compass and check the cardinal directions, we see the desert in the south, and the great, grassy steppe to the east. What lies around the northern aimags? The taiga, a pine-scented quilt of coniferous forest that blankets the boggy ground from northern Mongolia to the edge of the Arctic circle.

But it's not only forest here. Indeed, much of the land is wild, rugged steppe country, or a transition zone, where fuzzy grasslands are riven by clumps of dark birch and larch. In other places, rocky mountain spines spread their snowy fingers into natural barriers, boundaries and basins, cupping ice-cold freshwater lakes that are as fiercely blue as the wide open Mongolian sky. The most famous body of water here is Lake Khövsgöl, the 'Mother Sea' of the nation, but beauty abounds across the region, especially in the Shangri-La-like isolation of the Darkhad Valley.

## When to Go
### Mörön

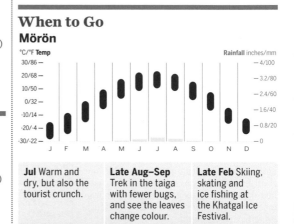

**Jul** Warm and dry, but also the tourist crunch.

**Late Aug–Sep** Trek in the taiga with fewer bugs, and see the leaves change colour.

**Late Feb** Skiing, skating and ice fishing at the Khatgal Ice Festival.

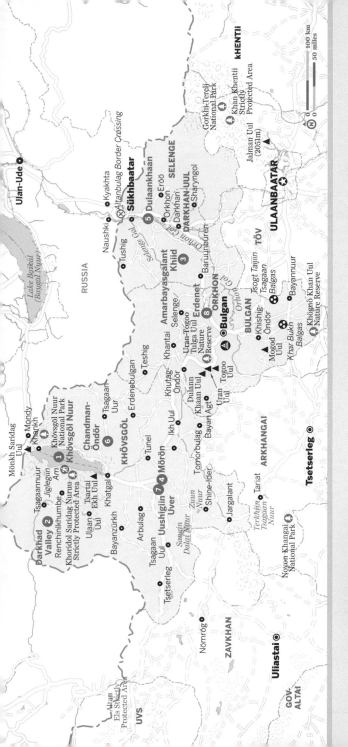

# Northern Mongolia Highlights

**1** Whiling away an afternoon fishing on Mongolia's loveliest alpine lake **Khövsgöl Nuur** (p135).

**2** Visiting the remote region's Tsaatan reindeer herders at **Darkhad Valley** (p142), the edge of the great Siberian taiga.

**3** Wandering the grounds of Mongolia's Buddhist architectural highlight, **Amarbayasgalant Khiid** (p125).

**4** Checking out culture and dining in energetic **Mörön** (p131).

**5** Patronising Dulaankhaan's traditional bow-and-arrow workshop in **Khuvchit Num** (p123).

**6** Journeying to little-visited region of **Chandman-Öndör** (p141) fish-filled streams, hot springs and sacred caves.

**7** **Uushigiin Uver** (p132) Studying curious deer stone carvings, some of the best examples of ancient rock art in Mongolia.

**8** **Erdenet** (p127) Enjoying excellent dining in this semi-cosmopolitan city, where Russia and Mongolia mingle.

## History

For thousands of years, northern Mongolia was the borderland between the Turkic-speaking tribes of Siberia and the great steppe confederations of the Huns, Uighurs and Mongols. Some of the Siberian tribes still survive in Mongolia, notably the Tsaatan people of northern Khövsgöl. Evidence of the steppe nomads can also found in Khövsgöl in the form of numerous burial mounds and deer stones (upright grave markers from the Bronze and Iron ages, on which are carved stylised images of deer).

Settled history really began in the 18th century under Manchu rule, when thousands of monks poured into the area from Tibet and China to assist in the construction of monasteries. As the nomads were converted to Buddhism, local shamans were harassed into giving up traditional practices. The largest religious centre, Amarbayasgalant Khiid (p125), had more than 2000 lamas.

Under communism, religious persecution boiled over into a 1932 rebellion that left thousands of monks and Mongolian soldiers dead. An attempt by monks to form an insurrectionist government ended in failure. Later, the Russians improved their standing with locals by developing a variety of industries: Darkhan and Selenge became important centres of agriculture, Bulgan became home to the Erdenet copper mine, and Khövsgöl developed thriving timber mills, fisheries and wool processing facilities. Khövsgöl Nuur served as an important gateway for Russia–Mongolia trade until the collapse of the Soviet Union.

### ℹ Getting There & Away

A good paved road runs from Ulaanbaatar (UB) all the way to the Russian border, and also west from Darkhan to Khatgal on the shores of Khövsgöl Nuur. Darkhan, Sükhbaatar and Erdenet can all be reached by rail from Ulaanbaatar. The quickest way to Khövsgöl Nuur is to fly from Ulaanbaatar to Mörön, and travelonwards for about 100km via car or 4WD.

To travel between Selenge aimag and the east, you'll have to come back through Ulaanbaatar first, or go by horse.

### ℹ Getting Around

Frequent buses, minibuses and shared taxis whiz along the paved roads between Darkhan, Sükhbaatar, Erdenet, Bulgan and Mörön. The fun starts when you travel off the highway into the rural *sums* (districts), with dirt roads, rocky terrain and bridges that come and go with the floods. In the Khövsgöl area, there are frequent minibuses between Mörön and Khatgal, with less frequent minibuses doing arduous overnight trips to Tsagaannuur, Renchinlkhumbe, and some destinations west and south. For everything else you'll need a 4WD, though if you're travelling light you may well be able to persuade locals with motorbikes to give you lifts.

In the region around Khövsgöl aimag, the terrain is mainly taiga (subarctic coniferous forest) of Siberian larch and pine trees, where there's plenty of rain (often 600mm a year). Snowfall can exceed 2m in some regions during winter. After winter, the lakes and rivers remain frozen until May; travel can be hazardous at this time, as trucks and 4WDs can fall through the thin ice. Travelling in winter means faster drive times, as vehicles won't get bogged in the mud.

## SELENGE   СЭЛЭНГЭ

POP 207,000 (INCL DARKHAN-UUL)

In a nation of nomads, Selenge stands out as an agricultural breadbasket. Throughout most of Mongolia, the land has a distinctly wild cast; on the steppe, the grass has been grazed, but rarely has the soil been tilled. Not so in Selenge. Here, you'll pass rolling wheat fields and shady apple orchards, rows of cabins and relatively few gers. This is a prosperous province, and in towns such as Darkhan and Sükhbaatar, you'll glimpse a possible preview of Mongolia's future – a nation of nomads, perhaps, but nomads a generation or more removed from the steppe, settled into the city.

And yet, the Mongolia of ger camps and guardian deities is still here for now. Towards the north, thunderhead clouds gather on the forested mountains that crowd the Russian border, and near an impossibly beautiful valley, travellers will find the sublime Amarbayasgalant Khiid (p125), a masterpiece of Mongolian Buddhist art and architecture.

## Sükhbaatar   Сухбаатар

📅 7036, 01362 / POP 22,240 / ELEV 626M

Sükhbaatar, the capital of Selenge aimag, is a pint-sized, friendly town anchored by a main square capped with a statue of its namesake general. As aimag capitals go, it's a prosperous if sleepy spot that makes for an uneventful stopover for travellers heading into or out of Russia.

# ⦿ Sights

### Eej Mod
RELIGIOUS SITE

(Ээж Мод, Mother Tree; GPS: N 50°09.2417', E 106°12.0913'; ⓜ fines.comrades.resigning; T500 parking fee; ⓟ) Locals frequently come to this sacred tree (10km south of Sükhbaatar) to pray to the spirits that inhabit it; a rite that predates Buddhism. According to shamanic beliefs, the spirits have the power to grant wishes, on the condition that the devotee visits three times. Whatever your beliefs, it's hard not to feel like there's *some* sort of power in the spindly plant, especially when it's crowned by squawking ravens.

### Khutagt Ekh Datsan
BUDDHIST MONASTERY

(Хутагт Эх Дацан; Tsagaan Eregiin Gudamj, ⓜ perky.sedative.spades; ⊘10am-2pm Wed-Mon) This small temple near the town square has a woman for a head lama, unusual for a Mongolian monastery.

# 🛏 Sleeping

### Station Hotel
HOTEL $

(☑ 2362 40371; ⓜ lunge.snuggled.wins; s/d/lux T15,000/25,000/70,000) No-frills rooms with shared facilities in a building attached to the train station (p122); travellers can take a room and pay per hour (s/d T2500/4000). The lux room is effectively its own large furnished apartment, complete with en suite bathroom. Wi-fi only works on the first two floors.

### Hotel Nine
HOTEL $$$

(☑ 7036 3433; www.hotelnine.mn; ⓜ ants.progress.collides; s/d/tr T69,000/85,000/105,000; ⓟ🛜) This lime-green hotel is a swish little stay if you're headed north. Rooms are decorated in soothing pastel shades and there's on-site pampering in the form of sauna, Jacuzzi and massage. Little English spoken.

# ✕ Eating & Drinking

### Khairkhan
MONGOLIAN $

(Хайрхан; ☑ 9973 2664; ⓜ cigar.happy.redouble; meals T3500-9000; ⊘9am-10pm Mon-Fri, from 10am Sat & Sun) Popular restaurant near the town square gets packed at lunchtime with locals. The extensive picture menu features hearty soups, good dumplings and meat-and-rice dishes.

### Modern Nomads
MONGOLIAN $$

(☑ 7036 3433; Hotel Nine; ⓜ ants.progress.collides; mains T5000-24,000; ⊘7am-11.30pm; 🅙) This branch of the popular Modern Nomads chain restaurant is a breath of fresh air in a

## Sükhbaatar

## Sükhbaatar

town where, frankly, good eateries are thin on the ground. If you can get the nervous staff to serve you, you can choose from meat dishes, soups, dumplings and even vegetarian-friendly salads. Located at Hotel Nine.

# ⓘ Information

**Khan Bank** (Хаан Банк; ⓜ instilled.habits. catapult; ⊘9am-7pm Mon-Fri, 10am-3pm Sat) Changes money and has an ATM.

# ⓘ Getting There & Away

### BUS & TAXI

The road to Ulaanbaatar (311km) through Darkhan (92km) is well paved. The bus, minivan and **taxi station** (☑ 9908 1866; ⓜ functions. vowing.recount) is located just outside the train station. Buses leave for Ulaanbaatar at 8am and 5pm (T12,200, six hours) and Darkhan (T4600, two hours). Shared cars leave for UB when full

(T25,000 per person) and Altanbulag (T3500, 30 minutes).

If you're heading to Russia, buses (T18,000, six hours) leave for Ulan-Ude at 5.30am Thursday to Sunday.

### TRAIN

International trains going to/from Moscow, Irkutsk or Běijīng stop at Sükhbaatar for two or more hours (usually in the evening) while customs and immigration formalities are completed.

Direct local trains leave Sükhbaatar for Ulaanbaatar at 7.15am (hard seat/hard sleeper/soft sleeper T7900/17,200/25,400, about 10 hours), with a stop at Darkhan (hard seat/hard sleeper/soft sleeper T3350/6850/9750, about four hours).

The **train station** (☑ 2362-40124; ⅲ flagged.unusable.martini) sells local tickets as well as tickets for Ulan-Ude (T57,160), Irkutsk (T111,310) and Moscow (T389,810); to purchase them you'll need a Russian visa. The ticket office opens up an hour or two before the train leaves.

# Altanbulag   Алтанбулаг

☑ 3641 / POP 4700

Altanbulag is a small, peaceful border town opposite the Russian city of Khyakhta with an immediately noticeable golden-domed church. Both Khyakhta and Altanbulag are of some historical importance to Mongolians. In 1915 representatives from Russia, China and Mongolia met in Khyakhta to sign a treaty granting Mongolia limited autonomy. At a meeting in Khyakhta in March 1921, the Mongolian People's Party was formed by Mongolian revolutionaries in exile, and the revolutionary hero Sükhbaatar was named Minister of War.

## ☉ Sights

**Selenge Aimag Museum**                    MUSEUM
(Аймгийн Музей; ⅲ inflate.landline.multicultural; admission T3000; ☉ 9am-2pm & 3-5pm Mon-Fri) The surprisingly entertaining aimag museum features exhibits dating back to Mongolia's independence movement of 1921. Standout relics include heroic Soviet-style mosaics of puppet dictator Sükhbaatar, a life-sized golden statue of the man meeting Lenin, and some of Sükhbaatar's personal effects – his boots, gun and even his desk. Sükhbaatar's office was allegedly in the small red building outside the museum.

## 🛏 Sleeping & Eating

**Dolphin Hotel**                    HOTEL $
(☑ 9969 7436, 9584 1650; ⅲ embedding.enraged. photograph; d T20,000; 🅿) You're as likely to spot a dolphin in Altanbulag as a unicorn, but this is a good-value hotel, with spic and span rooms that have en-suite bathrooms, cutesy art on the walls and a friendly front desk. The on-site **restaurant** (Dolphin Hotel; ⅲ embedding. enraged.photograph; mains T3500-12,000; ☉ 9am-8pm) serves Mongolian and Russian cuisine. The hotel is on the main Altanbulag road, within walking distance of the border.

## ℹ Getting There & Away

Altanbulag is located 24km northeast of Sükhbaatar. Minivans (T3500) run between Sükhbaatar and Altanbulag at various times during the day, or you could charter a taxi (from T10,000).

### BORDER CROSSINGS

The Mongolia–Russia border is open 24 hours and is located right at the edge of Altanbulag. If you're heading into Russia, you cannot cross on foot. That said, the border guards can pair you up with any private car that has room, and after you go through the border formalities, you can then catch a bus to Ulan-Ude.

It should go without saying, but you need to have your Russian visa sorted before attempting the border crossing.

# Dulaankhaan   Дулаанхаан

POP 2000

This tiny village, 47km south of Sükhbaatar, is worth a stop if you have your own vehicle. Dulaankhaan is home to a traditional bow-making workshop, one of the last in Mongolia.

To find the workshop, cross the railway tracks to enter the village then look for the long, decrepit-looking warehouse located near the Government House. To be fair, many local buildings look like decrepit warehouses; if you're lost, track someone down and show them the words 'ХӨВЧИТ НУМ' (Khuvchit Num, the name of the workshop), which ought to do the trick.

## ℹ Getting There & Away

The village is 6km west of the Sükhbaatar–Darkhan Hwy along a newly paved road. Public transportation out here isn't reliable; you could take a Sükhbaatar–Darkhan minivan and walk from the main highway, drive if you have your own wheels, or hire a taxi from Sükhbaatar (T40,000 to 50,000) or Darkhan (T50,000 to 60,000).

## CENTRAL ASIAN RECURVED BOWS

Some say the English longbow was the height of archery technology; others argue for the enormous Japanese yumi bow. These are cute positions, but only one civilisation's bow facilitated the conquest of the largest land empire in history, and that was the recurved Central Asian composite bow.

Shorter than the longer, well, longbow, a recurved composite bow is a deceptively simple piece of technology – a bow formed from wood layered with animal sinew. The organic muscle allows the bow to store more energy for the same length of wood; effectively, a short composite bow has equal to or greater stopping power than a larger longbow, which is formed solely from wood.

Why the need for a shorter bow? Because such a weapon can be carried and shot on horseback. While a European knight had force and mobility, and a medieval archer possessed ranged weaponry, a Mongol mounted archer had mobility *and* firepower. It was this marriage, plus excellent tactics and administration of logistics, that fuelled the Mongol conquests of most of Eurasia.

Many modern bows are made from fibreglass and can be ordered online. But true traditional Central Asian recurved composite bows, made with cattle sinew and horn and wood logged from the taiga, are very rare. You can find them made in the traditional fashion in the **Khuvchit Num** (Хөвчит Нум; bow-making workshop; ☑ 9913 1491; www.facebook. com/mongolianbow.archery; GPS: N 49°55.1072; E 106°11.2818'; ⓜ devotion.track.invariable; ⊘ hours vary) workshop in Dulaankhaan.

# Darkhan  Дархан

☑ 7037, 01372 / POP 97,700

Mongolia's second-largest city sprawls across a few hills and dusty smatterings of steppe. It's not our first pick for must-see tourism destination of the 21st century, but Darkhan does make an appealing short stop en route to Amarbayasgalant Khiid (p125) or the Russian border.

The city was created by the Soviets in the 1960s as an industrial base for the north. Under communist rule it worked as a model urban cooperative of factory workers, tractor drivers, coal miners and government officials. The economy took a nosedive in the early 1990s following independence, but is slowly picking up again, thanks to grain production and coal mining.

## ◉ Sights

**Museum of Darkhan-Uul**  MUSEUM

(☑ 7037-3020; ⓜ nearly.nests.caravans; admission T1500; ⊘ 9am-1pm & 2-6pm Mon-Fri) This appealing little museum contains a well-laid-out collection of archaeological finds, traditional clothing, religious artefacts and taxidermied examples of aimag wildlife. You may spot a jade chess set and a wind instrument made of a human femur, but the museum's most valued piece is an original painting of Lenin meeting Sükhbaatar, a classic work of communist pictorial hagiography painted by B. Tsultem in 1953.

**Morin Khuur Statue
& Seated Buddha**  MONUMENT

(ⓜ rectangle.upshot.beckons; ℗) Two monuments, linked by a (worryingly wobbly) pedestrian bridge, cross a busy road and form two ends of an arch, as it were, spanning the gap between old and new Darkhan. Locals come here to socialise at sunset and enjoy a view across the city's skyline.

## 🛏 Sleeping

**Rich Hotel**  HOTEL $

(☑ 7037-7205; ⓜ decide.stopwatch.voice; r T40,000-50,000; �🛜) Besides some fantastically strange artwork of pop-culture celebrities decorating the halls, the main appeal of the RIch is a good location near Darkhan's best restaurants and clean – if identikit – rooms. There's wi-fi, but it only works on the first floor.

**Kharaa Hotel**  HOTEL $$

(☑ 9147 0069; kharaa.hotel@yahoo.com; ⓜ disarmed.afternoon.barmaid; r/lux incl breakfast from T40,000/60,000; @🛜) Renovated rooms are clean and feature efficient yet comfortable furnishings, making this midrange option ultimately very good value for money. It's set back behind the Comfort hotel. The bar on the ground floor adds a bit of spice to this compact hotel; unless you're a night owl, ask for a room upstairs.

# Darkhan

## Darkhan

★**Comfort Hotel**                              HOTEL **$$$**
(📱7037-9090; Naadamchid Gudamj, ///bota-
nists.placed.remake; d/ste from T55,000/85,000;
🛜) This lovely hotel has spotless, well-
maintained, and large if unmemorable

rooms decorated in pastel shades. There's a
decent **restaurant**, a fitness centre to help
burn off the calories, a sauna to steam in
and friendly staff who speak some English.
Wi-fi is temperamental. Book ahead.

## ✖ Eating & Drinking

**Sondor Bakery & Cafe**                        CAFE **$**
(📱9509 9772; ///canines.slicer.cavalier; meals
T4000-14,000; ⊙9am-10pm) This cute cafe
and bakery serves up pizzas, pastas, tasty
cakes and other baked goods. There's an at-
tached pub where you can sink a drink; it's
open until midnight.

★**Bulgogi Family**                            KOREAN **$$**
(📱7037-7300; ///applause.banks.captions; meals
T8500-22,000; ⊙10am-midnight; 🛜) Bright,
friendly, genuine Korean restaurant featuring *bulgogi* (grilled meat), spicy soups, tasty
*bibimbap* (rice topped with meat, vegetables and an egg, choice of hot or cold) and

noodle dishes. Mains are accompanied by an array of obligatory little side dishes. Alternatively, cook your own meal on the teppanyaki grill in the middle of your table. Picture menu; some English spoken.

**Texas Pub**                    AMERICAN, MONGOLIAN **$$**
(⏱7037-4008; ⧉comply.clusters.tangling; meals T5000-24,000; ☺8am-midnight Mon-Fri, from 11am Sat & Sun; ☎) Though Texans are about as common in Darkhan as Mongolians who can't ride a horse, the menu at this darkwood, modern bar features plenty of burgers, fries, steaks and sandwiches – yeehaw. Wednesday is cocktail night and there's live music Monday and Saturday.

## ❶ Getting There & Away

### BUS

From the main **bus station** (Авто Вокзал; ⧉walking.inactivate.ticket), buses depart hourly between 8am and 8pm for Ulaanbaatar (T10,100, 3½ hours). Two buses a day leave for Erdenet (T10,000, three hours) at 11am and 5pm. Buses leave for Mörön (T32,500, 13 hours) once every two days (you can catch daily buses from Erdenet if need be).

### MINIVAN, TAXI & 4WD

Plenty of shared taxis (T15,200) do the three-hour run to Ulaanbaatar, departing from the bus station in the new town. The station also has share taxis to Erdenet (T15,200, 2½ hours).

For Sükhbaatar (T10,000, two hours), 4WDs leave from a **stand** (⧉camps.futile.jabbing) outside the market in the new town; there are signs for different destinations (in Mongolian). You can hire your own car or 4WD here for a full day (car/4WD T150,000/200,000) – useful if you want to get to **Amarbayasgalant Khiid**. Bargain hard.

### TRAIN

Darkhan is the only train junction in northern Mongolia: all northern trains to/from Ulaanbaatar, and all trains to/from Erdenet stop at this **station** (GPS: N 49°29.0971', E 105°55.8508'; ⧉wowed.superbly.misjudge).

The express service to Ulaanbaatar (hard seat/hard sleeper/soft sleeper T5500/13,500/15,300) leaves Darkhan at 2.10pm, arriving in Ulaanbaatar at 6pm.

The daily five-hour trip between Darkhan and Erdenet (hard seat/soft seat/soft sleeper T5050/11,450/16,150, five hours) leaves Darkhan at an ungodly 3am.

Two daily Ulaanbaatar–Sükhbaatar trains leave Darkhan for Sükhbaatar at 5.30pm and 2.30am (hard seat/hard sleeper/soft sleeper T2600/4700/6900, about three hours).

# Amarbayasgalant Khiid
Амарбаясгалант Хийд

Mongolia is not a nation that tends to be included on the global 'famous religious buildings tourism' circuit (we're pretty sure that's a thing), yet deep in an impossibly gorgeous valley within the wilds of Selenge aimag, you'll find one of the world's great Buddhist temples, not to mention one of the nation's most attractive and intact architectural complexes.

## ◉ Sights

### ★ Amarbayasgalant Khiid                    BUDDHIST MONASTERY
(Амарбаясгалант Хийд; GPS: N 49°28.672', E 105°05.121'; ⧉picketing.inflicts.tourists; T5000; ☺10am-7pm summer, hours vary at other times; 🅿) Amarbayasgalant Khiid was built between 1727 and 1737 by the Manchu emperor Yongzheng, and dedicated to the great Mongolian Buddhist and sculptor Zanabazar, whose mummified body was moved here in 1779. The design references Manchu style, down to the inscriptions, symmetrical layout, imperial colour scheme and roof guardians on every roof corner.

Despite extensive restoration by Unesco, there's a sense of genteel decay and a gradual takeover by nature that adds to the allure of the place.

From the faded wooden beams thickly coated in bird droppings, and riotous greenery blocking some entrances, to the scurrying marmots and cawing jackdaws that seem to rule the place, the exterior of the complex radiates a lost-in-time sense of magic. The interior of the main temple is far more vigorous; enormous banners painted in riotous colours descend from the high, airy ceiling, while similarly vibrant pillars climb up to it. All throughout, hundreds of Buddhas, bodhisattvas and guardian deities keep watch over visitors and the resident lamas.

The monastery was largely spared during the 1937 purge, possibly because of sympathetic and procrastinating local military commanders. These days, about 30 monks live in the monastery, compared with more than 2000 in 1936.

Most of the temples in the monastery are normally closed, so if you want to see any statues or *thangkas* (scroll paintings), you'll have to find the monks with the keys in the monks' quarters, the yellow concrete buildings on the right side (east) of the monastery.

NORTHERN MONGOLIA AMARBAYASGALANT KHIID

This isn't an uncommon request, so don't feel too awkward about asking. The main gates to the temple are supposed to be open from 10am to 7pm during the summer, although these times seem a little fluid in practice. During winter, you'll usually have to ask at the dorms for the keys.

The richly decorated **main temple**, Tsogchin Dugan, has a disturbingly lifelike, life-sized statue of Rinpoche Gurdava, a lama from Inner Mongolia who lived in Tibet and Nepal before returning to Mongolia in 1992 and raising much of the money for the temple's restoration. Photography inside the temple seems to be allowed, but it's disrespectful to turn your back to the deities.

Ceremonies are usually held at 10am, so arrive early or stay overnight to see them.

A couple of newer monuments – a golden Buddha statue and a stupa – are situated on the hills behind the monastery. You could continue hiking up the mountains for even better views of the valley.

## ✦✦ Festivals & Events

**Gongoriin Bombani Hural**　　RELIGIOUS
(⊙mid-Aug) The most interesting time to visit Amarbayasgalant Khiid is when the Gongoriin Bombani Hural is held. As part of the rituals, locals hike up to the eight white stupas in the hills around the monastery. Festivalgoers usually camp in the fields near the monastery – like a Buddhist version of Woodstock, only minus the illegal substances.

## 🛏 Sleeping

There are excellent camping spots all around Amarbayasgalant Khiid.

★ **IF Tour Ger Camp**　　TOURIST GER CAMP $$
(☎9119 0808, 9918 9981; iftour@yahoo.com; ✉siege.megabyte.scale; ger & r/cabin T50,000/60,000; ⊙May-Oct; P) This camp, furthest west from the temple complex, is the one with the best facilities. Choose between a cosy ger with electricity, an individual cabin or a bright room inside the lodge.

## Amarbayasgalant Khiid

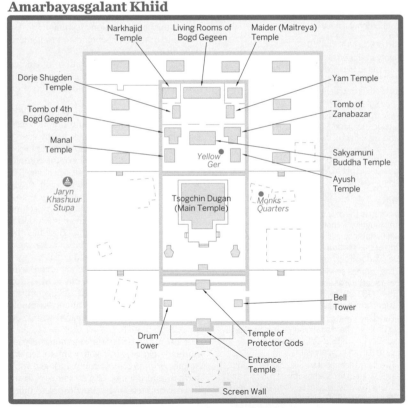

## ZANABAZAR: THE MICHELANGELO OF THE STEPPES

Zanabazar, an artist, statesman and Living Buddha, is today considered one of the greatest Renaissance artists in all of Asia. He was born in 1635, and at the tender age of three he was deemed to be a possible *gegeen* (saint); when he turned 14 he was sent to Tibet to study Buddhism under the Dalai Lama. Known in Mongolia as Öndör Gegeen, he was proclaimed the reincarnation of the Jonangpa line of Tibetan Buddhism and became the first Bogd Gegeen (reincarnated Buddhist leader of Mongolia).

When he returned from his studies in Tibet, the artist-lama kickstarted a Mongolian artistic renaissance. Besides sculpting and painting, he also invented the *soyombo* (the national symbol of Mongolia) and reformed the Mongolian script. A political figure, Zanabazar's struggle with the Zungar leader Galdan led to Mongolia's submission to the Manchus in 1691.

Zanabazar died in Běijīng in 1723; his body was later entombed in a stupa in **Amarbayasgalant Khiid** (p125). You will see many of Zanabazar's creations in monasteries and museums in Mongolia, and there is a fine collection of his art in the **Zanabazar Museum of Fine Arts** (p61) in Ulaanbaatar. You can recognise images of Zanabazar by his bald, round head, the *dorje* (thunderbolt symbol) he holds in his right hand and the bell in his left hand.

For more on Zanabazar, look for the *Guidebook to Locales Connected with the Life of Zanabazar*, by Don Croner.

It's clean, comfortable, offers hot showers and flushing toilets and serves hearty meals (dinner around T13,500). Some English and German spoken.

### ⓘ Getting There & Away

From Ulaanbaatar, travel north by jeep to the T-intersection for Erdenet (just short of Darkhan). Take the Erdenet road for 90km and then turn right on to a dirt road; look for the **sign** (GPS: N 49°12.814', E 104°59.131') that says 'Amarbayasgalant 35km'. Altogether, the journey to or from Ulaanbaatar takes around five or six hours. If you don't have your own car you could charter one from Darkhan; if you bargain, you can negotiate a day rental for around T150,000.

## BULGAN                БУЛГАН

POP 160,800 (INCLUDING ORKHON)

Most visitors to northern Mongolia charge through Bulgan aimag en route to more popular sights such as Khövsgöl Nuur (p135) and Amarbayasgalant Khiid (p125). But travellers with a bit of time on their hands can find some interesting, rarely visited sights in Bulgan, as well as beautiful scenery that makes for nice cycle touring. A small mountain range, the **Bürengiin Nuruu**, bisects the aimag; though only reaching a maximum altitude of 2058m, it provides plenty of lush habitat for wild animals and livestock.

Technically not part of Bulgan, Erdenet – the third largest city in the nation – is the capital of Orkhon aimag. That province was carved out from Bulgan and basically encompasses Erdenet's urban footprint.

## Erdenet                Эрдэнэт

⏺ 7035, 7039 / POP 95,000

It's fair to say that Mongolia, in the minds of her visitors, is characterised by wild spaces and nomadism. Yet Erdenet, the country's third largest city, is an enjoyable little urban enclave worth a day of your time. This friendly town has many of the amenities of Ulaanbaatar without – by and large – the crippling traffic and smog.

### ◉ Sights

**Museum of Orkhon Aimag**                MUSEUM
(Орхон Аймгийн Музей; ⏺ 7035-0041; 🌐 dominate.allies.dugouts; admission T1500; ⊙ 9am-5pm)
Hidden in a concrete complex on the right side of the **Marx mural** (🌐 freezers.recruited.denote), this small museum has an eclectic range of exhibits, from Khalkha, Kazakh and Buriat national costumes, traditional musical instruments and snuff bottles made of semi-precious stones to a model of the copper mine (see it in 'day' or 'night') and another of a modern ger with a TV inside. Look out for the two-headed calf, and the demented expressions on the faces of the taxidermied wildlife.

# Erdenet

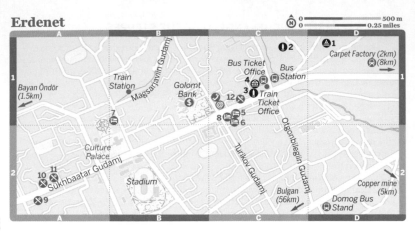

## Erdenet

**Friendship Monument**  MONUMENT
(⌽ relating.talents.spud) This communist monument, located northeast of the bus station, depicts Russian and Mongolian women united in chaste appreciation of hard work, planned economies and traditional dress. How to get here? On the way from the town centre, you'll pass a fine mural of Karl Marx and the ever-recognisable profile of Lenin bolted to the wall (near the bus ticket window). Keeping walking northeast for about 100m.

## 🛏 Sleeping

**Molor Erdene**  HOTEL $$
(Молор Эрдэнэ;  ☑ 7035-0309;  ⌽ yesterday.wide.flicked;  d/half-lux/lux incl breakfast T50,000/70,000/100,000; P 🛜) Rooms at the Molor Erdene are large and comfortable, and boast somewhat reliable – if slow – wifi. There's a decent breakfast of eggs, toast and sausage, plus an excellent on-site hot-pot restaurant.

**★Erdenet Inn**  HOTEL $$$
(☑ 7035-3715;  ⌽ flicks.reversed.cuddling;  s/lux T60,000/80,000;  P 🛜) The renovated east wing of the monolithic Soviet-style complex is an excellent spot to lay your head. Expect crisp white bed linen, modern bathrooms with heated towel racks and reliable wi-fi throughout. Good cafe right by the entrance, too. The complex also includes the **Gold Hotel** (☑ 7035-2868;  ⌽ mend. withdraws.scripted;  s/lux from T50,000/77,000; P 🛜) and the **Selenge Hotel** (Сэлэнгэ Зочид Буудал;  ☑ 7035-8882;  ⌽ cargo.person. assembles;  d/semi-lux/lux incl breakfast from T40,000/60,000/80,000;  P 🛜).

## ✗ Eating

**★Eternal Springs**  BAKERY $
(Мөнхийн Булаг;  ☑ 7035-6004; Sükhbaatar Gudamj, ⌽ clasp.envies.headband; meals T3200-5000, pizza T18,000;  ◷ 10am-7pm Tue-Sat;  ⌽) Vegetarians rejoice! This tiny, cute-as-a-button Swedish-American bakery not only offers a daily selection of vegetable soups (pumpkin, broccoli), but has meatless pizzas, great baked goodies and an extensive loose-leaf tea selection. Located on the ground floor of an apartment-block complex. If you need to ask directions, use the restaurant's Mongolian name (Mönkhiin Bulag).

**Traktir** RUSSIAN $$
(Трактир; ☑9955 4090; Sükhbaatar Gudamj, ⎚deprive.accented.dine; mains T6000-20,000; ☺noon-11pm) A magnet for visiting Russians, Traktir serves up the likes of *borscht* (beetroot soup), fried liver and grilled meats with mushroom sauce, with welcome helpings of vegetables on the side. The cosy dining room is decked out with photos of ye olde Russia, and there are good acoustics for singing once you've downed a few too many vodkas.

**Modern Nomads** MONGOLIAN $$
(☑7035-4422; Sükhbaatar Gudamj, ⎚blotting.an-aerobic.history; mains T7000-27,000; ☺11am-midnight Mon-Sat, to 11pm Sun) A branch of this ever-popular chain restaurant is one of the most popular dining fixtures in Erdenet, bringing you large portions of Mongolian dishes, salads and soups selected from a traveller-friendly picture menu.

## 🛍 Shopping

**Carpet Factory** HOMEWARES
(☑7035-9517; GPS: N 49°02.0866', E 104°05.0454'; ⎚costly.novels.spinners; ☺9am-7pm Mon-Fri, from 10am Sat & Sun) If you've come to Mongolia for a carpet, this might be the store you've been waiting for (although we stress 'might'). Most of the carpets aren't traditional, and some may seem garish (pixellated Mongol cavalry charge on a rug, anyone?), but there are some okay finds, and a nice selection of cashmere and silk products.

## ℹ Information

ATMs are not hard to find; many are near main roads and the **Nomin Supermarket** (⎚usurper.cascading.excerpts; ☺8.45am-10.30pm Mon-Fri, from 9am Sat, 9am-10pm Sun).
**Golomt Bank** (Голомт Банк; ⎚carbonate.spooned.princes; ☺8am-7.30pm Mon-Fri, 9am-5.30pm Sat & Sun) Changes US dollars and euros.
**Internet Cafe** (Sükhbaatar Gudamj, ⎚consumed.issued.inspects; per hr T800; ☺9am-7pm) at the **Telecom** (cnr Sükhbaatar Gudamj & Natsagorjiin Gudamj, ⎚consumed.issued.inspects; ☺24hr) office.

## ℹ Getting There & Away

**BUS, MINIVAN & 4WD**
Erdenet's **bus station** (Авто Вокзал; GPS N 49°01.9708', E 104°03.5874'; ⎚continues.polite.stars) is a car park at the foot of the **Friendship Monument** from which daily buses

(T15,000, six hours) depart to Ulaanbaatar's Dragon Avto Vaksal bus stand on the hour from 9am to 4pm, and at 5.30pm. Private vans (T15,000) and shared taxis (T25,000) also depart for Ulaanbaatar when full from 9am until 8pm. There are also buses to Darkhan (T10,000, 2½ hours) leaving at 8am and 2pm, as well as vans (T13,000) and shared taxis (T15,000), which leave from 8am until 2pm.

You can buy train and bus tickets at the **bus ticket office** (⎚sushi.irony.meant), located across the street from the bus station.

Shared minibuses to Mörön (Хөвсгөл; T28,000, 10 to 15 hours) leave when full from the **minivan stand** (Домог Вокзал; ⎚seasick.repeating.stereos) in front of the small grocery store in the southeast part of town.

**TRAIN**
The train to Ulaanbaatar (via Darkhan) leaves Erdenet at 6.35pm, arriving in UB at 6am (hard seat/hard sleeper/soft sleeper T8400/18,000/27,400). If you're just heading to Darkhan (hard seat/soft seat/soft sleeper T5050/11,450/16,150), expect a five-hour journey (at least). If you're heading to Sükhbaatar, change trains in Darkhan.

The same train goes on to Zamyn-Üüd, on the Chinese border along the southeastern edge of the country (hard seat/soft seat/soft sleeper T11,950/22,850/35,550). Expect the train to arrive at the border at 2am two days after you depart.

One train leaves for Moscow on Tuesdays at 3.30pm. There's a flat fare of T443,850.

Want a ticket? It's easiest to queue on the day of, or before, departure at the **ticket office** (⎚countries.articulated.bundles; ☺8am-6pm) across from the **bus station**. You can also buy train tickets at the window within the bus station from 8am to 6pm.

The **train station** (⎚unreserved.navigators.invented) is located around 9km east of the centre. Minibuses (T1000) meet arriving trains or you can take a taxi (T15,000). Buses to the train station leave from the car park opposite the train ticket office.

### NATIONAL PARKS OF BULGAN

**Khögnö Khan Nature Reserve** (469 sq km) Its rocky semi-desert terrain is home to wolves, ibex and various birds of prey. Located off the main Ulaanbaatar–Kharkhorin Hwy.

**Uran-Togoo Tulga Uul Nature Reserve** (58 sq km) A protected area of undulating hills and grassland, encompassing three extinct volcanoes.

# Bulgan City Булган Хот

☎ 7034, 01342 / POP 12,100 / ELEV 1208M

By day, Bulgan City is so sleepy it might as well be snoring, and you're as likely to see horses as cars on the lazy main street. At night, the poorly lit streets might put you in mind of a horror movie – but hey, at least there's atmosphere. This very compact town is friendly enough, and at the end of the day, Bulgan's dilapidated charm makes it an offbeat (but hardly necessary) stopover if you are travelling between Mörön and Ulaanbaatar.

## ◉ Sights

### Dashchoinkhorlon Khiid
BUDDHIST MONASTERY

(Дашчойнхорлон Хийд; GPS: N 48°47.821', E 103°30.687'; ⏳dilute.adequate.blaring; P) FREE Like most monasteries in Mongolia, Dashchoinkhorlon Khiid (1992) is the replacement of an older version; the original, Bangiin Khuree, was destroyed in 1937. About 1000 monks lived and worshipped at Bangiin Khuree before they were arrested and, presumably, executed. The remains of several stupas from the old complex can be seen nearby. The modern monastery features a painting of the former layout and statues of Tsongkhapa (founder of the Yellow Hat sect of Tibetan Buddhism) and Sakyamuni (the historical Buddha).

### Bulgan Aimag Museum
MUSEUM

(Булган Аймгийн Музей; ☎7034-2589; ⏳gritting.flickered.overhearing; admission T2000; ◷9am-6pm) This museum on the main street has some information on obscure sights in the aimag; a display on J Gurragchaa (Mongolia's first man in space), war photos and a few musical instruments, including the ol' human-femur-turned-wind-instrument (known as a *kangling* or *ganlin*). The ethnography section features a red-eyed wolf and a demented-looking lynx; elsewhere there are a few period surgical instruments that'll make you glad you live in the 21st century, plus some *airag* (fermented mare's milk) churners and saddles.

You can ask for the key to the **Khatanbaatar Magsarjav Mausoleum** (Хатанбаатар Магсаржавын Бунхан; GPS N 48°48.2173', E 103°31.5439'; ⏳whispered.relents.schoolbag; P) FREE here.

### Bulgan City

**◉ Sights**
1 Bulgan Aimag Museum .......................A1

**⊟ Sleeping**
2 Bulgan Hotel .......................................A1
3 Khantai Hotel .....................................A2

**ⓘ Information**
4 XacBank .............................................A1

### Museum of the West Road Military Unit
MUSEUM

(Баруун Замын Тусгай Ангийн Штаб; ☎7034-2589; GPS: N 48°47.6416', E 103°32.0496'; ⏳controls.propagates.precocious; admission T1000; ◷9am-5pm; P) The West Road Military Unit was a key force in freeing Mongolia from White Russian rule in 1921. Its history is described in this small museum, 2.5km south of Bulgan. Choibalsan and Khatanbaatar Magsarjav both stayed here during Mongolia's military campaigns of the early 20th century. The museum contains, among other things, Choibalsan's saddle and sword. If the museum is closed, find the caretaker at the ger next door.

## 🛏 Sleeping

### Khantai Hotel
B&B $$

(☎9605 4780; ⏳invariable.foreign.jotted; per person with/without toilet T60,000/30,000; P) This small B&B offers spotless double rooms, one with a nice balcony overlooking the park. The bathroom and shower are both downstairs and there is 24-hour hot water. The friendly owner sometimes offers breakfast (eggs, bread and rice milk) for an extra cost.

### Bulgan Hotel
HOTEL **$$**

(☎7034-4040, 9994 6897; ⊡slathering.desperate.tonics; r T30,000-60,000; 🕸) While this hotel looks a little ratty from the outside, the rooms are clean, the shared toilets are sparkling, the owners are friendly and there's working wi-fi on the first floor. Not to be confused with the other Bulgan Hotel overlooking the park.

### ℹ️ Information

**Internet Cafe** (⊡embarrassed.thicken.discount; per hr T800; ⊙9am-9pm) In the same building as Telecom (⊡navigating.purchased.archduke; ⊙9am-9pm). Connections are spotty.

**XacBank** (Хас Банк; ⊡delegated.disarming.running; ⊙9am-5pm Mon-Fri) Exchanges US dollars and has an ATM.

### ℹ️ Getting There & Away

#### BUS, MINIVAN & 4WD

A **bus** (⊡tooth.insulating.schmoozed) departs Bulgan for Ulaanbaatar daily at 10am (T16,800, seven hours). Minivans go between Bulgan and Ulaanbaatar (T25,000, six hours) on demand, but most people take a minivan to Erdenet (T5000, one hour, 55km) and then take the bus or overnight train. Shared taxis (T5000) run to Erdenet on demand several times a day; if you're in a hurry, just pay the fare for the entire taxi (T25,000).

To get to Mörön (or anywhere else), go to Erdenet first, as minivans, cars and 4WDs all tend to leave from there.

There are two routes between Ulaanbaatar and Bulgan City: the rougher but more direct southern route (318km) via Dashinchilen, or the paved northern route (434km) via Darkhan and Erdenet. To visit **Amarbayasgalant Khiid** (p125), the northern route is the way to go.

# KHÖVSGÖL    ХӨВСГӨЛ
POP 128,000

The southern edge of Siberia kisses the northern mountains of Mongolia in Khövsgöl, and the resulting marriage is a sweep of dark pine forests, snow-capped mountains, frozen lakes, wet bogs and icy winds that could have been imagined by a fantasy author on a productive day.

This is a land of yaks, reindeer and clouds of black-furred goats (so coloured, locals say, to keep themselves warm during the frigid Khövsgöl winter). Khalkh Mongols dominate the south, while pockets of minority ethnic groups, including the Uriankhai, Khotgoid, Darkhad and Tsaatan reindeer herders, are found elsewhere.

## Mörön    Мөрөн
☑0138, 7038 / POP 38,000 / ELEV 1283M

Imagine a loose, spread-out grid of streets surrounded by green hills, with a wrestling stadium here, a large dusty park there, a couple of multi-storey hotels, a busy labyrinthine market, a few gers and a temple complex on the outskirts. That's Mörön (pronounced *mu*-roon not 'moron'), a transport hub in northern Mongolia that's also the centre of civilisation in this part of the country (think internet, an actual tourist information office and a couple of half-decent restaurants). It comes alive in summer when tourists pass through on

NORTHERN MONGOLIA MÖRÖN

---

**WORTH A TRIP**

### DASHINCHILEN  ДАШИНЧИЛЭН

The Dashinchilen district in Bulgan aimag's south is home to two unique ruins worth seeking out if you're travelling between Ulaanbaatar and Tsetserleg, via Ögii Nuur.

On the western side of the Tuul Gol, about 35km northeast of Dashinchilen, are the impressive ruins of **Tsogt Taijiin Tsagaan Balgas** (GPS: N 48°01.422′, E 104°21.091′; ⊡parched.bowlful.narrated), a 17th-century fort that was home to the mother of Prince Tsogt, a 17th-century poet who fought against Chinese rule. There is a **stone stele** nearby.

About 12km west of the *sum* (district) capital, the ruined **Khar Bukh Balgas** (Khar Bakhin Fortress; GPS: N 47°53.198′, E 103°53.513′; ⊡puffy.wittiest.reassembly) is just a few kilometres north of the main road. The fortress, inhabited by the Kitan from 917 to 1120, is sometimes known as Kitan Balgas. A small **museum** nearby is unlocked by a caretaker when visitors arrive.

their way to Khövsgöl Nuur (p135), and if you're exploring the area, you'll probably find yourself lingering here a day or two. This is a good spot to stock up on supplies, grab a hot shower, sit down on a functioning toilet and generally enjoy life's little luxuries.

## ◉ Sights

### ★ Uushigiin Uver    ARCHAEOLOGICAL SITE
(Уушигийн Өвөр; GPS: N 49°39.334', E 99°55.701'; 🌐 lobby.shame.lavish; T3000; ⊙24hr; 🅿) ✍ On an arid plain about 20km west of Mörön, 14 deer stones have survived both howling winds and history, and now constitute one of the most enchanting Bronze Age archaeological sites in the country. Some of the stones have vibrant white designs etched against an ochre-coloured background. The most unique, **stone 14**, is topped with the head of a woman; there is only a handful of such deer stones in Mongolia. The carved stones are 2500 to 4000 years old.

### Danzandarjaa Khiid    BUDDHIST MONASTERY
(Данзандаржаа Хийд; GPS: N 49°38.3278', E 100°08.7257'; 🌐 taller.nights.decompose; 🅿) FREE An eerie dusty plain and the ruins of arched gates make for a dramatic backdrop to this monastery. The original structure (Möröngiin Khuree) was built around 1890 and housed some 2000 monks. It was rebuilt and reopened in June 1990 and now has around three dozen monks of all ages. The concrete ger contains a great collection of *thangkas* (Buddhist scroll paintings). No set visiting hours, but even if the monastery is closed, the exterior and grounds are attractive.

### Khövsgöl Aimag Museum    MUSEUM
(Хөвсгөл Аймгийн Музей; 🕿 7038-8630; GPS: N 49°38.2422', E 100°09.6948'; 🌐 serenade.released.qualified; admission T1000; ⊙10am-2pm & 3-6.30pm daily Jun-Oct, closed Sat & Sun Nov-May) Given the variety of wildlife in the aimag, stuffed animals such as the ibex and the lynx are, not surprisingly, the main feature of the museum; there's also a large tusk from a woolly mammoth dating back at least 40,000 years. Highlights of the ethnographic display include a beriboned shaman's outfit, a wooden Tsaatan saddle and furry skis, a Choijin robe with a skull-bedecked headpiece, and a rare *sukh khuur* (swan's-head fiddle).

## 🛏 Sleeping

### ★ Bata Guesthouse    GUESTHOUSE $
(🕿 9809 7080, 9138 7080; bata_guesthouse@yahoo.com; GPS: N 49°39.063', E 100°10.030'; 🌐 modem.crash.backup; per person incl breakfast T10,000; 🛜) The friendly English-speaking owner, Bata, can help arrange transport and homestays with nomad families (around US$20 per night), and is one of the better tourism fixers in Mörön. There's an excellent little ger cafe and lounge on-site that is a good spot for backpacker socialising; it also serves vegetarian meals and coffee made from actual beans.

Showers cost T3000, and there are clean pit toilets on site. The guesthouse is a 20-minute walk from the centre, 400m past the market. Turn right at the water pump house and walk for another 150m; it's on the left, marked 'Bata Guesthouse'.

### ★ Baigal Guesthouse    GUESTHOUSE $
(🕿 9938 8408; baigal99mn@yahoo.com; GPS: N 49°38.176', E 100°10.798'; 🌐 valley.disengage.glimmers; per person incl breakfast T15,000) About 600m east of the wrestling stadium, you'll spot a bright purple gate inscribed with the words 'guest house'. Inside there are neat guest gers and the friendly, English-speaking Baigal, who feeds you breakfast with eggs from under her own chickens, plus fresh yoghurt and jam. She's also an expert at assisting with travel logistics. Hot showers are T2000.

### ★ Saraa's Guesthouse    GUESTHOUSE $$
(🕿 9938 5577; www.taigatrip.com; GPS: N 49°38.6950', E 100°11.4997'; 🌐 label.readjust.skim; dm/r incl breakfast T15,000/20,000; 🅿🛜) ✍ Friendly, knowledgeable Saraa is a gracious host and a font of information on the region. She is a well-regarded contact with the Tsaatan reindeer people, and can arrange horse tours, cycling trips, treks – you name it. Guests can lounge in the front yard and bunk in cheerful dorms or private rooms; every stay includes a shower.

### 50° 100° Hotel    HOTEL $$$
(🕿 7038-2000; GPS: N 49°38.2393', E 100°09.5472'; 🌐 coder.latitudes.poster; d/lux from T70,000/80,000; 🅿🛜) The 50° 100° has modern rooms with reliable hot water and cable TV (wi-fi isn't as consistent, but is present). Friendly staff will help with luggage, and some English is spoken, but the rooms don't all live up to their price point.

# Mörön

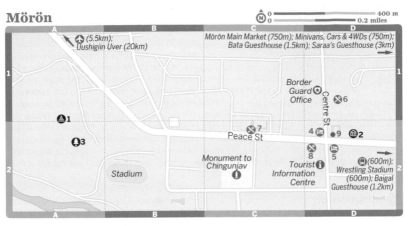

It's named after a particular geographical phenomenon in Khövsgöl, where the 50° north latitude meets 100° east longitude.

## 🍴 Eating

**And Restaurant**  MONGOLIAN $
(☑9511 5869; GPS: N 49°3290, E 100°09.6142'; ✉perfumes.prancing.mute; mains T4000-15,000; ☺9am-midnight Mon-Fri, from 10am Sat & Sun) The menu at this standby consists mostly of solid Mongolian standards, but exotica comes in the form of a few salads, excellent *kimchi* soup and even 'shpagetti' and 'mousaka'.

**Jargalan Restaurant**  KOREAN, MONGOLIAN $$
(☑7038-8080; GPS: N 49°38.2598', E 100°09.3156'; ✉pushes.human.triathlon; T5000-25,000; ☺10am-10pm Mon-Fri, from noon Sat & Sun) One of Mörön's more popular offerings, Jargalan has plenty of delicious Korean hot pots and Mongolian variations on fried mutton. There are a few tasty dumpling soups on the menu too.

**50° 100° Hotel**  MONGOLIAN, INTERNATIONAL $$
(✉coder.latitudes.poster; mains T7000-23,000; ☺9am-midnight; ☑) This hotel restaurant serves a good range of Mongolian and Western mains, including pretty fine pizzas that only take about five hours to prepare (we're exaggerating, but order in advance). The menu features a range of vegetarian salads, imaginative dishes including beef in plum sauce, and Korean offerings such

## Mörön

as *bibimbap* (white rice with vegetables, chilli paste and meat).

## 🛍 Shopping

**Mörön Main Market**  MARKET
(3ax; GPS: N 49°38.7531', E 100°09.9408'; ✉mild.noodle.joyously; ☺9am-7pm Tue-Sat, from 11am Sun) If you've forgotten any expedition gear, check out the market; you'll find torches, tents, stoves, fishing equipment, bags and bike parts. Quality and variety won't be great but it'll do in a pinch. Close to the market is a strip of **vehicle repair shops** that can help if you need to fix a flat or pick up spare car parts.

NORTHERN MONGOLIA MÖRÖN

## DEER STONES

Found across Mongolia, deer stones are ancient markers that date from the Bronze Age; there are several theories as to why they exist. The ancient steppe tribes believed that after death, a soul departed this world and ascended to the sky on the backs of deer. The deer carved on to the stones seem to be representational of this act. However, since human remains have never been found near deer stones, they do not appear to be gravestones, but rather serve some sort of religious or spiritual purpose. Many deer stones were also carved with an image of a belt, from which hung various tools including axes and spears; these accessories would have been required for successfully navigating the afterlife. Of the 700 deer stones known to exist worldwide, 500 are located in Mongolia. The best collection of deer stones is at Uushigiin Uver (p132).

## ℹ️ Information

ATMs are plentiful in Mörön; you'll find a few lining Peace St in front of the **Chinggis Hotel** (Чингис Төв; ☑ 7038-3999; GPS N 49°38.2217', E 100°09.6253'; ⓜ pies.albums.petition; s/d/lux from T35,000/50,000/70,000; @ 🛜) and the **supermarket** (GPS N 49°38.2229', E 100°09.5005'; ⓜ plus.reserve.conforms; ⊘ 9am-9pm).

**Border Guard Office** (☑ 1382-24662, 1382-24136; ⓜ starters.chatters.asking; ⊘ 9am-noon & 2-6pm Mon-Fri) Can issue permits for border towns such as Tsagaannuur, but only if you have a Mongolian-speaking local with you posing as your guide. Otherwise, get your pass in **Ulaanbaatar** (p84).

**Tourist Information Centre** (☑ 9938 2050; www.huvsgul.wix.com/info; ⓜ submits.loved. sometimes; ⊘ 9am-6pm) This helpful office, affiliated with the ever-busy Saraa (☑ 9938 5577; www.taigatrip.com), can put you in touch with local guides, provide maps of town, and help organise accommodation and onward travel. Also maintains a non-commercial website dedicated to providing accurate information on the region. It's around 200m south of the 50° 100° Hotel.

## ℹ️ Getting There & Away

### AIR

Both **Aero Mongolia** (☑ 9997 7705; khuvsgul@aeromongolia.mn; ⊘ hours vary) and **Hunnu Air** (☑ 7038-4411; www.hunnuair.com; Mörön airport, ⓜ frisks.shippers.caterer; ⊘ hours vary) offer flights marked at similar prices to Ulaanbaatar; between the two airlines there should be at least two flights a day in summer. Winter schedules are cut back.

Mörön **airport** (MXV; ⓜ frisks.shippers. caterer) is about 5.5km from the centre of town. A taxi will cost around T5000.

### BUS

Three daily direct buses depart Mörön for Ulaanbaatar (T32,600, 15 hours) at 8am, 3pm and 6pm. Buy your ticket well in advance in late summer when the buses fill up with students headed for the capital. The same buses stop in Erdenet (T28,500, six hours). You can also catch buses to Darkhan (T30,500, 10 hours), which leave at 3pm.

Minivans run between Mörön and Ulaanbaatar daily (T50,000, 17 hours, 671km), departing at around 1pm. Minivans also run to Erdenet (T25,000, 12 hours) and Darkhan (T30,000, 15 hours); there's usually one daily, departing at around 4.30pm; which can drop passengers off in Bulgan (same price as Erdenet) on request. Buses and minibuses leave from the concrete **bus station** (Авто вокзал; GPS N 49°38.1424', E 100°10.2508'; ⓜ guarding.gladiators.compacts), diagonally across from the wrestling stadium.

From Mörön, it's 273km to Tosontsengel in Zavkhan aimag and 353km to Bulgan City.

### MINIVAN & 4WD

The local 4WD and minivan **stands** (GPS N 49°38.7531', E 100°09.9408'; ⓜ mild.noodle. joyously) to *sums* (districts) around Khövsgöl are located in and around the market. Vehicles to Tsagaannuur (T50,000) and Renchin-lkhumbe (T50,000) leave daily around noon; don't expect to arrive until night, or possibly the next morning (the trip takes eight hours if you're lucky). Vehicles leave when full for Khatgal (T20,000 per person, one hour), either from the market or from a separate parking area just off the main road opposite the clothing stalls.

# Khövsgöl Nuur National Park
## Хөвсгөл Нуур Үндэсний Цэцэрлэгт Хүрээлэн

Transparent in some places, midnight blue in others, tropical aquamarine in stretches, yet frozen for much of the year, **Khövsgöl Nuur** (Хөвсгөл Нуур; [🎙]sleeved.sheaf.branches) (Lake Khövsgöl) is an extraordinary natural wonder in a country with no shortage of physical beauty. As with its larger sibling across the border, Siberia's Lake Baikal, superlatives don't really do this immense, mountain-fringed lake justice. Its moody waters, surrounded by silent, eerie groves of pine-fresh taiga, attract thousands of Mongolian and international tourists every year.

The lake is full of fish, such as lenok and sturgeon, and the **national park** (Хөвсгөл Нуур Үндэсний Цэцэрлэгт Хүрээлэн; [🎙]sleeved.sheaf.branches; admission T3000) that surrounds it is home to argali sheep, ibex, bears, sables, moose and a few wolverines, plus some 200 species of birds.

The region hosts three unique peoples: the Darkhad, Buriat and Tsaatan (aka Dukha). Shamanism – the real thing – is practised in these parts, along with traditional Mongolian Buddhism.

## 🌣 Sights

### Khatgal Хатгал
Cheerful Khatgal (Хатгал) is a scattering of colourful roofs, dirt alleyways and wooden houses, spread out beneath the foothills and along the narrow arm of Khövsgöl Nuur that funnels into the Egiin Gol. The southern gateway to the lake, Khatgal is the largest town in the area, with some of the best budget accommodation in Mongolia.

It is a good launching pad for multi-day adventures in the area, as well as hiking, biking, kayaking and horse riding. The **Khatgal Ice Festival** (🕙 late Feb) takes place in late February, and includes Ice fishing, cross-country skiing, ice skating and horse sledding competitions.

For a good view of the lake, just climb the hill immediately north of Nature's Door (p140) camp. You can also check out the **Mogoi Mod** (Snake Tree; GPS: N 50°27.080', E 100°07.274'; [🎙]elbowed.blithely.discounts) (snake tree), 4km from town, past the defunct airport and towards Jankhai Davaa. This tree, which curves into a unique spiral, is honoured with *Hadaks* (ritual scarves).

### Western Shore
A paved road – expected to be completed in 2018 – will connect Khatgal all the way to the Toilogt (p139) ger camp. Once completed, tourism in the area will likely expand exponentially, placing a significant infrastructure strain on the park which is not prepared for. Already, trash is piling up near ger camps. While there is some enforcement aimed at curbing this sort of activity, for now it feels like a case of too little, too late. Tourists are already ubiquitous on the western shore of the lake, and their numbers seem likely to greatly expand in the near future.

At the time of research, a good, packed gravel road first heads southwest before swinging northeast across several dry riverbeds and over the pass, **Jankhai Davaa**, 17km from Khatgal, where you'll come across a few minor **ovoos** (GPS: N 50°34.023', E 100°07.797'; [🎙]driftwood.personalities.chill) (shamanistic collections of stones, wood or other offerings to the gods) and a cluster of reindeer herders selling handicrafts. These few Tsaatan (nicknamed 'business Tsaatan' by locals), sometimes accompanied by a so-called shamaness, have been lured down to the lake by the promise of tourist tögrög; their token, miserable reindeer are adversely affected by the lowland climate.

Over the pass, the road, lined with ger camps, continues past the gorgeous headlands of **Jankhai** and Toilogt (p139) to a geologic **research station** (GPS: N 50°45.613', E 100°13.407'; [🎙]unpacking.pursed.dejectedly). The road then deteriorates into a swampy mess. Even local Mongolian drivers don't attempt to drive past here, although you can carry on up the coast on horseback.

About 30km north of Toilogt is **Khar Us** (GPS: N 50°56.07', E 100°14.57'; [🎙]jingly.indirect. waterfall), a series of springs surrounded by meadows of beautiful wildflowers. In June, locals flock here to eat the bailius fish for its medicinal properties; these fish are smoked and served with wild green onions, or sometimes boiled.

Almost exactly halfway up the western shore lies **Jiglegiin Am** (GPS: N 51°00.24', E 100°16.002'; [🎙]confines.professes.deodorants), from where a westbound road of varying

## Khövsgöl Nuur National Park

0 ———— 20 km
0 ———— 10 miles

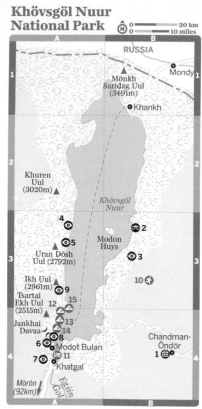

## Khövsgöl Nuur NP

### ◉ Sights
1 Alan Goa Museum ........................... B4
2 Borsog ............................................. B3
3 Ikh Santiin Davaa ......................... B3
4 Jiglegiin Am .................................... A3
5 Khar Us ............................................ A3
6 Khövsgöl Nuur ............................... A4
   Khövsgöl Nuur National Park ......(see 6)
7 Mogoi Mod ...................................... A4
8 Ovoos ............................................... A4
9 Research station ........................... A3

### ⊕ Activities, Courses & Tours
10 Bulnai Hot Springs ........................ B3

### 🛏 Sleeping
   Ashihai ........................................(see 6)
   Bulnai Tour Camp ....................(see 10)
11 Garage 24 ....................................... A4
12 Grand Tour Camp .......................... A4
   Huvsgul Dalai .............................(see 6)
13 Misheel Ger Camp ......................... A4
   Mongol Ujin ...............................(see 11)
   MS Guesthouse ..........................(see 11)
14 Nature's Door ................................ A4
15 Toilogt .............................................. A4

### ✖ Eating
   Garage 24 ...................................(see 11)
   MS Guesthouse ..........................(see 11)

### ℹ Information
   Information Centre ....................(see 11)
   Khan Bank ...................................(see 11)

### ℹ Transport
   Khatgal Car Stand ......................(see 11)

condition runs to Renchinlkhumbe, on the way to Tsagaannuur. Be warned: this track is often impassable for vehicles.

To get a ride up the western shore, you have to pay for a taxi from Khatgal. At the time of research, the price was anywhere from T70,000 to T100,000 depending on the state of the road, but this rate will drop significantly once the way is completely paved. If you're travelling solo and travelling light, ask at your guesthouse if anyone can give you a ride on the back of a motorbike.

### Eastern Shore
The eastern shore is less mountainous than the west, but offers spectacular views across Khövsgöl Nuur (p135). It gets far fewer visitors than the western shore, making it a great destination for travellers seeking an off-the-beaten-path experience. The main drawback to this side of the lake is the appalling road that heads up to Khankh. Ex-

pect mud, rocks, roots and the odd collapsed bridge. There is a chance this road will be impassable outside of winter.

From Khatgal, head for the bridge over the Eigin Gol. The trail meanders over some hills and continues past a prominent *ovoo* at the **Ikh Santiin Davaa** (Их Сантын Даваа; GPS: N 50°52.37′, E 100°41.11′; [≡]scowling.tribunals.greedily) to a gorgeous spot called **Borsog** (Борсог; GPS: N 50°59.40′, E 100°42.59′; [≡]socks.collages.nettle), six hours by 4WD and 103km from Khatgal.

If your spine hasn't suffered permanent damage, you could carry on further to a couple of gers that dot an area known as **Sevsuul**. The road actually improves a little here, then hugs the lake and is usually passable all the way to Khankh.

From Khatgal, allow at least 11 hours by 4WD (less by motorcycle) to travel about 200km to **Khankh**, a former depot for oil tankers headed to and from Siberia. Khankh is more Buriat and Russian than Mongolian, as most visitors are Russian holidaymakers from Irkutsk.

Remember that if you reach Khankh, you will have to come *all* the way back along the same bone-crunching eastern road: there is no way any vehicle can get from Khankh down the western shore. During the winter, some vehicles do drive directly from Khatgal to Khankh *over* the frozen lake, a trip that takes about two hours. There are apparently more than a few rusting cars and trucks littering the bottom of Khövsgöl Nuur, which we think speaks volumes about the safety of making this journey.

At the time of research, going all the way around the lake was only possible by boat or horse. The nearby border crossing with Russia is closed to third-country nationals.

## 🏃 Activities

### Fishing

If your idea of heaven is sitting utterly still for hours on end and contemplating the bobbing of your line in the water, well, welcome to Eden! If you don't have fishing gear already, the Buren Khaan shop in Khatgal has the best selection.

Around a dozen species of fish inhabit the lake, including salmon, grayling, omul, Siberian roach, perch and lenok. A **fishing permit** costs T15,000 and is valid for three days or 10 fish, whichever comes first. You can get them from the park rangers, MS Guesthouse (p138) or Khatgal's Government House (ask for directions at your accommodation). Fishing is not allowed between 15 April and 15 June. The fine for fishing illegally depends on what you've caught; it's worked out using the value of the fish multiplied by 10, with a US$40 fine on top of that.

### Hiking

One of the best ways to see the lake and the mountains surrounding it is on your own two feet. You will need to be self-sufficient, although there are a few gers in the area from which to buy some meat or dairy products. The trails around the lake are easy to follow.

Of the mountains in the southwestern region, the most accessible is **Tsartai Ekh Uul** (2515m), immediately west of Jankhai, where the hiking is excellent. Also try the numerous other mountains of the Khoridol Saridag Nuruu, such as **Khuren Uul** (3020m), not far north of the trail to Renchinlkhumbe; **Ikh Uul** (2961m), a little northwest of Toilogt; and the extinct volcano of **Uran Dösh Uul** (2792m).

Longer treks are possible around the **Ikh Sayani Nuruu**, which has many peaks over 3000m. It's right on the border with Russia, so be careful not to accidentally cross it or you may be shot at by border guards. A popular hike is up the western shore of the lake from Khatgal to Renchinlkhumbe via Jiglegiin Am (p135); it takes roughly a week.

### Horse Riding

The only place to organise a horse trek around the lake is in Khatgal. The guesthouses here can arrange everything within 24 hours. Prices are negotiable but reasonable at about T25,000 per horse per day, and about the same per day for a guide. Ger camps along the lake can organise horse hire for day trips.

A guide is recommended for horse-riding trips in the region and, in fact, park regulations stipulate that foreigners should have one local guide for every four tourists. Even if you have great equestrian skills, there are concerns that tourists riding solo may get lost or have their horses stolen. Guides will expect you to provide food while on the trail.

A complete circuit of the lake on horseback will take from 15 to 21 days. A return trip by horse from Khatgal to Tsagaannuur, and a visit to the Tsaatan, will take 14 to 20 days, most of which will be spent in the saddle, giving you only a day or two with the Tsaatan themselves.

An interesting two-week trip could take you east of the lake to Chandman-Öndör and Dayan Derkhiin Agui, a sacred cave. A trip to the Bulnai hot springs (p140) would take eight to nine days.

> ### ℹ️ DON'T PEE HERE
>
> We really wish this went without saying, but enough local ger camp and guesthouse owners asked us to include the warning, so here goes: don't pee in Khövsgöl Nuur. Besides being sacred to Mongolians, the lake is the source of the region's fresh water. If you're spotted taking a leak in the lake, there will likely be violent repercussions from locals.

Shorter trips include one to Toilogt, through the mountainous Khoridol Saridag Nuruu Strictly Protected Area, or up to Khar Us (p135) and back in five or six days.

## Kayaking & Boating

The lake is full of glorious coves that are perfect for kayaking. Nomadic Expeditions (p40) in Ulaanbaatar runs kayaking trips in the region, while Garage 24 and MS Guesthouse rent kayaks for about T50,000 per day. MS Guesthouse also offers the fun option of sending you downriver along Egiin Gol and agreeing on where to fish you out; you can kayak for up to 100km and come back by 4WD (T100,000).

Almost exactly in the middle of the lake lies **Modon Huys**, a picturesque little island surrounded by turquoise, tropical-looking waters. Several guesthouses, including MS Guesthouse and Garage 24, own motorboats; the latter can run travellers up to its camp and beyond to the island and the northern reaches of the lake. Other boat owners are happy to whisk three to four passengers up to a smaller island near Khatgal (around two hours return). For something a bit longer, ask about the two-day boat trip to Jiglegiin Am (p135) (T600,000 to T800,000 for up to five people, including meals).

In summer (July to mid-August) the **Sükhbaatar passenger ferry** (Сухбаатар Усан Онгоц; ☑9811 3550; adult/child T22,900/10,000; ☉Jul–mid-Aug) does daily 90-minute scenic/party boat trips, to the loud accompaniment of Mongolian pop and with plenty of passenger 'fuel' in the form of beer.

## 🛏 Sleeping

### Khathal

If you have a tent, you can camp along the shores of the Egiin Gol.

At the beginning of the season, the main ger camps in town set a standard price which tends to be the same across the board. At the time of research the price was T20,000 per person for a ger and T5000 for camping.

Beware of small-scale family operations that undercut official ger camps by running small, unofficial 'ger camps' that are not environmentally friendly. These are particularly prevalent on the western shore of the lake.

At the time of writing, a new law had been passed that all ger camps must be located at least 200m away from the lake's waterline. Enforcement of the law seems spotty, and some older ger camps built near the lake seem to have been given a pass.

★**MS Guesthouse**　　TOURIST GER CAMP $
(☑9979 6030, 8836 7666; www.facebook.com/msghmongolia; GPS: N 50°26.019, 100°09.674, ⠿folding.railroad.interestingly; per person

---

## THE REINDEER HERDERS

Not far from **Khövsgöl Nuur** (p135) live the Tsaatan (literally 'Reindeer People'). Their entire existence is based on their herds of reindeer, which provide milk for making cheese, antlers for carving and medicine, transport (the males can carry up to 90kg) and, very occasionally, meat.

The Tsaatan are part of the Tuvan ethnic group, which inhabits the Tuvan Republic of Russia, and they speak both Tuvan and Mongolian. There are only about 400 Tsaatan in total (around 250 live in the taiga, the rest in small towns), spread over 100,000 sq km of northern Mongolian taiga landscape. Taiga Tsaatan are truly nomadic, often moving their small encampments (ail) in search of the special types of grass and lichen loved by the reindeer. The Tsaatan do not use gers, but prefer orts, similar to Native American tepees, traditionally made from birch bark but now from store-bought canvas. Shamanism plays an important part in Tsaatan life; the shaman also acts as a healer, providing traditional remedies for ailments.

When the president of Mongolia visited the Tsaatan in the winter of 2012, he decreed that elders and families with many children would receive a stipend from the government. Before communism and forced collectivisation, the Tsaatan were completely self-sufficient, with enough reindeer per family to feed themselves. These days, in autumn the Tsaatan gather berries, pine nuts and wild potato, and fish and hunt when possible as further means of subsistence. January to March is the hungriest time of all.

T20,000, camping T5000; ℗ 🛜) This year-round camp, in the extreme south of town, is perhaps the most congenial of lodgings around Khatgal. English-speaking owner Ganbaa makes visitors feel at home, with communal meals (T1500) in the lodge and plenty of advice on hiking and horse trekking in the area. There are hot showers, clean pit toilets and a lounge with cold beer.

★ **Garage 24**  LODGE $
(📋 9838 0004; www.naturesdoor.mn; GPS: N 50°27.383, E 100°09.970, 🌐 equipment.floodlight. rural; per person with shower access T25,000; ℗ ) This environmentally conscious backpacker hang-out occupies the grounds of a reclaimed Soviet-era truck garage just north of Khatgal. Choose between staying in a ger or a dorm with comfy bunks in the fireplace-warmed lodge, and take some of the finest food in Khövsgöl out onto the veranda. Kayaks, horses and camping gear are available for hire. English is spoken.

**Mongol Ujin**  TOURIST GER CAMP $
(📋 9906 1921; www.facebook.com/MongolUjin-camp; GPS N 50°26.2666, E 100°10.2, 🌐 tempt. consoling.reeling; ger or cabin per person incl breakfast/3 meals T25,000/45,000; ℗ ) Friendly Ujin, who speaks good English, runs this lovely Khatgal ger camp. Ujin has a decade and a half of tour-guide experience and knows what travellers need. The range of tours and activities offered here (horse treks, bike treks, visits to nomadic families, etc) are well organised and come highly recommended, as do the comfortable gers and cabins.

**Modot Bulan**

**Huvsgul Dalai**  TOURIST GER CAMP $$
(📋 9927 5028; www.travelsmongolia.com; GPS: N 50°29'619, E 100°09.610, 🌐 separators.disclaims. cloves; ger with/without meals T90,000/50,000, cabins T120,000; ℗ ) On a raised bit of land just up from the western shore, this few-frills ger camp offers regimental rows of two- and three-person gers, a sauna and a dining hall serving solid Mongolian standards. Cabins come with en suite toilets.

**Ashihai**  TOURIST GER CAMP $$$
(📋 9926 4484, 7000 5459; www.ashihai.mn; GPS: N 50°29.915, E 100°09.871, 🌐 wetsuit.sailed. decoders; per person with/without meals gers T180,000/110,000, cabins T270,000/200,000; ℗ ) Elevated on wooden platforms, these beautifully decorated gers on the lake's west side are embroidered with traditional patterns; interiors contain exquisitely carved furniture. Gers and cabins offer tranquil lake views; gers have heated floors for chilly nights. Meals are served in the dining room of the appealing wooden lodge. Enjoy massages and sauna sessions in between motorboating and horse riding.

## Western & Eastern Shores

There are numerous ger camps on the western shore; the main group starts where the road meets the lake, after descending from Jankhai Davaa. The new paved road will likely bring electrical power lines with it.

Secluded camping spots are surprisingly difficult to come by along the stretch of western shore lined with ger camps. If you have your own 4WD, the best spot to camp on the eastern shoreline is Borsog (p136).

★ **Misheel Ger Camp**  TOURIST GER CAMP $
(📋 9977 3835, 9998 1422; GPS: N 50°36.254, E 100°11.824, 🌐 backboard.granted.brushed; T20,000; ℗ ) At first glance, this camp on the western shore resembles many other ger camps around the lake. What sets Misheel apart is having owners with long histories as tourism guides – they can provide well-mannered horses for treks, rent bicycles to guests (T5000) and cook good meals. The camp has hot showers (T3000) and modern toilets.

The owners go out of their way to make your visit a memorable one.

**Grand Tour Camp**  TOURIST GER CAMP $$
(📋 9692 0141; GPS: N 50°39.0616, E 100°12.404, 🌐 transfer.gangway.arranged; ger/cabin incl meals T60,000/90,000; ℗ ) A sweet spot on a hill overlooking the western shore of the lake, and a large, kid-friendly dining hall are the hallmarks of this clean ger camp. It frequently hosts events throughout the summer tourism season, making it popular with Mongolian holidaymakers. Some English is spoken. Has modern toilets, showers and a sauna.

★ **Toilogt**  TOURIST GER CAMP $$$
(📋 9999 9802, 9909 2273; www.hovsgoltravel.com; GPS: N 50°39.31, E 100°15.22, 🌐 matey.sobered. facsimile; per person tepee & ger/cabin incl meals T170,000/180,000; ℗ 🛜) 🌿 This eco-conscious camp is in a splendid location on its own little peninsula north of the other ger camps. Accommodation is a mix of tepees, gers and adorable wooden cabins (which come with en suite toilet). English is spoken, and the dining room is a hive of activity in the evenings. All stays come with meals.

WORTH A TRIP

## BULNAI HOT SPRINGS

The Soviet-era resort of **Bulnai Hot Springs** (Булнайн Рашаан; GPS: N 50°46.5250', E 100°47.8583'; [w]workbench. preheat.reacquaint; per person T10,000) has wood cabins over hot springs, some of which reach 48°C. Locals believe a dip here will cure gastrointestinal ailments, relieve high blood pressure and basically refresh the soul. The springs are located about 60km northwest of Chandman-Öndör village; **MS Guesthouse** (p138) in Khatgal arranges trips here.

**Bulnai Tour Camp** (GPS: N 50°46.5241', E 100°47.9762'; [w]phrased. knowledge.sabotages; per person T25,000) rustic cabins provide simple, modest accommodation for travellers looking to rest at the hot springs.

★**Nature's Door**　　　TOURIST GER CAMP $$$
([☑]9838 0004; www.naturesdoor.mn; GPS: N 50°35.546, E 100°10.882, [w]rappers.wardrobes. commentary; per person incl meals lodge/ger US$70/50; [P][🛜]) [🍴] Popular with backpackers and foreign hikers, this western-shore spot has plush cabins, a lodge, English-speaking staff, pizza and pasta on the menu, and happy hours (beer and wine), not to mention some of the best hot showers in northern Mongolia. Even if you're staying in one of the gers, you get access to the airy lounge with games.

An eco-conscious camp, Nature's Door gets high marks for composting and recycling. You can rent bicycles or kayaks (T20,000/25,000 per hour).

It's affiliated with Garage 24 (p139) in Khatgal.

### Khankh

**Northern Gate**
**Ger Guesthouse**　　　　　GUESTHOUSE $
([☑]9979 6030, 8836 7666; per person T20,000) Operated by the people from MS Guesthouse (p138) in Khatgal. It's just outside Khank (within walking distance) but can be hard to find. Call for directions.

**Last Frontier**　　　　TOURIST GER CAMP $$$
(Саян Радиан; [☑]8808 9141; www.sayan-radian. ru; GPS N 51°30.566', E 100°39.296'; per person incl 3 meals ger T66,000, r from T87,000; [P]) A cluster of gers surrounding an appealing wooden lodge on the lake's eastern shore. Most of the wood-panelled rooms have their own bathrooms. Activities on offer range from horse riding to fishing and hunting. Caters to a predominantly Russian clientele.

## 🍴 Eating

**MS Guesthouse**　　　　　　MONGOLIAN $
([w]folding.railroad.interestingly; meals around T5000; [⊙]hours vary) MS is a nice place to eat and will occasionally prepare *khorkhog* (a mutton dish cooked using hot stones) and authentic Mongolian barbecue for guests and visitors. They also whip up some of the best *buuz* (dumplings) in town.

**Garage 24**　　　　　　INTERNATIONAL $$
([w]equipment.floodlight.rural; meals T5000-20,000; [⊙]hours vary; [P]) Garage 24 has a Western-oriented menu (the chef trained in the UK) that will come as a welcome break after a few days of roughing it in the wilderness. The English breakfast includes bacon, toast, beans and sausage. Lunch and dinner menus include surprisingly good shepherd's pie and pizza. Give some advance warning as preparations take around an hour.

## ℹ️ Information

On the main road, 12km south of Khatgal, you'll be required to pay the park entrance fee (T3000) at a gate to the **national park** (p135). If there's no one there you can buy permits at the **information centre** (GPS N 50°26.1532', E 100°09.5959', [w]longer.sparkler.waxy; [⊙]10am-6pm) or from a ranger patrolling the lakeside on horseback. With your permit you should receive a visitors' pamphlet explaining how to limit your impact on the lake. Hang on to the ticket as you may be asked to show it.

**Khan Bank** (Хаан Банк; [w]starstruck.macho. typically; [⊙]9am-1pm & 2-5pm Mon-Fri) Changes cash. The closest guaranteed ATM is in Mörön.

## ℹ️ Getting There & Away

### MINIVAN & 4WD

You can fly into **Mörön** (p134) from UB, which easily cuts a huge chunk of potential travel time to the lake. Minivans and 4WDs regularly make the trip between Mörön and Khatgal (one hour) for T20,000 per person or T80,000/100,000 per car/4WD. Enquire at the **stand** (p134) at the northern end of the **market** (p133) in Mörön and around Khatgal's car stand.

Transport also meets the Ulaanbaatar flight at Mörön airport to take passengers directly to Khatgal. Some 4WD owners try to charge foreigners up to US$100 for the run; local drivers with the 'ХӨ' at the beginning of their license plate are likely to be more fair. Any of Mörön's backpacker-oriented guesthouses can arrange Khövsgöl transportation and tours.

A chartered 4WD should cost around T1000 per km. There are plenty of 4WDs in Mörön but few in Khatgal, where it is best to ask at the guesthouses. Khatgal is 101km from Mörön via paved road.

The **Khatgal Car Stand** (GPS N 50°26.4708', E 100°09.7819', [w]magical.kitty.sequence) is surrounded by small businesses and convenience stores.

# Chandman-Öndör
Чандмань-Өндөр

Nestled between pine-clad mountains and consisting almost entirely of log cabins, the village of Chandman-Öndör sits in one of the most picturesque locations in the country. The surrounding area, with its clear streams, alpine forests and wildflowers, is ideal horse-riding country.

Every three years (the next is in August 2018) a large **naadam** is held here to honour the locally revered folk heroine Alan Goa. It attracts Mongols from Inner Mongolia, Kalmyks, Tuvans and Buriats, as well as a host of Khalkh Mongols.

## ◉ Sights

**Alan Goa Museum**                                    MUSEUM
([w]flimsy.pendants.reconciles; T1000; ⊘hours vary) Housed inside a ger-shaped log cabin is this museum dedicated to the legendary Alan Goa – supposed ancestor of Chinggis Khaan, major figure in *The Secret History of the Mongols* and locally revered folk heroine.

## 🛏 Sleeping & Eating

There are some guest gers and a hotel in Chandman-Öndör, but they are pretty dire. If you do decide to shack up in town, expect to pay around T10,000-20,000 for a bed. You're better off camping, which can be done in any of the foothills or open spaces outside of town.

You can find some meat and bread in local *guanzes* (canteens) and supply stores. There's not much else, although locals apparently sell fresh strawberries in season.

---

### DRIVING TOUR: EAST OF CHANDMAN-ÖNDÖR

Heading east of Chandman-Öndör village, the road follows the Arig Gol. After 41km you'll pass a row of 13 **ovoos** (GPS: N 50°30.727', E 101°17.478', [w]unshaven.complicit.regularly) made from assemblages of wood and scarves. After another 18km you'll reach the town of **Tsagaan-Uur**, with basic shops and *guanzes* (canteens) and curious faces – foreigners don't tend to come out this way. The road to Tsagaan-Uur is notoriously rough, and it can take up to six hours to drive from Chandman-Öndör.

Around 38km past Tsagaan-Uur (97km past Chandman-Öndör) is the **Dayan Derkh Monastery** (Даян Дэрх Хийд; GPS: N 50°26.804', E 101°53.328'; [w]refolded.swooped.dexterity) FREE, set on a beautiful bend of the Uur Gol. Another 15km east of the temple is the **Dayan Derkhiin Agui**, a cave considered holy by local Buddhists and shamanists. In theory, you need a border permit to visit Tsagaan-Uur and Dayan Derkhiin Agui. The enforcement of this policy is spotty; if you're staying in Khatgal or Mörön, your accommodation owners may be able to fill you in on the permit situation. Permits can be gathered in UB or from the **border station** (p134) in Mörön, although you may get a raised eyebrow if you seek your permit out at the latter office.

About 26km downstream from the monastery, you'll see the confluence of the Eg and Uur rivers; despite their monosyllabic names, this makes for a dramatic sight. Head west at the Eg, and after about 35km you'll reach the 'town' of **Erdenebulgan**, from where it is possible to double back to Mörön.

The road from Dayan Derkh Monastery to Erdenebulgan has been made easier by bridges across the two river crossings, but these are old wooden structures subject to being flooded by high water levels. There is talk of installing new bridges in the region, but this is just that (talk) for now.

This entire trip involves driving on some excruciatingly rough roads that can become nigh on impassable in the wake of rain. Assuming that you're stopping to rest at night, bank on this journey taking at least two days.

## VISITING THE TSAATAN

This nomadic nation is primarily known for horse herders working the steppes, but deep in the taiga that lines the Russian border, one can find the reindeer herders of the forest. That's not some lost script page from *Game of Thrones*; the Tsaatan, or Dukha, people are some of the world's last reindeer nomads, and visiting them is a highlight of many Mongolian adventures.

The trick is visiting them responsibly. Though the Tsaatan are relatively used to outsiders by now, part of the draw of visiting them is seeing a unique society that does not exist for the sake of tourism. Of course, as more tourists seek out out this 'authentic' experience, the more the experience itself can be watered down, or worse, threatened by exposure and exploitation. This isn't to say the Tsaatan don't want visitors – many believe tourism is an important economic engine that allows them to maintain their traditional ways. But they do ask visitors to come with care and respect.

The Tsaatan are happy to receive visitors who are genuinely interested in learning about their way of life. They'd rather not have visitors who are not interested in talking with them and are only keen to take photos (which makes them feel like zoo exhibits), or those who wash their clothes and dishes in the Tsaatan's drinking water and drop trash. Tour companies are often at fault as well, discouraging clients from bringing spending money, encouraging them to bring tents when there are guest tepees available, and bringing horses that are not used to reindeer.

You can visit the Tsaatan year-round. Their winter camps are reachable by 4WD, whereas at other times you must come on horse (or reindeer!). How long the horse trek takes depends on the condition of local roads around Tsagaannuur. The Tsaatan live in two groups, known as the east (*zuun*) and west (*baruun*) taiga; this is a little confusing as the west taiga is actually southwest of the east taiga. The communities communicate via two-way radio.

Most visitors head for the east taiga. From Tsagaannuur, it can take four to 12 hours to reach either the west or east taiga by horse; the camps move and come closer to town as the summer ends (many Tsaatan children attend school in Tsagaannuur in winter, living in dorms during these months).

The **Tsaatan Community & Visitors Centre** (TCVC; ☑ 9525 8500, 9977 0480; www. visittaiga.org; ⓜ insinuates.jockeying.invent; ⊙ hours vary) can provide guides (but not interpreters), hire horses and offer information about the location of the Tsaatan camps. The centre is fully owned and operated by the Tsaatan and works to both help travellers and give the Tsaatan a chance to control tourism in their community. Arrangements can also be made with the assistance of **Zaya** (zaya_004@yahoo.com), the English-speaking member of the community. She checks her email weekly, though the community has no phone

## ❶ Getting There & Away

Shared 4WD vehicles going to Chandman-Öndör (T15,000) occasionally leave from the northern side of the **market** (p133) in Mörön. If you have your own wheels, a road winds its way around green hills and lush meadows to Chandman-Öndör via the village of Tunel. From Khatgal there are two roads to Chandman-Öndör. The one that approaches it from the south is particularly rough, muddy and boggy and can take up to five hours; don't attempt it after heavy rain. The slightly shorter road that branches off the main lakeside road to the north of Khatgal is easier to drive; there's a turn-off for the **Bulnai Hot Springs** (p140) halfway along.

In the rainy season, the best way to Chandman-Öndör is by horse; the trek from Khatgal takes four to five days. The route is spectacular, though marred by swarms of flies.

## Darkhad Valley
### Дархадын Хотгор

There are few more dramatic landscape shifts in...well, anywhere, than the moment you crest the mountain pass that leads from Khövsgöl into the wild basin of the Darkhad Valley. Hidden by the ice-carved borders of the Khoridol Saridag and Ulaan Taiga mountains, the valley is roughly the same size as Khövsgöl Nuur (p135) – fitting, as the region was formed by a glacial lake scooping out the earth.

reception between mid-June and mid-August. The folks at **Erdene's Guesthouse** (p144), plus **Saraa** (p134) and **Baigal** (p132) in Mörön, also enjoy good working relationships with the Tsaatan.

When you visit, behave like a responsible guest. Give the community advance warning of your arrival (book at least a week – ideally 10 days – in advance). Bring your hosts a useful gift (toothpaste, good batteries, soap, colouring books for children, make-up for women, small torches, mementos from your home country, etc). Do not bring sweets as there's no dentist here. Also make sure you rent horses that are have visited the Tsaatan before: there have been incidents when horses (from Khatgal and elsewhere) that were not used to reindeer have freaked out and crippled some of the Tsaatan reindeer, the livelihood of the herder.

Once you've left Tsagaannuur, figure on the following costs:

➡ T20,000 per day for a TCVC guide. This is not applicable if you bring your own guide, who you work out your own rate with. We recommend bringing your own guide/interpreter in any case; the TCVC can arrange one, but English skills will likely be lacking.

➡ T20,000 per day for *each* horse or reindeer – usually one for you, one for your guide and one for your bags.

➡ T10,000 per person per night for accommodation.

Be self-sufficient and carry more than enough food for yourself; the Tsaatan have horror stories to tell about visitors who turn up without food and deplete the Tsaatan's already meagre supplies. Bring a tent (just in case), camping supplies and 100% DEET to keep the bugs at bay. Bring small denomination tögrög (not dollars!) in case you wish to purchase some handicrafts. Show a willingness to engage in everyday activities; they'll be happy to put you to work! People typically stay for a couple of days, but you can stay longer if you're really interested in the Tsaatan way of life.

Getting to the Tsaatan involves a wonderfully picturesque horse (or reindeer) trek through pristine forest and mountains. You'll have to determine a meeting point, from where the Tsaatan will send a guide to meet and escort you to their camp. If you are intent on making the trip, check up about permits with the General Office of Border Protection (p84) in UB, as you'll need one to travel to this border area.

One final note: there really is a good chance that you can ride a reindeer with the Tsaatan. It's actually a pretty comfortable experience (it beats the hell out of wooden saddles on Mongolian horses, as we can attest), but if you weigh more than 82kg, you may be too heavy for the little beasts.

**NORTHERN MONGOLIA** DARKHAD VALLEY

The difficulty in reaching the region ensures the unique Tsaatan people are able to continue their traditional lifestyle here. The area is also one of Mongolia's strongest centres of shamanism – the genuine kind, not the let's-pose-for-tourists kind.

The entrance to the region is most dramatic, marked with a **gate** (GPS N 50°34.645', E 099°08.567'; [///]creasing.recoils.accredit) and a number of large *ovoos* sprinkled with food.

The valley is also known as the Darkhad Depression (Дархадын Хотгор).

To enter the Darkhad Valley, you ostensibly have to pay a national park fee of T5000. We were never charged during our visit, but travellers report that they have been assessed the fee in Ulaan Uul, the first town you encounter driving north.

## ❶ Getting There & Away

Getting into the Darkhad involves driving northwest of Mörön and navigating a series of disastrously maintained dirt tracks that lead to a white-knuckle mountain pass road that eventually descends into the valley. The roads actually improve a wee *(wee)* bit in the valley, depending on where you are, though there are still some extremely rough patches.

Public transportation originates in and heads to Mörön, where you can catch minivans to Tsagaannuur (T50,000) and Renchinlkhumbe (T50,000). These leave daily (at noon from Mörön; when full from Darkhad Valley towns) and take anywhere from eight hours to about half a year. Just kidding! Eight hours *is* the minimum, though, and many of these minivans won't arrive until the next morning.

## ⓘ Getting Around

To visit the Tsaatan during the warmer months, you'll have to come by horse. After arranging your visit, a Tsaatan guide (or guides) will arrange to meet you at an exchange point that is accessible by motor vehicle. From this point, you will mount horses (or reindeer!). The subsequent ride to the Tsaatan taiga camp could take anywhere from a few hours to a day, and potentially even longer. The location of the exchange point will vary depending on where the Tsaatan are camped, and how far vehicles can travel into the taiga, which is itself dependent on how wet the ground is.

For more information, see Visiting The Tsaatan. (p142)

## Renchinlkhumbe   Рэнчинлхумбэ

Mountain-fringed Renchinlkhumbe is 42km west of the Jiglegiin Am (p135) trailhead on Khövsgöl Nuur (p135), an adventurous two-day journey on foot or horseback; it's otherwise reachable by a fairly rough road via Ulaan-Uul.

Renchinlkhumbe hosts an excellent local **naadam** in July.

## 🛏 Sleeping

**Saridag Inn**   TOURIST GER CAMP $
(☑ 9914 0965; GPS: N 51°06.852', E 099°40.135'; ⩚complying.comprehend.lawn; camping/r/ger per person T5000/15,000/20,000) This local camp consists of homey gers and musty rooms inside the main lodge building, with stupas on its property. Its hot-water showers and sit-down toilets are legendary. The owners can arrange basic meals for breakfast, lunch and dinner (soup, rice porridge, dumplings and the like) for around T5000.

### BLUE VALLEY AWARDS FESTIVAL

Held annually in the Darkhad Valley, the **Blue Valley Awards Festival** (⊘mid-Jun) cultural festival features traditional horse games and singing competitions. The venue moves between the four towns of Renchinlkhumbe, Ulaan Uul, Arbulag and Bayanzürkh; check the location in advance at the **tourist office** (p134) in Mörön.

## ⓘ Getting There & Away

A minivan (T50,000) leaves Mörön around noon for Renchinlkhumbe, but there's no reason to come here if your goal is to visit the Tsaatan; in that case, head straight to Tsagaannuur. Most folks coming to Renchinlkhumbe will have trekked or ridden horses from Khövsgöl Nuur.

## Tsagaannuur   Цагааннуур

☑ 3858 / POP 1400
About 40km beyond Renchinlkhumbe is Tsagaannuur, the northernmost town in Mongolia and last stop before the Tsaatan encampments in the taiga. Besides its picturesque lakeside location, there's little here other than a few small grocery stores and a couple of guesthouses. That said, it's a friendly little spot where you can kill a day before hopping on a reindeer.

## 🛏 Sleeping

**Egshiglen**   CABIN $
(☑ 8992 1007, 9538 5646; ⩚apparent.scrolled.socked; cabin T15,000; ℗) This lakeside sleeping spot includes a nice on-site restaurant (open 9am-9pm; meals T3000 to 10,000) where you can snack on fresh fish, and several different cosy cabins. The owner can arrange boat trips (T40,000 for 20 minutes, boat can hold seven passengers) and a private lift to Mörön (around T350,000). She also does tyre repairs – why not?

**Erdene's Guesthouse**   GUESTHOUSE $
(☑ 9950 8657, 8826 8075; ⩚whoops.afterbirth.licks; incl breakfast T15,000; ℗) A friendly option consisting of a basic bed-and-breakfast deal. The owner's wife speaks English, and the couple is always willing to negotiate on rates. They're also well connected to the Tsaatan and can arrange English- and Russian-speaking guides, as well as horse treks (T20,000 per day). You can order meals for around T2500.

## ⓘ Information

Permission from **Ulaanbaatar** (p84) is required to visit Tsagaannuur and you have to register at the local **checkpoint** (Хилийн 0258 Дугаар Тусгай Салбар; ⩚absorption.attended.blouses; ⊘hours vary).

It's best to bring a guide and interpreter who can help smooth out any permit issues. It may be possible to obtain a permit from the **border guards** (p134) in Mörön, but as this requires the assistance of your guide, or a local posing as your guide, it's best to get permits in Ulaanbaatar. You must also register in Mörön – many guesthouses are willing to take on all of this legwork for a small fee (T10,000).

Border permits are free and are processed in one to three working days. You'll need a travel itinerary and passport copies. In a pinch, guesthouses can arrange the permit in Khatgal through their Mörön contacts. This involves handing over your passport for a few days, which many travellers are unwilling to do.

### 🛈 Getting There & Away

#### HORSE
There is really only one way to get to the taiga in the warmer months: by horse. Horses can be hired in Tsagaannuur for T20,000 per day. Some travellers make the journey all the way from Khatgal: a return trip from Khatgal to Tsagaannuur, with a day's visit to the Tsaatan, will take from 14 to 20 days. You could go from Khatgal to Tsagaannuur on an easy trail in about five days, bypassing **Jiglegiin Am** (p135) and **Khövsgöl Nuur** (p135). If you do come from Khatgal, consider switching to fresh horses in Tsagaannuur via the **Tsaatan Community & Visitors Centre** (p142); their horses will be accustomed to taiga trekking and the presence of reindeer.

#### MINIVAN & 4WD
You can get to Tsagaannuur from Mörön by 4WD in a bone-crunching, nine-hour (minimum) drive, depending on the state of the road. Contact the guesthouses in Mörön and ask if they can set you up with a vehicle, or arrange one through a UB tour operator.

With your own wheels, you can drive here from Mörön, but there is no clearly signposted way to the Darkhad Valley or, once you're in the valley, to Tsagaannuur. The first town you'll reach in the valley is the small crossroads settlement of Ulaan-Uul. From here you'll arrive at a the **fork** (GPS: N 50°50.453', E 099°18.407') which branches towards Renchinlkhumbe and Tsagaannuur. There is an old logging road that cuts through the mountains pretty much directly to Renchinlkhumbe from around the Jankhai pass, but even locals wouldn't attempt this drive at the time of research.

Minivans run between Tsagaannuur and Mörön and Renchinlkhumbe and Mörön, departing Mörön from a **stand** (p134) near the main market. A seat to either destination will cost around T50,000, and journeys take an absolute minimum of eight hours; many minivans won't arrive until the next morning. Ask at the 4WD stand in Mörön.

### 🛈 TOP UP ON PETROL
As the towns in the Darkhad Valley in particular are subject to frequent power cuts, top up on petrol whenever you get the opportunity when travelling in the region. Sometimes there's no electricity for days, petrol pumps do not function and you can be stuck in some one-horse town for an interminable period of time.

## Shine-Ider & Jargalant
### Шинэ-Идэр, Жаргалант

The borderlands between Khövsgöl and Arkhangai aimag largely constitute a series of dry, rocky valleys and raw, ochre upcountry. You can make a nice drive here, passing through towns such as **Shine-Ider** (Шинэ-Идэр) and pretty **Jargalant** (Жаргалант); the latter occupies a lovely position near the confluence of the Ider and Khonjil rivers. The road south out of Khövsgöl threads this harsh landscape like a needle through a hot, dusty quilt.

The *sum* (district) these towns occupy is perhaps most famous for being the homeland of a herder named Öndöör Gongor (Tall Gongor, 1879–1931), who was 2.57m tall.

### ⊙ Sights

Around 30km south of Shine-Ider, right off the main road, is an area of **standing rocks and graves** (GPS: N 48°45.808', E 99°23.084'; ⌗defeat.pharmacists.wrangling). A further 8km brings you to a scenic pass and the 1890 stupa, **Gelenkhuugiin Suvraga** (Гэлэнхүүгийн Суврага; GPS: N 48°41.182', E 99°22.650'; ⌗refreshes.housemates.polkas). From this pass, it's an easy 19km to Jargalant.

About 6km south of Jargalant are several **burial mounds** (GPS: N 48°32.0956', E 99°22.2157'; ⌗defeat.pharmacists.wrangling), including one with a tree growing from it. Some 26km south of Jargalant there is a small ger hotel and, on the hill behind it, a Buddhist temple constructed in 2001 to replace an older temple on the same spot. About 46km from Jargalant is **Orokhiin Davaa** (Орохийн Даваа; GPS: N 48°17.484', E 99°23.130'; ⌗converging.choreograph.observed), the final pass on the way to Terkhiin Tsagaan Nuur. There is a delicious cold water **spring** (GPS: N 48°18.7883', E 99°23.7031'l ⌗undramatic.grasshoppers.

shortsighted) by the road on the north side of the pass.

**Zuun Nuur** LAKE
(Зуун Нуур; GPS: N 49°03.727', E 99°31.096'; ⏚rebutted.jock.shushing) This large lake is the scenic highlight of Khövsgöl's far south. There is excellent camping all around, or you can stay at the **Dalai Vam Ger Camp** (☑8914 0217; GPS: N 49°02.870', E 99°29.359'; ⏚aground.episode.swelled; with/without meals US$35/25), located on a hill overlooking the southern shore. This blue dollop of water is located 13km north of Shine-Ider village and about 100km southwest of Mörön.

## 🛏 Sleeping

★ **Jargal Jiguur** TOURIST GER CAMP $$
(Жаргал Жигүүр; ☑9909 6776; jargaljiguur @yahoo.com; GPS: N 48°33.615', E 99°22.061'; ⏚comments.controls.moles; per person with/without meals T80,000/30,000) This excellent place is run by the infectiously bubbly Jargal. It's located at the foot of beautiful mountains, and is based around a mineral spring pool that feeds into on-site natural baths. Throw in some modern toilet blocks and great cuisine at its **restaurant**, and you've got a winner of a ger camp.

## ❶ Getting There & Away

**Minivans** (GPS: N 48°56.9268', E 99°32.1715'; ⏚amble.infeasible.traitors) run to Shine-Ider from Mörön and back when full (T50,000, five hours). Note that it can take a long time for them to fill up. You could ask to be dropped off on the main road if you wanted to trek to **Zuun Nuur**; the road comes near the lake, but even at the closest point it's a 10km hike. Buses run from Jargalant's **bus station** (GPS: N 48°34.9882', E 99°21.0772'; ⏚funk. photographic.nerds) to Ulaanbaatar at 3pm (T40,000, 16 hours).

If you're driving, it's a rough road from Mörön to Terkhiin Tsagaan Nuur; bank on the trip taking around six to eight hours.

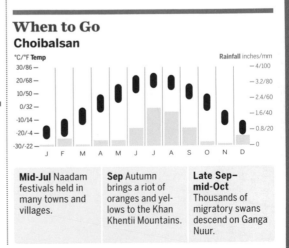

# Eastern Mongolia

POP 208,000

## Best Places to Eat

➡ Ikh Ursgal (p158)

➡ Ezent Guren (p151)

➡ Azure Restaurant (p158)

➡ Khanburged (p151)

## Best Places to Stay

➡ Khanburged Hotel (p150)

➡ Onon Khurkh Urguu Ger Camp (p153)

➡ Olikhon Hotel (p158)

➡ Ezent Guren (p151)

➡ Buir Nuur Ger Camp (p160)

## Why Go?

In Brazil, there is the deepest jungle heart of the Amazon. In the Arctic, there are swathes of untouched tundra. And in Mongolia's eastern aimags, another ecosystem reaches its apotheosis – the steppe. This is where you'll find the grassy ocean that was the ecological backbone of the great horse nomadic empires of history; indeed, Khentii aimag lays claim to being the birthplace of Chinggis Khaan. There's both table flatlands and upland elevation here; in the north, the taiga forest envelopes the hills in a pine-scented cradle, but everywhere is grass, grass, grass and herders who have carved a life out of the marriage of livestock and prairie.

These wide horizons demand to be explored by horseback, but said adventures are rarely easy. This is by far the most remote, least visited part of Mongolia, and a venture into its depths is a challenge to even the most experienced of travellers.

## When to Go
### Choibalsan

**Mid-Jul** Naadam festivals held in many towns and villages.

**Sep** Autumn brings a riot of oranges and yellows to the Khan Khentii Mountains.

**Late Sep–mid-Oct** Thousands of migratory swans descend on Ganga Nuur.

# Eastern Mongolia Highlights

❶ Spending a few days around log cabins and Chinggis Khaan legends in **Dadal** (p153).

❷ Paying your respects to the local deities with an ascent of the sacred peak of **Shiliin Bogd Uul** (p163).

❸ Touring **Dariganga's** (p162) cultural relics and eerie volcanic landscapes.

❹ Contemplating **Khalkhiin Gol's** (p159) war memorials and impressive stone statues.

❺ Travelling across the steppe to watch the sun rise

and set over the immense remote **Buir Nuur** (p160).

❻ Seeking out **Baldan Bereeven Khiid** (p154) and getting blessed by a local lama.

❼ Marvelling at the treasures housed in **Khentii Ethnography Museum** (p149) in Chinggis, the 18th-century home of the Tsetseg Khan.

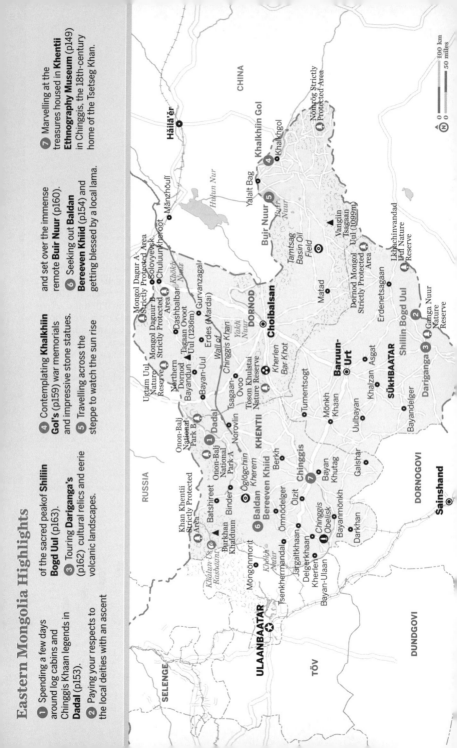

## History

The Tamsagbulag Neolithic site in Dornod, active more than 4000 years ago, is proof that agriculture predated nomadic pastoralism on the eastern steppes. But it was the Khitan, a Manchurian tribal confederation, which made the first big impression on the region, building forts and farming communities, including Kherlen Bar Khot (p156) in Dornod. Other buildings date as far back as the 10th century.

Another Manchu tribe, the Jurchen, deposed the Khitan in the early 12th century, renamed itself the Jin, and returned eastern Mongolia to its warring ways. It wasn't until Chinggis Khaan united the fractured clans in 1206 that peace was restored.

It was from Avarga (modern Delgerkhaan) that Chinggis launched expeditions south towards China. When the capital was moved to Karakorum in 1220, the region withdrew into obscurity. It wasn't until 1939 that eastern Mongolia was again in the headlines, this time as a battlefield between Japanese and joint Soviet–Mongolian forces. Heavy losses forced the Japanese military machine south, a crucial turning point in WWII.

The discovery of zinc and oil in the region in the 1990s brought the promise of development, with change hot on its heels. These natural resources have altered the local landscape, with oil wells and other mining infrastructure now permanent fixtures on the Dornod landscape.

### ℹ Getting There & Away

Paved roads connect Ulaanbaatar (UB) to all of the aimag capitals in eastern Mongolia. Other towns and attractions are connected by dirt roads and shallow tracks, which are often boggy after heavy rains. Note that there are few street signs, and those that exist are in Cyrillic. There are limited air connections to **Choibalsan** (p159) from UB.

Buses for Chinggis, Baruun-Urt and Choibalsan depart from Ulaanbaatar's **Bayanzürkh Avto Vaksal** (p85) bus station. Private vehicles wait at UB's **Naran Tuul** (p81) 4WD station. Another route into the region is through northern Khentii – daily minivans from Naran Tuul travel to Dadal via Binder; these services are not well advertised so you may need a local to help you contact the drivers.

### ℹ Getting Around

Public transport can get you to most towns in the region provided you're armed with the patience of an angel. But if you want to see what the region really has to offer, you'll need your own transport.

# KHENTII　ХЭНТИЙ

POP 72,600 / AREA 80,300 SQ KM

Even in a country of considerable natural beauty, Khentii stands out. The Mongol people believe they are descendants of the blue wolf and the white doe – a fusion of the steppe and the forest, respectively – and few aimags link those environments like Khentii. Here, the blue sky soars above mountains furred in dark groves of larch, and rolling steppe sliced into partitions by icy cold rivers. This landscape gave the world Temujin, the boy who would become Chinggis Khaan, and much of the tourism in the region revolves around sites associated with the controversial man's life.

The true joy of exploring here is felt when history and physical beauty merge into one experience; the rushing waters of the Onon river and the pine-clad peaks of the Khentii Mountain Range are beautiful on their own, but doubly fascinating when you consider they were the backdrop of the Great Khaan's childhood.

---

## Chinggis　Чингис

☑ 7056, 01562 / POP 21,500 / ELEV 1027M

As aimag capitals go, Chinggis, previously known as Öndörkhaan (Өндөрхаан; Supreme Emperor), is a pretty pleasant place that's worth a day of sightseeing. Tree-lined streets, scattered Chinggis Khaan monuments and a small collection of well-preserved 18th-century buildings sit alongside some of the region's best museums, along with some good-value hotels. The city sits on the northern bank of the Kherlen Gol, which provides a fishing hole for locals and riverside camping spots for travellers.

### ⊙ Sights

★ **Khentii Ethnography Museum**　MUSEUM
(Summer Palace Museum; ☑ 1562-22187; ⦿ hound. refreshed.glorified; admission T3000; ⊙ 8am-5pm Tue-Sat) This excellent museum occupies the 18th-century home of the Tsetseg Khan, who governed most of eastern Mongolia during the Manchu reign. Standout exhibits include ethnic costumes and Khalkh silver jewellery, a shaman outfit complete with skull and feathers, a 1923 portrait of the last Tsetseg Khan, handmade chess sets, and wooden spiral puzzles. Exhibits are treated with obvious care and attention, and the integration of the palace space with museum galleries is seamless.

**Shadavdarjaliin Khiid**  BUDDHIST MONASTERY

(Шадавдаржаалийн Хийд; ⌨scorpions.distorts.charging; ⊙hours vary) Shadavdarjaliin Khiid, in the western part of town near the Sports Palace, is a freshly painted, walled temple complex with some *ovoo* (shamanistic offering) trees and a dozen monks. The original monastery in this area was built in 1660 and housed the first Buddhist philosophy school in Mongolia; at its peak, before the Stalinist purges of 1938, the monastery was home to more than 1000 monks.

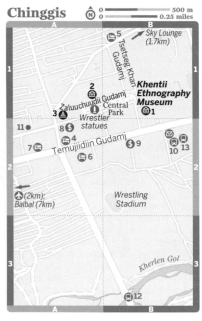

**Chinggis**

**Balbal**  MONUMENT

(GPS: N 47°16.722', E 110°36.096'; ⌨bakes.fogey.outlived) A well-preserved Turkic-era *balbal* (stone grave marker) is 7km west of Chinggis. The squat-figured statue is covered in blue silk *Hadaks* (ritual scarves) and has a disproportionately large head with pronounced eyebrows and deep-set eyes. His long hair is curled behind his ears, an unusual feature for this type of statue.

**Khentii Aimag Museum**  MUSEUM

(Аймгийн Музей; Museum of Local Research; ⌨dabbling.stables.bristle; admission T2000; ⊙8am-5pm Mon-Fri, 9am-6pm Sat) The small Aimag Museum features a mastodon tusk, a protoceratops skull, Chinggis Khaan–era armour and an array of stuffed local wildlife. In the central park across the road, you'll find statues of famous local wrestlers (and their prominent buttocks) – a popular photo stop for locals.

The museum's future is in doubt, given low amounts of funding and visitors.

## 🛏 Sleeping

**Negdelchin Hotel**  HOTEL $$

(Нэгдэлчин Төв; ☎9952 3701; ⌨caressing.plots.dame; d/ste from T30,000/65,000; P) Although it looks a little grim from the outside, the Negdelchin boasts decent if faded rooms. All have basic beds and enough comfort to take the ache off a few days of being on the road, but beware – the cheapest chambers don't have bathrooms. Try a suite for a little more space.

⭐**Khanburged Hotel**  HOTEL $$$

(☎9890 6867, 8924 7337; www.facebook.com/Khanburgedhotel; ⌨pokers.pollution.formation; d T55,000-85,000; P🛜) This excellent, professionally run place comes with all the bells

## ℹ️ DIY EASTERN MONGOLIA

For independent travellers, eastern Mongolia is both a godsend and a logistical nightmare. You're certainly not likely to be tripping over ger-loads of Gobi-lovers here, but making your solitary way across this region requires a considerable amount of patience, effort and forward planning.

You can't just wing it, as the region's biggest highlights lie in the border area and even non-local Mongolians require permission to travel here. You must have a set itinerary if you wish to travel beyond the major cities, and you must obtain permission in advance from the General Office of Order Protection (p84) in Ulaanbaatar. Make the itinerary as detailed as possible and specify the order in which you wish to visit the proposed locations.

Easy enough? On the road, you will have to register at police stations or military bases in Batshireet, Dadal, Choibalsan, Khalkhgol and other areas. As rules change from time to time, find out in Ulaanbaatar exactly where you have to register – and register you must. If you fail to do so at one of your set itinerary points and then try to register at your next destination, the police could, in theory, send you back to your previous destination to register before you can proceed further. If you don't speak Mongolian, registering can be tricky, as can hiring a horse and anything else that requires language skills. A translation app on your phone may help, assuming you get service.

Always carry your passport, as there are several military checkpoints, particularly in the easternmost part of the region, and a photocopy just won't do.

All of the region's highlights require you to have your own wheels (or hooves). It's possible to rent 4WDs with drivers in several towns, though it's easiest in Ulaanbaatar. As northern Khentii tends to suffer from muddy roads bad enough to sink a 4WD, the best way to explore the region is on horseback; both Batshireet and Dadal are good places from which to launch an expedition. A GPS is essential for finding more remote sites. Unless you're supremely confident of your equestrian abilities and have a GPS, it's not advisable to go off without a guide. That's about it. Not put off yet? Then you qualify for our 'most intrepid traveller' award.

and whistles, including a marble-floored lobby, helpful receptionists, reliable hot water in the modern bathrooms, and stylish rooms decked out in creams and browns. In a great central location.

### ✖️ Eating

**Jonon Lounge**  ASIAN $

(〽️dined.perused.nuzzling; mains T4000-12,000; ☺noon-midnight) A pan-Asian menu of stir-fries and finger foods features prominently at this smart lounge, incongruously located on the ground floor of the semi-ratty **Jonon Hotel** (Жонон Төв; ☎9956 9119; 〽️dined. perused.nuzzling; r T40,000; 🅿️🛜). You can grab drinks here too; dancing and karaoke carry on in the lounge area on weekends.

**Ezent Guren**  MONGOLIAN $$

(〽️laying.rural.year; mains T5000-20,000; ☺9am-9pm) This **hotel** (☎7056-2778, 7056-3678; 〽️laying.rural.year; s/d/ste from T65,000/90,000/195,000; 🅿️🛜) restaurant probably has the most diverse menu in town, supplementing the usual Mongolian slate of grilled and roasted meats and dumplings with big bowls of soup, which are pretty tasty.

**Khanburged**  MONGOLIAN $$

(〽️pokers.pollution.formation; mains T6000-18,000; ☺8am-9pm) The usual Mongolian suspects – dumplings and animal protein – are staples here. The hotel restaurant does a mean plate of fried liver, and serve decent salads that don't feel like an afterthought.

### 🍷 Drinking & Nightlife

**Sky Lounge**  LOUNGE

(www.facebook.com/SkyLoungeChinggis; 〽️undergo.lioness.pendulum; ☺noon-11.30pm daily) This bar, which occupies the top floor of a high-rise apartment block, goes all in for the high-roller-in-a-penthouse vibe, with varying degrees of success. The views are expansive, and while the dusty urban blocks of Chinggis city may not wow you, the cocktails might.

## ℹ️ Information

**Khas Bank** (⧉quicker.crimson.rigs; ⊘ATM 24hr) Has an ATM.

**XacBank** (Хас Банк; ⧉gown.bedrock.esti-mates; ⊘9am-5pm Mon-Fri) Changes dollars and has an ATM.

## ℹ️ Getting There & Away

### BUS, MINIVAN & 4WD

From the **bus station** (⧉budgeted.galloped. shade), two daily buses head to Ulaanbaatar (T13,500, five hours) at 8am and 2pm. Daily buses to Choibalsan and Baruun-Urt both orig-inate in Ulaanbaatar, so they're often full by the time they arrive. Still, you can try and hitch a ride by waiting by the **toll station** (⧉organs.harm-lessly.trailing) at the southern bridge; the buses pass through town around 1.30pm, 5pm, 7.30pm and 11.30pm. An open seat on a Baruun-Urt bus costs T12,000 (four to five hours); expect to pay T17,000 for a seat on a Choibalsan bus (six to seven hours).

Daily **minivans** (⧉echo.bunkers.paler) go between Ulaanbaatar and Chinggis (T20,000, five hours, 331km). To go further east, your best bet is to wait for the bus. You can also rent a car or 4WD at the minivan station; expect to pay T200,000 for a car to Baruun-Urt, or T250,000 for a car to Choibalsan. Local drivers here also rent 4WDs (from T150,000 per day).

Early morning **postal trucks** (⧉recliner. force.wove) run to Dadal at 8am (T16,600, eight to nine hours) on Monday and to Batshireet, also at 8am (T12,300, four to five hours) on Monday and Thursday; afternoon trucks head to Binder at 4pm (T12,000, four to five hours) on Monday, Wednesday and Friday.

# Binder      Биндэр

At the confluence of the Khurkh and Onon Gols, the village of Binder is a good place to rustle up some horses for an expedition to Burkhan Khalduun (p152), or to dine at one of the *tsainii gazars* (teahouses) on your way to or from Dadal.

Don't miss **Rashaan Khad** (GPS: N 48°22.763', E 110°17.950'; ⧉cynic.mothership.galas), a site which, if placed anywhere else in the world, it would be the centrepiece of an archaeological

---

### WORTH A TRIP

## BURKHAN KHALDUUN

For the nomads of Chinggis Khaan's generation – and for many 21st-century Mongolians – the land and sky are holy, the abode of spirits and fonts of power. In a land of flat, wind-lashed grass, mountains assume a particular importance; of those mountains, **Burkhan Khalduun** (Бурхан Халдуун; GPS: N 48°45.728', E 109°00.629'; ⧉burrito.rewired.will) stands above all other contenders, in some cases physically, but always spiritually. Many Mon-golians believe this peak to be the cradle of their nation, as did Chinggis Khaan himself, who returned to this forested massif whenever he sought spiritual guidance from the Eternal Blue Sky.

Because of these connections, locals climb the mountain, topped with many *ovoos* (shamanistic collections of stones, wood or other offerings to the gods; GPS: N48° 45.430', E109° 00.300'), to gain strength and good luck. Climbing it is forbidden to for-eigners, who may only travel as far as the foot of the mountain; there are plans to create an observation route to make visits worthwhile.

You can camp in the shadow of the mountain, but foreigners may not proceed up its slopes.

**Khalun Us Rashant** (Hot Water Springs; GPS: N 48°57.206', E 109°00.217'; ⧉aubergine. microscope.consulate) This site has more than a dozen hot springs, a collection of log bathhouses and a small **Buddhist temple** built in honour of Zanabazar (the third holi-est leader in the Tibetan Buddhist hierarchy), who frequented the site.

It's located around 22km due north (as the falcon flies) of Burkhan Khalduun.

Burkhan Khalduun is in an exceedingly isolated corner of Mongolia. To get here, you'll need to head to Möngönmorit in Töv, and then travel north along the Kherlen Gol; this is often only possible during the winter months, when the ground freezes. The dirt roads are often washed out during spring and summer. You could come on horseback (in which case it makes sense to approach from Binder or Batshireet). The easiest option would be to organise a trip out here from UB. Whatever you decide, make sure to ask about ground conditions; during our research, a Mongolian truck was literally swept down a river while trying to drive to Burkhan Khalduun.

museum. In Mongolia, it is a largely forgotten rock – albeit a rock carved with some 20 different petroglyphs portraying ancient wildlife and mysterious symbols. The adjacent stone formations, which crust a ridge line that looks out over the great Khentii steppe, are also studded with ancient carvings.

A couple of cheap hotels (rooms around T20,000 to 30,000 per person) are in the middle of town; they're serviceable, but don't expect much more. You can camp outside of Binder near the banks of the rivers.

An excellent place to stay is the luxurious **Onon Khurkh Urguu Ger Camp** (☑7733 5588; GPS: N 48°34.891', E 110°41.545'; [w]hexagonal.dozen.thundered; 4-person ger with/without meals US$50/20; [P]). Each comfortable bed has its own mosquito net, there are hot showers and the dining room serves hot meals on request. You'll need to summon up your nerve and plunge your vehicle into the shallow part of the river to reach the camp (follow the other 4WD tracks).

If you are travelling on to Dadal you'll need to cross the Onon Gol. A hilly road leads down to the **pontoon dock** (GPS: N 48°35.835', E 110°43.419'; [w]restrooms.basecamp.thermos; T10,000; ☺24hrs). A ferryman pulls the small car ferry across the river using a cable. Alternatively, there's a **bridge** across the river a few kilometres south of Binder. Binder sits roughly halfway between Baldan Bereeven Khiid (p154) and Dadal, and makes for a natural stop between either destination.

---

# Dadal     Дадал

☑5649 / POP 2800

Chinggis Khaan conquered more of the world than any human being who has ever existed, but his origins – as a refugee and hunter-gatherer living off of berries and mice – can be traced to the junction of the Onon and Balj rivers. Here in Dadal *sum* (district), near the town of the same name, the man who would be khaan (emperor) was born in an area that was remote even during his lifetime. A patchwork of dark pine forests, clear rivers and howling winds – the latter a playground for enormous ravens – was the geographic heritage inscribed on the memory of the future khaan.

Modern Dadal encompasses several sites associated with Chinggis, plus hiking opportunities, log cabins and a population of ethnic Buriats. With its shadowy blanket of taiga forest and deep blue skies, it's one of the highlights of a trip to eastern Mongolia.

---

**NATIONAL PARKS OF KHENTII**
...................................................
**Khan Khentii Strictly Protected Area**
(12,000 sq km) Situated mostly in Töv aimag, the strictly protected area includes the northwest corner of Khentii, protecting taiga forest, steppe and the sacred mountain Burkhan Khalduun (p152).

**Onon-Balj National Park** (4157 sq km) Protects taiga and steppe along the Mongolia–Russia border. It's divided into two parts; part A is west of Dadal and part B covers the area to the northeast.

---

## ◎ Sights

The countryside around Dadal is technically part of 4157-sq-km Onon-Balj National Park, which extends north from Dadal towards Russia. Within this forested wilderness, you can camp, fish and spot wildlife. The 'park' has very limited infrastructure; to really get the most out of a trip, it's best to arrange a tour or guide with the WWF office (p155), which will also charge you the T3000 national park fee.

★**Deluun Boldog**          MONUMENT
(Дэлүүн Болдог; GPS: N 49°03.0542', E 111°38.3933'; [w]economy.resurfaces.tumbling; [P]) In a boundary zone of steppe and taiga some 3.5km north of Dadal village, you'll find a grouping of rounded hills and shallow gullies intercut with clear mountain streams known as Deluun Boldog. On top of one of the hills is a stone marker (p153), erected in 1990 to commemorate the 750th anniversary of the writing of *The Secret History of the Mongols*, inscribed with a simple message: Chinggis Khaan was born here in 1162.

**Museum of Temujin's Childhood**     MUSEUM
(GPS: N 49°01.232', E 111°37.4901'; [w]bangles.distribution.ticklish; admission T5000; ☺hours vary) The entertaining village museum includes a wooden ger with a statue of young Temujin out front, and paintings of the grown-up Chinggis and his descendants inside, along with black stallion tail-hair pennants (the most prestigious kind!), a map depicting Mongol empire conquest and a model of a massive ger, pulled by scores of oxen. Standout exhibits inside the second building include a particularly creepy artistic depiction of Chinggis Khaan, Buriat swan-head fiddles and an intricately carved horse-sweat scraper.

## WORTH A TRIP

## BALDAN BEREEVEN KHIID

Resembling a piece of Lhasa, Tibet, that got lost in the Khentii foothills, **Baldan Bereeven Khiid** (Балдан Бэрээвэн Хийд; GPS: N 48°12.0296', E 109°25.9257'; [m]gestured.edibility. deductible; admission T5000; ⊙hours vary) was one of Mongolia's largest and most important monasteries prior to the violent purges of the 1930s. Today the site is a shadow of its former size and grandeur, but its historical importance and gorgeous position in a raw, rocky valley makes it an alluring Khentii destination. There's an otherworldly beauty to this place, which perhaps amplifies the belief, held by many Mongolians, that this area is haunted by the spirits of their murdered countrymen.

There are maybe a dozen lamas here, attended by around two to three times that many pilgrims. The main temple, with its beautifully painted beams and dragon motifs, was revamped in 2010; it also features a massive prayer hall and a 2nd-floor balcony that is closed to all visitors (even local lamas can access this floor only on certain holy days). By the gateway to the temple complex is a map of a walking loop that takes in the most important *ovoos* (offerings to the gods), the Eej (Mother) Cave, which acts a purifying place for anyone who passes through it, and a hilltop viewpoint with spectacular views of the buildings and the plain below.

About 24km east of Baldan Bereeven Khiid, on the dirt track that leads to Binder, you'll pass through the green mountains and squiggly river of the **Khurkh Valley** (GPS: N 48°11.5416', E 109°45.3550'; [m]driving.breakers.columnists). What's here? Nothing. As in, no people. Or fences. Or anything man-made. It's simply an exceptionally beautiful place in very sparsely populated country. Go ahead. Camp. Pick your nose. No one is watching.

There is no public transportation to Baldan Bereeven Khiid; for that matter, there are barely any roads. It's rough going over mud tracks in the steppe, so approach with caution. Many travellers come here as part of a package deal from UB; it's possible to reach Baldan Bereeven Khiid in a day from the capital, and many go on from here to Dadal.

**Stupa Memorial**     MEMORIAL
(GPS: N 49°01.085', E 111°36.761'; [m]manliness.twilights.respectable) This memorial, comprising three stupas, was built to honour the 607 people from Dadal – mainly Buriats – who died during the political repressions of the 1930s. The list of names is printed on prayer wheels, which adds a touch of Buddhist poignancy. It's worth noting that the Buriats were treated much more harshly than Khalkh Mongols during the purge era, largely due to old-fashioned prejudice and rumours that some Buriats were in league with the Japanese.

**Chinggis Khaan Obelisk**     MONUMENT
(GPS: N 49°02.0064', E 111°39.2841'; [m]equestrian. publics.foolproof; [P] ) This not-so-subtle, enormous wedge-shaped white rock was placed in the middle of a ger camp in 1962 to commemorate the 800th anniversary of Chinggis' birth. This was at the height of the communist era, when Chinggis was officially viewed as a reactionary, but somehow the monument was allowed to stand.

## 🏃 Activities

### Fishing

There is good fishing in the area. Get a permit (T10,000, good for five days) at the Government House next to the Temujin Museum (p153), or with the help of a licensed tour operator.

### Hiking & Horse Riding

There are several hiking and horse-riding routes out of Dadal. Locals recommend the 30km hike to the junction of the Onon and Balj rivers, or the 45km trek further along the Onon Gol to the gorge at the confluence of the Onon and Agats rivers. You'll need to inform the border patrol (the WWF can help track them down) of your itinerary and it would be wise to take a local guide; ask at the ger camps or track down Dorjsuren, who runs the eponymous homestay, or Mr Gansukh (also of a self-named homestay).

## ✨ Festivals

Dadal is a great place to be for **naadam** (11 and 12 July). You can get up close and personal with archers and jockeys, and perhaps make up the numbers in the wrestling tourney!

## 🛏 Sleeping

This is perfect camping country; just find a secluded spot away from the village. Otherwise, there are a few tourist ger camps scattered about.

**Gansukh Homestay**               HOMESTAY $
(☑9567 7777; GPS: N 49°01.1652, E 111°38.6203'; �🌐selflessly.neutrals.congregate;  r from T10,000; P ) Friendly **Mr Gansukh** (☑9567 7777), a local Buriat who has worked with the WWF, allows visitors to stay in rustic cabins on his property, located at the edge of the taiga. He might make you artichoke tea or chop up some mutton for a barbecue. There are pit toilets and good vibes on-site, and meals can be arranged.

**Dorjsuren's Homestay**            HOMESTAY $
(☑9822 4720, 9580 4720; dorjsurengalsan 2009@yahoo.com; GPS: N 49°01.280', E 111°38.562'; �🌐commended.nightfall.wristbands; per person with/without meals T10,000) **Dorjsuren** (☑9822 4720, 9580 4720), a friendly elderly Buriat, has a small log cabin for guests next to his home, consisting of a rather cramped but tidy dorm and a hot-water shower block (T3000). There's a cast-iron stove for cooking and Dorjsuren can provide a breakfast of tea, homemade bread and clotted cream (and wild strawberry jam in summer!) for T3000.

It is a 10-minute walk southeast of the centre, across the river. There is no sign, so ask for directions (everyone knows where Dorjsuren lives).

**Altargara**                 TOURIST GER CAMP $$
(Алтаргана; ☑9191 0221, 9972 3629; altargana.camp@yahoo.com; GPS: N 49°02.2625', E111°39.7264'; wbumble.obstructions.lotions; per person with/without breakfast US$24/19; P ) This cheerful collection of log cabins and gers occupies a beautiful clearing in the taiga. English is spoken (a bit) and there are reliable hot showers and a chill-out picnic area with tables. Hot meals can be ordered in advance from the dining room.

## ℹ️ Information

Dadal is in a sensitive border area so it's best to register with the police – if you can find them, as the local police officers are often away. If you are heading any further out of town, it's also a good idea to register with the border guards; the folks at the WWF office can help you track them down.

The closest thing Dadal has to a tourist information centre is the **WWF office** (GPS: N 49°01.771', E 111°38.410'; �🌐destroyer.cycled. unbuckles; ⊙9am-6pm Mon-Fri) located between the village and **Chinggisiin Gurvan Nuur** (Чингисийн Дэлүүн Нуур; ☑9861 2494; GPS: N 49°02.233', E 111°39.646'; ⌐unladylike.marquees.submissions; per person with/without meals T40,000/25,000; P ) ger camp. Staff here sell T3000 tickets to Onon-Balj National Park.

## ℹ️ Getting There & Away

A postal truck travels to Dadal from Chinggis (T16,600) every Monday at around 8am, returning to Chinggis on the same day. The trip takes about eight to nine hours over awful 'roads' – good times.

Ask around the shops for the few vehicles for hire. Expect to pay at least T100,000 per day, depending on your route, plus petrol.

For travel from Dadal to Chinggis or Dornod (but not Binder), you'll need to cross the Onon Gol at a lone bridge crossing (GPS: N 48°50.403', E 111°38.746').

# DORNOD                   ДОРНОД

POP 76,500 / AREA 123,600 SQ KM

Eastern Mongolia is a sea of grass; in most of its aimags, that sea has hills and elevation. That's not really the case in Dornod: this is is pure steppe, with pancake-flat grasslands and an overbearing sky evident in all directions for days on end. It's an inhospitable land for humans, with few water sources and fewer places to ask for directions. An especially remote region in a country where the word 'remote' can so easily be overused, Dornod presents a challenge even to the most experienced of travellers.

The main attractions are the enormous dollop of blue beauty that is Buir Nuur lake, and the gritty prairies that run alongside the Khalkhiin Gol, where a Soviet-Mongolian alliance stopped a Japanese invasion and changed the course of history's largest war – all before said war officially started.

# Khökh Nuur   Хөх Нуур

According to *The Secret History of the Mongols,* it was at **Khökh Nuur** (Хөх Нуур, Blue Lake; GPS: N 48°01.0549', E 108°56.7883'; ⌗flaming.throttle.depositing) that Temujin first proclaimed himself khaan (emperor) of the Mongol tribe. It's an aptly stirring place for a coronation; the imaginatively named Blue Lake nestles at the foot of a peak known as **Heart-Shaped Mountain.**

## 🛏 Sleeping

You can camp in the woods on the southwest side of the lake, or alteratively sleep in one of the ger or cabin camps set up by the water.

**Mandal**   TOURIST GER CAMP **$$**
(☑9860 0408, 9860 0407; GPS: N 48°01.096', E 108°56.8403'; ⌗brighter.doctored.vocational; ger T60,000; ℗) Clean gers cluster at the water's edge; cabins were being constructed at the time of research. Meals can be ordered for T4000.

**Khar Zurkhnii Khukh Nuur**   CABIN **$$$**
(Хар Зурхний Хөх Нуур; ☑9917 1675; GPS: N 48°01.042', E 108°57.029'; ⌗curated.wheezing.nectarines; 6-person cabin with meals T120,000; ℗) This camp consists of two-storey log cabins. It's popular with locals, and can get rowdy on weekends.

## ❶ Getting There & Away

The lake is about 35km northwest of Tsenkhermandal, off the Ulaanbaatar–Chinggis Road. Roads can be muddy and you'll need your own transport and a driver who knows where the lake is. If you're approaching from the west, a small Хөх Нуур sign several kilometres west of the Tsenkhermandal turn-off indicates a shortcut.

# Choibalsan   Чойбалсан

☑0158 / POP 43,000 / ELEV 747M

Mongolia's easternmost capital is a welcome sight if you're craving a hot shower, a decent bed and an opportunity to eat something other than *tsuivan* (noodles) cooked over a stove. That said, by any objective measure, Choibalsan is a dreary town, decked out in full-on

WORTH A TRIP

### NORTHERN DORNOD

A loop around northern Dornod makes for a good, offbeat three- or four-day 4WD trip. From the starting point of Choibalsan, what looks like a main road on the map is in fact a dirt track that loosely parallels the railway line that runs to the Russian border.

About two-thirds along the way, near the village of Gurvanzagal, keep an eye out for the **Wall of Chinggis Khaan** (Чингисийн Хэрэм). Despite the name, it was probably built during the Liao (Khitan) dynasty to prevent rampaging Mongol hordes from heading east. Locals know it as the Chingissiin Zam, or Chinggis' Rd, which gives some indication of just how worn down the wall has become; it's not quite as impressive as that other, more famous wall built by the Chinese.

The road continues northeast to **Khökh Nuur**, a medium-sized freshwater lake at an altitude of 560m, the lowest point in Mongolia. There's a desolate beauty to this home of waders and shore birds.

From Khökh Nuur you could head northwest to **Mongol Daguur B Strictly Protected Area**; if you're lucky, you may come across a roaming herd of gazelle. The nearest town is Chuluunkhoroot, near the border crossing with Russia – an unappealing mess of ramshackle concrete buildings, gers and junkyards.

A good dirt road leads west from Chuluunkhoroot through the village of Dashbalbar and the mountainous **Ugtam Uul Nature Reserve**, the home of deer, situated along the Ulz Gol. If you take the turn-off from the main road into the hills, you'll soon come across some mysterious **monastery ruins** (GPS: N 49°17.175', E 113°46.196'; ⌗tribunals. pageant.kneel). It's not known exactly when the monastery was built, but some effort has been made to stop it from disintegrating completely.

4WD tracks lead further west along the main road to Bayandun and Bayan-Uul, both fine areas for camping and horse riding. There is a good road from Bayan-Uul back to Choibalsan (187km, 3½ hours) or you could take the rough road further west to Dadal via Norovlin (140km, four hours).

# Choibalsan

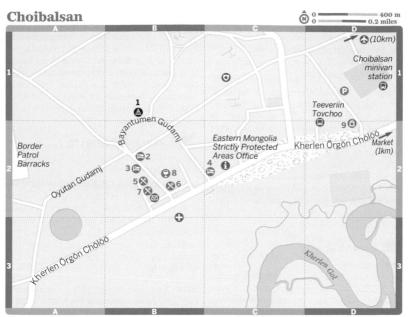

massive-apartment-block chic. It doesn't help that looting devastated the western half of the city when the Russians upped and left in 1990.

Centuries ago, this town – the fourth-biggest in Mongolia – was a trading centre and part of a caravan route across Northeast Asia. In 1941 it was named after the Stalinist stooge Khorloogiin Choibalsan, an honour bestowed while the dictator was still in power.

## ◎ Sights

★**Dornod Aimag
Museum & Gallery**                    MUSEUM
(⧉streaking.cape.masts; incl Natural History Museum T3000; ◷10am-5pm Mon-Fri, to 3pm Sat & Sun) Inside the former Government House, the comprehensive collections here stampede through the aimag's history, from Stone Age and Bronze Age finds to the communist years and beyond. Standout exhibits include a painting of Chinese-era capital punishment (one of which involves a man wearing female underwear), fascinating war photos, Choibalsan (the dictator) memorabilia including his desk and shortwave radio (a real antique gem), and fine examples of national costume, including a shaman's outfit and an elaborate headdress weighing 6kg.

# Choibalsan

◎ **Sights**
1 Danrig Danjaalin Khiid ..........................B1

🛏 **Sleeping**
2 Chadanguud ..........................................B2
3 Olikhon Hotel ......................................B2
4 To Van Hotel .......................................C2

🍴 **Eating**
5 Azure Restaurant ................................B2
6 Ikh Ursgal ...........................................B2
7 Khishig Supermarket ..........................B2

🍷 **Drinking & Nightlife**
8 Winners Pub ........................................B2

🛍 **Shopping**
9 Market.................................................D2

ℹ **Information**
Golomt Bank .................................(see 5)

**Danrig Danjaalin Khiid**      BUDDHIST MONASTERY
(Данриг Данжаалин Хийд; ⧉bearings.factually. agreeable; ◷hours vary) This monastery, built around 1840, was once one of the most active holy sites in eastern Mongolia. Though it contained three northern temples and four southern temples, less than half of the resident 800 monks could be accommodated

at one time; most had to pray outside. Communist clampdowns shut the temple in 1937. The monastery reopened in 1990, and now has two small temples where about a dozen monks worship. It's located about 400m behind the Kherlen Hotel.

**Mongolian Heroes' Memorial**  MONUMENT
(Ⓜromantics.football.cycled) Like a socialist realist lightning bolt, this masterpiece of Stalinist monument-chic features a soldier on horseback flying straight towards the enemies of the motherland. Behind the monument, a horseshoe arch decorated with mosaic tilework depicts cavalry stampeding into battle, and brave soldier wives holding down the home front. A small Soviet tank next to the monument saw action during the 1939 Khalkhiin Gol war.

## 🛏 Sleeping

**Chadanguud**  HOTEL $$
(Чадангууд; ☑9957 7427; Ⓜgalloping.flop.edge; s/d T40,000/60,000; ℗🛜) Spacious rooms (all with wi-fi) and powerful hot showers equal happy stays at the Chadanguud. That said, some rooms have weird wall stains and peeling paint – a small inconvenience, by our measure. The hotel has been undergoing renovations; you'll definitely want to ask for one of the newer rooms.

**To Van Hotel**  HOTEL $$
(Зочид Буудал; ☑8958 3555; Kherlen Örgön Chölöö, Ⓜcapacity.defected.drawn; s/d/lux incl breakfast from T30,000/50,000/120,000; ℗🛜) The To Van used to be one of the more stylish options in Choibalsan, but it's been scaled back into a midrange accommodation choice and is beginning to show its age. Still, you'll find well-lit rooms and wi-fi that (pretty much) functions, which is a blessing in this part of the world.

**Olikhon Hotel**  HOTEL $$$
(Ольхон зочид буудал; ☑9902 8287, 9958 9530; Olikhon@yahoo.com; Ⓜspring.promotion. merit; s/d T55,000/90,000; ℗🛜) A central location, semi-reliable wi-fi, and clean rooms that have a slightly more cosy atmosphere than the average corporate, midrange Mongolian hotel are all votes in the Olikhon's favour. A slightly inflated price point is a strike against.

## 🍴 Eating & Drinking

⭐**Ikh Ursgal**  MONGOLIAN, INTERNATIONAL $$
(Их Урсгал; ☑7058 4666; Ⓜdefensive.laces. scooped; dishes T8000-15,000; ⊘9am-9pm) We found great grilled chicken, fried mutton ribs and decent French fries at this local favourite. The kitchen pushes out delicious meat dishes sure to satisfy carnivorous Mongolians; there are also some Chinese stir-fries on the menu, which has pictures (but no English).

**Azure Restaurant**  CHINESE $$
(☑7058 2839; wwimp.combos.disco; mains T8000-12,000; ⊘9am-10pm) Pop into this hang-out for spicy Chinese pork, ginger-inflected stir-fries or just about anything plucked from an enormous menu that specialises in Mongolian favourites and dishes from nearby northern China. The Azure is attached to the Olikhon Hotel and has a pretty extensive bar on-site as well.

**Winners Pub**  PUB
(Ⓜassist.consumed.segmented; ⊘10am-midnight Mon-Sat) This vaguely footy-and-beer-themed pub sports English Premier League paraphernalia on the walls and comfy red leather sofas. It also serves a variety of Western and Mongolian dishes.

---

### KHERLEN BAR KHOT

The small-scale ruins of **Kherlen Bar Khot** (Хэрлэн Бар Хот; GPS: N 48°03.287', E 113°21.865'; Ⓜissues.rephrasing.consequences), consist of the remnants of four temples and eroded pedestals of statues, as well as the reconstruction of a 10m-high brick tower. This isis all that remains of a 12th-century fortress town that was once part of the ancient state of Qidan.

Kherlen Bar Khot is about 90km west of Choibalsan, on the main road between Choibalsan and Chinggis. It is worth a look only if you have your own vehicle and are heading that way.

## KHALKHIIN GOL

At the far eastern edge of Mongolia, the region of Khalkhiin Gol (Халхын Гол) is best known to travellers – and the world – as the site of a pre-World War II battle (p225) that significantly changed the course of Mongolian (and arguably, world) history. This is a land of sharp grass, rounded ridges and big vistas overlooking the Khalkhiin River and the hills that mark the Chinese border beyond. Most folks come to soak up the history of the battlefield and check out the many Soviet-style military monuments that dot the grasslands. The one outpost of civilisation – besides some border patrol posts – is the desolate settlement of Khalkhgol (Халхгол). The people are friendly, but fields of trash, crumbling apartment blocks, and clouds of steppe dust make for the sort of town even Mad Max might think is a little too rough.

Numerous war memorials, built to honour the Soviet and Mongolian dead, are scattered about the area, most of them on the road to Khalkhgol (town). There are some real socialist masterpieces; the most impressive are the **Yakovlev Chuudiin Tank Khoshuu** (Яковлевчуудын Танк Хөшөө, Monument for Yakovlev Tank Brigade; GPS: N 47°48.813', E 118°32.856'; ⊞bran.taxing.breakable; ℗), a Soviet tank on a pedestal 23km northwest of the town, and the 10m-high **Yalaltiin Khoshuu** (Ялалтын Хошуу, Victory Monument; GPS: N 47°38.091', E 118°35.944'; ⊞grievances.pouch.gauze; ℗) (Victory Monument) just outside Khalkhgol, with a stylised Mongolian maiden on one side and grim-faced Soviet and Mongolian soldiers on the reverse.

Beyond the **Museum guesthouse** (☑8954 7779; ⊞spoonful.stretching.resisting; per person T10,000) and a decent enough **hotel** (☑8843 1311; GPS N 47°37.9340', E 118°37.3342'; ⊞blast.onslaughts.prototypes; d/tr T25,000/37,000; ℗), there aren't many accommodation options in Khalkhgol.

Khalkhiin Gol is near the Chinese border and a military base, and there is one military checkpoint en route from Choibalsan along the main road to Buir Nuur. As well as requiring a border permit, you technically have to register at the military base in Khalkhgol, although this rule wasn't enforced when we visited.

Khalkhgol is about 325km from Choibalsan, at least a nine-hour drive over some of the worst roads eastern Mongolia has to offer (and that's saying something). It's best to hire your own vehicle in Choibalsan, as shared vans (T25,000, nine to 10 hours) to Khalkhgol still can't deliver you to the local sites. Vans return to Choibalsan when full, and usually leave between 11am and 1pm from the **town centre** (⊞artfully.imperious.wooing).

## 🛍 Shopping

**Market**        MARKET
(Зах; ⊞bibs.plankton.tall; ⊙9am-7pm) Choibalsan's proximity to China means that its market is well stocked. Purchase anything from fresh produce, dried dairy products and a local relish made of spring onion and garlic (great for livening up that mutton!) to saddles, Mongolian hats and boots. Note that the market closes on one day towards the end of each month – the date changes monthly.

## ℹ Information

**Eastern Mongolia Strictly Protected Areas Office** (☑9866 7161, 7058 3461; Sanjaadoo@yahoo.com; ⊞mercy.daylight.salaried; ⊙8am-5pm Mon-Fri) Provides information on visiting protected areas in both Dornod and Sükhbaatar aimags. Arranges permits and sells tickets to protected areas and nature reserves. If you stop by to enquire about visiting protected areas, they will probably make you pay the T5000 protected area fee, just in case.

**Golomt Bank** (Голомт Банк; Kherlen Örgön Chölöö, ⊞harmony.hologram.slate; ⊙Hours vary) Next to **Khishig Supermarket** (Хишиг; ⊞bribing.ambushed.subway; ⊙9.30am-10pm Mon-Fri, 9am-9pm Sat & Sun).

## ℹ Getting There & Away

### AIR

**Hunnu Air** (p85) flies to/from Ulaanbaatar. The **airport** (⊞waveform.emotionless.annotation) is about 10km east of Choibalsan's centre.

### BUS, MINIVAN & 4WD

Buses (T31,600, 13 hours, 655km) depart for the **Bayanzürkh Avto Vaksal** (p85) bus station in Ulaanbaatar daily at 8am and 4pm from **Teevriin Tovchoo** (Тээврийн Товчоо; ☑9866 1845; ⊞broke.meals.reckoned) at the eastern end of town. From the same station it's also possible to get a seat in a minivan to Ulaan-baatar (T40,000) or to Chinggis (T18,000), which doesn't have a specific departure time but generally leaves when full.

Private minivans and 4WDs run between Ulaanbaatar and Choibalsan daily (T36,000), departing near Ulaanbaatar's **Naran Tuul 4WD station** (p81). Minivans from Choibalsan market depart to UB when full. Private vans and 4WDs (also from the market) go to Chinggis (T22,000, 324km) and Baruun-Urt (T27,000, 191km).

If you want to hire a car and driver, locals will charge around T100,000 per day plus petrol.

A minivan to Khalkhiin Gol (T25,000, 10 hours) leaves daily around 1pm from a separate **station** (⌖ tailback.melon.instructive).

## Buir Nuur   Буйр Нуур

You may never see sunsets like those that utterly inflame Buir Nuur. Situated amidst a land of utterly flat, endless horizons, perhaps it is no surprise the dusk on this vast 40km lake is so incredibly vivid, a veritable bonfire of pink and orange.

But you have to get here first. And getting here, in a word, sucks. The area around Buir Nuur is Mongolia's equivalent of Arabia's Empty Quarter – a seriously remote and seemingly endless arid sea.

The lake is located by Mongolia's eastern thumb and is well known for its large stocks of fish and birdlife, particularly in the north-east area around the Khalkhiin Gol delta. Given that the northern shore of Buir Nuur is in China, most of the fish end up on the plates of Chinese restaurants – a source of much bitterness on the Mongolian side.

### 🛏 Sleeping

**Buir Nuur Ger Camp**   TOURIST GER CAMP **$$**
(☑ 9958 5588, 8811 5499; www.facebook.com/buir lake; GPS: N 47°51.6635, E 117°53.4799'; wrooftops. insecurity.mufti; d/q/ger T20,000/40,000/40,000; ℗) This longtime standby of the Buir Nuur tourism game offers comfortably decked-out gers and clean, plain hotel rooms attached to a low-slung compound with a kitchen that cranks out good meals. The owner can help arrange horse treks and similar activities in the area.

**Buir Lake Complex Resort**   RESORT **$$$**
(☑ 8808 5387; www.buirlake.com; GPS: N 47°48.8251, E 117°52.7751'; wplucking.prattled.greases; ger/cabin/lux ger T80,000/200,000/250,000; ℗🛜) Is this the most unexpected beach resort in the world? Sitting as it does thousands of miles

from any ocean, we have to guess it's a contender. There is, in fact, a sandy beach here, as well as beachy cabins, volleyball nets and fold-out chairs. Perhaps even more unexpected is the working electricity and wi-fi. Attracts mainly Chinese guests.

### ❶ Getting There & Away

Getting around eastern Mongolia can be a slog, but during our research, no journey felt as long, tedious and bone crunching as the drive to Buir Nuur. And drive you must: the only way to get here is by 4WD from Choibalsan, 285km away over dirt roads that cross utterly flat, featureless expanses of endless steppe. Allow at least nine hours, and be prepared for the bone-jostling bumps of a lifetime.

Before following the eastern shore of the lake, the road passes through two military check-points (make sure your paperwork is in order) and skirts an oil field that looks ripped out of Dante's *Inferno*.

## SÜKHBAATAR
### СУХБААТАР

POP 59,000 / AREA 82,300 SQ KM

If Khentii aimag represents the transition between taiga and steppe, pancake-flat Sükhbaatar synthesises the Gobi Desert with the pure steppes of Dornod. In the southwest, you'll find shifting sand dunes and barren rock faces, while in the east, knee-high grass brushes against the haunches of gazelle in huge herds.

The highlight of the province is the southern *sum* (district) of Dariganga, home to some 20 extinct volcanoes and several sacred mountains. This is one of the most beautiful corners of eastern Mongolia, a legendary region of horse thieves who hail from a landscape dappled with caverns and ancient circular ice caves.

## Baruun-Urt   Баруун-Урт

☑ 7051, 01512 / POP 19,700 / ELEV 981M

Baruun-Urt, Sükhbaatar's capital, is a compact place, the sort of town that reminds you that, in Mongolia, a provincial centre is as big as a mid-sized neighbourhood in many other nations. The burg sits smack in the middle of a fairly desolate hollow carved out of eastern Mongolia's vast plains where there's no river, no lake, no trees, the winters are ferocious and the summer feels like scorching hell. Despite it all, this is a cheerful little spot, where the main square buzzes with families at sunset, and folks seem quick with a smile.

All that said, there *is* a high level of sulphur in the soil, so consider buying some bottled water.

## Sights

**★ Baruun-Urt Ethnography Museum** MUSEUM
(patch.gobbling.stung; admission T3000; 8am-5pm Mon-Fri) Baruun-Urt's museum has a fine collection of costumes representing the three ethnic groups that inhabit the region: the Khalkh (the majority), the Dariganga (around 30,000 live in the south of Sükhbaatar aimag) and the Uzemchin (about 2000 live in Dornod and Sükhbaatar aimags). Look out for a brass-studded Uzemchin wrestling jacket.

There are also beautiful crafts made by Dariganga's renowned silversmiths and blacksmiths, stuffed gazelle, and two rooms dedicated to the famed poet, author and politician Ochirbatyn Dashbalbar (1957–99).

**Erdenemandal Khiid** BUDDHIST MONASTERY
(Эрдэнэмандал Хийд; sugar.managers.showrooms; hours vary) Erdenemandal Khiid was originally built in 1830, about 20km from the present site. At the height of its splendour, there were seven temples and 1000 monks in residence; the 1938 Stalinist purges put an abrupt end to that. The new monastery, surrounded by a wall topped with 108 stupas and fluttering strings of prayer flags, is about 400m west of the square. If you wander into the courtyard during warmer months, you may catch groups of crimson-robed monks chanting outside.

## Sleeping

**Zotol Mandal Hotel** HOTEL $$
(Зотол Мандал; 9495 5687, 9412 9898; crucially.ratty.lands; r incl breakfast T45,000; P) This would be our top hotel choice in Baruun-Urt if it wasn't annoyingly located about a 15- to 20-minute walk to the centre. Still, it's a good option: rooms are clean, there's reliable wi-fi, breakfast is included and half of the rooms have en-suite toilets. Also, there's a big Chinggis Khaan poster decorating the place – bonus.

**Tansag Hotel** HOTEL $$
(7051-2444, 7051-2644; filer.qualifier.bless; s T30,000-50,000, d T35,000-50,000; P) The bright yellow Tansag, decorated with fabulously ridiculous Egyptian-themed wallpaper, is located in a newish building on the east side of the main square. The lux rooms are somewhat bigger than the compact half-lux options; all have fancy showers with fairly reliable hot water. Wi-fi is erratic.

## Eating

**Tansag** MONGOLIAN $
(filer.qualifier.bless; mains T4000-16,000; 7.30am-midnight) There will be few surprises with the mutton-heavy menu at the Tansag Hotel's on-site restaurant, but they do serve a decent kimchi soup.

**Gun Bulag Zoog** CHINESE $
(Гүн Булаг Зоог; fact.shining.plankton; mains T3500-14,000; 9am-midnight) Gun Bulag Zoog offers a few Chinese dishes, along with beer and karaoke. It's along the street that runs from the northwest corner of the square.

## Drinking & Nightlife

**Smile Pub** BAR
(Смайл Зоогийн Газар; central.immune.cloud; 9am-midnight) The youngsters patronise this place, which has a small disco upstairs from a restaurant. Off the street that runs west from the northwest corner of the square.

## Information

**Khan Bank** (Хаан Банк; breakfast.ballroom.customers; 9am-1pm & 2-5pm Mon-Fri) Just to the west of the main square. Has an ATM.

**Telecom Office** (nitrate.puncture.complies; 24hr) The post office is also located here.

## Getting There & Away

### BUS

Buses and minivans depart from the **bus station** (tins.twitching.clear) just to the northwest of the main square. Two daily buses (T21,600, 11 hours) depart for Ulaanbaatar at 8am and 5pm. The same buses can drop you in Chinggis (T11,500, four to five hours, 229km).

### MINIVAN & 4WD

Shared vehicles (4WDs, minivans and cars) congregate by the bus station and leave when full for UB (T25,000); the fare is officially around T18,000 to Chinggis (229km), but many drivers will want to charge the full fare all the way to UB. It's cheaper to take the bus.

You could hire a minivan (T100,000 per day) or 4WD (T120,000 per day) here as well; rates do not include petrol.

# Dariganga    Дарьганга

POP 3000

The vast grasslands of Dariganga are speckled with volcanic craters, small lakes and sand dunes, the sum of which makes the area one of the most scenic in eastern Mongolia. Before communism, this area was a haven of aristocracy and its grasslands were the royal grazing grounds of horses belonging to the emperor in Běijīng. Silversmiths and blacksmiths made their homes here, providing local women with elaborate fine jewellery that now features prominently in Ulaanbaatar's National Museum of Mongolia (p57). These days, Dariganga is all about sacred mountains, one in town, and the other – Shiliin Bogd Uul – a shortish drive away. With a 4WD and a good driver you can also explore the lakes, volcanoes, caves, sand dunes and ancient stones nearby.

## ◎ Sights

All around the village, you'll see **sand dunes** creeping to the edge of Dariganga's grid. These natural landscape features are known as Moltsog Els (Молцог Элс) and stretch for some 20km into the countryside.

In the steppe around the town there are dozens of broken *balbals* (stones carved into roughly human shape, believed to be Turkic grave markers) – mostly dating back to the 13th- or 14th-century Mongol period. According to tradition, you should place an offering of food in the cup held in the statue's left hand. The three main *balbal* sights, on the north edge of town, consist of the **King and Queen** (GPS: N 45°18.507', E 113°51.711'; ///potions.spitefully.posse), the nearby **Son** (GPS: N 45°18.541', E 113°51.221'; ///additions.unimproved.stoops) and, finally, a short walk away, the **Bride** (GPS: N 45°18.512', E 113°51.214'; ///motored.cushions.exuberantly), to whom women make offerings in the hope of having healthy babies.

★ **Ganga Nuur**    LAKE
(Ганга Нуур; GPS: N45° 15.994', E113° 59.874'; ///slumber.than.graphite; per person/car T1500/500; P ) From the end of September until mid-October, this lake is home to thouands of migrating swans. Along the shore, in a fenced compound, is delicious spring water that's safe to drink. If you don't fancy paying the car entry fee you can park by the gate and walk. Ganga Nuur is about 13km southeast of Dariganga.

**Altan Ovoo**    RELIGIOUS SITE
(Алтан Овоо, Golden Ovoo; GPS: N 45°18.690', E 113°50.180'; ///unjustly.afterschool.shrieks) The skyline of the neat little town of Dariganga is dominated by Altan Ovoo, an extinct volcano topped by a **stupa**, which only men are allowed to visit. The stupa was built in 1990 on top of the ruins of the original Bat Tsagaan stupa, which was built in 1820 and destroyed in 1937. It's a short but steep climb to the top.

The men-only rule is enforced here. At the base of the flat-topped hill there are a couple of stupas that women are allowed to visit, and they do so with gusto, making copious offerings.

**Toroi-Bandi Statue**    MONUMENT
(GPS: N 45°17.305', E 114°04.465'; ///orienteers.colossus.pimples) Looking like the bad-ass hero of an excellent action movie we really hope gets optioned one day, the seated figure of Toroi-Bandi – the Robin Hood of Mongolia – pointedly stares across the steppe to China. You can almost hear the sculpture whisper, 'I'll be back'. Bandi's claim to fame was stealing horses from the Manchurians, then eluding them by hiding at Shiliin Bogd Uul and in his cave.

The statue is located on the road between Dariganga and Shiliin Bogd, 8km past Ganga Nuur.

**Ovoon Khiid**    BUDDHIST MONASTERY
(Овоон Хийд; ///undulations.takeaway.fashioning; ◷ hours vary) In the village you can visit the small Ovoon Khiid, which was built in 1990 (and has probably not been repainted since) and is served by a handful of monks.

## ⊨ Sleeping

**Gangar Khun Tourist Camp**    TOURIST GER CAMP $$
(✆ 9821 0922, 9604 0696; gangar_hun@yahoo.com; GPS: N 45°17.0149', E 113°57.8513'; ///markings.generic.acquitting; ger & cabin from T40,000; P ) This enormous ger camp, located between Dariganga village and Ganga Nuur, includes rows of well-appointed gers, cabins, clean outhouse facilities, working shower blocks and a decent kitchen for Mongolian meals. The chatty owners don't speak English, but they love foreign guests. They can arrange horse treks in the area (from T10,000 per hour).

# ⓘ Information

Permits are required for Dariganga; you'll hit checkpoints on the roads leading into town, so have paperwork in order and register yourself with the border guard.

If you are coming from Dornod you shouldn't have any trouble getting to Shiliin Bogd and on to Dariganga; this allows you to travel directly from the Khalkhiin Gol area and Dornod Mongol Strictly Protected Area, bypassing Choibalsan and Baruun-Urt. This is the most scenic drive in eastern Mongolia and will be faster than heading back through Choibalsan. Make sure you have this route listed on your border permit.

## ⓘ Getting There & Away

Shared 4WDs (T15,000, four hours) connect Dariganga with Baruun-Urt on Wednesday, Friday and Sunday (provided there's enough demand). A postal truck runs every Thursday from Baruun-Urt at 8am; you should reserve a ticket the day before.

If you're driving here from Dornod, you'll pass a weird stretch of paved road that exists solely for the benefit of a local oil field.

One or two 4WDs (T100,000 per day) should be available to hire if you ask around the 4WD stand in the centre of town.

# Shiliin Bogd Uul
### Шилийн Богд Уул

The plains of Dariganga are littered with the calderas of extinct volcanoes, lonely mountains that have been rounded into soft cupolas by the omnipresent wind. It's a dramatic landscape, one that feels powerfully raw to both visitors and Mongolians; for the latter, no area is more holy than the 1778m **Shiliin Bogd Uul** (Шилийн Богд Уул; GPS: N 45°28.509', E 114°35.909'; � ///truly.frictional.captioning), one of the most sacred mountains in Mongolia. This peak and the rolling steppe that proceeds from it form a gorgeous panorama. The only drawback is the gender rule that ostensibly keeps women from climbing to the top of Shiliin Bogd Uul.

# ⊙ Sights & Activities

**Taliin Agui**                                      CAVE
(Талын Агуй; GPS: N 45°35.417', E 114°30.044'; ///speckled.arrogantly.unlicensed) Imagine a cave of utter darkness where the walls glitter like lost stars and the interior feels like an icebox, even in the heart of summer. This, folks, is the reality of Taliin Agui, one of the largest caves in the nation. To access the cave's grandest chambers, you have to scrabble on hands and knees through a narrow crack – if you're claustrophobic, this is a sure recipe for a potentially very dangerous panic attack.

The odd glow of the cave's walls is caused by ice crystals, which are evident up until late spring. You'll need a torch for exploration. The cave is believed to project positive energy, and is visited by wrestlers seeking victory. It is located about 15km from Shiliin Bogd Uul. Assuming that you have a 4WD to get to Shiliin Bogd Uul in the first place, good hiking can be done on the Taliin Agui loop tour: depart Dariganga, take in Ganga Nuur on the way to Shiliin Bogd Uul, then stop by Taliin Agui on the way back to Dariganga.

## ⌷ Sleeping

**Taliin Agui Ger Camp**      TOURIST GER CAMP $$
(☑ 9926 1659, 9606 1659; GPS: N 45°35.376', E 114°29.869'; ///resented.chevrons.artful; ger from T40,000; ℗ ) This large ger camp is located next to the cave of the same name. The gers are basic and comfy, there are pit toilets onsite, and horse treks can be arranged. Meals are also available, or you can cook your own food in the lodge.

## ⓘ Getting There & Away

The only two roads to Shiliin Bogd start from Erdenetsagaan (70km) and Dariganga (70km). If you are coming from the Buir Nuur/Khalkhgol area, once you've passed Tamsagbulag, a sometimes muddy shortcut road cuts across the countryside to the main road leading to the Chinese border near Erdenetsagaan. It runs close to the border of the Eastern Mongolia Nature Reserve, home of the endangered gazelle, and runs through an oil field (also, alarmingly, located near said nature reserve).

# The Gobi

POP 288,300

## Best Places to Eat

➡ Three Camel Lodge (p184)
➡ IkhNart Wilderness Camp (p175)
➡ Uran Khairkhan (p187)

## Best Places to Stay

➡ Three Camel Lodge (p184)
➡ IkhNart Wilderness Camp (p175)
➡ Secret of Ongi Tourist Camp (p171)

## Why Go?

The Gobi reveals itself in pockets of amazing scenery, bridged by vast stretches of desolation where smartphone signals die and silence saturates. It can be daunting to be this far out in such harsh conditions, but this is where desert foliage shimmers in greens and golds, and where Tibetan lamas etched ancient messages on red rock cliffs. You'll watch horses romp and gazelles sprint, hear goats and sheep cry, and commiserate with camels huddling in fierce winds that gather and roll across the steppe. At night galaxies erupt on the domed sky.

No wonder it's one of Mongolia's top-draw regions, promising colossal sand dunes, ice-filled canyons, dinosaur fossils, camel treks, and hospitable nomadic herders who will shower you with warmth, and more than a little milky tea. So choose one of those criss-crossed two-wheel tracks and follow it ever deeper into the mystery.

## When to Go
### Dalanzadgad

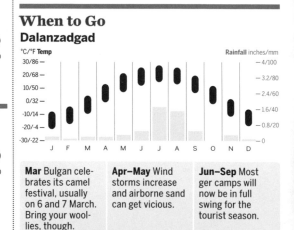

**Mar** Bulgan celebrates its camel festival, usually on 6 and 7 March. Bring your woollies, though.

**Apr–May** Wind storms increase and airborne sand can get vicious.

**Jun–Sep** Most ger camps will now be in full swing for the tourist season.

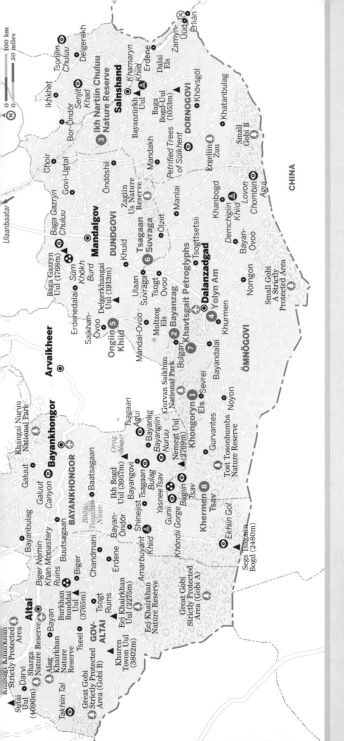

## The Gobi Highlights

**1** Taking one step forward and sliding three steps back on awesome sand dunes at **Khongoryn Els** (p180).

**2** Going fossil hunting at the beautiful 'flaming cliffs' of **Bayanzag** (p177), rich in dinosaur bones and fossil eggs.

**3** Scrambling up rock formations and searching for argali (mountain sheep) at **Ikh Nartiin Chuluu** (p175).

**4** Looking out for ibexes as you trek through **Yolyn Am** (p180), an ice-filled canyon with vultures soaring above.

**5** Camping by the river before picking your way through **Ongiin Khiid's** (p170) ruins.

**6** Taking in the mineral-streaked sandstone majesty of the White Stupa at **Tsagaan Suvarga** (p170).

**7** Searching for prehistoric rock carvings that overlook the desert at **Khavtsgait Petroglyphs** (p181).

**8** Getting truly off the beaten track and venturing south to **Khermen Tsav** (p186) a canyon spossibly more spectacular than Bayanzag.

## ❶ Getting There & Away

There are plenty of shared minivans, taxis and jeeps, as well as the (normally) daily public buses, heading from Ulaanbaatar (UB) to all the Gobi aimag (province) capitals. Remember the travel times given are indicative only and don't take into account breakdowns and time spent in *guanz* (canteens) drinking *airag* (fermented mare's milk) and watching sumo. Flying is also an option to Dalanzadgad (daily) and Altai (once weekly). If you are travelling on local trains from China, it's possible to enter Mongolia at Zamyn-Üüd and continue on to Gobi towns such as Sainshand, although organising Gobi tours is best done in UB.

## ❶ Getting Around

There are good paved roads connecting Dalanzadgad, Bayankhongor and Altai to Ulaanbaatar, but in general, Gobi infrastructure is almost nonexistent. Still, the lack of roads does not prevent vehicles from getting around. On the contrary, the rock-hard jeep trails are the best in the country, and sometimes jeeps, Landcruisers and those old Russian vans reach speeds of 100km/h, eliciting thrills if an unexpected rise sends them airborne.

Breakdowns in the Gobi can be deadly, and you shouldn't think of setting off without a reliable vehicle and driver, a good sense of direction and plenty of water.

Annoyingly, public transport between aimag capitals is practically nil, and rarer still out to national parks and other attractions. As it's easier to get off a bus heading back to Ulaanbaatar than trying to hop on an already full one on its way out, a good plan is to travel to your furthest destination first and work your way back to the capital.

If you are hitching, you will have the best chance of success if you ask around at markets, bus stations or any places selling petrol. Hitching is never entirely safe, and we don't recommend it. Travellers who hitch should understand that they are taking a small but potentially serious risk.

# DUNDGOVI    ДУНДГОВЬ

POP 38,500 / AREA 75,000 SQ KM

Dundgovi (middle Gobi) is something of a misnomer. The aimag would be best described as 'northern Gobi', as this area is the northernmost extent of the Gobi Desert. Lying just a few hours' drive south of Ulaanbaatar, it's also one of the most convenient Gobi regions to explore.

Dundgovi's allure lies in its mysterious rock formations, which mainly appear at two locations: Baga Gazryn Chuluu (p168)

and Ikh Gazryn Chuluu (Их Газрын Чулуу; Ⓜ descend.rescheduled.fudgy; T5000). At both you'll find large granite pinnacles and winding canyons that make for fantastic hiking and bouldering. The water that manages to collect in these areas supports wildlife such as argali sheep and ibexes.

---

# Mandalgov    Мандалговь

Ⓙ 01592, 7059 / POP 13,660 / ELEV 1427M

Mandalgov came into existence in 1942 and originally consisted of only 40 gers. Today it's a sleepy, rather charmless town that offers the usual amenities for an aimag capital: a hotel, a monastery, a surprisingly good museum and a few shops. A walk to the top of Mandalin Khar Ovoo, just north of the town centre, affords sweeping views of the bleak terrain. There is more to see in western Dundgovi, but Mandalgov can be a useful stop-off on the overland route to Dalanzadgad. You don't need to spend the night, however.

## ◉ Sights

**Byamba's Tree Nursery**    PARK

(Ⓙ 9959 8468; www.gobioasis.com; Ⓜ herbivorous.grabby.frowning) ✒ Retired forest engineer and local conservationist Byamba Tseyen helped establish, and now maintains, this small tree-planting nursery on the edge of town, in an attempt to fend off desertification from the Gobi's shifting sands. She and her family have planted more than 10,000 trees and shrubs here, and you can help their cause by planting one of your own. The equivalent of US$10 will get you lunch at their family home, and a sapling, which they will then help you plant.

**Mandalgov Museum**    MUSEUM

(Ⓙ 1592-23690; Buyan Emekhiin Gudamj, Ⓜ contagious.headsets.splinters; T2000; ☉ 8am-6pm) This enjoyable and informative museum is divided into two main sections: a taxidermy-heavy natural history section and a more interesting ethnography and historical section where you'll peruse a collection of priceless *thangkas* (scroll paintings), old flintlock rifles, bronze arrowheads, silver snuffboxes, pipes, chess sets carved out of ivory, and an unnerving collection of, ahem, castration knives.

# Mandalgov

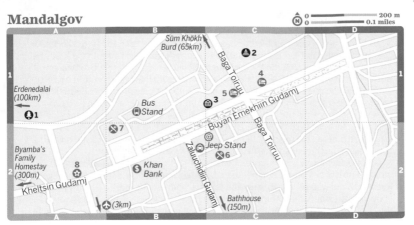

Süm Khökh
Burd (65km)

Erdenedalai
(100km)

Bus
Stand

Byamba's
Family
Homestay
(300m)

Kheltsin Gudamj

(3km)

Khan
Bank

Jeep Stand

Zaluuchiidiin Gudamj

Baga Toiruu

Buyan Emekhiin Gudamj

Baga Toiruu

Bathhouse
(150m)

200 m
0.1 miles

---

**Dashgimpeliin Khiid**     BUDDHIST MONASTERY
(Дашгимпэлийн Хийд; [M]subset.forged.soils; ⊘closed Thu) In 1936 there were 53 temples in Dundgovi; a year later the Mongolian KGB reduced nearly all to ash and rubble. In 1991 Dashgimpeliin Khiid was opened for the people of Mandalgov. Around 30 monks now serve the monastery, and services are held most days at around 10am and 2pm. It's 300m northeast of **Hotel Mandal** (☑8833 9111; www.mandalhoteldundgobi.mn; Baga Toiruu, [M]seeping.expanding.defensively; s/tw/q T40,000/60,000/85,000, lux tw T150,000; ⊛).

## 🛏 Sleeping

⭐**Byamba's Family Homestay**    HOMESTAY $
(☑9876 3202, 9959 8468; www.gobioasis.com; A 6-13 Kheltsin Gudamj, [M]narrowed.patches.rebuts; per person with meals & tree $50, without meals T20,000; ⊛) 🖉 Byamba Tseyen, who manages the nearby tree nursery (p166), also opens up her family compound to guests. Accommodation is inside one of two guest gers located in her yard. Both are clean, comfortable and come with a warm welcome and tasty home-cooked meals. As part of the package, guests are given a tree sapling to plant in the nursery.

**Gobi Hotel**      HOTEL $$
(☑9115 2771, 1592-23690; Buyan Emekhiin Gudamj, [M]shameful.fishing.chopping; s/d T30,000/50,000; ⊛) The building is past its prime and those rooms aren't ageing well either, but they are clean with plenty of light, though some ceilings have water stains. Doable for a night.

## Mandalgov

◎ **Sights**
1 Byamba's Tree Nursery .....................A1
2 Dashgimpeliin Khiid ..........................C1
3 Mandalgov Museum .........................C1

🛏 **Sleeping**
4 Gobi Hotel ..........................................C1
5 Hotel Mandal......................................C1

⊗ **Eating**
6 Gobi Anu............................................C2
7 Urgoo Restaurant.............................B2

⊕ **Entertainment**
8 Central Mongolian Concert
    Theatre ...............................................A2

## ✕ Eating

⭐**Urgoo Restaurant**      KOREAN $
([M]sublimated.snaked.haggis; mains T5000-8000; ⊘9am-7pm) This Korean restaurant, the best in town, is set on the 1st floor of a permanent ger structure behind the main government building off the main square. They offer a mix of hotpots, and fried, sweet chicken and pork dishes, served up on prim tables decorated with fake flowers in a dining room with parquet floors.

**Gobi Anu**      MONGOLIAN $
([M]snapping.amends.inhaling; mains T4000-5000; ⊘9am-10pm) This clean and friendly *guanz* (canteen) knocks out all the usuals: *buuz* (dumplings), *khuushuur* (fried mutton pancakes), *tsuivan* (fried noodles). No English menu or sign, but there is (lukewarm) beer.

## MONGOLIA'S PRODIGAL SON

In the 1930s, with the socialist-led purges gathering steam, a beloved Mongolian *Rinpoche*, Jambal Dorje, fled to Tibet to study and work alongside the Dalai Lama. In the 1950s he and much of the Tibetan Buddhist community would flee again, this time to Dharamsala. But India didn't feel like home and he would soon land in Jersey City and start a temple.

His presence there helped sprout a Mongolian community that flourished in Manhattan's long shadow. One of their own, Jalsa Urubshurow, who arrived as a toddler and grew up poor, became one of the most successful building contractors on the east coast of the US. Once the Cold War ended, Urubshurow launched a second career, as a tour leader and hotelier. His mission, then as now, is to use a revitalised tourist industry to help provide much-needed jobs for young Mongolians.

When Urubshurow first returned home in 1990, Mongolia received roughly 100 foreign tourists per year. He remembers the shops being bare in the city. That good Russian bread was gone, with only salt for sale wherever he looked. Things were better in the countryside, where nomadic herder families took him in. He would soon launch the North American Mongolian business council and start Nomadic Expeditions, his tour company. In 2002 he opened Three Camel Lodge (p184), arguably the finest hotel in the country. In addition to providing jobs, he has built wells that water 17,000 goats, sheep, camels and horses belonging to area herders. He's also helped launch the Eagle Festival in west Mongolia, and has become one of Mongolia's most effective tourism ambassadors.

## 🛈 Information

Like most second (or third) tier cities in Mongolia, Mandalgov has an **internet cafe** (per hour T900; ⊙ 9am-10pm) in the local Telecom office. **Khan Bank** (⊙ 9am-6pm Mon-Fri, 10am-4pm Sat) changes US dollars and has an ATM.

## 🛈 Getting There & Away

### BUS

A **bus** leaves every day at 8am and 2pm for Ulaanbaatar (T13,200, four to five hours, 260km). The bus from Ulaanbaatar on its way to Dalanzadgad (nine hours, 293km) passes sometime between noon and 3pm. If there's room, tickets cost T13,200.

### JEEP & MINIVAN

Daily shared jeeps to Ulaanbaatar (T15,000, four hours) leave when full from the **jeep stand** near the Telecom office. You're unlikely to find a shared jeep to Dalanzadgad (T20,000, seven hours), but Dalanzadgad-bound jeeps coming from Ulaanbaatar might be able to squeeze you in. Wait for these at the petrol station at the south end of town.

## Baga Gazryn Chuluu Nature Reserve

### Бага Газрын Чулуу

The spectacular granite-rock formations of **Baga Gazryn Chuluu** (Бага Газрын Чулуу; *//*/lightbulbs.donation.stateless; T5000) – which translates as 'rocks in a small place' – rise in the middle of the dusty plains, and once sheltered Zanabazar during conflicts between the Khalkh and Oirat Mongols. In the summer, these red rock mountains are dusted with lichen and provide a dramatic contrast against the light-green grasslands and stark blue sky. Lucky visitors may glimpse the odd ibex rambling among the rocks. If you're headed south from Ulaanbaatar this is where the real business of the Gobi begins, and it's quite a gateway.

## ◉ Sights

**Süm Khökh Burd**                     RUINS
(Сум Хөх Бүрд; GPS: N 46°09.621', E 105°45.590'; *//*/emotions.stalemated.supremely) The ruined 10th-century temple Süm Khökh Burd sits on an island in the middle of a seasonal lake, and was built from rocks that can only be found more than 300km away. It was abandoned and left in ruins a few centuries later and 300 years ago a palace was built in its place. When that too fell into disrepair, the writer Danzan Ravjaa built a stage here. Makes sense. The setting is that dramatic.

Behind it, enough of the temple and palace remain to give you some idea of their previous magnificence. Even in ruins, with needle grass sprouting between the stones, it's an impressive sight, thanks largely to its remote location. In the evening when guests are on the premises, the ruins are lit up magnificently. However, it's largely the domain of luxury tour groups and Buddhist scholars, and outside of July the grounds may be locked (we hopped the fence, which is easily done). During peak season, you may be lucky enough to stumble upon a naadam performance staged on the concrete amphitheatre which fronts the ruins.

The lake itself, **Sangiin Dalai Nuur**, only encircles the palace after heavy rains, but the perennial marsh provides good **birdwatching**. Various species of eagle, goose and swan come to this spring-fed lake in summer and autumn.

The temple is located 72km northeast of Erdenedalai, 65km northwest of Mandalgov and 21km west of Baga Gazryn Chuluu.

### Usan Bolortiin Agui                    CAVE

(GPS: N 46°12.686' E 106°01.717'; [///] clump.khakis. trekking) This cave has a funnel-like opening through which you can squeeze into a ger-sized cavern 18m below. One hundred years ago it glowed with quartz crystal, but Chinese miners plundered the bounty in the 1920s. Still, the odd quartz rock may be found glowing amid the rubble. There's also a tiny **freshwater spring** (GPS: N 46°12.249' E 106°01.135'; [///] hourly.frameless.stouts) nearby.

## 🏃 Activities

The highest peak in the area, **Baga Gazryn Uul** (1768m), takes about an hour to climb. The freshwater springs (if you can find them) and gnarled Siberian elm trees in the region make it a great spot to camp, and there are plenty of rocky hills topped by *ovoos* (shamanistic offerings to the gods) to explore.

## 🛏 Sleeping

### Naarka Family Ger Camp           HOMESTAY $

([✆] 9819 0868; [///] tinker.remand.prestige; per person $10) Three tidy if basic guest gers are situated behind this nomadic family's summer campsite, which they've used for eight generations. There are petroglyphs on the rocks behind the gers, and their children speak some basic English. No showers. Food is available for a couple of dollars per meal.

### Baga Gazar Camp           TOURIST GER CAMP $$

([✆] 9959 5555; [///] towers.hosting.blinding; per person with/without meals US$35/16; ⊙ Apr-Oct) Opened in 2013, here are 20 tidy gers set on stone foundations, surrounding a main bathhouse and a hexagonal dining room where you can tuck into vegetarian meals if

### THE LOST TREASURE OF DANZAN RAVJAA

Tall tales about Noyon Khutagt Danzan Ravjaa (1803–56), a hot-headed rebellious monk, a writer and popular leader of Mongolia's Red Hat Buddhists, are legion. It is said that he could fly to Tibet in an instant, disappear into thin air and turn water into whisky. At age six he was proclaimed the Fifth Gobi Lord, even though the Manchus had forbidden another after executing his predecessor.

Danzan Ravjaa would spend months in solitude writing, either in caves or in his ger, and his fame as a writer, artist and social critic spread far and wide. He was also an expert at martial arts, tantric studies, yoga and traditional medicine.

His mysterious death came at the hands of either the rival Yellow Hat Buddhist sect or a jealous queen who failed to gain his love. During his life, Danzan Ravjaa amassed a collection of statues, paintings, original manuscripts, opera costumes and ritual objects. It eventually fell to a man called Tuduv, the hereditary *takhilch* (caretaker) of Danzan Ravjaa's legacy, to protect these treasures during the 1937 communist purges. Every night, under the cover of darkness and in total secrecy, Tuduv buried a crate of treasure in the shifting sands of the Gobi. He only had time to bury 64 of the 1500 crates before the Khamaryn Khiid (monastery) was destroyed.

The only man alive today who knows the location of the buried crates is Zundoi Altangerel (Tuduv's grandson and the fifth *takhilch*), and in 1990 he retrieved all but 17 of them to found the Museum of Danzan Ravjaa in Sainshand (p172). Then in 2009, much to the delight of a worldwide audience courtesy of a live webcast (www.gobi-treasure.com), Altangerel dug up two more crates. In 2013 the ninth reincarnation of the Noyon Khutagt, a young man named Danzan Luvsan Tudev, was identified and installed as the head of the monastery in an elaborate ceremony that attracted more than 10,000 people.

For more information on Danzan Ravjaa, pick up a copy of his biography *Lama of the Gobi* (Blacksmith Books, 2010), by Michael Kohn.

THE GOBI BAGA GAZRYN CHULUU NATURE RESERVE

## TSAGAAN SUVARGA

Imagine a 400m-long jigsaw of white-sand cliffs, striped pastel shades of purple, orange and red, and the thrumming beat of swallows' wings as they zoom toward the cliffs, veering off at the last heartbeat before impact. Now, move toward the edge (be careful not to get too close to an eroding overhang). Look down, and you'll see more of the same: white sand, streaked with minerals formed into a rolling landscape of colour, before finally flattening into big sky plains. That's the scene awaiting you at **Tsagaan Suvarga** (Цагаан Суварга; White Stupa; ⓜ learnt.lonesome.tramway), a sight similar to Bayanzag, but with much more colour and a sliver of the tourism footprint.

Most visitors merely walk along the cliff top, then find a trail down to the mounds that roll along the valley floor. The photo ops are tremendous and there are two sleeping options nearby too.

**Gobi Suvarga** (☑ 9998 3003; per person with/without meals T90,000/50,000) A basic midrange ger camp at research time, with 20 tidy gers each sleeping up to three guests.

**Zorigoo Homestay** (☑ 9865 7233; per person T10,000) The gers here are clean and cheery, although some smell better than others.

Tsagaan Suvarga is set in the desert, east of the highway connecting Ulaanbaatar to Dalanzadgad. It's roughly 180km south of Mandalgov and 160km northeast of Dalanzadgad. There is no public transport option; you'll need to have your own wheels.

arranged in advance. This is the best tourist camp in the area. Each ger offers one to four beds, so couples can cuddle up here.

### ❶ Getting There & Away

Baga Gazryn Chuluu is about 60km north by northwest of Mandalgov, and about 21km east of Süm Khökh Burd.

## Erdenedalai   Эрдэнэдалай

Erdenedalai, a seasonal camel-herding community in the middle of nowhere (114km northwest of Mandalgov), is known for the shape-shifting old monastery **Gimpil Darjaalan Khiid** (ⓜ fuzzily.pleads.lobs; T5000), which survived Stalin's purges by becoming a warehouse and shop. The small, dusty town that sprouted up around it has rudimentary tourist facilities, including a bathhouse and a decent supermarket.

There are a couple of very basic guesthouses (per person T20,000) here, but basic places in tiny *sums* like these are seldom well looked after, and may not be in any condition to sleep in when you arrive. Our advice? Bring camping supplies or find a ger in which to nest.

About 25km north of Erdenedalai, the **Middle Gobi Camp** (☑ 9912 8783; GPS: N 46°08.816', E 105°11.013'; ⓜ ducking.grooms.piggyback; per person with/without meals from US$40/20; ☺ May-Sep) is not a bad place to spend the night if you are headed in this direction.

There is no restaurant of note in Erdenedalai.

Although Erdenedalai is small, it is on a major jeep trail so a few vehicles come through every day. You may be able to find passage to Mandalgov (114km, two hours).

## Ongiin Khiid   Онгийн Хийд

Once a place of devotion and Buddhist scholarship, Ongiin Khiid houses the largest and most important ruins in the Gobi. Nearly a century ago, and for more than 120 years before that, this mountainous nook, nestled on the Ongiin Gol River, was home to 28 Buddhist temples and four universities. All that changed once socialism arrived in the 1930s. Soon after, soldiers showed up to massacre 200 lamas and destroy the entire complex. What's left are monochromatic ruins and an eerie energy that may move you. It's set in the western *sum* (district) of Saikhan-Ovoo and, despite its dark history, makes a pleasant stop en route to the southern Gobi.

### ❍ Sights

★ **Ongiin Khiid**                    BUDDHIST MONASTERY
(Онгийн Хийд; GPS: N 45°20.367', E 104°00.306'; ⓜ roofs.unwise.dislodges; T3000) The bend in the river here marks the remains of two ruined monasteries which are today considered one vast complex known as Ongiin Khiid. **Bari Lam Khiid** was built in 1810 on the north bank, the same side of the river

as the area's tourist ger camps. **Khutagt Lam Khiid** was built in 1760 on the south. It was formerly one of the largest monasteries in Mongolia, and home to over a thousand monks.

In the monasteries' heyday there were 17 temples on the northern side of the river and 11 on its southern bank, along with four Buddhist universities. After the murder and destruction of the 1937 Communist purges, other lamas suffered forced conscription into the communist army and still others ran away to become herders and hopefully live in peace.

After the temple was destroyed the river was soon rerouted to support local mines run by the communist government, and when the river dried up local herders were forced out of the area in search of water. Happily, once the Cold War ended in 1990 a small but growing contingent of monks arrived to set up shop amid the ruins, completing a small temple in 2004 and incorporating some original beams from the old ruined monastery in the new structure. A few monks live here full-time, and every morning, before an altar flickering with candles and graced with a framed photo of the Dalai Lama, they worship and chant. Services begin at roughly 9am and last until about noon. You are welcome to join them. In summer their numbers swell.

The ger beside the temple houses a small but interesting **museum** showcasing some artefacts found at the site, many of which were hidden by monks to save them from the purges. Views of the monochromatic mudbrick ruins and the surrounding area are impressive from the ibex monument at the top of the complex, where you can find broken original roof tiles.

**Khutagt Lam Khiid** can only be accessed when the water level of the river is low, or when the river is iced over in winter.

## Sleeping

**Ongiin Khiid Camp** TOURIST GER CAMP **$**
(☎8600 5256, main camp phone 8816 7078, reservations 9666 5256; ///situated.radars.switchboards; ger per person T15,000; P) The smallest and best-value ger camp at Ongiin Khiid features a canteen built to look like a castle. It stays open year-round and has clean, comfortable gers, with four beds and hand-painted doors overlooking a bend in the river. They offer hot showers (T5000) and meals (T7000 to T8000) to all comers.

**Ongi Energy Camp** TOURIST GER CAMP **$$**
(☎8919 8980; www.facebook.com/ongienergytouristcamp; ///mucking.magnifier.blanking; per person with/without meals T80,000/35,000) This recently rebranded camp features a small restaurant with fine river views, and a games building with table tennis and a pool table. They have showers, and 30 well-kept gers decorated with floral tapestries and connected by stone and concrete paths. The staff are warm and speak some English.

**★ Secret of Ongi Tourist Camp** TOURIST GER CAMP **$$$**
(☎9888 6800; www.mongoliansecrethistory.mn; ///magnets.nagging.intricate; s/d with meals $90/160, s/d without meals US$50/82, mains T8000-12,000; P @) This is the most comfortable place to stay. The big draw is the log-and-stone restaurant-bar, reminiscent of a Chinese-style temple, the smart gers with curved wooden doors, and some of the cleanest toilets and showers in the Gobi, though some of the gers are showing their age. Nonguests can use the showers (T5000), sauna (T20,000) and massage services (T35,000 to T60,000).

## Getting There & Away

Ongiin Khiid is set 180km due north of Bayanzag, and 190km southwest of Mandalgov. It is not served by public transport – you'll have to charter private transportation.

# Ikh Gazryn Chuluu

From afar, the remote Gobi nature reserve Ikh Gazryn Chuluu looks jumbled and its jagged peaks part of a close-knit mountain range, but drive closer and you'll see independent rock formations, some rounded like giant boulders, others elongated and stacked like abstract totems, as if the gods themselves worshipped Picasso. It almost feels like another planet, one that's pock-marked with caves, run through with canyons and blessed with excellent rock-climbing opportunities.

There are four main caves in the area. **Ehynumay Cave** (GPS: N 45°44.389', E 107°13.271'; ///admits.mockery.unglued), 'mother's vagina', is set just 2.5km southwest of the park ranger's camp; if you'd like to be born again, step inside, climb up and out a small skylight and ramble down the rocks to the valley floor. **Toonotaguy Cave** also has great views from its mouth and a chute that leads to an opening with more amazing views on the other side.

About 1.5km south of the ranger's camp is a rather surreal open-air theatre. **Norovbanzad Theatre** (GPS: N 45°43.913', E 107°15.005'), named in honour of a famous Mongolian long-song singer, holds concerts during the local naadam festival. There's also a **monument** to Norovbanzad, set atop a windswept hill, which is crowned with a monolith carved with a dedication in Mongolian script. The views from here are breathtaking.

You can overnight at the comfortable **Töv Borjigan Ger Camp** (☑9976 9266; GPS: N 45°45.664', E 107°15.977'; per person with/without meals US$60/50). Two kilometres away, just over the rocks to the southwest, the park ranger has a couple of basic **guest gers** (☑9589 4489; GPS: N 45°44.902', E 107°14.902'; ⓜdescend.rescheduled.fudgy; per person T10,000) in his family home. The camping around here is magnificent too.

# DORNOGOVI ДОРНОГОВЬ

POP 57,930 / AREA 109,500 SQ KM

Dornogovi (eastern Gobi) unfurls like film through a viewfinder past the train window, where a seemingly infinite landscape of green and gold grasses rolls by. This steppe teems with camels and horses, goats and sheep, and sprouts with the occasional hard scrabble *sum* punctuated by decaying socialist relics. Through it all the bucking, rocking rhythm of the coach will lull you like a baby's carriage, until it all feels like a peaceful dream.

Such is the first taste of Mongolia experienced by many overlanders, as the train line from Běijīng to Ulaanbaatar blazes straight through the eastern Gobi. The railway supports local trade while the rest of the economy rides on the back of uranium development, coal and small-scale oil extraction. It is the transport links that attract most foreign visitors, but there is a spectacular nature reserve here too, and it is not to be missed.

## Sainshand     Сайншанд

☑01522, 7052 / POP 20,515 / ELEV 938M

The aimag capital of Sainshand seems to rise out of the dust. It's divided into two parts: a cluster of homes and businesses around the train station, and the more developed centre, 2km south, where you'll find most of the action. It is not a tourist town by any conceivable measure, but a nearby monastery and a couple of museums in town are worth a look. Plus, the sunsets ooze pastels. Daily trains barrel through carrying coal and flesh, energy and blood, to the Chinese border, less than three hours away.

## ◉ Sights

**Museum of Danzan Ravjaa**     MUSEUM
(☑1522-23221; www.danzanravjaa.org; ⓜswirls.shavers.sackful; T2000; ◉9am-8pm) The life and achievements of Noyon Khutagt Danzan Ravjaa (1803–56), a well-known Mongolian writer, composer, painter and medic who was born about 100km southwest of Sainshand, are honoured in this small but well-put-together museum. Look out for the glass jar which contains Danzan Ravjaa's bones; his mummified body was burned along with his monastery in the 1930s.

**Sainshand Natural**
**History Museum**     MUSEUM
(☑1522-22657; ⓜcurvature.capful.privileges; T2000; ◉9am-1pm & 2-6pm) This well-appointed museum houses plenty of stuffed Gobi animals, and a collection of seashells and marine fossils (Dornogovi was once beneath the sea). There is also an impressive skeleton of a Protoceratops and a dinosaur egg. Upstairs, look out for the wooden breastplate used by a Mongol soldier in the imperial days.

## 🛏 Sleeping & Eating

**Ikh Soyon Hotel**     HOTEL $
(ⓜfixture.truths.watchdog; d T35,000; @🛜) The decent, modern rooms have high ceilings, but are otherwise a bit cramped. Nice touches include wall-mounted flat screens and wood furnishings. It's right next to the market and jeep stand, and remains a solid choice, even if some rooms smell like an airport smoking lounge. The 2nd-floor Chinese **restaurant** (ⓜfixture.truths.watchdog; mains T10,000-21,000) is among the best in town.

★**Lux Hotel**     HOTEL $$
(☑9962 6152; ⓜannoyance.vendor.expensively; d T45,000-55,000; 🅿❄🛜) Boasting the most polished exterior of the hotels in town, Lux has a small spa and sauna on-site and good-sized rooms with recessed lighting, wood

furnishings and air-con. There's a hot-water kettle too. Easily the best hotel in town, even if service is a bit sour.

**Best Restaurant**              MONGOLIAN $
(✆ 9925 5579; ⌨ puns.hollered.disdains; meals T5000-10,000; ☺ 10am-11pm) Clean and friendly, this local favourite doles out excellent Mongolian dishes; they recommend the *bainshte shöl* (dumpling soup). Ask for the English menu – they only have one, and it sometimes takes a while to find. There's no sign but it's above a small supermarket.

## ❶ Information

**Internet Cafe** (⌨ kippers.allowances.jammy; per hour T900; ☺ 8am-10pm) In the Telecom building, along with the post office.

There are plenty of ATMs around town, at the local banks and in the lobby in the Telecom building.

**Khan Bank** (⌨ shopkeeper.complainant.elaborate) Has an ATM and changes US dollars.

**Trade & Development Bank** (⌨ huggable. crusaded.cornmeal; ☺ 9am-5pm Mon-Fri) Changes US-dollar travellers cheques and gives cash advances on MasterCard and Visa.

## ❶ Getting There & Away

Because at least two trains link Sainshand with Ulaanbaatar every day, there are no flights here. The well-maintained paved road connecting UB and Zamyn-Üüd makes catching a shared taxi to either possible.

### CAR & MOTORCYCLE

**Shared jeeps and taxis** (⌨ logo.jauntily. amber) park themselves by the market. Ask here for a taxi to Khamaryn Khiid (T50,000 to T60,000 return).

There are also shared taxis to Zamyn-Üüd (per person T20,000, 2½ hours). You can charter the whole taxi for T80,000.

### TRAIN

Departure times here are based on the summer schedule (May to September), and are subject to slight variations each year.

**UB to Sainshand** Train 286; departs 9.35am daily; arrives 8.15pm

**Sainshand to UB** Train 285; departs 9pm daily; arrives 8.05am

**UB to Zamyn-Üüd** Train 276; departs UB 4.30pm daily; arrives in Sainshand 1.38am

**Zamyn-Üüd to UB** Train 275; departs Sainshand 11pm daily; arrives in UB 9.25am

Tickets from Ulaanbaatar cost 9100/18,000/28,700 for hard seat/hard sleeper/soft sleeper.

# Sainshand

# Sainshand

If you book your ticket more than a day ahead there is a T800 to T1200 fee, although we found it fairly easy to buy same-day tickets to Ulaanbaatar from here. If you want to guarantee a private compartment, you'll have to buy up all four seats.

The Trans-Mongolian Railway and the trains between Ulaanbaatar and Èrlián (Ereen; just over the Chinese border) and Hohhot (in Inner Mongolia) stop at Sainshand, but you cannot use these services just to get to Sainshand unless you buy a ticket all the way to China.

## ❶ Getting Around

A shared taxi from the train station to the town centre costs T1000 per person during the day or night. You can walk the 2km in around 30 minutes. Walk away (south) from the station, turn right at the T-junction, then take the next left and keep walking up and over the hill.

# Khamaryn Khiid
## Хамарын Хийд

You'll hear desert winds whip the prayer flags on the campus of this expanding reconstructed **monastery** (Хамарын Хийд; GPS: N 44°36.038', E 110°16.650'; [m]misguided. likening.timely; ⊘ 9am-1pm & 2-6pm) an hour's drive south of Sainshand. Temples are colourful and alive with monks and their scrolls and drums. Halls smell of incense, and winds shift desert sands that bury paths between buildings. It's atmospheric to say the least and it developed around the cult of writer and leader of Mongolia's Red Hat Buddhists, Danzan Ravjaa (p169), who many locals believe was a living god. The original monastery and three-storey theatre, built by Danzan Ravjaa in 1821, was destroyed in the 1930s.

Beyond the campus is Ravjaa's revered **Shambhala** (T5000) site, where local followers come to chant and pray and feel his spirit. If you cross their paths you may be swept up in the moment and feel...something, even if it's just a contact high.

**Bayanzürkh Uul** (GPS: N 44°41.644', E 110°02.707'; [m]subjunctive.responsive.mildness) is the mountain home of the spirit of the third Noyon Khutagt (a predecessor of Danzan Ravjaa). The temple halfway up the mountain is as far as local women are allowed to go (no one seems to mind if foreign women go to the top). At the summit (1070m) you are required to make three wishes at the so-called 'wishing *ovoo*', and circle the peak. It's located around 23km northwest of Khamaryn Khiid.

## 🛏 Sleeping

If you plan on making anything other than a day trip to Khamaryn Khiid, it is worth noting that the monastery has only very basic facilities. You'll probably need a tent.

**Gobi Sunrise**
**Tavan Dohoi**                           TOURIST GER CAMP **$$**
(📞 9908 0151; GPS: N 44°45.418', E 110°11.236'; with/without meals US$45/12; 🅿) Set in the middle of a vast, deserted landscape, this comfortable ger camp has flush toilets and clean showers with hot water. To arrange transport to the camp, which is about 16km south of Sainshand, on the way to Khamaryn Khiid, ask **Altangerel** (📞 9909 0151), the curator at the Museum of Danzan Ravjaa (p172). He speaks English.

A taxi from town costs around T20,000 to T30,000 one way.

## ❶ Getting There & Away

A taxi from Sainshand to Khamaryn Khiid costs T50,000 to T60,000 return, including waiting time.

# Ikh Nartiin Chuluu

As you hike through its canyons and scramble up navigable rock towers in the Ikh Nartiin Chuluu Nature Reserve you'll notice the red earth is so mineral-rich, crystals gleam at your feet, which only magnifies the valley's beauty until it glows in your mind like a place of pure, almost spiritual, magic. Join the club. Here are prayer flags looped around *ovoo* and rock outcrops, there are prayer beads left as offerings beneath swallows nests. This is probably because it was once set on a spur of

---

**LOCAL KNOWLEDGE**

### RITUALS AT SHAMBHALA

There are several rituals to observe when you enter the Shambhala site. Try to do them in the following order.

➡ Write a bad thought on a piece of paper and burn it in the rocks to the left.

➡ Write down a wish, read it, throw some vodka in the air and drop some rice in the stone circles on the ground (representing the past, present and future).

➡ Take a white pebble from the ground, place it on the pile of other white pebbles and announce your family name.

➡ Take off your shoes and lie down on the ground, absorbing the energy of this sacred site.

➡ Circle the *ovoo* three times.

the Silk Road, and in the 19th century there was a Buddhist monastery here, home to 3000 lamas. The monastery was destroyed in the purges, but at a natural amphitheatre you'll still see Tibetan script carved into the rock. It reads: *Om Mani Padme Om* (for the sake of all sentient beings).

## ⊙ Sights

### ★ Ikh Nartiin
### Chuluu Nature Reserve                       NATURE RESERVE
(Ikh Nart, Их Нартын Чулуу; www.ikhnart.com; GPS: N 45°34' E108°38'; ⎙ verge.confusedly.compounds) This 670-sq-km nature reserve, only a four-hour drive from Ulaanbaatar, at an elevation of 2200m, is home to hundreds of ibexes (mountain goats), argali (big-horn sheep), gazelles, black vultures, wolves and other wildlife. There are 10 nomadic herder families living in the park, which is studded with spectacular glacial rock formations, their winter corrals built into red cliffs. Aside from the remote location, one of the reasons there is so much wildlife here is because of the water.

### Ikh Nartiin Chuluu
### Burial Mounds                               HISTORIC SITE
(GPS: N 45°75.546', E 108°65.454') There are several ancient burial mounds found throughout the park.

### Ikh Nartiin Chuluu Petroglyphs          ROCK ART
(GPS: N 45°60.787', E 108°57.201'; N 45°60.237', E 108°55.959'; N 45°59.175', E 108°61.397') Tibetan petroglyphs can be found throughout the park.

## 🛏 Sleeping

### ★ IkhNart
### Wilderness Camp                    TOURIST GER CAMP $$$
(🖉11-330 360; www.nomadicjourneys.com; GPS: N 45°39.830', E 108°39.204'; ⎙ verge.confusedly.compounds; per night incl meals US$125-135; 🅿) ✦ Nomadic Journeys (p40) operates this splendid tourist camp in the reserve, about 50km drive from Shiveegobi train station. Guided wildlife walks, multiday camel treks and jeep tours are available to guests, and the main camp offers true glamping, with 15 gers supported by gorgeous hand-painted pillars, and furnished with a dung-burning oven, a private sink and reading chairs.

## ➊ Getting There & Away

You can access the reserve by taking a southbound train from Ulaanbaatar and getting off at Shiveegobi, Tsomog or Choir train stations.

However, you'll have to arrange pick-up, as there will be no taxis awaiting your arrival. The best plan is to book with IkhNart Wilderness Camp. They will arrange for a local driver to meet you at the train station and escort you into the park.

## Zamyn-Üüd    Замын-Үүд
🖉 02524, 7052 / POP 13,300

The Trans-Mongolian Railway line serves as the lone life-sustaining artery for the small and shrinking town of Zamyn-Üüd in the Gobi Desert. Be warned: this is hardly the multicultural Sino-Mongo mingling you may have hoped for, partly because this border is political and not cultural. The Chinese province of Inner Mongolia, on the other side of the line, is an extension of the Gobi and Mongolians consider its residents their brothers and sisters.

Most of the town's activity can be found around the square in front of the train station. The chief attractions here are the disused water fountain, some outdoor pool tables and grabbing a bite at one of the many eateries that cater to transit travellers killing time. The town seems perpetually under construction with scaffolds on torn-up buildings, workers swarming everywhere, but not much work getting done. Still, the droves do pass through.

## 🛏 Sleeping & Eating

### Nomgon Hotel                                   HOTEL $
(⎙granny.chomps.pedometers; standard/deluxe T30,000/55,000; 🕾) Set right on the train platform, deluxe rooms are large and bright with wood floors and flat screens, though wallpaper may be peeling. Standard rooms are smaller but still clean and doable. There's no sign out front and no air-con either. It's next to the old Zamyn-Üüd Hotel, which was under construction at research time.

### Khan Buuz                                   MONGOLIAN $
(⎙expiring.fastening.squabbles; mains T5000-6500; ⏱24hr) On the train station platform is this branch of the dependable canteen chain, Khan Buuz. No English menu, but some photos to point at. Does *buuz* (obviously), as well as *tsuivan,* various soups, *khuushuur* and warming mugs of *süütei tsai* (salty milk tea).

## ➊ Information

The train station's new ticket office is on the station platform and contains several ATMs that accept international cards. Money changers are on hand outside the station to change your tögrögs or Chinese rénmíbì.

## ❶ Getting There & Away

Train tickets are bought on the 2nd floor of **Zamyn-Üüd's train station** ([⊞]objects.galaxies.attainments; [☎]).

**Zamyn-Üüd to UB** Train 275; departs 6.05pm daily; arrives 9.25am; seat/hard-sleeper/soft-sleeper to UB T11,000/22,600/38,550; to Sainshand T4500/9300/14,300.

**Èrlián to UB** Train 21; departs Zamyn-Üüd 9.25pm Monday and Friday; arrives UB 10.35am; hard-/soft-sleeper to UB T22,100/39,200; to Sainshand T13,500/22,050. Otherwise there are two daily buses to Ulaanbaatar (T56,000 incl a meal; 10-12 hours), departing at 10am and 1pm.

There's also a Sunday 'express' train (No 43), which leaves Zamyn-Üüd for Ulaanbaatar at 9.25pm, and a train (No 33) which originates in China's Hohhot and leaves Zamyn-Üüd for Ulaanbaatar at the same time on Tuesdays and Saturdays.

In short, there are trains from Zamyn-Üüd to Ulaanbaatar at 6.05pm daily, and at 9.25pm on Monday, Tuesday, Friday, Saturday and Sunday. Departure and arrival times are based on the summer schedule (May to September) and are subject to slight variations each year.

The well-maintained paved road connecting Zamyn-Üüd and Ulaanbaatar means catching a share taxi (per person T60,000) or a ride with a trader may be possible.

Luggage storage is available for T1000 per item in the basement of the train station's ticket office.

# ÖMNÖGOVI  ӨМНӨГОВЬ

POP 60,900  /  AREA 165,000 SQ KM

Ömnögovi (southern Gobi) is the largest aimag in Mongolia, and has a population density of only 0.4 people per square kilometre. With an average annual precipitation of just 130mm a year, and summer temperatures reaching an average of 38°C, this is the driest, hottest and harshest region in the entire country. Tourists love it, however, and there are plenty of ger camps throughout the aimag thanks to its epic sand dunes, that icy gorge and those flaming cliffs. Far more important from a dollars and cents perspective, however, is the mining industry, and in particular the massive Oyu Tolgoi copper and gold deposit in Khanbogd *sum*, and Tavan Tolgoi, one of the world's largest coking and thermal coal deposits. But with every mountain top removed and precious stream or spring polluted, life for nomadic herders and local wildlife only gets harsher.

## TO & FROM CHINA

Jeeps, trains and buses all trundle to and from the Chinese border town of Èrlián (Ereen).

If you are on a Trans-Mongolian train, or the service between Ulaanbaatar and Hohhot or Èrlián (both in China), you will stop at Zamyn-Üüd for an hour or so while Mongolian customs and immigration officials do their stuff – usually in the middle of the night.

If you're on a train that only goes as far as the border, then you'll need to find a vehicle in which to cross the border (you can't walk or cycle across), before catching onward transport from the other side. It's best to catch the public bus (from Mongolia T8000 per person, from China ¥50 per person). This shuttles between the car park outside Zamyn-Üüd train station and the main bus station in Èrlián, via the border post. Shared jeeps/minivans offer the same service for T20,000, although you may need to negotiate. There are also two daily direct buses that run to/from Èrlián (T56,200; 10 to 12 hours).It may also be possible to catch a long-distance, luxury bus to Beijing (¥220) from the main square. You'll need to change your money before buying a ticket. They generally meet the train from UB and will take you if they are not yet sold out.

Heading into Mongolia, the bus leaves Èrlián bus station at 1.30pm and 3pm. If you catch the 1.30pm bus across the border, you should have plenty of time to get a ticket for the 6.05pm train from Zamyn-Üüd to Ulaanbaatar (apart from around nadaam season in July, when things get very busy). In Zamyn-Üüd, the public bus to Èrlián is usually there to meet passengers as they get off trains from Ulaanbaatar. Otherwise there's a daily direct bus to UB from Èrlián that departs at 10am and 1pm (¥180, 10-12 hours). You'll need to pay a ¥5 departure tax in either direction, unless you're crossing the border on a train.

Once in Èrlián, it's almost always easiest to catch a long-distance bus to your next destination in China as trains are usually fully booked days in advance.

For details on your onward travel, head to shop.lonelyplanet.com to purchase a downloadable PDF of Lonely Planet's *China* guide.

## BATTLE OF THE TOST MOUNTAINS

In March 2017 the Mongolian government set aside 8163 sq km of critical snow leopard habitat as the **Tost Tosonbumba Nature Reserve** (⧉enjoying.conditional.pens), building a de facto wildlife corridor that bridges **Small Gobi A Strictly Protected Area** and **Gurvan Saikhan National Park** (p179). It was a victory for a coalition of environmentalists that included a team of Mongolian grassroots organisers and researchers with the Snow Leopard Trust (www.snowleopard.org) in Ulaanbaatar, all of them women, who have made inroads with local herders and persuaded them to help protect cats that historically have preyed upon their goats and sheep. Their incentives include a unique livestock insurance program that helps herders mitigate the loss of a sheep or goat whose valuable wool is exported all over the world as cashmere.

However, theirs was not a complete victory. The new reserve boundaries are most notable for what was not included. Namely, a pair of mountain oases that 25 herder families and local farmers have relied on since 2001, when Memorandums of Understanding (MOUs) granted them grazing and farming rights for 15 years. When those MOUs expired in 2015 they were not renewed. Soon enough, around the time that the nature reserve was made official, two mining companies set up camps to survey near those oases, and local herders worry that soon they will begin to exploit the land looking for coal.

Mining, which has contributed to the development of Mongolia with cash and capital projects, is king in Gurvantes, where a total of eight mining operations, owned by both Mongolian and foreign interests, dig for coal, copper and gold. Coal is the main prize, and nearly all of that mineral wealth is transported out of the country by road and rail to nearby China. The form of mining conducted here is called mountain-top removal. Using explosives, mining companies blow up the top of a peak, flatten it out, and dig into the core for whatever they are after. It's water-intensive, so their activities typically drain the aquifer and pollute streams. In some areas where this type of mining persists, goats have died and been found to have been infected with black lung thanks to the abundance of coal dust. Obviously, if the oases are polluted it won't just be the farmers, herders and their livestock that suffer, but endemic wildlife too, including the snow leopard.

The families have not given up the fight, nor have they vacated their land as ordered, and with the help of the Snow Leopard Trust (who, in addition to community organising, also collar and monitor snow leopards and help restore habitat in Mongolia, China, India and Pakistan) they continue to lobby government officials in the hope that they will once again be granted rights to the oases that have supported their flocks and families for so many years. Of course, the mining companies are well connected politically and show no signs of backing down either. In 2017 it appeared that a showdown was looming.

---

# Dalanzadgad    Даланзадгад

🖊 01532, 7053 / POP 18,740 / ELEV 1465M

The capital of Ömnögov, Dalanzadgad is a speck of civilisation in the desert, sitting in the shadow of the mountainous Gurvan Saikhan National Park. You'll find decent hotels here, with good restaurants and bars, so it's not a bad place to recharge before you explore the region's big draws: the monstrous sand dunes known as Khongoryn Els (p180) and the 'Flaming Cliffs' of **Bayanzag** (Баянзаг, Flaming Cliffs; GPS: N 44°08.311′, E 103°43.667′; ⧉accuracy.accelerator.rejection; T2000). Both are within a half-day's drive.

## ◉ Sights

**South Gobi Museum**      MUSEUM
(🖊1532-23871;   ⧉daring.lion.race;   T2000; ⊙9am-6pm Mon-Fri) Surprisingly, this museum has little on dinosaurs – just a few legs, arms and eggs. (All of the best exhibits are in Ulaanbaatar or in other museums around the world.) There are a few nice paintings, a huge stuffed vulture and a display of scroll paintings and other Buddhist items. Look out for the unusual jade flute.

## ⌗ Sleeping & Eating

**Bayan Govi Hotel**      HOTEL **$**
(🖊8853 9211;   ⧉caked.linens.fastening;   r T25,000-40,000; 🛜) This friendly, motel-like place is the town's best budget choice.

# Dalanzadgad

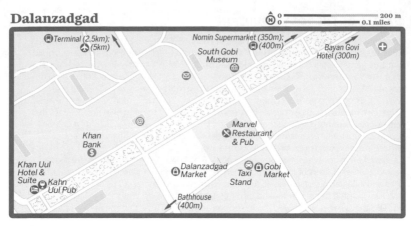

Rooms are simple, but clean and bright, and management are welcoming to foreigners despite not speaking English. Rooms sleep up to three and have wood floors, cable TV and plenty of light. You'll have to forgive the wonky ceilings.

They do not have air-con, however, and that is an issue in the summertime.

**Khan Uul Hotel & Suite** HOTEL $$$
(☑ 7053 4999; www.khanuul-hotel.mn; ⚏cases. natively.search; d standard T120,000, d deluxe T200,000-280,000; 🛜)More business-oriented, smarter and better-run than any other hotel in town. Staff here speak some English, and the **pub lounge** (www.khanuul-hotel.mn; ⚏thereof.bathed.utensils; ⊘noon-midnight) was the hippest spot in DZ when we came through. The 2nd-floor restaurant serves a nice roast chicken dinner.

**Marvel Restaurant & Pub** KOREAN $
(☑ 7053 3035; ⚏Illusionist.toadstools.oboe; mains T6000-7500; ⊘9am-midnight; 🛜) A tiny yet hip pub set down a pedestrian lane, with a nice menu of Mongolian favourites and Korean classics, including kimchi stew. They do some Western dishes, can arrange special-order vegetarian meals, and the Golden Gobi draughts are icy. It turns into a popular karaoke bar after dark. There is no English-language menu.

## ⓘ Information

**Internet Cafe** (⚏chatters.mouthy.illiteracy; per hour T900; ⊘8am-10pm Mon-Fri, 9am-10pm Sat & Sun) In the Telecom office.
**Khan Bank** (⊘9am-6pm Mon-Fri, to 4pm Sat) Changes cash and has a foreign-card-friendly ATM; on the same side of the road as the Telecom office.

## ⓘ Getting There & Away

### AIR
➤ The airport is 5km north of town, along a paved road. Taxis cost about T10,000 one way.
➤ At least one flight a day connects Dalanzadgad and Ulaanbaatar (from T250,000).

### BUS
➤ A twice-daily bus travels between Dalanzadgad and Ulaanbaatar (T23,000, nine hours, 553km), departing at around 8am and 6pm and travelling via Mandalgov (T12,200, five hours).
➤ Tickets are only available at the **bus terminal** (⚏wanderers.underdog.aspiration; ⊘7.30am-6pm), set just under 3km from the town centre. There is no reliable bus stop in town any longer, so you'll have to board here too.
➤ A taxi from town to the terminal could cost between T5000 and T10,000, depending upon your negotiation skills.

### MINIVAN & TAXI
➤ Minivans leave for Ulaanbaatar (T30,000) via Mandalgov (usually same price) when full. They gather outside the Gobi Market.
➤ Hiring a taxi is fairly straightforward, even though few people here speak much English. Look for drivers at the **taxi stand** (⚏thistle. companywide.inhibited) outside the **Gobi Market** (⚏stencils.eddied.manufacturing; ⊘10am-10pm).
➤ A day trip to Yolyn Am with three hours of waiting time costs T100,000. An overnight return trip, taking in Yolyn Am, Khongoryn Els and the Flaming Cliffs, will set you back between T250,000 and T300,000. One-way taxis to Mandalgov cost T60,000 to T70,000.

# Gurvantes

Gurvantes is a market town in the south-western Gobi, home to hundreds of herder families who winter in their small homes with yards defined by reused tin and wood fencing. It's also a *sum* centre that encompasses both vital habitat for snow leopards and significant gold, copper and (especially) coal mining interests. Oh, and it's a stone's throw from the Chinese border (though the border is closed to foreign visitors). In other words, life is complicated in Gurvantes. It's here that local herders, led mostly by women, and Mongolian snow leopard conservationists are working hardest to protect the last of these mysterious cats who gather in and roam the Tost Mountains. Some earned protection in 2017 when the Tost Tosonbumba Nature Reserve (p177) was set aside by the central government in Ulaanbaatar.

Most international visitors work for multinational mining companies or come to study the cats in the autumn when the animals are often collared and tracked. There are no tourist facilities here.

Travellers should note that there is no public transport to and from Gurvantes, which is 350km west of Dalanzadgad.

# Gurvan Saikhan National Park
Гурван Сайхан

With its iconic sand dunes, ice canyon and stunning mountain vistas, Gurvan Saikhan National Park is understandably one of Mongolia's most popular national parks. Most travellers see only a fraction of it, sticking to the main sites. With more time, though, it's possible to drive to the remote western area – an eerie landscape so lacking in life that you may feel as if you've landed on Mars.

**Gurvan Saikhan National Park** (Three Beauties; [m] mulberries.boss.apprehends; T5000), protected from development since 1963, is named after three of its ridges (though there are four). Besides its spectacular natural beauty it contains more than 200 bird species, including the Mongolian desert finch, cinereous vulture, desert warbler and houbara bustard. The park also has 600 or more types of plants, which help support the black-tailed gazelles, Kozlov's pygmy jerboas, wild asses and endangered species of wild camel, snow leopard, ibex and argali sheep.

## CAMELS

Known as ships of the desert, Mongolian Bactrian camels are two-humped beasts with shaggy wool coats. They can still be seen today, hauling goods and people across the Gobi, as they have done for centuries.

Your first encounter with a camel may be a daunting experience: it may bark, spit and smell like a sweaty armpit. But, excusing its lack of graces, the camel is a versatile and low-maintenance creature: it can last a week without water and a month without food; it is strong enough to carry a lot of gear (up to 250kg – equal to 10 full backpacks); it provides wool (on average 5kg per year) and milk (up to 600L a year); and it is a source of (somewhat gamey) meat. The camel also produces 250kg of dung a year – invaluable for fuel.

Monitoring the hump is an important part of camel welfare. A firm and tall hump is a sign of good health, while a droopy hump means the camel is in need of food and water. If a thirsty camel hasn't had a drink for some time, it can suck up 200L of water in a single day. Most camels are tame, but male camels suffer from surging hormones and can get mean during the mating season in January and February – definitely a time to avoid approaching one.

Of the 260,000 camels in Mongolia, two-thirds can be found in the Gobi – 80,000 in Ömnögovi alone. They are related to the rare wild camel known as the *khavtgai*, of which only around 800 remain in Mongolia. These are all found in the Great Gobi Strictly Protected Area (Gobi A). For more information, see www.wildcamel.com.

Visitors from around the country and beyond descend on Ömnögovi for **Bulgan Camel Festival** (Temeenii Uraldaanii Bayar) for two days every March (usually the 6th and 7th) for camel polo, camel shearing and camel races, as well as demonstrations of how nomads look after their herds.

## ⊙ Sights

★**Khongoryn Els**                                    DUNES
(Хонгорын Элс; [*m*]replanted.migrated.viewer)
Khongoryn Els are some of the largest and
most spectacular sand dunes in Mongolia.
Also known as the Duut Mankhan (Singing
Dunes – from the sound they make when
the sand is moved by the wind), they are
up to 300m high, 12km wide and about
100km long. The largest dunes are at the
northwestern corner of the range. From
afar the dunes look painted on the south
horizon in front of those gorgeous granite
mountains.

Up close you get more texture as the sand
forms peaks that look like whipped meringue.
Getting to the top (45 minutes to one hour) is
exhausting; every step forward is followed by
a significant backslide, and as you approach
you may be sandblasted as the wind shears
the lip off the dune and showers you with
stinging sand, but the views of the desert
from the sandy summit are wonderful. The
dunes are also a popular place for organising
**camel treks** (per hour/day T10,000/30,000,
plus the same again for the guide fee). Most
local herders can arrange treks. You'll have to
walk the dunes yourself, but the camel can
carry your gear. A two- or three-day walk
through the dunes would likely be the highlight of your trip and its greatest challenge.
A mini naadam featuring horse racing and
wrestling is held here in August.

The dunes are about 180km from Dalanzadgad. There is no way to get here unless
you charter a vehicle or are part of a tour.

From Khongoryn Els it is possible
to follow desert tracks 130km north to
Bogd in Övörkhangai, or 215km northwest to Bayanlig in Bayankhongor. This
is a remote and unforgiving area and you
shouldn't undertake either trip without an
experienced driver and full stocks of food,
water and fuel.

---

### YOLYN AM

As you enter through the park gateway, past the Yolyn Am Nature Museum, the dirt road
continues to rise through the arid, rugged Altai range before winding into a valley, 10km
away, where the slopes are velvety with vegetation and the ridges crenellated like a castle. Eventually the road will dead-end at a parking area from where you can **hike**, **bike**
([*m*]panics.flourishing.negotiable; per person T5000) or **ride a horse** ([*m*]panics.flourishing.
negotiable; per person T12,000) into a narrow gorge made from black and brown granite,
gurgling with a glacial stream.

**Yolyn Am** (Ёлын Ам, Vulture's Mouth; [*m*]panics.flourishing.negotiable), the Vulture's
Mouth, was originally established to conserve bird life in the region. In February 2017
bearded vulture eggs were discovered in the canyon, so the system is working, but the
**gorge** is its most popular sight thanks to its dramatic cliffs, which provide enough shade
to allow sheets of blue-veined ice to survive well into the summer. In the Soviet heyday, it's
said that Russian military units used the gorge as a butchery and a kind of walk-in freezer
where their meat would remain preserved from autumn until summertime.

The ice gathers roughly 2km away from the car park. You'll have to dismount your
horse or mountain bike near where a few vendors gather to sell handicrafts in order to
walk far enough for photo ops of the stunning glacier. If you fancy a full-day hike, an experienced driver can pick you up on the other side of the gorge, roughly 8km away, but
be careful, the footing is quite slippery in places.

Along the way to and from the gorge, you'll see herds of shaggy yaks and, if you're
lucky, an ibex. Make sure to look out for white etchings on the rock walls – markings
from ibex hooves scraping the face as they climb, like a four-legged Alex Honnold, to the
ridge above. The surrounding hills offer opportunities for some fine, if strenuous, day
hikes where more ibexes and argali sheep roam the ridge line.

Before you leave, make sure to step into the small but interesting **Yolyn Am Nature
Museum** (GPS: N 43°32.872', E 104°02.257'; [*m*]defrost.resampling.pavilions; T2000; ⊙8am-
8pm 1 Jun–20 Oct), where you'll peruse crystals, taxidermy of local fauna and a small
collection of dinosaur eggs and other fossils discovered right here. There are also three
gers selling local **handicrafts**, including some vintage gems.

Yolyn Am is in the Zuun Saikhan Nuruu, 46km west of Dalanzadgad (return taxi
T120,000, one to two hours).

**Khavtsgait Petroglyphs** ROCK ART
(GPS: N 43°54.256; E 103°31.345; elev 1822m; ⦚raider.performances.dollhouses) If you take the main route from Dalanzadgad to Khongoryn Els, keeping the mountains to your left as you go, you can stop and hunt the hills for this exceptional collection of petroglyphs dating from between 8000 BC and 3000 BC. From the parking area **trail head**, a rocky path gains 120m in elevation as it winds up a ridge littered with art. In under an hour you'll see petroglyphs aplenty.

Highlights are listed below, but there are far more than those listed here to seek and discover. The **1st group** (N 43°54.207; E 103°31.514'; elev 1780m) includes depictions of antelope, ibexes and mountain sheep. Just beyond here the **2nd group** (GPS: N 43°54.208', E 103°31.464'; elev 1808m) features more antelope and ibexes and a man on horseback. The **3rd group** (GPS: N 43°54.201', E 103°31.377'; elev 1836m) includes a large red deer, an ibex, hunters stalking deer and a cat-like animal, possibly a snow leopard. The **4th group** (GPS: N 43°54.172', E 103°31.360'; elev 1831m) shows horses and hunters in a scene dominated by a mysterious spiral pattern.

Further along near the top of the hill is the **Gallery** (GPS: N 43°54.256', E 103°31.345'; elev 1822m), the highlight of this site. On a single 2m-wide rock face are a number of scenes: galloping horses, hunters, a rare depiction of a camel, wheeled carts and rudimentary gers. Not far away, towards the edge of the hill, overlooking the vast steppe is a **6th group** (GPS: N 43°54.267', E 103°31.336'; elev 1819m), which features, ahem, two wolves mating on one rock, and another rock with a majestic red deer with huge antlers. And there are still others, hundreds, in fact. Explore and discover for yourself, but please be respectful. There has been some defacing by tourists, which is as depressing as it is idiotic.

The trail head is up to your left as you drive west from Three Camel Lodge (p184), 12km away, on the main route from Dalanzadgad (about 75km) to Khongoryn Els (about 100km). There are no facilities here.

**Dugany Am** GORGE
If you are headed from Yolyn Am to Khongoryn Els, an adventurous and rough alternative route takes you through the Dugany Am, a spectacular and narrow gorge barely wide enough to allow a jeep to pass through that eventually leads to some spectacular

---

**PIKA-BOO**

The small, mouse-like creatures often seen darting between rock crevices at **Yolyn Am** are called pikas and are actually members of the rabbit family. They're incredibly cute and frustratingly difficult to photograph.

Surprisingly, pikas don't hibernate, but they do spend their summers preparing for winter by dragging grass into their burrows for winter consumption.

---

views and a small **stupa** (GPS: N 43°29.115', E 103°51.043') that has been built on the remains of a former temple.

The gorge is blocked with ice until July and can be impassable even after the ice has melted, so check road conditions with the rangers at the park entrance.

**Mukhar Shiveert** AREA
About 1km before arriving at the Yolyn Am gateway is an ice valley called Mukhar Shiveert; visitors may be required to pay an additional T3000 to visit the site.

## 🛏 Sleeping

There are two main areas to sleep in the park: the family ger camps around Yolyn Am, and the family and tourist camps sprinkled in the shadow of the dunes at Khongoryn Els. If you have your own tent, you can camp practically anywhere. Camps are open from May to mid-October. Be prepared: most guides and drivers favour their contracted family and tourist camps, so if you wish to sleep elsewhere, express your preference.

## 🛏 Khongoryn Els

**Baasanhuu Family Ger Camp** HOMESTAY $
(☑9701 1690, 9889 1690; ⦚beanbag.skier.pigments; per person T10,000; 📶) A family ger camp run by a teacher from Ulaanbaatar who decamps to the shadow of the dunes each summer. Gers are simple and clean, the hosts are a delight and her goat's milk tea comes with an extra pinch of salt. This is the only family camp with wi-fi in the national park.

**Boliry Homestay** HOMESTAY $
(☑8853 5557; ⦚sucky.violets.subjunctive; per person T10,000) Just 5km from the park gates are five tidy gers with wooden,

hand-painted beds and epic mountain views from the doorway. From this vantage point the Altai range is textured with shadow and light. No meals provided, so bring your own supplies.

**Gobi Discovery 2** TOURIST GER CAMP **$$**
(☎9838 7299, 11-312 769; www.gobidiscovery.mn; GPS: N 43°46.495', E 102°20.307'; ///catchable.devoting.pamper; per person with/without meals T65,000/25,000; ⊙May–mid-Oct; P) The best tourist camp in the area. The shower rooms and toilets are sparkling, the 37 gers are larger than most (some have queen beds), and though the new-build main lodge heats up during the day, it's comfortable at breakfast. Most importantly, the staff are terrific. It's set 2km from the dunes (10km from the tallest section).

**Gobi Erdene** TOURIST GER CAMP **$$$**
(☎8811 5701, Ulaanbaatar main office 7720 0333, camp phone 9898 6038; ///rehash.cornmeal.luxurious; ger per person with meals T110,000, d T160,000-190,000; ) The newest tourist camp is furthest (10km) from the dunes, but you will have more lodging options here than anywhere else. Bed down in one of 24 rooms with private baths, set in cute log-cabin duplexes, or duck into one of their 33 gers with blonde wood furnishings. They don't offer room-only rates. Meals served in the main lodge.

## Information

- You can pay the national park entry fee at the entrance to **Yolyn Am** (p180) or to the ranger at **Khongoryn Els** (p180). Keep your entry ticket as you may need to show it more than once, though that's unlikely.
- **Conservation Ink** (www.conservationink.org) publishes the excellent *Gobi Gurvan Saikhan National Park Map and Guide*, a satellite map with informative articles.



# Bayanzag Баянзаг

Bayanzag (p177) means 'rich in saxaul shrubs', so named for the tree-like shrubs dotting the surrounding landscape that vaguely resemble Joshua trees. It's more commonly known as the 'Flaming Cliffs' thanks to the reddish tint in the soil that glows as the sun falls. It was a name first penned by palaeontologist Roy Chapman Andrews, who arrived in 1922 to excavate the area.

Even if you're not a 'dinophile', the eerie beauty of the surrounding landscape is a good reason to visit. It's a classic desert of rock, red sands, scrub, sun and awesome emptiness. The cliffs look to be formed by great rifts in the earth, like a layer cake torn open, offset by the surprisingly green valley below. There's not much to do once you're here except explore the cliffs – both the rim and the base – or grab a cold drink from the souvenir sellers who hang out on the edge of the cliff.

## Sights

**Moltzog Els** DUNES
(///atom.redeeming.evidencing) The 5km stretch of 40ft-tall, sugary sand dunes that rises and falls in the desert 22km northeast of Bayanzag makes for some brief, breathless hikes and beautiful vistas. Worth a visit if you're not planning to visit Khongoryn Els (p180). A local herder family offers camel rides through the dunes for T10,000 per hour, T30,000 per day.

## Sleeping

Camping opportunities abound – the *zag* (scrub) forest, 5km from the cliffs, is one option. You can also camp at any of the tourist ger camps, then pay to use their facilities: showers, restaurant etc.

### FALLING FLAMES

Bayanzag is changing, and though it is more accessible than ever, that's not necessarily good news. For 90 years after Roy Chapman Andrews first began to dig for bones, the cliffs' elevation didn't change. They were stark and steep and much wider than they are today; but as a result of heavy winds, thanks to the Soviet deforestation of the area, and an increase in flash storms that can dump inches of rain in mere minutes, Bayanzag is eroding. Rock arches have crumbled, boulders have tumbled and crevasses have opened in the cliffs. All of which makes the site more navigable on foot, but is also perhaps yet another troubling sign of global climate change.

## JURASSIC CLIFFS: LAND OF THE DINOSAURS

In the early 1920s, newspapers brought news of the world's first discovery of dinosaur eggs in the southern Gobi Desert by American adventurer Roy Chapman Andrews (1884–1960). Andrews, a real-life Indiana Jones and the inspiration for the film version, led expeditions worldwide, but became best known for his expeditions to Bayanzag, which he famously renamed the 'Flaming Cliffs'. Over a period of two years his team unearthed over 100 dinosaurs, including *Protoceratops andrewsi,* which was named after the explorer. The find included several Velocipedes (swift robbers), subsequently made famous by *Jurassic Park*. He also found a parrot-beaked Oviraptor, though his name for the creature (egg robber) was a misnomer as later discoveries proved that the Oviraptors were not stealing eggs, but incubating their own.

Subsequent expeditions have added to the picture of life in the Gobi during the late Cretaceous period 70 million years ago. One of the most famous fossils unearthed so far is the 'Fighting Dinosaurs' fossil, discovered by a joint Polish–Mongolian team in 1971 and listed as a national treasure. The remarkable 80-million-year-old fossil is of a Protoceratops and Velociraptor locked in mortal combat. It is thought that this and other fossilised snapshots were entombed by a violent sandstorm or by collapsing sand dunes. One poignant fossil is of an Oviraptor protecting its nest of eggs from the impending sands.

To think this all started as an accident. Andrews originally arrived in Bayanzag from what was then Peking, intent on proving his hypothesis that early man originated in the Gobi. Alas, that mission failed and was usurped by a breakthrough of dino proportions, and as a result a picture of the prehistoric Gobi has emerged. It was a land of swamps, marshes and lakes, with stretches of sand studded with oases, and inhabited by a colourful cast of characters, including huge duck-billed hadrosaurs; Ankylosaurs, which were up to 7.6m tall, were armour-plated and had club-like tails that acted like a giant mace; long-necked, lizard-hipped sauropods such as Nemegtosaurus, which may have grown to a weight of 90 tonnes; and the mighty Tarbosaurus (alarming reptile), a carbon copy of a *Tyrannosaurus rex*, with a 1.2m-long skull packed with razor-sharp teeth up to 15cm long.

Apart from the famous sites of **Bayanzag** (p177) and nearby Togrigiin Shiree, the richest sites – **Bugiin Tsav** (p186), Ulaan Tsav, Nemegt Uul and **Khermen Tsav** (p186) – are all in the remote west of Ömnögovi aimag and impossible to reach without a sturdy 4WD vehicle and dedicated driver (or a helicopter). Locals may approach you at Bayanzag, the ger camps and even Dalanzadgad to try to sell you dinosaur bones and eggs. Remember that it is *highly* illegal to export fossils from Mongolia.

Today the finest collection of Gobi dinosaurs is housed in the **American Natural History Museum** (www.amnh.org) in New York City, which also has a fine website. Mongolia has recently opened a **Museum of Dinosaurs** in Ulaanbaatar, to show off its collection. As for books, check out *Dinosaurs of the Flaming Cliffs* by American palaeontologist Michael Novacek. For more information on Roy Chapman Andrews, read *Dragon Hunter*, by Charles Gallenkamp.

**THE GOBI** BAYANZAG

**Geleg-Araash's Family Ger**   HOMESTAY **$**
(📞 9860 3335; GPS: N 44°10.806', E 103°41.478'; ⒨ swirls.sporting.backstage; per person T10,000) Geleg-Araash, the father of Sainzaya from **Sainzaya's Family Ger** (📞 9822 0218; GPS: N 44°11.362', E 103°41.200'; ⒨ ducklings.blotting.disagreement; per person T10,000), offers 10 gers. Each sleep two to six people and are accented with hand-painted posts and beams. A shower building was under construction when we visited. It doesn't offer meals.

**Gobi Tour Camp**   TOURIST GER CAMP **$$**
(📞 9909 1258; GPS: N 44°07.367', E 103°43.793'; ⒨ extensions.shipment.warden; per person with/without meals US$50/20) The closest camp to the cliffs, this friendly place, fronted by a T-Rex statue and powered by the wind, is on the up-side of the cliffs and you can see them clearly, 2km away. Facilities include 30 tidy gers with double beds and hand-painted accents. The food is decent, and camel rides (per hour/day US$10/25) can be arranged.

★ **Three Camel Lodge** LODGE $$$
(☑9888 0930, 11-313 396; www.threecamellodge.
com; GPS: N 43°53.603', E 103°44.435'; ⓜshelling.
devices.reissue; s/d incl meals from US$560/725;
☺May-Oct; ℗) ✎ To experience Three Camels is to know the epitome of the upscale Mongolian ger camp experience. Visitors stay in luxurious gers, which are decorated with handmade wood furnishings, and step down into sunken baths with private toilet, sink and hot showers. Their spectacular three-ger suites include a living room.

The dreamy **bar and lounge** (www.three-camellodge.com; ⓜshelling.devices.reissue; ☺11am-late) is decorated with wonderful Mongolian handicrafts, and there's plenty of terraced seating with views over the steppe. There's also a bundle of activities on offer, including camel rides, mountain biking, massage and guided tours of Bayanzag, which usually include a sunset dinner at the cliffs. There's a screening room, a sunset viewpoint, and at night galaxies reveal themselves in the inky Gobi sky. They have an ecological ethos too: the property is 90% solar and they have their own organic greenhouse where they grow greens and herbs for their superlative kitchen, which caters to vegans and vegetarians. They also drilled a well that waters more than 17,000 animals belonging to local nomadic herders. You will enjoy watching them roam. This is that oasis in the desert, 66km northwest of Dalanzadgad (on the route towards Khongoryn Els) and 28km south of Bayanzag.

---

**WORTH A TRIP**

### AMARBUYANT KHIID

The ruined monastery of **Amarbuyant Khiid** (Амарбуянт Хийд; GPS: N 44°37.745', E 98°42.214'; ⓜdeliberates.scrabbled.fastened) once housed around 1000 monks until its destruction in 1937 by Stalin's forces. Its claim to fame is that the 13th Dalai Lama, while travelling from Lhasa to Urga in 1904, stayed here for 10 days. The extensive ruins today include temples, buildings and walls, and the main temple has been partially restored. Locals can also show you a small ovoo built by the Dalai Lama; out of respect no rocks were ever added.

It's located 47km west of Shinejist.

---

**Dream Gobi Camp** TOURIST GER CAMP $$$
(☑9890 5074; dreamgobicamp@yahoo.com; GPS: N 43°54.458', E 103°51.999'; ⓜwithdrew.timepiece.epoch; per person with lunch & dinner/breakfast only T435,000/360,000) The facilities here are a notch above most other ger camps, not least because this is the only camp in the Gobi where every ger has an attached bathroom with hot shower. It's on the main route between Bayanzag (28km) and Dalanzadgad (60km).

### ❶ Getting There & Away

Bayanzag is around 90km from Dalanzadgad. You'll need to charter a taxi or jeep from there.

## BAYANKHONGOR
## БАЯНХОНГОР

POP 77,800 / AREA 116,000 SQ KM

One of the most diverse aimags in the Gobi, Bayankhongor has mountains in the north, deserts in the south, a handful of lakes and rivers, hot springs and a real oasis in the far south of the province. Bayankhongor, which means 'rich chestnut' (named after the colour of horses), is also home to wild camels and asses and the extremely rare Gobi bear.

## Bayankhongor City
## Баянхонгор

☑01442, 7044 / POP 29,817 / ELEV 1859M

Though short on sights, Bayankhongor is a leafy, affluent aimag capital set on the languid Tüin Gol, making it a good place to rest for a night and stock up on provisions before continuing into the more remote regions. There is a T1000 fee for all vehicles entering the city gates.

### ⊙ Sights

**Lamyn Gegeenii Gon
Gandan Dedlin Khiid** BUDDHIST MONASTERY
(Ламын Гэгээний Гон Гандан Дэдлин Хийд; ⓜlounged.negating.tackling) The original monastery by this name, one of Mongolia's largest at the time, was located 20km east of Bayankhongor City. It was levelled by the communist government in 1937. The current version is a hub of activity where locals come to seek counsel from among the 30 resident lamas. There was a pop-up medical clinic serving low-income residents when we stopped by.

# Bayankhongor City

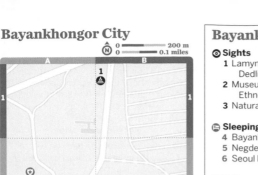

**⊙ Sights**

  **1** Lamyn Gegeenii Gon Gandan
      Dedlin Khiid ..........................................B1
  **2** Museum of History and
      Ethnography ..................................... B2
  **3** Natural History Museum ................... B3

**⊜ Sleeping**

  **4** Bayankhongor Hotel ........................... A2
  **5** Negdelchin Hotel ................................ B4
  **6** Seoul Hotel ......................................... A3

**⊗ Eating**

  **7** Baruun Bus .......................................... A5
  **8** Black Market ....................................... A4
  **9** Central Market .................................... A3
 **10** Ih Nomgon ........................................... A3
 **11** Jinchin Supermarket .......................... A2
 **12** Mammon .............................................. B3
 **13** Uran Khairkhan ................................... A3

old scroll paintings, and *tsam* (lama dance) masks and costumes.

**Natural History Museum**        MUSEUM
(⌨presenting.lactate.compatible; T2000; ⊙9am-6pm Mon-Fri) Filled with bad taxidermy, a replica Tarbosaurus skeleton and some fossils, including a 130-million-year-old fossilised turtle.

## 🛏 Sleeping

The best place to camp is by the Tüin Gol, a few hundred metres east of the city. Head to the river, then start walking north (left).

Not all midrange hotels offer air-conditioning, which makes for overheated nights in the summer.

**Negdelchin Hotel**        HOTEL **$**
(☑7044 2278; ⌨chattering.featured.spirited; s & d T40,000, tr T60,000) This long-standing Soviet-style cheapie is good value. Rooms have wood floors, high ceilings and private baths, are painted in pastels, yet remain extremely basic.

**Bayankhongor Hotel**        HOTEL **$$**
(☑7044 4000; ⌨surfer.contacting.trophies; s/d/deluxe T45,000/55,000/65,000; ℗❄☎) The most popular hotel in town, this place is smart throughout, and set opposite the leafy town square. The only frill in the so-called 'deluxe' rooms is a minibar. Standard rooms will do just fine. The restaurant comes well recommended. It's also one of the few hotels in town with air-conditioning – no small thing in the summer months.

Daily services start at 10am in the aromatic and atmospheric main 'brick ger' temple, which is suffused with incense and features a statue of Sakyamuni (the historical Buddha) flanked by a green-and-white Tara.

**Museum of History and
Ethnography**        MUSEUM
(⌨commissioner.lawfully.flatly; T1000; ⊙9am-6pm Mon-Fri) Formerly the Aimag Museum and set inside the sports stadium, the collection here is well laid-out and worth a quick look. There is a good display on Buddhist art, featuring two statues of Tara, some fine

**WORTH A TRIP**

## EXPLORING THE REMOTE GOBI

If you fancy yourself a bit of an Indiana Jones then you'll love the desert around Bayangovi. Few travellers make it this far, and any DIY explorers need to carry plenty of water, fuel and spare parts for their 4WD vehicle. The area around Khermen Tsav is particularly barren and as water is extremely scarce, virtually no one lives here. A minimum of two vehicles and an experienced guide are recommended for this area.

From north to south, areas to explore in Bayankhongor include the following:

**Galuut Canyon** (ⓜ parting.terminated.connotative) A 25m-deep canyon that narrows to around 1m wide in places. It is 20km southwest of Galuut *sum* centre, 85km northwest of Bayankhongor town.

**Böön Tsagaan Nuur** (GPS: N 45°37.114', E 99°15.350'; ⓜ scanty.marquees.footnote) A large, scenic saltwater lake at the end of Baidrag Gol with prolific bird-life, notably relic gulls, whooper swans and geese. The nearest *sum* centre is Baatsagaan. Locals from there sometimes come to swim in the lake. The east end of the lake is best for bird-watching. Camping is the only sleeping option.

**Ikh Bogd Uul** (ⓜ located.demolishes.leaping) The highest mountain (3957m) in the Gobi Altai range. It's possible to part-jeep, part-hike your way to the top for stupendous views. On Ikh Bogd's southern flank you'll also find the beautiful **Bituut rock**, formed after an earthquake in 1957.

**Tsagaan Agui** (White Cave; GPS: N 44°42.604', E 101°10.187; ⓜ deluded.phantom.timeline; T2000) This is a cave with a crystal-lined inner chamber that once housed Stone Age people. It is about 90km east of Bayangovi in a narrow gorge.

**Tsagaan Bulag** (GPS: N 44°35.156', E 100°20.733'; ⓜ weans.avenged.finalist) Also near Bayangovi, this white rock outcrop has the faint imprint of a strange helmeted figure, which locals believe was created by, um, aliens. Maybe they're right?

**Bayangiin Nuruu** (GPS: N 44°17.218', E 100°31.329'; ⓜ hydrate.stallion.jockeying) A canyon with well-preserved rock engravings and petroglyphs depicting hunting and agricultural scenes dating from 3000 BC.

**Yasnee Tsav** An eroded hilly region with some impressive buttes. Local guides claim they can point out authentic fossils at this site.

**Gunii Khöndii Gorge** A beautiful, 4km-long gorge with vertical walls. It is about 70km southwest of Bayangovi.

**Bugiin Tsav** (GPS: N 43°52.869', E 100°01.639'; ⓜ climates.headphones.tabs) A large series of rift valleys running parallel to the Altan Uul mountain range and famous for its dinosaur fossils.

**Khermen Tsav** (GPS: N 43°28.006', E 99°49.976'; ⓜ raindrop.concoction.faction) The most spectacular canyons in the area – some say more impressive than Bayanzag. The closest town is Gurvantes, where you can buy fuel.

**Sevrei Petroglyphs** (GPS: N 43°33.678', E 102°01.052'; ⓜ oversights.poaching.charcoal) These depict herds of animals including deer, ibexes and gazelles; 20km from the town of Sevrei.

**Seoul Hotel** HOTEL $$$
(☎ 7044 2754, 9144 6677; ⓜ pebbly.indecorous. disbanded; d from T110,000; @ 🛜) Smart, friendly and well-equipped, this is among the best choices in town, which is why it's frequently fully booked. Some staff speak English, all rooms have attached bathrooms, and breakfast is included. There's a restaurant, cafe and clothing boutique on the property, as well.

## ✕ Eating

**Baruun Bus** MARKET $
(ⓜ screened.cunningly.curtail; ⏱ 10am-8pm) This cavernous market, fragmented into stalls, offers the best produce selection in town, which makes it a good place to stock up on self-catering supplies. It's located just south of the **Black Market**.

★**Uran Khairkhan**　　　MONGOLIAN $
(⊞reference.empire.shameful; mains T5000-8500; ⊙9am-8pm) Enter through the ramshackle side entrance into jovial Uran Khairkhan, an atmospheric brick house with cosy booth dining. There's no English menu, but you'll find your usual favourites: *tsuivan*, goulash, *bif-shtek* (beef patty topped with a fried egg on rice), known collectively as *tsagaan khool* (white eats), along with a few Korean and Western dishes.

**Mammon**　　　MONGOLIAN $$
(⊞insolence.turf.phonetic; mains T6000-10,000; ⊙10am-midnight Mon-Sat) Bayankhongor's most pleasant restaurant is clean and family-friendly, but doesn't have an English menu. They have two or three chicken dishes *(takhia ny makh)* and the usual mutton offerings. Their *chinjutei makhan khuurag* (stir-fried meat, peppers and onions with rice) is supposedly tasty, and the *moogtei makhan khuurag* (fried mutton with mushrooms) is popular.

Walk down the left side of Khan Bank and it's on your left.

🛈 **Information**

**Khan Bank** (⊞opportunities.nougat.connect; ⊙9am-6pm Mon-Fri, to 4pm Sat) Changes US dollars and gives cash advances on Visa and MasterCard. There is an ATM next door.

There is an **internet cafe** (⊞carver.balsamic.wizards; per hour T900; ⊙9am-9pm) in the Telcom building on the main road.

🛈 **Getting There & Away**

AIR
The airport was defunct when we passed through, but given Mongolia's fluctuating transport connections it could be back up and running while you're in country, with possible flights between here and Ulaanbaatar.

BUS
Buses leave for Ulaanbaatar (T28,000, 15 hours, 630km) via Arvaikheer (T15,000, five hours, 200km) at 8am, 2pm and 6pm. These buses book up, so buy tickets the day before to ensure you snag a seat.

JEEP & MINIVAN
Shared minivans leave from the **bus stand** (⊞stepping.unalternable.minly) for Ulaanbaatar (T30,000) throughout the day, but most commonly just after the evening bus has left. You should also be able to catch a shared minivan to Altai (T30,000, 12 hours) most days, from where you can find onward transport to Khovd.

Shared vehicles also hang around outside the Black Market (p186).

# GOV-ALTAI　ГОВЬ-АЛТАЙ
POP 53,200 / AREA 142,000 SQ KM
Mongolia's second-largest aimag is named after the Gobi Desert and Mongol Altai Nuruu, a mountain range that virtually bisects the aimag to create a stark, rocky landscape. There is a certain beauty in this combination, but there is considerable heartbreak too. Gov-Altai is one of the least suitable areas for raising livestock, and therefore one of the most hostile to human habitation. Somehow a few Gobi bears, wild camels, ibexes and even snow leopards survive, protected in several remote national parks. Most of the population lives in the northeastern corner, where melting snow from Khangai Nuruu feeds small rivers, creating vital water supplies.

OFF THE BEATEN TRACK

**GREAT GOBI STRICTLY PROTECTED AREA**

Established more than 25 years ago, the Great Gobi Strictly Protected Area (Говийн Их Дархан Газар) has been nominated as an International Biosphere Reserve by the UN.

It's divided into 'Gobi A' (Southern Altai Gobi) and 'Gobi B' (Dzungarian Gobi). Gobi A is over 44,000 sq km in the southern part of the aimag, near Gurvantes; Gobi B is 8810 sq km in the southwest of Gov-Altai and neighbouring Khovd. Together, the area is the fourth-largest biosphere reserve in the world and protects wild asses, Gobi bears, wild Bactrian camels and jerboas, among other endangered animals.

For both parts of the **park** (Говийн Их Дархан Газар; ⊞Gobi A fencer.oafs.slings, Gobi B authentic.understates.solemn; T3000) you will need a very reliable vehicle and an experienced driver, and you must be completely self-sufficient with supplies of food, water and camping gear. A ranger will probably track you down and collect park entry fees.

## 🏃 Activities

Mountaineers and adventurous hikers with a lot of time on their hands might want to bag an Altai peak. Opportunities include **Khuren Tovon Uul** (3802m) in Altai *sum*, **Burkhan Buuddai Uul** (3765m) in Biger *sum*, and the permanently snow-capped peak of **Sutai Uul** (4090m), the highest peak in Gov-Altai, located right on the border with Khovd aimag. Most climbers approach Sutai Uul from the Khovd side.

## Altai Алтай

📞 01482, 7048 / POP 16,542 / ELEV 2181M

Altai, the aimag capital, is a dusty jumble of concrete and tin set between the mountains of Khasagt Khairkhan Uul (3579m) and Jargalant Uul (3070m). There's nothing too interesting here. It's a market and transport town with more petrol stations than functional hotels, but with one flight a week and bus service to UB it can be considered a transport hub. Most people simply pass through.

The dirt road out of town toward Biger from Altai takes you through a rugged landscape pock-marked with crude, unlicensed gold mines. You'll see families living out of tents, digging through spring-fed creek beds, hunting for gold flakes. In a parched region like this, it's not a happy sight.

## 🔘 Sights

**Khun Chuluu**  HISTORIC SITE
(GPS: N 46°15.830', E 96°16.484'; ⓜexits.revolved.delved) About 8km west of the main dirt tracks as you head south from Altai to Biger, and about 10km southwest of Altai itself, among the blemished land scarred by amateur gold miners, this single *khun chuluu* (which translates as stone figures or *balbal*) is said to date back to the 13th century (possibly earlier). You'll find it rooted into the ground, surrounded by stones. It looks as if it's praying at an invisible altar.

**Altai Museum**  MUSEUM
(📞1482-24213; ⓜoccults.fostered.chisel; T5000; ⊙9am-1pm & 2-6pm Mon-Fri) The Altai Museum shows off some excellent bronze statues, scroll paintings, genuine Mongol army chain-mail, and an interesting shaman costume and drum. Look out for the 200kg statue of Buddha, which was hidden

in a cave during the purges and recovered in 1965. The sturdy old building is worth a look in itself.

## 🛏️ Sleeping & Eating

**Zaiver Ger Camp**  TOURIST GER CAMP $
(📞9953 5404; GPS: N 46°14.391', E 96°21.682'; ⓜpropose.natively.munching; per person T10,000, meals T3000-5000; ⓟ) This pretty camp is nestled into the crook of a forested hillside, 16km south of Altai (west off the main road to Biger). Pick-up from town, and drop-off back again, is included in the price. There is no shower. This forest is the nicest place for camping in the area, too.

**Altai Hotel**  HOTEL $$
(📞7070 4444; ⓜlimo.panthers.reformation; s/d/tr T40,000/50,000/70,000; ⓐ) Rooms in this green-and-white-painted hotel have wood floors, flat-screen TVs, high ceilings, private baths and wi-fi. There's a decent lobby restaurant here too.

**★ Entum Hotel**  HOTEL $$$
(📞7048 3364; ⓜshops.solubility.underlie; r T65,000-95,000) The smartest and newest hotel in town at research time, Entum is set atop a hill, overlooking the city and just off the highway. All rooms have wood floors, tasteful wallpaper and flat screens; deluxe

versions come with a separate living area and a king-sized bed. There's no air-con.

## ℹ Information

**Internet Cafe** (per hour T900; ⊘9am-10pm) Inside the Telecom office, with the post office.

**Khan Bank** (🏧pamphlet.november.manicured; ⊘9am-6pm Mon-Fri) Currency exchange, an ATM (next door) and Western Union.

## ℹ Getting There & Away

### AIR

**Hunnu Air** (☎7000 1111; www.hunnuair.com; ⊘9am-6pm) flies to Ulaanbaatar (T190,000 to T300,000) on Fridays at 8am from Altai's adorable airport on the highway 2km outside town (T4000 in a taxi). Some staff speak English. Book tickets (in cash) in advance because thanks to the proximity of the mountains, flights have a weight limit and only take off if less than two-thirds full.

### BUS

Two **buses** (🏧roughing.texting.impartially) leave daily at 11am and 3pm for Ulaanbaatar (T40,700, 20 hours, 1000km) via Bayankhongor (371km), Arvaikheer (571km), several *guanz* stops, a couple of breakdowns and a small river crossing. You'll have to pay the full UB fare even if you disembark early, but they'll drop you anywhere along the route.

### THE ROAD TO BIGER

A remote back route takes you from Altai southeast to Biger, from where you can continue to Chandmani, Bayangovi and Khongoryn Els in Ömnögovi. The road cuts through the stark mountain-lined scenery of the Biger Depression, and passes a few rarely visited sights along the way, including an increasingly pock-marked landscape on the immediate outskirts of Altai thanks to crude, unlicensed gold mining. Biger is a small town known for producing yak-milk vodka, but has no reliable lodging options. If you come out this way, bring plenty of food and water, enough for three days at least, and your own camping supplies.

### MINIVAN & JEEP

Minivans leave from the **bus stand** (🏧overdue.span.icecap) when full for Ulaanbaatar (T50,000, 20 hours) and will reluctantly drop passengers in Bayankhongor (T30,000) and Arvaikheer (T40,500). Despite Altai being on the main road to Khovd, it is quite difficult to find transport west as passing buses/minivans are invariably full, but if there's capacity they will take you.

THE GOBI ALTAI

# Western Mongolia

POP 336,482

## Best Places to Eat

➡ Pamukkale (p195)

➡ Urguu Restaurant (p204)

➡ Han Hohii (p208)

➡ Arvin Restaurant & Pub (p195)

➡ Minj Restaurant (p204)

## Best Places to Stay

➡ Chinggis Hotel (p208)

➡ Eagle's Nest (p194)

➡ Zavkhan Hotel (p212)

➡ OT Tour Camp (p209)

➡ Bear Valley Ger Camp (p194)

## Why Go?

Raw, rugged and remote, this region has for centuries been isolated – both geographically and culturally – from the Mongolian heartland. With its glacier-wrapped mountains, shimmering salt lakes and hardy culture of nomads, falconry and horsemanship, western Mongolia is a timeless slice of Central Asia.

Squeezed between Russia, Kazakhstan, China and the rest of Mongolia, this region has long housed a patchwork of peoples including ethnic Kazakhs, Dörvöds, Khotons, Myangads and Khalkh Mongols. Traditional arts such as *khöömii* (Mongolian throat singing) and eagle hunting are still practised here, as they have been for thousands of years.

The wild landscape offers fabulous opportunities for trekkers and climbers on peaks that rise to more than 4000m. If that sounds too extreme, then just pick a lake, pitch a tent and have yourself a camping trip you'll never forget.

## When to Go

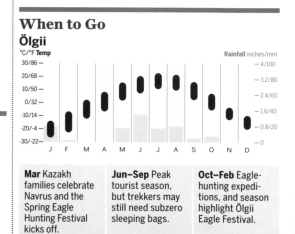

**Ölgii**

**Mar** Kazakh families celebrate Navrus and the Spring Eagle Hunting Festival kicks off.

**Jun–Sep** Peak tourist season, but trekkers may still need subzero sleeping bags.

**Oct–Feb** Eagle-hunting expeditions, and season highlight Ölgii Eagle Festival.

# Western Mongolia Highlights

**1** Climbing **Khuiten Uul** (p199) 4050m to Malchin Peak for stunning views of Mongolia's highest mountain.

**2** Pitching a tent beside beautiful **Khoton Nuur** (p199), dotted with Kazakh settlements around its shore.

**3** Rubbing shoulders with Kazakh eagle hunters at **Ölgii Eagle Festival** (p196); fast becoming western Mongolia's biggest tourist drawcard.

**4** **Üüreg Nuur** (p209) Experiencing the bewitching beauty of this lovely,

accessible freshwater lake surrounded by mountains.

**5** Trekking pristine glacial landscapes and enjoying the hospitality of nomads, including local eagle hunters, at **Tsambagarav Uul National Park** (p201).

## ❶ Getting There & Away

Transport between western Mongolia and Ulaanbaatar (UB) is mainly by plane: there are airports in **Ölgii** (p196), **Khovd City** (p204), **Ulaangom** (p208) and **Uliastai** (p213). Cheap seats fill up fast in summer: buy tickets a few weeks in advance if you can. Flights on and around the **Ölgii Eagle Festival** (p196) weekend sell out months in advance.

Transport by land from UB is improving every year. You'll likely end up on an air-conditioned, 45-seat Korean bus, but it'll still take you a good 36 hours to get all the way to Bayan-Ölgii.

More and more travellers are entering or leaving Mongolia at the Tsagaannuur border crossing with Russia (best accessed from Ölgii), but note that this closes on Sundays and during festivals. The less utilised border at Bulgan connects Khovd with China's Xinjiang province.

## ❶ Getting Around

Hiring a 4WD is a cinch in Ölgii but can be trickier elsewhere. The three westernmost aimag capitals are linked by decent 4WD trails; Uliastai is much further east, and less well connected to the west. You'll waste a lot of time hitching in the area: trucks will most likely be heading for the nearest border post and 4WDs will be packed full of people. You're better off with the buses and the shared jeeps and minivans that congregate at the markets of aimag centres. It's generally easier to get on a bus heading back to Ulaanbaatar than one coming in the other direction, so a good plan is to fly out and overland it back to the capital.

# BAYAN-ÖLGII
## БАЯН-ӨЛГИЙ

POP 100,172 / AREA 46,000 SQ KM

Travelling to Mongolia's westernmost aimag gives one the distinct feeling of having reached the end of the road, if not the end

---

**KAZAKH LANGUAGE**

Throughout Bayan-Ölgii aimag, and in parts of Khovd, Kazakh is the main language used for everyday conversation. Unsurprising considering the large majority of the population are ethnic Kazakhs. Though Mongolian is still the official language, in some areas it will be little used or understood, so a few words of Kazakh will go a long way. For more on the Kazakh Language, see p277.

---

of the earth. High, dry and wild, the isolated, oddly shaped Bayan-Ölgii follows the arc of the Mongol Altai Nuruu as it rolls out of Central Asia towards the barren wastes of the Dzungarian Basin.

Many peaks here are more than 4000m high and permanently covered with glaciers and snow. The valleys have some green pastures that support a few million head of livestock, with bears, foxes, wolves and ibex inhabiting the higher ground.

Unlike the rest of Mongolia, which is dominated by the Khalkh Mongols, about 90 per cent of Bayan-Ölgii's population is Kazakh. Travelling Mongolians liken coming here to visiting another country. Others who call Bayan-Ölgii home include the Khalkh, Dörvöd, Uriankhai, Tuva and Khoshuud ethnic groups.

---

# Ölgii                                  Өлгий

📞 01422, 7042 / POP 34,007 / ELEV 1710M

Ölgii city is a windblown frontier town that will appeal to anyone who dreams of the Wild West. It's a squat, concrete affair, straddling the banks of the Khovd Gol and surrounded by ger districts and rocky escarpments. Thunderclouds brew in the mountains above town, making for dramatic climatic changes throughout the day and brilliant light shows in the late afternoon.

The town is predominantly Kazakh, and you'll soon start feeling it has more in common with Muslim–influenced Central Asia than Buddhist Mongolia: there are signs in Arabic and Kazakh Cyrillic, several mosques, and the market – called a 'bazaar' rather than the Mongolian *zakh* – is stocked with goods from Kazakhstan.

## ◉ Sights

**Ölgii Aimag Museum**                    MUSEUM
(🌐 announced.guises.perform; admission T5000; ⏱ 9am-noon & 1-5pm Mon-Fri) The old-fashioned Ölgii Aimag Museum gives a basic overview of Kazakh culture and the geography of Bayan-Ölgii. The 1st floor has some terrifically bad taxidermy; the 3rd floor offers interesting ethnographic displays. A small **gift shop** sells Kazakh wall hangings, rugs and crafts.

## 🛏 Sleeping

Several tour operators have opened their own ger camps. Kazakh Tour, Blue Wolf and **Kobesh Travel** (📞 9910 7676, 9816 7676;

# Ölgii

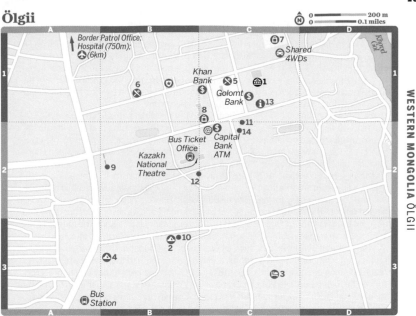

0 ————— 200 m
0 ————— 0.1 miles

# Ölgii

www.kobeshtravel.com; Ⓜ️rectangular.enough. played) were constructing hotels at time of research. Prices can increase significantly during the Ölgii Eagle Festival (p196), and beds book out months in advance.

To camp, walk east of the square to Khovd Gol and then head southeast, away from the market and ger suburbs. A clean and well-equipped **bathhouse** (Ⓜ️applause. simulates.delved; shower T1500; ⊙10am-10pm) is available in town.

★ **Blue Wolf**                      TOURIST GER CAMP **$**
(Ⓙ1422-22772, 9910 0303; www.bluewolftravel. com; Ⓜ️sentences.materials.unusually; per person incl breakfast T24,000; Ⓟ@ⓡ) Tour operator **Blue Wolf** (Ⓙ9911 0303, 9910 0303; www. bluewolftravel.com; wuser.trickled.exclusive) offers eight Kazakh–style gers sleeping two to four people each, and one larger ger with six beds, set in a walled and secure compound. Toilets and showers are communal. Breakfast is in the **Blue Wolf Restaurant**. The Blue Wolf tour office is in between the ger camp and the restaurant.

## EAGLE HUNTING: FACT, FICTION AND FALCONRY

BAFTA–nominated film *The Eagle Huntress* (2016) was the biggest thing out of Bayan-Ölgii since, well, ever. It tells the tale of Aisholpan, the 13-year-old daughter of a Kazakh *burkitshi* (eagle hunter) who longs to be the first female eagle hunter in 12 generations of her family.

Whether you go along with criticism that *The Eagle Huntress* was more of a fairy tale than a documentary, there's no doubt that it found a true star in the remarkable Aisholpan, who bravely overcomes the challenges set before her.

It's almost certain that the film exaggerated the weight of patriarchal hostility against Aisholpan, while at the same time ramping up the sporting drama to create its popcorn-friendly, girl power narrative. But it also brought the Kazakh pastime of eagle hunting to the attention of millions via its gorgeous shots of epic landscapes and soaring golden eagles – the ultimate gift to the tourism industry of Bayan-Ölgii.

The Ölgii Eagle Festival (p196) has always been tied to tourism. It came about in 1999 with funding from an American–run tour agency from Ulaanbaatar working in association with the then-newly formed Bayan-Ölgii Eagle Hunters Association. The festival has helped reignite the dwindling practice of eagle hunting and its associated customs, but as more tourists flock to Ölgii each October, its popularity is changing the nature of the pastime, from traditional winter hunting of wild foxes to demonstration falconry.

With this shift comes issues, such as eaglets being bought and sold for potential profiteering from tourist photographs, and not being returned to the wild when they reach breeding age. Even then, eagles taken from the nest before they could fly and be trained by their parents to hunt would have little chance of survival in the wild, according to American falconry expert Lauren McGough. Kazakh *burkitshi* claim the instincts an eagle needs to survive are inbuilt, but it's an issue that the Bayan-Ölgii Eagle Hunters Association admits requires more research, noting that during the Soviet period, accumulated knowledge on the rearing and care of eagles had been lost.

You can do your bit by visiting only established eagle hunters – usually descendants of a line of *burkitshi* who hunt in winter according to tradition and release their raptors after the proper tenure (five to seven years) when the eagle female reaches breeding age. 'Hunters' with eagles soliciting for photographs at the roadside are best avoided.

It's potentially less important that the eagle hunters you interact with are regular attendees of the festivals. Some say the best *burkitshi* don't compete because their birds, trapped or reared from an older age to be more effective wild hunters, would be too skittish and fearful in a festival environment.

At the time of research, Blue Wolf was building a 28-room hotel next door; it's due to be operational by 2018.

### ★ Traveller's
#### Guest House
TOURIST GER CAMP $

(☑ 9942 9696, 9942 8248; nazkanaa@gmail.com; ▥ wording.crows.teardrop; per person T15,000; [P][✿]) This no-frills, family-run operation offers good-value shared ger accommodation with a clean shower block and flushing toilets. The owner, Nazgul, who also works for **Kazakh Tour** (☑ 9942 2006; www.kazakhtour.com; NHU bldg, 2nd fl, ▥ dives.gurgled.partners), speaks English well and has extensive knowledge about the whole aimag. Mountain bike and motorcycle rental is available, and maps are for sale here. A restaurant is in the pipeline, but until then, no breakfast.

### Bear Valley Ger Camp
TOURIST GER CAMP $$

(☑ 9966 2324, 9460 1616; www.bearvalley adventures.com; ▥ cultivator.overpay.highlighted; per person with breakfast/three meals US$20/40; [P][✿]) Ger accommodation 7km outside Ölgii in a pleasant spot between mountains and a brook of the fast-flowing Khovd Gol. Each of the dozen gers sleeps two to three people; the restaurant is in a larger Kazakh ger. Owner Akhmaral is friendly, speaks English and can arrange local tours and activities. Free airport (p196) pick-ups.

### ★ Eagle's Nest
HOTEL $$

(☑ 9942 7003; www.altaiexpeditions.com; ▥ lakeside.saved.mainframe; tw incl breakfast US$25; [P][✿]) The best hotel in town has a cosy, hunting-lodge vibe and a quiet location, with 11 well-maintained twins all facing back on to the mountains. Rooms have bathtubs and include breakfast. Free airport (p196) pick-ups. The hotel, run by **Altai Expeditions** (📞9942 7003; www.altaiexpeditions.com; 🗺️ lakeside.saved.mainframe), is 1km south along Peace Avenue (in front of the big radio mast).

## ✖️ Eating

Dining in Ölgii is more varied and pleasurable than anywhere else in the west of Mongolia, with Kazakh and Turkic influences equating to tasty shashlik and shish kebabs, plus a smattering of Russian and Western fare. Ölgii's first cafes – even an Indian restaurant! – opened in 2017.

Self-caterers should head to the market or to one of the many supermarkets dotted about town.

### ★ Arvin Coffee & Book          CAFE $
(🗺️ fantastic.draining.broached; coffee from T3000, toast T3000; ⏱️8am-10pm Mon-Fri, from 11am Sat & Sun; 🛜) Stepping into the Starbucks-styled surrounds of Ölgii's first coffee shop is a bit like finding a pub on Mars. They'll even whizz you up a caramel, cream-topped frappeno, as Russian 4WDs bounce through potholes on the street below. Brunch bites include egg on toast and cereal. It's on the second floor above Arvin Restaurant.

### Arvin Restaurant & Pub   KAZAKH, MONGOLIAN $
(🗺️ fantastic.draining.broached; mains T4350-6500; ⏱️8am-midnight; 🛜) Genuinely friendly staff and some delicious Kazakh and Mongolian favourites (plus a few Western dishes) make this place popular with both locals and travellers. We recommend the Kazakh dish *sirne* (meat cooked in a pressure cooker). Beer from T2500. Photo menu.

### ★ Pamukkale          TURKISH $$
(🗺️ vertical.assemble.wealth; mains T4000-8500; ⏱️10am-11pm; 🛜) Smartly dressed staff greet you with a smile at this Turkish-run outfit, the nicest restaurant in town by a steppe mile. After a long trip, a juicy shish kebab with a side of fries really hits the spot. Also has soups, chicken dishes and authentic Turkish desserts. No alcohol but they do serve Turkish coffee.

## 🔒 Shopping

### Otau Shop          ARTS & CRAFTS
(🗺️ quits.tigers.bolts; ⏱️10am-6pm) Cosy arts and crafts shop selling Kazakh felt handicrafts (bags, purses, slippers, hats) as well as traditional clothing. Prices start at around T4000. The owners live on-site; ring the bell to get in. Look for the attractive blue-and-white building opposite the theatre (p196).

### Market          MARKET
(🗺️ fuses.merit.homeward; ⏱️10am-5pm Tue-Sun) Traditional Kazakh skullcaps, wall hangings and throws, knives and *dombra* (traditional Kazakh two-stringed lutes) can be found amid the chaos here. Also good for fruit and

---

### ONWARDS TO RUSSIA & KAZAKHSTAN

4WDs and/or minivans leave daily each morning at about 10am from around the market in Ölgii for the Russian border town of Kosh-Agach (T35,000 per person, 200km, time varies due to border crossing). From Kosh-Agach, there should be a morning bus to Gorno-Altaysk, the capital of Russia's Altai Republic region.

For Kazakhstan, a long-distance bus (T130,000 per person, 1862km) leaves Ölgii every Wednesday and Saturday in summer for Astana. The bus goes through Russia's Altai region so you'll need visas for both Russia and Kazakhstan. Kazakh Tour in Ölgii can help you buy the bus ticket (for a T20,000 commission). The bus first heads to the Mongolian border at Tsagaannuur (three hours), where you stay the night (a guesthouse here charges T10,000 per bed, including food). You then make the 30-hour trip to Astana from here. Privately operated shared minivans make the same trip pretty much every day from Ölgii.

Note that the border between Mongolia and Russia is open from 9am to 6pm and closed on Sundays (on the Russian side): it's wise to avoid crossing on Mondays when there may be a backlog of travellers. During the Naadam Festival public holiday around July 11-15, it can be closed for several days, leading to a mass of travellers wishing to cross; there have been reports of people having to wait for up to six days.

For further information, head to shop.lonelyplanet.com to purchase downloadable PDFs of chapters from Lonely Planet's *China* or *Russia* guides.

There are no international flights to or from Ölgii Airport (p196).

196

**DON'T MISS**

## ÖLGII EAGLE FESTIVAL

Hunting with eagles is a Kazakh winter hobby, not a profession, and it's estimated that there are about 400 practitioners living in Bayan-Ölgii. Every October, around a hundred of them converge at Sayat Tube (Hunter's Hill), 8km east of Ölgii, for this festival. With eagle antics and traditional horse games and camel races, it's the hottest ticket in the West.

**Ölgii Eagle Festival** (▥ scones.sneezed.jumpers; admission US$30; ⊘1st weekend Oct), often called the 'Golden Eagle Festival' or simply 'the Eagle Festival', has soared in popularity since the heroics of Aisholpan, a plucky 13-year-old Kazakh girl, were portrayed in the 2016 film *The Eagle Huntress*. That year, 800 foreign tourists descended on Ölgii for the festival, far outstripping the number of available beds. Since then, the town has been scrambling to catch up; four new hotels and several ger camps were being built at the time of research.

A photographer's dream, the programme kicks off around 10am on the Saturday with a fashion parade of sorts, as the mounted eagle hunters – resplendent in embroidered winter furs and brandishing their birds – are judged on their attire. The festival's various competitions and displays – including one called *shakhyru*, during which the eagle must catch a piece of fox fur pulled behind a galloping horse – are staggered over the weekend.

The festival culminates on Sunday, when a live fox (or sometimes a wolf pup) is released as bait for the top three eagles to hunt; note that some may find this somewhat distressing, as the fox or pup is killed.

The festival also includes traditional **horse games** and **camel races**. The most exciting are *kokpar* (a tug-of-war with an animal skin between two riders) and *tenge ilu* (a competition in which riders must swoop down to pick up a scrap of material from the ground at full gallop).

Although the tradition dates back about 2000 years (Marco Polo mentions it in his *Travels*), the practice of eagle hunting withered under Soviet rule, and the festival was held for the first time in 1999. Since then, its growing success has helped preserve the pastime, though it has also distorted the focus from seasonal hunting to camera-friendly display falconry. For the real thing, you need to go out on a winter hunt; the season starts after the festival.

Be sure to hang onto your festival admission ticket as it will get you into the Saturday night **traditional music concert** held in the **Kazakh National Theatre** (▥ natively. interviewer.skewed).

The easiest way to get to the festival grounds is on the bus (T5000 per person return) operated by **Kazakh Tour** (p194), or by taxi (T10,000 one way).

Other eagle festivals in western Mongolia include the **Altai Kazakh Eagle Festival** (p197), held in Sagsai on the third weekend of September, and the new **Spring Eagle Hunting Festival** (www.bluewolftravel.com; ▥ unclassified.hassle.afterbirth; ⊘21-22 Mar), which was in its infancy at the time of research.

vegetables. There are several cheap *guanzes* (canteens) here, including one run by a Uighur lady who makes Chinese–style noodles. The market doesn't really get going until the afternoon. Busiest on Saturdays.

## ℹ Information

**Mongolia Immigration** (INFC; ☎1422-22195, 9942 4338; ▥ treatable.steam.jugs; ⊘8am-noon & 1-5pm Mon-Fri) can register your passport and issue visa extensions (it takes half a day), as well as issue exit visas for Russia. Take a local to help you; staff have limited English.

There's a **Khan Bank** (▥ expecting.head-board.lease; ⊘8am-5.30pm Mon-Fri, 9am-3pm Sat) off the northwest of the square and a **Golomt Bank** (▥ mixers.overlaid.salsa) opposite the east side of the square; both may be able to change money. Foreign cards are accepted at the **ATMs** (▥ shining.taken.streaking) inside and outside the **Telecom Building** (▥ clincher. flashback.copes; ⊘9am-7pm).

### GETTING THERE & AWAY
#### Air

The **airport** (▥ forgotten.hillsides.slate) is 6km north of Ölgii's centre, on the opposite side of the river. There is no airport bus but you can find cars for hire at the **market** (p195) to take you there (T900 per km).

At the time of research, Hunnu Air was flying daily to UB, while Aero Mongolia was flying to UB on Tuesdays, Thursdays, Saturdays and Sundays between May and August. Their **ticket office** (📞 8808 0025; www.aeromongolia.mn; ⊙ 8am-5pm Mon-Sat) is on the 2nd floor of a three-storey block directly opposite **Pamukkale** (p195) restaurant.

Extra chartered flights are put on to cope with increased demand for the **Ölgii Eagle Festival**, but expect prices to skyrocket.

**Bus**

The non-stop bus to Ulaanbaatar (T81,000, 32 to 40 hours, 1636km) leaves Ölgii's **bus station** (▥ framework.altitude.revealing) daily at 3pm, and goes via Khovd (339km), Altai (635km), Bayankhongor (1006km) and Arvaikheer (1206km). Tickets for the latter destinations are rarely available; to secure a seat, you might have to pay the full UB fare. Go for the newer red-and-white 45-seat Korean buses rather than the old Greybird buses. The hard-to-find **ticket office** (▥ bake.zips.originals; ⊙ 8am-5pm) is in the basement of the **Kazakh National Theatre** (p196), in an annex building to the west. Duck in through the open doorway and you'll find the office down the corridor on the left.

**Minivan & Jeep**

Public **shared 4WDs** (▥ safety.grudge.stilted) and minivans leave for Khovd City from the **market** (p195) regularly throughout the day (T20,000, 339km, around five to seven hours, with minivans generally taking longer). They are far more frequent than those to Ulaangom (T40,000, 10 hours, 300km).

Hiring a random driver at the Ölgii **market** (p195) to embark on trips with is not a good idea – these drivers are not accountable to anyone and have a reputation for changing prices and itineraries mid-trip. The Mongol Altai Nuruu Protected Areas (MANSPAA) **administration office** (MANSPAA; 📞 9942 8858, 1422-22111; manspaa@mongol.net; ▥ vital. wished.orbited; ⊙ 9am-noon & 1.30-5pm Mon-Fri) and local tour companies have drivers more familiar with tourists' needs.

## Sagsai  Сагсай

📞 01422, 7042 / POP 5137

Squat Kazakh homesteads enclosed by walls of adobe bricks, and a location on the high desert steppe, give the sleepy community of Sagsai a distinctly Central Asian vibe.

A centre for eagle hunting, Sagsai is home to around 40 hunters, including three-time Eagle Festival champion Khizem.

Sagsai hosts the day-long Altai Nomad Festival (p198) each July, and a small eagle festival in September; there's talk of combining the two events in the future.

### 🏃 Activities

**Khizem Eagle Hunter Experience**  WILDLIFE WATCHING
(📞 9583 8188; ▥ contracted.desktop.pickled) Khizem is a celebrated Sagsai eagle hunter, a three-time medal winner at the region's eagle festivals since 2012. He welcomes visitors into his summer ger, decorated with fur pelts and medals (he's also a successful horse trainer), and will pose for snaps (for a fee) with his eagle.

**Altai Mountains School of Falconry**  WILDLIFE
(www.altaiexpeditions.com; ▥ underfunded.bewitch. oversights) Under development at the time of research, and slated to open in 2018, this winter wilderness is located 15km from Sagsai. It will offer two-day, five-day and longer programs that commence after the Ölgii Eagle Festival (p196) and run until spring. Students will train in falconry with local eagle hunters, eventually joining them on wilderness hunting expeditions.

### 🎉 Festivals & Events

⭐ **Altai Kazakh Eagle Festival**  CULTURAL
(▥ creditable.donkeys.shoving; per person US$30; ⊙ 3rd weekend Sep) This two-day festival, held about 6km southwest of Sagsai, is smaller than the Ölgii Eagle Festival,

---

### KAZAKH GER HOSPITALITY

If you find yourself inside a Kazakh ger at any time of day, you'll most likely be served a plate of *baursak* (puffy dough deep-fried in butter) with a bowl of *akh shai* (salty milk tea). Kazakhs also eat *kazy* (a type of cured horsemeat sausage), often as part of a *besh barmak* (literally 'five fingers'), a hands-on feast with five components: mutton, beef, horse, chewy noodles and potato. For special occasions, the platter is sometimes crowned with the head of a sheep or a goat, which is turned to face the guest of honour. Possibly you.

although it follows much the same program of eagle hunting competitions, horse events and camel races.

**Altai Nomad Festival**                    CULTURAL
(*III*creditable.donkeys.shoving; admission US$30; ⊘3rd weekend Jul (Sat)) Day-long festival featuring Kazakh horseplay, including *kyz kuar* ('kiss the girl', a race between a man and a woman on horseback); *buzkashi* (also known as *kokpar*), a horseback tug of war, and *tenge ilu,* where riders snatch flags from the ground at speed. Horse and camel races, and an awards ceremony, round out the afternoon.

A return trip from Ölgii in an eight-seater will cost US$90 per vehicle, if arranged through festival sponsors Blue Wolf Travel (p193).

### 🛏 Sleeping & Eating

Blue Wolf Travel (p193) in Ölgii can arrange homestays (with breakfast US$5-10 depending on group size, plus $12 for lunch and dinner) with local nomads nearby, including staying with competing eagle hunters during September's Altai Kazakh Eagle Festival. Book well in advance.

### ❶ Getting There & Away

A seat in a shared taxi from Ölgii should cost around T5000 one-way; the trip takes about an hour. **Blue Wolf Travel** (p193) can arrange return transport from Ölgii (US$90 per eight-seat vehicle).

# Altai Tavan Bogd National Park
Алтай Таван Богд

This stunning national park stretches south from the Tavan Bogd massif and includes the twin lakes of Khoton Nuur and Khurgan Nuur, which are the source of the Khovd Gol that flows to Khar Us Nuur in Khovd aimag. The lesser visited and rather less scenic Dayan Nuur is also found here.

Despite its remote location, the park and its beautiful scenery make it the premier attraction in western Mongolia. Divided from China and Russia by a high wall of snow-capped peaks, the area is a trekker's paradise.

The main entry to the **park** (Алтай Таван Богд; *III*primly.facsimile.inefficient; admission T3000) is by the bridge over the Khovd Gol, south of Tsengel, although travellers heading directly to the Tavan Bogd region go via Tsagaan Gol or Sogoog Gol. You can pay on entry or at the Mongol Altai Nuruu Protected Areas (MANSPAA) administration office (p197) in Ölgii. Border permits are required.

### ◉ Sights & Activities

#### Tavan Bogd Region
Tavan Bogd (Five Saints) is a soaring cluster of mountains that straddles the border between Mongolia, Russia and China. The range includes Khuiten (Cold Peak), Naran (Sun), Ölgii (Land), Bürged (Eagle) and Nairamdal (Friendship) mountains.

---

### NATIONAL PARKS OF BAYAN-ÖLGII
....................................................................

Most parks in Bayan-Ölgii come under the jurisdiction of the **Mongol Altai Nuruu Protected Areas Administration office**. (p197) At the time of research, park admission fees were due to increase to T10,000.

**Altai Tavan Bogd National Park** (6362 sq km) Fauna includes argali sheep, ibexes, *maral* (Asiatic red deer), stone martens, deer, elk, Altai snowcocks and eagles.

**Develiin Aral Nature Reserve** (103 sq km; p210) A remarkable habitat around Develiin Island in the Usan Khooloi and Khovd Rivers. It is home to pheasants, boars and beavers.

**Khökh Serkh Strictly Protected Area** (*III* commercially.animation.debug; admission T3000) (659 sq km) A mountainous area on the border with Khovd, protecting snow leopards, argali sheep and ibexes.

**Siilkhem Nuruu National Park** (*III* yesterday.unplugging.lengthy; admission T3000) (1400 sq km) This park has two sections, one around Türgen Uul, the other further west.

**Tsambagarav Uul National Park** (1110 sq km; p201) Protects glaciers and a snow-leopard habitat; borders on Khovd.

It's a compelling destination for serious mountaineers and trekkers, but you'll need a guide and equipment. The **Malchin Peak**, however, is a popular, non-technical climb that can be tackled by the reasonably fit.

### Tsagaan Sala                                            ROCK ART

(Baga Oigor; ⟦Ⅲ⟧shortness.blocking.muffle) The best petroglyphs in the area, if not all of Central Asia, can be found at Tsagaan Sala, in a river valley between Ulaankhus and Tavan Bogd. The carvings, more than 10,000 of them, are scattered over a 15km area; you'll need a guide to find the best ones.

### Sheveed Uul Petroglyphs                   ROCK ART

(⟦Ⅲ⟧curving.unsealed.trifling) Close to Tavan Bogd, the lower slopes of Sheveed Uul (3350m) and its surrounding valleys contain some fascinating petroglyphs depicting wild animals and hunting scenes. Keep your eyes peeled (and binoculars ready) for ibexes inhabiting the mountain above.

### ★Khuiten Uul                                       TREKKING

(Cold Peak; ⟦Ⅲ⟧ precludes.inky.shielding) The highest peak in the Tavan Bogd range (and the tallest mountain in Mongolia), Khuiten Uul (Cold Peak, 4374m) is of interest to professional climbers who are properly equipped with ice axes, crampons and ropes. The best time to climb is August and September, after the worst of the summer rains.

In 2006, the then-president of Mongolia climbed Khuiten and renamed it Ikh Mongol; however, no one seems to use this name.

Even if you are not a climber, it's worth trekking up to the **Tavan Bogd Ovoo** (⟦Ⅲ⟧words.maximum.shorn) or to the Khuiten Uul **base camp** (⟦Ⅲ⟧trouble.interstate.numberless), from where you'll have stunning views of all the Tavan Bogd peaks and the 12km-long Potanii Glacier, which tumbles out of the range. It's possible to walk onto the glacier, but be very careful of deep snow and crevasses. If you're not too exhausted, clamber to the top of **Malchin Peak** (4050m). The three-hour hike up is rewarded with stunning views of Russia, China and the surrounding mountains.

There are two trails to the base camp. One starts in the Sogoog Gol valley (north of Tsagaan Gol); from here it's 13km to the base camp via Tavan Bogd Ovoo. This trailhead has a ranger station (p200) with a ger shop and camping spots. Since 2014, a bone-rattling road (1½ hours, T15,000 per vehicle) has permitted vehicles to drive from the ranger station to the *ovoo* (shamanistic collection of stones, wood or other offerings to the gods), leading to an influx of local visitors. This has soured the serenity somewhat, though it does mean you can drive all the way to the mountain and back if all you want is photographs.

The other trail starts from the end of the road in Tsagaan Gol valley. From here it's a 16km trek to the base camp, passing well away from the *ovoo*. The trailhead has a ranger station and a place to camp. Across the river are some gers occupied by an extended family of Tuvans. You can hire horses (T20,000) from them, and one of the younger family members can guide you up to the base camp for around T25,000 with horse.

### Khoton Nuur Region

This is one of the most beautiful regions in the park, with the scenery growing more spectacular the further west you travel. The area is best explored on foot or horseback. In summer, you can hire horses from Kazakh families living around Khoton Nuur.

### ★Khoton Nuur                                          LAKE

(⟦Ⅲ⟧dwindled.obliging.scurrying) The southern shore along Khoton Nuur has excellent camping spots, especially around **Ulaan Tolgoi**, a spit of land that juts majestically into the lake. The northern tip of the lake is marked by **Aral Tolgoi** (Island Head), a hill surrounded by verdant pastureland and rocky escarpments. A border station at the northern end of the lake will check if your border permit is in order.

### Khoton Nuur to Tavan Bogd Trek       TREKKING

Northwest of Khoton Nuur, the mountains close in to offer some fine hiking possibilities. For experienced back-country walkers, it's possible to travel upriver to Tavan Bogd (110km, seven days). You'll need a local with you at all times or risk falling foul of border authorities.

## 🛏 Sleeping & Eating

There are no fixed ger camps set up for tourists in the Khoton Nuur region, but during summer, Tuvan and Kazakh families will often host trekkers in their gers for around T20,000 per person and may even supply a hot meal. Bring your own sleeping bag.

The best **camping spots** are around the lakes. Dayan Nuur has some nasty mosquitoes but the other two lakes are largely bug-free.

At Syrgal (☑austerely.prestigious.winningly), between the lakes, there's a couple of very basic shops selling sweets, vodka, water and little else. A ger shop at Tavan Bogd's north ranger station sells groceries.

**Cold Peak Camp**     TOURIST GER CAMP $$
(☑9842 0366; ☑conquered.sundial.clasp; per person T30,000; P) Rather than overnighting at the **north ranger station** (☑9821 1646; ☑celibates.theories.misspent; per person T30,000), this lovely spot 3km back down the trail has two five-bed gers with solar electricity and a toilet. It's run by Borsan, an affable Kazakh nomad who lives across the river. You can hire horses (T25,000 per day) from his family; they can also whip up a home-cooked meal (for a fee).

## ❶ Information

Border permits are required to enter the park and can be obtained in **Ulaanbaatar** (p84) or at the **Border Patrol office** (Khiliin Tserenk Alb; ☑1422-22341; ☑supporter.corporate.banks; ☺8-11am & 2-5pm Mon-Fri) in Ölgii. At the time of research, the permit was free to obtain (although this can change) and is good for an entire group, provided the group does not separate mid-trek.

Processing the permit takes between 10 minutes and an hour. You must bring your original passport (no photocopies accepted) and be prepared to describe your itinerary. The Border Patrol office is closed on weekends. Also note that the office will only deal with Mongolians so you'll need a local, your guide or a tour agency in Ölgii to apply on your behalf.

Border guards at Dayan Nuur, Tavan Bogd base camp, Aral Tolgoi (western end of Khoton Nuur) and Syrgal (the point where Khoton Nuur meets Khurgan Nuur) will all ask to see your paperwork (photocopies are not accepted); those without permits may be fined US$150 and possibly charged (around US$170) for the army to return them to Ölgii.

Most importantly, you cannot travel in Tavan Bogd National Park without a Mongolian accompanying you (this can be your driver). Your guide and driver will need their Mongolian passports.

Fishing permits cost T500 per day, and are only required if fishing before June 15. That said, in practice nobody seems to need them, or be able to get them.

### MAPS

**Traveller's Guest House** (p194) in Ölgii sells the excellent satellite map *Altai Tavan Bogd National Park Map & Guide* published by Conservation Ink (www.conservationink.org) for T15,000, and topographic 1:500,000 maps for

### KAZAKHS

Ask anyone in Kazakhstan for the best place to find genuine Kazakh culture, and they will most likely point to a small plot of land not in their own country, but in western Mongolia. Thanks to its isolation for most of the 20th century, Bayan-Ölgii is considered by many to be the last bastion of traditional Kazakh language, sport and culture.

Kazakhs first migrated to this side of the Altai in the 1840s to graze their sheep on the high mountain pastures during summer, returning to Kazakhstan or Xinjiang for the winter. After the Mongolian Revolution in 1921, a permanent border was drawn by agreement between China, the USSR and Mongolia, with the result that a large number of Kazakh nomads were technically living in Mongolia.

The word 'Kazakh' is said to mean 'free warrior' or 'steppe roamer'. Kazakhs trace their roots to the 15th century, when rebellious kinsmen of an Uzbek khaan broke away, and settled in present-day Kazakhstan.

Kazakh gers are taller, wider and more richly decorated than the Mongolian version. *Tush* (wall hangings) and *koshma* (felt carpets), adorned with stylised animal motifs, are common, while *chiy* (traditional reed screens) are becoming less so.

Kazakhs adhere rather loosely to Sunni Islam, but religion is not a major force. This is because of their distance from the centre of Islam, their nomadic lifestyle and suppression of the religion during the communist era. Islam is making a comeback in Bayan-Ölgii, thanks to the lifting of restrictions against religion, aid packages from other Muslim countries, the construction of mosques and the annual hajj pilgrimage to Mecca. The main Kazakh holiday is the pre-Islamic spring festival of **Navrus** (☺20, 21 or 22 Mar), celebrated around March 22.

Mongolian Kazakhs speak a Turkic language and write using a Cyrillic script of 42 letters; 33 are from the Russian alphabet, with nine additional letters that equate to sounds in the Kazakh language.

T18,000. A more basic map (T15,000) is available from the Mongol Altai Nuruu Protected Areas (MANSPAA) **administration office** (p197) in Ölgii.

## ⓘ Getting There & Away

The main road from Tsengel leads 45km south to the bridge over the Khovd Gol (T2000 toll) and then continues 33km to the junction of **Khoton** (p199) and **Khurgan** (⟦☷⟧kindling.picky.umpiring) nuurs, where there's a bridge across the wide water channel between the two lakes.

A more scenic route takes you from Sagsai over a pass and up the beautiful Khargantin Gol valley, past Tsengel, Khairkhan Uul and Khar Nuur right on the edge of the National Park, and then down to Dayan Nuur. A good option would be to enter the park this way and exit via the main road.

There are two main ways to access Tavan Bogd. One is via Tsengel and up the Tsagaan Gol (although fording the Khovd Gol after heavy rain can be tricky) to the **south ranger station** (⟦☷⟧pancakes.northbound.cellulose). The other is via Sogoog following the Sogoog Gol straight to Tavan Bogd via the **north ranger station**, or by going over the Hagiin Davaa (Hagiin Pass) that leads to Tsagaan Gol.

There is no public transport to the park. Theoretically you could arrange for a 4WD to drop you off and collect you at the end of your trek, but you will need a guide (this can be your driver) or risk getting turfed out of the park. This rule has been tightened since a party of hikers accidentally strayed into Russia a few years back.

A 4WD for one to five people from Ölgii to either ranger station typically costs around US$150.

# Tolbo                    Толбо

Travellers are drawn to this region by **Tolbo Nuur** (Толбо Нуур; ⟦☷⟧jungles.ripping.curses), an elevated lake that's popular for swimming in summer and ice fishing in winter. The lake is about 50km south of Ölgii on the main road to Khovd City.

The tiny settlement of Tolbo, 14km past the eastern edge of the lake and 3km off the main track, is a dusty strip of Kazakh houses and a single shop.

Tolbo *sum* (district) – along with Delüün *sum* to the south – is famous for its eagle-hunters (28 of them live here), and this is a good place to meet them. Craggy escarpments to the south are dotted with vertiginous nests that are plundered by Tolbo Kazakhs for their eaglets.

## ☆ Activities

**Urken Eagle Hunter Experience**                    WILDLIFE WATCHING
(⟦☷⟧complainer.inarguable.lower) A snarling wolf head hangs over the entrance to the winter home of Urken, a *burkitshi* (eagle hunter) training his young daughter Ahbota in the arts of eagle hunting. Urken can host winter hunting excursions, or you can stop by his cosy Toblo home for milk tea, photos and a chat (for a fee).

**Ice Fishing**                    FISHING
(Tolbo Nuur) Tolbo Nuur (p201), sheltering hefty Mongolian grayling and Altai osman, is becoming popular for ice fishing. Locals stage an **ice festival** in midwinter with activities including fishing, skating and traditional games. Talk to an Ölgii-based tour company for dates and more information.

## 🛏 Sleeping & Eating

**Tolbo Lake Ger Camp**          TOURIST GER CAMP $$
(☏9942 7003; www.altaiexpeditions.com; ⟦☷⟧celebrated.categorical.greyhound; per person with breakfast/full board US$20/40; 🅿) Each of this camp's five Kazakh–style gers sleeps four to five people; there are also three dorm cabins. The lake waters are shallow here for 15m, and good for swimming. The camp, operated by Altai Expeditions (p195), has a restaurant and showers but no wi-fi. Booking ahead is essential. Good camping spots nearby.

## ⓘ Getting There & Away

Shared taxis make the 50km trip (one hour) to Tolbo Nuur from Ölgii several times a day in summer, leaving from the market (p195). Look for vehicles marked Толбо Нуур. Expect to pay T5000 per person each way. You might be able to hitch a ride back into town, though hitching is never entirely safe, and we don't recommend it. Travellers who hitch should understand that they are taking a small but potentially serious risk.

# Tsambagarav Uul National Park
Цамбагарав Уул

This **national park** (Цамбагарав Уул; ⟦☷⟧haven.wingless.scooting; admission T3000) (1110 sq km) is named after the photogenic Tsambagarav Uul (4208m; p202), a permanently snow-capped peak that straddles the border between Khovd and Bayan-Ölgii aimags. It's a great place to visit eagle hunters, experience

WESTERN MONGOLIA TOLBO

pristine trekking (without the bother of pesky border permits) and see the summer camps of Uriankhai nomads. The park protects glaciers and is a snow leopard habitat.

The park is accessible from both Khovd and Bayan-Ölgii.

## 🏃 Activities

### ★ Aisholpan's
### Summer Camp                     WILDLIFE WATCHING
(☑ 9942 0519; Altan Tsogts, ⠿ guardians.drag. opportune) In a boulder-strewn valley in the Altan Tsogts *sum* (district) are the gers where Aisholpan, young star of *The Eagle Huntress*, lives between July and August. Aisholpan's father Agalai welcomes visitors for photographs and overnight stays (for a fee); after October he takes tourists on eagle hunting excursions into the wilderness from his winter camp in Oyin, 40km away.

### Sailay Eagle
### Hunter Experience               WILDLIFE WATCHING
(⠿ motionless.bankrupted.decamp) This well-watered valley overlooked by Tsambagarav Uul is the summer camping ground of local Kazakh nomads, including 60-year-old Sailay, one of the most experienced eagle hunters in the region. Visit in summer to meet his eagles and take photographs, or arrange a winter trip via one of Ölgii's tour operators to join Sailay on a wilderness hunt.

### Tsetsegt River Rafting          RAFTING
(www.bluewolftravel.com; ⠿ flagging.windscreen. breaker; per person incl gear, guide & meals (min two people) US$150) Rafting aficionados claim that the waters running through a canyon adjoining the Tsetsegt River adjoining the Khovd Gol serve up some of the best white water in Mongolia, with rapids up to Level Five. A local **rafting club** opened in Ölgii in 2016 – Blue Wolf (p193) acts as its agent for foreign tourists, adding on 15 per cent commission.

### Tsambagarav Uul                 CLIMBING
(⠿ issuers.sentiments.kerfuffle) The permanently snow-capped Tsambagarav Uul (4208m) is Bayan-Ölgii's second highest peak, and straddles the border between Khovd and Bayan-Ölgii aimags. Despite its altitude, the mountain's summit is relatively easy to climb compared with Tavan Bogd, but you'll need crampons and ropes. A neighbouring peak, Tsast Uul, is slightly lower at 4193m, and is also good for climbing.

## 🛏 Sleeping & Eating

From late June to late August, the massif is populated by nomad camps, and you might be able to organise a stay with the help of one of Ölgii's many tour agencies. Blue Wolf operates a small **ger camp** (☑ 9911 0303; www.bluewolftravel.com; ⠿ embedded.ambitious. potholed; per person incl breakfast/three meals US$15/35) in the north of the park, next to a family of Uriankhai nomads.

## ⓘ Getting There & Away

If coming from the southern side of Tsambagarav Uul (near the main Khovd–Ölgii Rd) you'll enter via the Namarjin valley, where there are outstanding views of the mountain. From here you can head west and then south to rejoin the main Khovd–Ölgii Rd, via several Kazakh settlements and a beautiful turquoise lake.

An alternative route from the Khovd side leads from the town of Erdeneburen, where you can see a *bugan chuluu* (deer stone; upright grave marker from the Bronze and Iron ages, on which is carved stylised images of deer) dating back to the pre-Mongol era, and up the mountainside to the Bayangol valley. The valley itself is nothing special but there are fine views southeast to Khar Us Nuur (p205), and you might be able to hire a horse for the hour-long ride to the Kazakh-populated Marra valley.

Entering the park from the Bayan-Ölgii (northern) side of the mountain is even more impressive. To reach the massif, a steep pass runs between Tavan Belchiriin Uul and Tsast Uul. From the glacier here, the road dips through some spectacular rocky gorges before finally tumbling down to Bayan Nuur, a small, slightly salty lake. From Bayan Nuur, a desert road travels east through a Martian landscape of red boulders and rocky mountains.

During summer, Blue Wolf (p193) operates a twice-weekly shuttle (US$100 for a six-seater, 2½ hours, 95km, Wednesdays and Sundays) from their Ölgii office to the Blue Wolf Tsambagarav Ger Camp (p202).

# KHOVD                              ХОВД
POP 84,486 / AREA 76,000 SQ KM

Khovd aimag has long been a centre for trade, business and administration in western Mongolia, a status that began during the Qing dynasty when the Manchus built a military garrison here. The aimag still does robust trade with China through the border at Bulgan. Its agricultural university is the largest of its kind in Mongolia outside Ulaanbaatar.

Besides its developing economy, Khovd is notable for being one of the most heterogeneous aimags in Mongolia; it's home to a Khalkh majority and the Khoton, Kazakh, Uriankhai, Zakhchin, Myangad, Oold and Torguud peoples. Its terrain is equally varied, with large salt lakes, fast-flowing rivers and the Mongol Altai Nuruu almost bisecting the aimag.

# Khovd City · Ховд

📞 01432, 7043 / POP 31,100 / ELEV 1406M

Khovd City is a pleasant, tree-lined place developed by the Manchus during their 200-year rule in Outer Mongolia. Though it's a small town, Khovd has slightly more going on than other cities in western Mongolia, with an agricultural university and some food processing and textile manufacturing plants.

Khovd offers a few sights to keep you busy for a day, and there are some great camping spots on the edge of town. Shops here are well stocked, and there are 4WDs to hire, making this a reasonable place from which to launch a trip to the Altai Mountains or the Great Lakes regions in Khovd and Uvs (though note that the vast majority of the region's tour operators are based in Ölgii). It's an eight- to ten-day journey from Khovd to the border at Bulgan, from where you can cross into China (provided you already have your Chinese visa).

## ◎ Sights

**Khovd Aimag Museum** — MUSEUM
(📞 9943 4502; 🌐 sage.seasonal.cakewalk; admission T5000; ⊙ 8am-noon & 1-5pm Mon-Fri) This museum has the usual collection of stuffed wildlife, plus excellent ethnic costumes, Buddhist and Kazakh art and a snow leopard pelt on the wall. One of the more interesting exhibits is a replica of the cave paintings of Tsenkheriin Agui (p206). There are also several examples of the many deer stones (upright grave markers from the Bronze and Iron ages, on which are carved stylised images of deer) scattered around the aimag, plus a model of Khovd's original fortress.

**Gandan Puntsag Choilon Khiid** — BUDDHIST MONASTERY
(🌐 glared.blackened.depleted) Officially opened in 2010, this is the largest monastery in western Mongolia. The compound is surrounded by a wall (with a path on top) and 108 stupas. Morning prayers are held from 9am until 3pm inside the main temple,

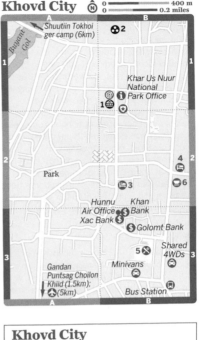

**Khovd City** N | 0 ——— 400 m | 0 ——— 0.2 miles

WESTERN MONGOLIA KHOVD CITY

## Khovd City

**◎ Sights**
1 Khovd Aimag Museum .......................... B1
2 Sangiin Kherem ................................... B1

**🛏 Sleeping**
3 Minj Hotel ........................................... B2
4 Urguu Hotel ........................................ B2

**🍴 Eating**
5 Market .................................................. B3
Minj Restaurant ............................... (see 3)
Urguu Restaurant ............................ (see 4)

**🍸 Drinking & Nightlife**
6 Coffee By The Boot ............................. B2

which features a statue of Buddha flanked by 10 divine protectors.

## 🛏 Sleeping & Eating

★ **Minj Hotel** — HOTEL $$$
(📞 7043-3968; 🌐 logo.unheated.pirates; s/tw/lux T45,000/60,000/80,000; 🅿 🛜) The staff here are cheerful, and rooms have extras including toothbrushes, reading lights and kettles, plus the best showers in Khovd. Twins are spacious and worth the higher outlay. Central, so can be noisy. *Minj* means 'beaver' in Mongolian.

OFF THE BEATEN TRACK

## DARA

This largely inaccessible and mysterious region is known simply as **Dara** (Дара; 'special place') by the Kazakh nomads who set their gers further down the valley. Little known and seldom visited (probably due to the bone-rattling drive over a sea of boulders required to get here), it rewards the intrepid with a rough and rugged beauty, and at least nine small **lakes** (Ⓜ haying.breathtaking.testify) scattered amid forbidding sawtooth mountains and vertiginous canyons.

About 60km west of Khovd City, Dara is accessible only by hired 4WD. The most scenic (yet arduous) route heads due west from Dund-Us *sum* (district) via a **natural spring** (Ⓜ infeasible.robots.unworthy), and then a spectacular *ovoo* (a shamanistic collection of stones, wood or other offerings to the gods) surrounded by at least eight Turkic **deer stones** (Ⓜ materials.plainest.emasculated). A faster, less scenic route turns northwest at Dund-Us and loops back around.

This wild region offers hiking, horse trekking, camping and fishing. **Dara Tour** (Khovd Handicraft & Tours; ☑ 9907 9485; www.facebook.com/MarkasShop) can arrange stays with Kazakh nomads in the area. Camping spots abound by the lakes.

★**Urguu**

**Restaurant** MONGOLIAN, INTERNATIONAL **$$**
(☑ 7043-8890; Ⓜ focal.space.stooping; mains from T5500; ⊙ 11am-10pm; Ⓟ 🛜) Tinted windows make this **hotel** (Ⓜ focal.space.stooping; s/tw/lux T45,000/60,000/80,000-100,000; Ⓟ 🛜) restaurant's dining room rather dreary (or romantic, depending on your point of view), but the dishes really shine. 'Fresh salad' (T4500) is made with leafy greens, cucumber and tomato, and is gloriously free of gloopy mayo. Chinese dishes include a large portion of lip-smacking fried chicken with chillies and peanuts (T12,500), served with white rice.

★**Minj**

**Restaurant** MONGOLIAN, INTERNATIONAL **$$**
(Ⓜ logo.unheated.pirates; mains from T6000; ⊙ 10.30am-9.30pm; Ⓟ 🛜) Minj Hotel (p203) has a bright, spotless restaurant that serves local and international dishes but the menu is in Mongolian only. *Frants takhia* ('T11,000, literally 'French chicken') is fried chicken with pineapple and veg, while *tackturetan* (T7500) is spicy Korean chicken with rice. They also have *bulgogi* (Korean-style grilled beef strips). A well-stocked bar serves spirits, wine and beer.

### 🍷 Drinking & Nightlife

★**Coffee By The Boot** CAFE
(☑ 8899 0181; Ⓜ nosedive.cosmic.hint; ⊙ 9am-9pm; 🛜) Named for its location next to a 3½m-high Mongolian *gutul* (traditional riding boot), this cosy spot is decorated with murals of snow leopards and argali sheep. It has the best (only?) real coffee in the aimag,

brewing the full gamut of caffeinated treats from espressos (T2000) to Americanos (T2500) to hazelnut lattes (T3500). It also has tea, juice and shakes.

### ℹ️ Information

**Telecom Office** (Ⓜ attitudes.dome.dialect; per hr T600; ⊙ 8am-10pm Mon-Fri, to 8pm Sat & Sun)

**Golomt Bank** (Ⓜ plod.developer.standing; ⊙ 9am-5pm Mon-Fri)

**Khan Bank** (Ⓜ chipper.emulated.harshest; ⊙ 8am-5pm Mon-Fri)

**Xac Bank** (Ⓜ advice.templates.done)

### ℹ️ Getting There & Away

#### AIR

Both Hunnu Air and Aero Mongolia have daily flights to and from UB. The **Hunnu Air office** (☑ 7043-8889; www.hunnuair.com; 2nd fl, Xac Bank, Ⓜ advice.templates.done; ⊙ 9am-6pm Mon-Sat) is on the second floor of **Xac Bank** near the market. The **airport** (Ⓜ upland.hips.unacceptable) is 5km south of the city.

#### BUS

Air-conditioned 45-seater buses leave twice a day (10am and 1pm) for the long slog to Ulaanbaatar (T66,000, about 30 hours, 1425km) via Altai and Bayankhongor; you'll likely have to pay through to UB to secure a seat for the prior stops. The small ticket office is just to the north of the **bus station** (Ⓜ oppositely.gremlin.timetables). Buy in advance.

#### MINIVAN & JEEP

**Minivans** (Ⓜ impersonated.quart.aimed) to regional destinations including Ölgii (T20,000, five to six hours, 339km), Ulaangom (T25,000, six to seven hours, 369km) and Bulgan (T30,000, eight to ten hours, 404km) congregate in a compound 200m north of the **bus station**. Ticket prices are fixed and must be bought from the small ticket office at the rear of the compound.

4WDs cost around T600 per km (including petrol) around town. **Shared 4WDs** (⟨*w*⟩mouthpieces.encodes.tightened) and taxis to local *sums* (districts) including Chandmani (T10,000, three to four hours) leave from the south of the market (note this location can change every year).

Marima, at **Dara Tour**, can help travellers arrange local taxi rides and 4WDs to other destinations.

# Khar Us Nuur National Park   Хар Ус Нуур

Khar Us Nuur (Dark Water Lake) is the second largest freshwater lake in Mongolia and the centrepiece of Khar Us Nuur National Park, an enormous area that also takes in smaller lakes, the twin peaks of **Jargalant Khairkhan Uul** (⟨*w*⟩persuader.spatulas.verifiably) (3796m) and Yargaitin Ekh Uul (3464m), and the Tsenkherlin Agui caves (p206).

The Khovd Gol flows into Khar Us Nuur, creating a giant marsh delta, the perfect habitat for wild ducks, geese, wood grouse, partridges and seagulls, including rare relict gulls and herring gulls.

In 2004, 22 *takhis* (Mongolian wild horses also known as Przewalski's horses) were introduced into the **Khomyn Tal** buffer zone, becoming the third herd of this critically endangered horse to be re-established in Mongolia.

A permit is technically required to visit the park, obtainable in Khovd City at the Khar Us Nuur National Park Office, (⟨*w*⟩dozed.imply.innovator; park permit T3000; ☉8am-5pm Mon-Fri) but there's a slim to no chance of anyone checking.

## ◉ Sights

**Dörgön Monastery**   BUDDHIST MONASTERY
(⟨*w*⟩crammed.roundups.resurface; T5000) Several brightly painted Buddhist temples have been erected on this hilltop in Dörgön *sum* (district) on the northeastern shore of Khar Us Nuur; the temples serve as a monastery. The site was established by Megjin, an elderly local woman who spent years here planting trees and shrubs and clearing out charnel ground said to be infested with demons. For her efforts, she was officially recognised as a Green Tara (Buddha of enlightened activity) in 2006 by the Mongolian Government.

## 🛏 Sleeping & Eating

A **ger camp** 5km from the **watchtower** (⟨*w*⟩flitting.inventive.rats) usually sets up shop in early spring, but closes for summer when the mosquitoes start raging. It reopens again in October.

UB–based tour operator Nomadic Journeys (p40) partners with local nomads for stays in and around the lake area for spring and autumn bird-watching trips.

The surrounding *sum* centres of Dörgön and Chandmani have a few shops and *guanzes* (canteens).

**Dörgön Zochid Budal**   HOTEL $
(⟨*w*⟩collections.cornfield.tapestry; bed T10,000; **P**) If you need to stay in Dörgön for the night, this place is five minutes' walk down the hill from the monastery, in the centre of the town. Meals T4000. No shower.

## ❶ Getting There & Away

It takes about an hour to drive from Khovd City to the watchtower on the western shore of Khar Us Nuur, and a further hour to continue around the southern tip of the lake, where the track closes to within 200m of the shore. Hiring a 4WD and driver for a half-day excursion from Khovd should set you back about T40,000 (plus fuel).

## Tsenkheriin Agui   Цэнхэрийн Агуй

Tsenkheriin Agui is famous for its cave paintings, some of which depict long-extinct fauna including mammoths and ostrich-like birds. This area is known as a great place to spot saiga antelopes, especially along the road to Chandmani.

The surrounding valleys are excellent for camping (if you can bear the mosquitoes) and short hikes.

---

### TO CHINA FROM KHOVD

It is possible to travel from Khovd to Ürümqi in China's Xinjiang province, via the Mongolian border town of Bulgan, but you will need to arrange your own transport. Note that at the time of research, the border was closed on weekends.

## ⊙ Sights & Activities

★ **Tsenkheriin Agui**                                    CAVE
(Khoid Tsenkher; [///]bodyguards.righteously.admission; per person/vehicle T3000/10,000) This huge cave looks deceptively small from the parking area. But once you scramble up the loose rock path, you realise its true size and how it must have afforded considerable shelter to the prehistoric humans who lived here.

Unfortunately, the Palaeolithic art (c 13,000 BC) has inspired others, with recent graffiti (c AD 2001) destroying much of it. In 2005 the area was incorporated into the Khar Us Nuur National Park (p205), and some of the paintings 'restored'.

To explore the cave you will need a strong torch and whatever kind of footwear you feel copes well with the dusty bird poo that blankets parts of the cave floor.

The paintings are very difficult to spot. There seem to be far fewer than the tourism spiel promotes, and we couldn't find the famed woolly mammoth paintings. The easiest to find are some antelope and bird paintings in the first cavern to your left as you descend the path into the main cave: most of them are found within a small conical recess here. Beside this, you can squeeze through a hole in the wall to see more animal figures.

Exiting the main cave, you can turn left and climb slightly higher to find the entrance to another, deeper cave, although it does not contain paintings.

The cave is about 100km southeast of Khovd City.

## 🛏 Sleeping

A **ger camp** ([☑]9943 9377, 9868 9377, 9525 9501, 9900 9377; gurvansenkher@yahoo.com; [///]proposals.mufti.mouth; per person incl meals T75,000; [P]) close to the cave serves travellers. Be warned: the mosquitoes here can be indescribably bad during summer.

## ℹ Getting There & Away

No shared transport goes to Tsenkheriin Agui, so your best bet is to arrange your own car and driver. It takes about two or three hours to reach the cave from Khovd City, making it a doable day trip, or as a stop-off when travelling between Khovd and Gobi-Altai aimags.

---

# Chandmani                    Чандмань
[☑]01432, 7043 / POPULATION 2916

Chandmani sits in the centre of a sun-baked plain, halfway between the blue strip of **Khar Nuur** in the east and the dramatic Jargalant Khairkhan Uul massif (p205) to the west. The *sum* (district) is a renowned centre for *khöömii* (throat singing): around 200 practitioners are said to live in the area.

It's also one of the better equipped *sum* centres, with a tiny handful of shops, a couple of banks, several *guanzes* (canteens) and a hospital.

## ⊙ Sights & Activities

**Petroglyphs**                                      ROCK ART
([///]incomes.flashy.stylishly) A pair of hillocks 3km west of town have a few petroglyphs etched into the boulders on top, and more in the narrow canyon between them. Performances are sometimes held here during the town's *khöömii* festival held every two years in July.

---

### KHÖÖMII (THROAT SINGING)

Thanks to some resident *khöömii* (throat singing) masters, such as **Tserendavaa** ([☑]8843 6510, 8892 6510; [///] endows.pressed.checkout; T120,000 per day), it is sometimes possible to arrange an impromptu demonstration (around T30,000 per group), and training (around T50,000 per hour). Apparently *khöömii* isn't as difficult to learn as you might imagine, although to attain any degree of proficiency you will need at least a week.

If you're lucky, your visit may coincide with one of the small concerts that are held in the purpose-built **Khöömii Ordon** ([///] incinerated.plant.orderings), although your best chance of this is during the third week of July when a **khöömii competition** is held as part of a biennial festival celebrating traditional Mongolian arts; the next festival is due to take place in 2018.

Locals claim Chandmani is a natural centre for *khöömii* because of the winds that sweep down from the mountain to the reedy marshes of **Khar Nuur** nearby, creating a throat-singing-like euphony.

## Camel and Horse Treks  HORSE RIDING

With a bit of notice, you can arrange horses or camels through Tserendavaa or one of the other throat singers for treks at **Dörgön Nuur**, about an hour's drive from Chandmani. The lake is also good for swimming.

## 🛏 Sleeping

Chandmani has a couple of single-room dormitory hotels. The throat singer Tserendavaa has a spare room in his house for which he charges T40,000 per person including meals. You can also sleep in a ger in his yard. Chandmani's best camping spots are around the small wooded groves south of town.

## 🔒 Shopping

**Bisness Enkhbator Töv**  ARTS & CRAFTS
(☑ 9511 8485; ⊞ slangy.soybeans.watering; ◴ 9am-5pm) A women's cooperative workshop that sells handmade felt and camel-wool items including cosy slippers, saddle covers for horses and camels, and woven *shagai* (a dice game using anklebones) fortune-telling boards.

## ℹ Getting There & Away

It takes about four hours to drive the 150km to Chandmani from Khovd City. The most scenic route is to turn off the paved Khovd–Altai Rd just south of Khar Us Nuur and travel around the southern tip of the lake, following the road between marshy shore and mountain until it turns east to hop over the northern tip of the **Jargalant Khairkhan Uul** (p205) massif. Then it's a straight shot south along lone and level plains to Chandmani, with several 600-year-old **burial mounds** (⊞ slideshow.accused.broadcaster) en route; they're marked by circles of standing stones.

Alternatively, you can stay on the paved road for longer and traverse around the southern tip of the Jargalant Khairkhan Uul range. This is also the way if you're coming up from Gobi-Altai.

Shared 4WDs/taxis (T10,000 per person, three to four hours, 150km) leave daily from Chandmani to Khovd in the afternoon when the vehicle is full.

# UVS  УВС

POP 81,278 / AREA 69,000 SQ KM

Uvs aimag is a land of extremes, a little-visited region bordering Russia to the north where desert steppes and great lakes collide. Here you'll find some of the world's most northerly sand dunes, Mongolia's largest lake by area, the country's lowest winter temperatures and a whole lot of high desert.

---

### ONE HOUR BEHIND

Note that the three westernmost aimags in Mongolia – Bayan-Ölgii, Khovd and Uvs – are in a different time zone from the rest of the country: they are one hour behind.

Zavkhan aimag is on Ulaanbaatar time.

---

The defining features of Uvs are its lakes, which come in all shapes, sizes and levels of salinity. The biggest, **Uvs Nuur**, is more like an inland sea, while spellbinding Üüreg Nuur (p209) might be the most gorgeous body of water in Mongolia. The lakes and the surrounding deserts make up the Ikh Nuuruudin Khotgor, the 39,000 sq km **Great Lakes Depression** that includes parts of neighbouring Khovd and Zavkhan aimags.

The twin peaks of **Kharkhiraa Uul** (4037m) and **Türgen Uul** (3965m) are also Uvs drawcards. From them spill permanent glaciers, fast-flowing rivers and verdant plateaus; the hiking opportunities are excellent.

## ℹ Getting There & Away

Aero Mongolia operates daily flights between Uvs and Ulaanbaatar from the **airport** (p208) at Ulaangom; at the time of research, Hunnu Air was running flights between the cities on Tuesdays to Sundays.

---

# Ulaangom  Улаангом

☑ 01452, 7045 / POP 30,688 / ELEV 939M

Ulaangom (Red Sand) slumbers halfway between the vast, shimmering and inaccessible waters of Uvs Nuur and the snow-capped peak of Türgen Uul. It's rather more spaced out than other aimag capitals

Ulaangom is just 120km from the Russian border, so you may encounter visiting Uriankhai from Russia's Tuva Republic.

## ◉ Sights

**Uvs Aimag Museum**  MUSEUM
(☑ 1452-24720; ⊞ defensive.hero.zeal; admission T4000; ◴ 8am-noon & 1-5pm Mon-Fri, 8.30am-noon & 1pm-5.30pm Sat) This okay museum has the usual dusty exhibits, plus a section on the 16th-century Oirad leader Amarsanaa (the chain-mail jacket is supposedly his). There's also a wing dedicated

solely to the reign of one-time dictator Yu Tsedenbal (who was born in Uvs), featuring photos of the man with other communist leaders including Fidel Castro and Ho Chi Minh.

**Dechinravjaalin Khiid**          BUDDHIST MONASTERY
([W]thin.skis.scrubbing) Dechinravjaalin Khiid was originally founded in 1738 and housed seven temples and 2000 monks; the place was pulverised in 1937, thanks to Stalin. Its current incarnation consists of a concrete ger and about 20 welcoming monks.

## 🛏 Sleeping & Eating

**★Chinggis Hotel**                    HOTEL $$
([☎]9945 8118; [W]nags.prepare.seasons; tw&d/half-lux/lux incl breakfast T40,000/80,000/100,000; [P][📶]) Chinggis is the undisputed grand khaan of Uvs hotels, slaying its rivals not with sword and bow but with surprisingly stylish rooms (especially the cosy 'half-lux' suites with comfy sofas and rugs), bathrooms with separate shower stalls and amenities, and a central location. Includes breakfast. No English spoken.

**★Grand Hotel**                      HOTEL $$$
([☎]9945 4435; [W]faced.beakers.prefect; tw/d&tr/half-lux/lux   T40,000/60,000/80,000/100,000; [P][📶]) Occupying the 3rd and 4th floors of this 2015 brick block in the north of town, the Grand has immaculate rooms with shower cubicles, toiletries, fridges and flat-screen TVs. The design is rather business-like, but when it's this fancy, who's complaining? Includes breakfast.

**★Han Hohii**                      INTERNATIONAL $$
([☎]9906 4559; 2nd fl, [W]intend.outdone.shunning; mains from T6500; [🕐]11am-11pm; [P][📶]) The top contender for date night in Uvs, with bow ties on the staff, chandeliers and a globetrotting menu that includes Greek salads (T6000), udon noodle soup (T7000), chicken tacos (T12,000), fish and chips (T14,000) and pizza slices from the bakery downstairs. They can do cappuccinos, though the machine was broken on our visit. In a bright orange building.

## ℹ Information

**Internet Cafe** ([W]community.cost.flaked; per hr T600; [🕐]8am-8pm Mon-Sat)

**Khan Bank** ([W]racks.simulator.voltages; [🕐]8am-5.30pm Mon-Fri)

**Hospital** ([W]warned.resorting.supplied)

## ℹ Getting There & Away

### AIR

Both Hunnu Air and Aero Mongolia have flights to and from UB most days of the week. Aero Mongolia also flies from Khovd City to Ulaangom, though not the other way. Ulaangom's **airport** ([W]shaded.monitor.honking) is 15km northwest of town. A taxi will cost T10,000-15,000 one way.

### BUS

The **bus ticket office** ([W]waddled.skid.booms; [🕐]9am-7pm summer, 10am-6pm winter), which is a kiosk inside the white building at the **bus station** ([W]camera.shielding.adopters), sells tickets for the 45-seater bus service to UB (T63,500, 32 hours), via Tosontsengel, departing at 10am and 3pm. In summer there are sometimes three buses a day.

---

### THE STRONG MEN OF UVS

Maybe it's something in the water, but they grow them big in Uvs, home to a disproportionate number of beefy wrestling champions. Khorloogiin Bayanmönkh is one such Uvs legend, winning the national championships a record 10 times, and even picking up a silver medal in the 1972 Olympics. A statue of Khorloo was erected in Ulaangom in 2015, close to the naadam stadium. Arms aloft, he towers over a lion (*arslan*) and an elephant (*zaan*) to show that he is *Titan* (number one). He stands on the crest of a wave, presumably to represent his home *sum* (district) of Khyargas, famous for the lake swells that crash against the rocks at Khetsuu Khad (p211).

In Naranbulag *sum*, just off the paved highway between Ulaangom and Khyargas Nuur, another statue of a wrestler looms over the steppe ([W]hastening.earplug.diplomat). He is S. Sukhbaatar, who earned the title of *zaan* by reaching the semi-final in the national naadam.

# Ulaangom

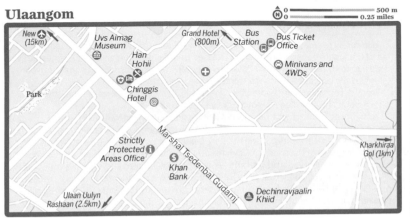

## CAR & MOTORCYCLE

Ulaangom is relatively easy to reach by car from Khovd (252km, five hours), with paved roads for about half the journey. Ölgii (307km) is a more substantial journey over rougher roads, taking the better part of a day at a push, but better spaced out over two days. Travelling to or from isolated Uliastai in Zavkhan (631km), you'll need a sturdy vehicle to navigate the unforgiving desert steppe, and should allow two days for the journey.

## JEEP & MINIVAN

If you're heading to Ölgii, it's generally easier to catch a shared **4WD or minivan** (marinated. scouted.amuses) to Khovd (T30,000, seven to eight hours, 339km) and make your way from there, as vehicles heading directly to Ölgii are few and far between. Even rarer are vans heading to Mörön (about 20 hours, 680km); if there is nothing available, consider riding a UB-bound minivan as far as Tariat (T35,000, 22 hours, 700km) and then attempting to bum a lift to Mörön from other backpackers at Terkhiin Tsagaan Nuur.

# Üüreg Nuur   Үүрэг Нyyp

'Spellbinding' is the word that best evokes **Üüreg Nuur** (Үүрэг Нyyp; trainees.duster. clatters), a freshwater lake encircled by a jade panorama of mountains and empty miles of rolling steppe. With an elevation of 1425m, it couldn't be more different from its marshy, sandy, much lower neighbour, Uvs Nuur.

The 3000m-plus surrounding peaks include Tsagaan Shuvuut Uul (3496m), part of the **Uvs Nuur Strictly Protected Area** (raincoat.marinated.negotiation; permit T3000) which provides a haven for snow leopards and other mammals.

The lake is great for swimming (albeit a little chilly) and locals say it has plenty of fish. It's one of the few mosquito-free lakes in the region.

The freshwater lake contains some unidentified minerals, and is designated as 'saltwater' on some maps; it's best to boil or purify all water from here.

## ⊙ Sights

★**Waterfall**                    WATERFALL
(scrolls.inarguable.patient) High up in the protected area of mountains north of Üüreg Nuur, a 14m waterfall cascades over black rocks. It's a 10km slog (most people drive this bit) up from the lake's shore to the start of the **river valley** (whacked.strikeout. neared), and then a 4km hike over rough ground to the waterfall. En route you'll pass through '**Love Street**' (stepson.tasteful. fierce), where snow leopards come to mate – try to spot the claw marks on the trees here.

## ⊨ Sleeping

★**OT Tour Camp**         TOURIST GER CAMP **$$**
(9913 6772, 8900 6772, 8948 4812; Contact@ ottour.com; bankers.doting.installed; Ger bed per person without/with meals US$22/52, tent pitch US$15) Most gorgeously situated camp in all of Mongolia? We may have a winner. It's nestled in the groove of a steep valley overlooking Üüreg Nuur, some 20km away, with nothing but rolling steppe in between. There's a dozen or so stylishly decorated gers and nine log cabins, a toilet and shower block, and a well-equipped **restaurant** with bar.

## ULAANGOM TO ÖLGII

This leisurely two-day 4WD journey begins on a 40km tarmac road heading northwest out of Ulaangom before turning left onto a jeep trail just past Türgen village. The jeep trail heads up to **Ulaan Davaa** (Red Pass; elevation 1972m), notable for its enormous *ovoo* (shamanistic collection of stones, wood or other offerings to the gods).

From the pass there are two routes. One heads due south and then southeast to Khökh Nuur, The other leads west to lovely Üüreg Nuur (p209).

From Üüreg Nuur, cargo trucks take a less rugged but longer route (301km) via **Bohmörön village**, where you can check out the 8th-century Turkic *balbal* (stone figure believed to be a Turkic grave marker). Light vehicles (4WDs and vans) bypass Bohmörön and take the shortcut (254km) over the steep **Bairam Davaa**. Look out for several **ancient graves and balbals** (Ⓜ literalist.contemplated.bustle) on this route a few kilometres south of Üüreg Nuur. The 8th-century *balbals* represent either local heroes or, possibly, enemies killed in battle. Another set of **graves and balbals** (Ⓜ freehand.hills. promotion) is a further 550m south. The circular piles of stones in the area are *kurgans* (burial mounds).

On the south side of Bairam Davaa, the road passes more *kurgans* and standing stones (thin, stone pillars used as grave markers). The most impressive, 7km north of Khotgor, include two **mounds** (Ⓜ largeness.invitingly.temptation) surrounded by concentric circles and radiating spokes.

**Khotgor** is a desolate coal-mining village, but long-distance cyclists take note: this is the only place to pick up supplies between Ulaangom and Ölgii. Most maps show no road via Bairam Davaa but you can make it with a halfway decent vehicle or bike (and the lungs of a yeti).

From Khotgor you could opt for a detour into the **Yamaat Valley**, which leads to Türgen Uul. Otherwise, continue south for 60km to the Achit Nuur bridge (p211). From here, it's another 75km to Ölgii. The road passes the surprisingly lush riverside forests of the **Develiin Aral Nature Reserve** (Ⓜ layouts.wharf.anyway; admission T3000), a 16km stretch along the fast-flowing Khovd Gol.

## ❶ Information

You should buy a permit (T3000) at the **Strictly Protected Areas Office** (☏ 9145 6666; javzansuren2017@gmail.com; Ⓜ patrolled. heartache.poets; ⊙ 8am-5pm Mon-Fri) in Ulaangom (although the ranger didn't check ours when we met him).

## ❶ Getting There & Away

It takes about two hours by car from Ulaangom to reach Üüreg Nuur, by first heading west out of town then crossing **Ulan Davaa** (Red Pass).

Note that the turn-off to OT Tour Camp is marked by a **boulder** (Ⓜ reignited.hideaway. heartaches).

## Kharkhiraa Uul & Türgen Uul
Хархираа Уул Ба Түргэн Уул

ELEV KHARKHIRAA UUL (4037M);
TÜRGEN UUL (3965M)

The twin peaks of Kharkhiraa Uul and Türgen Uul dominate the western part of the Uvs aimag. The mountains are vital sources of the Uvs Nuur, and part of the Uvs Nuur Strictly Protected Area (p209).

In summer, the area offers some excellent hiking opportunities and the chance to meet Khoton nomads who graze their flocks here. Khoton people are the only ethnic Mongols to practise Islam.

The village of **Tarialan** (Тариалан) makes a good base for exploration. It's 9km off the main Ulaangom–Khovd Rd, about 20km out of **Ulaangom** (Ⓜ indelicate.fizzed.knowledgeable – watch for the blue sign). The Strictly Protected Areas office in Ulaangom sells permits for the protected area.

## ⊙ Sights

### Khökh Nuur                                    LAKE
(Хөх Нуур, Blue Lake; Ⓜ crocheting.scrubby. thankful) This pretty alpine lake is surrounded by mountains and makes a great destination on foot or by horse from Tarialan; the trip is about 15km up Davaan Uliastai (one valley north of **Kharkhiraa Gol**). It's possible for a car to reach the lake in a very roundabout manner (120km), though

only an experienced driver could do it; the route involves driving up Ulaan Davaa (from Ulaangom), sweeping around the mountains close to Üüreg Nuur, and then heading southeast.

## ☞ Tours

Hunt down **Shinee** (☑9949 3110; shine bayars667@gmail.com; guide services per day T60,000), a local guide who lives in his family ger at the mouth of the valley which leads from Tarialan up into the hills. To find him, head to the small **naadam stadium** (⚏highlights.begin.injuries) at the far western edge of the village, then keep walking for a couple of hundred metres up the valley.

Shinee and his father **Dash** (☑9421 1004; guide services per day T60,000) are both experienced guides and can take you on some fabulous treks (T60,000 per day) ranging from a few days to two weeks. They can arrange horse or camel rides for around T20,000 per person per day, plus the same again for an animal-spotting guide. You'll have to bring your own food and camping equipment, although water is plentiful here. Shinee can also help arrange a car transfer – to or from Ulaangom, for example – for around T70,000 per day plus petrol.

Shinee is an English teacher so communication won't be a problem, but Dash doesn't speak English. It might be wise to email Shinee ahead of time to set things up.

Alternatively, a number of UB–based tour companies run walking trips through this area.

## 🛏 Sleeping & Eating

Camping spots abound along the shoreline of Khökh Nuur.

You'll need to be self-sufficient, so best to stock up in Ulaangom. Tarialan has a couple of basic shops if you've forgotten anything.

## ➊ Getting There & Away

Shared minivans between Ulaangom and Tarialan cost around T5000 per person, although if you've come here for hiking it wouldn't be out of the question to walk to Tarialan from Ulaangom.

Hitching as far as the Tarialan turn-off isn't out of the question either, though hitching is never entirely safe, and we don't recommend it. Travellers who hitch should understand that they are taking a small but potentially serious risk.

# Achit Nuur  Ачит Нуур

The largest freshwater lake in Uvs, Achit Nuur (Ачит Нуур) is on the border of Uvs and Bayan-Ölgii aimags, and is an easy detour between Ulaangom and Ölgii. It offers stunning sunsets and sunrises and good fishing.

The lake is home to flocks of geese, eagles and other bird-life. One drawback is the plethora of mosquitoes during the summer; locals claim they are almost bearable by October.

A **bridge** (⚏unzip.ministries.roundups) just south of the lake allows for relatively steady traffic between Ulaangom and Ölgii.

The small Kazakh encampment on the southeastern edge has a *guanz* (canteen).

# Khyargas Nuur National Park  Хяргас Нуур

**Khyargas Nuur National Park** (Хяргас Нуур; ⚏godfather.though.meteorites; park fee T3000) wraps around **Khyargas Nuur**, an impressive saline lake some 75km wide that shimmers amid scorched desert and scattered patches of scrub grass. Connected to Ulaangom by paved road, the lake's northwest shore has what amounts to a 'beach' of greyish gravel running down to the water's edge, and is popular with locals coming to picnic and swim. Consequently it has a litter problem, but the rest of the park is untouched, providing an attractive summer home for bird-life, especially around **Khetsuu Khad** (Хэцүү Хад; ⚏radiology.subpart.trappers), a dramatic rocky outcrop on the southern shore.

The national park fee (T3000) applies around the lake, though you'd be lucky (or unlucky) to find a ranger to pay it to.

## 🛏 Sleeping & Eating

★**Khyargas Nuur Tourist Camp**  TOURIST GER CAMP $$
(☑9898 9077; ⚏informed.swerved.foxgloves; 4-bed ger T40,000, cabin T50,000; ℗) About 30km east of the relative hubbub at **Khar Temis** (☑9307 2513, 9579 3419; ⚏inarguable.cronyism.formed; tr/tw T30,000/60,000, 5-bed ger T50,000-90,000, 8-bed ger T100,000; ℗) hotel, this Mongolian-run camp is on a lovely, isolated spur of land that dangles out into the lake. Four-bed gers and cabins are clean, tidy and include use of a shower and toilet block. It's about 3km off the paved road, marked by a sign.

**Khar Temis Restaurant**　　MONGOLIAN $
(◪ deviation.substantial.untiring; mains from T5000; ℗) The most interesting thing on the menu at this small restaurant inside the hotel (p211) is a riff on the ubiquitous *khuushuur* pancakes (T1000) filled not with mutton but lake fish; unfortunately they aren't always available. A fridge full of ice-cold beers does the trick. English spoken.

### ❶ Getting There & Away

It takes about two hours to reach the lake when driving from Ulaangom, on paved roads all the way. If travelling to Khetsuu Khad, you'll need another hour and a sturdy 4WD to make it over the sand. In summer you might be able to bag a seat in a shared car for T5,000 one way.

# ZAVKHAN　　ЗАВХАН

POP 70,546 / AREA 82,000 SQ KM

Zavkhan aimag occupies a transitional zone between the well-watered Khangai mountain range of central Mongolia and the harsh Great Lakes Depression of the west. Straddling the two regions, Zavkhan has its own microclimates and a varied terrain that ranges from snowy peaks to steppes to lakes surrounded by sand dunes.

The aimag is in an awkward, tricky-to-reach location and very few travellers are likely to pass through much or any of Zavkhan. This is a pity because the scenery is some of the most dramatically varied in the country; one minute you are travelling verdant valleys and hills, the next you're in the midst of desert reminiscent of *Lawrence of Arabia*.

### ❶ Getting There & Away

Hunnu Air flies between Ulaanbaatar and the aimag capital Uliastai twice a week, but seats are few and book out early. It's probably easier to reach by road. In the north of the aimag, Tosontsengel, Zavkhan's second city, is connected to UB by paved road all the way (11 hours, 815km).

# Uliastai　　Улиастай

☑ 01462, 7046 / POP 15,756 / ELEV 1760M

Along with Khovd, Uliastai is one of Mongolia's oldest cities, founded by the Manchus during their reign in Mongolia. Sadly, the old garrison is long gone, save for some ruins on the outskirts of town. Two rivers flowing nearby and a lush valley surrounded by mountains complete the picture and offer a number of great spots to camp.

If you've travelled here from other western aimags, note than you're now back on Ulaanbaatar time (one hour ahead of Ölgii).

## ◉ Sights

**Zavkhan History Museum**　　MUSEUM
(☑ 1462-23097; ◪ submits.threading.newlywed; admission T4000; ⊙ 9am-6pm Mon-Fri) This decent aimag museum contains the bone of a mammoth, some fine religious art and a coral *tsam* mask, worn during lama dances. There are also a few photographs of Uliastai taken in the early 20th century, a wall map depicting Uliastai's layout when it was a garrison, and some grisly reminders of the Manchu era in the form of shackles and torture devices.

## 🛌 Sleeping & Eating

**Uliastai Hotel**　　HOTEL $$
(☑ 8993 4004, 7046-2414; ◪ proposes.boating. wasps; s/tw/half-lux/lux T20,000/30,000/40,000-60,000/100,000-120,000; ℗) Though it looks and feels a little jaded, the Uliastai is a well-run operation with a good **restaurant** (◪ proposes.boating.wasps; mains T4000-9000; ⊙ 7am-9pm) and bar attached, and a Khan Bank ATM inside the entrance. The cheaper standard rooms have a flushing toilet and washbasin but no shower (common shower available). Sells tourist maps of Zavkhan (T5000, Mongolian only).

**★ Zavkhan Hotel**　　HOTEL $$
(☑ 7046-3046, 9546 3146; ◪ dampen.emporium.breezes; d/tw/lux T60,000/80,000/120,000; ℗ 🛜) Simply getting to isolated Uliastai can be a slog, so thank Chinggis there's a hotel as nice as the Zavkhan waiting for you. Rooms are spotless and modern with quality linen and clean bathrooms. All the little details are in place: plug points, mirrors, blackout curtains, thunderous showers and even a sausage with your breakfast egg. Bravo.

**★ Udwal Bakery and Coffee Shop**　　BAKERY $
(☑ 9999 0542; ◪ ringside.hissing.ruffling; dishes from T4000; ⊙ Mon-Sat 9am-8pm, Sun from 10am) Expect a warm, English–speaking welcome from Amarzaya, the owner of this homely cafe. She can brew you up a latte (T4000) or cappuccino using a Nespresso machine; milkshakes, freshly made sandwiches, beef

# Uliastai

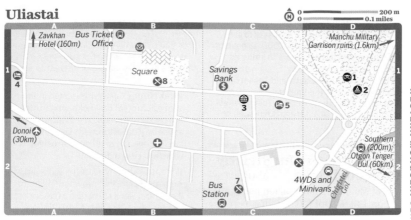

stew, tiny pizzas and awesomely gooey cinnamon rolls are also available. The only downside is the lack of wi-fi.

**Zagasan Nud Restaurant**            MONGOLIAN $
(⧉ track.lamplight.stole; mains T4000-9000; ⏰ 10am-10pm; ☎) Pair your meaty Mongolian fare with fresh salad dishes at this cosy restaurant attached to the **hotel** (☎ 9946 3000; ⧉ track.lamplight.stole; d/tw/lux T60,000/80,000/100,000; P☎) of the same name. It can also serve up a roast leg of sheep (T80,000) or whole fish (T30,000) with advance notice. English photo menu.

## ℹ️ Information

**Savings Bank** (⧉ reprints.clenching.tingled; ⏰ 9am-6pm Mon-Fri)
**Telecom Building** (⧉ braked.crafts.novelists)

## ℹ️ Getting There & Away

### AIR

Hunnu Air flies to UB twice a week from **Uliastai Donoi Airport** (⧉ unworthy.valuation.studio), 33km west of town, but seats are very limited and book out early.

### BUS

Ulaanbaatar–bound 45-seater buses (T48,800, 20 hours) leave twice a day (11am and 4pm). The morning bus leaves from a **depot** (⧉ quest. muffin.duet) just south of the market; the 4pm bus leaves from a **car park** (⧉ handicaps. garages.obstinate) south of town, a little way over the Chigistei Gol bridge. The **ticket office** (⧉ shorthand.episode.promising) is in a different location entirely, in the centre of town just west of the square.

The buses go via **Tosontsengel** (five hours, 181km), though if you want to alight there, be prepared to fork out for the full UB fare.

### MINIVAN & JEEP

Shared **minivans and 4WDs** (⧉ sideboard. wording.steers) congregate opposite the **Bayan Burd Supermarket** (⧉ upwardly.stir.torched; ⏰ 10am-6pm).

Note that it is virtually impossible to find a vehicle heading north to Mörön, south to Altai or even west to Ulaangom, although that doesn't stop people trying. Locals mostly organise their regional travel via a Mongolian–language Facebook group – Zaya at **Udwal Bakery** (☎ 9999 0542; amarzayag2000@ya-hoo.com; ⧉ ringside.hissing.ruffling) can tell you if there's a vehicle headed where you want to go. If not, you may be forced to hire a 4WD privately (around T80,000 per day plus fuel).

In the last week of August, it is easy to get a ride to Khovd City (around T40,000, 18 hours, 480km) when minivans fill up with students headed back to university.

The road between Uliastai and Tosontsengel was being paved at the time of research, and is easy to follow. The turn-off to Tosontsengel is 148km north of Uliastai and 33km west of Tosontsengel.

## Otgon Tenger Uul Strictly Protected Area Улиастай

One of Mongolia's most sacred mountains, **Otgon Tenger Uul** (4031m), has been the spiritual abode of the gods since the days of Chinggis Khaan, and is an important place of pilgrimage for many Mongolians. The mountain, 60km east of Uliastai, is the highest peak in the Khangai Nuruu and part of the **Otgon Tenger Uul Strictly Protected Area** (Отгон Тэнгэр Уул; 🕮 solicitors.underwriters.optimist; admission T3000).

Trekking opportunities abound, although climbing sacred Otgon Tenger Uul itself is prohibited, and attempting to do so could incur the wrath of the authorities in Uliastai. Most travellers content themselves with viewing the peak from the smaller **Dayan Uul** (Даян Уул; 🕮 reviving. unrelated.timeliness), with the option of continuing down to **Khökh Nuur** (Хөх Нуур; 🕮 heartbreak.temper.desiccation) for swimming, horse trekking and camping.

Camping opportunities abound all along the route between Uliastai and Otgon Tenger. There is a single, two-bed ger at the **ranger station** (🕮 toolmakers.icebreaker.prying), should you need to overnight and don't have a tent.

OFF THE BEATEN TRACK

### WESTERN ZAVKHAN

If you're travelling overland from Uliastai to western Mongolia (or vice versa) there are a few places of interest to stop on the way.

**Khar Nuur** (Хар Нуур) Located in the *sum* (district) of Erdenekhairkhan, this is a pretty freshwater lake bordering on alpine and desert zones. Most of the lake is ringed by sand dunes, making vehicle access difficult.

**Ikh Khairkhan Nuruu** (Их Хайрхан) An area of cliffs that provides shelter for ibexes and wolves. There are caves in the area, including **Ikh Agui** (Big Cave; 🕮 compost.tarantula.minnows), one of the largest caves in Mongolia.

**Ereen Nuur** (Эрээн Нуур) A beautiful lake surrounded by rolling sand dunes, some of them high enough to resemble small mountains. It's technically in Gov-Altai aimag but most travellers reach the lake via Uliastai.

### ℹ️ Getting There & Away

From Uliastai, it's a two-hour drive (or a two-three day hike) to the ranger station at the foot of Dayan Uul, following the gurgling Bodgin Gol for most of the way. Note the grand burial mound enclosed by a quadrangle of **boulders** (🕮 clinicians.headliners.enticed) en route.

A second route into the area is via the town of Otgon, 138km southeast of Uliastai, where a decent road heads up the Buyant Gol towards the southeastern flank of the mountain. This route is littered with impressive pre-Mongol-era burial mounds.

Zaya at **Udwal Bakery and Coffee Shop** (p213) can organise a day trip to Dayan Uul and back for US$70.

# Understand Mongolia

# Mongolia Today

**Mongolia may be a little fish in the big pond of globalisation but its importance on the world stage has only just started to grow. 'Mine-golia', as it's sometimes called, has enormous mineral wealth, including vast reserves of coal and copper. Despite its potential for a solid economy, there have been downturns, as various governments overspent mining revenues. Having learned some hard lessons, Mongolia now seems more committed to fiscal stability, cautious spending and diversification away from mining to focus on other sectors, including agriculture and tourism.**

## Best on Film

**The Story of the Weeping Camel** (2003) Docu-drama that follows a camel herder family in the Gobi.
**Mongol** (2007) Dramatic depiction of the rise of Chinggis Khaan.
**Tracking the White Reindeer** (2009) Docu-drama on reindeer herders, available online.
**The Eagle Huntress** (2016) Docu-drama about a 13-year-girl and her quest to become the first female champion in Bayan-Ölgii's eagle-hunting competition.

## Best in Print

**Ghengis Khan and the Making of the Modern World** (Jack Weatherford; 2005) Groundbreaking book and a bestseller on the Mongol empire.
**When Things Get Dark** (Matthew Davis; 2010) Raw examination of life in Tsetserleg from an American teacher.
**Hearing Birds Fly** (Louisa Waugh; 2003) Recollections of a year spent in remote Bayan-Ölgii by a British teacher.
**Wild East** (Jill Lawless; 2000) Slices of Mongolian life written by a Canadian expat editor of the UB Post.
**Mörön to Mörön** (Tom Doig; 2013) Wacky adventures of two Aussies travelling across Mongolia on pushbikes.
**Sky Shamans of Mongolia** (Kevin Turner; 2016) A shaman's eye-opening account of his encounters with a Mongolian counterpart.

## The Great Leap Forward

Mongolia's biggest driver of growth is the US$10-billion Oyu Tolgoi copper and gold underground mine, developed by the Anglo–Australian company Rio Tinto, but 34% owned by the Mongolian government. When complete in around 2021, the mine could account for one-third of the country's total GDP. The hope is that this single world-class deposit will lift the whole country up by the bootstraps. The nearby Tavan Tolgoi mine, another big revenue earner, exports coking coal to China, where it's used in the production of steel.

China is a ready market for Mongolia's raw materials, and the government is rapidly trying to build up its infrastructure to deliver the goods. New rail and road links to China are being built, and in a bid to diversify its markets, Mongolia is also planning a 1000km railway from the southernmost Gobi all the way to Russia (via Choibalsan).

Mongolia's political leaders seem keenly aware of the need to invest the new-found wealth back into the country. A copper smelter, an oil refinery and coal-washing plants are a few of the planned factories. A new international airport is expected to open in 2018. The government is also planning to construct enormous power plants to export energy to China, Korea and Japan. While most of these plans include dirty coal-fired plants, Mongolia insists that by 2030, more than 20% of its energy will come from renewable sources including solar and wind farms.

## Bankrupt Nation

Mongolians went to the polls in June 2016 and gave the Mongolian People's Party (MPP) a decisive victory over the ruling Democrats. The MPP took over a country nearly bankrupt after the Democrats spent the country's mineral wealth on populist projects, including subsidised mortgages, cash handouts and highways.

When the mining boom ended around 2012, the central bank quickly burned through its foreign reserves to pay the bills. At the same time the government found itself locked in a series of disputes with foreign banks and mining companies over broken contracts. Many investors packed their bags and headed for the exits.

In 2017 the International Monetary Fund (IMF) and other partners bailed Mongolia out of debt with a long-term loan worth US$5.5 billion, an amount nearly half the country's GDP.

To receive the massive loan, Mongolia agreed to cut spending and raise taxes, particularly on vehicles, petrol, cigarettes and alcohol. Income taxes shot up for higher earners, and state executives saw salaries cut by up to 50%. While the loan was under negotiation, protestors on Sükhbaatar Sq in Ulaanbaatar demanded officials get out of debt by repatriating monies hidden in offshore bank accounts. The organisers claimed some US$16 billion had been embezzled overseas.

The MPP also faces numerous social challenges, especially in Ulaanbaatar, where public anger over air pollution and lack of modern housing has boiled over to street protests. In response, the government has promised to redevelop the ger districts and ban the use of raw coal for heating. In the countryside, officials are promising more jobs by developing meat and dairy farms that will export products to China. In mid-2017 Battulga Khaltmaa became Mongolia's fifth president after an unprecedented two rounds of voting.

### The Future

Mongolia's journey over the past three decades since the fall of the Iron Curtain has been a two-step-forward, one-step-back process. One of its greatest successes is the establishment of an open society. Its people are now increasingly online, obsessed with social media and using new technologies to better society. Young Mongolians are forging unique identities, often driven by nationalist ideas.

Mongolia wants to expand its network of railways and highways. Mineral processing factories, coal-fired power plants and farms are also planned. The challenge lies in growing the industrial sector without causing harm to the environment. Mongolia is already suffering from wildlife habitat loss and desertification due to poorly enforced mining and agriculture regulations.

While increased industrialisation will bring jobs, revenue and prosperity, it will be some time before the benefits reach low-income households. In poor areas, schools are overcrowded, public hospitals are crumbling and basic infrastructure is generally nonexistent. While the government has been slow to address infrastructure needs in poor areas, the private sector has turned pockets of Ulaanbaatar into self-sustaining gated communities.

Despite the challenges ahead, public surveys show widespread support for the economic reforms. There is strong optimism among most of the population, but the country still has a long way to go before it can claim success.

POPULATION: **3,140,000**

GDP: **US$3870 PER CAPITA (2015)**

GDP GROWTH: **1% (2016)**

LITERACY RATE: **98%**

NUMBER OF LIVESTOCK: **73,000,000**

INFLATION: **2.5%**

### if Mongolia were 100 people

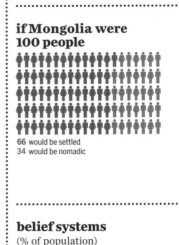

**66** would be settled
**34** would be nomadic

### belief systems
(% of population)

74 Buddhist
9 Shamanic believers
9 none
5 Christian
3 Muslim

### population per sq km

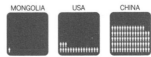

MONGOLIA   USA   CHINA

♦ ≈ 2 people

# History   *Dulmaa Enkhchuluun & Jack Weatherford*

Throughout history, hordes of warriors rode their horses down from the Mongolian plateau to challenge and transform the world. The steppe warriors not only conquered nations, they swept up whole civilisations and reassembled them into intercontinental empires of a scale never seen before. The legends of these ancient soldiers – including the greatest of them all, Chinggis Khaan – are seen as the recent past in Mongolia; the nation is rebranding itself with that same warrior spirit.

## People of the Sun

Dulmaa Enkhchuluun graduated from Augsburg College in Minnesota and now works to promote culturally and environmentally responsible tourism and commercial development in Mongolia.

The first of the steppe nomads to make an impact beyond Mongolia were the Hunnu, whom the Mongols now call the 'People of the Sun', better known as the Huns. They created the first steppe empire in 209 BC under Modun, a charismatic leader who took the title *shanyu* (king) and ruled until his death in 174 BC. Modun created a disciplined and strong cavalry corps personally devoted to him, and used the corps to overthrow and kill his father, the tribal chief.

Between the creation of the Qin dynasty in China in 221 BC and the collapse of the Han dynasty in AD 220, the Chinese became the dominant economic power in East Asia. Even still, under the Huns, the steppe tribes grew into a great military power. During this period, the Chinese and the Huns vied for dominance through protracted wars with intermittent truces, during which the Chinese lavished the steppe warriors with tributes of goods and women, including imperial princesses (in exchange the Huns agreed not to slaughter them all). Using the merchandise extracted from the Chinese, the Huns extended their trade routes, connecting the civilisations around them.

Anthropologist Jack Weatherford wrote *Genghis Khan and the Making of the Modern World*, for which he received the Order of the Polar Star, Mongolia's highest state honour.

Following the collapse of the Hun empire in the 4th century AD, various newly independent tribes left the Mongolian homeland, wandering from India to Europe in search of new pastures and new conquests. By the 5th century, one of these branches reached Europe and created a new Hun empire that stretched from the Ural Mountains to Germany. Under their most famous leader, Attila the Hun, they threatened Rome and ravaged much of Western Europe. Mounted archers

| TIMELINE | 209–174 BC | AD 552–744 | 744–840 |
|---|---|---|---|
| | Reign of Modun as *sha-nyu* (king) of the Huns; the first great steppe empire of Mongolia stretches from Korea to Lake Baikal in Siberia and south into northern China. | Succession of two Turkic empires whose greatest ruler is Bilge Khagan. Following his death in 734, a monument is erected near Ölgii Nuur. | The Uighur empire occupies central Mongolia until it's expelled by the Kyrgyz tribe; the Uighur move south into western China and control the Silk Route for nearly 1000 years. |

## CHINGGIS KHAAN

Known to the world as a conqueror, Mongolians remember Chinggis Khaan as the great law-giver and proudly refer to him as the Man of the Millennium (a title bestowed on him by the *Washington Post* in 1995). His laws derived from practical considerations more than from ideology or religion.

After the abduction of his wife Borte, Chinggis recognised the role of kidnapping in perpetuating feuds among clans and outlawed it. Similarly, he perceived religious intolerance as being a source of violence in society, and so decreed religious freedom for everyone and exempted religious scholars and priests from taxes.

To promote trade and communications, Chinggis built an international network of postal stations that also served as hostels for merchants. He decreased and standardised the taxes on goods so that they would not be repeatedly taxed. Under these laws, the Mongol empire formed the first intercontinental free-trade zone.

In an era when ambassadors served as hostages to be publicly tortured or killed during times of hostilities, Chinggis Khaan ordered that every ambassador be considered an envoy of peace. This law marked the beginning of diplomatic immunity and international law. Today nearly every country accepts and promotes, at least in theory, the ideas and policies behind the 'Great Law of Chinggis Khaan'.

HISTORY DESCENDANTS OF THE WOLF

from the Mongolian steppe created an intercontinental reputation for their fierceness and tenacity in battle.

## Descendants of the Wolf

In the 6th century, a new sense of order returned to the Mongolian Plateau with the rise of a series of tribes speaking Turkic languages. These tribes claimed descent from a boy who was left for dead but was saved and adopted by a mother wolf who raised him and then mated with him, creating from their offspring the ancestors of the various steppe clans. Compared with both the Huns before them and the Mongols after them, the literate Turks sought to blend traditional nomadic herding with a life of agriculture, urbanisation and commerce; consequently, they left more physical remains than the others in the ruins of Turkic cities and ceremonial centres. Along the Orkhon Gol in central Mongolia, they built their small cities of mud, the most famous of which were erected during the time of the Uighurs, the last of the great Turkic empires of Mongolia. The Turkic era reached its zenith in the early 8th century under Bilge Khagan and his brother Kultegen, the military general. Their monuments near the Orkhon Gol are probably the oldest known examples of writing in a Turkic language.

*Khan* means chief or king. *Khaan* means emperor or great khan. *Khagan* is the Mongol script version and the old Turkic version (*Khagan* is the origin of *Khaan*).

| 1162 | 1204 | 1206 | 1235 |
|---|---|---|---|
| Birth of Temujin, the child destined to become Chinggis Khaan, near the Onon Gol. According to legend, Temujin emerges with a blood clot clutched in his fist. | Chinggis Khaan establishes the Mongolian state script based on the Uighur alphabet; it has Semitic origins but is written vertically from top to bottom. | Chinggis Khaan calls a massive conclave at Kherlen Gol and creates his empire – he calls it the Great Mongol Nation. | Ögedei Khaan (son of Chinggis) completes the imperial capital at Karakorum. In addition to a great palace, the city has Muslim mosques, Christian churches and Buddhist temples. |

Like the Huns before them, the Turks moved down off the Mongolian Plateau, spreading from what is today China to the shores of the Mediterranean. Another invading Turkic tribe, the Kyrgyz, overthrew the Uighur empire in AD 840, destroying its cities and driving the Uighur people south into the oases of western China. But the Kyrgyz showed no inclination to maintain the cities or the empire they had conquered. With the expulsion of the Uighurs came another period of decentralised feuding and strife, before the greatest of all Mongolian empires arose at the beginning of the 13th century: the rise to power of Chinggis Khaan.

At Noyon Uul in Selenge aimag archaeologists have made curious finds inside Hunnu–era tombs. Unearthed objects include Hellenistic mirrors and jewellery from Afghanistan. Historians believe these were brought from Persia or Central Asia and traded by steppe nomads until they reached the Siberian border.

## Children of the Golden Light

The decline of the Turkic tribes gave the opening for a new tribe to emerge. Scholars offer varying explanations for when and where these new people arrived, but the Mongols ascribe their origins to the mating of a blue wolf and a tawny doe beside a great sea, often identified as Lake Baikal (in Russia). They further credit the origin of Chinggis Khaan's own clan to a mysterious and sacred woman called Alan Goa, who gave birth to two sons during her marriage, and had an additional three sons after her husband died. The elder sons suspected that their younger brothers had been fathered by an adopted boy (now a man) whom their mother had also raised and who lived with her.

Upon hearing of their suspicions and complaints, Alan Goa sat her five sons around the hearth in her ger and told them that the three younger sons were fathered by a 'Golden Light'. She then handed each an arrow with the command to break it. When they had done this, she handed each a bundle of five arrows with the command to break them all together. When the boys could not do so, she told them that it mattered not where the brothers came from so long as they remained united.

A Mongol is a member of the Mongol ethnic group; a Mongolian is a citizen of Mongolia. Kazakhs of Bayan-Ölgii are Mongolians but not Mongols; the Kalmyks of New Jersey are Mongols but not Mongolians.

No matter what the Mongol origin, the story of Alan Goa has had a persistent and profound influence on the development of Mongolian culture, on everything from the role of women and attitudes towards sexuality to the political quest for unity and the herder's value of practical action over ideology or religion.

## The Mongol Empire

The Mongols were little more than a loose confederation of rival clans until the birth of Temujin in 1162. Overcoming conditions that would have crushed lesser men, Temujin rose to become the strongest ruler on the steppe, and in 1206 founded the Mongol empire and took the title Chinggis Khaan (p219). He was already 44 years old at this stage, but since the age of 16, when his bride was kidnapped, he had been fighting one clan

| 1258 | 1260 | 1271 | 1368 |
|---|---|---|---|
| Mongolian soldiers destroy Baghdad and kill some 100,000 people. The siege marks the end of the 500-year-old Abbasid Caliphate. | The end of Mongol expansion with their defeat by the Mamluk army of Egypt at the Battle of Ayn Al-Jalut near the Sea of Galilee. | Kublai Khaan claims the office of great khan and also makes himself Emperor of China by founding the Yuan dynasty. | Yuan dynasty collapses in China but the Mongol government returns to Mongolia, refusing to submit to the newly created Ming dynasty. They continue ruling as the 'Northern Yuan'. |

feud and tribal war after another. Frustrated with the incessant chaos, he began killing off the leaders of each clan as he defeated them and incorporating the survivors into his own following. Through this harsh but effective way, Chinggis Khaan forced peace onto the clans around him.

## WARRIOR QUEENS OF MONGOLIA

Chinggis Khaan's greatest disappointment in life was the quality of his sons, but his greatest pride was in his daughters. He left large sections of his empire under the control of his daughters, although they did gradually lose power to his sons.

Mongol women presented a strange sight to the civilisations they helped conquer – they rode horses, shot arrows from their bows and commanded the men and women around them. In China, the Mongol women rejected foot-binding; in the Muslim world, they refused to wear the veil.

At the death of Ögedei (Chinggis Khaan's second son), in 1241, probably in an alcoholic stupor, his widow Töregene assumed complete power. She replaced his ministers with her own, the most important of whom was another woman, Fatima, a Tajik or Persian captive from the Middle Eastern campaign. In addition to the rule of Töregene and Fatima from Karakorum in Mongolia, two of the other three divisions of the empire also had female governors – only the Golden Horde of Russia remained under male rule. Never before had such a large empire been ruled by women.

Töregene passed power on to her inept son Guyuk in 1246, but he died mysteriously within 18 months and was replaced by his widow Oghul Ghamish, who had to face Sorkhokhtani, the most capable woman in the empire. With the full support of her four sons, whom she trained for this moment, Sorkhokhtani organised the election of her eldest son, Möngke, on 1 July 1251. So great was her achievement that a Persian chronicler wrote that if history produced only one more woman equal to Sorkhokhtani, then surely women would have to be judged the superior sex.

While Kublai Khaan ruled China, his cousin Khaidu continued to fight against him from Central Asia and, true to the Mongol tradition, Khaidu's daughter Khutlun fought with him. According to Marco Polo, who called her Aiyaruk, she was both beautiful and powerful. She defeated so many men in wrestling that today Mongolian wrestlers wear an open vest in order to visibly distinguish the male from the female wrestlers.

After the fall of the Mongol empire, in 1368, the men returned to squabbling over sheep and stealing horses, but the women kept the imperial spirit alive. In the late 15th century, a new conqueror arose, determined to restore the empire. Known to the grateful Mongols as Manduhai the Wise Queen, she took to the battlefield and united the scattered tribes into a single nation. She fought even while pregnant and was once injured while carrying twins; she and the twins survived, and her army won the battle.

Faced with Manduhai's tenacity and skill, the Chinese frantically expanded the Great Wall. Although she left seven sons and three daughters, the era of the great warrior queens of Mongolia passed with her death. Even so, Mongolians still wait for a new Manduhai.

| 1395 | 1448 | 1449 | 1586 |
|---|---|---|---|
| Geoffrey Chaucer's *The Canterbury Tales*, recognised as the first book of poetry written in English, includes an early account of Chinggis Khaan in 'The Squire's Tale'. | Birth of Mongolia's greatest queen, Manduhai the Wise Queen, who reunites Mongolia by the end of the century. | Esen Taishi defeats the Chinese and captures the Ming emperor. His reign marks the rise of western Mongolia and the Oirat people as major powers of inner Asia. | Founding of Erdene Zuu Khiid, the first Buddhist monastery in Mongolia, at the site of the Mongol capital, Karakorum (modern Kharkhorin). |

## MINING LEGION

Twenty-thousand mounted Mongols crossed Poland toward Western Europe in 1241. Urged by the pope to defend the Christian world, Henry II of Silesia conscripted thousands of Saxon miners to make their mining tools into weapons to fight the Mongols. In April, at the Battle of Liegnitz and a nearly simultaneous one in Hungary, the Mongols permanently crushed European knighthood and killed Henry, and they transported the captive miners and their tools to work the mines in greater Mongolia.

In 1245, fearing growth of the mining and arms industry in Asia, Pope Innocent IV sent Giovanni of Plano Carpini, a surviving companion of Francis of Assisi, in search of the lost legion of Saxon miners. He returned with little news of the miners but with Guyuk Khaan's stern command for the pope's submission. Another expedition sent by French King Louis IX under William of Rubruck in 1253 produced little information about the lost miners other than a tantalising encounter with a captured Parisian goldsmith whom the Mongols commissioned to build a silver tree fountain in Karakorum.

After the Mongol decline, commercial development, including mining, was forbidden until the end of the 19th century, when mining engineer (and future US president) Herbert Hoover arrived on horseback to meet the Bogd Khan and open Mongolia to the world. Despite an American trading post compound at American Denj, the European firm Mongol Ore secured the main mining concessions. Following heavy investment in German equipment transported via railway and ox cart, the company failed to persuade Mongolians to work as miners and had to rely on thousands of labourers from China. In WWI and the ensuing financial chaos, Mongol Ore disappeared into the Mongolian dust like the Lost Legion of Saxon Miners.

---

The English word 'horde' derives from the Mongol *ordu,* meaning 'royal court'.

Russian Cossacks adopted the Mongol battle cry of 'hurray!' and spread it to the rest of the world.

He named his new state Yeke Mongol Ulus (Great Mongol Nation). His followers totalled probably under a million people, and from this he created an army of nine units of 10,000 and a personal guard of another 10,000. With a nation smaller than the workforce of a large modern multinational corporation, and an army that could fit inside a modern sports stadium, the Mongols conquered the greatest armies of the era and subdued hundreds of millions of people.

In battle, Chinggis Khaan was merciless, but to those who surrendered without fighting, he promised protection, religious freedom, lower taxes and a heightened level of commerce and prosperity. His law did more to attract people into his empire than his military power. Based on military success and good laws, his empire continued to expand after his death until it stretched from Korea to Hungary and from India to Russia.

| 1603 | 1634 |
|---|---|
| A descendant of Chinggis Khaan and great-great grandson of Queen Manduhai is enthroned in Lhasa, Tibet, as the fourth Dalai Lama, the only Mongolian Dalai Lama. | Death of Ligden Khaan, the last of Chinggis Khaan's descendants to rule as great khan. Eastern Mongolia becomes part of the Manchu empire, but western Mongolia holds out. |

YURY BIRUKOV/SHUTTERSTOCK ©

➜ Erdene Zuu Khiid, Kharkhorin

## The Peak of Power

After Chinggis Khaan's death, his second son, Ögedei, ruled from 1229 to 1241, followed by Ögedei's widow Töregene Khatun (p221) and the brief 18-month reign of Ögedei's son Guyuk from 1246 through 1248. Tensions began to develop among the branches of his descendants, and broke into open civil war in 1259 when Ariq Böke and Kublai each claimed the office of great khan after the death of their brother Möngke. Ariq Böke controlled all of Mongolia, including the capital Karakorum, and enjoyed widespread support from the ruling Borjigin clan. Yet Kublai controlled the vast riches of northern China, and these proved far more powerful. Kublai defeated his brother, who then perished under suspicious circumstances in captivity.

Kublai had won the civil war and solidified his hold over China, but it had cost him his empire. Although still claiming to be a single empire, the nation of Chinggis Khaan had been reduced to a set of often-warring sub-empires. The Mongols of Russia became in effect independent, known later as the Golden Horde, under the lineage of Chinggis Khaan's eldest son Jochi. Persia and Mesopotamia drifted off to become the Ilkhanate, under descendants of Kublai's only surviving brother Hulagu, the conqueror of Baghdad.

Kublai went on to create a Chinese dynasty named Yuan, took Chinese titles and, while still claiming to be the great khan of the Mongols, looked southward to the remaining lands of the Song dynasty, which he soon conquered.

Mongolians have in recent years built a number of statues of Chinggis Khaan to honour the great warlord. These statues can be seen at Sükhbaatar Sq in UB, on the Ulaanbaatar–Khentii road, in Chinggis (Khentii) and in Dadal.

HISTORY THE PEAK OF POWER

## Fall of the Empire

Much of Central Asia, including Mongolia, pursued an independent course and acknowledged the Yuan dynasty only when forced to by military invasion or when enticed with extravagant bribes of silk, silver and other luxuries. By 1368 the subjects had mostly overthrown their Mongol overlords, and the empire withdrew back to the Mongolian steppe where it began. Although most Mongols melted into the societies that they conquered, in some distant corners of the empire, from Afghanistan to Poland, small vestiges of the Mongolian empire still survive to the present.

In 1368 the Ming army captured Běijīng, but the Mongol royal family refused to surrender and fled back to Mongolia with the imperial seals and their bodyguards. Much to the frustration of the Ming emperors in China, the Mongols continued to claim to be the legitimate rulers of China and still styled themselves as the Yuan dynasty, also known as the Northern Yuan. However, even within Mongolia, the imperial court exerted little power. Unaccustomed to the hardships of the herding life, and demanding vast amounts of food, fuel and

The best source for information on the life of Chinggis Khaan is The Secret History of the Mongols, which was written in the 13th or 14th century and not made public until the 20th century.

| 1639 | 1644 | 1696 | 1911 |
|---|---|---|---|
| Zanabazar, a direct descendant of Chinggis Khaan and the greatest artist in Mongolian history, is recognised as the first Jebtzun Damba, the supreme religious leader of Mongolia. | The Manchus expel the Ming dynasty and with the support of their Mongolian allies create the Qing dynasty in China. | The Manchus defeat Galdan Khan of Dzungaria and claim western Mongolia for the Qing dynasty, but some western Mongolians continue to resist foreign rule for several generations. | Mongolia declares independence from the dying Manchu empire and sets up religious leader as the Bogd Khan as the head of state. |

other precious resources for their large court and retainers, the Mongol rulers devastated their own country, alienated the increasingly impoverished herders and eventually became the captive pawns of the imperial guards.

In the 15th century the Mongols united with the Manchus, a Tungusic people related to Siberian tribes, for a new conquest of China and the creation of the Qing dynasty (1644–1911). Initially, the ruling Manchus treated the Mongols with favour, gave them an exalted place in their empire and intermarried with them. Gradually, however, the Manchus became ever more Sinicised by their Chinese subjects and less like their Mongol cousins. The Mongols were reduced to little more than a colonised people under the increasingly oppressive and exploitative rule of the Manchus.

## Revolutions

In 1911 the Qing dynasty crumbled. The Mongols broke away and created their own independent country under their highest Buddhist leader, the Jebtzun Damba (Living Buddha), who became both spiritual and temporal head of the nation as the Bogd Khan (Holy King). When the Chinese also broke free of the Manchus and created the Republic of China, the new nation did not recognise Mongolia's independence, claiming portions of the Manchu empire, including Tibet and Mongolia. In May 1915 the Treaty of Kyakhta, which granted Mongolia limited autonomy, was signed by Mongolia, China and Russia.

The Russian Revolution of October 1917 came as a great shock to Mongolia's aristocracy. Taking advantage of Russia's weakness, a Chinese warlord sent his troops into Mongolia in 1919 and occupied the capital. In February 1921 retreating White Russian (anti-communist) troops entered Mongolia and expelled the Chinese. At first the Bogd Khan seemed to welcome the White Russians as saviours of his regime, but it soon became apparent that they were just another ruthless army of occupiers.

Chinggis Khaan did not leave a monument to himself, nor a temple, pyramid, palace, castle or canal, and even his grave was left unmarked in the remote area where he grew up and hunted as a boy.

### INNER MONGOLIA

The existence of two places – Mongolia and Inner Mongolia – can be confusing. The latter is a province of China bordering the independent republic of Mongolia. The naming conventions and map borders are legacies of the complex, intertwined history of the Mongol and Chinese empires, which vied for control of the whole region for centuries. A divide-and-conquer policy during the Qing dynasty (1636–1912) led to the creation of 'Inner' and 'Outer' Mongolias. Modern Mongolia gained independence in 1921, with backing from the USSR.

| 1915 | 1921 | 1924 | 1937 |
|---|---|---|---|
| The Treaty of Kyakhta is signed by Mongolia, China and Russia, granting Mongolia limited autonomy. | The mad Russian baron, Roman von Ungern-Sternberg, briefly conquers Mongolia, but the Red Army and Mongolian forces under Damdin Sükhbaatar defeat him. | The Bogd Khan, the eighth reincarnation of the Jebtzun Damba, dies. The People's Republic of Mongolia is created on 26 November. | Khorloogiin Choibalsan's Buddhist purge leaves 700 monasteries destroyed and 27,000 monks and civilians dead. |

## THE BATTLE OF KHALKHIIN GOL

The battle of Khalkhiin Gol (Халхын Гол), also known as the Battle of Nomonhan and the Nomonhan Incident, may well be the most important battle – especially from World War II – that you've never heard of.

After occupying Manchuria (which borders Mongolia's eastern Dornod province as well as Siberia) in 1931, Japan turned its attention to the west. It seems that Japan's intention was to integrate Siberia into its territory and overrun Mongolia, creating a buffer zone between itself and the Soviet Union – and what better means of getting tanks into Northeast Asia than via the Mongolian grasslands? Skirmishes were fought on both sides of the Khalkhiin Gol throughout the summer of 1939, until the under-supplied Japanese forces were destroyed by a joint Soviet–Mongolian effort led by Georgy Zhukov at the end of August.

At the end of the day, the Japanese had been dealt a bloody nose, and they abandoned the idea of conquering Russia. A non-aggression pact was signed by Japan and the Soviet Union; the latter subsequently signed the Molotov–Ribbentrop Pact with Germany. As a result, Hitler was given the green light to invade Poland – and the USSR never feared an invasion on its eastern flank during World War II. Had Mongolia joined forces with Japan, the outcome of that war may have been markedly different, with the Soviet Union potentially boxed in by invasions on either border. The battle also gave the military career of Zhukov a huge boost – he would go on to command the Russian armies that eventually ground Berlin under their tank treads.

Side note: while local monuments and museums give the impression that the joint Soviet–Mongolian force was a 50/50 sort of affair, the vast majority of soldiers were Russian, supplemented by some Mongolian auxiliaries. This isn't to take away from the bravery of those Mongolian soldiers; rather, visitors should recognise that the 'Team Soviet–Mongolia' narrative pushed by the monuments in the Khalkhiin Gol area is focused propaganda meant to deepen ties between the former USSR and its then client-state.

Mongolian nationalists believed their best hope for military assistance was to ask the Bolsheviks for help. The White Russians disappeared from the scene when their leader, Baron von Ungern-Sternberg (p226), was captured, tried and shot. In July 1921, Damdin Sükhbaatar, the leader of the Mongolian army, marched uncontested into Urga (modern-day Ulaanbaatar) alongside Bolshevik supporters. The People's Government of Mongolia was declared and the Bogd Khan was retained as a ceremonial figurehead with no real power. Led by a diverse coalition of seven revolutionaries, including Sükhbaatar, the newly formed Mongolian People's Party (MPP), the first political party in

| 1937 | 1939 | 1945 | 1956 |
|---|---|---|---|
| Former Mongolian prime minister Peljidiin Genden is tried in Moscow on trumped-up espionage charges, found guilty and executed by firing squad on 26 November. | Japan invades Mongolia from Manchuria in May. With help from the Soviet Union, and after heavy fighting along the Khalkh Gol, the Mongols defeat Japan by September. | In a UN–sponsored plebiscite, Mongolians vote overwhelmingly to confirm their independence, but the USA and China refuse to admit Mongolia to the UN. | The Trans-Siberian Railway through Mongolia is completed, connecting Běijīng with Moscow. The Chinese and Russian trains still operate on different gauges, requiring the train wheels to be swapped at the border. |

## THE MAD BARON

Baron Roman Nikolaus Fyodirovich von Ungern-Sternberg, an unusual character in Mongolia's history, was a renegade officer of a group of White Russians (anti-communists), who believed he was the reincarnation of Chinggis Khaan, destined to restore the Mongol warlord's previous empire. Contemporaries paint a fine picture of Baron von Ungern-Sternberg, later known as the Mad Baron, describing him as haunted-looking, with a psychotic stare that fixed on people like an animal in a cave. He spoke with a high-pitched voice and his bulging forehead bore a huge sword scar, which pulsed with red veins whenever he grew agitated. As a finishing touch, one of his eyes was slightly higher than the other.

The Bolshevik victory in Russia forced the baron east, and he slowly accumulated a desperate army of renegade mercenaries. He enforced discipline with a reign of terror, roasting deserters alive, baking defiant prisoners in ovens and throwing his rivals in locomotive boilers. He was also a fervent Buddhist, convinced that he was doing his victims a favour by packing them off to the next life sooner rather than later.

With an army of 6000 troops (and the tacit backing of the Japanese), the baron crossed the Mongolian border in the summer of 1920 with the aim of establishing a pan–Mongol empire. By October his forces attacked Urga, but were driven back four times before finally taking the city. He freed the Bogd Khan (who had been imprisoned by the Chinese), but Mongol joy turned to horror as the next three days saw an orgy of looting, burning and killing. In May 1921 the baron declared himself the emperor of Russia.

After only a few months, the Bolshevik advance forced the baron to abandon Urga. Out on the steppes, his own followers tried to kill him, shooting him in his tent, but he managed to escape. A group of Mongolian herders later found him wounded in the grass, tortured by biting ants. He was eventually taken by the Bolsheviks, deported to Novosibirsk and shot on 15 September 1921, presumed mad.

Dr Ferdinand Ossendowski, a Polish refugee living in Mongolia in the early 1920s, offers an excellent account of the Mad Baron in his book *Beasts, Men and Gods*. For a more recent account, read James Palmer's *The Bloody White Baron*, published in 2009.

the country's history (and the only one for the next 69 years), took the reins of power. Soon after its birth the MPP adopted a new name, the Mongolian People's Revolutionary Party (MPRP). The party reinstated the original name in 2010.

## Soviet Control

After Lenin's death in Russia in 1924, Mongolian communism remained independent of Moscow until Stalin gained absolute power in the late 1920s. Then the purges began in Mongolia – MPRP leaders were disposed of until Stalin finally found his henchman in one Khorloogiin Choibalsan.

| 1961 | 1981 | 1990 | 1996 |
|---|---|---|---|
| Mongolia is admitted to the UN as an independent country, but the Soviet Union continues to occupy Mongolia with troops and runs the country as a satellite state. | On 22 March Jügderdemidiin Gurragchaa, a pilot in the Mongolian air force, becomes the first Mongolian in space. The cosmonaut spends seven days and 20 hours in orbit. | Democracy demonstrations break out in Ulaanbaatar. In June the first free, multiparty elections are held, with the Mongolian People's Revolutionary Party (MPRP) winning 85% of the vote. | The Democratic Coalition becomes the first non-communist government to win an election (although a series of scandals causes the fall of four successive governments). |

Following Stalin's lead, Choibalsan seized land and herds from the aristocrats, which was then redistributed to nomads. Herders were forced to join cooperatives, and private business was banned. The destruction of private enterprise without time to build up a working state sector had the same result in Mongolia as in the Soviet Union: famine. Choibalsan's policy against religion was just as ruthless – in 1937 some 27,000 people were executed or never seen again (3% of Mongolia's population at that time), 17,000 of whom were monks.

Choibalsan died in January 1952 and was replaced by Yumjaagiin Tsedenbal – no liberal, but not a mass murderer – and Mongolia enjoyed a period of relative peace. With the Sino–Soviet split in the early 1960s, the Mongolians sided with the Soviet Union. The Mongolian government expelled thousands of ethnic Chinese, and all trade with China came to a halt.

Throughout the 1970s, Soviet influence gathered strength. Young Mongolians were sent to the USSR for technical training, and Tsedenbal's wife, a Russian woman of modest background named Filatova, attempted to impose Russian culture – including food, music, dance, fashion and even language – on the Mongolians.

## The Great Transition

The unravelling of the Soviet Union resulted in decolonisation by default. In March 1990, in subzero temperatures, large pro-democracy protests erupted in the square in front of the parliament building in Ulaanbaatar. Hunger strikes were held, and in May 1990 the constitution was amended to permit multiparty elections in July of the same year.

The political liberation of Mongolia from the Soviets came as an economic disaster for Mongolia because of the heavy subsidies that the Soviets had paid to keep Mongolia as a buffer state between itself and China. The Mongols lost much of their food supply and, unable to pay their electrical bills to the Russian suppliers, the western districts were plunged into a blackout that lasted for several years. The economy of Mongolia withered and collapsed.

The harsh conditions called for stringent measures, and Mongolians created a unique approach to the new challenges. They began a radical privatisation of animals and large state-owned corporations. Unlike the other Soviet satellites in Eastern Europe and Central Asia that expelled the communist party, the Mongolians created a new democratic synthesis that included both the old communists of the MPRP and a coalition that became known as the Democrats. Freedom of speech, religion and assembly were all granted – the era of totalitarianism had ended.

HISTORY THE GREAT TRANSITION

During WWII, Mongolia donated 300kg of gold and more than six million animals to Soviet and Allied forces. More than 2000 Mongolians died fighting Japan.

Rivers in Mongolia are female and may be called *eej* (mother). A river, spring or lake that never runs dry is called a *khatun* (queen).

| 1998 | 2008 | 2008 | 2012 |
|---|---|---|---|
| On 2 October the 'Golden Magpie of Democracy', Sanjaasurengiin Zorig, credited with leading the 1990 democratic revolution, is assassinated in his home. To this day the murder remains unsolved. | In hotly contested parliamentary elections the MPRP narrowly defeats the Democratic Coalition. Protestors allege vote-rigging, and subsequent riots end with four people shot dead and hundreds arrested. | Naidan Tuvshinbayar wins Mongolia's first ever Olympic gold medal while competing in judo at the Běijīng summer Games. Enkhbat Badar-Uugan, a boxer, also wins gold in Běijīng. | Former president Nambaryn Enkhbayar is sentenced to two and a half years in prison for corruption. |

## THE MONGOL WHO SLAPPED STALIN

In 1932 Peljidiin Genden became the ninth prime minister of Mongolia, using the slogan 'Let's Get Rich!' to inspire Mongolians to overcome the troubled fighting that had been going on since the break-up of the Manchu empire and the establishment of an independent country. Mongolia was the second communist state, after the Soviet Union, but at this time Genden was trying to establish Mongolia as an ally of the Soviets rather than a colony or satellite.

Genden, standing up to Stalin, resisted demands that Mongolia purge the Buddhist monks and charged the Russians with 'red imperialism' for seeking to send Soviet troops into Mongolia. Amid much drinking at a reception in the Mongolian embassy in Moscow in 1935, the two men clashed, literally. Stalin kicked Genden's walking stick and Genden slapped Stalin and broke Stalin's trademark pipe, which always accompanied him.

Stalin held Genden under house arrest until he was convicted as a Japanese spy and executed by firing squad on 26 November 1937 – a day of great symbolic importance to the Mongols because it was the date of their declaration of independence and the creation of the Mongolian People's Republic.

In 1996 Genden's daughter, Tserendulam, opened the Victims of Political Persecution Memorial Museum (p63) in Ulaanbaatar in memory of her father and all those who died in defence of Mongolian independence.

In the mid-1950s, Howard Hughes cast John Wayne as Chinggis Khaan in *The Conqueror*, one of the worst films ever made by Hollywood.

The Mongolians gradually found their way towards the modern global economy and embraced their own brand of capitalism and democracy that drew heavily on their ancient history while adjusting to the modern realities of the world around them. Despite difficult episodes, such as the unsolved murder of the Democratic leader Sanjaasurengiin Zorig in 1998 (which resulted in a false conviction in 2016) and some heated clashes between government and citizens, Mongolia managed to move forward with tremendous cultural vigour. While maintaining staunch friendships with old allies such as North Korea, Cuba and India, Mongolia reached out to Europe, South Korea, Japan and, particularly, to the USA, which they dubbed their 'Third Neighbour' in an effort to create a counterpoint to China and Russia.

**2013**

The first stage of the US$6.6-billion Oyu Tolgoi mine is completed and copper concentrate shipments begin to China. One month later the company fires 1700 workers amid a dispute over funding the mine's underground phase.

**2017**

After an election victory the Mongolian People's Party acknowledges severe debts, declares a financial crisis and accepts a US$5.5-billion economic bailout from the IMF to stabilise the economy over the next decade.

# The Mongolian Way of Life

Every Mongolian, no matter how long he or she has lived in a city, is a nomad at heart. The nomadic way of life was born out of necessity as herders were forced to range their animals over vast distances in search of grass. While today, more than ever, Mongolians are lured to the city in search of work, some are choosing to stay on the land with their animals, unable to give up the freedom and independence afforded to them by their traditional lifestyle.

## Ingredients for Life

The nomadic way of life is defined largely by the ger and a family's livestock. The ger is a portable shelter that allows the family to move with the seasons, while the animals provide all of life's necessities, including food (mutton and beef), milk, fuel (in the form of dung) and transportation.

Mongolians are attached to their animals in the same way that Westerners feel a certain affinity for their cars. The horse in particular is a much beloved animal, forming an intimate part of the Mongolian lifestyle. It was the horse that allowed ancient tribes to spread across the steppes and cover their great distances. Later, it was the horse that carried the Mongol tribes across Asia as they built their empire. An old Mongolian proverb says: 'A man without a horse is like a bird without wings.'

Today you'll see symbolic images of horses everywhere, from the tops of fiddles to the tail of MIAT aeroplanes. It is frequently stated that Mongolian children start riding a horse at the age of two; in fact the horse riding begins earlier, essentially from birth, as parents will carry babies in their *dels* (traditional coat or dress) when they need to travel by horse.

The device used in ceremonial milk rituals is a tsatsal, a wooden spoon decorated with carved symbols, which may be Tibetan Buddhist, mythical, animistic or zodiacal. The spoon is used to flick milk into the air as a spiritual offering. Such offerings are nearly always made by women.

### A WOMAN'S WORLD

Women enjoy a great amount of freedom in Mongolian society. They always have, dating back to a time when Mongol queens helped rule the great Mongolian empire.

In the countryside Mongolian women are often in charge of managing household activities, such as selling sheep, bartering for flour and rice or managing the family cash reserves. These responsibilities usually fall upon the woman of the house because the men are often busy herding livestock, making repairs around the home or travelling to market.

Women also tend to achieve higher levels of education because, on average, they go to school longer than men (80% of higher-education students are women). Men often need to stay behind in the countryside to take care of ageing parents and their livestock. As a result of this lopsided male-female ratio, it's estimated that women hold some 70% to 80% of skilled jobs in Ulaanbaatar.

# Forces of Nature

Nomadic peoples are, for all intents and purposes, on a lifelong camping trip. As such, they are greatly affected by the climate and other natural forces around them. Reverence towards the land, a product of their shamanic beliefs, has attuned them to nature; the thought of degrading the land or altering nature strikes many Mongols as profane. Nature is not something that must be tamed or dominated, but something that thrives on balance and harmony.

Mongolia's reverence towards nature can still be seen in modern daily ritual. For example, the act of flicking milk into the sky is seen as an offering to the sky spirits. Tossing a rock on an *ovoo* (a shamanistic collection of stones) and walking around it three times is a way to bless earthly spirits. In the modern world some compromises do need to be made – for example, pits need to be dug for buildings and mines. In such cases lamas are often summoned not only to bless the project but also to pray for the damaged earth.

Reverence of nature is seen in all aspects of Mongolian culture, especially song, dance and art. Ride in a van full of Mongolians and you'll soon hear them break into song, crooning about the clear rivers and high mountains. These influences seem to have also affected the very nature of the Mongolian character. A Mongolian is typically humble, stoic and reserved; it is unusual to see a Mongolian express emotions vocally or in public. These personality traits must surely be rooted in the quiet, motionless steppes that remain unchanged through the aeons of time.

Seasons also shape Mongolian life. Spring in particular is a crucial time for Mongolians. Spring is usually dry, dusty, windy and unforgiving. This is the time when the weaker animals die and, it is said, when people die. Despite the severe temperatures, it is during winter that Mongolians feel most comfortable. After a difficult summer filled with chores and tending to livestock, winter is generally a time of relaxation.

One Mongolian tradition you might see is the annual horse-branding ceremony in September or early October, which involves rounding up the foals for branding. Following the special ceremony, the family and their invited guests will sit down to a night of singing, feasting and drinking.

# Steppe Rules

Mongolia's vast, open steppes and great distances have made hospitality a matter of sheer necessity rather than a social obligation. It would be difficult for anyone to travel across the country without this hospitality, as each ger is able to serve as a guesthouse, restaurant, pub and repair shop. As a result, Mongolians are able to travel rapidly over long distances without the weight of provisions. This hospitality is readily extended to strangers and usually given without fanfare or expectation of payment.

Nomads tend to move two to four times a year, although in areas where grass is thin they move more often. One nuclear family may live alone or with an extended-family camp of three or four gers (known as an *ail*);

## FUNERARY RITES

Up until the early 20th century Mongolians typically disposed of their dead by leaving them out in the elements, where dogs, birds and wild animals would devour the body. The practice followed the tradition of sky burial, common in Tibet. This act was seen to be the best way to return a body to the natural world, while the soul could safely be reincarnated into another body (either human or animal). When the Russians forbade the practice, Mongolians began following their tradition of burying their dead. In the post-communist era, some families are reverting to the old method of sky burial, although this is still quite rare. The more popular option now is cremation, and several crematoriums have been built around Ulaanbaatar in recent years.

## MONGOL GAMES

Day-to-day life may be a struggle on the steppes but families will still find time for games and leisure activities. In the evenings, children (and sometimes adults) play with *shagai* (ankle bones), which have four distinct sides representing horse, sheep, goat and camel. There are numerous *shagai* games but the most common is *moir uraldulakh* (horse race), which entails rolling four *shagai* (like dice) and then moving your 'horse *shagai*' a certain number of moves depending on the roll (roll four camels, move four spaces). The first person to reach the end of their ger wins the race. Other indoor games include ankle-bone shooting (like darts but with *shagai*), *shatar* (chess), *hözör* (cards) and *duu dulakh* (singing songs).

any more than that would be a burden on the grassland. A livestock herd should contain around 300 animals per family to be self-sustaining. These days it's not uncommon for wealthy herders to have 2000 or more animals.

Mongolia's nomads are surprisingly well-informed. Nearly all families have a short-wave radio to get national and world news. Many can receive satellite TV, and everyone reads newspapers when they are available (literacy is 98%). In winter, children go to school in the nearest town, where they live in dormitories, visiting their parents during holidays and summer. These days, mobile phones are ubiquitous at nomad camps, allowing herders to stay in touch with friends, family and business associates.

Life on the steppes is by no means easy or idyllic. Constant work is required to care for the animals, cook food and collect dung and water. It is also a precarious life – one bad winter can kill an entire herd, instantly wiping out a family's fortune. Life is even harder in the Gobi Desert, where grass is sparse and just one dry summer can threaten livestock.

## City Slickers

Mongolians have carried their rural traditions with them into the city. The unplanned ger districts around the capital seem just a step away from the countryside. Mongolia's strong democratic values are another reflection of nomadic traditions and their basic tenets – freedom, independence and pluralism.

However, life in the city is changing as more Mongolians become accustomed to an urban lifestyle. Ger districts in Ulaanbaatar, once considered a regular part of the fabric, are on their way out as developers transform these areas into modern apartment complexes. A government campaign called 'Friendly Ulaanbaatar' has also improved driving habits, queueing and other courtesies.

Youth culture is highly influenced by Western TV, music, movies and social media. A thriving culture of rap music exists in Ulaanbaatar. You'll also spot skaters, Harley Davidson biker gangs, girl bands, punks and a handful of neo-Nazis. But the traditional Mongolian lifestyle is far from dead. In fact, its restoration is a unique blend of foreign trends and Mongolian culture. There may be plenty of tattoos now, but many are traditional Mongolian designs and symbols.

In Ulaanbaatar many locals look like they've just stepped off the streets of New York or London, so convincing is their Western fashion sense. But talk to them and you'll soon realise that their hopes and dreams lie not only in the West but also in the future of Mongolia, its success, prosperity and the continuation of its unique culture.

The 'haircut ceremony' (*usnii nair*) is a traditional rite of passage for Mongolian children. Their heads are shaved (girls at the age of two and boys at the age of three) and a special party is held in their honour. Afterwards, the hair is usually burnt.

# Traditional Gers

The Mongolian ger is versatile and perfectly adapted for nomadic people living in a land of weather extremes. These domiciles are warm in winter and easily transported on the backs of two or three camels. The exterior of a ger looks simple, but the interior is well furnished and contains a stove at its centre. While traditions are fading in other countries where yurts are found, use of the ger is still common in Mongolia. For travellers, a visit inside a ger is central to the Mongolian experience.

## Structural Integrity

The outermost and innermost material of the ger is usually canvas, with an insulating layer of felt sandwiched in between (more layers in winter and fewer in summer), supported by a collapsible wooden frame. Ropes made from horsehair are cinched around the perimeter to hold the ger together. The roof tends to be low, which helps in deflecting wind. During hot weather the sides can be rolled up and mosquito netting added. Anchoring ropes held down with rocks are set in strong wind.

The felt *(esgi)* is made in the autumn by stretching out several layers of sheep's wool on the ground, sprinkling it with water, adding grass and rolling it up tight, wetting it again and then rolling the whole thing back and forth over the steppe. As the wool dries the threads tighten up and harden into a stiff (yet still flexible) mat. The poles traditionally come from Mongolia's forests but recent limits on wood use have forced ger makers to acquire timber from Russia.

Timothy Allen of BBC Earth filmed the set-up of a ger using time-lapse photography. Check out the 80-second clip on YouTube – search 'Timothy Allen BBC Earth'.

## Inside a Ger

The internal layout of the ger is universal throughout Mongolia. Anywhere from Khovd to Dornod you will see the same set-up and go through the same motions. The door always faces south, primarily because the wind comes from the north and a south-facing door will catch the most sunlight. Visitors should not step on the threshold as they enter, as this is symbolic of stepping on the neck of the ger patriarch.

Once inside, men move to the left (to the west, under the protection of the great sky god, Tengger), women to the right (east, under the protection of the sun). Towards the back, and a little to the west, is the place of

## GER CARTS

It is said that the great Mongol khaans (emperors) had enormous gers that they placed on ox carts to be pulled around their empire, like some sort of ancient Winnebago. This is depicted on some Mongolian banknotes. Some modern scholars, however, dispute this story. Whatever the case, the Mongols certainly did use their gers everywhere they went, only rarely adopting the life of the settled peoples they conquered. It is even said that the Mongols never lived in their own capital, Karakorum. Instead they parked their gers on the grasslands outside the city walls, used to the freedom they provided. The city itself was inhabited by foreign artisans, traders, labourers and priests, accustomed to the stone houses and to life within the city walls.

## 21ST CENTURY GERS

Some gers today sport many of the mod cons found in apartments. Most have a TV, radios are common and some have DVD players. Many families also own a generator (sometimes small solar panels or mini-windmills), which allows them to watch TV and DVDs, charge their mobile phones and use electric lights. At a ger we stopped by in Dornogov, 100km from any town, the owners said they use their phones to keep in touch with relatives in Los Angeles and Chicago.

The ger itself has not changed much, although at some tourist camps (fancy ones), you may see gers built with windows cut in the sides. Hand-crafted gers with delicate wood carvings made for celebrations and naadams are also growing in popularity. These can be seen pitched on Sükhbaatar Sq in summer or set up at the horse race area during Naadam.

honour set aside for guests. After two or three ger visits, this routine becomes like clockwork, and you'll be amazed how everyone in your group easily falls into the same place during each ger visit.

The back of the ger is the *khoimor,* the place for the elders, where the most honoured people are seated and treasured possessions are kept. On the back wall is the family altar, decorated with Buddhist images and family photos (mostly taken during trips to Ulaanbaatar). Near the door, on the male side are saddles, ropes and a big leather milk bag and churn, used to stir *airag* (fermented mare's milk). On the female side of the door are the cooking implements and water buckets. Around the walls there are two or three low beds and cabinets. In the centre sits a small table with several tiny chairs. Hanging in any vacant spot, or wedged between the latticed walls, are toothbrushes, clothes, children's toys and slabs of raw mutton.

An average ger weighs about 250kg and can be carried by two camels. These days most families tend to hire a truck to transport their ger to a new location.

## Building Your Ger

The small cartwheel-shaped opening at the top, called a *toon,* allows smoke to exit and sunlight to enter. It is covered with an *örkh,* which can be adjusted from the ground using ropes. The wooden roof poles *(uni)* are orange (the colour of the sun); the concertina-like latticed walls are called *khan.*

Most gers have five *khan,* although they can be bigger or smaller depending on the preference (and sometimes wealth) of the family. Each wall has about 10 to 15 roof poles. Depending on the mobility and wealth of the family, the ger is placed on a wooden platform or bare earth floor.

The first part of the ger to be assembled is the floor (if there is one). Next, the stove is placed in the centre. It is symbolic of the ritual fire worship practised by Central Asian nomads for centuries, and is therefore considered holy. The walls and the brightly painted door *(khaalga)* are erected along with the two central columns that support the roof. Once the frame is put together, the felt coverings are wrapped around the ger.

Everyone in the family is expected to contribute to this process in some way. However, once the ger is set up it's the sole responsibility of the woman of the home to hang the curtain *(khushig)* that covers the lattice frame.

Although the ger is a nomad dwelling, there are a number of gers right in central Ulaanbaatar, including two inside the Government House and one large ger on Seoul St.

The ger plays a vital role in shaping both the Mongolian character and family life. The small confines compel family members to interact with one another, to share everything and work together, tightening the bond between relatives. The ger prevents privacy but promotes patience and reduces inhibitions. It also creates self-sufficiency; ger dwellers must fetch their own water and fuel, and subsist on the food they themselves produce.

## DOS & DON'TS IN THE GER

### Do

➡ Sleep with your feet pointing towards the door.

➡ Say hello (*sain bain uu*) when you first arrive, but don't repeat it when you see the same person again.

➡ Try to converse in Mongolian as much as possible (have a phrasebook handy) and avoid long conversations in your own language.

➡ Bring a gift (even if it's just small) for the family or children. Your host will likely accept it humbly, so don't feel bad if they don't look too thrilled.

### Don't

➡ Touch another person's hat (even to move it out of the way).

➡ Whistle.

➡ Lean against the support column.

➡ Touch a child's (or anyone else's) head.

➡ Open drawers (or look at personal items).

➡ Serve yourself (wait for the host to serve you).

Nomads tend to move two to four times a year, although in areas where grass is thin they move more often. One nuclear family may live alone or with an extended-family camp of three or four gers (known as an *ail*); any more than that would be a burden on the grassland.

## Staying Overnight

If you are particularly fortunate you may be invited to spend a night or two out on the steppes in a genuine ger, rather than a tourist ger camp. This is a wonderful chance to experience the 'real' Mongolia.

If you are invited to stay in a family ger, only in very rare cases will you be expected to pay for this accommodation. Leaving a gift is strongly recommended. While cash payment is usually OK as a gift, it's far better to provide worthwhile gifts for the whole family, including the women (who look after the guests). Cigarettes, vodka and candy are customary gifts, but with some creativity you can offer more useful items. Welcome gifts include sewing kits, multi-tools, fleece sweaters, T-shirts, toothbrushes/toothpaste, Mongolian–language books and newspapers, and hand-powered torches and radios. Children will enjoy colouring books, pens, paper, puzzles and postcards from your home country.

Your host may offer to cook for you; it is polite for you to offer to supply some food, such as biscuits, bread, fruit, salt, rice and pasta. Pack out any garbage or packaging left over from these items. Mongolians love being photographed. If you take pictures of your host family, remember to take down their name and mail them a copy. For address purposes, you'll need their name, *sum* (district) and aimag.

The easiest way to organise such a visit is through a tour company, which can find you a homestay (for a fee). If travelling independently, don't take advantage of nomad hospitality by expecting a free night in a ger. Always have a tent handy in order to sleep separately from families you encounter.

Gers are growing in popularity in the US and Europe, where they often serve as accommodation at national parks. In the US they are produced by Oregon–based Pacific Yurts (www.pacificyurts.com).

# Spiritualism in Mongolia

**Mongolians are a deeply spiritual people. This, however, is not always apparent, as organised religion is but one small part of the spiritual matrix. Spirituality comes in many other forms, much of it day-to-day rituals rooted in Mongolia's shamanic past. The ancient animist beliefs of the Siberian and steppe tribes who worshipped the sun, earth and sky are still very much alive, woven intimately into the fabric of modern Mongolia.**

## Shamanism

Mongol tribes have long believed in the spirit world as their shamans described it to them. Their cosmic view of the universe did not differentiate between the worlds of the living and dead, nor did they consider themselves any greater than other creatures in this or other worlds. Any imbalance between the human and natural world could cause calamity.

Shamanism is based around the shaman – called a *bo* if a man or *udgan* if a woman – who has special medical and religious powers (known as *udmyn* if inherited, *zlain* if the powers become apparent after a sudden period of sickness and apparitions).

*Religions of Mongolia*, by Walther Heissig, provides an in-depth look at the Buddhist and shamanist faiths as they developed in Mongolia.

### THE NINTH JEBTZUN DAMBA

In 1924 the eighth Jebtzun Damba ('Bogd Khan' in Mongolian) passed away, marking the end of two centuries of Buddhist rule in Mongolia. Soon after his death Mongolia was declared a republic, and the then-communist government forbade the recognition of a ninth Jebtzun Damba. But the great lamas of Tibet had other plans. Tradition held that new incarnations of the Jebtzun Damba would be found in Tibet, so when the time was right, the regent of Lhasa recognised a ninth incarnation. His identity was kept secret to protect him from Russian secret agents, who were busy ridding Mongolia of its Buddhist clergy. The young Jebtzun Damba, named Jampal Namdrol Chokye Gyaltsen, was born in 1932 and undertook Buddhist studies at Drepung Monastery for 14 years.

At the age of 21 he left the monastery to live as a hermit, practising meditation at sacred caves throughout central Tibet. When he was 29 he fled Tibet for India, following the Dalai Lama and thousands of other Tibetans escaping Chinese persecution. The Jebtzun Damba lived in obscurity for decades until being re-recognised by the Dalai Lama in 1991.

In 1999, at the age of 67, he travelled unannounced to Ulaanbaatar, having received a tourist visa in Moscow. (One can only imagine the customs form: 'Occupation: Reincarnation of Tibetan deity Vajrapani'!) He stayed in Mongolia for two months, visiting monasteries in Ulaanbaatar and the countryside. Although mobbed by adoring fans wherever he went, he was deemed persona non grata by the Mongolian government, which at the time was unsure of his motives. He was finally pressured to leave after overstaying his visa.

In 2010 he was allowed to return to Mongolia, where a more confident government welcomed him and even granted him Mongolian citizenship. The Jebtzun Damba spent his remaining days at Gandan Monastery, where he died in March 2012. Speculation persists that the 10th incarnation will eventually be found in Mongolia.

For more information on Mongolia's spiritual leader, see www.jetsundhampa.com.

Two of a shaman's main functions are to cure sickness caused by the soul straying, and to accompany souls of the dead to the other world. As intermediaries between the human and spirit worlds, they communicate with spirits during trances, which can last up to six hours.

Shamanist beliefs have done much to shape Mongolian culture and social practices. For example, nomads today still fill in the holes left by their horse posts when they move camp, inherited from an old shamanic custom of returning the land to its natural state. The fact that Mongolia's landscape is being torn up in search of minerals is inexcusable according to shamans, and may lead to retribution from *tenger* (heaven).

Sky worship is another integral part of shamanism; you'll see Mongolians leaving blue scarves (representing the sky) on *ovoos*. Sky gods are honoured by flicking droplets of vodka in the air before drinking.

The word 'shaman' derives from the word 'saman' in the Evenk language, later passed on to the Western world in the late 1600s by Dutch traveller Nicolaes Witsen, who came into contact with Tungistic–speaking tribes of Siberia.

Shamanism has seen an explosion in popularity in recent years, and hundreds of shamans now offer their healing and consultation services in Ulaanbaatar and other cities. On weekends, shamans gather south of the Tuul Gol (river), about 1km east of Marshall Bridge (near Ikh Tenger valley). All over Mongolia, on cars in particular, you'll see swastikas, which may look offensive to Westerners but are symbols of ancient shamanism for Mongolians.

## Buddhism

The Mongols had limited contact with organised religion before their great empire of the 13th century. It was Kublai Khaan who first found himself with a court in which all philosophies of his empire were represented, but it was a Tibetan Buddhist, Phagpa, who wielded the greatest influence on the khaan (emperor).

In 1578 Altan Khaan, a descendant of Chinggis Khaan, met the Tibetan leader Sonam Gyatso, was converted, and subsequently bestowed on Sonam Gyatso the title Dalai Lama (*dalai* means 'ocean' in Mongolian). Sonam Gyatso was named as the third Dalai Lama and his two predecessors were named posthumously.

*Ovoos*, the large piles of rocks found on mountain passes, are repositories of offerings for local spirits. Upon arriving at an *ovoo*, walk around it clockwise three times, toss an offering onto the pile (another rock should suffice) and make a wish.

Mass conversions occurred under Altan Khaan. As young Mongolian males became monks instead of soldiers, the centuries of constant fighting seemed to ease (much to the relief of China, which subsequently funded more monasteries in Mongolia). This shift from a warring country to a peaceful one persists in contemporary society – Mongolia is a UN–sanctioned 'nuclear-weapons-free nation'. Buddhist opposition to needless killing reinforced strict hunting laws already set in place by shamanism. Today Buddhist monks are still influential in convincing local populations to protect their environment and wildlife.

Buddhism in Mongolia was nearly wiped out in 1937 when the communist government, at the urging of Stalin, launched a purge that destroyed most of the country's 700 monasteries. Up to 30,000 monks were massacred, and thousands more sent to Siberian labour camps. Freedom of religion was only restored in 1990, shortly after the democratic revolution.

While Christianity was the fastest growing religion in Mongolia in the 1990s and early 2000s, Buddhism is making a comeback thanks to renewed nationalism. Even the government (which ostensibly separates church and state) has supported Buddhist activities, including the Danshig Naadam, held each year in August.

## Islam

In Mongolia today, there is a significant minority of Sunni Muslims, most of them ethnic Kazakhs, who live primarily in Bayan-Ölgii. Because of Mongolia's great isolation and distance from the major Islamic centres of the Middle East, Islam has never been a major force in Bayan-Ölgii. However, most villages have a mosque, and contacts have been established with Islamic groups in Turkey. Several prominent figures in the community have been on a hajj to Mecca. Besides the Kazakhs, the only ethnic Mongols to practise Islam are the Khoton tribe, who live primarily in Uvs aimag.

## Christianity

Nestorian Christianity was part of the Mongol empire long before the Western missionaries arrived. The Nestorians followed the doctrine of Nestorious (AD 358–451), patriarch of Constantinople (428–31), who proclaimed that Jesus exists as two separate persons: the man Jesus and the divine son of God. Historically the religion never caught hold in the Mongol heartland, but that has changed in recent years with an influx of Christian missionaries, often from obscure fundamentalist sects. In Mongolia there are an estimated 65,000 Christians and more than 150 churches.

In 1903, when the British invaded Tibet, the 13th Dalai Lama fled to Mongolia and spent three years living in Gandan Khiid in Urga (modern-day Ulaanbaatar).

### IMPORTANT FIGURES & SYMBOLS

This brief guide to some of the deities of the Tibetan Buddhist pantheon will allow you to recognise a few of the statues you'll encounter in Mongolia, usually on temple altars. Sanskrit names are provided as these are most recognised in the West; Mongolian names are in brackets.

**Sakyamuni** The Historical Buddha was born in Lumbini in the 5th century BC in what is now southern Nepal. He attained enlightenment under a bodhi (peepul) tree and his teachings set in motion the Buddhist faith. Statues of the Buddha include 32 distinctive body marks, including a dot between the eyes and a bump on the top of his blue hair. His right hand touches the earth in the *bhumisparsa mudra* hand gesture, and his left hand holds a begging bowl.

**Maitreya (Maidar)** The Future Buddha, Maitreya is passing the life of a bodhisattva (a divine being worthy of nirvana who remains on the human plane to help others achieve enlightenment) and will return to earth in human form 4000 years after the disappearance of Sakyamuni to take his place as the next earthly buddha. He is normally seated with his hands by his chest in the *mudra* of turning the 'wheel of law'.

**Avalokitesvara (Janraisig)** The Bodhisattva of Compassion is either pictured with 11 heads and 1000 pairs of arms (Chogdanjandan Janraisig), or in a white, four-armed manifestation (Chagsh Janraisig). The Dalai Lama is considered an incarnation of Avalokitesvara.

**Tara** The Saviour, Tara has 21 different manifestations. She symbolises purity and fertility and is believed to be able to fulfil wishes. Statues of Tara usually represent Green Tara (Nogoon Dar Ekh), who is associated with night, or White Tara (Tsagaan Dar Ekh), who is associated with day. White Tara is the female companion of Avalokitesvara.

**Four Guardian Kings** Comprising Virupaksa (red; holding a snake), Dhitarastra (white; holding a lute), Virudhaka (blue; holding a sword) and Vaishrovana (yellow; sitting on a snow lion), the kings are mostly seen guarding monastery entrances.

### The Symbols & Objects

**Prayer Wheel** These are filled with up to a mile of prayers and are turned manually by pilgrims to gain merit.

**Wheel of Life** Drawings of the wheel symbolise the cycle of death and rebirth, held by Yama, the god of the dead.

**Stupas (Suvrag)** Originally built to house the cremated relics of Sakyamuni, they have become a powerful symbol of Buddhism. Later stupas became reliquaries for lamas and holy men.

# Mongolian Cuisine

The nomadic Mongols have lived off their herds for centuries. Meat and milk are the staples, while (traditionally, at least) vegetables were written off as feed for animals. Seasoning is not used in traditional cooking, although Mongolians have long added salt to their foods (including tea). Mongolians typically cook with a wok, so most foods are stir-fried or boiled. A steamer is usually available for cooking dumplings. In Ulaanbaatar and other large cities there's a surprisingly cosmopolitan restaurant scene.

## Staples & Specialities

Almost any Mongolian dish can be created with meat, rice, flour and potatoes. Most meals consist of *talkh* (bread) in the towns and cities and *bortzig* (fried unleavened bread) in the gers, and the uncomplicated *shölte khool* (literally, soup with food) – a meal involving hot broth, pasta slivers, boiled mutton and a few potato chunks. Two of the most popular menu options you'll find in restaurants are *buuz* (steamed dumplings filled with mutton and sometimes slivers of onion or garlic) and *khuushuur* (fried mutton pancakes). Miniature *buuz*, known as *bansh,* are usually dunked in milk tea. *Tsuivan* is a Mongolian version of pasta made from steamed flour noodles, carrots, potato and mutton chunks.

The classic Mongolian dinner staple, especially in the countryside, is referred to simply as *makh* (meat) and consists of boiled sheep bits (bones, fat, various organs and the head) with some sliced potato and/or carrots. The other highlight of Mongolian cuisine is *khorkhog,* made by placing hot stones from an open fire into an urn with chopped mutton, some water and sometimes vodka. The container is then sealed and left on the fire. While eating this, it's customary to pass the hot, greasy rocks from hand to hand, as this is thought to be good for your health.

In summer, Mongols snack on *tsagaan idee* (dairy products; literally 'white foods'): yoghurt, milk, delicious fresh cream, cheese and fermented milk drinks. When you visit a ger, you will be offered dairy snacks such as *aaruul* (dried milk curds). Finally, if you get a chance, don't miss the opportunity to try *boodog,* blow-torched marmot (prairie dog), a delicacy of the steppes.

Because of his failing health, the advisors of Ögedei Khaan (a son of Chinggis) suggested that he halve the number of cups of alcohol he drank per day. Ögedei readily agreed, then promptly ordered that his cups be doubled in size.

## Celebrations

Tsagaan Sar, the Mongolian New Year, is a festival for a new beginning. A full belly during Tsagaan Sar is said to represent prosperity in the year ahead; *buuz* are prepared and consumed in their thousands during the holiday. The central meal of the holiday must be the biggest sheep a family can afford; pride is at stake over how much fat and meat appears on the table. During Tsagaan Sar, food is even part of the decoration: the centrepiece is made from layers of large biscuits called *ul boov.* Young people stack three layers of biscuits, middle-aged couples five layers and grandparents seven layers.

At Mongolia's other big holiday, naadam, the customary food is *khuushuur.* Food stands all around the Naadam Stadium and the horse race fields sell stacks of the meat pancakes.

The well-researched www.mongolfood.info includes notes on Mongolian cuisine, plus cooking techniques and recipes, dispelling the myth that Mongolian menus stop at boiled mutton.

### Dos & Don'ts At the Table

#### Do

➡ Cut food towards your body, not away; pass knives by offering the handle.

➡ Accept food and drink with your right hand; use the left *only* to support your right elbow if the food is heavy.

➡ Drink tea immediately; don't put it on the table until you have tried some.

➡ Take at least a sip, or a nibble, of the delicacies offered, even if they don't please you.

➡ Hold a cup by the bottom, not by the top rim.

#### Don't

➡ Get up in the middle of a meal and walk outside; wait until everyone has finished.

➡ Cross your legs or stick your feet out in front of you when eating – keep your legs together if seated, or folded under you if on the floor.

## Habits & Customs

While traditions and customs do surround the dinner table, Mongolian meals are generally casual affairs, and there is no need to be overly concerned about offending your hosts.

In a ger in the countryside, traditional meals such as boiled mutton do not require cutlery or even plates; just trawl around the bucket until a slab catches your fancy. Eat with your fingers and try to nibble off as much meat and fat as possible; Mongolians can pick a bone clean and consider leftovers to be wasteful. There should be a pocket knife for slicing off larger chunks. Most other meals in the rest of Mongolia are eaten with bowls, knives, forks and spoons.

It is always polite to bring something to contribute to the meal; drinks are easiest, or in the countryside you could offer rice, bread or fruit. 'Bon appétit' in Mongolian is *saikhan khool loorai*.

Meals are occasionally interrupted by a round of vodka. Before taking a swig, there's a short ritual to honour the sky gods and the four cardinal directions. There is no one way of doing this, but it usually involves dipping your left ring finger into the vodka and flicking into the air four times before wiping your finger across your forehead.

> It is customary to flick spoonfuls of milk in the direction of departing travellers, whether they are going by horse, car, train or plane.

---

### WHAT'S YOUR DRINK?

Mongolians are big tea drinkers and will almost never start a meal until they've had a cup of tea first, as it is said to aid digestion.

*Süütei tsai*, a classic Mongolian drink, is milk tea with salt. The taste varies by region; in Bayan-Ölgii it may even include a dollop of butter. *Khar tsai* (black tea), is often available, served with sugar but no milk.

Alcoholic drinks are never far away, and Mongolians can drink you under the table if challenged. There is much social pressure to drink, especially on males – those who refuse to drink *arkhi* (vodka) are considered wimps. Chinggis black-label vodka, just US$8 a bottle, is popular. Jalam Khar (Dark Horse), GEM, Altan Gobi, Chinggis, Borgio and Senguur are popular local beers.

While it may not be immediately apparent, every countryside ger doubles as a tiny brewery or distillery. One corner of the ger usually contains a tall, thin jug with a plunger that is used for fermenting mare's milk. The drink, known as *airag*, has an alcohol content of about 3%. Go easy on it at the start or your guts will pay for it later.

# Tribal Mongolia

Mongolia is an ancient tribal society that can be broken down into more than a dozen ethnic subgroups. To this day, Mongolia still counts around 20 different *undesten* (nations), with numerous subclans. Most of these ethnic groups are located along the borders of modern Mongolia, and in some cases they spill over the borders into Russia and China. Inner Mongolia (in China) also has a tribal order that persists today.

## Tribal Groups

A thousand years ago clans regularly squared off against each other in seasonal warfare and bouts of bride theft. They went by the names of Kerait, Tatar, Merkit and Naiman, to list a few; linked by culture, they were divided by old feuds and rivalries. The clans were united during the great Mongol empire (1206 to 1368) but after its demise they went back to their periodic squabbles.

The clans of modern Mongolia lack the political, economic or social independence that one might encounter in tribal areas of Pakistan, southern Africa, India or the Americas. However, many Mongols still associate closely with their clannish roots. The Buriats, for example, sponsor the biannual Altargana Festival, which draws Buriats from all over the country as well as Buriats from Russia and China.

In the 1990s, when the government of Mongolia asked its citizens to choose a clan name, 20% of the population adopted the name 'Borjigin', the clan of Chinggis Khaan.

While it can be difficult to differentiate between some of these peoples, a few are starkly unique. The Tsaatan, who live in *orts* (tepees), speak a distinct Turkic language and herd reindeer, are one of the most identifiable ethnic groups. The Khoton people in western Mongolia are also easily distinguished as the only Mongols to practise Islam.

When meeting minority groups, ask about their traditional clothing, which can be quite distinctive, as is the case with the Dariganga peoples of Sükhbaatar aimag. The Kazakhs, who live primarily in Bayan-Ölgii aimag, are a Turkic tribe with cultural roots in Islamic Central Asia.

### Tribes in Modern Mongolia

The following is a list of some of the main ethnic groups you may encounter:

**Barga** Originally from the Lake Baikal region of Siberia, the Barga number about 2000 and live in remote border areas of Dornod aimag. Many Barga also live in Inner Mongolia (China) around Dalai Nuur and Hailar. Barga consider themselves descended from Alan Goa, a mythical figure described in *The Secret History of the Mongols.*

**Bayad** Descendants of Oirat Mongols; about 50,000 live in the Malchin, Khyargas and Züüngov *sums* of Uvs aimag. The most famous Bayad was the 13th-century princess Kököchin (Blue Dame), whom Kublai Khaan betrothed to the Il-Khanate khan Argun. It was Marco Polo who was selected to escort Kököchin on her journey to Persia.

**Buriat** There are around half a million Buriats in North Asia (around 50,000 live in Mongolia, with others in Russia and China), making them the largest ethnic minority in Siberia. Buriats are known for their strong associations with shamanism. Among

Mongols, they are also unique in their lifestyle; most live in log cabins instead of gers. You'll meet many Buriats in northern Khentii and Dornod aimags.

**Dariganga** During the Qing dynasty era, this ethnic group received special recognition from the emperor. They were responsible for supplying horses to the emperor in Běijīng and today they are still regarded as excellent horse breeders. During the Qing era, the Dariganga also gained skills as blacksmiths and silversmiths. Their traditional headdress, chock-full of silver, is considered the most elegant and valuable of its kind.

**Darkhad** This 20,000-member tribe can be found in the Darkhad Valley in northern Khövsgöl aimag. During the Qing era, they served as ecclesiastical serfs to the Bogd Gegeens and were required to perform services such as pasturing animals. Darkhads are known as powerful shamans but are also beloved for their great sense of humour. A pastime is to sing humorous songs about each other; ask politely and they may make one up about you!

**Dörvöd** There are around 66,000 Dörvöds in western Mongolia. In the 17th century a group of Dörvöds split from the main clan and trekked west to settle in the Volga region of Russia. Historically, the Dörvöd have sometimes clashed with Khalkh Mongols (during the communist era some proposed ceding their territory to the Soviet Union). Former prime minsters Yu Tsedenbal (r 1954–84) and Jambyn Batmönkh (r 1984–90) were both Dörvöd.

**Khalkh** The majority (about 86%) of Mongolians are Khalkh Mongolians. The origin of the word Khalkh is a topic of great debate: some believe it means shield, while others suggest it's derived from the Turkic word Halk, which means people.

**Torguud** About 7000 live in Khovd aimag. Originally from northern Xinjiang, a large group of them moved to the Volga to become the core Kalmyks. Today most Torguuds in Mongolia live in Bulgan *sum*.

**Tsaatan** About 500 of these reindeer herders live in northern Khövsgöl.

**Uriankhai (Tuvans)** About 21,000 Uriankhai live in western Mongolia – you'll meet some if you visit Tsengel Sum, near Altai Tavan Bogd National Park. The Uriankhai are renowned for their throat-singing abilities. Today, most Uriankhai live in the Tuva region of Russia.

**Uzemchin** Most Uzemchin live in Inner Mongolia. In 1945 about 2000 of them migrated to Outer Mongolia and they can still be found in some remote corners of Dornod aimag. Uzemchin are well known for their elegant embroidered *dels* (traditional coat dresses). During naadam, Uzemchin wrestlers wear leather jackets with brass studs.

Traditionally, clans names were passed down orally, with young family members required to remember seven generations of a clan's genealogical chart.

## THE MONGOLIAN NAME GAME

In the 1920s Mongolia's communist government forbade the use of clan names, a dedicated effort to stamp out loyalties that might supersede the state.

In the 1990s, after the fall of communism, few families were able to recall their own clan name. When the government ordered citizens to add a clan name to their official registry, it sparked a boom in amateur genealogy, with families contacting relatives to uncover possible clan names.

Authorities encouraged creativity, and people who could not retrace their name simply made one up – usually after a hobby, profession, favourite mountain or nickname. Mongolia's lone spaceman, Jügderdemidiin Gurragchaa, named his family 'Cosmos'. Another clan name currently up for grabs is 'Family of Seven Drunks', which hasn't had many takers.

Despite official efforts to use the names, the plan failed to resonate with citizens, and most Mongolians today still use their father's name as their surname. However, there is no uniform way to order the names so on business cards you might see a person's given name listed either first or second. If one of the names is in capital letters, that is their given name.

# Wild Lands & Wildlife

Mongolia is the sort of country that naturalists dream about. With the world's lowest population density, huge tracts of virgin landscape, minimal infrastructure, varied eco-systems and abundant wildlife, Mongolia is rightfully considered to be the last bastion of unspoilt land in Asia. Mongolia's lack of urban development, along with shamanic prohibitions against defiling the earth, have for centuries protected the country from degradation. Traditional beliefs, however, are always at odds with modern economics.

## The Land

A zud (extremely harsh winter) is a natural phenom-enon that occurs in Mongolia every five to 10 years. Zud typically means extreme cold for extended periods or heavy snows. A particu-larly bad zud in 2000 and 2001 killed over 10 million animals.

Mongolia is a huge landlocked country. At 1,566,500 sq km in area, it's about three times the size of France. The southern third of Mongolia is dominated by the Gobi Desert, which stretches into China. Only the southern sliver of the Gobi is 'Lawrence of Arabia'–type desert with cliffs and sand dunes. The rest is desert steppe and has sufficient grass to support scattered herds of sheep, goats and camels. There are also areas of desert steppe in low-lying parts of western Mongolia.

Much of the rest of Mongolia is covered by grasslands (or mountain forest steppe). Stretching over about 35% of the country, these steppes are home to vast numbers of gazelles, birds and livestock. The far north-ern areas of Khövsgöl and Khentii aimags are essentially the southern reaches of Siberia and are covered by larch and pine forests known by the Russian word 'taiga'.

### PROTECTED AREAS

The Ministry of Nature and Tourism and its Department of Special Protected Areas Man-agement control the national park system with an annual budget of around US$5 million. The 102 protected areas in Mongolia now constitute an impressive 17.9% of the country. The strictly protected areas of Bogdkhan Uul (p91), Great Gobi (p187), Uvs Nuur Basin, Dornod Mongol and Khustain (p101) are biosphere reserves included in Unesco's Man and Biosphere Network.

The government has a goal of protecting 30% of Mongolia (potentially creating the world's largest park system). This goal, however, has stalled in recent years as the gov-ernment has favoured expanding mining operations and the sale of mining rights.

The Ministry of Nature and Tourism classifies protected areas into four categories (from most protected to least):

**Strictly Protected Areas** Very fragile areas of great importance; hunting, logging and development are strictly prohibited and there is no established human influence.

**National Parks** Places of historical and educational interest; fishing and grazing by no-madic people is allowed and parts of the park are developed for ecotourism.

**Natural & Historical Monuments** Important places of historical and cultural interest; development is allowed within guidelines.

**Nature Reserves** Less important regions protecting rare species of flora and fauna, and archaeological sites; some development is allowed within certain guidelines.

## NATIONAL PARKS

| NATIONAL PARK | FEATURES | ACTIVITIES | TIME TO VISIT |
| --- | --- | --- | --- |
| **Altai Tavan Bogd National Park** | mountains, glaciers, lakes; argali sheep, ibexes, snow leopards, eagles, falcons | mountaineering, horse trekking, backpacking, fishing, eagle hunting (winter) | Jun–Sep |
| **Gorkhi-Terelj National Park** | rugged hills, boulders, streams | river rafting, hiking, mountain biking, rock climbing, camping, cross-country skiing, horse riding | year–round |
| **Gurvan Saikhan National Park** | desert mountains, canyons, sand dunes; Gobi argali sheep, ibexes, black-tailed gazelles | hiking, sand-dune sliding, camel trekking, bird-watching | May–Oct |
| **Khorgo-Terkhiin Tsagaan Nuur National Park** | lake, mountains; wolves, deer, foxes | fishing, hiking, horse trekking, bird-watching | May–Sep |
| **Khövsgöl Nuur National Park** | lake, mountains, rivers; fish, moose, wolverines, bears, sables, elk, roe deer | mountain biking, kayaking, fishing, hiking, horse trekking, bird-watching | Jun–Sep |
| **Khustain National Park** | rugged hills, Tuul Gol (river); *takhi* horses, gazelles, deer, wolves, lynxes, manul wild cats | trekking, wildlife spotting | Apr–Oct |
| **Otgon Tenger Uul Strictly Protected Area** | mountains, rivers, lakes; argali sheep, roe deer, wolves | horse trekking, hiking, swimming | May–Sep |

Near the centre of Mongolia is the Khangai Nuruu range, with its highest peak, Otgon Tenger Uul, reaching 3905m. On the northern slope of these mountains is the source of the Selenge Gol, Mongolia's largest river, which flows northward into Lake Baikal in Siberia. Just to the northeast of Ulaanbaatar is the Khentii Nuruu, the highest mountain range in eastern Mongolia and by far the most accessible to hikers. It's a heavily forested region with meandering rivers and impressive peaks, the highest being Asralt Khairkhan Uul (2800m). The range provides a major watershed between the Arctic and Pacific oceans.

Mongolia has numerous saltwater and freshwater lakes, which are great for camping, bird-watching, hiking, swimming and fishing. The largest is the low-lying, saltwater Uvs Nuur, but the most popular is the magnificent Khövsgöl Nuur, the second-oldest lake in the world, which contains 65% of Mongolia's (and 2% of the world's) fresh water.

## Wildlife

In Mongolia, the distinction between domestic and wild (or untamed) animals is often blurry. Wild and domesticated horses and camels mingle on the steppes with wild asses and herds of wild gazelles. In the mountains there are enormous (and horned) wild argali sheep and domesticated yaks along with wild moose, musk deer and roe deer. Reindeer are the only domesticated deer in the world and small herds are kept by Tsaatan people north of the Darkhad Valley. They can be ridden and will return to the same tent each night for a salt lick.

The Wildlife Conservation Society's Mongolia program strives to address wildlife conservation issues through various approaches that reach local communities, wildlife biologists, provincial governments and national ministries. Read more at www.wcs.org/mongolia.

## ECO-WARRIOR

Tsetsegee Munkhbayar, a herder from central Mongolia, is Mongolia's most famous eco-warrior. In 2007 he won the prestigious Goldman Environmental Prize for his efforts to block aggressive mining on the Ongii Gol (river). Munkhbayar has since become increasingly radical, leading a group called Gal Undesten (Fire Nation) on periodic 'eco-terrorism' stunts. Several times the group has shot up equipment at mining sites and in 2011 members shot arrows at the parliament building in UB, in protest of government mining policies. In 2014 Munkhbayar was arrested and imprisoned for two years on charges of domestic terrorism after brandishing rifles and hand grenades at a mining protest in Ulaanbaatar.

## Animals

Despite the lack of water in the Gobi, numerous species (many of which are endangered) somehow survive. These include the Gobi argali sheep (argal), wild camel (khavtgai), Asiatic wild ass (khulan), Gobi bear (mazaalai), ibex (yangir) and black-tailed gazelle (khar suult zeer).

In the wide-open steppe you may see the rare saiga antelope, Mongolian gazelle (tsagaan zeer), several species of jerboa (alag daaga; a rodent endemic to Central Asia), and thousands of furry marmots (tarvaga), waking up after their last hibernation or preparing for the next. Further north in the forests live the wild boars (zerleg gakhai), brown bears (khuren baavgai), roe deer (bor görös), wolves (chono), reindeer (tsaa buga), elk (khaliun buga), musk deer (khuder) and moose (khandgai), as well as plenty of sables (bulga) and lynx (shiluus), whose fur, unfortunately, is in high demand. Most of the mountains are extremely remote, thus providing an ideal habitat for argali sheep, ibexes, the very rare snow leopard (irbis), and smaller mammals such as foxes, ermine and hares.

The takhi (wild horse) also goes by the name Przewalski's horse. It was named after Colonel Nikolai Przewalski, an officer in the Russian Imperial Army who made the horse's existence known to Europe after an exploratory expedition to Central Asia in 1878.

## Birds

Mongolia is home to 469 recorded species of bird. In the desert you may see desert warblers, saxaul sparrows (boljmor) and McQueen's bustards (toodog), as well as sandgrouse, finches (byalzuuhai) and cinereous vultures (tas).

On the steppes, you will certainly see the most charismatic bird in Mongolia – the demoiselle crane (övögt togoruu) – as well as the hoopoe (övöölj) and the odd falcon (shonkhor), vulture (yol), and golden and steppe eagle (bürged). Other steppe species include upland buzzards (sar), black kites (sokhor elee) and some varieties of owl (shar shuvuu) and hawk (khartsaga). Some black kites will even swoop down and catch pieces of bread in midair if you throw the pieces high enough. These magnificent raptors, perched majestically on a rock by the side of the road, will rarely be disturbed by your jeep or the screams of your guide. But following the almost inaudible click of your lens cap, these birds will move and almost be in China before you have even thought about apertures.

The International Crane Foundation (www. savingcranes.org) works to preserve important crane habitats and wetland areas in Mongolia.

In the mountains, you may be lucky to spot species of ptarmigan (tsagaan yatuu), bunting (khömrög byalzuuhai), woodpecker (tonshuul), owl and endemic Altai snowcock (khoilog). The lakes of the west and north are visited by Dalmatian pelicans (khoton), hooded cranes (khar togoruu), relict gulls (tsakhlai) and bar-headed geese. Eastern Mongolia has several species of crane, including the hooded and Siberian varieties and critically endangered white-naped cranes (tsen togoruu), of which only 5000 remain in the wild.

### Fish

Rivers such as the Selenge, Orkhon, Zavkhan, Balj, Onon and Egiin, as well as dozens of lakes, including Khövsgöl Nuur, hold 76 species of fish. They include trout, grayling *(khadran)*, roach, lenok *(zebge)*, Siberian sturgeon *(khilem)*, pike *(tsurkhai)*, perch *(algana)*, the endemic Altai osman and the enormous taimen, a Siberian relative of the salmon, which can grow up to 1.5m in length and weigh up to 50kg.

### Plants

Mongolia can be roughly divided into three zones: grassland and shrub land (55% of the country); forests, which only cover parts of the mountain steppe (8%); and desert (36%). Less than 1% of the country is used for human settlement and crop cultivation.

Forests of Siberian larch (sometimes up to 45m in height), Siberian and Scotch pine, and white and ground birch cover parts of northern Mongolia. In the Gobi saxaul shrub covers millions of hectares and is essential in anchoring the desert sands and preventing degradation and erosion. Saxaul takes a century to grow to around 4m in height, creating wood so dense that it sinks in water.

Khentii aimag and some other parts of central Mongolia are famous for the effusion of red, yellow and purple wildflowers, mainly rhododendrons and edelweiss. Extensive grazing is the major threat to Mongolia's flowers, trees and shrubs; more than 200 species are endangered.

Mongolians consider wolf parts and organs to have curative properties. The meat and lungs are reputedly good for respiratory ailments, the intestines aid in digestion, powdered wolf rectum can soothe the pain of haemorrhoids and hanging a wolf tongue around one's neck will cure gland and thyroid ailments.

## Environmental Issues

Due to its sparse population and vast territory, there are huge tracts of untouched landscape in Mongolia. However, some pockets of the country are on the verge of an eco-disaster. A rising threat on the steppes is overgrazing by livestock, especially sheep and goats. A 2013 environmental report said that 70% of the grassland had been degraded and 12% of Mongolia's biomass had disappeared over the previoul two decades.

### ENDANGERED SPECIES

According to conservationists, 28 species of mammal are endangered in Mongolia. The more commonly known species are wild asses, wild camels, argali sheep and ibexes; others include otters, wolves, saiga antelopes and some species of jerboa. The red deer is also in dire straits; over the past two decades its numbers have plunged from 130,000 to around 20,000. Poachers prize brown bears for their gall bladders, which are used in traditional medicine. The mammal closest to extinction is the Gobi bear, the world's only desert-dwelling bear. With just 27 *mazaalai* left in the wild, they are in a precarious state. Mongolia's government declared 2013 the 'Year of Saving the Mazaalai' and established special reserves for the bears.

There are 22 species of endangered birds, including many species of hawk, falcon, buzzard, crane and owl. Until 2013 the government was exporting 150 falcons a year to buyers in Kuwait and the United Arab Emirates. The illegal export of these birds still occurs, albeit on a much smaller scale. There are an estimated 6800 breeding pairs left in Mongolia.

One positive news story is the resurrection of the *takhi* (wild horse). The *takhi* was actually extinct in the wild in the 1960s. It has been successfully reintroduced into three special protected areas after an extensive breeding program overseas.

In preserved areas of the mountains, about 1000 snow leopards remain. They are hunted for their pelts (which are part of some shamanist and Buddhist traditional practices), as are the leopards' major source of food, marmots.

Each year the government sells licences to hunt ibexes, argali, red deer, gazelles and roe deer. In 2012 the hunting permits netted the government T3.5 billion.

## RENEWABLE ENERGY

For centuries Mongolians have been fighting against the elements; now they are trying to harness nature's power to develop a giant renewable-energy infrastructure. The country's first foray into renewables was a 50-megawatt wind farm 75km southwest of Ulaanbaatar. Each year the farm saves 122,000 tons of coal and 1.6 million tons of water, and eliminates 180,000 tons of carbon-dioxide emissions. It generates around 5% of the energy needed by the central grid. Mongolia has set a goal to get 30% of its energy from renewables by 2030. In 2017 Mongolia opened its first large solar power farm, a 10-megawatt facility in Darkhan, with investment from Japan.

More wind and solar farms are planned for the Gobi Desert. Experts say wind in the Gobi could generate 300,000 megawatts of wind power and the sun could yield 11 gigawatts, and Mongolia could one day export power to an 'Asia Super Grid' that might share energy from Japan to India.

Forest fires, nearly all of which are caused by careless human activity, are common during the windy spring season. The fires destroy huge tracts of forest and grassland, mainly in Khentii and Dornod aimags.

Perhaps the biggest concern is mining, which has polluted 28 river basins in eight aimags. As one mining executive told us, parts of the Tuul Gol near the village of Zaamar look like a WWI battlefield. Water usage by mines in the Gobi has prompted a backlash by local communities. The huge Oyu Tolgoi mine in Ömnögov requires the use of 360L of water *per second,* prompting some locals to call for a ban on underground water usage.

China's appetite for minerals is opening up new mines but another threat lies in China's hunt for the furs, meat and body parts of endangered animals. Chinese demand has resulted in an 80% decline in the number of marmots and an 85% drop in the number of saiga antelope.

Urban sprawl, coupled with a demand for wood to build homes and for heating and cooking, is slowly reducing the forests. This destruction of the forests has also lowered river levels, especially that of the Tuul Gol near Ulaanbaatar. Large-scale infrastructure projects are further cause for concern. The 18m-tall Dörgön hydropower station, built on the Chon Khairkh Gol in Khovd, has submerged canyons and pastures. The dam threatens fish and will only operate in summer when electricity is in lower demand compared with winter. The planned Egiin Gol hydropower station in northern Mongolia has experienced fierce opposition from Russia as its waters flow to Lake Baikal.

Conservationists are also concerned about the expansion of paved roads and railways, which are cutting across important animal migration routes in eastern Mongolia and the Gobi Desert. These new routes increase mining and commerce inside fragile ecosystems.

Ulaanbaatar has its own distinct environmental problems. The air pollution is ranked among the worst in the world (particularly in winter) and toxic chemicals and coal dust have polluted the soil and water. The sudden rise of consumerism has also resulted in mountains of garbage and construction waste. Efforts to enforce waste management have seen mixed results and large piles of trash are still commonly found in playgrounds and parking lots. On the city outskirts, garbage dumps are inhabited by gangs of human scavengers who pick through the piles in search of scrap metal.

Mongolians collect various wild herbs and flowers for their medicinal properties: yellow poppies to heal wounds, edelweiss to add vitamins to the blood, and feather grass to cure an upset stomach.

In 2012 ex-President Tsakhiagiin Elbegdorj was awarded the 'Champion of the Earth' award by the United Nations Environmental Programme for his efforts to fight climate change.

# Survival Guide

# Directory A–Z

## Accommodation

Mongolia has a limited range of accommodation, and booking ahead is a good idea, especially in midsummer and around naadam. Consider also that many places close in winter.

➡ **Hotels** While many hotels are relics from the Soviet era, there are a growing number of international chains, especially in Ulaanbaatar.

➡ **Guesthouses** These are mainly located in Ulaanbaatar.

➡ **Ger Camps** Privately run camps where tourists stay in gers; some of them are quite luxurious. Most are found in remote locations, with some on the outskirts of small towns. Have a phone handy to call ahead for directions and meal preparation.

### Booking Services

In the countryside, traditional accommodations are limited, but many travellers can find places to stay on the usual home-sharing services.

➡ **Lonely Planet** (lonelyplanet.com/mongolia/hotels) Recommendations and bookings.

➡ **Mongolian Properties** (mongolia-properties.com/rent) Offers long-term rents.

### Ger Buudals

Ger *buudals* (homestays) are found in popular tourist destinations, including Khövsgöl Nuur National Park, Terkhiin Tsagaan Nuur and Terelj. These are family-run operations and usually consist of an extra ger next to the family's ger. Basically, these are homestays with local families. They are very basic: no toilets, no showers and thin bedding.

Expect to pay T10,000 to T15,000 per night. Lunch or dinner costs around T6000, while breakfast is around T3000.

Be aware that some families running ger *buudals* might not be able to cope with the trash you produce and may dispose of it improperly. For this reason, the rangers at Khövsgöl Nuur National Park and Gorkhi-Terelj will hand you a plastic bag when you enter the park (you're expected to carry your own rubbish out of the park). Bags are not handed out at other national parks, so bring a few of your own if you plan to camp or stay at a ger *buudal*.

### Ger Camps

One unique option, particularly popular with organised tours, is to stay in tourist gers, which are like those used by nomads – except for the hot water, toilets, sheets and karaoke bars.

The camps are found all over Mongolia. They may seem touristy and are often surprisingly expensive, but if you are going into the countryside, a night at one is a great way to experience a Western–oriented 'traditional

---

### SLEEPING PRICE RANGES

The following price ranges are for a standard double room in the summer high season (May to September). Tax (10%) is almost always built into the price.

Outside Ulaanbaatar accommodation price ranges are defined as follows:

**$** less than T50,000

**$$** T50,000–T80,000

**$$$** more than T80,000

In Ulaanbaatar accommodation price ranges are defined as follows:

**$** less than US$50 (T122,500)

**$$** US$50–US$100 (T122,500–T245,000)

**$$$** more than US$100 (T245,000)

Mongolian nomadic lifestyle' without the discomforts or awkwardness of staying in a private ger.

A tourist ger camp is a patch of ground consisting of several (or sometimes dozens of) traditional gers, with separate buildings for toilets, hot showers and a ger-shaped restaurant-bar. Inside each ger, there are usually two to four beds, a table, tiny chairs and a wood stove that can be used for heating during the night – ask the staff to make it up for you.

Note that a staff member may periodically come to your ger unannounced to light the fire (especially in the early morning).

**Toilets** Usually the sit-down types, though they may be (clean) pit toilets.

**Price** Often depends on the location. Where there is lots of competition, ie Khövsgöl Nuur, Kharkhorin and Terkhiin Tsagaan Nuur, you can find basic camps for around T10,000 per night. Better camps or camps in remote areas may charge US$40 to US$50 per person per night, including three meals. The cheapest camps charge US$20 to US$25 per person without meals. Activities such as horse or camel riding will cost extra. As meals add so much to the bill, you can save considerable cash by bringing your own food.

**Meals** Taken in a separate restaurant ger. Camp food is often Mongolian meals of meat, rice and potatoes, although improvements have been made in recent years and Western or East Asian meals are now often available. On the downside, meals can take a long time to arrive as wood-fired stoves need to be prepared first. Give the camp at least one hour's notice (two hours if possible) and call ahead if you are still on the road. Most camps have a bar (and sometimes satellite TV).

**Bring** If you plan to stay in a ger camp, you may want to bring a torch for nocturnal visits to the toilets, candles to create more

ambience than stark electric lights (though not all have electricity), towels (the ones provided are invariably smaller than a handkerchief) and toilet paper (it may run out).

**Seasons** Except for a handful of ger camps in Terelj, most ger camps are only open from June to August, although in the Gobi they open a month earlier and close a little later.

## Guesthouses

Ulaanbaatar now has around 15 guesthouses firmly aimed at foreign backpackers. Most are in apartment blocks and have dorm beds for around US$6 to US$8, cheap meals, a laundry service, internet connection and travel services. They are a great place to meet other travellers to share transportation costs, but can get pretty crowded before and during Naadam (11 and 12 July).

Outside Ulaanbaatar only a handful of places, including Kharkhorin and Khatgal, have accommodation aimed at backpackers.

## Hotels

For cheap digs in Ulaanbaatar, try the guesthouses. If you plan to stay in budget hotels in the countryside, you should bring a sleeping bag. An inner sheet (the sort used inside sleeping bags) is also handy if the sheets are dirty. Blankets are always available, but are generally dirty or musty.

Midrange places are generally good but rather overpriced, charging US$60 to US$120 for a double in Ulaanbaatar. These rooms will be comfortable and clean and probably have satellite TV. Hot water and heating is

standard for most buildings and hotels in Ulaanbaatar, and air-conditioning is rarely needed. A private room or apartment, available through guesthouses, may be a better idea.

**Prices** May be quoted in either dollars or tögrög. Either way, you should pay in tögrög because it is now the law, though some hotels will act as money changers. Payment for accommodation is usually made upon checkout, but some receptionists will ask for money upfront.

**Facilities** In the countryside, most hotels are generally empty and very basic, though facilities continue to improve and almost every aimag capital will have one decent new place. Even at the best places you should be prepared for dodgy plumbing, broken locks, rock-hard beds and electrical outages. Service can be pretty lacklustre. The quality of hotels in the countryside is reason enough to take a tent and go camping.

**Bathing** If the hotel has no hot water (most likely outside UB) or no water at all, it's worth knowing that most aimag capitals have a public bathhouse.

**Security** Always keep your windows and door locked (where possible). Err on the side of caution by keeping your valuables with you, or at the very least lock up valuables inside your luggage. Most hotels have a safe where valuables can be kept.

**CLASSES OF ROOM**

Most zochid buudals (hotels) in the countryside (and budget hotels in Ulaanbaatar) have three types of rooms:

**Lux (deluxe) rooms** Include a separate sitting room, usually with TV and private bathroom.

**Khagas lux (half-deluxe or half-lux)** Only a little smaller but often much cheaper.

**Engiin (simple) room** Usually with a shared bathroom.

Sometimes *niitiin bair* (dorm-style) rooms are available, but are rarely offered to foreigners. Invariably, hotel staff will initially show you their deluxe room, so ask to see the standard rooms if you're on a budget. Simple rooms cost around T25,000 per person per night. In *sum* (district) centres, expect to pay around T10,000 per person.

## Rental Accommodation

Apartment rental (p248) is really only an option in Ulaanbaatar. Guesthouse owners may have long-term rental options or could help navigate the Mongolian–language apartment rental websites.

# Children

Children can be a great ice-breaker and are a good avenue for cultural exchange with the local people. In Mongolia, children often like the thrill of camping, for a night or two at least. There are also lots of opportunities to sit on yaks, horses and camels, and plenty of opportunities to meet playmates when visiting gers. On the downside, long jeep rides over nonexistent roads are a sure route to motion sickness (stick to destinations with paved roads), and the endless steppe landscape may leave your children comatose with boredom. Check out Lonely Planet's *Travel with Children* for more general tips on keeping the kids entertained.

## Practicalities

→ Items such as formula, baby food, nappies (diapers) and wipes are sold in nearly every supermarket in Ulaanbaatar, and many of these items are now available in other cities too. In the countryside, the best place to get milk is directly from a herder, but make sure it has been boiled.

→ It's unlikely that your tour company will have a child seat for the vehicle. This is something to clarify when booking your tour. Chinese–made safety seats are sold in some Ulaanbaatar shops. Another option is to bring your own car seat. Note that Air China and MIAT will weigh the car seat and count it as part of your luggage (some other airlines won't count it against your luggage allotment).

→ When travelling in the countryside, deluxe hotel rooms normally come with an extra connecting room, which can be ideal for children.

→ Many restaurants in Ulaanbaatar have a high chair available. This will be rare in the countryside.

→ Nappy-changing facilities are rare.

→ Breastfeeding in public is common in the countryside but slightly rarer in the city.

→ There are several kids' soft play places in Ulaanbaatar – the largest (and priciest) is at the **Shangri-La** (Map p58; ☑7010 9911; www. shangrilacentreub.mn; Olympic St 19A-C, ⌨ sapping.beams. dice).

# Discounts Cards

An ISIC student card will get you a 25% discount on train tickets plus discounts with some tour operators. Check the ISIC website (www.isic card.com) for updates.

A student price might not always be listed but may be available; it's a good idea to inquire if you've got a student card on you.

# Electricity

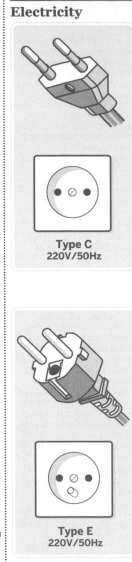

**Type C**
**220V/50Hz**

**Type E**
**220V/50Hz**

# Embassies & Consulates

## Mongolian Embassies & Consulates

You'll find a full listing of Mongolia's embassies and consulates at: embassy.goabroad. com/embassies-of/mongolia.

## Embassies & Consulates in Mongolia

A growing number of countries operate embassies in Ulaanbaatar, though for some nationalities the nearest embassy is in Běijīng. If your country has an embassy in Ulaanbaatar, it's a good idea to register with it if you're travelling into the remote countryside, or in case you lose your passport.

Note that the German embassy also looks after the interests of Dutch, Belgian, Greek and Portuguese citizens. The British embassy can handle normal consular duties for Commonwealth countries that do not already have an embassy or consulate in Mongolia.

**Australian Embassy** (Map p58; ☑7013 3001; www.mongolia. embassy.gov.au; Seoul St 21, 4F, Naiman Zovkhis Bldg, ⓜ coiling.handover.guidebook; ⓧ9.30am-4.30pm Mon-Fri)

**Canadian Embassy** (Map p58; ☑11-332 500; www.canada international.gc.ca/mongolia-mongolie; Peace Ave, Central Tower, 6th fl, ⓜ devoured. village.trooper; ⓧ9am-noon Mon-Fri)

**Chinese Embassy** (Map p58; ☑11-323 940; http://mn.china-embassy.org; Zaluuchuudyn Örgön Chölöö 5, ⓜ adults. reputable.breathy; ⓧvisas 9.30am-noon Mon, Wed & Fri)

**French Embassy** (Map p58; ☑11-324 519; www.amba france-mn.org; Peace Ave 3, ⓜ broker.overdrive.glimmers; ⓧ8.30am-12.30pm & 1.30-5pm Mon-Fri)

**German Embassy** (Map p58; ☑11-323 915, 11-323 325; www. ulan-bator.diplo.de; United Nations St 16, ⓜ scan.redeeming. regaining; ⓧ8.30am-12.30pm & 1-5pm Mon-Thu, 8.30am-12.30pm Fri)

**Japanese Embassy** (Map p58; ☑11-320 777; www.mn.emb-japan.go.jp; Embassy Rd 10, ⓜcarriage.parsnips.shut; ⓧ9am-1pm & 2-4.45pm Mon-Fri)

**Kazakh Embassy** (☑11-345 408; ulaanbaatar@mfa.kz; Zaisan St 31/6, Khan Uul District, ⓜ forgets.indicated. fantastic)

**Russian Embassy** (Map p58; ☑11-326 037; www.mongolia. mid.ru/en; Peace Ave 6A, ⓜ prime.slant.beaker; ⓧvisas 9am-noon Mon-Fri)

**South Korean Embassy** (☑7007 1020; http://mng. mofa.go.kr; Mahatma Gandhi St 39, ⓜ tilts.liquid.farmland; ⓧ9am-noon & 1.30-6pm Mon-Fri)

**Swiss Consulate** (Map p58; ☑11-331 422; www.eda.admin. ch/mongolia; Embassy Rd, Sky Plaza Business Centre, ⓜ pioneered.honest.rules; ⓧ9am-5pm Mon-Fri)

**UK Embassy** (Map p67; ☑11-458 133; www.gov.uk/world/ mongolia; Peace Ave 30, ⓜ nets.cases.dummy; ⓧ8.30am-1pm & 2-5pm Mon-Thu, to 1.30pm Fri)

**US Embassy** (Map p67; ☑7007 6001; https://mn.usembassy. gov; Denver St 3, ⓜ craftsman. memo.rags; ⓧ8.30am-5pm Mon-Fri)

## Gay & Lesbian Travellers

While homosexuality remains a fairly taboo topic in Mongolia, attitudes towards the LGBT community are changing, especially in Ulaanbaatar. Homosexuality was decriminalised in 2002, and in 2013 the LGBT community hosted its first **Pride Week** (ⓧSept), with a film festival, workshops and a parade (all in a private venue). Harassment by police is becoming less of a problem, and the gay community has become better organised; an **LGBT centre** (☑7011-0323) opened in 2007.

D Otgoo, the head of the LGBT centre in Ulaanbaatar, explained to us that Mongolia's youthful, tolerant and adaptable society has led to a better understanding and acceptance of the LGBT community.

Meeting places come and go quickly, so you'll need to tap into the scene and ask. At the time of writing the best gathering spots were

**D.d/h.z** (Map p58; ☑9400 8658; www.facebook.com/didihzub; Baga Toiruu, w flame.blogs.pipe; ⊙6pm-late) and **18cm** (☑9990 4255; Seoul St, w cinemas.disbanded. celebrate; ⊙8pm-4am), both in Ulaanbaatar. As you never know what sort of reaction you'll get from a Mongolian in person, try making contacts through the web. Check out the LGBT centre (Mongolia) Facebook page for more details.

## Health

For information on Health in Mongolia, see p273.

## Insurance

A policy covering loss, theft and medical expenses, plus compensation for delays in your travel arrangements, is essential for Mongolia. If items are lost or stolen you'll need to show your insurance company a police report. You may also need to prove damage or injury, so make sure to take photos. All policies vary, so check the fine print.

Worldwide travel insurance is available at www.lonelyplanet.com/bookings. You can buy, extend and claim online any time – even if you're already on the road.

## Internet Access

A handful of internet cafes can be found in Ulaanbaatar and other cities. Signs are often in English or Mongolian (Интэрнэт Кафэ). Wi-fi hotspots are just about everywhere in bigger cities. In villages you'll need to ask around.

**Internet cafes** Every aimag capital has an internet cafe at the central Telecom office. Some *sum* centres also have internet access. Expect to pay around T1000 per hour at internet cafes, double or triple that for hotel business centres.

**Wi-fi and cable** In our reviews, places with wi-fi, or internet-connected computers, are indicated with an icon. Some hotels will just have an internet cable sticking out of the wall but require you to have your own laptop; if this is the case, it is described in the hotel listing.

**ISPs** Internet service providers such as Skytel charge T44,000 for 5mbs of internet service per month.

**Mobile broadband** 3G is available in places where you can get a mobile-phone connection. Use sparingly as it does tend to drain your phone units.

## Legal Matters

Foreigners' rights are generally respected in Mongolia.

**Drugs** If caught, drug use will give you a peek into Mongolia's grim penitentiary system.

**Borders** The most common offence committed by foreigners is straying too close to a border without a permit. Violators end up paying a fine, and a few unlucky souls have been imprisoned for a few days. If you run into serious trouble, ask to contact your embassy.

**Police** The police get mixed reviews. Some travellers have reported fast response and results, while others have been let down with lacklustre work. Overall, police are harmless, but can be unreliable when you really need them. In Mongolia, it is often the victim who is blamed (because of 'carelessness'), so never expect much sympathy from the police in any given circumstance.

## Maps

Among the maps produced outside Mongolia, the best is the 1:200,000 *Mongolia* map published by Gizi Maps (www.gizimap.com). The map is in both Latin and Cyrillic letters, handy for both you and your driver. It's available at **Seven Summits** (Map p58; ☑9942 9989, 11-317 923; www.activemongolia.com; btwn Peace Ave & Seoul St, /// absorb.inkjet.whisk; ⊙10am-7pm Mon-Fri, to 6pm Sat & Sun) in Ulaanbaatar for T34,000.

While shopping for maps in Ulaanbaatar, look out for the 1:1,500,000 *Road Network Atlas* (T36,000) produced by MPM Agency. Another handy map is the 1:2,500,000 *Road Map of Mongolia* (T13,600). It has the most accurate road layout and town names and usefully marks the kilometres between all towns. Also useful is the *Tourist Map of Mongolia* (T8100), which marks

---

### ETIQUETTE

⇒ **Touching shoes** Should you accidentally step on someone's foot, quickly shake their hand.

⇒ **Meeting seniors** When meeting a senior citizen, always ask about their health before beginning a conversation.

⇒ **Bargaining** Mongolians usually don't bargain – the price stated is generally what you are expected to pay.

⇒ **Gift giving** Guests are usually expected to bring a gift when visiting a home; even flowers or sweets will suffice.

⇒ **Dress** Mongolians dress with pride; holes in clothing, especially socks, are considered to bring bad luck.

⇒ **Demeanour** Mongolians rarely show anger towards one another to get something accomplished. Always try to keep your cool.

a host of obscure historical, archaeological and natural sights, as well as ger camps. Most maps are updated every couple of years.

Explorers will want to check out the 1:500,000 series of topographic maps, which covers Mongolia in 37 maps. Each sheet costs around T10,000 to T12,000, but don't count on all being available. The topographic maps are particularly useful if travelling by horse or foot or using a GPS, but they can get expensive. A cheaper alternative is a series of all 21 aimag maps (T25,000, or T1500 per sheet).

You will also spot handy regional maps (from T7000 to T10,000 each) of the most popular tourist areas, including Khövsgöl Nuur (1:200,000), Gobi Gurvan Saikhan (1:200,000) and Terelj (1:100,000).

Conservation Ink (www. conservationink.org) produces maps (US$8) using satellite images combined with useful information on culture, wildlife and tourist facilities. The national park series includes Altai Tavan Bogd, Khövsgöl Nuur, Gobi Gurvan Saikhan, Gorkhi-Terelj and Khustain.

Chinggis Khaan junkies will want to check out the *Chinggis Khaan Atlas*, available around Ulaanbaatar for about T8000, which maps his every presumed movement in obsessive detail.

## Money

ATMs are widely available. Credit cards are accepted in most hotels, restaurants and shops. Money changers are easily accessible and give better rates compared to hotels.

The tögrög has been a quite unstable currency in recent years. IMF assistance from 2017 should help the currency to stabilise. ATMs are everywhere, but only a few accept debit cards with a microchip. Credit cards are

widely accepted at shops, hotels and restaurants.

**Currency** The Mongolian unit of currency is the tögrög (T), often spelled tugrik because this reflects the pronunciation more accurately. It comes in notes of T5, T10, T20, T50, T100, T500, T1000, T5000, T10,000 and T20,000. (T1 notes are basically souvenirs.) The highest-value note is worth around US$8.

**Money changers** Banks and exchange offices in Ulaanbaatar will change money with relative efficiency. Banks in provincial centres are also fine; they change dollars and give cash advances against debit and credit cards.

**Payments** When paying out large sums of money (to hotels, tour operators and sometimes airlines), it's fine to use either US dollars or tögrög; the merchant will act as a money changer, though the rate will not generally be very good. Other forms of currency aren't usually accepted, although the euro is probably the next best. Cash offers the best exchange rates and you won't be paying any commission charge, but for security purposes you can also use debit cards.

**Travellers cheques** These are no longer accepted anywhere in Mongolia.

**Leaving Mongolia** Remember to change all your tögrög when leaving the country, as it's worthless elsewhere.

**Depreciation** Bear in mind that the tögrög fluctuates widely against the dollar, and local businesses often raise prices to keep up with the changes. Prices are likely to adjust upwards if the currency continues to devalue.

### ATMs

➡ Golomt, Trade & Development Bank, Khan Bank and XacBank all have ATMs in their Ulaanbaatar and countryside branches. ATMs are also found in many shops and malls. These ATMs accept Visa and MasterCard and work most of the time, allowing you to withdraw up to T800,000 per day, although the amount may depend on your home bank. Chip cards are not accepted at most ATMs – try the XAAH Bank ATMs. You could also visit the HQ of Trade & Development Bank on Peace Ave.

➡ Before leaving home check with your bank about fees for making ATM transactions overseas. A 3% charge is standard nowadays but some banks will only charge 1%. If you plan to use your debit card a lot, it may be worth opening an account with a bank that has the lowest ATM fees.

### Credit Cards

➡ Credit cards are becoming more widely accepted across the country – card readers are available even in small grocery shops and cafes. Bring one that won't charge a foreign-transaction fee. Note that some merchant names might appear as a series of numbers on your statement, so retain your receipts if you are keeping track of your accounts.

➡ Banks can give cash advances on credit cards, although a fee of 3% usually applies.

## Tipping

Traditionally, Mongolians don't tip. However, Mongolians working in tourism-related fields (guides, drivers, bellhops and waiters at restaurants frequented by foreigners) are now accustomed to tips. If you do feel service was good, a 10% to 20% tip is appreciated.

## Exchange Rates

| Australia | A$1 | T1785 |
|---|---|---|
| Canada | C$1 | T1778 |
| China | Y1 | T344 |
| Euro zone | €1 | T2636 |
| Japan | ¥100 | T21 |
| New Zealand | NZ$1 | T1710 |
| Russia | R1 | T39.8 |
| UK | UK£1 | T3003 |
| USA | US$1 | T2357 |

For current exchange rates, see www.xe.com.

# Opening Hours

Operating hours in Ulaanbaatar are generally consistent. In the countryside they are more loosely followed, and banks, museums and other facilities may close for an hour at lunch, some time between noon and 2pm.

**Banks** 9am–6pm Monday to Friday. Main branches remain open on weekends.

**Museums** Reduced hours and normally closed an extra couple of days a week in winter.

**Restaurants** 10am–8pm (to 10pm in UB) Monday to Saturday. Some remain open on Sunday.

**Shops** 9am–6pm (to 10pm in UB) Monday to Saturday.

# Photography

Mongolia's remote and beautiful landscapes make for some incredible photography, but it's this same remoteness that requires extra planning when taking pictures. For professional tips on how to take better photos, check out Lonely Planet's *Travel Photography*, by Richard I'Anson.

**Digital photography** As you may go several days in a row without seeing a shop, internet cafe or electrical outlet, you'll need extra batteries and memory cards for your digital camera. These are best bought at home or in Ulaanbaatar as electronic goods in aimag centres can be hard to find. Once you reach an aimag capital you can go to an internet cafe and upload your pictures to the cloud.

**Light** In summer, days are long, so the best time to take photos is before 10am and between 6pm and 8pm, when Mongolia basks in gorgeous light. As bright, glaring sunshine is the norm, a polarising filter is essential.

**Dust** If you do a jeep trip on an unsurfaced road, you can expect plenty of dust, so keep the camera well sealed in a plastic bag.

## Photographing People

Always ask before taking a photograph. Keep in mind that monks and nomads are not photographic models, so if they do not want to be photographed, their wishes should be respected. Point a camera at an urban Mongol on the street and chances are they will cover their face. Don't try sneaking around for a different angle as this may lead to an argument. Markets are also places where snap-happy foreigners are often not welcome.

On the other hand, people in the countryside can be happy to pose for photographs if you ask first. If you have promised to send them a copy, please do it. One way to do this is to print out the photos at an aimag centre or in Ulaanbaatar. To simplify matters, bring blank envelopes and ask them to write their address on the outside. On the inside, make a note to yourself about who they were in case you forget.

When Mongolians pose for a portrait they instantly put on a face that looks like they are in mourning at Brezhnev's funeral. You may need to take this Soviet–style portrait in order to get a more natural shot later. 'Can I take your photograph?' in Mongolian is *Bi tany zurgiig avch bolokh uu?*

## Restrictions

➡ Photography is prohibited inside monasteries and temples, although you may photograph building exteriors and monastery grounds. You can sometimes obtain special permission to take photographs for an extra fee.

➡ Don't photograph potentially sensitive areas, especially border crossings and military establishments.

# Post

**Service** The postal service is generally reliable. Allow at least a couple of weeks for letters and postcards to arrive home from Mongolia.

**Stamps** You can buy stamps in post offices (and top-end hotels) in Ulaanbaatar and aimag capitals.

---

### PHOTOGRAPHY CHARGES IN MUSEUMS

In most museums throughout the country you need to pay an extra fee (often outrageously high) to use your still or video camera. The fees tend to vary, between T12,000 and T25,000 for photos and from T25,000 to T50,000 for videos. It is best to have a look around first before you decide whether to fork out the extra tögrög.

**Poste restante** The poste restante at the **Central Post Office** (CPO, Töv Shuudangiin Salbar; Map p58; ☑11-313 421; cnr Peace Ave & Sükhbaataryn Gudamj, ⃞ wicked.greet. conjured; ⊙7.30am-9pm Mon-Fri, 9am-8pm Sat & Sun) in Ulaanbaatar seems to work quite well; bring along your passport as proof of identification. Don't even think about using poste restante anywhere else in the country.

**Couriers** The more reliable courier services include DHL and FedEx.

**Postal rates** Normal-sized letters cost T1320 and postcards cost T1100 to all countries. A 1kg airmail parcel to Europe or the USA is around T70,000.

# Public Holidays

The Naadam Festival and Tsagaan Sar each warrant three days off, plus there's a day off for Children's Day, New Year and Chinggis Khaan's birthday. Most tourist facilities remain open during holidays, but shops and offices will close down. The following holidays are observed:

**Shin Jil** (New Year's Day) 1 January

**Constitution Day** 13 January; to celebrate the adoption of the 1992 constitution (generally a normal working day).

**Tsagaan Sar (Lunar New Year)** January/February; a three-day holiday celebrating the Mongolian New Year.

**Women's Day** 8 March (generally a normal working day).

**Mothers' & Children's Day** 1 June; a great time to visit parks.

**Naadam Festival** 11 and 12 July; also known as National Day celebrations.

**Chinggis Khaan's Birthday** Early November; the date is the first day of the first winter month, based on the lunar calendar. Most government offices and banks are closed.

# Safe Travel

Mongolia is a reasonably safe country in which to travel, but given the infrastructure of the country, the state of the economy and other development problems, you are bound to run into bumps along the way. With a bit of patience, care and planning, you should be able to handle just about anything.

# Telephone

It's easy to make international or domestic calls in Ulaanbaatar and the aimag capitals. Technology is still lagging in many *sum* centres; however, it's now possible to use mobile (cell) phones in most of the country.

**Calling Mongolia** To make a call *to* Mongolia, dial the international access code in your country (normally 00) and then the Mongolian country code (976). Then, for a landline number, dial the local code (minus the '0' for Ulaanbaatar, but include the '0' for all other areas) and then the number. If you are calling a mobile phone, dial the country code (976) without the area code. Be aware, though, that there are different requirements for area codes if you're using a mobile phone.

**Calling out of Mongolia** If you are calling *out of* Mongolia and using an IDD phone, dial 00 and then your international country code. If you have a mobile phone and you are roaming on your regular plan, add the + sign, then country code and the number.

For ease of use and lower costs, you can also use Skype, Viber or a similar VoIP app.

**Operator** In Ulaanbaatar, the domestic operator's number is 109. Outside normal working hours, call 1109.

## Mobile Phones

Local SIM cards can be used in whatever phone you bring. You can also keep your own SIM card if you have a plan that allows roaming, but be wary of roaming charges.

The main companies are Mobicom, Skytel, Unitel and G-Mobile. Mobicom and Unitel operate on GSM (Global System for Mobile communication) 900/1800. G-Mobile and Skytel are both on the CDMA network. (Make sure you buy a SIM card appropriate for your phone.)

➡ Buying a SIM card in Mongolia will probably work out cheaper than paying roaming charges on your home country network.

➡ Mobicom booths can be found in the **Central Post Office** (CPO, Töv Shuudangiin Salbar; Map p58; ☑11-313 421; cnr Peace Ave & Sükhbaataryn Gudamj, ⃞ wicked.greet. conjured; ⊙7.30am-9pm Mon-Fri, 9am-8pm Sat & Sun) and on the 5th floor of the **State Department Store** (Их Дэлгүүр; Map p58; ☑1800 2888; www.nomin. mn; Peace Ave 44, ⃞ bravo. hexes.steamed; ⊙8.45am-10pm Mon-Fri, 9am-10pm Sat, to 9.30pm Sun). Buy a SIM card (around T7000), and top up with units as needed. It is free to receive calls, and text messaging charges are almost negligible.

➜ Every aimag capital (and many *sum* centres) has mobile-phone service, and calls are fairly cheap, making this a good way to keep in touch with home. If a *sum* centre is not covered by Mobicom, it probably will be covered by an alternative network, such as G-Mobile.

➜ It's a good idea to have a phone while travelling in the countryside, as it allows you to communicate with your tour operator should problems arise on your trip. You can also use it to call ger camps or hotels to make a reservation.

➜ If you have a smartphone (Edge, 3G or 4G), you should be able to access the internet with a local SIM card.

➜ New and used mobile-phone shops are everywhere in UB and also in some rural cities. The cheapest phones will cost around US$20. In UB, try the Tedy Centre on Baruun Selbe Gudamj.

## Satellite Phones

If you're planning a serious mountaineering or horse-trekking expedition, considering bringing or renting a satellite phone, which isn't too bulky and can be used anywhere. If you haven't already purchased one in your home country, these are available for sale in Ulaanbaatar – make inquires at the Mobicom office in the **State Department Store** (Их Дэлгүүр; Map p58; ☑1800 2888; www.nomin.mn; Peace Ave 44, ⓜ bravo.hexes. steamed; ⏱8.45am-10pm

Mon-Fri, 9am-10pm Sat, to 9.30pm Sun).

## Area Codes

➜ Numbers starting with 99, 96, 95, 91, 88, 77, 94 or 81 are mobile numbers and therefore don't require an area code.

➜ Every aimag has its own area code.

➜ Ulaanbaatar has several area codes: 11 is the most widely used. If a phone number begins with a 23, 24 or 25, then the area code is 21. If the phone number begins with a 26, the code is 51.

➜ If calling from a landline to a number in Ulaanbaatar, add a '0' before the phone code.

➜ If you are calling from a mobile phone, just dial the number in the listing. Note that Mongolia has two types of phone codes:

**New codes** Have four digits (which always start with 70) followed by another four digits.

**Old codes** Those in Ulaanbaatar have two digits (followed by six-digit phone numbers) while in the countryside the codes have five digits (followed by five-digit phone numbers).

## Time

**Time zones** Mongolia is divided into two time zones: the three western aimags of Bayan-Ölgii, Uvs and Khovd are one hour behind Ulaanbaatar and the rest of the country.

**Daylight saving** Mongolia does not observe daylight-saving time, which means that the sun can rise at very early hours in summer.

**Standard time** The standard time in Ulaanbaatar is UTC/GMT plus eight hours. This puts Ulaanbaatar in the same time zone as Běijīng, Hong Kong, Singapore and Perth. When it's 1pm in Ulaanbaatar it's 6am in London and 10.20pm (the day before) in Los Angeles.

**24-hour clock** The 24-hour clock is used for plane and train schedules.

## Toilets

**Pit toilets** In most hotels in Ulaanbaatar and aimag capitals and most ger camps, toilets are the sit-down European variety. In other hotels and some more remote ger camps, you will have to use pit toilets and hold your breath.

**Outdoors** In the countryside, where there may not be a bush or tree for hundreds of kilometres, modesty is not something to worry about – just do it where you want to, but away from gers. Also, try to avoid such places as *ovoos* (sacred cairns of stones), rivers and lakes (water sources for nomads) and marmot holes.

**Toilet paper** The plumbing is decrepit in many of the older hotels, and toilet paper can easily jam up the works. If there is a rubbish basket next to the toilet, this is where the waste paper should go. Toilet paper in the basic hotels resembles industrial-strength cardboard, or may be scraps of newspaper or old books. To avoid paper cuts, stock up on softer brand toilet paper, available in the larger cities.

## Tourist Information

➜ There are two tourist information desks in Ulaanbaatar: at the **Ulaanbaatar Bank building** (Map p58; ☑7010 8687; www.tourism.ub.gov.mn; Baga Toiruu W 15, ⓜ float.unscathed. snippets; ⏱8am-5pm Mon-Fri) and the **Guide Tourist Information Centre** (Map

---

### MARGASH & YOU

There is another form of 'Mongolian time': add an hour to any appointments you make. Mongolians are notorious for being late, although this is more a problem in the countryside than in the city. Often events and meetings are simply put off until the next day. The Mongolian version of *mañana* (tomorrow) is *margash*.

p58; ☎7010 1011; www.touristinfocenter.mn; Peace Ave, State Department Store, 1st fl, /// bravo.hexes.steamed; ⏰9am-9pm Mon-Fri, 10am-9pm Sat & Sun May-Sep, to 6pm Oct-Apr) inside the State Department Store. Each is run by a separate entity.

➡ Outside UB, there is a **tourist information centre** (Map p133; ☎9938 2050; www.huvsgul.wix.com/info; /// submits.loved.sometimes; ⏰9am-6pm) in Mörön.

# Travellers with Disabilities

Mongolia is a difficult place for independent travellers in wheelchairs. While the infrastructure is getting better, pavements are rough, and buildings and buses are generally not wheelchair-accessible.

It's best to travel with a private guide who can assist with transport. Travel to Ulaanbaatar and 4WD trips to places such as Khustain National Park shouldn't cause too many insurmountable problems.

If any specialised travel agency might be interested in arranging trips to Mongolia, the best bet is the US company Accessible Journeys (www.disabilitytravel.com) in Pennsylvania. At the very least, hire your own transport and guide through one of the Ulaanbaatar agencies. If you explain your disability, these agencies may be able to assist you.

Download Lonely Planet's free Accessible Travel guides from http://lptravel.to/AccessibleTravel.

# Visas

**Tourist visas** A 30-day tourist visa is required for most countries and can be easily obtained at any Mongolian embassy, consulate, consulate-general or honorary consul.

**Visa on arrival** If you are travelling to Mongolia from a country that has no Mongolian consulate, you can pick up a 30-day tourist visa on arrival at the airport in Ulaanbaatar. You'll need T108,000 (or dollar equivalent) and two passport photos – you should also have a pre-approval letter from an organisation or company in Mongolia.

**90-day visa-free nationalities** Citizens of the following countries can stay in Mongolia for up to 90 days without a visa: Belarus, Brazil, Kazakhstan, Kyrgyzstan, Macau, Serbia, Ukraine and USA. If they stay less than 30 days, nothing needs to be done, other than having their passport stamped when they enter and leave the country. If they stay more than 30 days, they need to register.

**Other visa-free nationalities** Citizens of Canada, Germany, Israel, Japan, Laos, Malaysia, Russia, Thailand and Turkey can stay visa-free for up to 30 days; Philippines passport-holders can stay for 21 days without a visa, and Hong Kong citizens can stay visa-free for up to 14 days.

**Registration** All visitors who plan to stay more than 30 days must be registered within seven days of their arrival.

**Extension** Visitors can extend on a per-week basis. A one-week extension is T22,000. A 30-day extension is T108,000. If you overstay your visa the fine is also T108,000. When requesting an extension, you may be asked for a flight itinerary printout.

**Regulations** To check current regulations, try the website of the Mongolian embassy in Washington DC at www.mongolianembassy.us. Other websites to check include www.immigration.gov.mn and mfa.gov.mn.

## Tourist Visas

**Cost** Standard tourist visas generally last 30 days from the date of entry, and you must enter Mongolia within three months of issue. Each embassy or consulate sets its own price. For single-entry/exit visas you can expect to pay: A$230 in Canberra, UK£40 in London, C$90 in Ottawa and Y405 in Běijīng.

**Issuing time** Visas normally take several days, or even up to two weeks, to issue. If you want your visa quicker, possibly within 24 hours, you will have to pay an 'express fee', which is double the normal cost. If you want to stay longer than 30 days, tourist visas can be extended in Ulaanbaatar.

**Multiple-entry visas** Multiple-entry/exit tourist visas are usually only issued to foreign residents who do a lot of travel.

## Transit Visas

These visas last 72 hours from the date of entry. This period will only allow you to get off the Trans-Mongolian train for a very short time before catching another train to Russia or China. A single-entry/exit transit visa costs between US$25 and US$60, depending on where you apply for it, and cannot be extended. You will need to show the train or plane ticket and a visa for the next country (Russia or China).

## Visa Extensions

If you have a 30-day tourist visa, you can extend it by another 30 days. For extensions, go to the **Office of Immigration, Naturalisation & Foreign Citizens** (INFC; ☎1900 1882; Airport Rd, Ulaanbaatar; ⏰9am-1pm & 2-6pm Mon-Fri). The only catch is that if you stay longer than 30 days you have to be registered at this office (which you should have done within seven days after arrival).

The office is located about 1.8km east of Ulaanbaatar airport (next to the large sports arena), an inconvenient 15km trek from the city centre. The office can get quite busy, so try to arrive early to avoid the lines. There is a small cafe here that serves meals if you get stuck during the lunch hour. An information desk with English–speaking staff can help answer your questions and point you to the correct line.

The INFC office is a branch of the main visa office of the Ministry of External Relations (www.mfa.gov.mn). You may be sent to the ministry if your visa situation is complicated (ie you require a work permit). The entrance is on the west side of the building. In Mongolian it's known as: Gadaadiin Irgen Haryatiin Asuudal Erhleh Gazar (Гадаадын Иргэн Харьяатын Асуудал Эрхлэх Газар).

If you have already registered, you should apply for an extension about a week before your visa expires. It costs T3600 per day and the minimum extension is seven days. You will need a passport-sized photo and must pay a T5000 processing fee. The extension will be issued on the same day. Credit cards may be accepted, but it's best to bring cash in case the machine isn't working.

Several guesthouses in Ulaanbaatar will take care of visa extensions (and registration) for a small fee. If you don't have a letter of support, you can write your own (handwritten is OK); the letter should state the date of your arrival, the date of extension and the reason for travel.

Getting a visa extension outside Ulaanbaatar is difficult, as officials would need to send your passport back to Ulaanbaatar. In an extreme situation this might be possible at the **INFC office** (INFC; Map p193; ☑1422-22195, 9942 4338; [画] treatable.steam.jugs; ⊗8am-noon & 1-5pm Mon-Fri) in Ölgii.

### Exit Visas

Transit and tourist visas are good for one entry and one exit (unless you have a double or multiple-entry/exit visa). If you are working in Mongolia, or if you obtained your visa at an

honorary consul, you are usually issued a single-entry visa (valid for entry only). In this case, another visa is required to *leave* the country. These visas are available from the **INFC office** (INFC; ☑1900 1882; Airport Rd, Ulaanbaatar; ⊗9am-1pm & 2-6pm Mon-Fri).

The exit visa situation in particular applies to Israeli and US passport-holders (who usually enter without visas). Israelis need an exit visa if they stay more than 30 days and Americans need one if they stay more than 90 days.

**Cost** For most nationalities the exit visa costs around US$15, plus an additional US$2 per day that you stay beyond the expiry of your entry visa.

**Duration** It is valid for 10 days, which means that you can stay 10 days after your normal visa has expired.

### Registration

If you intend to stay in Mongolia for more than 30 days, you must register before the end of your first seven days of being in the country (although this rule is sometimes overlooked and you might be able to register in the first 30 days). Note that you can only register twice per calendar year at the INFC office.

**Requirements** Registration takes place at the **INFC office** (INFC; ☑1900 1882; Airport Rd, Ulaanbaatar; ⊗9am-1pm & 2-6pm Mon-Fri). The process is free, but you have to pay T1000 for the one-page application. You'll need one passport-sized photo. Most guesthouses can rustle up an invitation to Mongolia for you if you require one.

**Signing out** As a formality, the registration also needs to be 'signed out'; however, the official you are dealing with will usually do this when you register so you won't have to come back. A specific date is not needed; just set the exit date as far out as possible and

you can leave any time before that date.

**Ölgii office** If you've arrived in western Mongolia from Russia, the **INFC office in Ölgii** (INFC; Map p193; ☑1422-22195, 9942 4338; [画] treatable.steam.jugs; ⊗8am-noon & 1-5pm Mon-Fri) can get you registered.

**Fine** If you don't register, you are liable for a fine (theoretically from US$100 to US$300) when you leave the country.

### Long-Term Stays

The only way to remain in Mongolia on a long-term basis (ie more than three months) is to get a work or study permit. The company or organisation you are working for should handle this for you, but if you are working independently you need to go it alone. You will almost certainly need a letter from an employer providing a legitimate reason for your stay. Registration typically takes place at the **INFC office** (INFC; ☑1900 1882; Airport Rd, Ulaanbaatar; ⊗9am-1pm & 2-6pm Mon-Fri) near the airport.

## Volunteering

Some organisations and companies are anxious to receive help from qualified people, particularly in education, health and IT development. Agencies are more interested in committed people who are willing to stay two years or more, although short-term projects are available. In most instances, you will be paid in local wages (or possibly a little more). Besides the following, a good starting reference is Go Overseas (www.gooverseas.com/volunteer-abroad) and Projects Abroad (www.projects-abroad.org/volunteer-destinations/volunteer-mongolia/). Contact the following to inquire about opportunities:

**Khustain National Park** (www.hustai.mn)

**Australian Volunteers for International Development Program** (www.volunteering. scopeglobal.com)

**Peace Corps** (www.peacecorps. gov)

**UN Development Program** (www.undp.mn)

**Asral** (☑11-304 838, 9595 2272; www.asralmongolia.org; ⓦ trade.bond.nicely)

**Meg's Adventure Tours** (☑9964 3242; www.meg mongolia.com)

---

## Work

Work options for foreigners in Mongolia typically include teaching English and working for a development organisation or NGO. The pay for teaching can be decent (compared to typical local salaries). If you have specialised skills the best money is paid by mining companies.

**Contacts** If you are keen to work in Mongolia and are qualified in teaching or health, contact volunteer organisations, network through the internet or check the English–language newspapers in Ulaanbaatar.

**Permits** Permission to work is fairly easy to obtain if you have been hired locally. In most cases, your employer will take care of this for you.

## Language Teaching

Many Mongolians are hungry to learn a second language, particularly English, so there is a demand for teachers. Colleges and volunteer agencies are always on the lookout for qualified teachers who are willing to stay for a few terms (if not a few years), not just for a week or two.

In Ulaanbaatar try the following options:

**American School of Ulaanbaatar** (☑11-348 888; www. asu.edu.mn; Zaisan Hill 11, Khan Uul District, ⓦ hails.shirtless. mend)

**International School** (☑7016 0010; www.isumongolia.edu. mn; Ikh Mongol State St, ⓦ intervene.apt.crib)

**National University of Mongolia** (NUM; Map p58;☑7730 7730; www.num.edu.mn; Ikh Surguuliin Gudamj 1, ⓦ dreams.lives.months)

**TalkTalk English** (Map p58; ☑7013 5135; www.talktalk english.mn; Baga Toiruu North, ⓦsnipe.incur.monkey; ⊘7am-9pm Mon-Fri, 9am-3pm Sat)

DIRECTORY A–Z WORK

# Transport

## GETTING THERE & AWAY

Mongolia has become more accessible in recent years, with more flights arriving from more destinations. MIAT still holds a monopoly, however, so room for expansion is somewhat limited.

Flights, cars and tours can be booked online at lonely planet.com/bookings.

## Entering the Country/Region

When entering Mongolia, by land or air, fill out the straightforward entry form. You'll have to register if you plan to be in Mongolia for more than 30 days. Registering in Ulaanbaatar (UB) is fairly straightforward, and it's also possible in Ölgii if you arrive in western Mongolia.

## Passport

Make sure that your passport is valid for at least six months from your date of arrival. If you lose your passport, your embassy in Ulaanbaatar can replace it, usually in one day.

## Air

### Airports & Airlines

Ulaanbaatar's **Chinggis Khaan Airport** (☑1900 1980; http://en.airport.gov.mn; ⓘ inspects.roaring.nags; ☎) is Mongolia's major international airport; the code is ULN. At the time of writing a new airport was under construction 52km southwest of Ulaanbaatar. It is expected to be complete in 2018.

Flights to/from Ulaanbaatar can be pricey, as there is a limited number of carriers. The main carriers are **MIAT** (☑in UB 011-333 999; www.miat.com), **Air China** (☑in UB 7000 9933; www.airchina.cn), **Korean Air** (☑in UB 011-317 100; www.koreanair.com), **Turkish Airlines** (☑in UB 7014 6161; www.turkishairlines.com) and **Aeroflot** (☑in UB 011-320 720; www.aeroflot.ru). Apart from to major cities like Běijīng, Seoul and Moscow, there are flights to smaller destinations in China, Russia and Kyrgyzstan. These include an **Aero Mongolia** (☑in UB 7010 3030; www.aero mongolia.mn) flight to/from Hohhot four times a week for US$125 one way. Other regional flights to places like Mǎnzhōulǐ, Ulan Ude and Èrlián, however, change with the seasons.

High-season (June to August) prices for midweek travel are cheaper than on the weekend (Monday and Tuesday flights are generally cheaper than Friday and Saturday flights). In July and August, most flights are full, so book well in advance.

### CLIMATE CHANGE & TRAVEL

Every form of transport that relies on carbon-based fuel generates $CO_2$, the main cause of human-induced climate change. Modern travel is dependent on aeroplanes, which might use less fuel per kilometre per person than most cars but travel much greater distances. The altitude at which aircraft emit gases (including $CO_2$) and particles also contributes to their climate change impact. Many websites offer 'carbon calculators' that allow people to estimate the carbon emissions generated by their journey and, for those who wish to do so, to offset the impact of the greenhouse gases emitted with contributions to portfolios of climate-friendly initiatives throughout the world. Lonely Planet offsets the carbon footprint of all staff and author travel.

## FLIGHTS TO/FROM ULAANBAATAR

| FROM | AIRLINE | FREQUENCY | ONE-WAY/ RETURN FARE |
|---|---|---|---|
| Běijīng | Air China | daily | US$193/330 |
| Běijīng | MIAT | daily | US$189/325 |
| Berlin | MIAT | 2 weekly (via Moscow) | US$560/1024 |
| Bishkek | Turkish Airlines | 3 weekly | US$470/850 |
| Èrilián | Hunnu | 4 weekly | US$58/102 |
| Frankfurt | MIAT | 3 weekly (summer only) | US$475/820 |
| Hohhot | AeroMongolia | 5 weekly | US$125/250 |
| Irkutsk | AeroMongolia | 4 weekly | US$141/248 |
| Istanbul (via Bishkek) | Turkish Airlines | 3 weekly | US$590/1050 |
| Mǎnzhōulǐ | Hunnu | 3 weekly (summer only) | US$126/216 |
| Moscow | Aeroflot | daily (summer), 3 weekly (winter) | US$490/760 |
| Moscow | MIAT | 2 weekly | US$533/787 |
| Seoul | Korean Air | 6 weekly | US$325/510 |
| Seoul | MIAT | 6 weekly | US$339/478 |
| Tokyo | MIAT | 4 weekly | US$454/666 |
| Ulan Ude | Hunnu | 2 weekly (summer only) | US$336/454 |

## Tickets

Airfares to Mongolia peak between June and August. Overlanders should consider purchasing an open-jaw ticket. This option could involve, for example, flying into Běijīng and then flying out of Moscow. This allows you to travel slowly along the Trans-Siberian Railway.

## Land

There are two main land border crossings open to foreigners. The main border with China is at Èrlián (Ereen) and Zamyn-Üüd. The main border with Russia has two points – the Kyakhta-Altanbulag border point is for vehicles, and 26km away the Naushki-Sükhbaatar point is where trains cross. While most traffic passes through these borders, smaller border points with both countries also exist (but are usually not available to third-country travellers).

## China

### BORDER CROSSINGS

There are currently two border points open to foreigners, the main one being between Zamyn-Üüd and Èrlián.

### ZAMYN-ÜÜD/ÈRLIÁN

Most travellers end up in the Chinese border town of Èrlián (二连) in the middle of the night when passing through on an international train. Zamyn-Üüd, on the Mongolian side, is not an interesting place, so you aren't missing anything if you are on the overnight train. Alternatively there's a direct bus that runsfrom Èrlián to Ulaanbaatar, taking around 10 hours.

**Opening hours** The Zamyn-Üüd–Èrlián crossing is open daily, but note that on holidays only the train (not the road) crossing will operate. For vehicles the border is open 8am to 6pm.

**Processing** Mongolian customs and immigration officials take about two hours to process all the train passengers.

**Walking** It's not possible to walk across the border.

**Change money** If you have just come from Mongolia, change any remaining tögrög here or you'll be keeping it as a souvenir.

**Onward travel** Remember that if you are carrying on to the Chinese interior there is no need to go to Běijīng first. From Èrlián you can travel to the rail junction at Dàtóng and then catch trains or buses to Píngyáo, Xī'ān and points south. For western China and Tibet, get off at Jíníng where you can change to Hohhot, Lánzhōu and beyond. Read Lonely Planet's *China* guide for details on connections from these cities.

### BULGAN/TǍKÈSHÉNKÈN

After Zamyn-Üüd–Èrlián (p261), the other main border crossing with China is in a remote corner of

(p261)

### DEPARTURE TAX

Departure tax is included in the price of a plane ticket.

## TRANSITING AT BEIJING OR INCHEON

Flying to Mongolia usually requires one or two stops en route, and you are likely to spend some time in either Běijīng International Airport (PEK) or South Korea's Incheon International Airport (ICN). Moscow's Sheremetyevo International Airport (SVO) and Istanbul's Ataturk Airport (IST) are possible stops if you are coming from Europe. Here is what you need to know while in transit:

➡ Your luggage allowance is determined by the airline that provides the longest segment of the journey. This applies only if you check your baggage *all the way through* to Ulaanbaatar. If you pick up your luggage midway through the journey you will be subject to luggage restrictions when you check in with MIAT or Air China.

➡ With an onward ticket, most nationalities can now stay in China for 72 hours without a visa. Luggage storage is available at the airport in Běijīng for about Y30 per bag. Terminal 3 also has a small, scruffy hotel on the arrivals level where you can stay in between flights (rooms start from Y100 per hour). Better hotels are a short bus ride away. The airport is open all night. A free shuttle bus connects Terminal 3 and Terminal 2. Free internet is available but you'll need to get a password from the information desk.

➡ If you want to pop into Běijīng for a few hours, take the Airport Line light rail (Y25), which runs every 15 minutes to Dongzhimen subway station.

➡ Incheon airport is amazingly transit-friendly. It has a comfortable lounge with big sofas where you can sleep, free internet, free showers and even free city tours that can last from two to six hours! The airport also has a hotel – see www.airport.kr for details.

➡ When leaving Mongolia, if you are catching a connecting flight via Běijīng, you must be able to show proof of your onward ticket at the counter in Ulaanbaatar and in Běijīng (so have a printout handy). If you cannot show an onward ticket and you have no visa for China, you won't be allowed on the flight.

western Mongolia where Bulgan (Khovd aimag) meets Tăkèshénkěn (Xīnjiāng).

**Opening hours** This border is open year-round (except Mongolian and Chinese holidays) Monday to Friday from 9am to 6pm. The border can close for lunch so arrive as early as possible.

**Processing** Expect multiple passport checks on both sides of the border. On the Chinese side there are extensive bag searches and they will probably also want to inspect photos on your camera.

**Walking** Travellers are allowed to cross by foot and bicycle.

**Bulgan** The village of Bulgan is a five-hour drive from Khovd on a newly paved road. Taxis to Bulgan depart from the jeep stand in Khovd. Hunnu Air used to have a flight from UB to Bulgan, although this service was suspended at the time of research. Bulgan has no hotel so you just need to ask your driver for a homestay, or camp. A taxi ride to the border from Bulgan

should cost T5000 per person. The 30-minute ride is on a paved road.

**Time difference** Khovd is one hour behind Xīnjiāng.

**Onward travel** Once across the border into China, there are share taxis to Ürümqi (seven hours, Y250). Buses are also available for Y250, but these are slower and require at least one change.

**Entering Mongolia** Heading in the other direction (from China to Mongolia), there are two buses per day from Ürümqi to Qinghe (清河; 10 hours, Y140). From Qinghe, there are minivans and taxis to Takeshiken (塔克什肯; two hours, Y60), from where you can take a taxi to the border (20 minutes, Y20 per person). Once in Mongolia, find a shared vehicle to Bulgan and wait around for any vehicle continuing to Khovd.

### CAR & MOTORCYCLE

As long as your papers are in order there is no trouble crossing the China–Mongolia

border in your own car. Driving around Mongolia is a lot easier than China, where drivers require a guide and Chinese driving permit.

### MINIVAN

➡ Minivans shuttle between the train stations of Zamyn-Üüd and Èrlián. Either way the trip is Y50 for a seat in a jeep.

➡ When the train arrives in Zamyn-Üüd there is a frantic rush for minivans and then a jockeying for position at the border as Mongolian traders race to be the first into China for a full day of shopping. Note that the first jeeps charge about Y30 more than the ones in the back of the line.

➡ In Èrlián, jeeps assemble at the bus station and the market; ask the Mongolian drivers. There is a Y5 tax that you need to pay going either way (you can pay the driver in tögrög or yuan and they will pay the tax for you).

## TRAIN

Mongolia has trains to both Russia and China. Getting a ticket in Ulaanbaatar can be very difficult during the summer tourist season, so you need to plan ahead.

**Ticket office** The **International Railway Ticket Office** (☑2124 4367, 2124 3848; Narny Gudamj, 2nd fl, ⓦ engrossed.veal.abacus; ◷8am-8.20pm) is located on the 2nd floor of the train ticket sales building, next to the main railway station.

**Buying tickets** You'll need your passport to buy a ticket. The office is open from 8am to 8.20pm. There's no English spoken here so you may want to bring along a translator to help purchase a ticket. There is no departure tax if travelling on the train.

**Advance bookings** You can book a ticket for international trains out of Ulaanbaatar up to one month in advance, but for the Moscow–Běijīng or Běijīng–Moscow trains you will have to scramble for a ticket on the day before departure (although you could try asking two days in advance). If you have trouble booking a berth, ask your guesthouse manager or hotel reception desk for assistance.

**Getting there** A taxi between Sükhbaatar Sq and the train station costs about T5000. It's about a 25-minute walk from the square.

## DIRECT TRAINS

Most travellers catch the direct train between Běijīng and Ulaanbaatar.

➜ There are two direct trains a week each way between Běijīng and Ulaanbaatar. One of these (K3 and 4) is the Trans-Mongolian Railway, which runs between Běijīng and Moscow. It's easier to get a ticket for the other train (K23 and 24). However, Mongolia Train Tickets gets positive reviews for securing tickets along the Trans-Mongolian line from UB to Beijing or Moscow, and at cheaper rates than the bigger companies.

➜ The K23 changes its departure day each year (depending on whether it's run by China or Mongolia railways). The Chinese train typically departs Běijīng on Tuesday, while the Mongolian train typically departs Běijīng on Saturday. Note that the Chinese and Mongolians switch operating duties in May.

➜ The K23 summer train is an extra train service put on for the summer holiday season (it usually runs mid-June to early October). When operated by Mongolia it will most likely depart Běijīng on a Monday, when run by China it will most likely depart Běijīng on Saturday.

➜ Train K23 passes through Jíníng at 4.56pm, Èrlián at 9.48pm and Zamyn-Üüd at 1.25am.

➜ It is also possible to travel directly between Ulaanbaatar and Hohhot twice a week, allowing you to either bypass Běijīng completely or catch a train or flight (Y660) on to Běijīng from there.

➜ Trains leave from **Běijīng Train Station** (☑8610-5101 9999). If your luggage weighs more than 35kg, on the day before departure you'll have to take it to the Luggage Shipment Office, which is on the right-hand side of the station. The excess is charged at about US$11 per 10kg, with a maximum excess of 40kg allowed.

➜ With China International Travel Service (CITS) it is possible to book one month in advance for trains originating in Běijīng, and you can collect your ticket from one week to one day before departure. A booking fee applies.

➜ CITS only sells tickets from Běijīng to Moscow or Ulaanbaatar – no stopovers are allowed. Tickets to Ulaanbaatar cost Y1222/1833 in hard/soft sleeper. Prices can change slightly depending on which country is operating the train.

➜ You can also buy train tickets privately; they will be more expensive than at CITS, but you may also be able to arrange a stopover and visas. In Hong Kong, Monkey Shrine (www.monkeyshrine.com) can put together all kinds of stopovers and homestay programs. The company has a lot of experience in booking international trains for independent travellers.

➜ Note that the Russian embassies in most countries only accept visa applications from official residents. So it's best to apply for your Russian visa in your home country (or country where you have a residency card).

## ULAANBAATAR–CHINA TRAINS

Prices are for Chinese trains. Deluxe cars are not available on Mongolian trains. Mongolian trains are about 5% to 10% cheaper for 1st class.

| DESTINATION | 2ND CLASS HARD SLEEPER (T) | 1ST CLASS SOFT SLEEPER (T) | DELUXE COUPE (T) |
| --- | --- | --- | --- |
| Běijīng | 254,250 | 405,750 | 359,950 |
| Èrlián (Ereen) | 171,850 | 270,350 | 243,150 |
| Hohhot | 236,150 | 382,750 | 336,950 |

## TRAIN SCHEDULES TO/FROM MONGOLIA

Schedules change from one summer to another; services reduce in winter, and can increase in summer.

| TRAIN | TRAIN NO | DAY OF DEPARTURE | DEPARTURE TIME | DURATION FROM/ TO UB (HR) |
|---|---|---|---|---|
| **China–Mongolia** | | | | |
| Běijīng–Ulaanbaatar | K23 | Tue or Sat | 11.22am | 30 |
| Běijīng–Ulaanbaatar– (Moscow) | K3 | Wed | 11.22am | 30 |
| Èrlián–Ulaanbaatar | 21 | Mon, Fri | 5.10pm | 14 |
| Hohhot–Ulaanbaatar | 33 | Mon, Fri | 9.50pm | 37 |
| **Mongolia–China** | | | | |
| Ulaanbaatar–Běijīng | 24 | Thu or Fri | 7.30am | 30 |
| (Moscow)–Ulaanbaatar– Běijīng | 4 | Sun | 7.30am | 30 |
| Ulaanbaatar–Èrlián | 22 | Thu, Sun | 8.45pm | 12 |
| Ulaanbaatar–Hohhot | 34 | Mon, Fri | 10.45pm | 25 |
| **Mongolia–Russia** | | | | |
| Ulaanbaatar–Irkutsk | 263 | daily | 10.35pm | 36 |
| Ulaanbaatar–Moscow | 5 | Tue, Fri | 3.22pm | 70 |
| (Běijīng)–Ulaanbaatar– Moscow | K3 | Thu | 3.22pm | 100 |
| **Russia–Mongolia** | | | | |
| Irkutsk–Ulaanbaatar | 264 | daily | 4.32pm | 24-36 |
| Moscow–Ulaanbaatar | 6 | Wed, Thu | 11.45pm | 70 |
| Moscow–Ulaanbaatar– (Běijīng) | 4 | Tue | 11.45pm | 100 |

Visa rules at the Russian embassy in Ulaanbaatar are relaxing a little for some nationalities but it's often the case that applications are handled on a case-by-case basis.

### LOCAL TRAINS

If you're on a tight budget it's possible to take local trains between UB and Běijīng. This will save some money but involves more hassle and time. Unless you have booked your seats weeks in advance, the local train may be your only option during the peak summer travel period. However, express buses in China may end up getting you more quickly to your destination.

➡ The first option is train 21 or 22, which runs between Ulaanbaatar and Èrlián just inside China. Mongolian train 22 leaves Ulaanbaatar at 8.45pm on Thursday and Sunday and arrives in Èrlián at about 10.25am the next morning, after completing immigration and customs formalities. In reverse, train 21 leaves Èrlián on Monday and Friday at 5.10pm and arrives the next day. The schedules for this train change regularly.

➡ The second option is to take local trains to Zamyn-Üüd in Mongolia and then cross the border by minivan or jeep. From Èrlián you can go deeper into China by either train, bus or plane.

➡ From Běijīng, the K617 for Hohhot departs at 10.24am and passes through Jíníng at 5.09pm. The train from Jíníng to Èrlián departs at 5.08pm and takes six hours. (Alternatively, a 7am bus takes just four hours.) If you have to stay the night in Jíníng, there's a budget hotel on the right (south) side of the plaza as you walk out of the train station.

If you need help with the logistics of train travel, a good contact is freelance guide **Daka Nyamdorj** (⌨9984 4844; www.happy mongolia.net), who specialises in tours by train.

## Russia
### BORDER CROSSINGS

Most travellers go in and out of Russia at the Naushki–Sükhbaatar train border crossing.

**Naushki** You can have a look around Naushki, but there is little to see and the train border crossing usually takes place in the middle of the night. Surprisingly, you may have difficulty finding anyone at the Naushki station to change money, so wait until Sükhbaatar or Ulaanbaatar, or somewhere else in Russia. (Get rid of your tögrög before you leave Mongolia, as almost no one will want to touch them once you are in Russia.)

**Sükhbaatar** The train may stop for one or two hours at the pleasant Mongolian border town of Sükhbaatar. You may be able to buy some Russian roubles or Mongolian tögrög from a money changer at the train station, but the rate will be poor. If there aren't any money changers, you can use US dollars to get by until you can change money elsewhere.

**Road crossings** There are two road crossings: Tsagaannuur–Tashanta in Bayan-Ölgii aimag and Altanbulag–Kyakhta (near Sükhbaatar) in Selenge. The crossings are open from 9am to noon and 2pm to 6pm daily except holidays. The Khankh–Mondy border in northern Khövsgöl and the Ereentsav–Solovyevsk crossing in Dornod are not open to third-country nationals.

**Processing** Both the road and rail crossings are slow but at least on the road journey you can get out and stretch your legs. Train travellers have been stranded for hours on the Russian side, spending much

of this time locked inside the train wagons. Procedures on the Ulaanbaatar–Moscow train are faster than on the local trains. Heading out of Russia, you will be asked to fill out a customs declaration form. You should note on the form how much currency you are taking out of the country.

**BUS**

Bus is probably the fastest form of public transport between Mongolia and Russia.

**From Mongolia** A daily bus operated by **Vostok Trans** (☑9906 0734; Dragon Station) departs Ulaanbaatar bound for Ulan Ude. It departs Wednesday, Friday and Saturday at 7.30am (and Sunday at 7am), and the journey takes 12 hours and costs T67,000. Buses leave from the **Dragon Bus Terminal** (Dragon Avto Vaksal; ☑1900 1234; www.eticket.transdep. mn; Peace Ave, ⅢⅢ outs.solve. enlarge; ⏰7.30am-7.30pm). Tickets are sold inside the domestic railway ticket office on the 1st floor. You can buy a ticket one week in advance. Tickets are also available online at teever. gov.mn, in Mongolian.

**To Mongolia** An Ulan Ude bus (R1800) departs at the same time for Ulaanbaatar, leaving from the fountain/Opera House in Ulan Ude. In Ulan Ude contact Trio-Impex (www.trio-impex.com) or **Buryat-Intour** (☑3012-

216 954; www.buryatintour.ru; ul Ervanova 12).

**CAR & MOTORCYCLE**

It's possible to drive between Russia and Mongolia at Tsagaannuur (Bayan-Ölgii) and Altanbulag (Selenge).

**Processing** These road crossings can be difficult and time-consuming – up to six hours if traffic is backed up or if you have visa problems.

**Paperwork** In order to speed things up, it may help to have a letter written by the Mongolian consular (or Russian consular if you are headed that way) when you get your visa. The letter should state that you are authorised to take a car or motorcycle across the border. A carnet (passport for your car) may be useful but is not necessary.

**Walking** Foreigners are currently not allowed to 'walk' across the Kyakhta–Altanbulag border, but they are allowed to pass through in a car or even on a motorcycle, so you may have to pay someone to drive you across.

**TRAIN**

Besides the Trans-Mongolian Railway connecting Moscow and Běijīng, there is a direct train twice a week connecting Ulaanbaatar and Moscow, which is easier to book from Ulaanbaatar. The epic trip takes four days.

**Lake Baikal** If you are headed to Lake Baikal, there is a daily

## ULAANBAATAR–RUSSIA TRAINS

Exact costs depend on whether the train is Russian, Chinese or Mongolian; we have listed the most expensive.

| DESTINATION | 2ND CLASS (T) | 1ST CLASS (T) |
| --- | --- | --- |
| Irkutsk | 118,300-172,350 | 218,550 |
| Krasnoyarsk | 248,850 | 328,750 |
| Moscow | 458,750 | 618,450 |
| Naushki | 77,450 | 90,550 |
| Novosibirsk | 285,750 | 379,650 |
| Omsk | 317,950 | 424,350 |
| Perm | 390,650 | 524,850 |
| Ulan Ude | 115,350 | 144,150 |
| Yekaterinburg | 374,150 | 501,550 |

train between Ulaanbaatar and Irkutsk, which stops in Darkhan. These trains stop at every village, however, and train 263 travels past Lake Baikal at night, so if you are in a hurry or want to see the lake, take the Ulaanbaatar–Moscow train (5) as far as Irkutsk. Note that departure and arrival times at Irkutsk are given in Moscow time, although Irkutsk is actually five hours ahead of Moscow.

**Staged travel** This trip can be done more cheaply by travelling in stages on local trains (eg from Ulan Ude to Naushki, Naushki to Sükhbaatar, and Sükhbaatar to Ulaanbaatar). However, this route is covered much more quickly by shared taxi.

**Tickets** In Moscow you can buy tickets at the building on Ulitsa Krasnoprudnaya 1, next door to the Yaroslavl train station, from where the trains to Ulaanbaatar and Běijīng leave. **Unifest Travel** (http://unifest.ru/en.html) in Moscow is a reliable travel agent that can sell train tickets on the Trans-Siberian Railway. In Irkutsk, you can try **Irkutsk Baikal Travel Inc** (⌨3952-200 134; www.irkutsk-baikal.com; 1a Cheremhovsky Ln). For tickets to Moscow along the Trans-Mongolian line, try **Mongolia Train Tickets** (⌨8880 6963; www.mongolia traintickets.com) in Ulaanbaatar, who offer rates that are more competitive than most operators.

### Kazakhstan
At the time of writing a bus travelled between Bayan-Ölgii and Astana in Kazakhstan.

## Sea
As a landlocked nation, Mongolia has no border points with the sea.

# GETTING AROUND

Public transport in Mongolia is slow, and destinations are limited to cities and towns. You'll still need to hire a guide

and driver to go beyond the cities and towns to reach places of interest. Jumping on a tour at the last minute is very difficult, so streamline your trip by booking a tour several weeks prior to arrival. Note that occasional outbreaks of the plague and foot-and-mouth disease can quarantine areas and affect travel plans.

**Train** Useful for getting in and out of the country but unnecessary for domestic travel. One exception is for a side trip to Sainshand (for Khamaryn Monastery). Local trains are also good for a trip to Zamyn-Üüd for travellers heading to the Chinese border.

**Car** The main way to get around the countryside. Hiring a car and driver is actually cheaper than hiring a car without a driver. Drive on the right. A 4WD is essential for most destinations outside the capital.

**Bus** The provincial capitals are accessible by bus and services run daily to most cities. Connections to the western aimags are less regular.

## Air

Mongolia, a vast, sparsely populated country with very little infrastructure, relies heavily on air transport. There are 16 paved airstrips across the country.

Almost all of the destinations are served directly from Ulaanbaatar, so flying from, say, Dalanzadgad to Bayan-Ölgii is impossible without first returning to UB.

### Airlines in Mongolia
**Aero Mongolia** (⌨in UB 7010 3030; www.aeromongolia.mn) Operates three Fokker aircraft. Routes change but at last check it flew domestic services to Ölgii, Dalanzadgad, Mörön, Ulaangom, Gov-Altai and Khovd. Baggage allowance is only 15kg (including hand luggage); any kilogram over the limit costs around T3000. Credit card and cash payments are accepted. Aero Mongolia

also serves Hohhot in China, and Irkutsk in Russia.

**Hunnu Airlines** (⌨in UB 7000 1111; www.hunnuair.com) Operates Fokker 50 and ATR 72 aircraft. Domestic destinations include Donoi (Uliastai), Dalanzadgad, Khovd, Mörön, Choibalsan, Bayankhongor and Altai. In summer they often add a flight to Ulan Ude in Russia. Baggage allowance is 15kg.

**MIAT** (⌨in UB 011-333 999; www.miat.com) The state-owned airline that once flew to every corner of the country. It no longer operates any domestic routes.

### Checking In
Get to the airport at least one hour before your flight. Even if you have a ticket, flight number and an allocated seat number, don't assume the plane won't be over-booked. Try to make certain your luggage has gone on the plane. Gas canisters are not allowed on any flight.

### Costs
➡ Aero Mongolia and Hunnu Air prices are similar and change based on availability; a one-way fare from UB to Dalanzadgad costs around US$160 while a flight to Bayan-Ölgii goes for about US$137. This is good value, considering the overland alternative to Ölgii is a 42-hour trip in an overstuffed van.

➡ Children aged between five and 16 years pay half; under fives fly free. If you've come on a student visa you can get 25% to 50% off the cost of the ticket. Ticket fares may increase during the summer holiday season.

➡ Ask about baggage allowances when you buy your aeroplane ticket. Some airlines allow you to carry 20kg without extra charges.

### Reservations & Tickets
**E-tickets** It's now possible to buy a domestic airline e-ticket with Mongolia's domestic carriers

(Hunnu and Aero Mongolia). Airlines can usually hold a reservation for two or three days.

**One-way tickets** If you wish to fly in one direction and return by road in the other (for example to Mörön), it's best to fly from Ulaanbaatar, where you are more likely to get a ticket and a seat, and then go back overland – otherwise you may wait days or more for a flight and ticket in Mörön.

**Peak seasons** Seats can be difficult to get in summer, especially in the July tourist peak and in late August as students return to college. Book flights as soon as you can.

## Bicycle

For keen cyclists with a sense of adventure, Mongolia offers an unparalleled cycling experience. The vast, open steppes make for rough travel but if you're properly equipped there is nothing stopping you from travelling pretty much anywhere (although travel in remote areas of the Gobi could only be done with vehicle support). Bikes are hard to store on long-distance buses due to lack of room.

Biking is relatively safe due to the light traffic in the countryside; just be careful on paved roads, which may be narrow. The main danger is the dogs that will chase you when passing a ger. Ulaanbaatar has a few bike lanes now, although these are often used by pedestrians too.

## Boat

➡ Although there are 397km of navigable waterways in Mongolia, rivers aren't used for transporting people or cargo.

➡ The biggest boat in the country is the *Sükhbaatar*, which has daily tours around Khövsgöl Nuur in summer.

➡ Some ger camps at Khövsgöl Nuur also own small boats that can be chartered.

### TAKING A GPS

When travelling around the featureless plains, a global positioning system (GPS) can be very useful in determining where exactly you are, as long as you have a reliable map on which to pinpoint your coordinates.

A GPS won't help you every time, as you'll still need to know which road to take, even if you know the rough direction. Every few kilometres you'll come upon a fork in the road and if you start heading off in the wrong direction a GPS can help you correct.

Most smartphones also have GPS capability (and you can download GPS navigation apps). But be aware that the coordinates displayed on a mobile phone (which uses mobile phone towers to determine a location) are less accurate than those given by a dedicated GPS unit (which uses satellites).

It is always a good idea to ask about road conditions at gers along the way. Often a good-looking road will become impassable, running into a river, swamp or wall of mountains; herders can offer good info on the best route to take.

If all else fails, you can always rely on Mongolian GPS (ger positioning system), which requires following the vague sweep of the ger owner's hand over the horizon, until you reach the next ger.

## Bus

Private bus companies connect Ulaanbaatar to the other aimag capitals. Large buses that can accommodate 40-plus passengers make a daily run to most cities. However, cities in the far west such Bayan-Ölgii and Uvs are served by minivans less frequently.

The benefit of the regularly scheduled buses and vans is that they leave on time and drive non-stop to their destination, as opposed to private vans, which run on 'Mongolian time' (ie whenever they have crammed in enough passengers) and make stops on the way to drop off and pick up passengers. With the government buses you also get an assigned seat.

However, the official buses have their share of discomforts. One problem is that there seems to be no restriction on luggage, so boxes and bags tend to pile up in the aisles, which makes getting on and off the bus at breaks

a real chore. Try getting a seat closer to the front of the bus to avoid the pile.

Note that in winter, the heater will be turned to maximum, which is fine if you're up front or in the back (the heater is in the middle). However, if you are unfortunate enough to get the seat over the heater it will feel like you are hovering over a blast furnace.

No matter what time of year it is, the driver will probably crank up the music. This is bearable for an hour or two, but if you want to get some sleep (or maintain sanity) consider bringing noise-cancelling headphones.

## Car & Motorcycle

**Private cars** (p42) are the best way to get around the countryside. Four-wheel-drive vehicles are almost essential for any long-distance road trip to the main tourist sites, although an improved number of paved roads means that compact cars can

# GPS Coordinates Table

The table shows latitude and longitude coordinates for various locations in Mongolia, in degrees, minutes and decimal minutes (DMM). To convert to degrees, minutes and seconds (DMS) format, multiply the number after the decimal point (including the decimal point) by 60. The result is your seconds, which can be rounded to the nearest whole number. The minutes is the number between the degree symbol and the decimal point. For example: 43°52.598' DMM is equal to 43°52'36" DMS.

| CENTRAL MONGOLIA | Latitude (N) | Longitude (E) |
| --- | --- | --- |
| Arvaikheer | 46°15.941 | 102°46.724 |
| Bat-Ölzii | 46°49.028 | 102°13.989 |
| Battsengel | 47°48.157 | 101°59.040 |
| Bayan Önjuul | 46°52.859 | 105°56.571 |
| Bayan-Öndör | 46°30.018 | 104°05.996 |
| Bayangol | 45°48.505 | 103°26.811 |
| Bayantsagaan | 46°45.806 | 107°08.709 |
| Bogd | 44°39.971 | 102°08.777 |
| Burenbayan Ulaan | 45°10.276 | 101°25.989 |
| Chuluut | 47°32.830 | 100°13.166 |
| Delgerkhan | 46°37.097 | 104°33.051 |
| Eej Khad (Mother Rock) | 47°18.699 | 106°58.583 |
| Erdenemandal | 48°31.445 | 101°22.265 |
| Erdenesant | 47°19.071 | 104°28.937 |
| Guchin Us | 45°27.866 | 102°23.726 |
| Gunjiin Süm | 48°11.010 | 107°33.377 |
| Ikh Tamir | 47°35.221 | 101°12.413 |
| Jargalant | 48°43.716 | 100°45.120 |
| Khandgait | 48°07.066 | 106°54.296 |
| Khangai | 47°51.553 | 99°26.126 |
| Kharkhorin | 47°11.981 | 102°50.527 |
| Khashant | 47°27.034 | 103°09.708 |
| Khotont | 47°22.196 | 102°28.746 |
| Khujirt | 46°54.225 | 102°46.545 |
| Khustain National Park | 47°45.459 | 105°52.418 |
| Mandshir Khiid | 47°45.520 | 106°59.675 |
| Möngönmorit | 48°12.192 | 108°28.291 |
| Naiman Nuur | 46°31.232 | 101°50.705 |
| Ögii Nuur | 47°40.319 | 102°33.051 |
| Ögii Nuur (Lake) | 47°47.344 | 102°45.828 |
| Ölziit | 48°05.573 | 102°32.640 |
| Ondor Ulaan | 48°02.700 | 100°30.446 |
| Orkhon Khürkhree | 46°47.234 | 101°57.694 |
| Övgön Khiid | 47°25.561 | 103°41.686 |
| Stele of Tonyukuk | 47°41.661 | 107°28.586 |
| Tariat | 48°09.574 | 99°52.982 |
| Terelj | 47°59.193 | 107°27.834 |
| Tögrög | 45°32.482 | 102°59.657 |
| Tövkhön Khiid | 47°00.772 | 102°15.362 |
| Tsakhir | 49°06.426 | 99°08.574 |
| Tsenkher | 47°26.909 | 101°45.648 |
| Tsetseguun Uul | 47°48.506 | 107°00.165 |
| Tsetserleg City | 47°28.561 | 101°27.282 |
| Tsetserleg Soum | 48°53.095 | 101°14.305 |
| Ulaanbaatar | 47°55.056 | 106°55.007 |
| Uyanga | 46°27.431 | 102°16.731 |
| Zaamar | 48°11.843 | 104°46.629 |
| Züünbayan-Ulaan | 46°31.176 | 102°34.971 |
| Zuunmod | 47°42.357 | 106°56.861 |

| EASTERN MONGOLIA | Latitude (N) | Longitude (E) |
| --- | --- | --- |
| Asgat | 46°21.724 | 113°34.536 |
| Baldan Baraivun Khiid | 48°11.910 | 109°25.840 |
| Baruun-Urt | 46°40.884 | 113°16.825 |
| Batnorov | 47°56.952 | 111°30.103 |
| Batshireet | 48°41.405 | 110°11.062 |
| Bayan Tumen | 48°03.076 | 114°22.252 |
| Bayan Uul | 49°07.550 | 112°42.809 |
| Bayandun | 49°15.276 | 113°21.565 |
| Binder | 48°36.967 | 110°36.400 |
| Chinggis Statue | 47°06.157 | 109°09.356 |
| Choibalsan | 48°04.147 | 114°31.404 |
| Chuluunkhoroot | 49°52.163 | 115°43.406 |
| Dadal | 49°01.291 | 111°37.598 |
| Dashbalbar | 49°32.794 | 114°24.720 |
| Delgerkhaan | 47°10.735 | 109°11.423 |
| Erdenetsagaan | 45°54.165 | 115°22.149 |
| Galshar | 46°13.324 | 110°50.606 |
| Khalkhgol | 47°59.565 | 118°05.760 |
| Khalzan | 46°10.019 | 112°57.119 |
| Kherlen Bar Khot | 48°03.287 | 113°21.865 |
| Khökh Nuur (Blue Lake) | 48°01.150 | 108°56.450 |
| Matad | 46°57.007 | 115°16.008 |
| Mönkh Khaan | 46°58.163 | 112°03.418 |
| Norovlin | 48°41.449 | 111°59.596 |
| Öglöchiin Kherem | 48°24.443 | 110°11.812 |
| Ömnödelger | 47°53.469 | 109°49.166 |
| Chinggis Khot (Öndörkhaan) | 47°19.416 | 110°39.775 |
| Ongon | 45°21.509 | 113°08.297 |
| Shiliin Bogd | 45°28.350 | 114°35.349 |
| Sükhbaatar | 46°46.285 | 113°52.646 |
| Sümber | 47°38.174 | 118°36.421 |
| Tsagaan Ovoo | 48°33.864 | 113°14.380 |
| Tsenkhermandal | 47°44.673 | 109°03.909 |
| Uul Bayan | 46°30.036 | 112°20.769 |

| NORTHERN MONGOLIA | Latitude (N) | Longitude (E) |
| --- | --- | --- |
| Altanbulag | 50°19.225 | 106°29.392 |
| Amarbayasgalant Khiid | 49°28.672 | 105°05.121 |
| Arbulag | 49°54.949 | 99°26.537 |
| Baruunburen | 49°09.753 | 104°48.686 |
| Bayangol | 48°55.472 | 106°05.486 |
| Borsog | 50°59.677 | 100°42.983 |
| Bugat | 49°02.874 | 103°40.389 |
| Bulgan City | 48°48.722 | 103°32.213 |
| Chandman-Öndör | 50°28.436 | 100°56.378 |
| Chuluut and Ider | 49°10.415 | 100°40.335 |
| Darkhan | 49°29.232 | 105°56.480 |
| Dashchoinkhorlon Khiid | 48°47.821 | 103°30.687 |
| Dashinchilen | 47°51.179 | 104°02.281 |
| Dulaankhaan | 49°55.103 | 106°11.302 |
| Erdenebulgan | 50°06.880 | 101°35.589 |
| Erdenet | 49°01.855 | 104°03.316 |
| Five Rivers | 49°15.475 | 100°40.385 |
| Gurvanbulag | 47°44.499 | 103°30.103 |

| | Latitude (N) | Longitude (E) |
|---|---|---|
| Jiglegiin Am | 51°00.406 | 100°16.003 |
| Khangal | 49°18.810 | 104°22.629 |
| Khankh | 51°30.070 | 100°41.382 |
| Khar Bukh Balgas | 47°53.198 | 103°53.513 |
| Khatgal | 50°26.517 | 100°09.599 |
| Khishig-Öndör | 48°17.678 | 103°27.086 |
| Khötöl | 49°05.486 | 105°34.903 |
| Khutag-Öndör | 49°22.990 | 102°41.417 |
| Mogod | 48°16.372 | 102°59.520 |
| Mörön | 49°38.143 | 100°09.321 |
| Orkhon | 49°08.621 | 105°24.891 |
| Orkhontuul | 48°49.202 | 104°49.920 |
| Renchinlkhumbe | 51°06.504 | 99°40.234 |
| Saikhan | 48°39.448 | 102°37.851 |
| Selenge | 49°26.647 | 103°58.903 |
| Shine-Ider | 48°57.213 | 99°32.297 |
| Sükhbaatar | 50°14.196 | 106°11.911 |
| Teshig | 49°57.649 | 102°35.657 |
| Toilogt | 50°39.266 | 100°14.961 |
| Tosontsengel | 49°28.650 | 100°53.074 |
| Tsagaan Uur | 50°32.391 | 101°31.806 |
| Tsagaannuur (Khövsgöl) | 51°21.778 | 99°21.082 |
| Tsagaannuur (Selenge) | 50°05.835 | 105°25.989 |
| Tsetserleg | 49°31.959 | 97°46.011 |
| Ulaan Uul | 50°40.668 | 99°13.920 |
| Uran Uul | 48°59.855 | 102°44.003 |
| Züünkharaa | 48°51.466 | 106°27.154 |

| THE GOBI | Latitude (N) | Longitude (E) |
|---|---|---|
| Altai City | 46°22.388 | 96°15.164 |
| Altai Soum | 44°37.010 | 94°55.131 |
| Altanshiree | 45°32.046 | 110°27.017 |
| Baatsagaan | 45°33.266 | 99°26.188 |
| Baga Gazryn Chuluu | 46°13.827 | 106°04.192 |
| Bayan Dalai | 43°27.898 | 103°30.763 |
| Bayanbulag | 46°48.223 | 98°06.189 |
| Bayangovi | 44°44.017 | 100°23.476 |
| Bayankhongor | 46°11.637 | 100°43.115 |
| Bayanlig | 44°32.555 | 100°49.809 |
| Bayan-Ovoo | 42°58.607 | 106°06.994 |
| Bayan-Uul | 46°59.129 | 95°11.863 |
| Bayanzag | 44°08.311 | 103°43.667 |
| Biger | 45°42.583 | 97°10.354 |
| Bömbogor | 46°12.279 | 99°37.234 |
| Böön Tsagaan Nuur | 45°37.114 | 99°15.350 |
| Bugat | 45°33.440 | 94°20.571 |
| Bulgan | 44°05.312 | 103°32.297 |
| Buutsagaan | 46°10.411 | 98°41.637 |
| Choir | 45°47.994 | 109°18.462 |
| Dalanzadgad | 43°34.355 | 104°25.673 |
| Delger | 46°21.074 | 97°22.011 |
| Delgerekh | 45°48.157 | 111°12.823 |
| Erdenedalai | 46°00.418 | 104°56.996 |
| Erdentsogt | 46°25.080 | 100°49.234 |
| Galuut | 46°42.061 | 100°07.131 |
| Govi-Ugtal | 46°01.916 | 107°30.377 |
| Gurj Lamiin Khiid | 43°29.030 | 103°50.930 |
| Gurvantes | 43°13.759 | 101°03.360 |
| Jargalant | 47°01.480 | 99°30.103 |
| Khamaryn Khiid | 44°36.038 | 110°16.650 |
| Khanbogd | 43°12.000 | 107°11.862 |
| Khatanbulag | 43°08.882 | 109°08.709 |
| Khökhmorit | 47°21.248 | 94°30.446 |
| Khövsgöl | 43°36.314 | 109°39.017 |
| Khüreemaral | 46°24.523 | 98°17.037 |
| Mandakh | 44°24.122 | 108°13.851 |

| | Latitude (N) | Longitude (E) |
|---|---|---|
| Mandalgov | 45°46.042 | 106°16.380 |
| Mandal-Ovoo | 44°39.100 | 104°02.880 |
| Manlai | 44°04.441 | 106°51.703 |
| Nomgon | 42°50.160 | 105°08.983 |
| Ondorshil | 45°13.585 | 108°15.223 |
| Ongiin Khiid | 45°20.367 | 104°00.306 |
| Orog Nuur | 45°02.692 | 100°36.314 |
| Saikhan-Ovoo | 45°27.459 | 103°54.110 |
| Sainshand | 44°53.576 | 110°08.351 |
| Sevrei | 43°35.617 | 102°09.737 |
| Shinejist | 44°32.917 | 99°17.349 |
| Süm Khökh Burd | 46°09.621 | 105°45.590 |
| Taihshir | 46°42.671 | 96°29.623 |
| Takhi Research Station | 45°32.197 | 93°39.055 |
| Tsagaan Agui | 44°42.604 | 101°10.187 |
| Tseel | 45°33.266 | 95°51.223 |
| Tsogt | 45°20.813 | 96°37.166 |
| Tsogt-Ovoo | 44°24.906 | 105°19.406 |
| Tsogttsetsii | 43°43.541 | 105°35.040 |
| Ulaanbadrakh | 43°52.598 | 110°24.686 |
| Yolyn Am | 43°29.332 | 104°04.000 |
| Zag | 46°56.168 | 99°09.806 |
| Zamyn-Üüd | 43°42.967 | 111°54.651 |

| WESTERN MONGOLIA | Latitude (N) | Longitude (E) |
|---|---|---|
| Altai | 45°49.115 | 92°15.497 |
| Altantsögts | 49°02.700 | 100°26.057 |
| Batuunturuun | 49°38.578 | 94°23.177 |
| Bulgan (Bayan-Ölgii) | 46°55.559 | 91°04.594 |
| Bulgan (Khovd) | 46°05.486 | 91°32.571 |
| Chandmani | 47°40.100 | 92°48.411 |
| Darvi | 46°56.181 | 93°37.158 |
| Deluun | 47°51.553 | 90°44.160 |
| Dörgon | 48°19.768 | 92°37.303 |
| Erdeneburen | 48°30.131 | 91°26.811 |
| Erdenkhairkhan | 48°07.228 | 95°44.229 |
| Khökh Nuur | 47°37.207 | 97°20.546 |
| Khovd (Uvs) | 49°16.720 | 90°54.720 |
| Khovd City | 48°00.430 | 91°38.474 |
| Mankhan | 47°24.557 | 92°12.617 |
| Möst | 46°41.626 | 92°48.000 |
| Naranbulag | 49°23.164 | 92°34.286 |
| Nogoonuur | 49°36.923 | 90°13.577 |
| Ölgii (Uvs) | 49°01.306 | 92°00.411 |
| Ölgii City | 48°58.070 | 89°58.028 |
| Öndörkhangai | 49°15.849 | 94°51.154 |
| Otgon | 47°12.488 | 97°36.391 |
| Sagsai | 48°54.688 | 89°39.429 |
| Telmen | 48°38.197 | 97°09.900 |
| Tes | 49°39.013 | 95°49.029 |
| Tolbo | 48°24.557 | 90°16.457 |
| Tolbo Nuur | 48°35.320 | 90°04.536 |
| Tosontsengel | 48°45.286 | 98°05.992 |
| Tsagaanchuluut | 47°06.531 | 96°39.497 |
| Tsagaankhairkhan | 49°24.209 | 94°13.440 |
| Tsagaannuur | 49°31.437 | 89°46.697 |
| Tsengel | 48°57.213 | 89°09.257 |
| Tsenkheriin Agui | 47°20.828 | 91°57.225 |
| Tüdevtei | 48°59.390 | 96°32.229 |
| Ulaangom | 49°58.764 | 92°04.028 |
| Ulaankhus | 49°02.525 | 89°26.929 |
| Uliastai | 47°44.591 | 96°50.582 |
| Urgamal | 48°30.653 | 94°16.046 |
| Üüreg Nuur | 50°05.236 | 91°04.587 |
| Zavkhan (Uvs) | 48°49.463 | 93°06.103 |
| Zavkhanmandal | 48°19.071 | 95°06.789 |

now travel safely between most cities. Cars can be hired through almost any hotel or guesthouse and will usually include a driver.

## Driving Licences

An international driving permit (or Mongolian driving licence) is required to drive in Mongolia if you plan to spend more than a month in the country. If you are in Mongolia for less than a month you can use a licence from your home country.

## Road Conditions & Rules

➡ Roads outside the capital are often of poor quality, although the network of modern highways is increasing. In rural areas, the roads are mainly 4x4 jeep tracks.

➡ Drivers need to be alert to animals on the road; this is even more of a hazard at night as few roads will be illuminated.

➡ Police stops occur periodically for breathalyser tests. You may also be stopped for running a red light or other illegal manoeuvres.

## Car & Motorcycle Hire

➡ Travelling across Mongolia on a motorbike is a great way to get around, and some tour operators offer motorcycle trips. **Drive Mongolia** (Map p58; ☎11-312 277, 9911 8257; www.drivemongolia.com; Bayangol District, 3rd Khoroo 24-1, ⊞ presuming.belief.insist) is one outfit that can rent out vehicles and motorbikes. **Sixt** (Map p58; ☎8600 7259; www.sixt.mn; Jamyn St, ICC Tower, ⊞ selection.pegged. dynamics; ◷8am-9pm) is another.

➡ Self-guided road trips will require considerable planning as the limited road network and road signs can easily result in getting terribly lost. Always travel with a good set of maps and a GPS unit.

# Camel & Yak

➡ For Mongolia's nomads, yaks and camels are recognised forms of transportation. Camels can carry the weight of an average-sized sumo wrestler. Yaks are also a useful and environmentally friendly way of hauling heavy cargo.

➡ At Ongiin Khiid and Khongoryn Els you can arrange camel treks. A few travel agencies include a ride on a camel or yak in their program. Otherwise, you can always ask at a ger.

# Hitching

Hitching is never entirely safe, and we don't recommend it. Travellers who hitch should understand that they are taking a small but potentially serious risk. Hitchers will be safer if they travel in pairs and let someone know where they are planning to go.

**Hitching in Mongolia** Because public transport is so limited, hitching (usually on trucks) is a recognised – and, often, the only – form of transport in the countryside. Hitching is seldom free and often no different from just waiting for public transport to turn up. In remote areas, the going can be very slow, especially if you're travelling in a truck. After breakdowns, fixing flat tyres and stopping for tea at gers, a truck can take 48 hours to cover 200km.

**Hazards** Hitching is not generally dangerous per se, but it is still hazardous (because getting stranded in remote areas is a real possibility) and often extremely uncomfortable. Don't expect much traffic in remote rural areas; you might see one or two vehicles a day and sometimes nobody at all for several days. In the towns, ask at the market, where trucks invariably hang around, or at the bus/truck/jeep station. The best place to wait is a petrol station on the outskirts of town,

where most vehicles stop before any journey.

**Limitations** If you rely on hitching entirely, you will just travel from one dreary aimag town to another. You still need to hire a jeep to see, for example, the Gobi Desert, the mountains in Khentii or some of the lakes in the far west.

**Payment** Truck drivers will normally expect some negotiable payment, which won't be much cheaper than a long-distance bus or shared jeep; figure on around T5000 per hour travelled.

**Bring** Take a water- and dust-proof bag to put your backpack in. The most important things to bring, though, are an extremely large amount of patience and time, and a high threshold for discomfort. Carry camping gear for the inevitable breakdowns, or suffer along with your travel mates.

# Local Transport

## Bus, Minibus & Trolleybus

In Ulaanbaatar, crowded trolleybuses and buses ply the main roads for T500 a ride (you'll need to buy a U-money swipe card at a kiosk near the bus stand). Cities such as Darkhan and Erdenet have minibuses that shuttle from one end of town to the other, but you are unlikely to need them because most facilities are located centrally.

## Share Minivan & Jeep

Share jeeps and minivans are the most common form of public transport in Mongolia.

**Destinations** Private vehicles go from Ulaanbaatar to all aimag capitals, major cities and tourist destinations. Less frequent and reliable services operate between most aimag capitals, but very few jeeps go to the *sums*.

**Bring** For a long-distance trip bring snacks and water; stops at a roadside *guanz* (canteen or cheap restaurant) can be few and far between.

**Breakdowns** You can expect at least one breakdown, and it would be a good idea to bring a sleeping bag and warm clothes just in case you have to spend the night somewhere.

**Discomfort** Long-distance travel of more than 15 hours is fiendishly uncomfortable. Most people who take a long-distance minivan to western Mongolia end up flying back. Trips to Mörön and Dalanzadgad are more bearable now that paved roads reach these towns.

**Cost** Minivan and jeep fares are usually about 10% more than a bus fare, largely because they tend to be faster than a bus.

**Postal vans** In the countryside, the post office operates postal vans, which accept passengers. They have fixed departure times, normally running once a week between an aimag capital and a *sum* capital. The local post office should have a list of departure times and fares.

## Private Minivan & Jeep

The best way to see the countryside of Mongolia independently is to hire your own minivan or jeep, which will come with a driver and, for a little extra, a guide. If you share the costs with others it doesn't work out to be too expensive. Guesthouses in Ulaanbaatar are the best places to ask.

Minivans, jeeps and SUVs are used for long- and short-distance travel in the countryside, and are mandatory when visiting more remote attractions. They can be shared among strangers, which is good for a group of people headed from one aimag centre to another (or usually to/from Ulaanbaatar). Alternatively, they can be hired privately.

**Furgon minivans** In most cases, the grey 11-seat Furgon minivans are used for longer cross-country trips that see a lot of traffic. Jeeps, khaki-coloured or green, are found in more remote areas

such as *sum* (district) centres. They are nicknamed *jaran yös* (shortened to *jaris*), which means '69' – the number of the original model.

**Toyota Land Cruisers** The large and comfortable Toyota Land Cruiser–style jeeps are owned by wealthy Mongolians and never used for share purposes (though some travel agencies might have them for hire, but expect to pay at least 30% more than for a good Russian jeep).

**Travelling speed** Off the paved roads, jeeps and minivans can typically only travel between 30km/h and 50km/h. Travel speeds in the Gobi tend to be a bit faster due to the flat, open landscape.

## Taxi

Mongolia's network of paved roads now extends from Ulaanbaatar to most aimag capitals, with the exception of cities in the far west. Taxis are only useful along these paved roads, eg from Ulaanbaatar north to Darkhan, Erdenet and Mörön (and Lake Khövsgöl), west to Kharkhorin, Tsetserleg and Bayankhongor, south to Dalanzadgad, Sainshand and Zamyn-Üüd and east to Choibalsan. However,

most sights worth seeing lie a considerable distance from the main roads, so even short trips require some off-roading. And if you are on a circular route a good part of your journey will be on jeep tracks. It should raise a big flag in your mind if a freelance guide tells you it's OK to tour the countryside in his brother's Toyota Prius taxi.

## Tours

Mongolia's limited public-transport network makes independent travel challenging because the sights can only be reached by private vehicle. Most travellers wisely opt for a tour in order to see more of the country in a limited period of time. Guided trips range from budget camping tours to high-end hot-air-balloon trips.

## Train

**Lines** The 1810km of railway line is primarily made up of the Trans-Mongolian Railway, connecting China with Russia. In addition, there are two spur lines: to the copper-mining centre of Erdenet (from Darkhan)

### THE MINIVAN WAITING GAME

A real problem with share vehicles is that they are privately operated and won't leave until they are packed tighter than a sardine tin. The waiting game sometimes has the effect of turning your hair grey.

In the countryside, most vans just park at the local market and wait for passengers to turn up, which means that if the van isn't already mostly full you'll be waiting around all day for the seats to fill up, if they ever do.

Typically, even after the 11-seat van has 20 or so passengers, the driver will vanish for an hour or two for lunch, or to find more cargo, spare parts and petrol.

One solution is to ask the driver to pick you up at your hotel or the local internet cafe when they are ready to go, which they usually agree to. If you have a mobile phone, give the driver your number and they will call you when they are ready to go.

The waiting time from Ulaanbaatar isn't as bad, but you can still count on two hours or more.

and the coal-mining city of Baganuur (from Ulaanbaatar). Another train runs weekly from Choibalsan, the capital of Dornod aimag, to the Russian border.

**Services** From Ulaanbaatar, daily express trains travel north to Darkhan, and on to Sükhbaatar or Erdenet. To the south, there are daily direct trains from Ulaanbaatar to Zamyn-Üüd, via Choir and Sainshand. You can't use the Trans-Mongolian Railway for domestic transport.

**Safety & Comfort** Trains in Mongolia are slow but safe. Book 2nd class for more comfort (four bunks per private cabin). In 3rd class seating there's less privacy and bunks are less comfortable. Food available on the local trains is usually of poor quality so it's best to bring snacks, fruit and instant noodles.

**Booking** If you're travelling from Ulaanbaatar, it is important to book a soft seat in advance – this can be done 60 days before departure. In general, booking ahead is a good idea for any class, though there will almost always be hard-seat tickets available. In summer, just getting a ticket on your own is difficult and will require standing in long lines. Your guesthouse or hotel can usually purchase the ticket for you, saving lots of headaches. For inquiries contact the **Ulaanbaatar train station** (Narny Gudamj, 🖳 ethic.pursuing. baking).

If you need additional assistance in booking a ticket, contact **Mongolia Train Tickets** (☎8880 6963; www. mongoliatraintickets.com).

**Getting a seat** When travelling in hard-seat class, you will almost certainly have to fight to get a seat. If you're not travelling alone, one of you can scramble on board and find seats and the other can follow with the luggage.

## Classes

There are usually three classes on domestic passenger trains: hard seat, hard sleeper and soft seat.

**Hard seat** In hard-seat class, the seats are actually padded bunks but there are no assigned bunks or any limit to the amount of tickets sold, so the carriages are always crowded and dirty.

**Hard sleeper** Called *platzkartnuu*, this looks just like the hard seat but everyone gets their own bunk and there is the option of getting a set of sheets and a blanket (T1500). Upgrades are available to soft seat if you decide you can't stand the hard seats.

**Soft seat** These are only a little bit softer, but the conditions are much better: the price difference (usually at least double the price of the hard seat) is prohibitive for most Mongolians. The soft-seat carriages are divided into compartments with four beds in each. You are given an assigned bed, and will be able to sleep, assuming, of course, that your compartment mates aren't rip-roaring drunk and noisy. If you travel at night, clean sheets are provided for about T1500, which is a wise investment since some of the quilts smell like mutton. Compared with hard-seat class, it's the lap of luxury, and worth paying extra for.

# Health

Mongolia's dry, cold climate and sparse human habitation means there are few of the infectious diseases that plague tropical countries in Asia. The rough-and-tumble landscape and lifestyle, however, presents challenges of its own. Injuries sustained from falling off a horse are common in the summer season. In winter, the biggest threats are the flu and pneumonia, which spread like wildfire in November. If you do become seriously ill in Mongolia, your local embassy can provide details of Western doctors. Serious emergencies may require evacuation to Seoul or Běijīng. If in the countryside, make a beeline for Ulaanbaatar to have your ailment diagnosed. The advice here is a general guide only; be sure to seek the advice of a doctor trained in travel medicine.

## BEFORE YOU GO

Prevention is the key to staying healthy while abroad. A little planning before departure, particularly for pre-existing illnesses, will save trouble later. See your dentist before going on a long trip, carry a spare pair of contact lenses and glasses, and take your optical prescription with you. Bring medications in their original, clearly labelled containers. A signed and dated letter from your physician describing your medical conditions and medications, including generic names, is also a good idea. Western medicine can be in short supply in Mongolia. Most medicine comes from China and Russia, and the labels won't be in English, so bring whatever you think you might need from home. Take extra supplies of prescribed medicine and divide it into separate pieces of luggage; that way if one piece goes astray, you'll still have a back-up supply.

## Insurance

**Adequate cover** If your health insurance does not cover you for medical expenses abroad, consider supplemental insurance. Check the Lonely Planet (www.lonelyplanet.com/travel-insurance) website for more information.

**Payment policy** While you may prefer a policy that pays hospital bills on the spot, rather than you paying first and sending in documents later, the only place in Mongolia that might accept this is the **SOS Medica Mongolia** (Map p67; 11-464 325, emergency 9911 0335; www.sosmedica. mn; Big Ring Rd, 4a Bldg, native.surround.trembles; 9am-6pm Mon-Fri) clinic.

**Pre-existing conditions** Declare any existing medical conditions to the insurance company; if your problem is pre-existing, the company will not cover you if it is not declared.

**Adventure activities** You may require extra cover for adventurous activities – make sure you are covered for a fall if you plan on riding a horse or a motorcycle. If you are uninsured, emergency evacuation is expensive, with bills over US$100,000 not uncommon.

## Medical Checklist

Following is a list of items you should consider including in your medical kit – consult your pharmacist for brands available in your country.

➡ Antibacterial cream (eg Mupirocin)

➡ Antibiotics (prescription only) – for travel well off the beaten track; carry the prescription with you in case you need it refilled

➡ Antifungal cream or powder (eg Clotrimazole) – for fungal skin infections and thrush

➡ Antinausea medication (eg Prochlorperazine)

➡ Antiseptic (such as povidone-iodine) – for cuts and grazes

➡ Aspirin or paracetamol (acetaminophen in the USA) – for pain or fever

➡ Bandages, Band-Aids (plasters) and other wound dressings

## RECOMMENDED VACCINATIONS

Ask your doctor for an International Certificate of Vaccination (otherwise known as the yellow booklet), which will list all of the vaccinations you have received, and take it with you. The World Health Organization (WHO) recommends the following vaccinations for travel to Mongolia:

**Adult diphtheria & tetanus** Single booster recommended if none in the previous 10 years. Side effects include sore arm and fever.

**Hepatitis A** Provides almost 100% protection for up to a year; a booster after 12 months provides at least another 20 years' protection. Mild side effects such as headache and a sore arm occur with some people.

**Hepatitis B** Now considered routine for most travellers, it provides lifetime protection for 95% of people. Immunisation is given as three doses over six months, though a rapid schedule is also available, as is a combined vaccination for Hepatitis A. Side effects are mild and uncommon, usually headache and a sore arm.

**Measles, mumps & rubella (MMR)** Two doses of MMR are recommended unless you have had the diseases. Occasionally a rash and flu-like illness can develop a week after receiving the vaccine. Many young adults need a booster.

**Typhoid** Recommended unless your trip is less than a week. The vaccine offers around 70% protection, lasts for two to three years and comes as a single dose. Tablets are also available, although the injection is usually recommended, as it has fewer side effects. A sore arm and fever may occur.

**Varicella** If you haven't had chickenpox discuss this vaccination with your doctor.

The following are recommended for long-term travellers (more than one month) or those at special risk:

**Influenza** A single jab lasts one year and is recommended for those over 65 years of age or with underlying medical conditions such as heart or lung disease.

**Pneumonia** A single injection with a booster after five years is recommended for all travellers over 65 years of age or with underlying medical conditions that compromise immunity, such as heart or lung disease, cancer or HIV.

**Rabies** Three injections are required. A booster after one year will then provide 10 years' protection. Side effects are rare – occasionally headache and a sore arm.

**Tuberculosis (TB)** A complex issue. High-risk, adult, long-term travellers are usually recommended to have a TB skin test before and after travel, rather than a vaccination. Only one vaccine is given in a lifetime. Children under five spending more than three months in China and/or Mongolia should be vaccinated.

➡ Calamine lotion, sting-relief spray or aloe vera – to ease irritation from sunburn and insect bites or stings

➡ Cold and flu tablets, throat lozenges and nasal decongestant

➡ Insect repellent (DEET-based)

➡ Loperamide or diphenoxylate – 'blockers' for diarrhoea

➡ Multivitamins – consider them for long trips, when dietary vitamin intake may be inadequate

➡ Rehydration mixture (eg Gastrolyte) – to prevent dehydration, which may occur during bouts of diarrhoea (particularly important when travelling with children)

➡ Scissors, tweezers and a thermometer – note that mercury thermometers are prohibited by airlines

➡ Sunscreen, lip balm and eye drops

➡ Water purification tablets or iodine (iodine is not to be used by pregnant women or people with thyroid problems)

## Websites

**Lonely Planet** (www.lonelyplanet.com) For further information this is a good place to start.

**MD Travel Health** (www.mdtravelhealth.com) A website of general interest; providing complete travel health recommendations for every country and is updated daily.

**World Health Organization** (www.who.int/ith) The WHO publishes a superb book called *International Travel & Health*, which is revised annually and is available online at no cost.

# Further Reading

**Traveller's Health** by Dr Richard Dawood.

**Travelling Well** by Dr Deborah Mills (www.travellingwell.com.au).

**Travel with Children** Lonely Planet guide, useful for families.

# IN MONGOLIA

## Availability & Cost of Health Care

**Advice** Health care is readily available in Ulaanbaatar, but choose your hospital and doctor carefully. Private hospitals with modern facilities are now available in the capital. The best advice will come from your embassy.

**Cost** Consultations cost around US$5, although **SOS Medica** (Map p67; ☎11-464 325, emergency 9911 0335; www. sosmedica.mn; Big Ring Rd, 4a Bldg, ⓘ native.surround. trembles; ⓘ9am-6pm Mon-Fri), a reliable clinic in Ulaanbaatar with Western doctors, charges around US$195.

**Medication** Most basic drugs are available without a prescription.

**Regional areas** Health services in the countryside are generally poor but are improving in some aimag capitals. Taking very small children to the countryside is therefore risky.

**Women's health** Female travellers will need to take pads and tampons with them, as these won't be available outside the main cities.

## Infectious Diseases

### Brucellosis

➡ The most likely way for humans to contract brucellosis is by drinking unboiled milk or eating homemade cheese. People with open cuts on their hands who handle freshly killed meat can also be infected.

➡ In humans, brucellosis causes severe headaches, joint and muscle pains, fever and fatigue. There may be diarrhoea and, later, constipation.

➡ The onset of the symptoms can occur from five days to several months after exposure, with the average time being two weeks.

➡ Most patients recover in two or three weeks, but people can get chronic brucellosis, which recurs sporadically for months or years and can cause long-term health problems. Fatalities are rare but possible.

➡ Brucellosis is a serious disease and requires blood tests to make the diagnosis. If you think you may have contracted the disease, seek medical attention, preferably outside Mongolia.

### Bubonic Plague

➡ Bubonic plague (which wiped out one third of Europe during the Middle Ages) makes an appearance in remote parts of Mongolia in late summer. Almost 90% of reported cases occur in August and September.

➡ The disease (also known as the Black Plague) is normally carried by rodents and can be transmitted to humans by bites from fleas that make their home on the infected animals. It can also be passed from human to human by coughing.

➡ The symptoms are fever and enlarged lymph nodes. The untreated disease has a 60% death rate, but if you get to a doctor it can be quickly treated.

➡ The best (but not only) drug is the antibiotic Gentamicin, which is available in Mongolia.

➡ During an outbreak, travel to infected areas is prohibited, which can greatly affect overland travel. All trains, buses and cars travelling into Ulaanbaatar from infected areas are also thoroughly checked when an outbreak of the plague has been reported, and vehicles are sprayed with disinfectant.

### Hepatitis

➡ Hepatitis is a general term for inflammation of the liver.

➡ The symptoms are similar in all forms of the illness, and include fever, chills, headache, fatigue and aches, followed by loss of appetite, nausea, vomiting, abdominal pain, dark urine, light-coloured faeces, jaundiced (yellow) skin and yellowing of the whites of the eyes.

➡ People who have hepatitis should avoid alcohol for some time after the illness, as the liver needs time to recover.

➡ Hepatitis A is transmitted by contaminated food and drinking water. You should seek medical advice, but there is not much you can do apart from resting, drinking lots of fluids, eating lightly and avoiding fatty foods.

➡ Hepatitis E is transmitted in the same way as hepatitis A; it can be particularly serious in pregnant women.

➡ Hepatitis B is endemic in Mongolia. It is spread through contact with infected blood, blood products or body fluids. The symptoms of hepatitis B may be more severe than type A and the disease can lead to long-term problems such as chronic liver damage, liver cancer or long-term carrier status.

➡ Hepatitis C and D are spread in the same way as hepatitis B and can also lead to long-term complications.

➡ There are vaccines against hepatitis A and B, but there are currently no vaccines against the other types of hepatitis.

### Rabies

➡ In the Mongolian countryside, family dogs are often vicious and can be rabid; it is their saliva that is infectious.

➡ Any bite, scratch or even a lick (if it's across broken skin) from an animal should be cleaned immediately and thoroughly. Scrub with soap and running water, and then apply alcohol or iodine solution.

→ Seek medical help promptly to receive a course of injections to prevent the onset of symptoms and death.

→ The incubation period for rabies depends on where you're bitten. On the head, face or neck it's as little as 10 days, whereas on the legs it's 60 days.

## Tuberculosis

→ Tuberculosis (TB) is a bacterial infection usually transmitted from person to person by coughing but which may be transmitted through consumption of unpasteurised milk.

→ Milk that has been boiled is safe to drink, and the souring of milk to make yoghurt or cheese also kills the bacilli.

→ Travellers are generally not at great risk as close household contact with an infected person is usually required before the disease is passed on. You may need to have a TB test before you travel, as this can help diagnose the disease later if you become ill.

# Environmental Hazards

## Heatstroke

→ This serious, occasionally fatal, condition can occur if the body's heat-regulating mechanism breaks down and the body temperature rises to dangerous levels.

→ Long, continuous exposure to high temperatures and insufficient fluids can leave you vulnerable to heatstroke.

→ The symptoms are feeling unwell, not sweating very much (or at all) and a high body temperature. Where sweating has ceased, the skin becomes flushed and red.

→ Victims can become confused, aggressive or delirious.

→ Get victims out of the sun, remove their clothing and cover them with a wet sheet or towel and fan continually. Give fluids if they are conscious.

## Hypothermia

→ In a country where temperatures can plummet to -40°C, cold is something you should take seriously.

→ Hypothermia occurs when the body loses heat faster than it can produce it and the body's core temperature falls.

→ If you are trekking at high altitudes or simply taking a long bus trip across the country, particularly at night, be especially prepared. Even in the lowlands, sudden winds from the north can send the temperature plummeting.

→ It is best to dress in layers; silk, wool and some of the new artificial fibres are all good insulting materials. A hat is important, as a lot of heat is lost though the head. A strong, waterproof outer layer is essential (as is a 'space' blanket for emergencies if trekking).

→ Carry basic supplies, including fluid to drink and food containing simple sugars to generate heat quickly.

## Bites & Stings

**Bees and wasps** Stings are usually painful rather than dangerous. Calamine lotion or sting-relief spray will give relief and ice packs will reduce the pain and swelling. However, people who are allergic to bees and wasps may require urgent medical care.

**Snakes** Mongolia has four species of venomous snakes: the Halys viper *(agkistrodon halys),* the common European viper or adder *(vipera berus),* Orsini's viper *(vipera ursine)* and the small *taphrometaphon lineolatum*. To minimise your chances of being bitten, wear boots, socks and long trousers where snakes may be present. Don't put your hands into holes and crevices, and be careful when collecting firewood.

**Bedbugs** These live in various places, but particularly in dirty mattresses and bedding, evidenced by spots of blood on bedclothes or on the wall. Bedbugs leave itchy bites in neat rows. Calamine lotion or a sting-relief spray may help.

**Lice** Lice make themselves at home in hair, clothing, or in pubic hair; causing itching and discomfort. You catch lice through direct contact with infected people or by sharing combs, clothing, etc. Powder or shampoo treatment will kill the lice, infected clothing should be washed in very hot, soapy water and left in the sun to dry.

## TAP WATER

→ Bottled water is generally safe – check that the seal is intact at purchase.

→ Tap water in Ulaanbaatar and other cities is considered bacteria-free, however antiquated plumbing means the water may contain traces of metals that won't be good for your long-term health.

→ Be cautious about drinking from streams and lakes, as they are easily polluted by livestock. Water is usually OK if you can get it high up in the mountains, near the source. If in doubt, boil your water.

→ The best chemical purifier is iodine, although it should not be used by pregnant women or those with thyroid problems.

→ Water filters should filter out viruses. Ensure your filter has a chemical barrier such as iodine and a small pore size (less than four microns).

# Language

Mongolian is the country's only official language, while Kazakh is spoken by many Kazakh minority groups in Western Mongolia, particularly around Bayan-Ölgii. Russian is also spoken by many people due to the country's Soviet history, and you'll find a growing number of people speak English.

## MONGOLIAN

Mongolian is a member of the Ural-Altaic family of languages, and as such it is distantly related to Turkish, Kazakh, Uzbek and Korean. It has around 10 million speakers worldwide. The traditional Mongolian script (cursive, vertical and read from left to right) is still used by the Mongolians living in the Inner Mongolia Autonomous Region of China. In 1944 the Cyrillic alphabet was adopted and it remains in use today in Mongolia and two autonomous regions of Russia (Buryatia and Kalmykia).

Mongolian also has a Romanised form, though the 35 Cyrillic characters give a better representation of Mongolian sounds than the 26 of the Roman alphabet. Different Romanisation systems have been used, and a loose standard was adopted in 1987 – so the capital city, previously written as Ulan Bator, is now Ulaanbaatar.

It's well worth the effort to familiarise yourself with the Cyrillic alphabet so that you can read maps and street signs. Otherwise, just read the coloured pronunciation guides given next to each word in this chapter as if they were English, and you'll be understood.

### WANT MORE?

For in-depth language information and handy phrases, check out Lonely Planet's *Mongolian Phrasebook*. You'll find it at **shop.lonelyplanet.com**, or you can buy Lonely Planet's iPhone phrasebooks at the Apple App Store.

Mongolian pronunciation is explained in the alphabet table on the next page. It's important to pronounce double vowel letters as long sounds, because vowel length can affect meaning. In our pronunciation guides the stressed syllables are in italics.

| | | |
|---|---|---|
| **Hello.** | Сайн байна уу? | sain *bai*·na uu |
| **Yes./No.** | Тийм./ Үгүй. | tiim/ü·*güi* |
| **Thank you.** | Баярлалаа. | ba·yar·la·*laa* |
| **You're welcome.** | Зүгээр. | zü·*geer* |
| **Excuse me.** | Уучлаарай. | uuch·*laa*·rai |
| **Sorry.** | Уучлаарай. | uuch·*laa*·rai |
| **Goodbye.** | Баяртай. | ba·yar·*tai* |

**What's your name?**
Таны нэрийг хэн гэдэг вэ? — ta·*ny* ne·*riig* khen ge·deg ve

**My name is ...**
Миний нэрийг ... гэдэг. — mi·*nii* ne·*riig* ... ge·deg

**Do you speak English?**
Та англиар ярьдаг уу? — ta an·*gliar yair*·dag uu

**I don't understand.**
Би ойлгохгүй байна. — bi *oil*·gokh·güi *bai*·na

## ACCOMMODATION

**Do you have any rooms available?**
Танайд сул өрөө байна уу? — ta·*naid* sul ö·*röö bai*·na uu

**How much is it per night/week?**
Энэ өрөө хоногт/ долоо хоногт ямар үнэтэй вэ? — e·ne ö·*röö* kho·nogt/ do·*loo* kho·nogt *ya*·mar ün·*tei* ve

**I'd like a single/double room.**
Би нэг/хоёр хүний өрөө авмаар байна. — bi neg/*kho*·yor khü·*nii* ö·*röö* av·*maar bai*·na

| **air-con** | агааржуулалт | a·*gaar*·*juul*·alt |
| **bathroom** | угаалгын өрөө | u·*gaal*·gyn ö·*röö* |

278

| cot | хүүхдийн ор | khüükh·*diin* or |
| dormitory | нийтийн байр | *nii*·tiin bair |
| hotel | зочид буудал | zo·chid *buu*·dal |
| window | цонх | tsonkh |
| youth hostel | залуучуудын байр | za·*luu*·chuu·dyn bair |

# DIRECTIONS

**Where's ...?**
... хаана байна вэ?  ... khaan *bai*·na ve
**How can I get to ...?**
... руу би яаж очих вэ?  ... ruu bi yaj o·chikh ve
**Can you show me on the map?**
Та газрын зураг дээр зааж өгнө үү?  ta gaz·*ryn* zu·rag deer zaaj ög·nö *üü*

| address | хаяг | *kha*·yag |
| behind | хойно | *khoi*·no |
| in front of | өмнө | *öm*·nö |
| straight ahead | чигээрээ урагшаа | chi·*gee*·ree u·rag·*shaa* |
| to the left | зүүн тийш | züün tiish |
| to the right | баруун тийш | ba·*ruun* tiish |

# EATING & DRINKING

**Can I have a menu, please?**
Би хоолны цэс авч болох уу?  bi *khool*·nii tses avch bo·lokh uu
**What food do you have today?**
Өнөөдөр ямар хоол байна вэ?  ö·*nöö*·dör ya·mar khool *bai*·na ve
**I'd like to have this.**
Би энэ хоолыг авъя.  bi en *khoo*·lyg a·*vi*
**I don't eat (meat).**
Би (мах) иддэггүй.  bi (makh) *id*·deg·gui
**Cheers!**
Эрүүл мэндийн төлөө!  e·*rüül* men·*diin* tö·*löö*
**The bill, please.**
Тооцоогоо бодуулья.  too·*tsoo*·goo bo·*duu*·li

## Key Words

| appetisers | хүйтэн зууш | *khüi*·ten zuush |
| bottle | шил | shil |
| breakfast | өглөөний хоол | ög·*löö*·nii khool |
| canteen | гуанз | guanz |
| cold | хүйтэн | *khüi*·ten |
| cup | аяга | a·*yag* |
| dessert | амтат зууш | *am*·tat zuush |
| dinner | оройн хоол | o·*roin* khool |
| dining room | зоогийн газар | *zoo*·giin ga·zar |
| dumplings | банштай | *ban*·shtai |

## CYRILLIC ALPHABET

| Cyrillic | Sound | |
|---|---|---|
| А а | a | as the 'u' in 'but' |
| Г г | g | as in 'get' |
| Ё ё | yo | as in 'yonder' |
| И и | i | as in 'tin' |
| Л л | l | as in 'lamp' |
| О о | o | as in 'hot' |
| Р р | r | as in 'rub' |
| У у | u | as in 'rude' |
| Х х | kh | as the 'ch' in Scottish *loch* |
| Ш ш | sh | as in 'shoe' |
| Ы ы | y | as the 'i' in 'ill' |
| Ю ю | yu | as the 'yo' in 'yoyo' |
| | yü | long, as the word 'you' |
| Б б | b | as in 'but' |
| Д д | d | as in 'dog' |
| Ж ж | j | as in 'jewel' |
| Й й | i | as in 'tin' |
| М м | m | as in 'mat' |
| Ө ө | ö | long, as the 'u' in 'fur' |
| С с | s | as in 'sun' |
| Ү ү | ü | long, as the 'o' in 'who' |
| Ц ц | ts | as in 'cats' |
| Щ щ | shch | as in 'fresh chips' |
| Ь ь | | 'soft sign' (see below) |
| Я я | ya | as in 'yard' |
| В в | v | as in 'van' |
| Е е | ye | as in 'yes' |
| | yö | as the 'yea' in 'yearn' |
| З з | z | as the 'ds' in 'suds' |
| К к | k | as in 'kit' |
| Н н | n | as in 'neat' |
| П п | p | as in 'pat' |
| Т т | t | as in 'tin' |
| Ф ф | f | as in 'five' |
| Ч ч | ch | as in 'chat' |
| Ъ ъ | | 'hard sign' (see below) |
| Э э | e | as in 'den' |

The letters ь and ъ never occur alone, but simply affect the pronunciation of the previous letter – ь makes the preceding consonant soft (pronounced with a faint 'y' after it), while ъ makes the previous consonant hard (ie not pronounced with a faint 'y' after it).

| food | хоол | khool |
| fork | сэрээ | se·*ree* |
| fried | шарсан | *shar*·san |
| fried food | хуураг | *khuu*·rag |
| glass | шилэн аяга | *shi*·len a·*yag* |
| hot | халуун | kha·*luun* |
| knife | хутга | *khu*·tag |
| lunch | үдийн хоол | ü·*diin* khool |
| market | зах | zakh |

LANGUAGE DIRECTIONS

| | | |
|---|---|---|
| menu | хоолны цэс | khool·ny tses |
| plate | таваг | ta·vag |
| restaurant | ресторан | res·to·ran |
| set dish | бэлэн хоол | be·len khool |
| spoon | халбага | khal·bag |
| tea shop | цайны газар | tsai·ny ga·zar |
| vegetarian | ногоон | no·goon |
| | хоолтон | khool·ton |

## Meat & Fish

| | | |
|---|---|---|
| antelope | цагаан зээр | tsa·gaan zeer |
| beef | үхрийн мах | ü·khriin makh |
| carp | булуу цагаан | bu·luu tsa·gaan |
| chicken | тахианы мах | ta·khia·ny makh |
| duck | нугас | nu·gas |
| fillet | гол мах | gol makh |
| fish | загас | za·gas |
| goat | ямаа | ya·maa |
| kebab | шорлог | shor·log |
| marmot | тарвага | tar·vag |
| meat | мах | makh |
| (fried) meat pancake | хуушуур | khuu·shuur |
| meat with rice | будаатай хуураг | bu·daa·tai khuu·rag |
| mutton | хонины мах | kho·ni·ny makh |
| mutton dumplings (steamed) | бууз | buuz |
| patty | бифштекс | bif·shteks |
| perch | алгана | al·gan |
| pike | цурхай | tsurh·kai |
| pork | гахайн мах | ga·khain makh |
| salmon | омуль | o·mul |
| sausage | хиам/зайдас/ сосик | khiam/zai·das/ so·sisk |
| sturgeon | хилэм | khi·lem |
| antevenison | бугын мах | bu·gyn makh |
| wild boar | бодон гахай | bo·don ga·khai |

## Fruit & Vegetables

| | | |
|---|---|---|
| apple | алим | a·lim |
| banana | гадил | ga·dil |
| cabbage | байцаа | bai·tsaa |
| carrot | шар лууван | shar luu·van |
| cucumber | өргөст хэмэх | ör·göst khe·mekh |
| fruit | жимс | jims |
| onion | сонгино | son·gin |
| potato | төмс | töms |
| radish | улаан лууван | u·laan luu·van |
| salad | салат | sa·lad |

| | | |
|---|---|---|
| tomato | улаан лооль | u·laan loo·il |
| turnip | манжин | man·jin |
| vegetable | ногоо | no·goo |

## Other

| | | |
|---|---|---|
| bread | талх | talkh |
| butter | цөцгийн тос | tsöts·giin tos |
| cake | бялуу | bya·luu |
| camel yogurt | хоормог | khoor·mog |
| cheese | бяслаг | byas·lag |
| cream | өрөм | ö·röm |
| dairy | цагаан-идээ | tsa·gaan i·dee |
| (dried) curds | ааруул | aa·ruul |
| egg | өндөг | ön·dög |
| honey | зөгийн бал | zö·giin bal |
| ice cream | зайрмаг | zair·mag |
| jam | жимсний чанамал | jims·nii cha·na·mal |
| noodle soup | гоймонтой шөл | goi·mon·toi shöl |
| pasta | хөндий гоймон | khön·diin goi·mon |
| pepper | поваарь | po·vaair |
| rice | цагаан будаа | tsa·gaan bu·daa |
| salad | ногоон зууш | no·goon zuush |
| salt | давс | davs |
| soup | шөл | shöl |
| sour cream | тараг/цөцгий | ta·rag/tsöts·gii |
| stewed fruit | компот | kom·pot |
| sugar | чихэр | chi·kher |
| sweets | цаастай чихэр | tsaas·tai chi·kher |
| with rice | будаатай | bu·daa·tai |

## Drinks

| | | |
|---|---|---|
| beer | пиво | piv |
| coffee | кофе | ko·fi |
| (buckthorn) juice | (чацарганы) шүүс | (cha·tsar·ga·ny) shüüs |
| koumiss (fermented mare milk) | айраг | ai·rag |

| Signs | |
|---|---|
| ГАРЦ | Exit |
| ЛАВЛАГАА | Information |
| ОРЦ | Entrance |
| ХААСАН | Closed |
| ХАДГАЛСАН | Reserved/Engaged |
| ЭРЭГТЭЙН | Men |
| ЭМЭГТЭЙН | Women |

| | | |
|---|---|---|
| lemonade | нимбэгний ундаа | nim·beg·*nii* un·*daa* |
| milk | сүү | süü |
| milk tea | сүүтэй цай | *süü*·tei tsai |
| milk with rice | сүүтэй будаа | *süü*·tei bu·*daa* |
| mineral water | рашаан ус | ra·*shaan* us |
| tea | цай | tsai |
| vodka | архи | a·rikh |
| wine | дарс | dars |

## EMERGENCIES

**Help!**
Туслаарай! — tus·*laa*·rai

**Go away!**
Зайл! — zail

**I'm lost.**
Би төөрчихлөө. — bi töör·chikh·*löö*

**There's been an accident.**
Осол гарчээ. — o·sol gar·*chee*

**Call a doctor/the police!**
Эмч/Цагдаа дуудаарай! — emch/tsag·*daa* duu·*daa*·rai

**I'm ill.**
Би өвчтэй байна. — bi övch·*tei bai*·na

**I'm allergic to (antibiotics).**
Миний биед (анти-биотик) харшдаг. — mi·*nii* bi·ed (an·ti·bi·o·tik) *harsh*·dag

## SHOPPING & SERVICES

**I'd like to buy ...**
Би ... авмаар байна. — bi ... av·*maar bai*·na

**I'm just looking.**
Би юм үзэж байна. — bi yum ü·zej *bai*·na

**Can you show me that?**
Та үүнийг надад үзүүлнэ үү? — ta *üü*·niig na·dad ü·*züü*·len üü

**I don't like it.**
Би үүнд дургүй байна. — bi üünd dur·*güi bai*·na

**How much is it?**
Энэ ямар үнэтэй вэ? — en ya·mar ün·*tei* ve

**That's very expensive.**
Яасан үнэтэй юм бэ? — yaa·san ün·*tei* yum be

**Can you reduce the price?**
Та үнэ буулгах уу? — ta ün *buul*·gakh uu

| | | |
|---|---|---|
| exchange rate | мөнгөний ханш | möng·*nii* khansh |

### Question Words

| What? | Юу? | yuu |
|---|---|---|
| When? | Хэзээ? | khe·*zee* |
| Where? | Хаана? | khaan |
| Which? | Ямар? | ya·mar |
| Who? | Хэн? | khen |

| | | |
|---|---|---|
| post office | шуудан | *shuu*·dan |
| public phone | нийтийн утас | *nii*·tiin u·tas |
| signature | гарын үсэг | ga·*ryn* ü·seg |
| travellers check | жуулчны чек | *juulch*·ny chek |

## TIME & DATES

**What time is it?**
Хэдэн цаг болж байна? — khe·den tsag bolj *bai*·na

**It's (nine) o'clock.**
(Есөн) цаг болж байна. — (yö·sön) tsag bolj *bai*·na

**It's half past (four).**
(Дөрөв) хагас болж байна. — (dö·röv) *kha*·gas bolj *bai*·na

| | | |
|---|---|---|
| morning | өглөө | ög·*löö* |
| afternoon | өдөр | ö·dör |
| evening | орой | o·roi |

| | | |
|---|---|---|
| yesterday | өчигдөр | ö·*chig*·dör |
| today | өнөөдөр | ö·*nöö*·dör |
| tomorrow | маргааш | mar·*gaash* |

| | | |
|---|---|---|
| Monday | даваа | da·*vaa* |
| Tuesday | мягмар | *myag*·mar |
| Wednesday | лхагва | *lkha*·vag |
| Thursday | пүрэв | *pü*·rev |
| Friday | баасан | *baa*·sang |
| Saturday | бямба | byamb |
| Sunday | ням | nyam |

Remember to add the word **cap** sar (literally 'month', 'moon') after each of the following words:

| | | |
|---|---|---|
| January | нэгдүгээр | neg·dü·*geer* |
| February | хоёрдугаар | kho·yor·du·*gaar* |
| March | гуравдугаар | gu·rav·du·*gaar* |
| April | дөрөвдүгээр | dö·röv·dü·*geer* |
| May | тавдугаар | tav·du·*gaar* |
| June | зургадугаар | zur·ga·du·*gaar* |
| July | долдугаар | dol·du·*gaar* |
| August | наймдугаар | naim·du·*gaar* |
| September | есдүгээр | yes·dü·*geer* |
| October | аравдугаар | a·rav·du·*gaar* |
| November | арваннэг-дүгээр | ar·van·neg·dü·*geer* |
| December | арванхоёр-дугаар | ar·van·kho·yor·du·*gaar* |

## Numbers

| 1 | нэг | neg |
|---|---|---|
| 2 | хоёр | *kho·*yor |
| 3 | гурав | *gu·*rav |
| 4 | дөрөв | *dö·*röv |
| 5 | тав | tav |
| 6 | зургаа | zur·*gaa* |
| 7 | долоо | do·*loo* |
| 8 | найм | naim |
| 9 | ес | yös |
| 10 | арав | *ar·*av |
| 20 | хорь | *kho·*ri |
| 30 | гуч | guch |
| 40 | дөч | döch |
| 50 | тавч | taiv |
| 60 | жар | jar |
| 70 | дал | dal |
| 80 | ная | *na·*ya |
| 90 | ер | yör |
| 100 | зуу | zuu |
| 1000 | мянга | *myang·*ga |

# TRANSPORT

## Public Transport

**What times does the ... leave/arrive?** ... хэдэн цагт явдаг/ирдэг вэ? ... *khe·*den tsagt *yav·*dag/*ir·*deg ve

| bus | Автобус | av·*to·*bus |
|---|---|---|
| plane | Нисэх онгоц | ni·seh on·gots |
| train | Галт тэрэг | galt te·reg |
| trolleybus | Троллейбус | trol·*lei·*bus |

**I want to go to ...**
Би ... руу явмаар байна.  bi ... ruu yav·*maar bai·*na

**Can you tell me when we get to ...?**
Бид хэзээ ... хүрэхийг хэлж өгнө үү?  bid khe·*zee* ... khu·re·*hiig* helj *ög·*nö uu

**I want to get off!**
Би буумаар байна!  bi *buu·*maar *bai·*na

| 1st class | нэгдүгээр зэрэг | neg·dü·*geer* ze·reg |
|---|---|---|
| 2nd class | хоёрдугаар зэрэг | kho·yor·du·*gaar* ze·reg |
| one-way ticket | нэг талын билет | neg ta·*lyn* bi·*let* |
| return ticket | хоёр талын билет | *kho·*yor ta·*lyn* bi·*let* |
| first | анхны | ankh·*ny* |
| next | дараа | da·*raa* |

| last | сүүлийн | *süü·*liin |
|---|---|---|
| airport | нисэх онгоцны буудал | ni·sekh on·gots·*ny* *buu·*dal |
| bus stop | автобусны зогсоол | av·*to·*bus·ny zog·*sool* |
| platform | давцан | *dav·*tsan |
| ticket office | билетийн касс | bi·le·*tiin* kass |
| timetable | цагийн хувaарь | tsa·*giin* khu·*vaair* |
| train | галт тэрэгний | galt te·re·ge·*nii* |
| station | буудал | *buu·*dal |

### Visiting the Locals

**We'd like to see inside a herder's yurt.**
Бид малчны гэрт орж үзэх гэсэн юм.  bid malch·*ny* gert orj *ü·*zekh ge·sen yum

**We'd like to drink some koumiss.**
Бид айраг уух гэсэн юм.  bid *ai·*rag uukh ge·sen yum

**I hope your animals are fattening up nicely.**
Мал сүрэг тарган тавтай юу?  mal *sü·*reg tar·gan tav·*tai* yü

**Please hold the dogs!**
Нохой хогио!  nok·*hoi* kho·ri·o

| I'd like to ride a ... | Би ... явах гэсэн юм | bi ... *ya·*vakh ge·sen yum |
|---|---|---|
| camel | тэмээгээр | te·*mee·*geer |
| horse | мориор | mo·*rior* |
| yak | сарлагаар | sar·la·*gaar* |

| camel | тэмээ | te·*mee* |
|---|---|---|
| chicken | тахиа | *ta·*khia |
| cooking pot | тогоо | to·*goo* |
| cow | үнээ | *ü·*nee |
| cowdung box | араг | *a·*rag |
| donkey | илжиг | *il·*jig |
| felt material | эсгий | es·*gii* |
| goat | ямаа | ya·*maa* |
| herding | мал аж ахуй | mal aj ak·*hui* |
| horse | морь | *mo·*ri |
| koumiss bag | хөхүүр | khö·*khüür* |
| pig | гахай | ga·*khai* |
| saddle | эмээл | e·*meel* |
| sheep | хонь | *kho·*ni |
| summer camp | зуслан | *zus·*lan |
| yak | сарлаг | *sar·*lag |
| yurt | гэр | ger |

## Driving & Cycling

**Excuse me, am I going in the right direction for ...?**
Уучлаарай, би ... руу    uuch·*laa*·rai bi ... ruu
зөв явж байна уу?    zöv yavj *bai*·na uu

**How many kilometres is it?**
Замын урт хэдэн    za·*myn* urt *khe*·den
километр вэ?    ki·lo·*metr* ve

| | | |
|---|---|---|
| **bicycle** | унадаг дугуй | *u*·na·dag du·*gui* |
| **map** | газрын зураг | gaz·*ryn* zu·rag |
| **mechanic** | механик | me·*kha*·nik |
| **motorcycle** | мотоцикл | mo·to·*tsikl* |
| **petrol** | бензин | ben·*zin* |

| Numbers – Kazakh | |
|---|---|
| 1 | bir |
| 2 | yeki |
| 3 | ush |
| 4 | tort |
| 5 | bes |
| 6 | alty |
| 7 | jeti |
| 8 | sakkiz |
| 9 | togyz |
| 10 | on |
| 100 | zhus |
| 1000 | myn |

# KAZAKH

Kazakh is spoken by almost 10 million people in nine countries. In Mongolia, it is spoken by around 101,000 Kazakhs – Mongolia's second largest ethnic group (after the Mongols), comprising 3-5% of the country's population. The vast majority of Mongolian Kazakhs live in the county's far west, in Bayan-Ölgii and Khovd aimags. Worldwide, Kazakh is spoken by almost 7 million people in Kazakhstan itself, as well as 1.2 million in Xīnjiāng, 850,000 in Uzbekistan, 650,000 in Russia; 92,000 in Turkmenistan, 40,000 in Kyrgyzstan and 12,000 in both Ukraine and Tajikistan.

The Kazakh language is written in Cyrillic script in Kazakhstan and a modified Persian-Arabic script in China. As with Kyrgyz, Chinese and Soviet governments imposed changes from a Persian-Arabic script to a Cyrillic or a Roman script in the hope of breaking Kazakhstan's ties to the Muslim world.

| | |
|---|---|
| **Peace be with you.** | assalamu aleykum |
| **And peace with you.** (response) | wagaleykum ussalam |
| **Hello.** | salamatsyz be |
| **Goodbye.** | kosh-sau bolyndar |
| **Thank you.** | rakhmet |
| **Yes./No.** | ia/zhok |
| **How are you?** | khal zhag dayynyz kalay? |
| **I'm well.** | zhaksy |
| **Do you speak English?** | agylshynsa bilesiz be? |
| **I don't understand.** | tusinbeymin |
| **Where is...?** | ... kayda? |
| **How much?** | kansha? |

| | |
|---|---|
| **airport** | auezhay |
| **bus station** | avtovokzal/avtobeket |
| **doctor** | dariger |
| **friend** | dos |
| **hospital** | aurukhana |
| **hotel** | konak uy/meymankhana |
| **police** | politsia |
| **restaurant** | ashana |
| **toilet** | daretkhana |
| **train station** | temir zhol vokzal/beket |

## EATING & DRINKING

| | |
|---|---|
| **bad** | zhaman |
| **boiled water** | kaynagan su |
| **bread** | nan |
| **expensive** | kymbat |
| **good** | zhaksy |
| **meat** | yet |
| **rice** | kurish |
| **tea** | shay |

## TIME & DATES

| | |
|---|---|
| **Monday** | duysenbi |
| **Tuesday** | seysenbi |
| **Wednesday** | sarsenbi |
| **Thursday** | beysenbi |
| **Friday** | zhuma |
| **Saturday** | senbi |
| **Sunday** | zheksenbi |

# GLOSSARY

**agui** – cave or grotto

**aimag** – a province/state within Mongolia

**airag** – fermented mare's milk

**am** – mouth, but often used as a term for canyon

**aral** – island

**baatar** – hero

**baga** – little

**balbal** – stone figures believed to be Turkic grave markers; known as *khun chuluu* (man stones) in Mongolian

**baruun** – west

**bodhisattva** – Tibetan-Buddhist term; applies to a being that has voluntarily chosen not to take the step to nirvana in order to save the souls of those on earth

**Bogd Gegeen** – the hereditary line of reincarnated Buddhist leaders of Mongolia, which started with Zanabazar; the third-holiest leader in the Tibetan Buddhist hierarchy; also known as *Jebtzun Damba*

**bulag** – natural spring

**Buriat** – ethnic minority living along the northern frontier of Mongolia, mostly in Khentii and Dornod

**chuluu** – rock; rock formation

**davaa** – mountain pass

**deer stones** – upright grave markers from the Bronze and Iron Ages, on which are carved stylised images of deer

**del** – the all-purpose, traditional coat or dress worn by men and women

**els** – sand; sand dunes

**erdene** – precious

**gegeen** – saint; saintlike person

**ger** – traditional circular felt dwelling

**gol** – river

**gov** – desert

**guanz** – canteen or cheap restaurant

**gudamj** – street

**ikh** – big

**Inner Mongolia** – a separate province within China

**Jebtzun Damba** – see *Bogd Gegeen*

**Kazakh** – ethnic minority, mostly living in western Mongolia

**khaan** – emperor; great *khan*

**khad** – rock

**Khalkh** – the major ethnic group living in Mongolia

**khan** – king or chief

**khar** – black

**kherem** – wall

**khiid** – Buddhist monastery

**khoid** – north

**khöömii** – throat singing

**khoroo** – district or subdistrict

**khot** – city

**khulan** – wild ass

**khuree** – originally used to describe a 'camp', it is now also in usage as 'monastery'

**lama** – Tibetan Buddhist monk or priest

**Living Buddha** – common term for reincarnations of Buddha; Buddhist spiritual leader in Mongolia (see *Bogd Gegeen*)

**man stones** – see *balbal*

**morin khuur** – horse-head fiddle

**MPRP** – Mongolian People's Revolutionary Party

**naadam** – games; traditional festival with archery, horse racing and wrestling

**nuruu** – mountain range

**nuur** – lake

**ömnö** – south

**örgön chölöö** – avenue

**Outer Mongolia** – northern Mongolia during Manchurian rule (the term is not currently used to describe Mongolia)

**ovoo** – a shamanistic collection of stones, wood or other offerings to the gods, usually found in high places

**rashaan** – mineral springs

**soyombo** – the national symbol of Mongolia, signifying freedom and independence; its components represent natural elements and virtues; legend has it that Zanabazar created the Soyombo in 1686

**stupa** – a Buddhist religious monument composed of a solid hemisphere topped by a spire, containing relics of the Buddha; also known as a pagoda, or *suvrag* in Mongolian

**sum** – a district; the administrative unit below an *aimag*

**süm** – Buddhist temple

**suvrag** – see *stupa*

**taiga** – subarctic coniferous evergreen forests (Russian)

**takhi** – the Mongolian wild horse; also known as Przewalski's horse

**tal** – steppe

**talbai** – square

**thangka** – scroll painting; a rectangular Tibetan Buddhist painting on cloth, often seen in monasteries

**tögrög** – the unit of currency in Mongolia

**töv** – central

**Tsagaan Sar** – 'white moon' or 'white month'; a festival to celebrate the Mongolian New Year (start of the lunar year)

**tsainii gazar** – teahouse/cafe

**tsam** – lama dances; performed by monks wearing masks during religious ceremonies

**tsuivan gazar** – noodle stall

**tugrik** – another spelling of tögrög

**ulaan** – red

**us** – water

**uul** – mountain

**yurt** – the Russian word for *ger*

**zakh** – market

**Zanabazar** – see *Bogd Gegeen*

**zochid buudal** – hotel

**züün** – east

# Behind the Scenes

## SEND US YOUR FEEDBACK

We love to hear from travellers – your comments keep us on our toes and help make our books better. Our well-travelled team reads every word on what you loved or loathed about this book. Although we cannot reply individually to your submissions, we always guarantee that your feedback goes straight to the appropriate authors, in time for the next edition. Each person who sends us information is thanked in the next edition – the most useful submissions are rewarded with a selection of digital PDF chapters.

Visit **lonelyplanet.com/contact** to submit your updates and suggestions or to ask for help. Our award-winning website also features inspirational travel stories, news and discussions.

Note: We may edit, reproduce and incorporate your comments in Lonely Planet products such as guidebooks, websites and digital products, so let us know if you don't want your comments reproduced or your name acknowledged. For a copy of our privacy policy visit lonelyplanet.com/privacy.

## OUR READERS

**Many thanks to the travellers who used the last edition and wrote to us with helpful hints, useful advice and interesting anecdotes:** Amanda Chilcott, Ashley M Karitis, Berangere Marceau, Betty Rebellato, Brenda Boucher, Carola Kehrle, Cindy Poole, Claudio Bollani, Dave Lamb, Domenico Grandoni, Dowshan Humzah, Elad Remer, Emma Dell, Enkhmandakh Khurel-Erdene, Fika Perié, Filipe Azenha, Fiona Fitzgerald, Folke Hermansson Snickars, Gantuya Badamgarav, Goyo Reston, Hayley Allen, Jesse White, Jo Lockart, Jongkug Kim, Leah Chapple, Margareta Gustafsson, Meghan Dougherty, Meghan Moorhouse, Narangarav Enkhtuya, Nick Freeland, Olly Reston, Pierre Piquemal, Rachel Donovan, Sanne Wurzer, Sophie Hunter, Susan Kassouf, Talia Young, Tanya and Sten Johansson, Tsetsegee Sumiya.

## WRITER THANKS

### Trent Holden

A massive thanks to Megan Eaves for giving me such a fantastic opportunity to work on this update. A big shout out to Tooro, Uyanga and Shagai for all your invaluable assistance! In Kharkhorin thanks heap to Tulgaa for getting me around the countryside. To Michael Kohn for all the tips, and the inhouse production team for putting this together. Finally lots of love to my family and my partner, Kate, who I was lucky enough to travel around with on this trip.

### Adam Karlin

Megan Eaves for getting me on this dream project, Anna Kaminski for encouraging me to pursue it, and Mike Kohn for helping me ground my feet. Thank you to everyone at home who helped keep said home humming along: Mark Matthews, Mike Robertshaw, Nora Ellersten and the usual New Orleans crew. Thanks to my guides and drivers and every Mongolian who offered us some hard candy and a piece of dried dairy; Marilyn in Mörön; Xavi and Cristina in the Darkhad Valley; the staff at MS Guesthouse, and many more. This is for Rachel and Sanda; the former for knowing how much this meant to me, and the latter for reminding daddy of the importance of adventure, home and the space they share.

### Michael Kohn

Thanks to my wife, Baigalmaa Kohn, and daughters Molly and Elizabeth for everything; to my fellow authors Trent Holden, Tom O'Malley, Adam Karlin and Adam Skolnick for the excellent support and information provided from the field; and to our Destination Editor Megan Eaves for bringing it all together. In Ulaanbaatar, many thanks to Olly Reston and Toroo for advice and help on the ground.

## Thomas O'Malley

I would like to thank Jan Wigsten for his advice, contacts and excellent choice of restaurants. Thanks also to Dosjan, Canat, Bek and many more in Olgii for their local knowledge and assistance. I'd also like to thank Marima in Khovd for introducing me to some special places, and finally, a big thanks for the ger hospitality, endless cups of milk tea and roadside assistance I experienced along the way.

## Adam Skolnick

Special thanks to Daniel Martinez and fam at Millie's Café, Jalsa Urubshurow and his amazing team in UB and the Gobi, Uugganaa, Amra and Toroo at Khongor Guesthouse, Jan Wigsten and Nomadic Journeys, Pujii and colleagues at Snow Leopard Trust, and the wonderful herders we met in the Gurvantes area who are fighting for their rights, and for the land, in the Tost Mountains. Thanks especially to my partner in travel and life, April Wong.

## ACKNOWLEDGEMENTS

Climate map data adapted from Peel MC, Finlayson BL & McMahon TA (2007) 'Updated World Map of the Köppen-Geiger Climate Classification', Hydrology and Earth System Sciences, 11, 163344.

Cover photograph: Shaman in an offering ceremony; Feije Riemersma/Alamy©

BEHIND THE SCENES

# THIS BOOK

This 8th edition of Lonely Planet's *Mongolia* guidebook was curated by Trent Holden, and researched and written by Trent Holden, Adam Karlin, Michael Kohn, Thomas O'Malley and Adam Skolnick. The previous edition was written by Charles Rawlings-Way, Brett Atkinson, Sarah Bennett, Lee Slater and Peter Dragicevich.

This guidebook was produced by the following:
**Destination Editor** Megan Eaves
**Product Editors** Jessica Ryan, Kate Chapman
**Senior Cartographers** Valentina Krema, Alison Lyall
**Book Designer** Gwen Cotter
**Assisting Editors** Imogen Bannister, Melanie Dankel, Kate James, Tamara Sheward, Ross Taylor, Saralinda Turner, Sam Wheeler.
**Cartographer** Rachel Imeson
**Cover Researcher** Naomi Parker
**Thanks to** Baigalmaa Batsukh, Heather Champion, Dan Corbett, Seb Neylan, Kirsten Rawlings, Alison Ridgway, Kate Sullivan, Angela Tinson, Amanda Williamson, Juan Winata.

# Index

# Map Legend

## Sights
- Beach
- Bird Sanctuary
- Buddhist
- Castle/Palace
- Christian
- Confucian
- Hindu
- Islamic
- Jain
- Jewish
- Monument
- Museum/Gallery/Historic Building
- Ruin
- Shinto
- Sikh
- Taoist
- Winery/Vineyard
- Zoo/Wildlife Sanctuary
- Other Sight

## Activities, Courses & Tours
- Bodysurfing
- Diving
- Canoeing/Kayaking
- Course/Tour
- Sento Hot Baths/Onsen
- Skiing
- Snorkelling
- Surfing
- Swimming/Pool
- Walking
- Windsurfing
- Other Activity

## Sleeping
- Sleeping
- Camping
- Hut/Shelter

## Eating
- Eating

## Drinking & Nightlife
- Drinking & Nightlife
- Cafe

## Entertainment
- Entertainment

## Shopping
- Shopping

## Information
- Bank
- Embassy/Consulate
- Hospital/Medical
- Internet
- Police
- Post Office
- Telephone
- Toilet
- Tourist Information
- Other Information

## Geographic
- Beach
- Gate
- Hut/Shelter
- Lighthouse
- Lookout
- Mountain/Volcano
- Oasis
- Park
- Pass
- Picnic Area
- Waterfall

## Population
- Capital (National)
- Capital (State/Province)
- City/Large Town
- Town/Village

## Transport
- Airport
- Border crossing
- Bus
- Cable car/Funicular
- Cycling
- Ferry
- Metro/MRT/MTR station
- Monorail
- Parking
- Petrol station
- Skytrain/Subway station
- Taxi
- Train station/Railway
- Tram
- Underground station
- Other Transport

## Routes
- Tollway
- Freeway
- Primary
- Secondary
- Tertiary
- Lane
- Unsealed road
- Road under construction
- Plaza/Mall
- Steps
- Tunnel
- Pedestrian overpass
- Walking Tour
- Walking Tour detour
- Path/Walking Trail

## Boundaries
- International
- State/Province
- Disputed
- Regional/Suburb
- Marine Park
- Cliff
- Wall

## Hydrography
- River, Creek
- Intermittent River
- Canal
- Water
- Dry/Salt/Intermittent Lake
- Reef

## Areas

- Airport/Runway
- Beach/Desert
- Cemetery (Christian)
- Cemetery (Other)
- Glacier
- Mudflat
- Park/Forest
- Sight (Building)
- Sportsground
- Swamp/Mangrove

*Note: Not all symbols displayed above appear on the maps in this book*

### Thomas O'Malley

Western Mongolia A lifestyle writer based in Beijing, Tom loves wine, food, walking, words, and train travel (in that order, and especially combined together). As well as writing LP guidebooks, Tom reviews hotels for the *Telegraph* and contributes travel and food stories to everyone from *Guardian* to *Playboy*. Under another guise, Tom is a former Marvel comics editor and comedy screenwriter, part of the Gorillaz writing team, and occasionally DJs (badly) as Hawaiian Brian (unsigned).

### Adam Skolnick

The Gobi Adam Skolnick's travel obsession bloomed while working as an environmental activist in the mid '90s. These days he's an award-winning journalist and travel writer who writes about travel, culture, human rights, sports and the environment for a variety of publications, including the *New York Times*, *Playboy*, Outside, BBC.com, *Wired*, ESPN.com and *Men's Health*, and he's authored or co-authored over 35 Lonely Planet guidebooks. An avid open-water swimmer and diver, he's also the author of the critically acclaimed narrative nonfiction book, *One Breath: Freediving, Death and the Quest to Shatter Human Limits* and *Indolirium*. He lives in Malibu, California. IG: @adamskolnick

### Contributing Writers

Dulmaa Enkhchuluun graduated from Augsburg College in Minnesota and now works to promote culturally and environmentally responsible tourism and commercial development in Mongolia.

Jack Weatherford Anthropologist Jack Weatherford wrote *Genghis Khan and the Making of the Modern World*, for which he received the Order of the Polar Star, Mongolia's highest state honour.

# OUR STORY

A beat-up old car, a few dollars in the pocket and a sense of adventure. In 1972 that's all Tony and Maureen Wheeler needed for the trip of a lifetime – across Europe and Asia overland to Australia. It took several months, and at the end – broke but inspired – they sat at their kitchen table writing and stapling together their first travel guide, *Across Asia on the Cheap*. Within a week they'd sold 1500 copies. Lonely Planet was born.

Today, Lonely Planet has offices in Franklin, London, Melbourne, Oakland, Dublin, Beijing and Delhi, with more than 600 staff and writers. We share Tony's belief that 'a great guidebook should do three things: inform, educate and amuse'.

# OUR WRITERS

### Trent Holden

Ulaanbaatar, Central Mongolia A Geelong-based writer, located just outside Melbourne, Trent has worked for Lonely Planet since 2005. He's covered 30 plus guidebooks across Asia, Africa and Australia. With a penchant for megacities, Trent's in his element when assigned to cover a nation's capital – the more chaotic the better – to unearth cool bars, art, street food and underground subculture. On the flipside he also writes books to idyllic tropical islands across Asia, in between going on safari to national parks in Africa and the subcontinent. When not travelling, Trent works as a freelance editor and reviewer, spending all his money catching live gigs. You can catch him on Twitter @hombreholden.

### Adam Karlin

Eastern Mongolila, Northern Mongolia Adam has contributed to dozens of Lonely Planet guidebooks, covering an alphabetical spread that ranges from the Andaman Islands to the Zimbabwe border. As a journalist, he has written on travel, crime, politics, archeology and the Sri Lankan Civil War, among other topics. He has sent dispatches from every continent barring Antarctica (one day!) and his essays and articles have featured in the BBC, NPR and multiple non-fiction anthologies. Adam is based out of New Orleans, which helps explain his love of wetlands, food and good music. Learn more at http://walkonfine.com/, or follow on Instagram @adamwalkonfine.

### Michael Kohn

Michael has been working as a travel writer for more than a decade. In 2003 he jumped in headfirst with Lonely Planet by taking on the Uzbekistan and Kazakhstan chapters of the *Central Asia* guidebook. Since then he has been exploring some of the remoter corners of Asia and the Middle East for LP, while also reporting the news for international media outlets. His LP titles include *Sri Lanka*, *Tibet*, *Mongolia*, *Israel & the Palestinian Territories* and *Trans-Siberian Railway*. Michael's particular area of interest is Mongolia, where he has covered the news for Bloomberg, the BBC and others. During his time in Mongolia he wrote *Lama of the Gobi*, a biography of the 19th century poet-monk Danzanravjaa, and *Dateline Mongolia*, a personal memoir about his time spent working as a reporter in Ulaanbaatar recounting misadventures and bizarre news events. When not on the road Michael can be found in the SF Bay Area. Michael wrote the Plan, Understand and the Survival Guide chapters of this book.

## 31901063576369

OVER PAGE MORE WRITERS

**Published by Lonely Planet Global Limited**
CRN 554153
8th edition – Jul 2018
ISBN 978 1 78657 572 2
© Lonely Planet 2018  Photographs © as indicated 2018
10 9 8 7 6 5 4 3 2 1
Printed in Singapore

Although the authors and Lonely Planet have taken all reasonable care in preparing this book, we make no warranty about the accuracy or completeness of its content and, to the maximum extent permitted, disclaim all liability arising from its use.